the Unofficial Guide® to

Florida

Also available from John Wiley & Sons, Inc.:

Beyond Disney: The Unofficial Guide to Universal, Sea World,
and the Best of Central Florida

Inside Disney: The Incredible Story of Walt Disney World
and the Man Behind the Mouse

Mini Las Vegas: The Pocket-Sized Unofficial Guide to Las Vegas

Mini-Mickey: The Pocket-Sized Unofficial Guide
to Walt Disney World

The Unofficial Guide to Bed & Breakfasts and Country Inns:
California   Great Lakes States   Mid-Atlantic
New England   Northwest   Rockies
Southeast   Southwest

The Unofficial Guide to Best RV and Tent Campgrounds:
California and the West   Florida and the Southeast
Great Lakes   Mid-Atlantic   Northeast   Northwest
Southwest   U.S.A.

The Unofficial Guide to Branson, Missouri

The Unofficial Guide to Central Italy: Florence, Rome,
Tuscany, and Umbria

The Unofficial Guide to Chicago

The Unofficial Guide to Cruises

The Unofficial Guide to Disneyland

The Unofficial Guide to Disneyland Paris

The Unofficial Guide to Golf Vacations in the Eastern U.S.

The Unofficial Guide to the Great Smoky
and Blue Ridge Region

The Unofficial Guide to Hawaii

The Unofficial Guide to Las Vegas

The Unofficial Guide to London

The Unofficial Guide to Maui

The Unofficial Guide to Mexico's Best Beach Resorts

The Unofficial Guide to New Orleans

The Unofficial Guide to New York City

The Unofficial Guide to Paris

The Unofficial Guide to San Francisco

The Unofficial Guide to Skiing and Snowboarding in the West

The Unofficial Guide to South Florida

The Unofficial Guide to Traveling with Kids:
California   Florida   Mid-Atlantic
New England   Southeast

The Unofficial Guide to Walt Disney World

The Unofficial Guide to Walt Disney World for Grown-Ups

The Unofficial Guide to Walt Disney World with Kids

The Unofficial Guide to Washington, D.C.

The Unofficial Guide to the World's Best Diving Vacations

the Unofficial Guide® to Florida

1st Edition

Pam Brandon

WILEY

Please note that prices fluctuate in the course of time, and travel information changes under the impact of many factors that influence the travel industry. We therefore suggest that you write or call ahead for confirmation when making your travel plans. Every effort has been made to ensure the accuracy of information throughout this book, and the contents of this publication are believed correct at the time of printing. Nevertheless, the publishers cannot accept responsibility for errors or omissions or for changes in details given in this guide or for the consequences of any reliance on the information provided by the same. Assessments of attractions and so forth are based upon the author's own experience, and therefore, descriptions given in this guide necessarily contain an element of subjective opinion, which may not reflect the publisher's opinion or dictate a reader's own experience on another occasion. Readers are invited to write the publisher with ideas, comments, and suggestions for future editions.

Published by:
John Wiley & Sons, Inc.
111 River Street
Hoboken, NJ 07030

Copyright © 2004 by Robert W. Sehlinger. All rights reserved. No part of this publication may be reproduced, stored in a retrieval system or transmitted in any form or by any means, electronic, mechanical, photocopying, recording, scanning or otherwise, except as permitted under Sections 107 or 108 of the 1976 United States Copyright Act, without either the prior written permission of the Publisher, or authorization through payment of the appropriate per-copy fee to the Copyright Clearance Center, 222 Rosewood Drive, Danvers, MA 01923, (978) 750-8400, fax (978) 750-4744, or on the web at www.copyright.com. You can contact the Publisher directly for permission by email at permreq@wiley.com or on the web at www.wiley.com/about/permission.

Wiley, the Wiley logo and Unofficial Guide are registered trademarks of John Wiley & Sons, Inc. in the United States and other countries and may not be used without written permission. Used under license. All other trademarks are the property of their respective owners. John Wiley & Sons, Inc. is not associated with any product or vendor mentioned in this book.

Produced by Menasha Ridge Press
Cover design by Michael J. Freeland
Interior design by Michele Laseau

For information on our other products and services or to obtain technical support please contact our Customer Care Department within the U.S. at (800) 762-2974, outside the U.S. at (317) 572-3993 or fax (317) 572-4002.

John Wiley & Sons, Inc. also publishes its books in a variety of electronic formats. Some content that appears in print may not be available in electronic formats.

ISBN 0-7645-3948-5
ISSN 1520-5584

Manufactured in the United States of America
5 4 3 2 1

Contents

List of Maps   vii
Acknowledgments   ix
About the Authors and Contributors   x

Introduction   1
About This Guide   1
How Information Is Organized   2
Planning Your Visit   6
The Best of Florida   10
Visiting Florida with Children   11

Part One   Accommodations   14
Deciding Where to Stay   14
Getting a Good Deal on a Room   20
Hotels and Motels: Rated and Ranked   63
The Best Deals   95

Part Two   The Florida Panhandle: Pensacola, Fort Walton, Destin, Panama City, and Tallahassee   100
Welcome to the Panhandle   100
Visiting the Panhandle   101
The Best Beaches   103
Outdoor Adventures and Sports   105
Pensacola and Pensacola Beach   111
Fort Walton, Destin, and the Beaches of South Walton   121
Panama City Beach   133
Tallahassee   141

Part Three   Northeast Florida: Amelia Island, Jacksonville, St. Augustine, and Gainesville   148
Welcome to Northeast Florida   148
Visiting Northeast Florida   149
The Best Beaches   151
Outdoor Adventures and Sports   152
Amelia Island and Fernandina Beach   159

Contents

Part Three   **Northeast Florida: Amelia Island, Jacksonville, St. Augustine, and Gainesville (continued)**

- Jacksonville   164
- St. Augustine   173
- Gainesville and Environs   189

Part Four   **The Space Coast: Daytona Beach, New Smyrna Beach, and Cocoa Beach   197**

- Welcome to the Space Coast   197
- Visiting the Space Coast   198
- The Best Beaches   201
- Outdoor Adventures and Sports   202
- Daytona Beach   209
- New Smyrna Beach   220
- Cocoa Beach and Surrounding Areas   225

Part Five   **Orlando: Walt Disney World, Universal, and Beyond   239**

- Introduction   239
- Visiting the Orlando Area   240
- Outdoor Adventures and Sports   242
- Walt Disney World   246
- Universal Orlando   269
- Greater Orlando Area   276

Part Six   **The Central Gulf Coast: Tampa, St. Petersburg, and Sarasota   300**

- Welcome to the Central Gulf Coast   300
- Visiting the Central Gulf Coast   301
- The Best Beaches   303
- Outdoor Adventures and Sports   306
- Tampa   312
- St. Petersburg and Clearwater   325
- Sarasota and Longboat Key   338

Part Seven   **The Gold and Treasure Coasts: Vero Beach, Palm Beach, and Greater Fort Lauderdale   347**

- Welcome to the Gold and Treasure Coasts   347
- Visiting the Gold and Treasure Coasts   349
- The Best Beaches   352
- Outdoor Adventures and Sports   353
- Vero Beach   361
- Palm Beach County   365
- Fort Lauderdale/Broward County   380

Part Eight   **Southwest Florida: Fort Myers, Sanibel and Captiva Islands, Naples, and Marco Island   396**

- Welcome to Southwest Florida   396
- Visiting Southwest Florida   397
- Island Hopping   400

The Best Beaches 403
Outdoor Adventures and Sports 405
Fort Myers and Fort Myers Beach 411
Sanibel and Captiva Islands 421
Naples and Marco Island 426

Part Nine Miami and Miami Beach 435

Welcome to Miami 435
Visiting Miami 440
The Best Beaches 444
Outdoor Adventures and Sports 445
What to See and Do in Miami 452

Part Ten Everglades National Park 478

Welcome to Everglades National Park 478
Visiting Everglades National Park 479
Touring the Park from the North 482
Touring the Park from the South 484
Touring the Park from the Gulf Coast 487

Part Eleven The Florida Keys and Key West 490

Welcome to the Keys 490
A Brief History 492
Visiting the Florida Keys 493
The Best Beaches 495
Outdoor Adventures and Sports 495
The Upper Keys 498
The Middle and Lower Keys 503
Key West 506

Accommodations Index 524
Subject Index 536

List of Maps

Florida Touring Zones 4–5
Pensacola and Pensacola Beach Accommodations 22–23
Fort Walton Beach Accommodations 24
Destin Area Accommodations 25
Santa Rosa Beach Area Accommodations 26
Panama City Beach Accommodations 27
Apalachicola Area Accommodations 28
Tallahassee Accommodations 29
Amelia Island/Fernandina Beach Accommodations 30
Gainesville Accommodations 31
Jacksonville Accommodations 32–33
St. Augustine and St. Augustine Beach Accommodations 34–35
Daytona Accommodations 36
The Space Coast Accommodations 37
South Orlando and Walt Disney World Accommodations 38–40
St. Petersburg–Clearwater Accommodations 41
Tampa Accommodations 42–43

Contents

List of Maps (continued)

Sarasota Accommodations   44
Vero Beach and the Treasure Coast Accommodations   45
Palm Beach County Accommodations   46
Miami Beach Accommodations   47
Broward County Accommodations   48–49
Miami Area Accommodations   50–51
South Beach Accommodations   52
The Florida Keys Accommodations   53
Key West Accommodations   54
Downtown Key West Accommodations   55
Fort Myers Accommodations   56
Fort Myers Beach Accommodations   57
Naples Accommodations   58
Sanibel and Captiva Accommodations   59
Marco Island Accommodations   60
Pensacola   112–113
Fort Walton Beach   123
Destin Area   124
Santa Rosa Beach Area   125
Panama City Beach   134
Downtown Tallahassee   142
Amelia Island/Fernandina Beach   160
Jacksonville   165
St. Augustine   174
Gainesville   190
Daytona   210
New Smyrna Beach   221
Cocoa Beach and Surrounding Area   226
Walt Disney World   248–249
Universal Orlando   270–271
The Orlando/Walt Disney World Area   278
Tampa   314–315
Downtown St. Petersburg   326
Clearwater   327
Sarasota   339
Vero Beach and the Treasure Coast   362
Palm Beach County   366
Greater Fort Lauderdale/Broward County   382–383
Fort Myers and Fort Myers Beach   412
Sanibel and Captiva Islands   422
Naples and Marco Island   428–429
Miami   436–437
South Miami Beach   438
Southern Miami–Dade County   439
Everglades National Park   480–481
The Florida Keys   491
Key West   507

Acknowledgments

The Florida peninsula covers an area roughly the size of England, with astounding diversity in destinations coast to coast. Traveling from the edge of the Panhandle to the Florida Keys took time—lots of time—and notebooks full of ideas. When it came time to pare down and compile the work, big thanks go to research assistant Doris Ramirez, who followed up on minute details. And to Erin Seabolt who jumped in to finish chapters that were only outlines. Special thanks to Lea Lane, Joe Surkiewicz, and Marcia Levin, authors of *The Unofficial Guide to South Florida,* for sharing information from that book. And to Joseph Mark Passov and C. H. Conroy, authors of *The Unofficial Guide to Golf Vacations in the Eastern U.S.,* for their comments about many of the Florida golf courses. Kudos to Trish Riley who spent months researching hotels to recommend. And to friends across Florida who work in the tourism industry—Wit Tuttle, Jayna Leach, Lee Rose, and others—for sharing their personal insights. Finally, special thanks to my husband, Steve, and my children, Katie and Will, who were so patient as I spent hours on the road and at my desk.

Last, but not least, I am grateful to the team at Menasha Ridge Press—Bob Sehlinger, Molly Merkle, Steve Jones, Annie Long, and especially to editor Nathan Lott for his patience and fine work.

About the Authors and Contributors

Pam Brandon, a freelance writer based in Winter Park, Florida, is a 25-year veteran of news and feature reporting. She began her journalism career in 1975 at *The Charleston Gazette* in Charleston, West Virginia, then relocated to Central Florida as news editor for *Orlando Magazine* and later as senior publicist for Walt Disney World. In 1995, she started her own company, Pam Brandon Editorial Services. Brandon is the author of *The Unofficial Guide to Florida with Kids,* and is a writer for the *Berlitz Florida Pocket Guide.* Her travel stories have appeared both online and in numerous local and national publications.

Trish Riley personally inspected and rated every hotel property in the guide. She is an independent journalist who writes about families, health, and environmental issues. Trish's work is published in many newspapers, magazines, and custom publications.

Introduction

About This Guide

In this new era of travel, when many vacationers are playing it safe, Florida moves to the top of the "favorite destinations" list. Even Floridians are rediscovering all that's great about the Sunshine State. The sea, sand, and Mickey Mouse are key reasons, but lots of travelers are finding another side to this beautiful state—its caves and springs, lakes and rivers, rich history and cultural breadth. The hardest part is parceling out exactly what you can cover in a week or two of vacation time (without going home exhausted). That's where we come in.

Start planning your trip by narrowing your options. Beaches, golfing, theme parks, resort hotels, deep-sea fishing, backcountry canoeing—Florida has it all. In this book, we've divided the state into ten regions and ordered them roughly from north to south: The Northwest and Panhandle, the Northeast, the Space Coast, Orlando, the Central Gulf Coast, the Gold and Treasure Coasts, Southwest Florida, Miami and Miami Beach, the Everglades, and the Keys.

Every region of Florida offers something special, from beaches and parklands to wonderful hotels and restaurants. There's world-class shopping, every kind of spectator sport, and an abundance of tourist attractions. This book will tell you where to find the best of the best. We'll point out the good values and tell you what we consider a waste of time and money, hopefully making your visit more fun, efficient, and economical.

Other *Unofficial* guidebooks that might also be helpful when planning your Florida vacation are the *Unofficial Guide to South Florida including Miami & the Keys*, the *Unofficial Guide to Florida with Kids*, the *Unofficial Guide to Walt Disney World*, and *Beyond Disney: The Unofficial Guide to Universal, SeaWorld, and the Best of Central Florida*.

How *Unofficial* Guides Are Different

The Unofficial Guide to Florida is for individuals and families traveling for fun as well as for business travelers and convention-goers. First-time visitors and Florida-vacation veterans alike will find the helpful tips and evaluations that add up to a (pleasantly) unforgettable vacation. Our readers are value-conscious, adventuresome adults, many with families, who seek a cost-effective but comfortable travel style. We simplify complicated destinations and attractions, giving you control even in the most unfamiliar environments.

We don't provide all the info possible, just the most accessible and useful—unbiased by affiliation with any organization or industry. Our authors and research team are completely independent from the attractions, restaurants, and hotels we describe. We work for you alone because we want you to have the best trip possible.

Comments and Suggestions from Readers

We learn from our mistakes, and from reader input. Many of you write with your own discoveries and lessons learned on Florida vacations. We appreciate both positive and critical input, and encourage you to continue writing.

How to Contact the Author:

Pam Brandon
The Unofficial Guide to Florida
P.O. Box 43673
Birmingham, AL 35243
unofficialguides@menasharidge.com

Be sure to put your return address on your letter as well as on the envelope—sometimes they get separated. And remember, our work takes us out of the office for long periods, so forgive us if our response is delayed.

How Information Is Organized

Where you choose a hotel (or condo) will shape your Florida vacation more than any other decision. Therefore, we devote an initial section to lodging options. To facilitate touring, we present information on attractions, restaurants, and nightlife geographically, dividing the state into ten areas.

The **Florida Panhandle** has sugar-white beaches and more than 50 miles of shoreline that invite you to slip off your shoes and step into sand so fine it squeaks (locals call it "barking") beneath your feet.

Northeast Florida offers authentic history lessons and the great outdoors in a region alive with meticulously re-created historic districts, natural springs, lush inland forests, tree-lined rivers, and wide beaches.

Daytona and the Space Coast, home to sand, surf, space shuttles, and the Speedway, stretch southward down the Atlantic coast.

Orlando is the state's number one destination, and most visitors flock there to experience one thing: Walt Disney World. But there's another side to Central Florida—one of the country's largest national forests, and more than 1,000 lakes and rivers.

The **Central Gulf Coast** has beautiful beaches, man-made attractions, sports, and history. Beaches boast an annual average of 361 days of sunshine, an average water temperature of 75 degrees, and glorious sunsets, which you miss on the Atlantic coast of Florida.

The **Gold and Treasure Coasts,** on Florida's eastern shore, were originally named for the sunken treasure of ships wrecked along the rocky shore. Today, wealthy, cosmopolitan cities like Palm Beach, Boca Raton, and Fort Lauderdale give the monikers a whole new meaning.

Southwest Florida is booming as a tourism and retirement destination, but one that emphasizes nature and ecology. With more than a million acres of nature sanctuaries, area tourists can still explore virginal Florida and observe wildlife thriving in natural settings.

Miami and **Miami Beach** comprise an international destination that doesn't require a passport, with remarkable cultural diversity. Likewise, Miami is a gateway for Latin Americans and Europeans visiting the United States and a major cruise embarkation point.

Everglades National Park is the paragon of outdoor Florida. The as-yet-unspoiled wetlands of the largest national park east of the Rockies are home to a dazzling array of flora and fauna.

The **Florida Keys** are filled with sights and activities to enjoy, including world-class diving and sport fishing, and Key West is a major cruise port, drawing more than a million visitors each year.

Florida Maps and Profiles

In order to help you assess your travel options throughout Florida, we've organized material, using several formats. Maps allow you to plan efficient touring. Easy-to-read profiles help you determine what to see and do.

Hotels With so many lodging choices, our maps, ratings, and rankings help you focus and decide. We concentrate on the major variables: location, size, room quality, services, amenities, and cost.

Golf Courses Golf is a major industry in the Sunshine State, so we've included thorough profiles of the best courses in each region, concentrating on those most accommodating to travelers.

Attractions We've provided detailed profiles of the best attractions in Florida. We rate each attraction by age group to help you decide which ones are right for you. And we provide recommendations on other things to do nearby so you can plan a full day of sight-seeing.

Restaurants We provide detailed profiles of a variety of the best restaurants in Florida—from informal to posh.

Entertainment and Nightlife We spotlight the best bars, clubs, and lounges throughout Florida, indicating what sorts of crowds, music, and prices to anticipate.

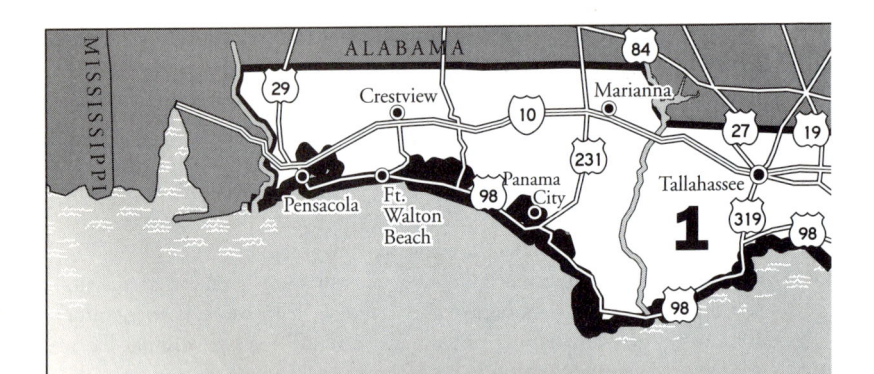

Florida Touring Zones

1 The Florida Panhandle — page 100
2 Northeast Florida — page 148
3 Daytona and the Space Coast — page 197
4 Orlando and Beyond — page 239
5 The Central Gulf Coast — page 300
6 The Gold and Treasure Coasts — page 347
7 Southwest Florida — page 396
8 Miami and Miami Beach — page 435
9 The Everglades — page 478
10 The Florida Keys — page 490

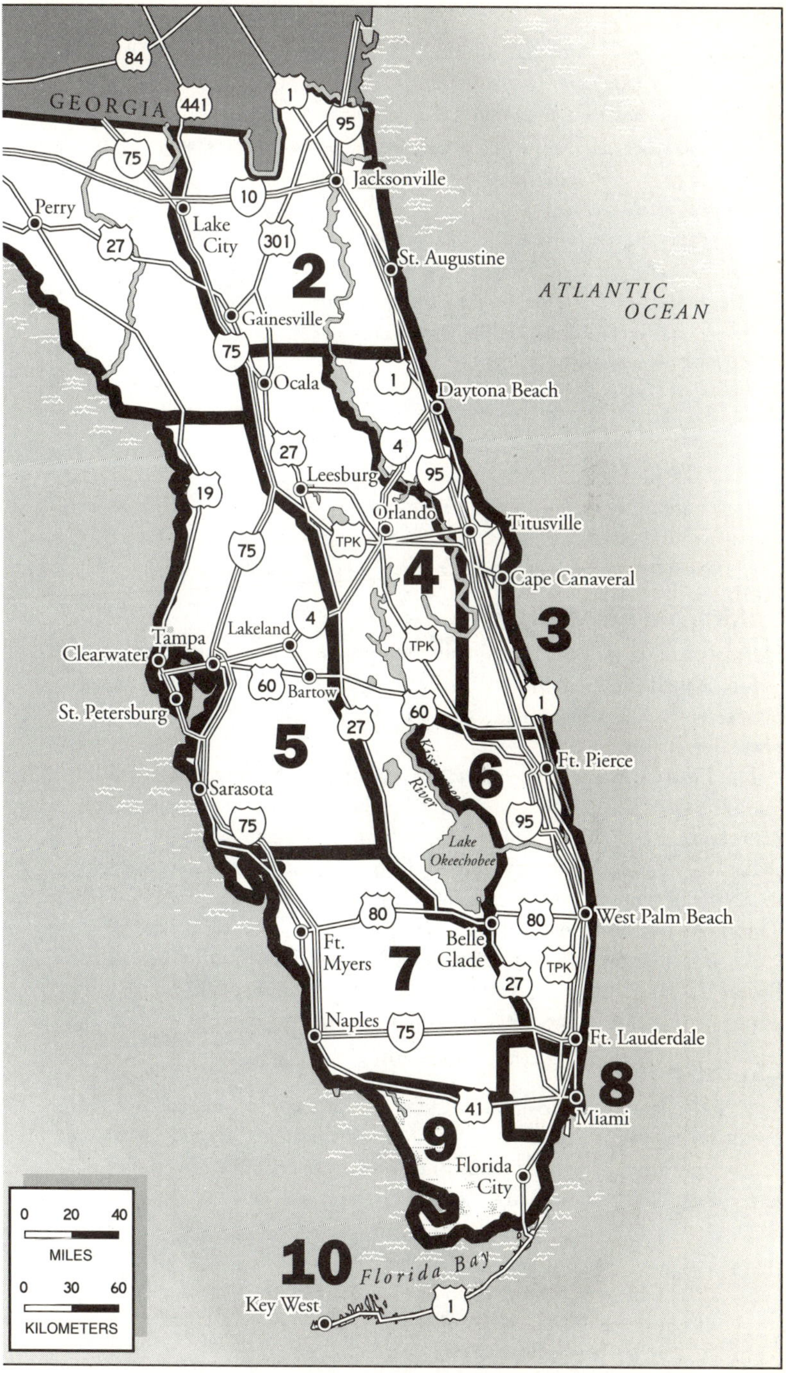
GEORGIA
84
441
1
95
75
10
Jacksonville
Perry
Lake City
301
27
St. Augustine
2
ATLANTIC OCEAN
Gainesville
75
Ocala
1
Daytona Beach
4
27
95
Leesburg
19
Orlando
Titusville
TPK
75
4
Cape Canaveral
3
4
Lakeland
Tampa
Clearwater
TPK
60
Bartow
1
St. Petersburg
60
27
5
Kissimmee River
6
Ft. Pierce
Sarasota
75
95
Lake Okeechobee
80
80
West Palm Beach
Ft. Myers
7
Belle Glade
TPK
27
Naples
75
Ft. Lauderdale
8
41
Miami
9
Florida City
0 20 40
MILES
0 30 60
KILOMETERS
10
Florida Bay
Key West
1

Special Features

Our goal is to give you what you need for a maximum Florida travel experience, so this *Unofficial Guide* offers:
- Easy-to-read hotel information and accompanying maps.
- Brief overviews of the history of each region, to put things in perspective.
- "Highlights"—savvy opinions on five top attractions in each region you don't want to miss.
- Well-organized, easy-to-read attraction profiles, keyed to your interests.
- Our favorite golf courses, restaurants, and nightclubs.
- Maps to help you find what you want, and avoid what you don't.
- Practical tips and inside information that locals know, but tourists usually don't, including the best places to shop.
- A detailed index.

Planning Your Visit

In each section, we include contact information for the region's major tourist bureaus, chambers of commerce, etc. We highly recommend contacting these organizations for information on area offerings and special events.

Before You Leave Home

Florida vacation guides are available in versions for the United States, the United Kingdom, Germany, France, and Spain from **Visit Florida Headquarters** (P.O. 1100, Tallahassee, FL 32302-1100; (888) 7-FLA-USA; www.flausa.com).

The **Florida Attractions Association** (P.O. Box 10295, Tallahassee, FL 32302; (850) 222-2885) has guide maps and information on museums, parks and natural areas, theme parks, cruises, and tours.

For hiking, biking, and canoeing information on **Florida's state parks,** write or call the Division of Parks and Recreation, Mail Station 536, 3900 Commonwealth Boulevard, Tallahassee, FL 32399-3000; (850) 488-9872.

For information on touring **Florida's historical sites,** write or call the Bureau of Historical Preservation, R. A. Gray Building, 500 South Bronough Street, Tallahassee, FL 32399-0250; (850) 245-6333.

On the Road

The State of Florida maintains Official Florida Welcome Centers for motorists on major arteries leading into and through the state. Besides a break from driving, these centers can provide travelers information on local attractions, help booking lodgings, and discount coupons.

- I-95 7 miles north of Yulee on I-95 South; phone (904) 225-9182; fax (904) 225-0064
- I-75 4 miles north of Jennings on I-75 South; phone (904) 938-2981; fax (904)-938-1292
- I-10 16 miles west of Pensacola on I-10 East; phone (850) 944-0442; fax (850) 944-3675

| US 231 | 3 miles north of Campbellton; phone/fax (850) 263-3510 |
| The Capitol Plaza Level | The Capitol, Tallahassee, 32301; phone (850) 488-6167; fax (850) 414-2560 |

Information and Access for Disabled Visitors

Most public places in Florida now offer facilities for disabled visitors, including wheelchair access. Even small hotels now offer elevators, ramps, and bathroom railings to make their rooms wheelchair accessible. Plus, many buses have lowering platforms that allow wheelchair-bound passengers to board. Even in Everglades National Park, all the walking trails are wheelchair accessible.

Florida State law requires guide dogs be permitted in all establishments. Also, motorists must yield to people with white canes and guide dogs.

Out-of-state vehicles displaying disability parking permits/plates issued by another state are allowed to park in spaces designated for persons with disabilities.

Websites Recommended by the Society for the Advancement of Travel for the Handicapped

www.access-able.com	Access-Able Travel Source
www.disabilitytravel.com	Accessible Journeys
www.accessiblevans.com	Accessible Vans of America
www.blvd.com/wg	Wheelchair Getaways

FLORIDA FAST FACTS

Nickname The Sunshine State

History Florida has belonged to five different nations—Spain, England, France, the Confederacy, and the United States. The state's first permanent European settlement was at St. Augustine, founded in 1565.

State Capital Tallahassee

Water, Water Everywhere There are 7,700 lakes, 34 major rivers, 320 springs, and a beach no more than 60 miles from any spot.

National Parklands The state has two national parks: Biscayne National Park and Everglades National Park, both in South Florida. And there are four national forests: Apalachicola, Choctawhatchee, Osceola, and Ocala.

Time Zones Most of the state is in the Eastern Time Zone. West of the Apalachicola River, the Panhandle is in the Central Time Zone.

Geography From Pensacola to Key West, the distance is 832 miles. It has the longest tidal coastline in the lower 48 states—1,197 miles of coastline with 663 miles of beaches. And the state has more than 4,000 islands ten acres or larger, more than any state except Alaska.

Weather and When to Go

Florida weather can be quite varied though South Florida rarely dips below the 70s, it snows on occasion in the Panhandle.

When to travel in the Sunshine State depends on what you plan to do. If you're here for the Central Florida attractions, the least crowded times (and the best weather) are January through March and late September through Thanksgiving. For camping, nothing beats the winter months, with cooler weather and hibernating mosquitoes. Summertime is best for inexpensive beach vacations and trips to the Panhandle and Northern Florida.

Average summertime temperatures range from the low to mid 80s, though they can soar into the 90s, especially in the south. The intense sun, high temperatures, and humidity can be oppressive, but the thermometer doesn't tell the whole story: Most natives pay more attention to a weather forecast's humidity levels than the day's high temperature (80% humidity is comfortable; the high 90s are not).

November through April offers the lowest humidity, blue skies, and plenty of sunshine. But it's also peak tourist season in the southern half of the state, starting just before Christmas and ending just after Easter. Lines get long at major tourist destinations; small attractions get inundated; and finding a hotel room that's both convenient and affordable is more difficult.

The "shoulder seasons"—during April and May and from September to November—are great times to visit any part of the state. Temperatures are milder, and hotel rates are lower. In general, popular tourist sights are busier on weekends than weekdays, and Saturdays are busier than Sundays.

AVERAGE TEMPERATURES (FAHRENHEIT/CELSIUS) IN VARIOUS FLORIDA CITIES

	Jan	Feb	Mar	Apr	May	Jun	July	Aug	Sept	Oct	Nov	Dec
Orlando	60/16	63/17	66/19	71/22	78/26	82/28	82/28	82/28	81/27	75/24	67/19	61/16
Miami	69/21	70/21	71/22	74/23	78/26	81/27	82/28	84/29	81/27	78/26	73/23	70/21
Tampa	60/16	61/16	66/19	72/22	77/25	81/27	82/28	82/28	81/27	75/24	67/19	62/17
Key West	69/21	72/22	74/23	77/25	80/27	82/28	85/29	85/29	84/29	80/27	74/23	72/22
Tallahassee	52/11	56/13	63/17	68/20	72/22	78/26	81/27	81/27	77/25	74/23	66/19	59/15

Warm Weather Precautions

For comfort, as well as crowd and thunderstorm avoidance, try to schedule touring, tennis, golf, and sight-seeing early in the day or late in the afternoon. Summer storms—complete with world-class lightning shows—can be a daily occurrence and usually strike in late afternoon. Plan your exercise and recreation for the morning to avoid storms as well the heat of mid-afternoon. Summer travelers should stash rain ponchos, sunscreen, and bottle water, no matter what the activity.

Keep in mind the afternoon thunderstorms if you plan to camp; unless you're on the ocean, it's extremely humid and mosquitoes can be unbearable. Still if you can stand the heat and humidity, bargains are plentiful at the beach.

Remember: South Florida shares the same latitude as the Sahara Desert. Always wear sunscreen and reapply it regularly, especially after swimming. Dehydration, like sunburn, is a constant threat in Florida's hot summer, but is as easily avoided. Carry a bottle of water around with you, and keep hydrated. Lastly, dress appropriately. You'll be much more comfortable in shorts than in jeans, and in pastels and whites than in darker hues.

Beach Precautions

On Florida beaches, red flags warn you not to swim, although beaches are rarely closed and swimmers may choose to ignore the warning. Yellow flags mean caution; ask the lifeguard to tell you the specific hazard (jellyfish, rip tide, etc.). However, the most common hazard on the beach isn't rough water or bad weather—it's the sun. Cloudy days pose a particular hazard because beach-goers often underestimate the exposure their skin receives and end up burned.

Rip tides, also called undertow, usually occur when winds are blowing ashore from 15 to 20 miles an hour, creating a break off-shore that drains water from the beach. Even if you're a strong swimmer, don't fight a rip tide. Rather, swim with the undertow parallel to the beach. Eventually, you'll break free.

Panic is far more dangerous than rip tides themselves. The same is true for cramps or other swimming hazards. Sometimes as tides come in, swimmers find themselves in deeper water, realize they can't touch bottom, and panic. It is wise to cast frequent glances ashore (or to children playing in the waves) and to position yourself near a lifeguard.

Pale, pink jellyfish can appear on Florida's shores at any time, but are more common in the winter. Portuguese men-of-war, bluish-purple translucent creatures as beautiful as Tiffany glass, are more common in the summer. Both have tentacles that sting. Yellow warning flags indicate their presence in the water. If they wash ashore, avoid stepping on them—the tentacles still sting. If you get stung, go to a lifeguard for help, or if you are feeling really unwell, a hospital emergency room. In the absence of help, scrape the tentacle away from the skin using a credit card or something similar (don't touch it) and treat the sting with vinegar.

Sea lice—actually the spores of Portuguese men-of-war—are invisible creatures that cause an itchy rash also called "swimmers' eruption." The rash lasts about a week and can be treated with cortisone lotion. Avoid seaweed or anything else floating in the water, since the spores usually come ashore on a host.

Stingrays, another potential hazard, bury themselves in the sand. Occasionally, swimmers step on them, and the barb on the end of a stingrays tail, while it isn't poisonous, is usually dirty and poses an infection risk.

Finally, what about everybody's beach fear: sharks? Shark attack is the least of your worries at the beach—in Florida or elsewhere. Attacks are very rare. Nevertheless, shark sightings are taken very seriously. Often the Coast Guard will investigate and clear nearby beaches.

Other hazards? Lots of children—and adults—manage to lose their bearings and are thus separated from their companions, cars, or possessions. Make note of some permanent landmark (a building, lifeguard stand, etc.) to use as a reference point. Likewise, take precautions not to roam when snorkeling and diving, and always mark your location with a diving flag so you're not run over by a boat. Lastly, don't exceed your physical limits by swimming too far from shore.

The Best of Florida

Florida touring has long been associated with sun, surf, and sport. Throughout the region, the standards for relaxation and recreation are high, but some are "the best." Below is our best-of list for Florida. For more information on each venue, see complete listings in each chapter.

Best Beaches
Bill Baggs Cape Florida Recreation Area (Miami and Miami Beach)
Caladesi Island State Park (Central Gulf)
Canaveral National Seashore (Space Coast)
Captiva Beach (Southwest)
Grayton Beach State Recreation Area (Panhandle)
John D. MacArthur Beach (Gold Coast and Treasure Coasts)
St. George Island State Park (Panhandle)

Best Shelling
Captiva Island (Lee Island Coast, Southwest)
Sanibel Island (Lee Island Coast, Southwest)
Shell Island (Central Gulf)

Best Views of Nature
Canaveral National Seashore (Space Coast)
Everglades National Park
Babcock Wilderness Adventures (Southwest)
J. N. "Ding" Darling National Wildlife Refuge (Southwest)
Ocala National Forest (Orlando and Walt Disney World)
Wakulla Springs State Park (Panhandle)

Best Golf
Doral Blue Course (Miami and Miami Beach)
Grand Cypress Resort (Walt Disney World and Orlando)
PGA National Golf Club (Gold and Treasure Coasts)
Walt Disney World Osprey Ridge Course (Walt Disney World and Orlando)
World Golf Village, Slammer and Squire Course (Northeast)

Best Sport Fishing
Florida Keys (Islamorada)
Gold and Treasure Coasts (Palm Beach)

Southwest Florida (The Coastal Islands)
Panhandle (Destin)

Best Museums for Adults
Billie Swamp Safari and Ah-Tah-Thi-Ki Museum, Big Cypress Reservation (Gold and Treasure Coasts)
Flagler Museum (Gold and Treasure Coasts)
Morse Museum of American Art (Walt Disney World and Orlando)
Norton Museum of Art (Gold and Treasure Coasts)
Ringling Museum Complex (Central Gulf)
Salvador Dali Museum (Central Gulf)
The Wolfsonian (Miami and Miami Beach)

Best Museum for Children
Colonial Spanish Quarter Museum (Northeast)
Imaginarium (Southwest)
The Museum of Discovery & Science/Blockbuster IMAX 3-D (Gold and Treasure Coasts)
Museum of Science and Industry (Central Gulf)
Orlando Science Center (Walt Disney World and Orlando)

Best Performing Arts Venues
Broward Theater of the Performing Arts (Gold and Treasure Coasts)
Kravis Center in Palm Beach (Gold and Treasure Coasts)
Performing Arts Center in Miami (Miami and Miami Beach)
Philharmonic Center for the Arts in Naples (Southwest)

Best Historic Sites
Castillos de San Marcos National Monument, St. Augustine (Northeast)
Edison's Winter Home and Museum (Fort Myers/Southwest)
Henry Morrison Flagler Museum (Palm Beach/Gold and Treasure Coasts)
Vizcaya Museum and Gardens, Coconut Grove (Miami and Miami Beach)

Best Dining Choices
Boss Oyster in Apalachicola (Panhandle)
California Grill at Walt Disney World (Walt Disney World and Orlando)
Columbia Restaurant in Ybor City (Central Gulf)
Criolla's in Grayton Beach (Panhandle)
Joe's Stone Crab (Miami and Miami Beach)
Mark's at Mizner Park in Boca Raton (Gold and Treasure Coasts)
Norman's in Coral Gables (Miami and Miami Beach)

Best Shopping
Bal Harbour Shops (Miami and Miami Beach)
Fifth Avenue South in Naples (Southwest)
Mall at Millenia (Walt Disney World and Orlando)
Sawgrass Mills (Gold and Treasure Coasts)

Visiting Florida with Children

Sunshine State vacation activities with big appeal for children range from theme parks to butterfly-watching, from nature walks among alligators to beaches, beaches, beaches.

12 Introduction

Most families with children visit Florida during the summer months, when the weather is hot and humid. So, before starting off on a day of touring or a visit to the beach, head off potential problems.

Sunburn, Overheating, and Dehydration Sunburn in young children can cause lifelong problems. Doctors advise putting sunscreen on every morning before breakfast. Sweat, friction, and rain dilute sunscreen, so it must be reapplied throughout the day.

SPF 15 and above is appropriate for tan skin and 30 and above for fair skin. Don't forget to put sunscreen on the neck, top of the shoulders, tops of feet, and scalp, if hair is thin or absent. Sunscreen should include the UVA blockers Parsol or Avobenzone. Remember sunglasses and hats, and be especially careful in the sun between 11 a.m. and 3 p.m.

Don't count on keeping small children properly hydrated with soft drinks and water fountains. Long lines at popular attractions often make buying refreshments problematic, and water fountains are not always handy. What's more, excited children may not inform you or even realize that they're thirsty or overheated. We recommend carrying plastic water bottles in your stroller.

The Beach Don't let kids swim alone; don't even leave them alone on the beach. Practice the buddy system (good advice even for adults); it's easy to become disoriented in the water. Pay attention to lifeguards, who warn of hazards like rip tides. For more information on the hazards of the beach and ocean swimming, see our section on beach safety above.

Blisters Wear comfortable, well-broken-in shoes or sandals. If you or your children are unusually susceptible to blisters, carry some precut moleskin bandages; they offer the best possible protection, stick great, and won't sweat off. When you feel a hot spot, stop, air out your foot, and place a moleskin patch over the area before a blister forms. Moleskin is available by name at drugstores.

Sometimes small children won't tell their parents about a developing blister until it's too late. We recommend inspecting the feet of preschoolers at least twice a day. Athletic socks absorb perspiration and might be your best bet.

Glasses If you want your smaller children to wear sunglasses, or if they wear prescription glasses, it's a good idea to affix a strap or string to the frames so the glasses won't get lost and can hang from the child's neck while indoors. Remember, ultraviolet coating is advised for sunglasses.

Top Attractions for Kids by Region

The Northwest and Panhandle
Old-fashioned amusement park rides at Miracle Strip, Panama City Beach
Glass-bottom boat ride at Wakulla Springs
A day at the ocean on St. George Island
A day at the ocean at Grayton Beach State Recreation Area
A guided tour of Florida Caverns State Park in Marianna

Visiting Florida with Children 13

Northeast Florida
Exploring Castillo de San Marcos National Monument in St. Augustine
A day at the secluded beach on Little Talbot Island State Park
Tubing down chilly Ichetucknee Springs
Wandering through real history in downtown St. Augustine
A climb to the top of the St. Augustine Lighthouse

The Space Coast
A visit to Kennedy Space Center
A night rocket launch (subject to launch schedules)
A day at Canaveral National Seashore
Daytona International Speedway and Daytona USA
Driving on the beach at Daytona Beach

Orlando and Beyond
The Magic Kingdom at Disney World
Islands of Adventure at Universal Orlando
Swimming with the dolphins at Discovery Cove
SeaWorld Orlando
Snorkeling, swimming, and canoeing in Ocala National Forest

The Central Gulf Coast
The roller coasters at Busch Gardens Tampa Bay
A day at Caladesi Island State Park
The Florida Aquarium in Tampa
A side trip to Weeki Wachee to see the mermaids
Clearwater Beach

The Gold and Treasure Coasts
A turtle walk on Hutchinson Island (May through August)
A day at John D. MacArthur Beach on Singer Island
Butterfly World
Lion Country Safari
A surfing lesson from the Surf School at Fort Pierce Inlet

Southwest Florida
Looking for seashells on Sanibel Island
Babcock Wilderness Adventures near Fort Myers
A canoe trip through the J. N. "Ding" Darling National Wildlife Refuge, Sanibel Island
Looking for shark's teeth on Venice Beach
Corkscrew Swamp Sanctuary, Naples

Miami and Miami Beach
Biscayne National Park
Miami Metrozoo
Miami Museum of Science/Space Transit Planetarium
Parrot Jungle and Gardens
Seaquarium

The Florida Keys
John Pennekamp Coral Reef State Park (Key Largo)
Swimming with the Dolphins at Dolphins Plus (Key Largo)
Fort Zachary Taylor State Historic Site (Key West)
Key West Aquarium
Tram Ride (Key West)

Part One

Accommodations

Deciding Where to Stay

Location, Location: An Overview of Your Options

Your motive for visiting Florida will naturally influence your choice of hotel. However, whether traveling for business or pleasure, to watch people or alligators, your primary consideration should be location. A lengthy commute to your meeting, to a museum, or, especially, to the beach is an unnecessary and unreasonable headache. While there are hotels all over Florida—some stuck in quite improbable places—we deal primarily with those hotels that are located in areas of concentrated tourist activity, business activity, or both. Besides your itinerary and budget, of course, a cursory knowledge of the various Florida communities with significant hotel concentrations will help you select the right location.

The Florida Panhandle: Pensacola, Fort Walton, Destin, Panama City, and Tallahassee

Pensacola is home to Eglin Air Force Base on Santa Rosa Island, as well as numerous hotels and motels near the airport and along highways. But it is also a gateway to Gulf Islands National Seashore, encompassing more than 135,000 acres of Florida and Mississippi shoreline along the coast of the Gulf of Mexico.

Pensacola itself is an older Florida town with a few great hotel values—especially compared to the nearby Gulf Shore offerings. The Seville historic district downtown dates back to the Civil War, and has been preserved by caring residents. Nearby is the small, historic New World Inn. Weekend deals are often available at the downtown Luxury Crowne Plaza Grand Hotel, a glass structure towering over the historic train station, which serves as part of the hotel lobby today and continues to function as a way station for trains, too.

Four-lane US 98 snakes between high-rise hotels, two-story motels, packed restaurants, and amusement attractions as it passes through **Destin,**

South Walton Beach, and the neighboring hamlets along the stretch of beach between Fort Walton Beach and Panama City. Many of the properties along this strip are managed by resort companies and include a selection of cottages and vacation homes. A few communities, such as **Seaside** and **Rosemary Beach,** reflect an architectural innovation called New Urbanism. Buildings are clustered together, cars are parked off premises (hidden in back lots and garages), and pedestrian paths and courtyards pass between buildings, creating what designers consider a friendlier community.

Apalachicola is a tiny fishing village. US 98 runs into town with a great flair—first a long, tall bridge over the Apalachicola River, then a quick twist brings all passersby right down into the heart of town. The historic village has begun a slow renaissance offering a few revitalized century-or-more-old buildings. Some have evolved into fine dining and accommodations, such as the stately three-story Gibson House.

Beach lovers may enjoy the rentals on **St. George Island,** but there's not much to do besides lounging on the soft white sand.

The **Panama City** area is known by some as the Redneck Riviera thanks to its popularity with spring breakers and summer vacationers from Southern and Midwestern states. The beachfront is crowded with low-priced motels, amusement parks, video galleries, and pizza joints.

Tallahassee, the seat of Florida's state government, has a surprising small-town feel. Quiet during the off-seasons, the town bustles when the legislature is in session. Roadside hotels are clustered along the highway interchanges and more sophisticated digs for politicos are found in the heart of town.

Northeast Florida: Amelia Island, Jacksonville, St. Augustine, and Gainesville

Amelia Island has an enchanting historical past as getaway for the rich and famous. Their homes have become an impressive collection of bed-and-breakfasts and guest houses in the downtown area, which caters to vacationers with interesting shops, excellent restaurants, and a convenient waterfront marina. Beachfront hotels are a fair distance from the historic district, with just a few restaurants to provide distraction from the sea. There is a good selection of vacation rental homes on the beach as well. On the southern tip of the island is a cluster of resort hotels, which offer luxurious vacations without stepping off the premises.

Jacksonville is a huge city geographically—the largest in the state in terms of square miles. Hotels are located all around the city along the highway bypass, I-295, as well as near the airport, downtown, and on the beach. Those in the busy downtown riverfront are sleek and modern, with easy access to city nightlife.

The historic and beach districts of **St. Augustine** are well tended and clean. The historic area is most amazing for its authentic appeal; although it is clearly a tourist zone, it is well preserved rather than re-created. Travelers can select from several hotels, bed-and-breakfasts, and even a hostel within the peaceful and educational historic district.

Home of the University of Florida, **Gainesville** is primarily a college town. The hotel scene reflects that, with a few campus-area hotels for prospective students and visiting parents. But most hotels line the road that runs from the school to the highway, Southwest 13th Street. Many of these hotels are older and their conditions vary. Newer hotel properties are clustered around the highway intersections.

The Space Coast:
Daytona Beach, New Smyrna Beach, and Cocoa Beach

Cocoa Beach has a tiny pier, quiet and surrounded by a few hotels and restaurants. There are not a lot of tourist attractions, which happens to be something that some tourists find attractive. The town offers a few blocks of quaint shops and a couple of excellent restaurants.

Daytona is a seasoned beach town, famous for its bikers, race fans, and spring breakers. Hardy locals drive their trucks along the wide, hard-sand beach lined with aging pubs and T-shirt parlors. The beachfront hotels suit the speed-demon crowds and good-time vacationers that frequent the area.

New Smyrna Beach is a clean, neat little beachside town with a tony historic district as well as slightly higher hotel prices. A great getaway destination when peace and quiet are on the agenda.

Titusville serves the space center with staff and military enrollees, but it's not a tourist town, except when visitors gather at riverside hotels for firsthand views of rocket launches.

Orlando and Central Florida

Although **Orlando** is best known for its endless amusement parks, the downtown area is a lovely, quaint town that has benefited from the economic boom of surrounding development. Grand hotels stand a few blocks from historic homes on tree-lined streets, with huge Lake Eola providing passive pleasure right in the heart of town. Airport hotels cater to the business crowd. Theme-park hotels, although not cheap, offer the significant advantage of proximity to the parks. Both Walt Disney World and Universal Orlando offer world-class hotels, though Disney's hotels cover a wider spectrum of quality and cost. A host of nearby properties, many on International Drive, range from bare-bones motels to themed resorts.

The Central Gulf Coast:
Tampa, St. Petersburg, and Sarasota

Despite its heavily congested urban area and attendant pollution, **Tampa** is a friendly town. The airport and downtown hotel districts both offer fine lodgings, though hotels in the downtown area and historic Ybor City nearby have more character.

Safety Harbor is just north of Tampa Bay, inland from Clearwater. It's a well-known getaway for fitness and history buffs. This scenic town is positioned over several mineral springs, purported to have healthful, restorative effects. A few shops dot its quaint downtown district.

St. Petersburg is a smaller city just across the bay from Tampa. The downtown area has been nicely restored and draws intellectuals as well as businesspeople thanks to the University of South Florida, Poynter Institute for Journalism, and the Salvador Dali Museum. West of the downtown area is Gulfport, a quiet bayside artists' community.

Off the coast of St. Petersburg, a claustrophobic cluster of rental properties lines Gulf Boulevard on Treasure Island, St. Petersburg Beach, and Indian Rocks Beach off Clearwater. Then the crowds give way to exclusive residential digs at Belleair Beach, with private homes and condos all the way to **Clearwater.** Then suddenly it's hotel heaven again, with several resorts and nicer hotels gathered near the causeway.

To the south, also famous for its arts community, is **Sarasota,** a bastion of wealthy and conservative Midwesterners with taste. Hotels are plentiful alongside I-75, downtown, near the airport, and on Longboat Key, a barrier island. Downtown boasts the fanciest selection for traveling businesspeople. The biggest bigwigs can stay at the Ritz-Carlton, vacation near St. Armand's Circle on Longboat, or on nearby Anna Maria Island.

The Gold and Treasure Coasts: Vero Beach, Palm Beach, and Fort Lauderdale

Vero Beach is a delightfully quiet, mostly residential community, with a few comfortable, non-touristy hotels on the beach. Southward, Fort Pierce is a working-class town famous for a Navy Underwater Demolition Teams/Seals training camp established in 1943. A few hotels serve tourists and anglers along the beachfront, and other, less appealing lodgings line US 1.

Farther south, the town of **Jensen Beach** offers beach hotels as well as cute cottages and a fish camp along the Indian River. The town of **Stuart** has a small, quiet historic district with a few shops, and **Jupiter** and **Juno** offer nice, undisturbed beach areas.

Palm Beach is home or getaway to some of the nation's wealthiest citizens, and many have lived or vacationed here for generations. The high-end hotels have a certain well-worn elegance and charm. A small shopping area offers fine dining and boutique shopping in a village atmosphere.

In **West Palm Beach,** downtown hotels offer the most excitement, or try nearby **Boca Raton** and **Delray Beach,** with a few, not-too-crowded beach hotels and a few exceptional historic bed-and-breakfasts and hotels. Boca is more ritzy, while Delray offers a pleasant, quaint downtown area that often comes alive with street fairs and festivals.

In northern Broward County, **Pompano Beach** offers good value and a wide, golden beach, while **Lauderdale-by-the-Sea** offers a quaint, convenient village atmosphere—great for vacationers without cars.

Fort Lauderdale Beach is a hot spot for the young crowd day and night. Well-heeled sophisticates enjoy shops and restaurants around Las Olas Boulevard, and the town's historic district has broad appeal with the

Broward Center for the Performing Arts, as well as a few good restaurants and night clubs.

Dania Beach is not fancy—just a quiet village known for its antique stores as well as its close proximity to the airport. **Hollywood's** renovated downtown area provides a pleasant stroll among shops and eateries, although some seem rather high-priced. Unfortunately, the downtown area is more than a walk from the beach, where there are only a few restaurants and T-shirt shops.

Miami and Miami Beach

Miami is a colorful, diverse city with pockets of dense, poor communities as well as world-class destinations. Although there is a variety of hotels near the airport, the most interesting areas for visitors are Coconut Grove, Coral Gables, and Miami Beach.

Hotels in downtown **Miami** are close to the Port of Miami, the Orange Bowl, city government, the airport, and Miami's business and financial center. The Miami Beach Convention Center is a 15-minute commute under optimal traffic conditions. Downtown Miami is not particularly active after business hours, however, and the choice of restaurants and nightspots is decidedly limited compared to Miami Beach, Coral Gables, or Coconut Grove. Hotels situated near the airport are convenient to Coral Gables, downtown Miami, major expressways, Pro Player Stadium (home of the Miami Dolphins), and Fort Lauderdale.

Coral Gables is about two miles south of the airport and four miles southwest of downtown. A banking and trade center as well as one of Miami's nicest residential areas, Coral Gables is also home to the University of Miami and the Miracle Mile shopping venues, and many of the city's finest restaurants. Miami Beach and the Miami Beach Convention Center are a complicated 30- to 50-minute commute from Coral Gables, however.

Coconut Grove is an upscale bayside community framed on the west and south by Coral Gables. Coconut Grove is convenient to a number of attractions, including Parrot Jungle, Miami Seaquarium, Fairchild Tropical Garden, and Vizcaya. Key Biscayne and various Biscayne Bay marinas are also easily accessible from Coconut Grove.

Miami Beach is situated on a barrier east of downtown Miami. The Art Deco District, extending from 5th Street northward along the beach to 15th Street, represents Miami Beach at its finest. Hotels here are small, independently owned, and architecturally distinctive in the Deco/Caribbean style of Miami Beach's original tourist boom. While parking is virtually nonexistent, dozens of restaurants and clubs are within easy walking distance—and so is the beach. The Miami Beach Convention Center is a 20- to 30-minute walk or a 5- to 10-minute cab ride away. Hotel rooms, and particularly baths, in the Art Deco District may be smaller than you would find in a chain hotel, but they are often beautifully appointed. On Miami Beach to the north of the official historic district (from 5th to 15th Streets), there are many hotels in the Art Deco style that eventually melt into larger hotels, and may or may not have been recently renovated. If you want to stay in the heart of the Art Deco District, confirm that your hotel is located across from Lummus Park (beach front) or on Collins Avenue (one block west of the beach) between 5th and 15th Streets.

In **North Miami Beach,** Collins Avenue north of Arthur Godfrey to the Kennedy Causeway (71st Street), is the home of Miami Beach's fabled hotel giants. Though many of the great hotels are gone and others have been renamed or replaced by skyward-stretching condominiums, the Fontainebleau and the Eden Roc, among others, still invite visitors to relive the zenith of Miami Beach's golden age. Huge, commanding, and magnificent after 40 years, these hotels offer elaborate swimming pools, landscaped gardens, meeting facilities, shopping arcades, and a variety of restaurants. The nightlife and restaurants of South Miami Beach are a 10- to 30-minute drive away, depending on traffic. The Miami Beach Convention Center is 10 to 20 minutes by cab or convention-sponsored bus.

Bal Harbour is an isolated oceanside bastion of affluence and beauty. Large, modern, well-maintained hotels alternate with equally imposing condominiums. The Bal Harbour Shops, one of the most diverse and tasteful shopping venues in the Southeast, is situated at the 96th Street end of the area. Nearby to the north is Haulover Park and Marina. The airport and Miami Beach Convention Center are about 40 to 55 minutes away by car.

Across the Haulover Cut (back on the mainland) are **Sunny Isles** and **Golden Shores.** This area was developed during the late 1950s and early 1960s and is characterized by small, motel-sized properties with exotic themes ranging from space travel to the Suez Canal. While there are some nice rooms, many of the properties have seen better days. The area is pretty remote unless you are bound for the Calder Race Track or Pro Player Stadium.

Southwest Florida: Fort Myers, Sanibel and Captiva Islands, Naples, and Marco Island

Fort Myers itself is an aged little town, faintly scenic along its waterfront, with an authentic village atmosphere downtown all the more charming for its lack of polish. Downtown hotels provide nice respite for business travelers, although the airport is located about half-an-hour away, southeast of the city. The airport is well served by the many hotels that line the highway, interstate I-75.

Pine Island and **Matlacha** are a pair of islands strung together off the coast of Fort Myers near Cape Coral. Matlacha provides an interesting land bridge to Pine Island, and is lined with funky hotels, galleries, shops, restaurants, and rustic cottages. Pine Island is still a rural farming community producing mangoes, avocadoes, and star fruit. Bokeelia, at the tip of the island that reaches into Charlotte Harbor, offers a few small rentals that provide a peaceful and remote island getaway.

Bonita Springs is a small city sandwiched between Naples and Fort Myers with just a few hotels overlooking vast preserves of oceanfront wetlands and parklands.

In contrast, **Fort Myers Beach** is terribly congested except toward the southern tip, a resort and residential area. It's a big getaway for Midwesterners, but it is also notable as a place with many European immigrants, particularly among those who own vacation properties.

Sanibel and **Captiva** are well-known vacation spots. Sanibel is well guarded by savvy residents who understand the great value of preserving the native growth of trees, grasses, and groundcover. The result is a peaceful oasis, with small hotels and cottages dotting the shorelines instead of wall-to-wall concrete that blocks the views and breezes. Captiva is much smaller than Sanibel and more crowded, although there are still a number of private residences lining the waterfront. In the village area near the western tip of the island, new development creates a glut of civilization.

Marco is a tidy, remote island village that serves as a popular winter residence for the wealthy. **Naples** was once a similar vacation haven, but is quickly evolving into a commercial city. Visitors can enjoy the finest in four- and five-star beach area hotels, as well as prime dining and shopping experiences. Yet the long-standing residential foundation of well-heeled citizens has protected the natural ambience of the fast-growing city. Vacationers can join eagles at the beach or commune with hundreds of passing flocks at the Audubon Society's Corkscrew Swamp Sanctuary bordering the Everglades.

The Everglades

Everglades City is a fishermen's village famous for its stone crabs and nefarious residents. Digs here are simple, many without phones, but some offer an aged charm. Folks are friendly and time passes gently if you enjoy exploring quiet, natural waterways filled with dolphins, manatees, and mullet.

The Florida Keys and Key West

Florida City is the gateway to the Florida Keys, most popular with fishers and those divers drawn to the coral reef . . . at least until you reach **Key West,** 100 miles from the mainland. Once a paradise for artists and writers, the city has evolved into a tourist destination especially popular among gays. Large hotels crowd the waterfront and their shops encroach on historic Duval Street, replacing some of the charm with modern buildings crowds. But many of the historic homes nearby have been renovated into guest houses, each with its own charm and style. As a tourist mecca, Key West offers many excellent restaurants to choose from, crafts created by local artisans, and millions of T-shirts.

Getting a Good Deal on a Room

High Season vs. Low Season

High season in most of Florida runs from Christmas through Easter. Additionally, some hotels observe a second high season from mid-June through mid-August, known as the family season. Room rates for many hotels are 25%–50% higher during these times of year. September, October, November (excluding the Thanksgiving holiday), and the first two weeks of December are the best times for obtaining low rates. Be aware, though, that large conventions can drive rates up regardless of the season. Check with your destination city's convention and visitors bureau to make sure your visit does not fall during a big meeting or trade show.

Special Weekend Rates

While well-located hotels typically charge higher rates, it's not impossible to get a good deal and a convenient location, at least relatively speaking. For starters, most downtown hotels that cater to business, government, and convention travelers offer special weekend discount rates that range from 15% to 40% below normal weekday rates. You can find out about weekend specials by calling the hotel or consulting your travel agent.

Getting Corporate Rates

Many hotels offer discounted corporate rates (5%–20% off rack rates). Usually you do not need to work for a large company or have a special relationship with the hotel to get these rates. Simply call the hotel of your choice and ask for their corporate rates. Many hotels will guarantee you the discounted rate on the phone when you make your reservation. Others may make the rate conditional on your providing some sort of bona fides, for instance a fax on your company's letterhead requesting the rate or a company credit card or business card on check-in. Generally, the screening is not rigorous.

Preferred Rates

If you cannot book the hotel of your choice through a half-price program, you may search for a lesser discount, often called a "preferred rate." A preferred rate could be a discount made available to travel agents to stimulate their booking activity or a discount initiated to attract a certain class of traveler. Most preferred rates are promoted through travel industry publications and are often accessible only through an agent.

We recommend sounding out your travel agent about possible deals. Be aware, however, that the rates shown on travel agents' computerized reservations systems are not always the lowest rates available. Zero in on a couple of hotels that fill your needs in terms of location and quality of accommodations, then have your travel agent call for the latest rates and specials.

Wholesalers, Consolidators, and Reservation Services

Wholesalers and consolidators buy rooms, or options on rooms (room blocks), from hotels at a low, negotiated rate. They then resell the rooms at a profit through travel agents, tour packagers, or directly to the public. The wholesaler's or consolidator's relationship with any hotel is predicated on volume. Thus, wholesalers and consolidators often offer rooms at bargain rates, anywhere from 15% to 50% off rack, occasionally sacrificing profit margin in the process, to avoid returning the rooms to the hotel unsold.

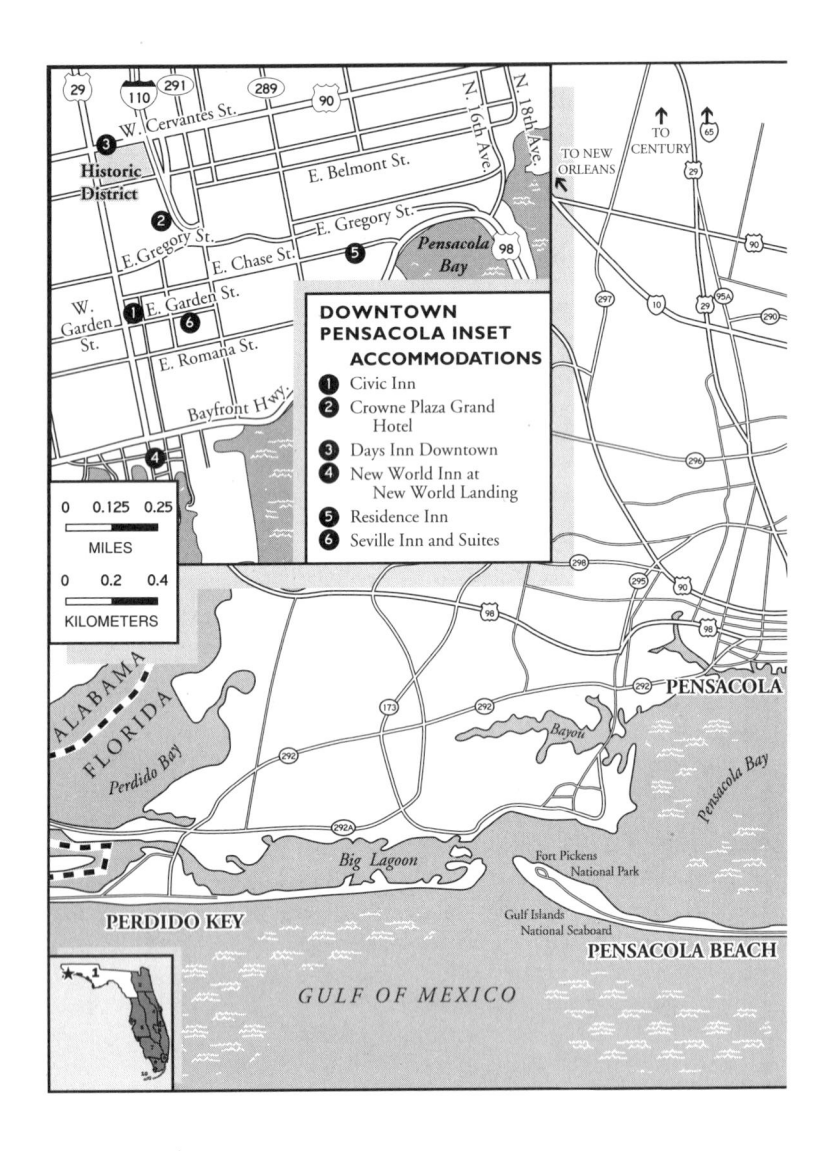

DOWNTOWN PENSACOLA INSET
ACCOMMODATIONS
1. Civic Inn
2. Crowne Plaza Grand Hotel
3. Days Inn Downtown
4. New World Inn at New World Landing
5. Residence Inn
6. Seville Inn and Suites

Pensacola and Pensacola Beach

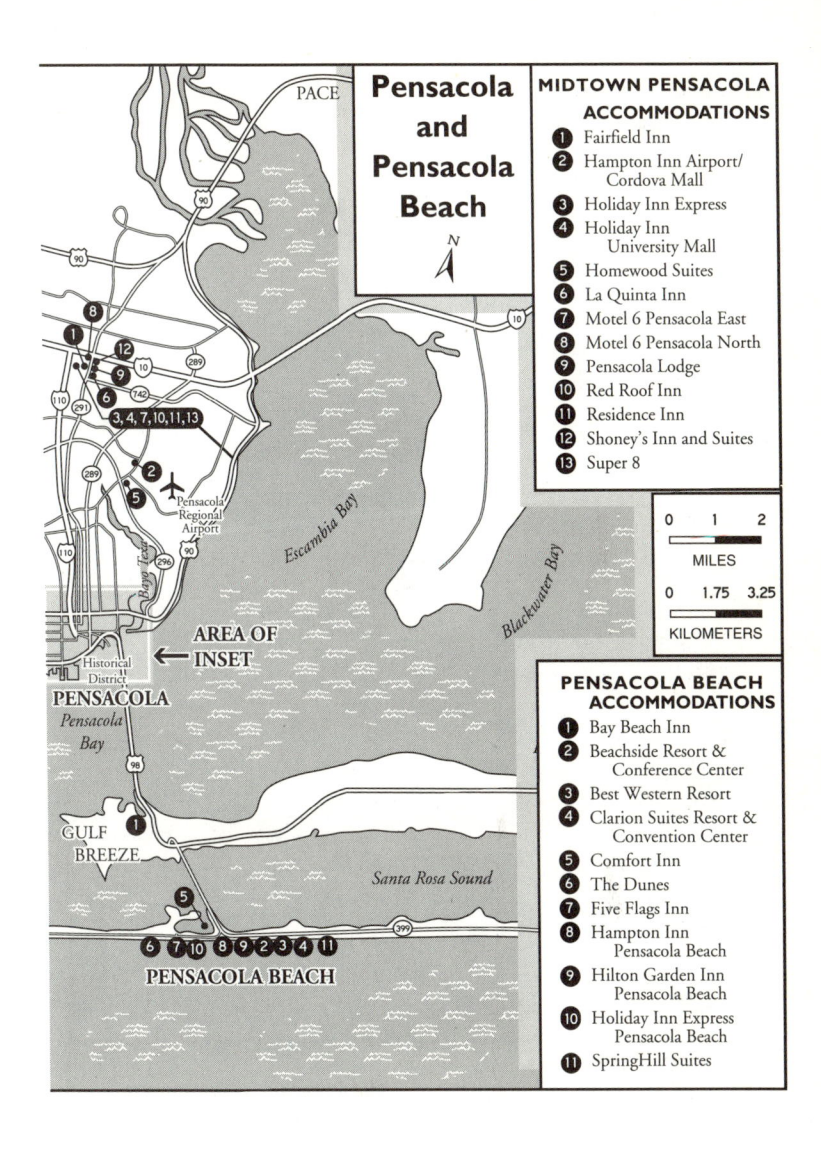

MIDTOWN PENSACOLA ACCOMMODATIONS

1. Fairfield Inn
2. Hampton Inn Airport/Cordova Mall
3. Holiday Inn Express
4. Holiday Inn University Mall
5. Homewood Suites
6. La Quinta Inn
7. Motel 6 Pensacola East
8. Motel 6 Pensacola North
9. Pensacola Lodge
10. Red Roof Inn
11. Residence Inn
12. Shoney's Inn and Suites
13. Super 8

PENSACOLA BEACH ACCOMMODATIONS

1. Bay Beach Inn
2. Beachside Resort & Conference Center
3. Best Western Resort
4. Clarion Suites Resort & Convention Center
5. Comfort Inn
6. The Dunes
7. Five Flags Inn
8. Hampton Inn Pensacola Beach
9. Hilton Garden Inn Pensacola Beach
10. Holiday Inn Express Pensacola Beach
11. SpringHill Suites

23

Fort Walton Beach

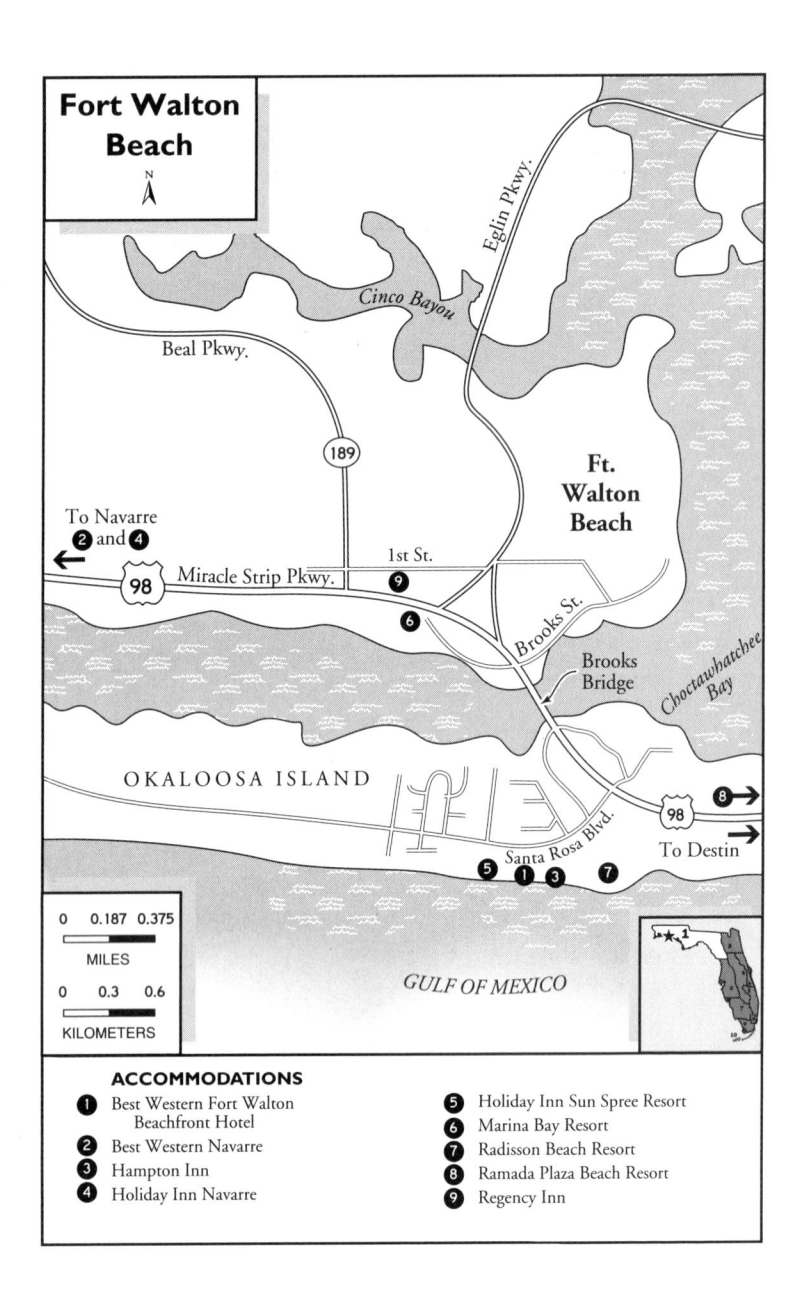

ACCOMMODATIONS

1. Best Western Fort Walton Beachfront Hotel
2. Best Western Navarre
3. Hampton Inn
4. Holiday Inn Navarre
5. Holiday Inn Sun Spree Resort
6. Marina Bay Resort
7. Radisson Beach Resort
8. Ramada Plaza Beach Resort
9. Regency Inn

Destin Area

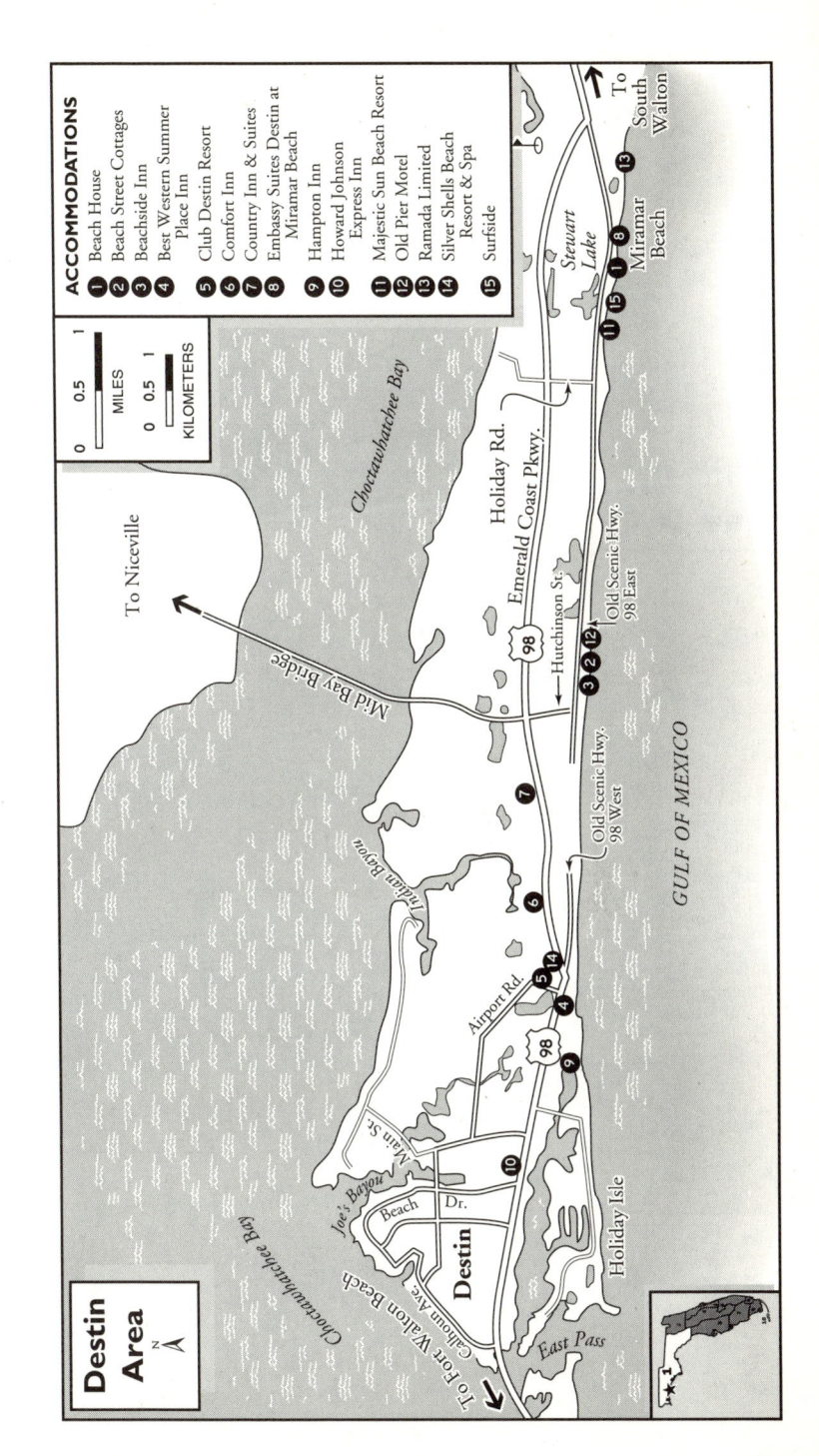

ACCOMMODATIONS

1. Beach House
2. Beach Street Cottages
3. Beachside Inn
4. Best Western Summer Place Inn
5. Club Destin Resort
6. Comfort Inn
7. Country Inn & Suites
8. Embassy Suites Destin at Miramar Beach
9. Hampton Inn
10. Howard Johnson Express Inn
11. Majestic Sun Beach Resort
12. Old Pier Motel
13. Ramada Limited
14. Silver Shells Beach Resort & Spa
15. Surfside

Santa Rosa Beach Area

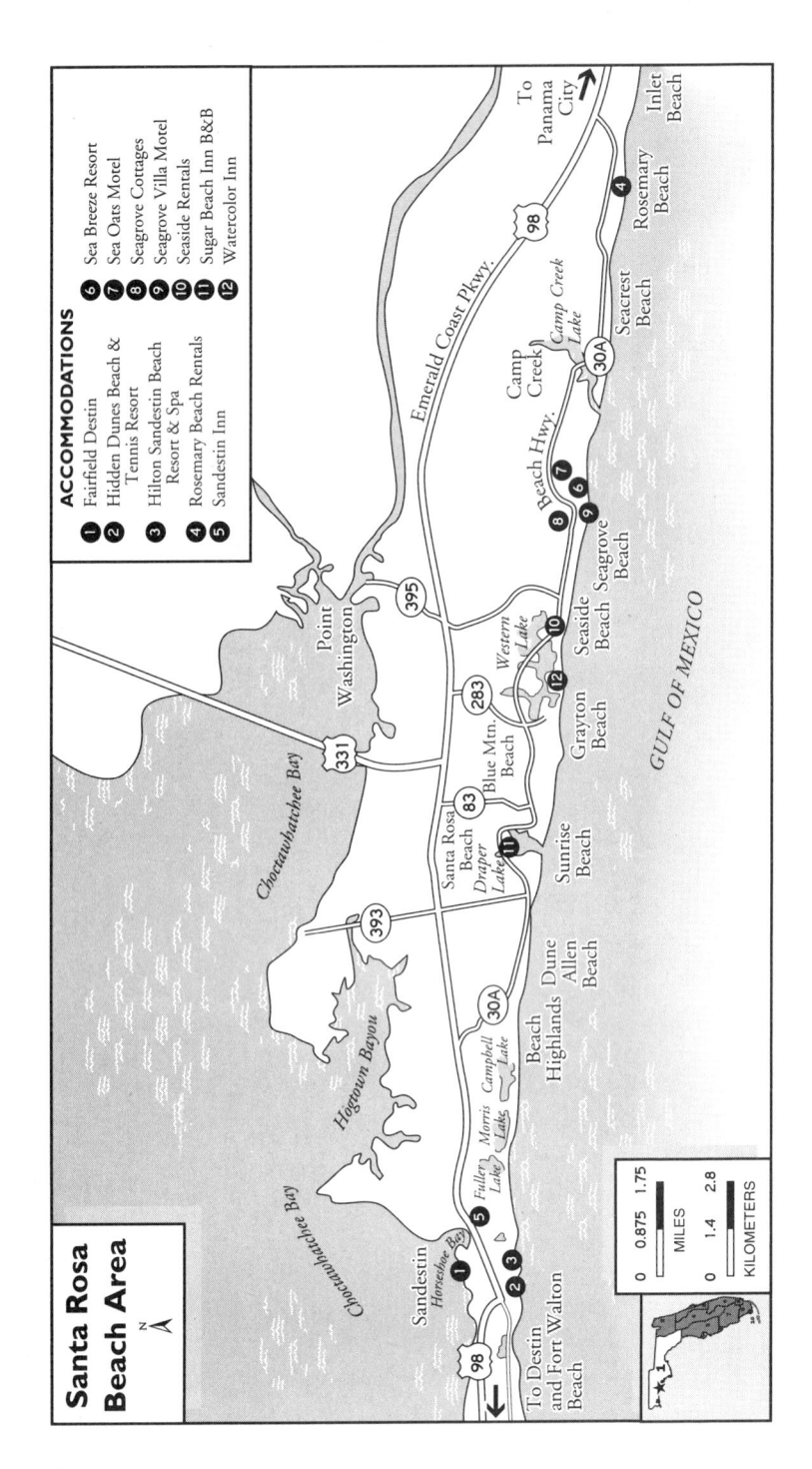

ACCOMMODATIONS

1. Fairfield Destin
2. Hidden Dunes Beach & Tennis Resort
3. Hilton Sandestin Beach Resort & Spa
4. Rosemary Beach Rentals
5. Sandestin Inn
6. Sea Breeze Resort
7. Sea Oats Motel
8. Seagrove Cottages
9. Seagrove Villa Motel
10. Seaside Rentals
11. Sugar Beach Inn B&B
12. Watercolor Inn

Panama City Beach

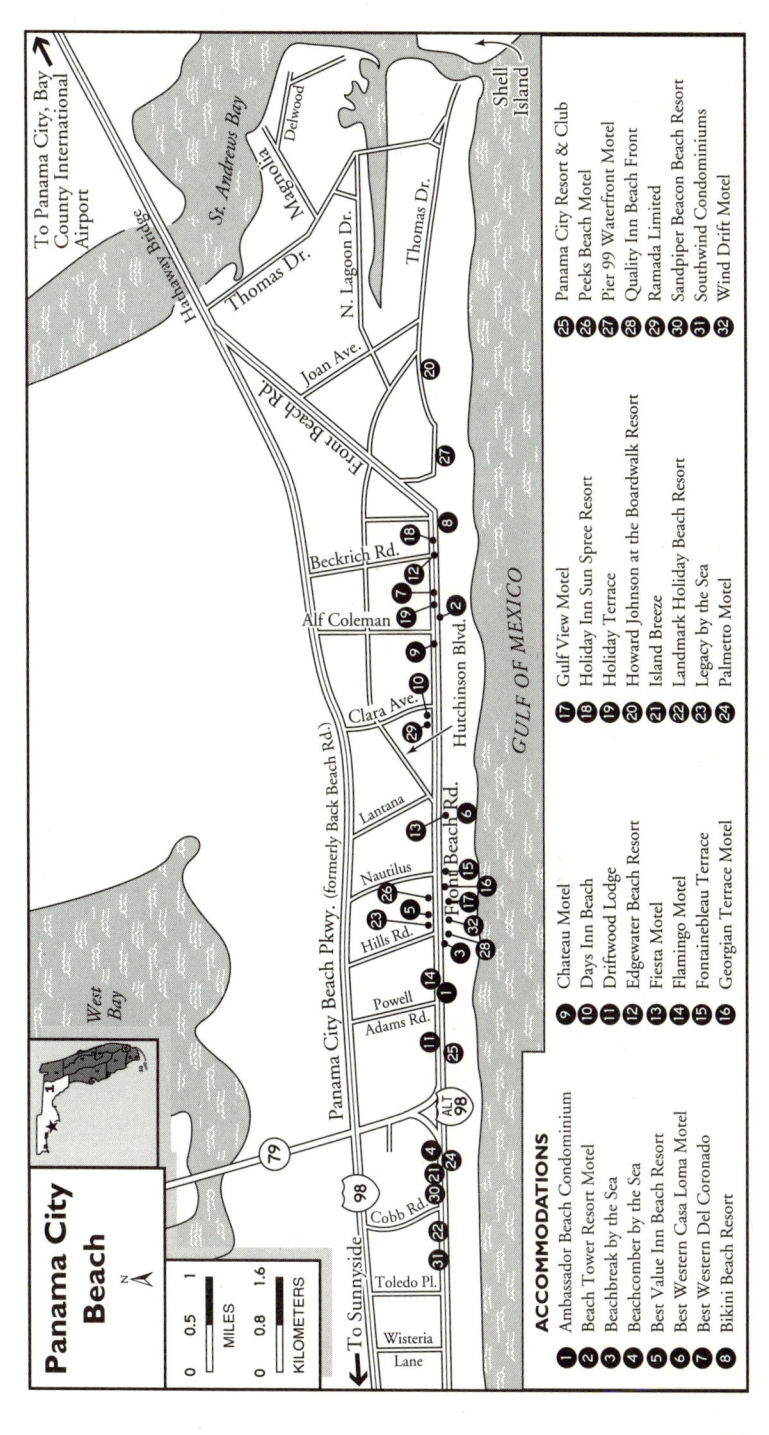

ACCOMMODATIONS

1. Ambassador Beach Condominium
2. Beach Tower Resort Motel
3. Beachbreak by the Sea
4. Beachcomber by the Sea
5. Best Value Inn Beach Resort
6. Best Western Casa Loma Motel
7. Best Western Del Coronado
8. Bikini Beach Resort
9. Chateau Motel
10. Days Inn Beach
11. Driftwood Lodge
12. Edgewater Beach Resort
13. Fiesta Motel
14. Flamingo Motel
15. Fontainebleau Terrace
16. Georgian Terrace Motel
17. Gulf View Motel
18. Holiday Inn Sun Spree Resort
19. Holiday Terrace
20. Howard Johnson at the Boardwalk Resort
21. Island Breeze
22. Landmark Holiday Beach Resort
23. Legacy by the Sea
24. Palmetto Motel
25. Panama City Resort & Club
26. Peeks Beach Motel
27. Pier 99 Waterfront Motel
28. Quality Inn Beach Front
29. Ramada Limited
30. Sandpiper Beacon Beach Resort
31. Southwind Condominiums
32. Wind Drift Motel

Downtown Apalachicola Inset

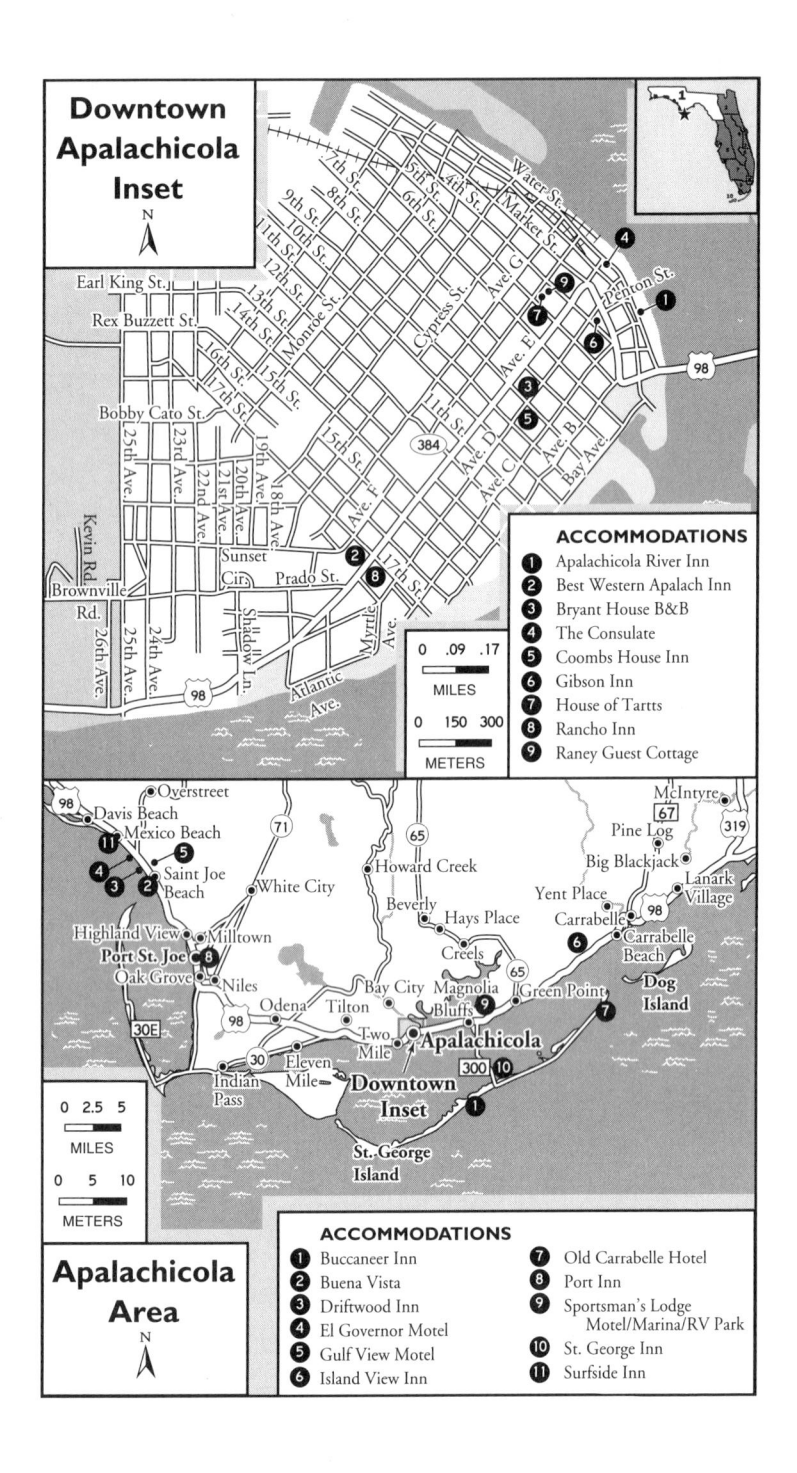

ACCOMMODATIONS
1. Apalachicola River Inn
2. Best Western Apalach Inn
3. Bryant House B&B
4. The Consulate
5. Coombs House Inn
6. Gibson Inn
7. House of Tartts
8. Rancho Inn
9. Raney Guest Cottage

Apalachicola Area

ACCOMMODATIONS
1. Buccaneer Inn
2. Buena Vista
3. Driftwood Inn
4. El Governor Motel
5. Gulf View Motel
6. Island View Inn
7. Old Carrabelle Hotel
8. Port Inn
9. Sportsman's Lodge Motel/Marina/RV Park
10. St. George Inn
11. Surfside Inn

Tallahassee

ACCOMMODATIONS
1. Best Western Seminole Inn
2. Comfort Inn
3. Days Inn North
4. Doubletree Hotel
5. Fairfield Inn
6. Governor's Inn
7. Hampton Inn I-10
8. Holiday Inn Northwest
9. Holiday Inn Select
10. Howard Johnson Express Inn
11. La Quinta Inn
12. Microtel Inn & Suites
13. Radisson Hotel Tallahassee
14. Ramada Inn
15. Shoney's Inn

Amelia Island/Fernandina Beach

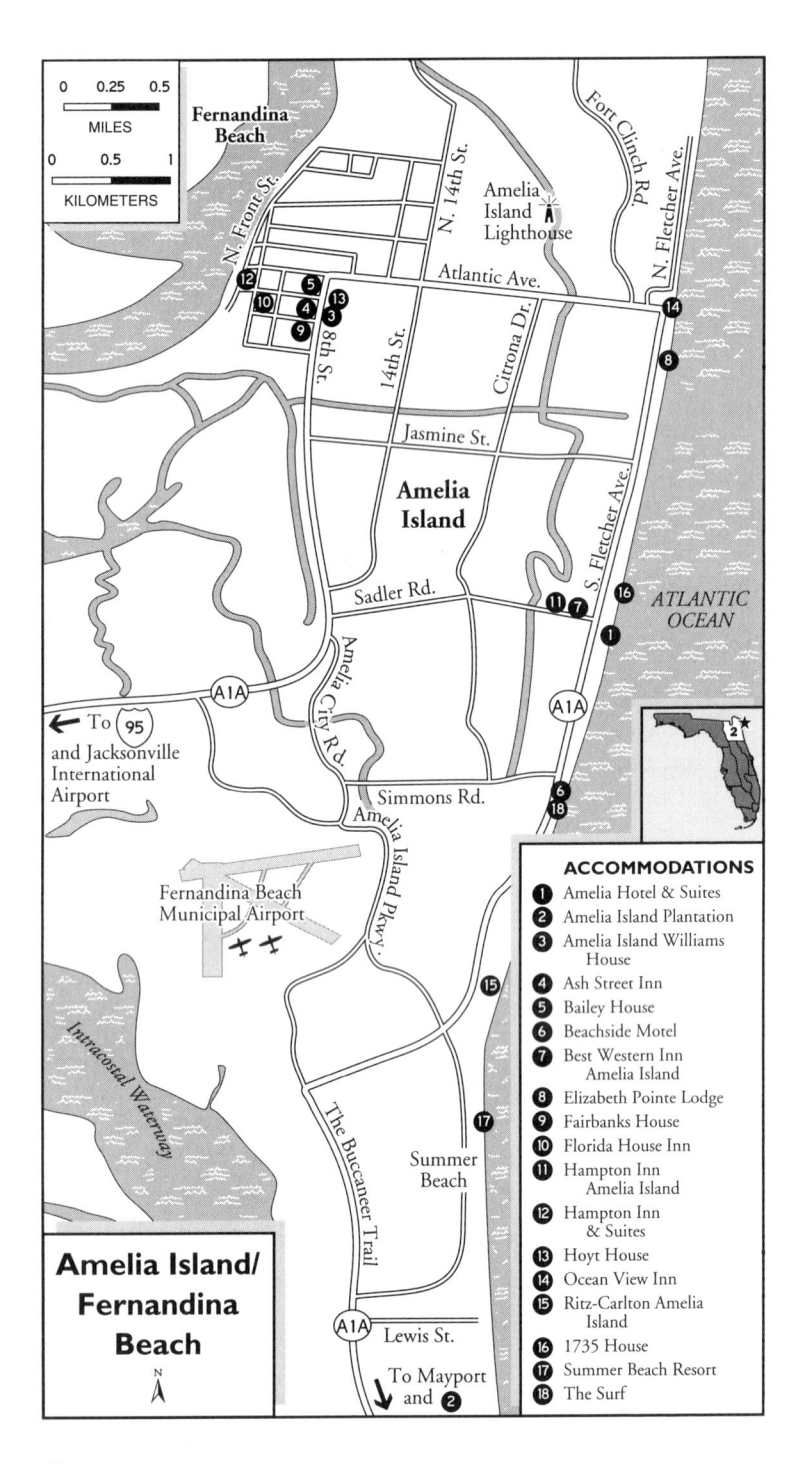

ACCOMMODATIONS

1. Amelia Hotel & Suites
2. Amelia Island Plantation
3. Amelia Island Williams House
4. Ash Street Inn
5. Bailey House
6. Beachside Motel
7. Best Western Inn Amelia Island
8. Elizabeth Pointe Lodge
9. Fairbanks House
10. Florida House Inn
11. Hampton Inn Amelia Island
12. Hampton Inn & Suites
13. Hoyt House
14. Ocean View Inn
15. Ritz-Carlton Amelia Island
16. 1735 House
17. Summer Beach Resort
18. The Surf

Downtown Gainesville

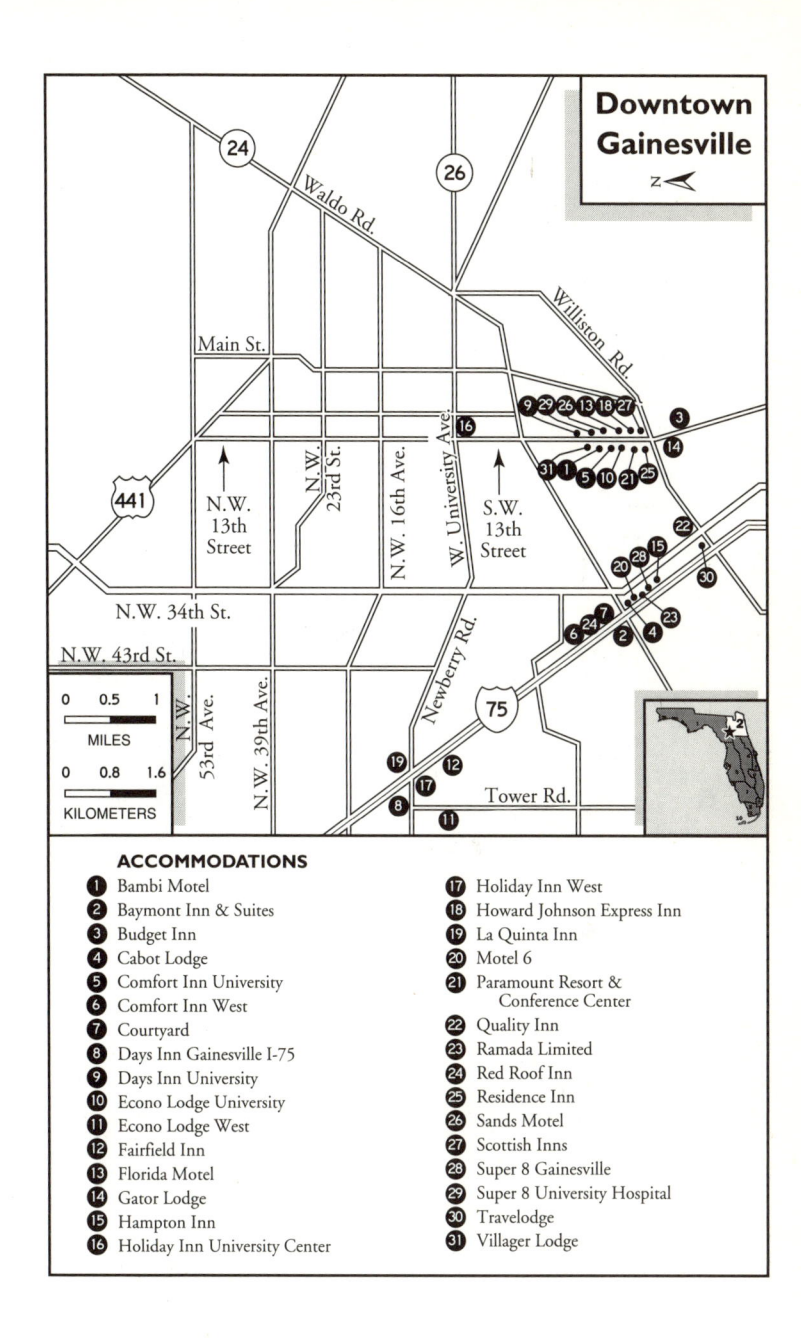

ACCOMMODATIONS

1. Bambi Motel
2. Baymont Inn & Suites
3. Budget Inn
4. Cabot Lodge
5. Comfort Inn University
6. Comfort Inn West
7. Courtyard
8. Days Inn Gainesville I-75
9. Days Inn University
10. Econo Lodge University
11. Econo Lodge West
12. Fairfield Inn
13. Florida Motel
14. Gator Lodge
15. Hampton Inn
16. Holiday Inn University Center
17. Holiday Inn West
18. Howard Johnson Express Inn
19. La Quinta Inn
20. Motel 6
21. Paramount Resort & Conference Center
22. Quality Inn
23. Ramada Limited
24. Red Roof Inn
25. Residence Inn
26. Sands Motel
27. Scottish Inns
28. Super 8 Gainesville
29. Super 8 University Hospital
30. Travelodge
31. Villager Lodge

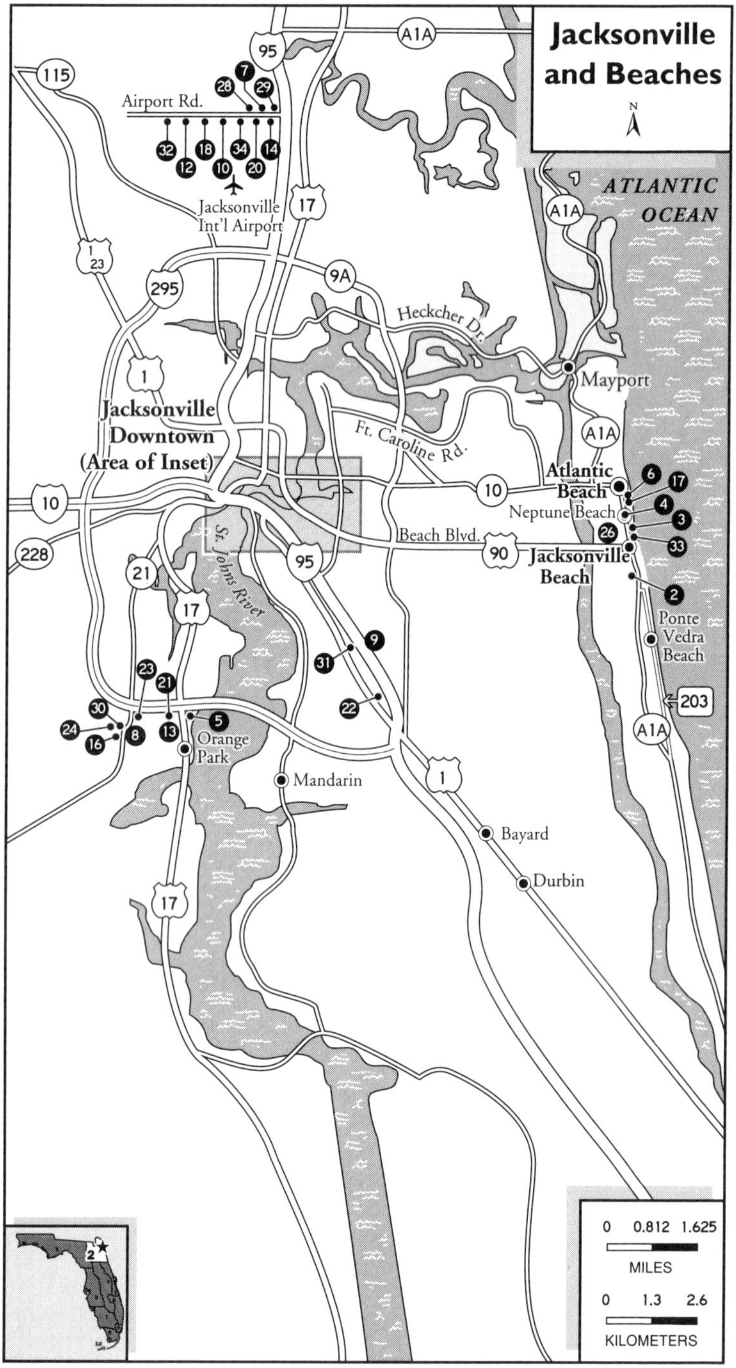
Jacksonville
and Beaches
N
ATLANTIC
OCEAN
Airport Rd.
Jacksonville
Int'l Airport
Heckcher Dr.
Mayport
Jacksonville
Downtown
(Area of Inset)
Ft. Caroline Rd.
Atlantic
Beach
Neptune Beach
Beach Blvd.
Jacksonville
Beach
St. Johns River
Ponte
Vedra
Beach
Orange
Park
Mandarin
Bayard
Durbin
0 0.812 1.625
MILES
0 1.3 2.6
KILOMETERS

ACCOMMODATIONS
- ❶ Adam's Mark Jacksonville Hotel
- ❷ Beach Landing Motel
- ❸ Best Western Oceanfront
- ❹ Casa Marina Inn
- ❺ Comfort Inn Orange Park
- ❻ Comfort Inn Oceanfront
- ❼ Comfort Suites Airport
- ❽ Country Inn & Suites
- ❾ Courtyard
- ❿ Courtyard Airport
- ⓫ Extended Stay America
- ⓬ Fairfield Inn Airport
- ⓭ Fairfield Inn Orange Park
- ⓮ Hampton Inn Airport
- ⓯ Hampton Inn Central
- ⓰ Hampton Inn Jacksonville Orange Park
- ⓱ Hillsmoore Oceanfront Inn
- ⓲ Hilton Garden Inn
- ⓳ Hilton Jacksonville Riverfront
- ⓴ Holiday Inn Airport
- ㉑ Holiday Inn Orange Park
- ㉒ La Quinta Inn Baymeadows
- ㉓ La Quinta Inn Jacksonville Orange Park
- ㉔ Motel 6
- ㉕ Omni Jacksonville Hotel
- ㉖ Quality Suites
- ㉗ Radisson Riverwalk Hotel & Conference Center
- ㉘ Ramada Limited Suites
- ㉙ Red Roof Inn Airport
- ㉚ Red Roof Inn Jacksonville Orange Park
- ㉛ Red Roof Inn Jacksonville Southpoint
- ㉜ Residence Inn Airport
- ㉝ Surfside Inn
- ㉞ Wingate Inn

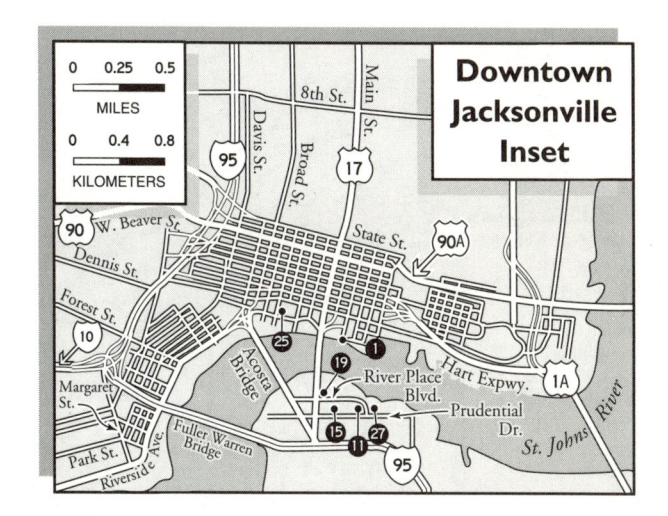

Downtown Jacksonville Inset

33

St. Augustine

To I-95 and
3, 7, 8, 11, 16, 17, 18

ACCOMMODATIONS
1. Agustin Inn
2. Best Western Historical Inn
3. Best Western St. Augustine I-95
4. Casa de la Paz B&B
5. Casablanca Inn B&B
6. Comfort Inn
7. Days Inn
8. Hampton Inn
9. Hampton Inn Historic
10. Holiday Inn & Suites St. Augustine
11. Holiday Inn Express
12. La Quinta Inn
13. Merida Motel
14. Pirate Haus Hostel
15. Ramada Inn St. Augustine
16. Ramada Limited St. Augustine
17. Scottish Inns
18. Super 8
19. Whale's Tale B&B

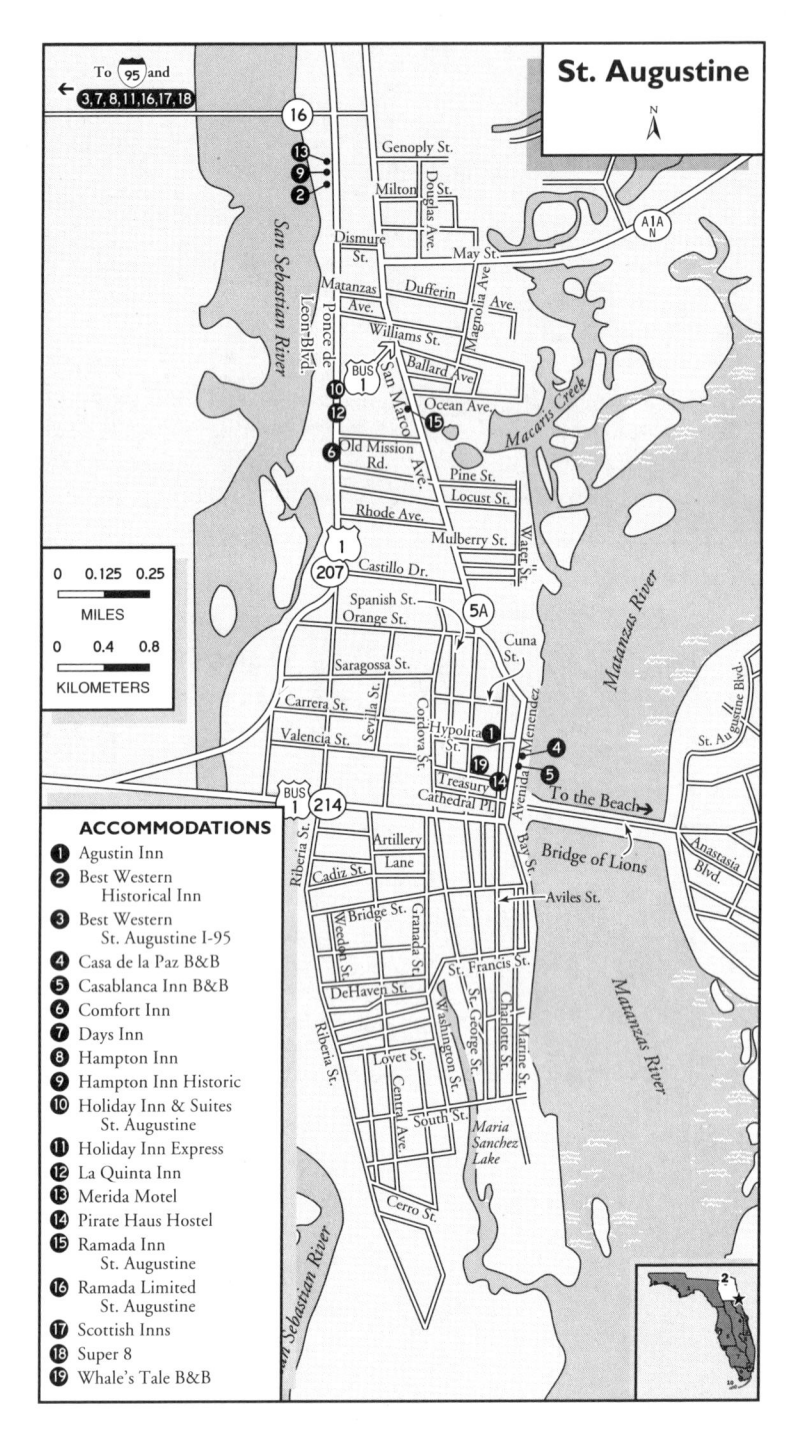

St. Augustine Beach

ACCOMMODATIONS
1. Anastasia Inn B&B
2. Anchorage Inn
3. Beacher's Lodge Oceanfront Suites
4. Budget Inn
5. Edgewater Inn
6. Hampton Inn St. Augustine Beach
7. Hilton Garden Inn
8. Historic Inn
9. Holiday Inn St. Augustine Beach
10. La Fiesta Ocean Inn & Suites
11. Lion Inn
12. Ramada Limited St. Augustine Beach
13. Regency Inn & Suites
14. Sleep Inn
15. St. Augustine Beach Front Resort
16. Sunrise Inn
17. Super 8 St. Augustine Beach

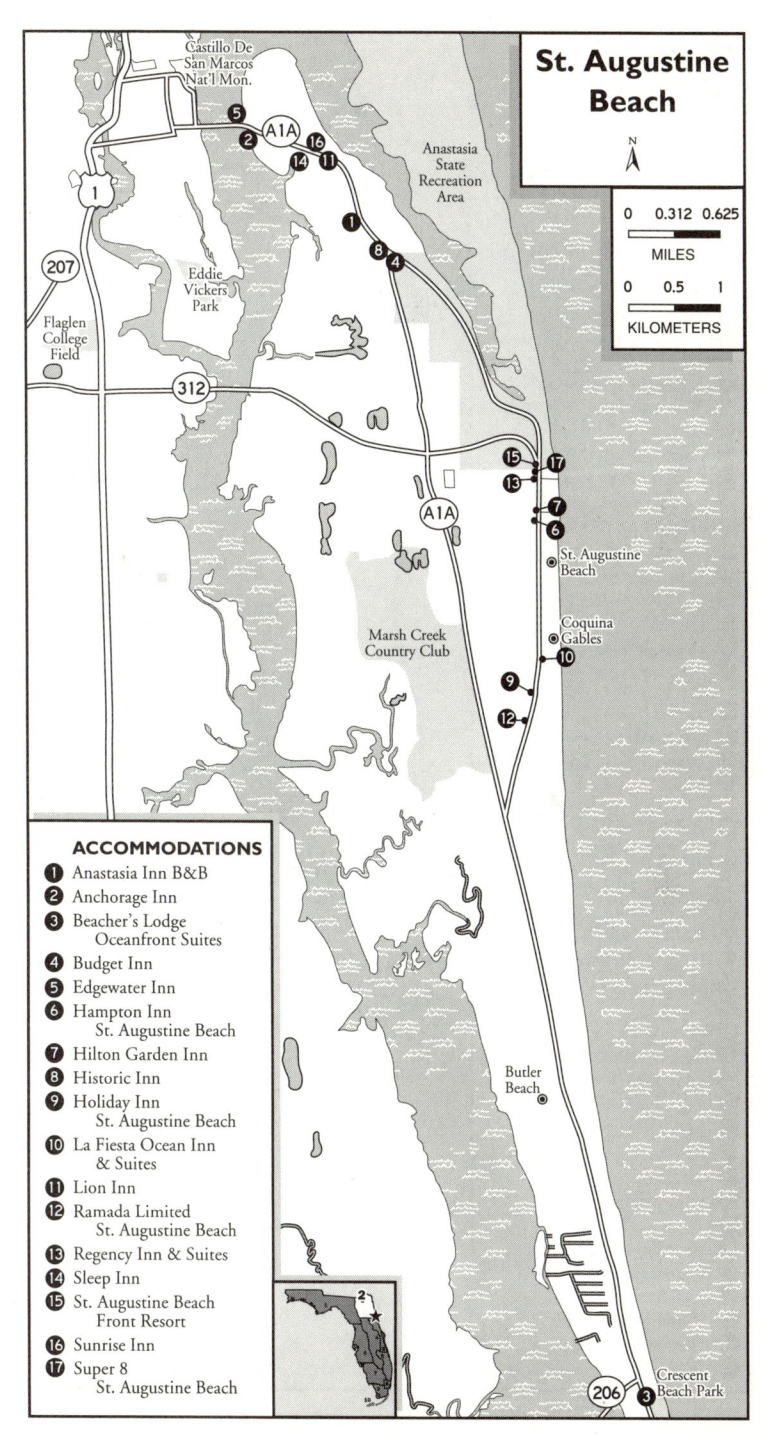

Daytona

N

ACCOMMODATIONS

1. Adam's Mark Daytona Beach Resort
2. Americano Beach Resort
3. Beachcomber Motel
4. Beachcomer
5. Beachside Motel
6. Best Western Mainsail Inn & Suites
7. Best Western Mayan Inn
8. Boardwalk Inn & Suites
9. Breakers Beach Oceanfront Motel
10. Cardinal Inn
11. Coconut Palms Beach Resort
12. Comfort Inn & Suites
13. Comfort Inn Ormond Beach
14. Coral Beach Resort
15. Cove Motel
16. Daytona Beach Ocean Jewels
17. Daytona Beach Regency
18. Desert Inn Resort
19. El Caribe Resort & Conference Center
20. Esquire Beach Motel
21. Grand Seas Resort
22. Harbour Beach Resort
23. Hilton Daytona Beach Oceanfront Resort
24. Holiday Inn Hotel & Suites Daytona Beach
25. Holiday Inn Hotel & Suites New Smyrna Beach
26. Ivanhoe Beach Resort
27. Magic Carpet Motel
28. Makai Beach Lodge
29. Maverick Resort
30. Ocean Inn
31. Ocean Walk Resort
32. Oceania Beach Club
33. Palm Plaza Oceanfront Resort
34. Plaza Resort & Spa
35. Radisson Resort Daytona Beach
36. Red Carpet Inn
37. Scottish Inns
38. Seagarden Inn
39. Seven Seas Resort
40. Silver Beach Club
41. Surfside Resort & Suites
42. Symphony Beach Club
43. Treasure Island Resort
44. Tropical Manor Motel
45. Tropical Winds Oceanfront Hotel

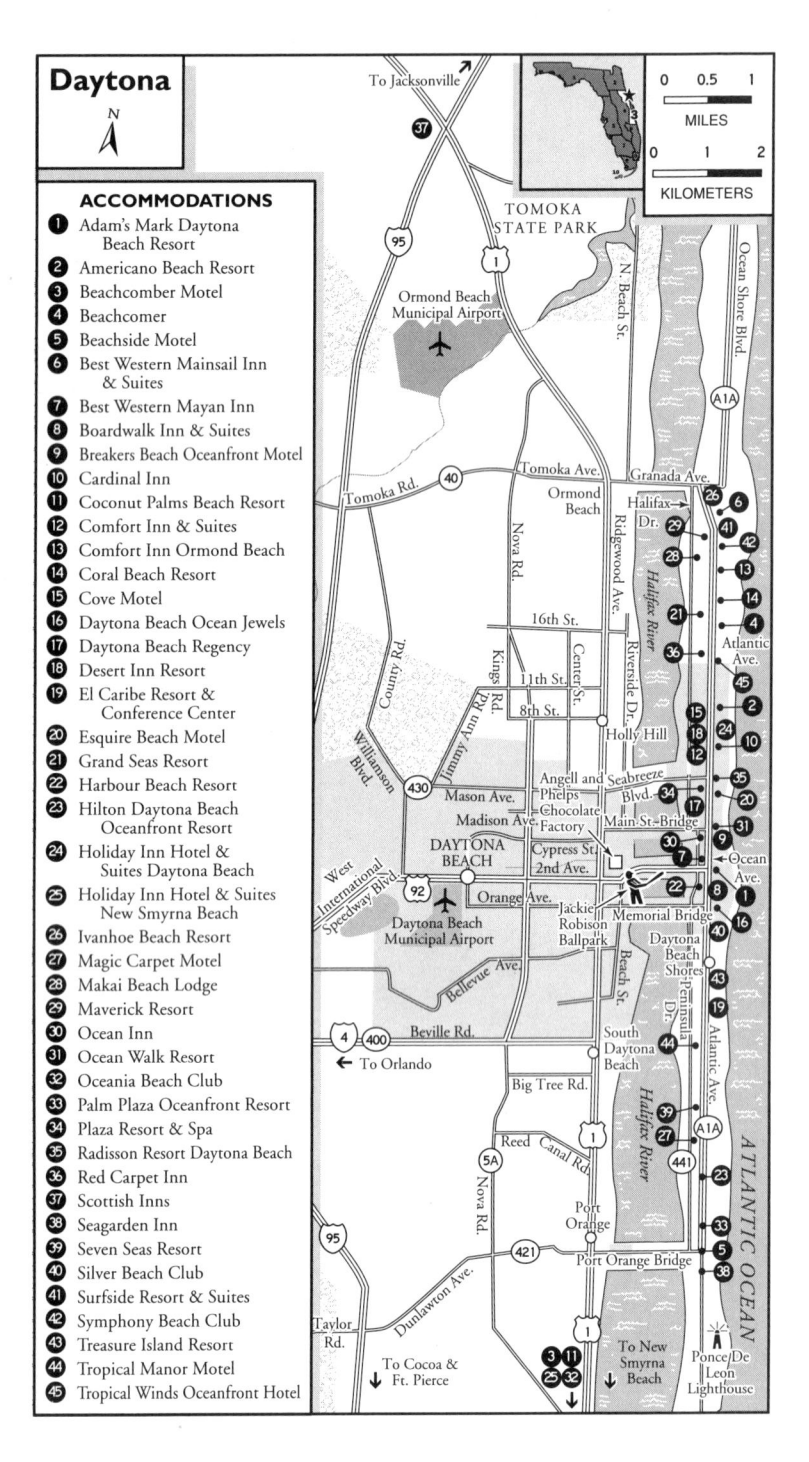

The Space Coast

N

0	1.625	3.25
MILES		

0	2.125	5.25
KILOMETERS		

ACCOMMODATIONS

1. Baymont Inn & Suites
2. Best Western Oceanfront Resort
3. Best Western Space Shuttle Inn
4. Clarion Hotel
5. Cocoa Beach Oceanside Inn
6. Comfort Inn
7. Courtyard
8. Days Inn Kennedy Space Center
9. Days Inn Oceanside
10. Doubletree Hotel
11. Econo Lodge
12. Fawlty Towers
13. Hampton Inn Cocoa Beach
14. Hilton Cocoa Beach Oceanfront
15. Holiday Inn Cocoa Beach Resort
16. Holiday Inn Express
17. Holiday Inn Kennedy Space Center
18. Howard Johnson Express Inn
19. Imperial's Hotel & Conference Center
20. Inn at Cocoa Beach
21. Luna Sea B&B Motel
22. Motel 6
23. Ocean Suite Hotel
24. Quality Inn
25. Radisson Resort at the Port
26. Ramada Inn Kennedy Space Center
27. Ramada Inn Satellite Beach
28. Randolph Inn
29. Resort on Cocoa Beach
30. Riverside Inn
31. Sea Aire Motel
32. Surf Studio Beach Resort
33. Wakulla Suites

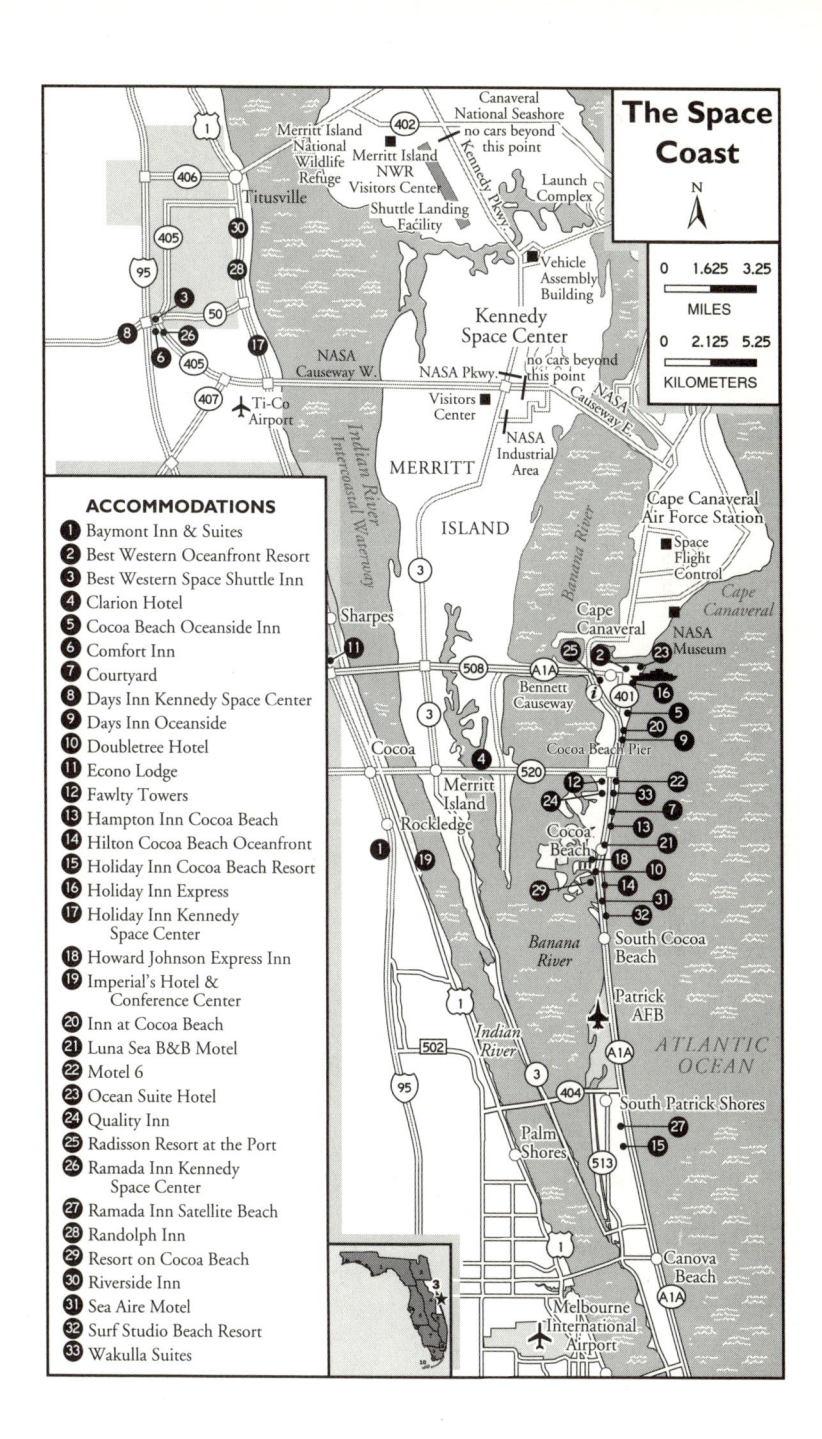

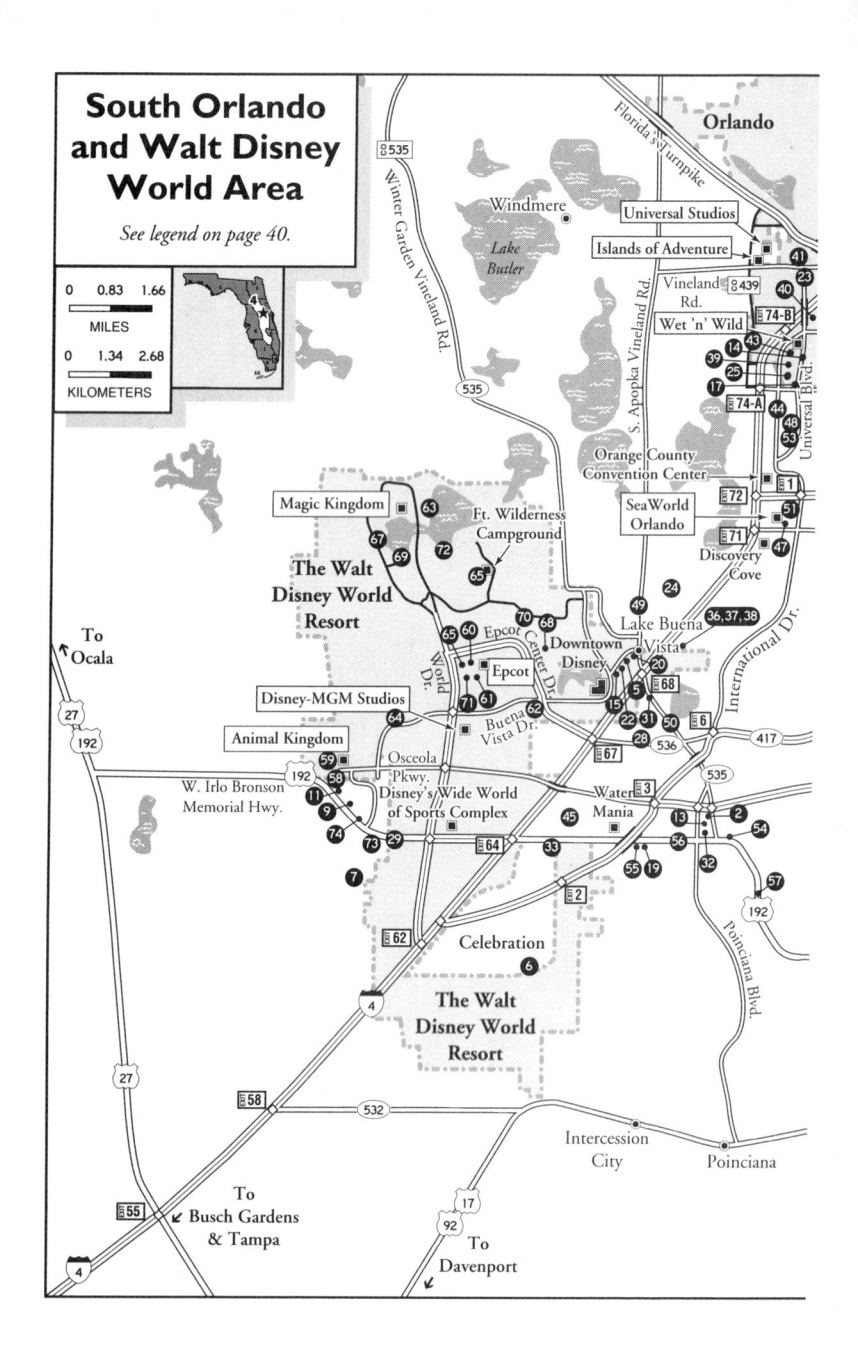

South Orlando and Walt Disney World Area

See legend on page 40.

ACCOMMODATIONS

1. Courtyard at Lake Lucerne
2. Courtyard Orlando Downtown
3. Embassy Suites Orlando Downtown
4. EO Inn Spa
5. Holiday Inn Orlando Downtown
6. Marriott Hotel Orlando Downtown
7. Travelodge
8. Westin Grand Bohemian Hotel

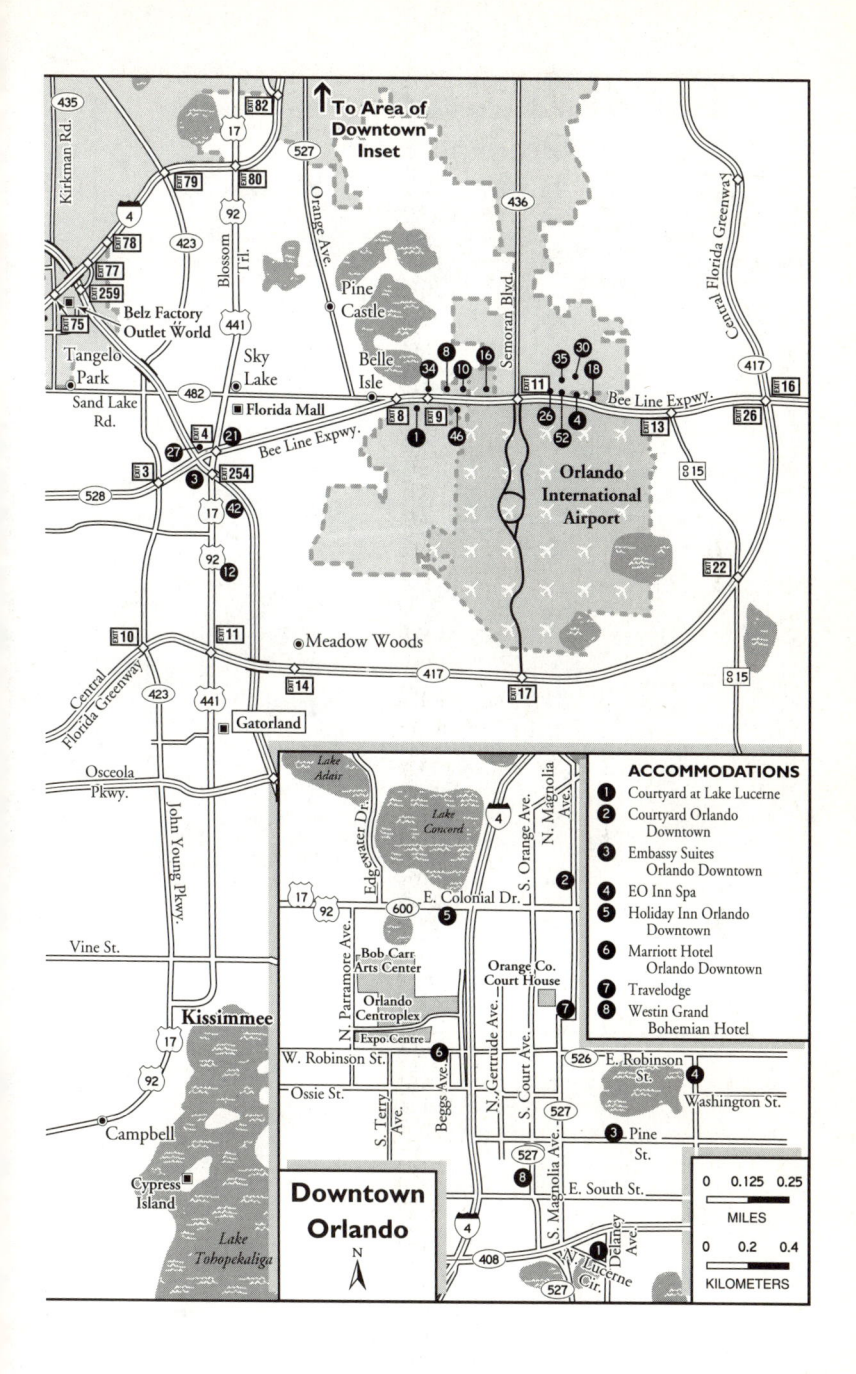

Downtown Orlando

South Orlando and Walt Disney Area Accommodations

1. AmeriSuites Airport
2. AmeriSuites Lake Buena Vista South
3. Baymont Inn & Suites
4. Best Western Airport Inn
5. Best Western Lake Buena Vista
6. Celebration Hotel
7. Celebration World Resort
8. Clarion Hotel Airport
9. Clarion Maingate
10. Comfort Suites Airport
11. Comfort Suites Maingate
12. Countryside Lodge
13. Country Inn & Suites
14. Country Inn & Suites Universal
15. Courtyard Disney Village
16. Crowne Plaza Airport
17. Crowne Plaza Universal
18. Days Inn Airport
19. Days Suites Maingate East
20. Doubletree Guest Suites
21. Fairfield Inn Airport
22. Grosvenor Resort
23. Hard Rock Hotel
24. Hawthorn Suites Lake Buena Vista
25. Hawthorn Suites Universal
26. Hilton Garden Inn
27. Holiday Inn Express Florida Mall
28. Holiday Inn Family Suites Resort
29. Holiday Inn Nikki Bird Resort
30. Holiday Inn Select Airport
31. Holiday Inn Sun Spree Resort
32. Howard Johnson EnchantedLand Resort Hotel
33. Hyatt Orlando
34. La Quinta Inn Airport
35. Marriott Hotels Resorts Suites
36. Marriott Village Courtyard
37. Marriott Village Fairfield Inn
38. Marriott Village SpringHill Suites
39. Microtel Inn & Suites
40. Motel 6 International Drive
41. Portofino Bay Hotel
42. Quality Inn & Suites Airport
43. Quality Suites International Drive
44. Radisson Barcelo Inn International
45. Radisson Resort Parkway
46. Renaissance Orlando Hotel Airport
47. Renaissance Orlando Resort
48. Residence Inn Convention Center
49. Sheraton Royal Safari
50. Sheraton Vistana Resort
51. Sheraton World Resort
52. Sleep Inn & Suites
53. SpringHill Suites
54. Super 8 Kissimmee Lakeside
55. Super 8 Maingate
56. Travelodge Suites Eastgate
57. Travelodge Suites Maingate
58. WDW All-Star Resort
59. WDW Animal Kingdom Lodge
60. WDW Beach & Yacht Club Resort & Beach Club Villas
61. WDW Boardwalk Inn & Villas
62. WDW Caribbean Beach Resort
63. WDW Contemporary Resort
64. WDW Coronado Springs Resort
65. WDW Dolphin
66. WDW Fort Wilderness Resort
67. WDW Grand Floridian Resort
68. WDW Old Key West Resort
69. WDW Polynesian Resort
70. WDW Port Orleans Resort
71. WDW Swan
72. WDW Wilderness Lodge & Villas
73. Westgate Resorts
74. Westgate Towers

Clearwater Beach

St. Petersburg–Clearwater

N

ACCOMMODATIONS
1. Anchor Court Apartments & Motel
2. Beach Suites Resort
3. Best Western Beachfront Resort
4. Best Western Sea Wake Beach Resort
5. Best Western Treasure Island
6. Bilmar Beach Resort
7. Don Cesar Beach Resort and Spa
8. Econo Lodge Clearwater Beach
9. Fiesta Motel
10. Gulf Strand Beach Front Resort
11. Hampton Inn
12. Hilton Clearwater Beach Resort
13. Hilton Tampa Bay N. Redington Beach
14. Holiday Inn Beachfront Resort
15. Holiday Inn Sun Spree Resort Clearwater Beach
16. Holiday Inn Sun Spree Resort St. Petersburg
17. Holiday Inn Treasure Island
18. Howard Johnson Resort Hotel
19. Jefferson Motel
20. Lorelei Resort
21. Miramar Resort
22. Peninsula Inn & Spa
23. Plaza Beach Resort Motel
24. Quality Hotel on the Beach
25. Quality Inn Clearwater
26. Radisson Suite Resort on Sand Key
27. Ramada Treasure Island
28. Sea Breeze Manor B&B Inn
29. Seahorse Cottages
30. Sheraton Sand Key Resort
31. Tahitian
32. TradeWinds Island Resorts

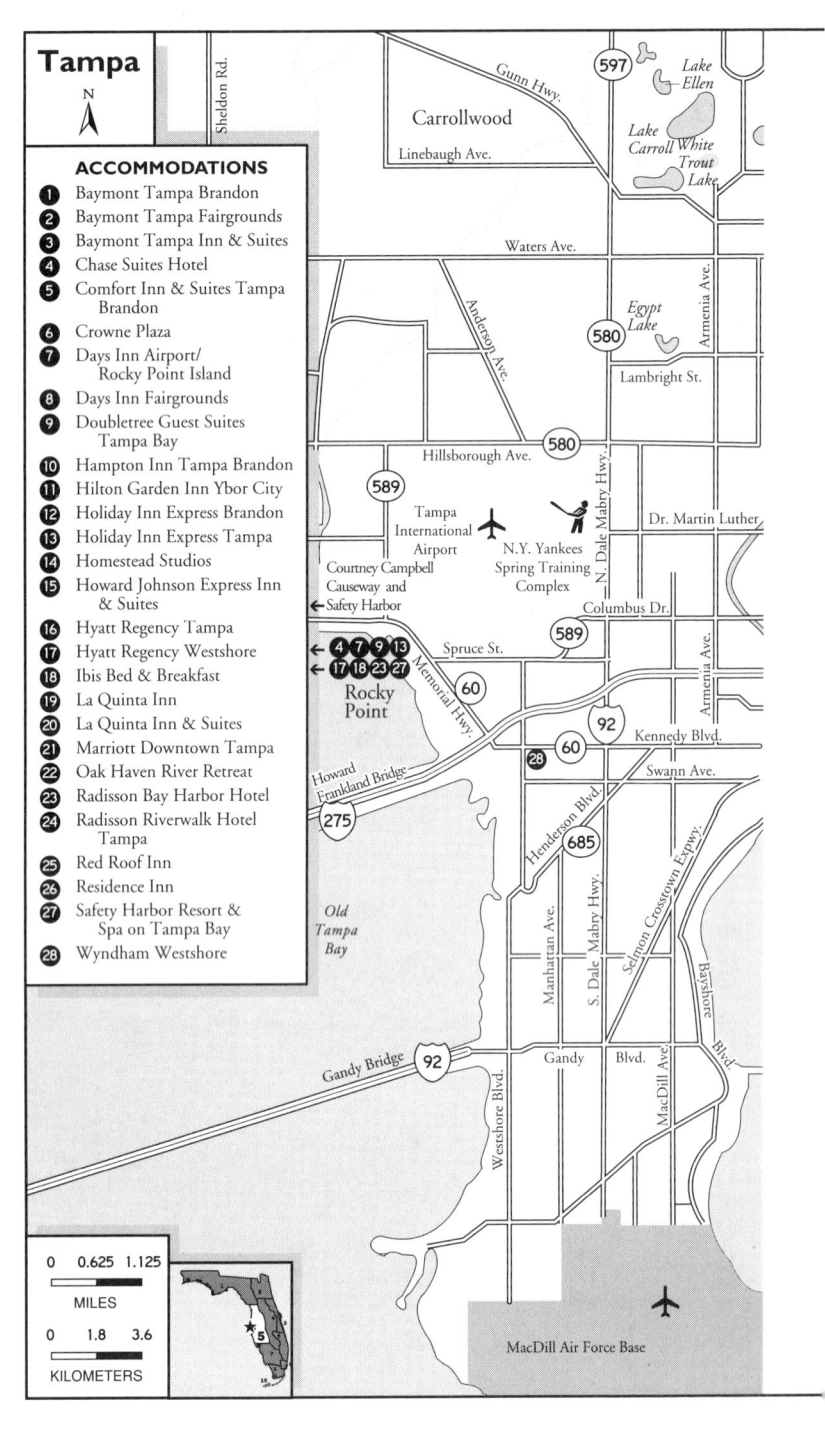

Tampa

N

ACCOMMODATIONS

1. Baymont Tampa Brandon
2. Baymont Tampa Fairgrounds
3. Baymont Tampa Inn & Suites
4. Chase Suites Hotel
5. Comfort Inn & Suites Tampa Brandon
6. Crowne Plaza
7. Days Inn Airport/Rocky Point Island
8. Days Inn Fairgrounds
9. Doubletree Guest Suites Tampa Bay
10. Hampton Inn Tampa Brandon
11. Hilton Garden Inn Ybor City
12. Holiday Inn Express Brandon
13. Holiday Inn Express Tampa
14. Homestead Studios
15. Howard Johnson Express Inn & Suites
16. Hyatt Regency Tampa
17. Hyatt Regency Westshore
18. Ibis Bed & Breakfast
19. La Quinta Inn
20. La Quinta Inn & Suites
21. Marriott Downtown Tampa
22. Oak Haven River Retreat
23. Radisson Bay Harbor Hotel
24. Radisson Riverwalk Hotel Tampa
25. Red Roof Inn
26. Residence Inn
27. Safety Harbor Resort & Spa on Tampa Bay
28. Wyndham Westshore

43

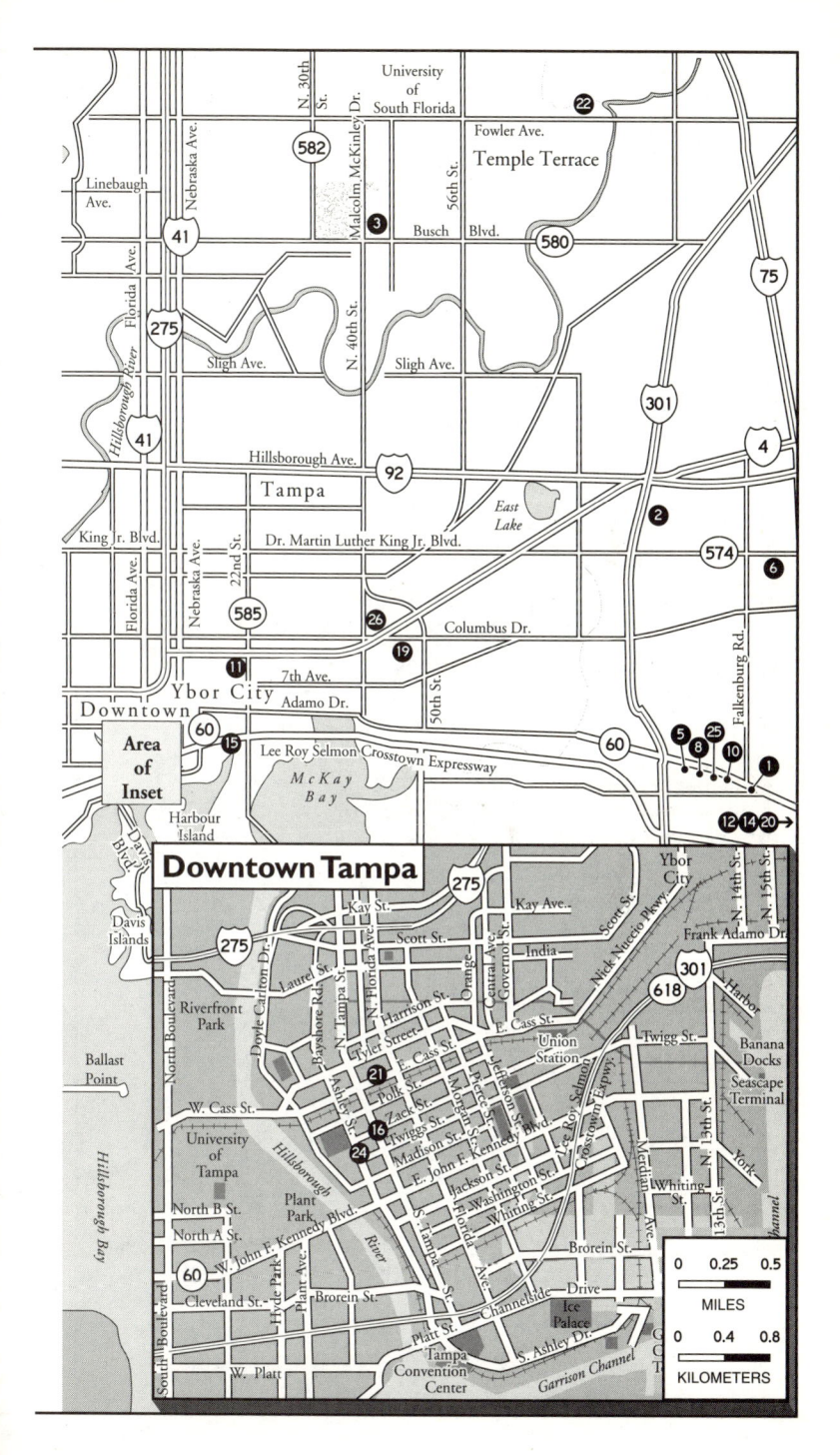

Sarasota

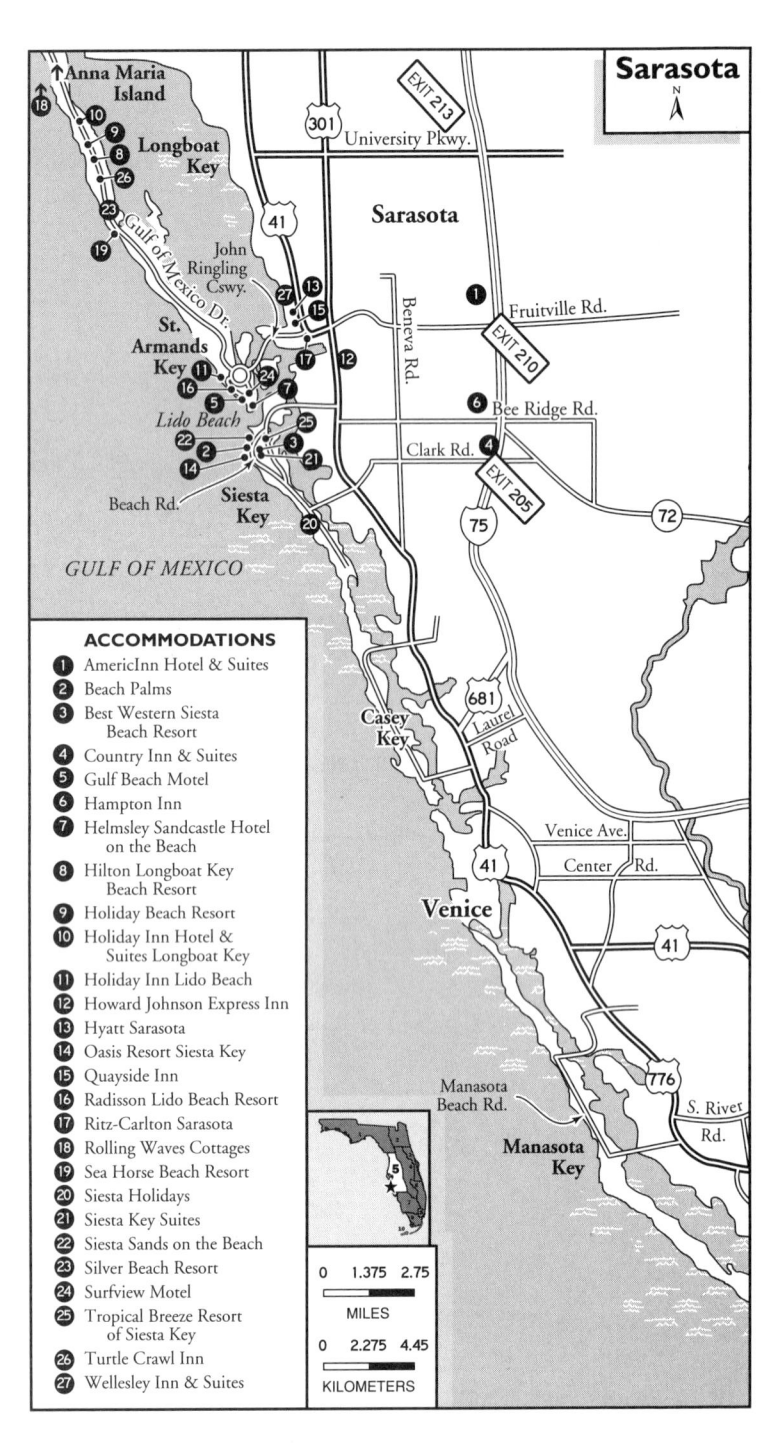

ACCOMMODATIONS
1. AmericInn Hotel & Suites
2. Beach Palms
3. Best Western Siesta Beach Resort
4. Country Inn & Suites
5. Gulf Beach Motel
6. Hampton Inn
7. Helmsley Sandcastle Hotel on the Beach
8. Hilton Longboat Key Beach Resort
9. Holiday Beach Resort
10. Holiday Inn Hotel & Suites Longboat Key
11. Holiday Inn Lido Beach
12. Howard Johnson Express Inn
13. Hyatt Sarasota
14. Oasis Resort Siesta Key
15. Quayside Inn
16. Radisson Lido Beach Resort
17. Ritz-Carlton Sarasota
18. Rolling Waves Cottages
19. Sea Horse Beach Resort
20. Siesta Holidays
21. Siesta Key Suites
22. Siesta Sands on the Beach
23. Silver Beach Resort
24. Surfview Motel
25. Tropical Breeze Resort of Siesta Key
26. Turtle Crawl Inn
27. Wellesley Inn & Suites

Vero Beach and the Treasure Coast

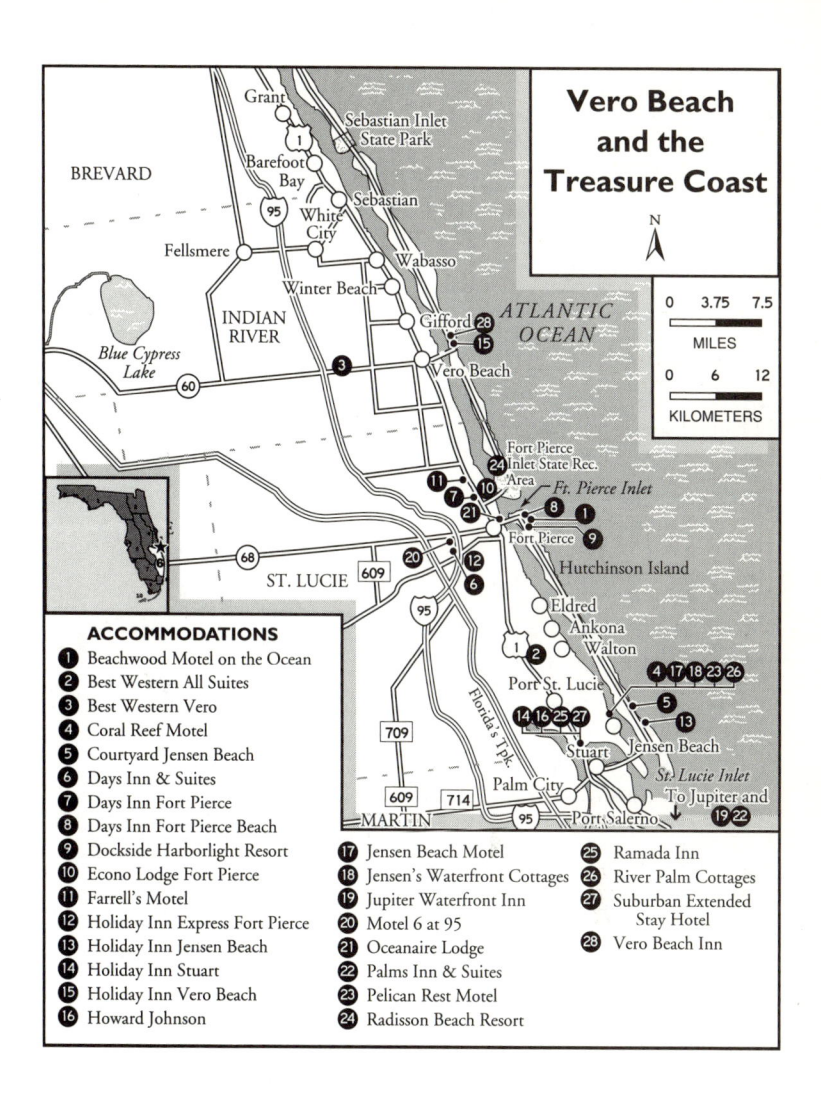

ACCOMMODATIONS
1. Beachwood Motel on the Ocean
2. Best Western All Suites
3. Best Western Vero
4. Coral Reef Motel
5. Courtyard Jensen Beach
6. Days Inn & Suites
7. Days Inn Fort Pierce
8. Days Inn Fort Pierce Beach
9. Dockside Harborlight Resort
10. Econo Lodge Fort Pierce
11. Farrell's Motel
12. Holiday Inn Express Fort Pierce
13. Holiday Inn Jensen Beach
14. Holiday Inn Stuart
15. Holiday Inn Vero Beach
16. Howard Johnson
17. Jensen Beach Motel
18. Jensen's Waterfront Cottages
19. Jupiter Waterfront Inn
20. Motel 6 at 95
21. Oceanaire Lodge
22. Palms Inn & Suites
23. Pelican Rest Motel
24. Radisson Beach Resort
25. Ramada Inn
26. River Palm Cottages
27. Suburban Extended Stay Hotel
28. Vero Beach Inn

Palm Beach County

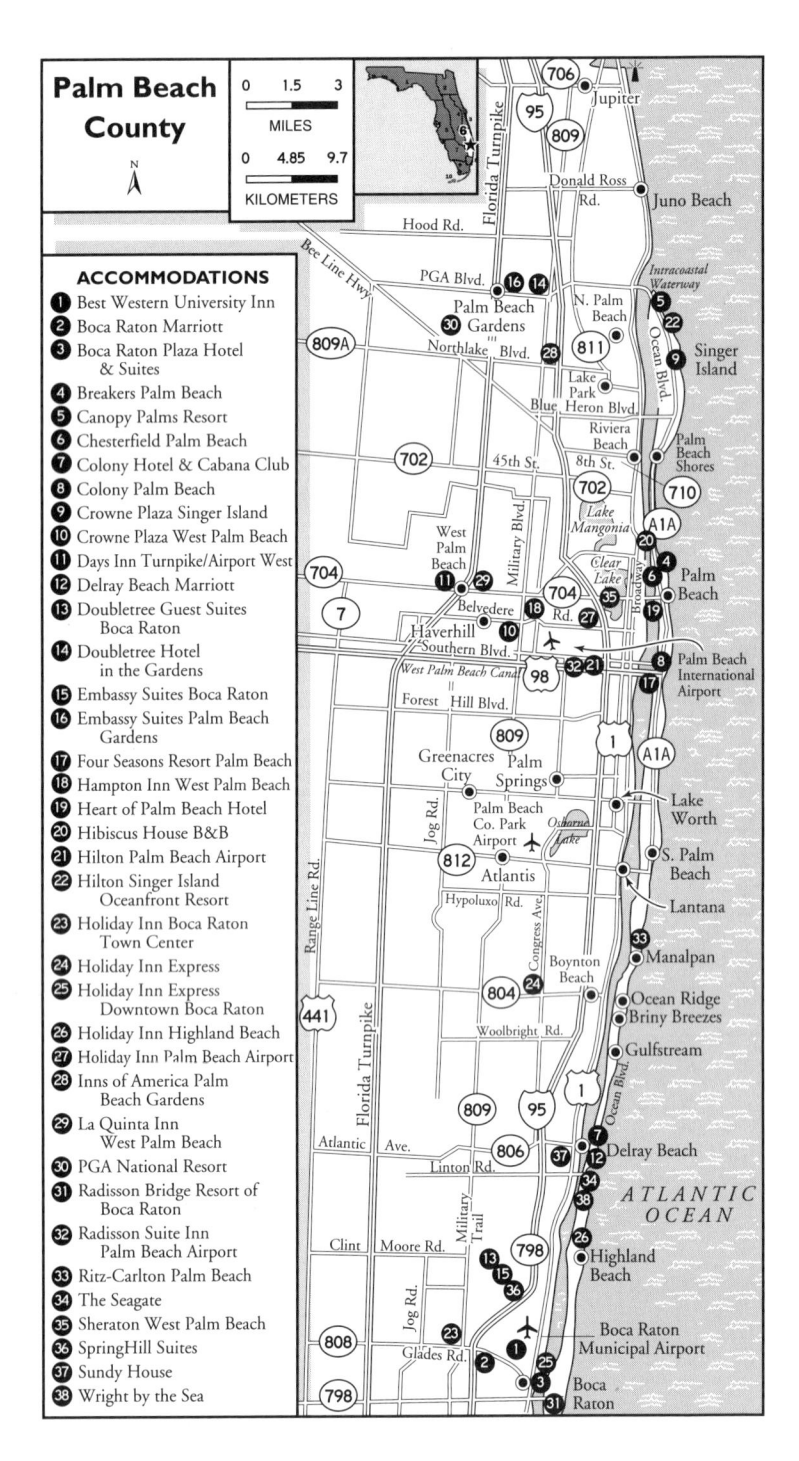

0 — 1.5 — 3 MILES
0 — 4.85 — 9.7 KILOMETERS

ACCOMMODATIONS
1. Best Western University Inn
2. Boca Raton Marriott
3. Boca Raton Plaza Hotel & Suites
4. Breakers Palm Beach
5. Canopy Palms Resort
6. Chesterfield Palm Beach
7. Colony Hotel & Cabana Club
8. Colony Palm Beach
9. Crowne Plaza Singer Island
10. Crowne Plaza West Palm Beach
11. Days Inn Turnpike/Airport West
12. Delray Beach Marriott
13. Doubletree Guest Suites Boca Raton
14. Doubletree Hotel in the Gardens
15. Embassy Suites Boca Raton
16. Embassy Suites Palm Beach Gardens
17. Four Seasons Resort Palm Beach
18. Hampton Inn West Palm Beach
19. Heart of Palm Beach Hotel
20. Hibiscus House B&B
21. Hilton Palm Beach Airport
22. Hilton Singer Island Oceanfront Resort
23. Holiday Inn Boca Raton Town Center
24. Holiday Inn Express
25. Holiday Inn Express Downtown Boca Raton
26. Holiday Inn Highland Beach
27. Holiday Inn Palm Beach Airport
28. Inns of America Palm Beach Gardens
29. La Quinta Inn West Palm Beach
30. PGA National Resort
31. Radisson Bridge Resort of Boca Raton
32. Radisson Suite Inn Palm Beach Airport
33. Ritz-Carlton Palm Beach
34. The Seagate
35. Sheraton West Palm Beach
36. SpringHill Suites
37. Sundy House
38. Wright by the Sea

Miami Beach

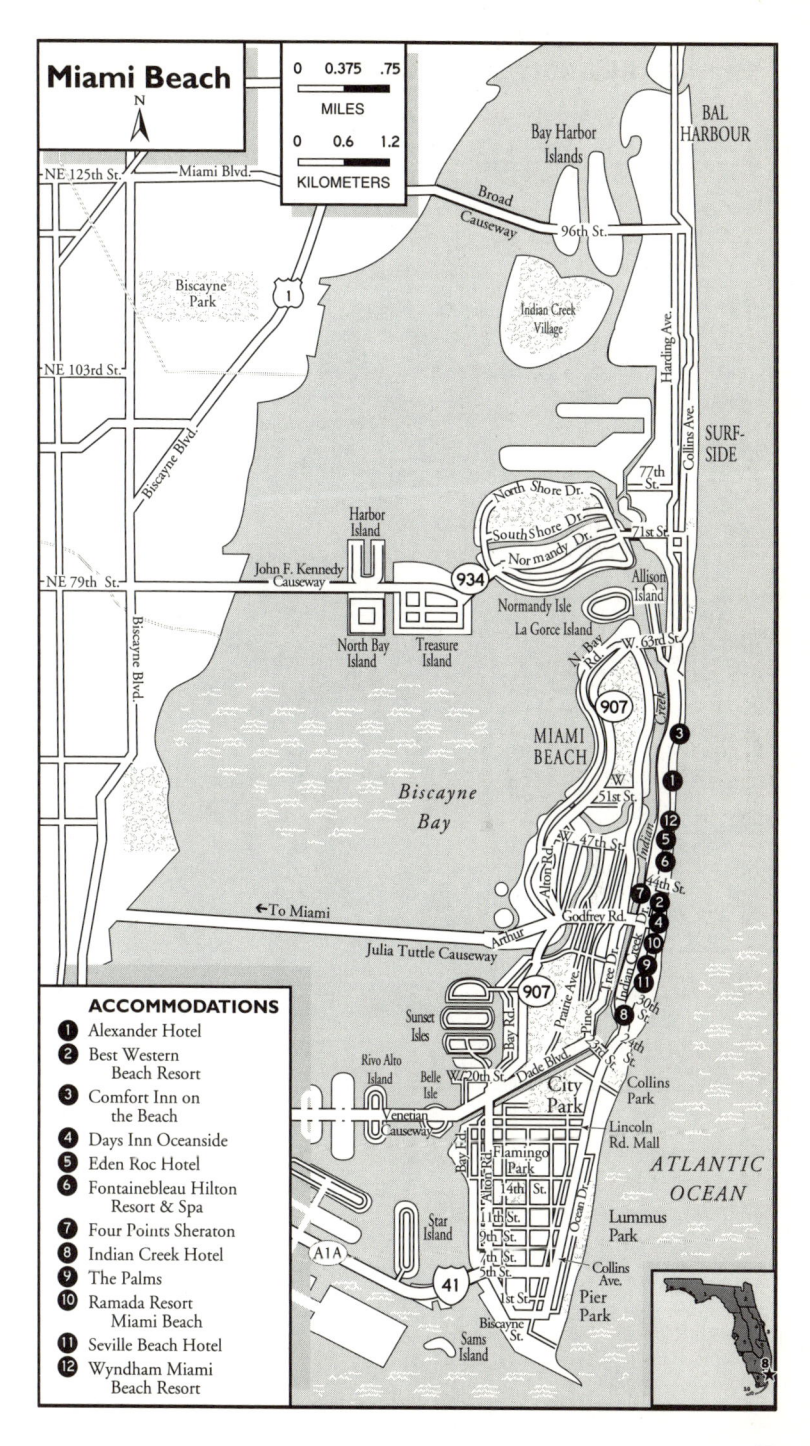

ACCOMMODATIONS
1. Alexander Hotel
2. Best Western Beach Resort
3. Comfort Inn on the Beach
4. Days Inn Oceanside
5. Eden Roc Hotel
6. Fontainebleau Hilton Resort & Spa
7. Four Points Sheraton
8. Indian Creek Hotel
9. The Palms
10. Ramada Resort Miami Beach
11. Seville Beach Hotel
12. Wyndham Miami Beach Resort

47

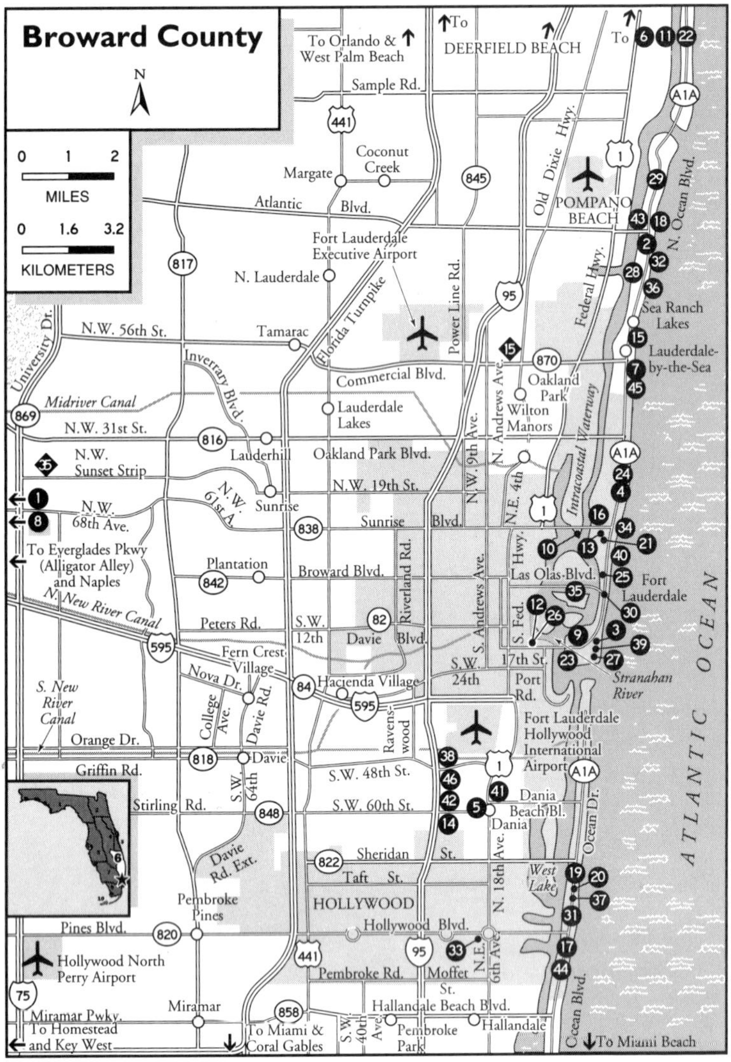
Broward County
N
0 1 2
MILES
0 1.6 3.2
KILOMETERS
To Orlando & West Palm Beach
To DEERFIELD BEACH
To 6 11 22
Sample Rd.
441
Coconut Creek
Margate
845
1
Old Dixie Hwy.
POMPANO BEACH
A1A
29
N. Ocean Blvd.
Atlantic Blvd.
43 18
2
32
28
36
Fort Lauderdale Executive Airport
817
N. Lauderdale
Florida Turnpike
Power Line Rd.
95
Federal Hwy.
Sea Ranch Lakes
15
Lauderdale-by-the-Sea
7
45
N.W. 56th St.
Tamarac
University Dr.
Inverrary Blvd.
Commercial Blvd.
870
Oakland Park
Wilton Manors
Midriver Canal
869
N.W. 31st St.
816
Lauderdale Lakes
N. Andrews Ave.
N.W. 9th Ave.
Intracoastal Waterway
N.W. Sunset Strip
35
Lauderhill
Oakland Park Blvd.
N.E. 4th
A1A
24
4
1
8
N.W. 68th Ave.
N.W. 61st A.
Sunrise
N.W. 19th St.
838
Sunrise Blvd.
16
34
21
10
13
40
25
Fort Lauderdale
To Everglades Pkwy (Alligator Alley) and Naples
Plantation
842
Broward Blvd.
Riverland Rd.
S. Andrews Ave.
Hwy.
Las Olas Blvd.
35
30
N. New River Canal
Peters Rd.
S.W. 12th
82
Davie Blvd.
S. Fed.
12
26
9
3
39
595
Fern Crest Village
17th St.
23
27
Stranahan River
S. New River Canal
Nova Dr.
84
Hacienda Village
S.W. 24th
Port Rd.
595
College Ave.
Davie Rd.
Ravenswood
Fort Lauderdale Hollywood International Airport
Orange Dr.
818
Davie
38
1
A1A
Griffin Rd.
S.W. 64th
S.W. 48th St.
46
41
Dania Beach Bl.
Stirling Rd.
848
S.W. 60th St.
42
5
Dania
14
Ocean Dr.
ATLANTIC OCEAN
Davie Rd. Ext.
822
Sheridan St.
N. 18th Ave.
West Lake
19
20
Taft St.
37
Pembroke Pines
HOLLYWOOD
31
Pines Blvd.
820
Hollywood Blvd.
33
N.E. 6th Ave.
17
Hollywood North Perry Airport
441
95
44
Pembroke Rd.
Moffet St.
75
Miramar
858
Hallandale Beach Blvd.
Miramar Pwky.
To Homestead and Key West
To Miami & Coral Gables
S.W. 40th Ave.
Pembroke Park
Hallandale
Ocean Blvd.
To Miami Beach

Broward County Accommodations

1. Baymont Inn & Suites Sunrise
2. Best Western Beachcomber
3. Best Western Oceanside Inn
4. Best Western Pelican Beach Resort
5. Comfort Inn Fort Lauderdale Airport
6. Comfort Inn Oceanside
7. Courtyard Villas on the Ocean
8. Crowne Plaza Sawgrass
9. Days Inn Bahia Cabana
10. Doubletree Guest Suites
11. Embassy Suites Deerfield Beach Resort
12. Embassy Suites Fort Lauderdale
13. Fort Lauderdale Beach Resort
14. Hampton Inn & Suites
15. High Noon Beach Resort
16. Holiday Inn Fort Lauderdale Beach
17. Holiday Inn Hollywood Beach
18. Holiday Inn Oceanside
19. Hollywood Beach Inn
20. Hollywood Sands
21. Howard Johnson Ocean's Edge Fort Lauderdale
22. Howard Johnson Plaza Resort
23. Hyatt Regency Pier Sixty-Six
24. Ireland's Inn Beach Resort
25. Marriott BeachPlace Towers
26. Marriott Fort Lauderdale Marina
27. Marriott's Harbor Beach Resort
28. Paradise Beach Resort
29. Quality Inn Pompano Beach
30. Radisson Bahia Mar Beach Resort
31. Ramada Inn Hollywood Beach Resort Hotel
32. Ramada Ocean Beach Resort
33. Ramada Plaza Hotel
34. Ramada Sea Club Resort
35. Riverside Hotel
36. Sea Castle Inn
37. Sheldon Ocean Resort
38. Sheraton Fort Lauderdale Airport
39. Sheraton Yankee Clipper
40. Sheraton Yankee Trader
41. Sleep Inn & Suites Fort Lauderdale Airport
42. SpringHill Suites
43. Villamar Inn
44. Westin Diplomat Resort & Spa
45. Windjammer Resort & Beach Club
46. Wyndham Fort Lauderdale Airport

Miami Area

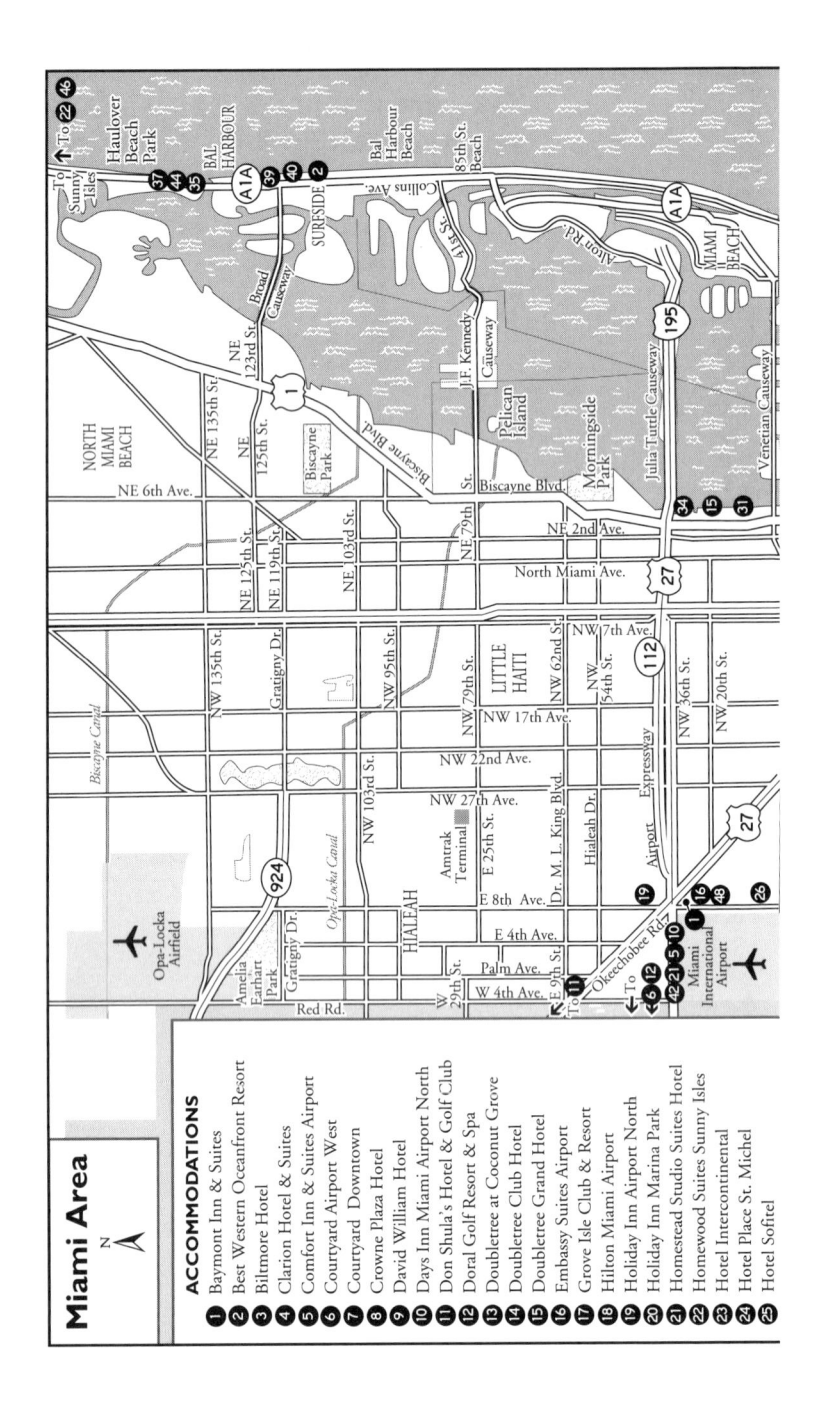

ACCOMMODATIONS

1. Baymont Inn & Suites
2. Best Western Oceanfront Resort
3. Biltmore Hotel
4. Clarion Hotel & Suites
5. Comfort Inn & Suites Airport
6. Courtyard Airport West
7. Courtyard Downtown
8. Crowne Plaza Hotel
9. David William Hotel
10. Days Inn Miami Airport North
11. Don Shula's Hotel & Golf Club
12. Doral Golf Resort & Spa
13. Doubletree at Coconut Grove
14. Doubletree Club Hotel
15. Doubletree Grand Hotel
16. Embassy Suites Airport
17. Grove Isle Club & Resort
18. Hilton Miami Airport
19. Holiday Inn Airport North
20. Holiday Inn Marina Park
21. Homestead Studio Suites Hotel
22. Homewood Suites Sunny Isles
23. Hotel Intercontinental
24. Hotel Place St. Michel
25. Hotel Sofitel

50

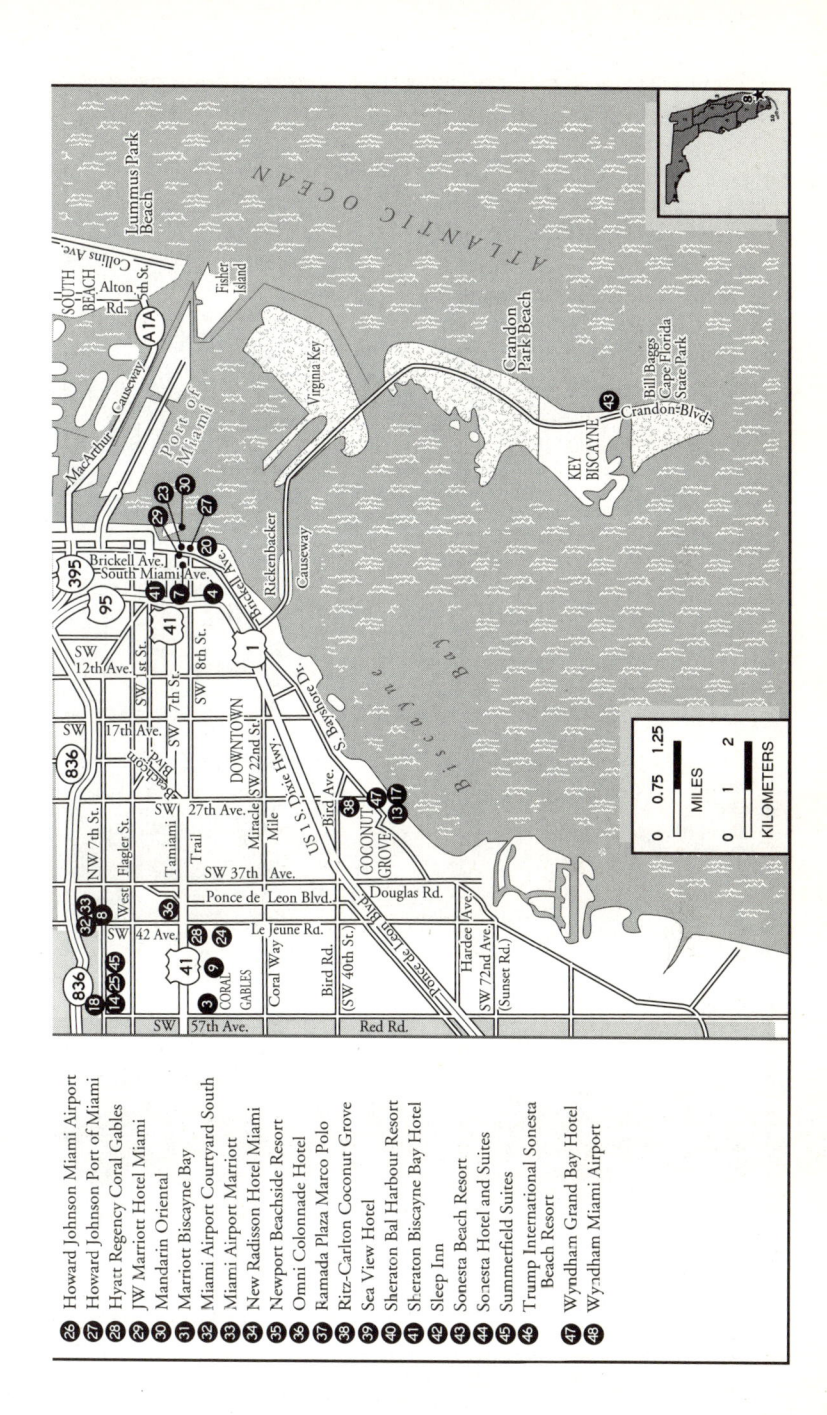

26 Howard Johnson Miami Airport
27 Howard Johnson Port of Miami
28 Hyatt Regency Coral Gables
29 JW Marriott Hotel Miami
30 Mandarin Oriental
31 Marriott Biscayne Bay
32 Miami Airport Courtyard South
33 Miami Airport Marriott
34 New Radisson Hotel Miami
35 Newport Beachside Resort
36 Omni Colonnade Hotel
37 Ramada Plaza Marco Polo
38 Ritz-Carlton Coconut Grove
39 Sea View Hotel
40 Sheraton Bal Harbour Resort
41 Sheraton Biscayne Bay Hotel
42 Sleep Inn
43 Sonesta Beach Resort
44 Sonesta Hotel and Suites
45 Summerfield Suites
46 Trump International Sonesta Beach Resort
47 Wyndham Grand Bay Hotel
48 Wyndham Miami Airport

51

South Beach

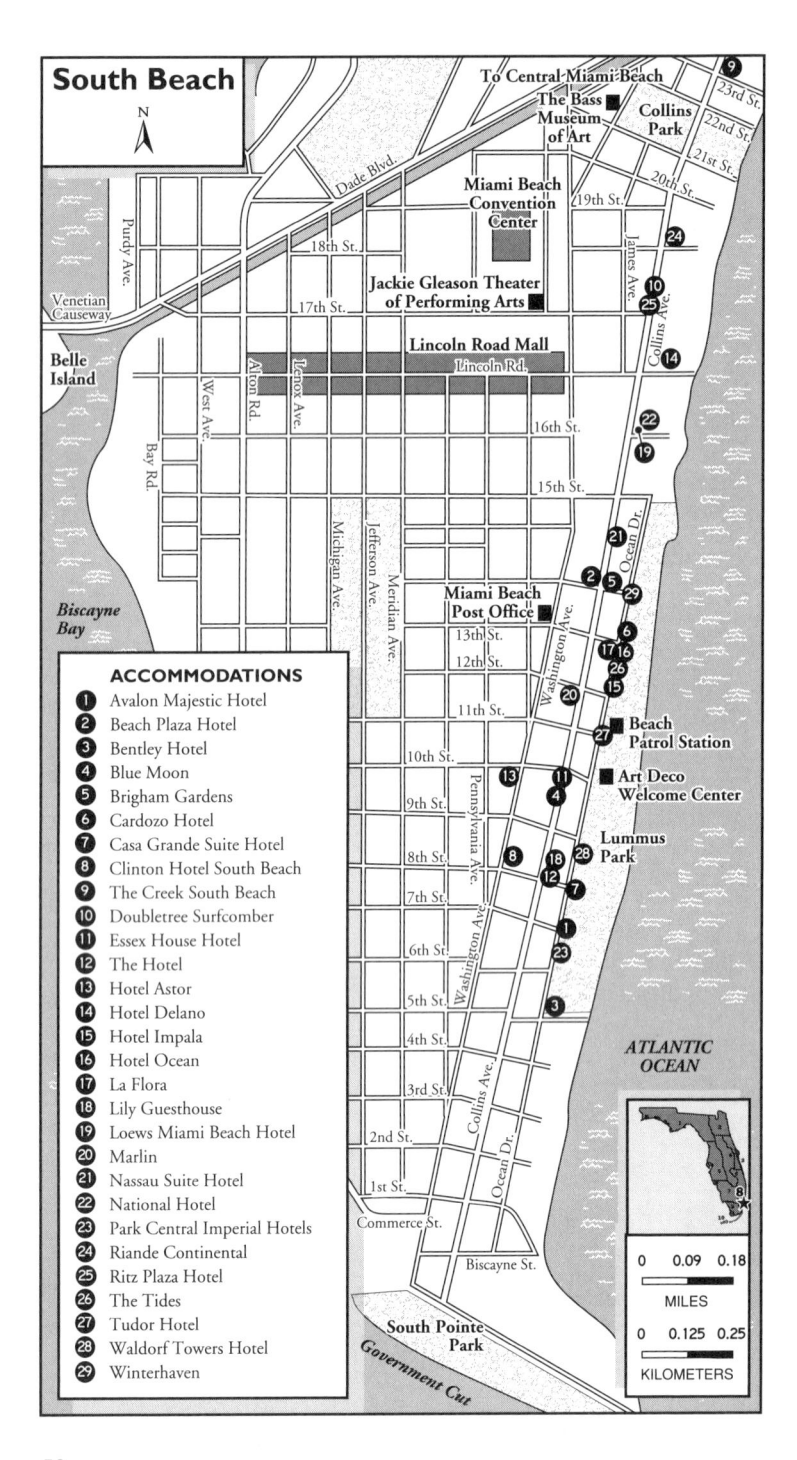

N

To Central Miami Beach
The Bass Museum of Art
Collins Park
Miami Beach Convention Center
Jackie Gleason Theater of Performing Arts
Lincoln Road Mall
Miami Beach Post Office
Beach Patrol Station
Art Deco Welcome Center
Lummus Park
South Pointe Park

Biscayne Bay
Belle Island
Venetian Causeway
Atlantic Ocean

Dade Blvd., Purdy Ave., West Ave., Bay Rd., Alton Rd., Lenox Ave., Michigan Ave., Jefferson Ave., Meridian Ave., Pennsylvania Ave., Washington Ave., Collins Ave., Ocean Dr., James Ave.

23rd St., 22nd St., 21st St., 20th St., 19th St., 18th St., 17th St., 16th St., 15th St., 13th St., 12th St., 11th St., 10th St., 9th St., 8th St., 7th St., 6th St., 5th St., 4th St., 3rd St., 2nd St., 1st St., Commerce St., Biscayne St., Government Cut

ACCOMMODATIONS

1. Avalon Majestic Hotel
2. Beach Plaza Hotel
3. Bentley Hotel
4. Blue Moon
5. Brigham Gardens
6. Cardozo Hotel
7. Casa Grande Suite Hotel
8. Clinton Hotel South Beach
9. The Creek South Beach
10. Doubletree Surfcomber
11. Essex House Hotel
12. The Hotel
13. Hotel Astor
14. Hotel Delano
15. Hotel Impala
16. Hotel Ocean
17. La Flora
18. Lily Guesthouse
19. Loews Miami Beach Hotel
20. Marlin
21. Nassau Suite Hotel
22. National Hotel
23. Park Central Imperial Hotels
24. Riande Continental
25. Ritz Plaza Hotel
26. The Tides
27. Tudor Hotel
28. Waldorf Towers Hotel
29. Winterhaven

0 0.09 0.18
MILES

0 0.125 0.25
KILOMETERS

52

The Florida Keys

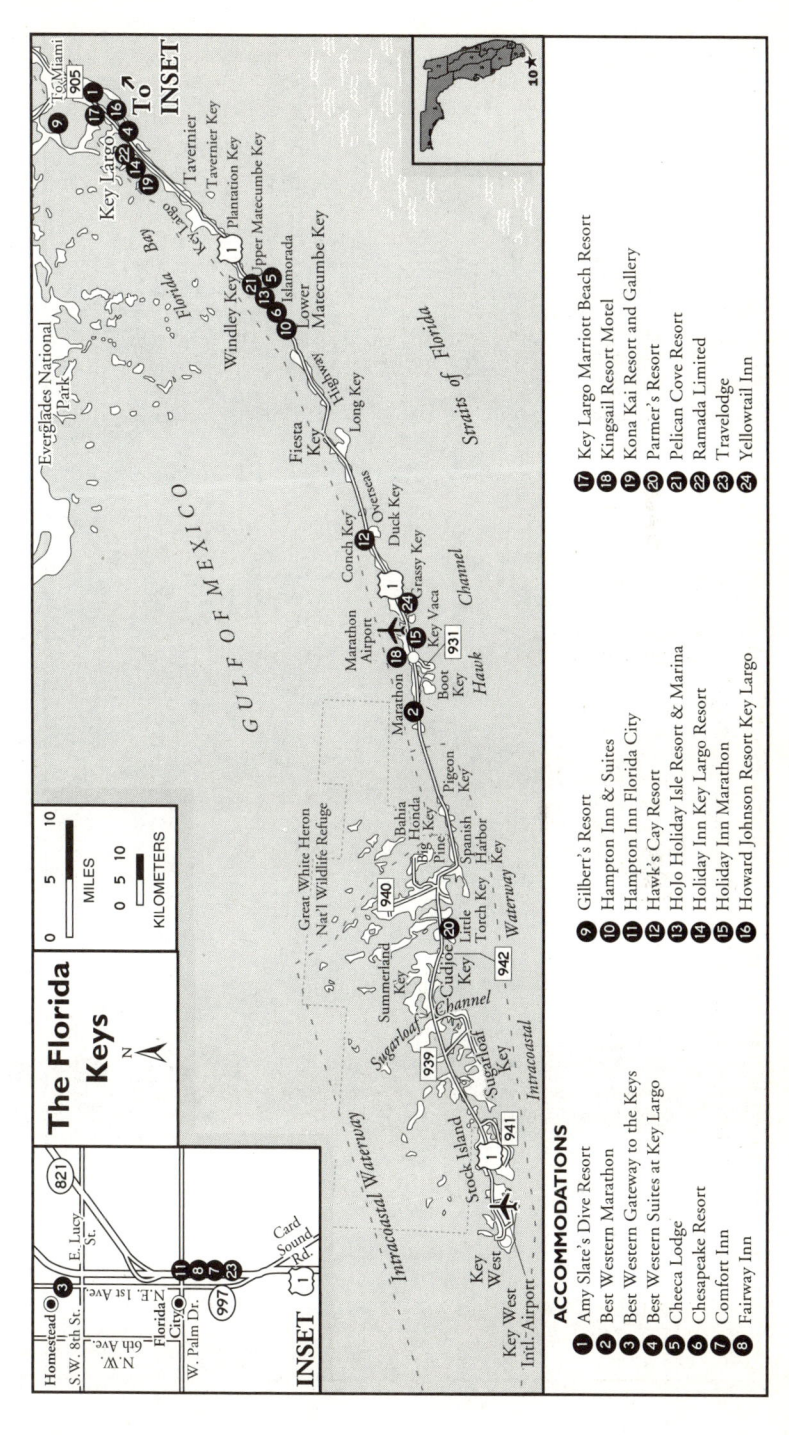

ACCOMMODATIONS

1. Amy Slate's Dive Resort
2. Best Western Marathon
3. Best Western Gateway to the Keys
4. Best Western Suites at Key Largo
5. Cheeca Lodge
6. Chesapeake Resort
7. Comfort Inn
8. Fairway Inn
9. Gilbert's Resort
10. Hampton Inn & Suites
11. Hampton Inn Florida City
12. Hawk's Cay Resort
13. Hojo Holiday Isle Resort & Marina
14. Holiday Inn Key Largo Resort
15. Holiday Inn Marathon
16. Howard Johnson Resort Key Largo
17. Key Largo Marriott Beach Resort
18. Kingsail Resort Motel
19. Kona Kai Resort and Gallery
20. Parmer's Resort
21. Pelican Cove Resort
22. Ramada Limited
23. Travelodge
24. Yellowtail Inn

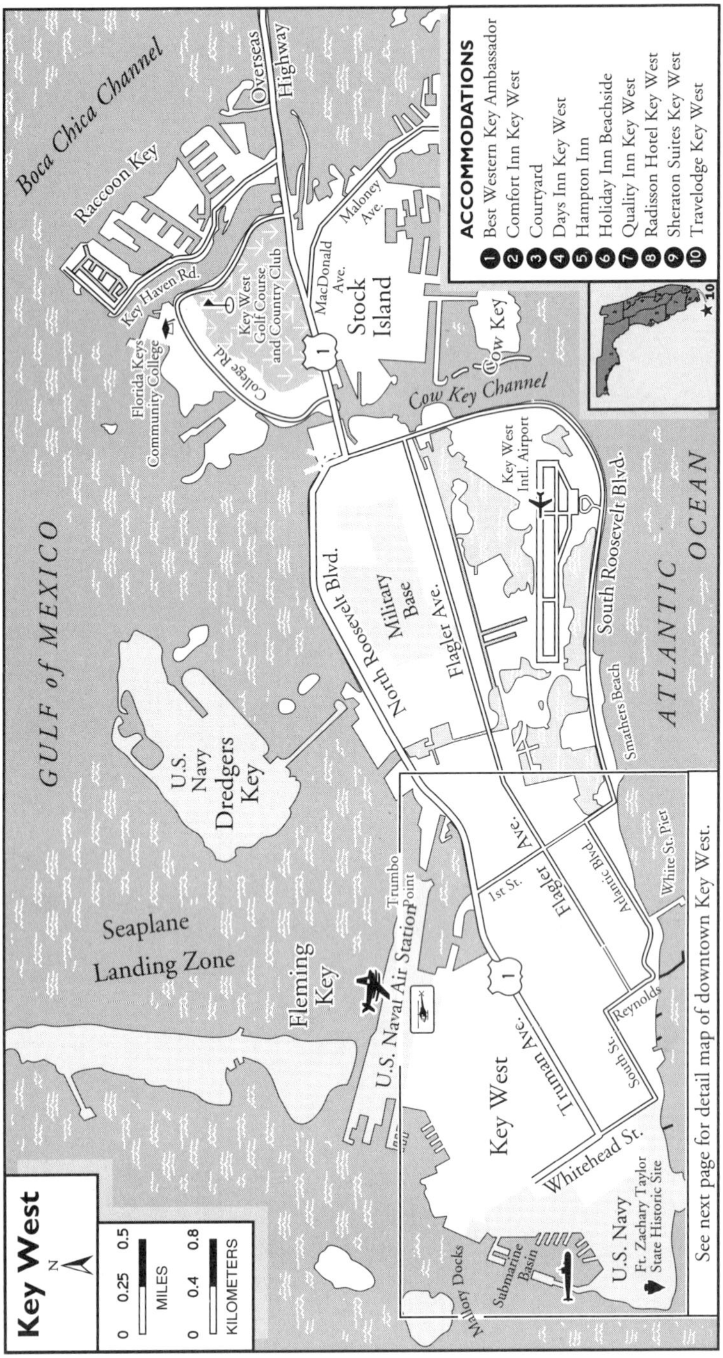
Key West
N
0 0.25 0.5
MILES
0 0.4 0.8
KILOMETERS
GULF of MEXICO
ATLANTIC OCEAN
Boca Chica Channel
Raccoon Key
Overseas Highway
Key Haven Rd.
Florida Keys Community College
College Rd.
Key West Golf Course and Country Club
MacDonald Ave.
Maloney Ave.
Stock Island
Cow Key
Cow Key Channel
Key West Intl. Airport
South Roosevelt Blvd.
North Roosevelt Blvd.
Military Base
Flagler Ave.
Smathers Beach
U.S. Navy Dredgers Key
Seaplane Landing Zone
Fleming Key
Trumbo Point
U.S. Naval Air Station
1st St.
Ave.
Flagler
Atlantic Blvd.
White St. Pier
Reynolds
South St.
Truman Ave.
Key West
Whitehead St.
Mallory Docks
Submarine Basin
U.S. Navy
Ft. Zachary Taylor State Historic Site
See next page for detail map of downtown Key West.
ACCOMMODATIONS
1 Best Western Key Ambassador
2 Comfort Inn Key West
3 Courtyard
4 Days Inn Key West
5 Hampton Inn
6 Holiday Inn Beachside
7 Quality Inn Key West
8 Radisson Hotel Key West
9 Sheraton Suites Key West
10 Travelodge Key West

Downtown Key West

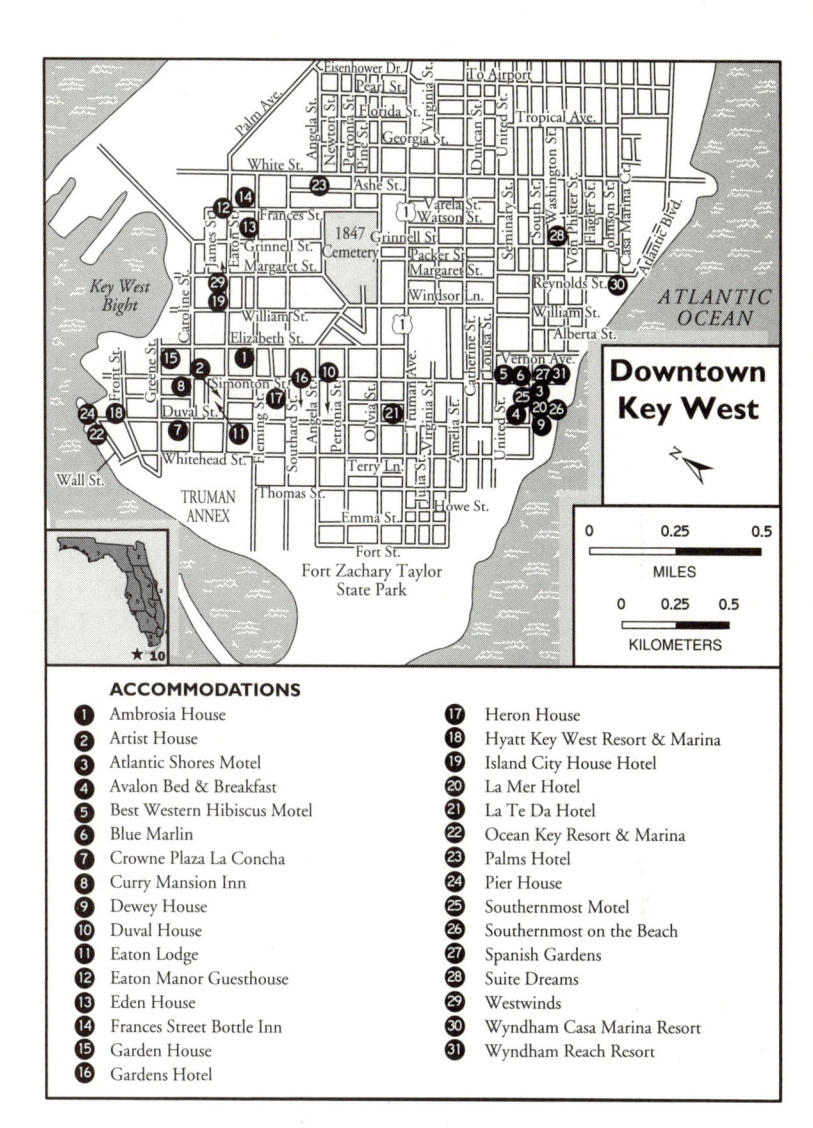

ACCOMMODATIONS

1. Ambrosia House
2. Artist House
3. Atlantic Shores Motel
4. Avalon Bed & Breakfast
5. Best Western Hibiscus Motel
6. Blue Marlin
7. Crowne Plaza La Concha
8. Curry Mansion Inn
9. Dewey House
10. Duval House
11. Eaton Lodge
12. Eaton Manor Guesthouse
13. Eden House
14. Frances Street Bottle Inn
15. Garden House
16. Gardens Hotel
17. Heron House
18. Hyatt Key West Resort & Marina
19. Island City House Hotel
20. La Mer Hotel
21. La Te Da Hotel
22. Ocean Key Resort & Marina
23. Palms Hotel
24. Pier House
25. Southernmost Motel
26. Southernmost on the Beach
27. Spanish Gardens
28. Suite Dreams
29. Westwinds
30. Wyndham Casa Marina Resort
31. Wyndham Reach Resort

55

Fort Myers

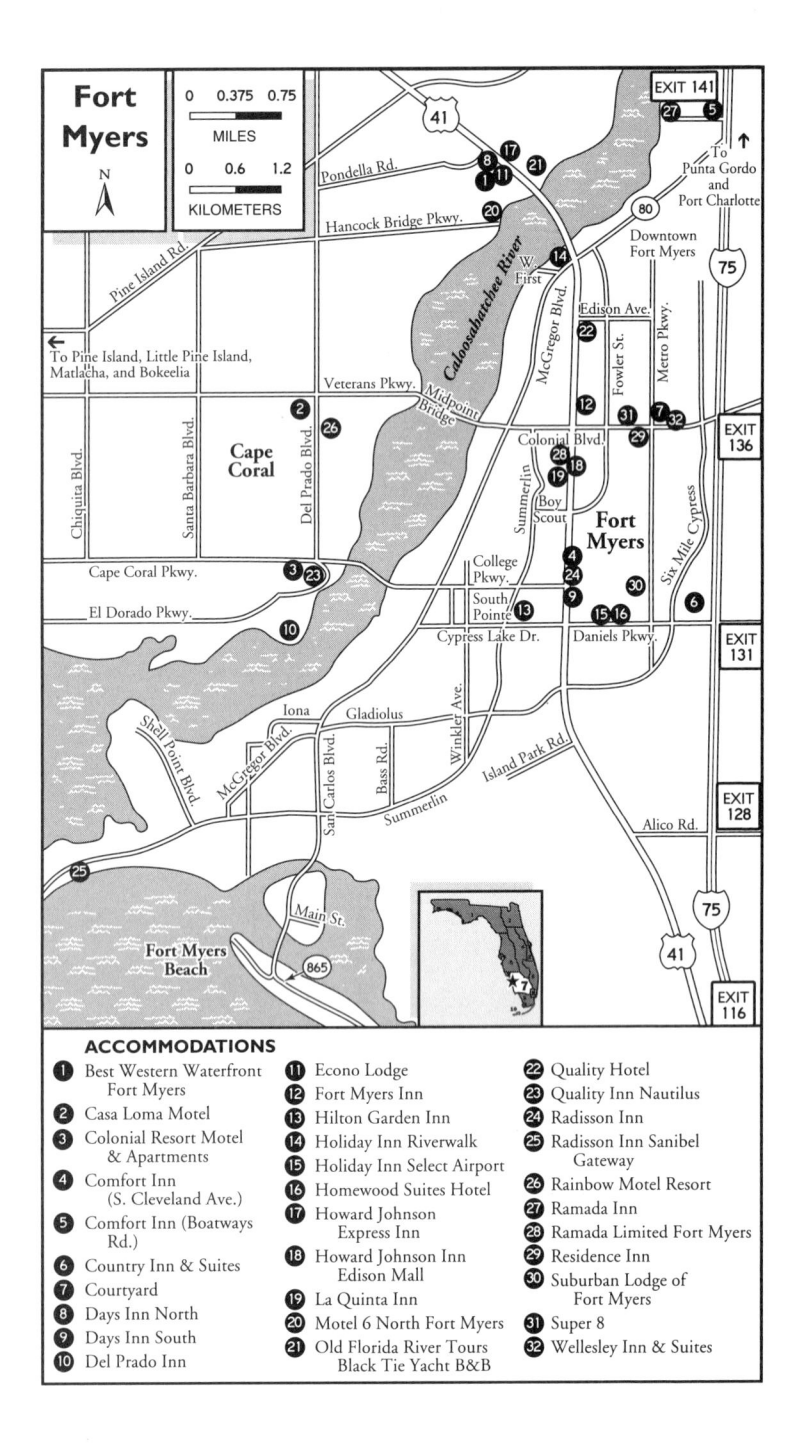

ACCOMMODATIONS

1. Best Western Waterfront Fort Myers
2. Casa Loma Motel
3. Colonial Resort Motel & Apartments
4. Comfort Inn (S. Cleveland Ave.)
5. Comfort Inn (Boatways Rd.)
6. Country Inn & Suites
7. Courtyard
8. Days Inn North
9. Days Inn South
10. Del Prado Inn
11. Econo Lodge
12. Fort Myers Inn
13. Hilton Garden Inn
14. Holiday Inn Riverwalk
15. Holiday Inn Select Airport
16. Homewood Suites Hotel
17. Howard Johnson Express Inn
18. Howard Johnson Inn Edison Mall
19. La Quinta Inn
20. Motel 6 North Fort Myers
21. Old Florida River Tours Black Tie Yacht B&B
22. Quality Hotel
23. Quality Inn Nautilus
24. Radisson Inn
25. Radisson Inn Sanibel Gateway
26. Rainbow Motel Resort
27. Ramada Inn
28. Ramada Limited Fort Myers
29. Residence Inn
30. Suburban Lodge of Fort Myers
31. Super 8
32. Wellesley Inn & Suites

Fort Myers Beach

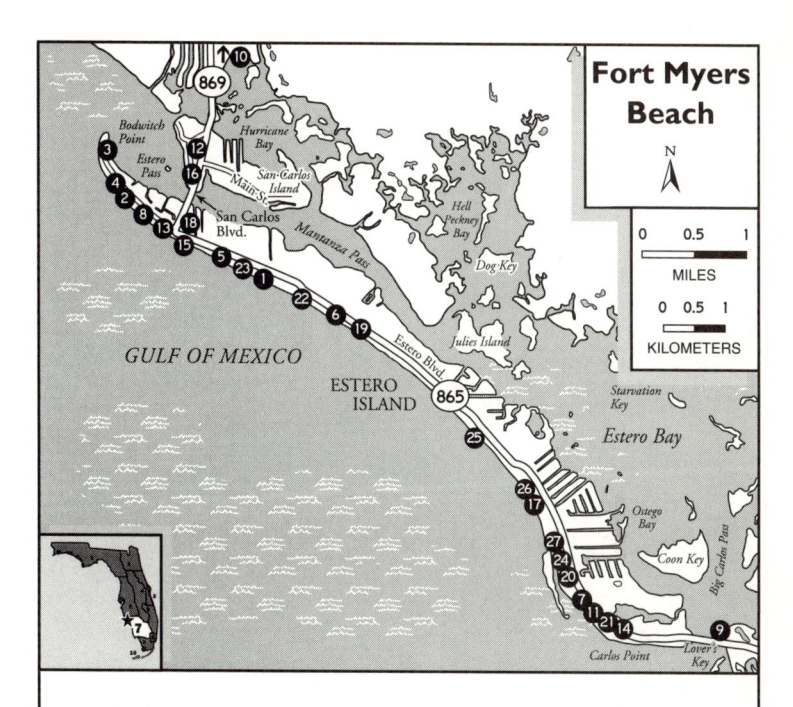

ACCOMMODATIONS

1. Beacon Motel & Gift Shop
2. Best Western Beach Resort
3. Best Western Pink Shell Beach Resort
4. Casa Playa Beach Resort
5. Days Inn Island Beach Resort
6. DiamondHead All Suite Beach Resort
7. Dolphin Inn
8. Edison Beach House
9. GrandView All Suite Resort
10. GuestHouse Inn Mariner's Lodge & Marina
11. Gullwing Beach Resort
12. Hidden Harbor Inn
13. Holiday Court Motel
14. Holiday Inn Fort Myers Beach
15. Howard Johnson Beachfront
16. Island Motel
17. Kahlua Beach Club
18. Lighthouse Island Resort
19. Neptune Inn
20. Outrigger Beach Resort
21. Pointe Estero Resort
22. Quality Inn & Suites at the Lani Kai
23. Ramada Inn Beachfront
24. Sandpiper Gulf Resort
25. Sandy Beach Hideaway
26. Ti Ki Resort
27. Tropical Inn Resort

57

Naples

N

0   0.5   1
MILES

0   0.8   1.6
KILOMETERS

ACCOMMODATIONS
1. Baymont Inn
2. Bel Mar Resort
3. Best Western Naples
4. Bonita Beach Resort Motel
5. Clarion Inn & Suites
6. Comfort Inn Bonita Springs
7. Comfort Inn Downtown Naples
8. Doubletree Guest Suites Naples
9. Flamingo Motel
10. Hampton Inn Bonita Springs
11. Hampton Inn Naples
12. Hawthorn Suites
13. Hilton Naples & Towers
14. Holiday Inn Express Hotel & Suites
15. Holiday Inn Naples
16. Hotel Escalante
17. Inn at Pelican Bay
18. Inn on Fifth
19. La Playa Beach Resort
20. Lemon Tree Inn
21. Lighthouse Inn
22. Naples Beach Hotel & Golf Club
23. Naples Courtyard
24. Quality Inn Gulfcoast
25. Ramada Plaza Hotel
26. Registry Resort
27. Residence Inn
28. Ritz-Carlton Naples
29. Sea Court Hotel
30. Staybridge Suites by Holiday Inn
31. Tradewinds
32. Trianon Bonita Bay
33. Vanderbilt Beach Resort House
34. White Sands Resort Club

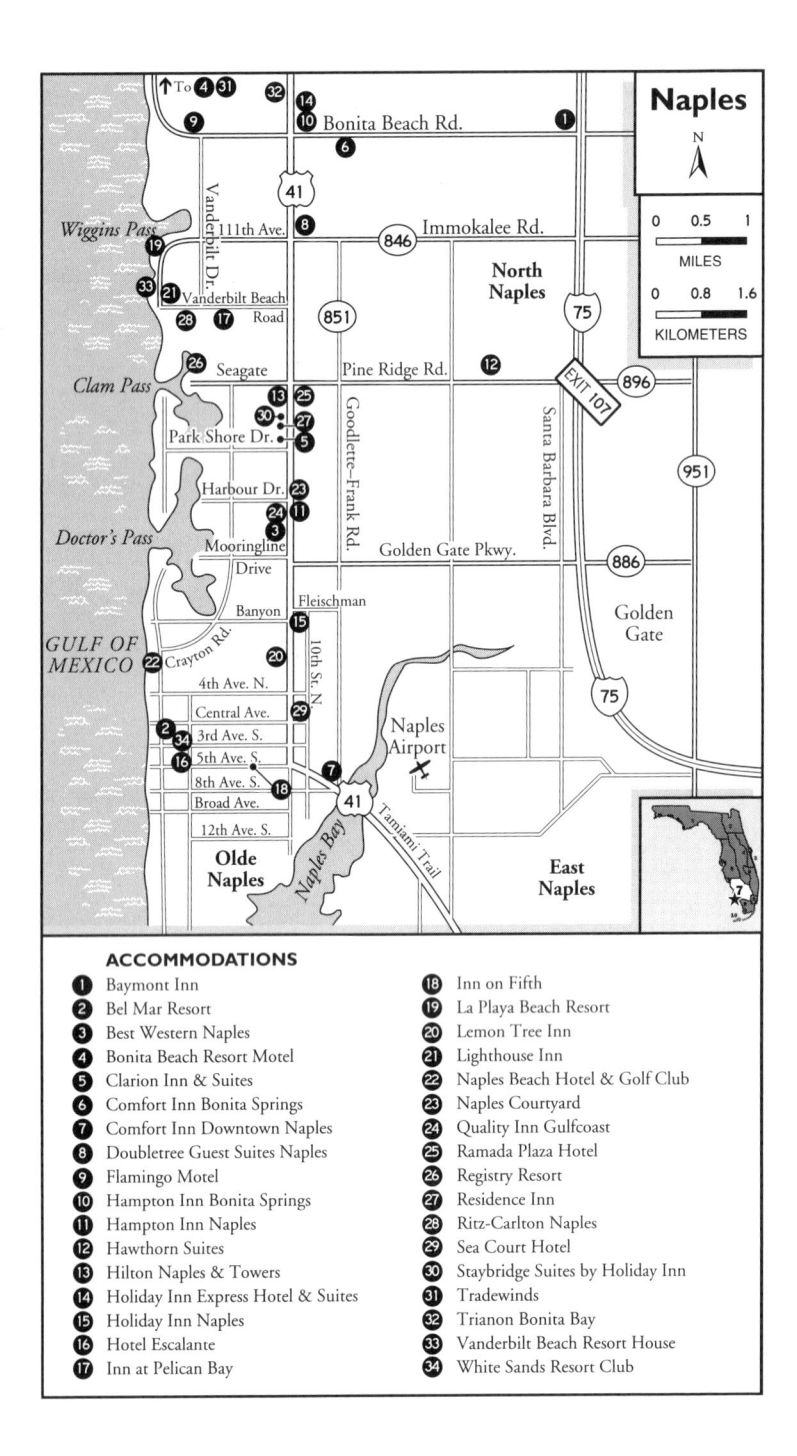

ACCOMMODATIONS

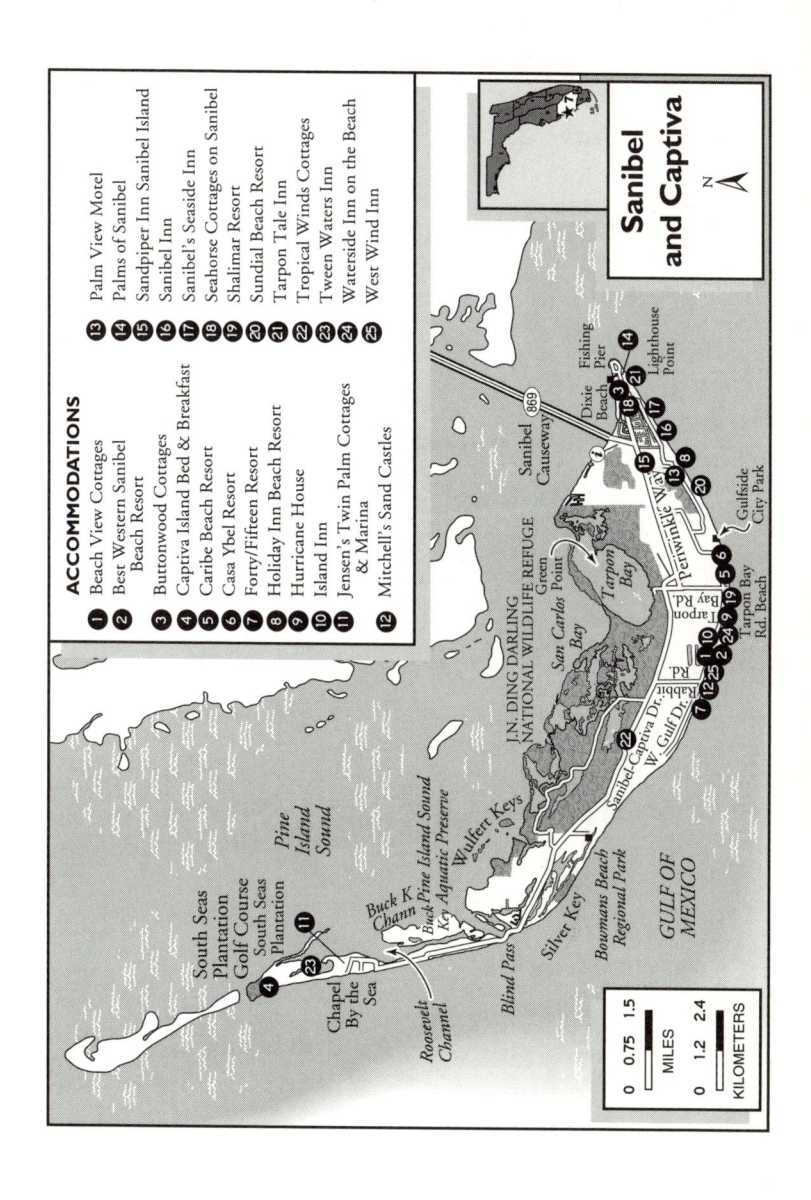

1. Beach View Cottages
2. Best Western Sanibel Beach Resort
3. Buttonwood Cottages
4. Captiva Island Bed & Breakfast
5. Caribe Beach Resort
6. Casa Ybel Resort
7. Forty/Fifteen Resort
8. Holiday Inn Beach Resort
9. Hurricane House
10. Island Inn
11. Jensen's Twin Palm Cottages & Marina
12. Mitchell's Sand Castles
13. Palm View Motel
14. Palms of Sanibel
15. Sandpiper Inn Sanibel Island
16. Sanibel Inn
17. Sanibel's Seaside Inn
18. Seahorse Cottages on Sanibel
19. Shalimar Resort
20. Sundial Beach Resort
21. Tarpon Tale Inn
22. Tropical Winds Cottages
23. Tween Waters Inn
24. Waterside Inn on the Beach
25. West Wind Inn

Sanibel and Captiva

59

Marco Island

ACCOMMODATIONS
1. Boat House Motel
2. Marco Beach Ocean Resort
3. Marco Island Hilton Beach Resort
4. Marco Resort & Club
5. Marriott Resort of Marco Island
6. Port of the Islands Resort
7. Radisson Suite Beach Resort

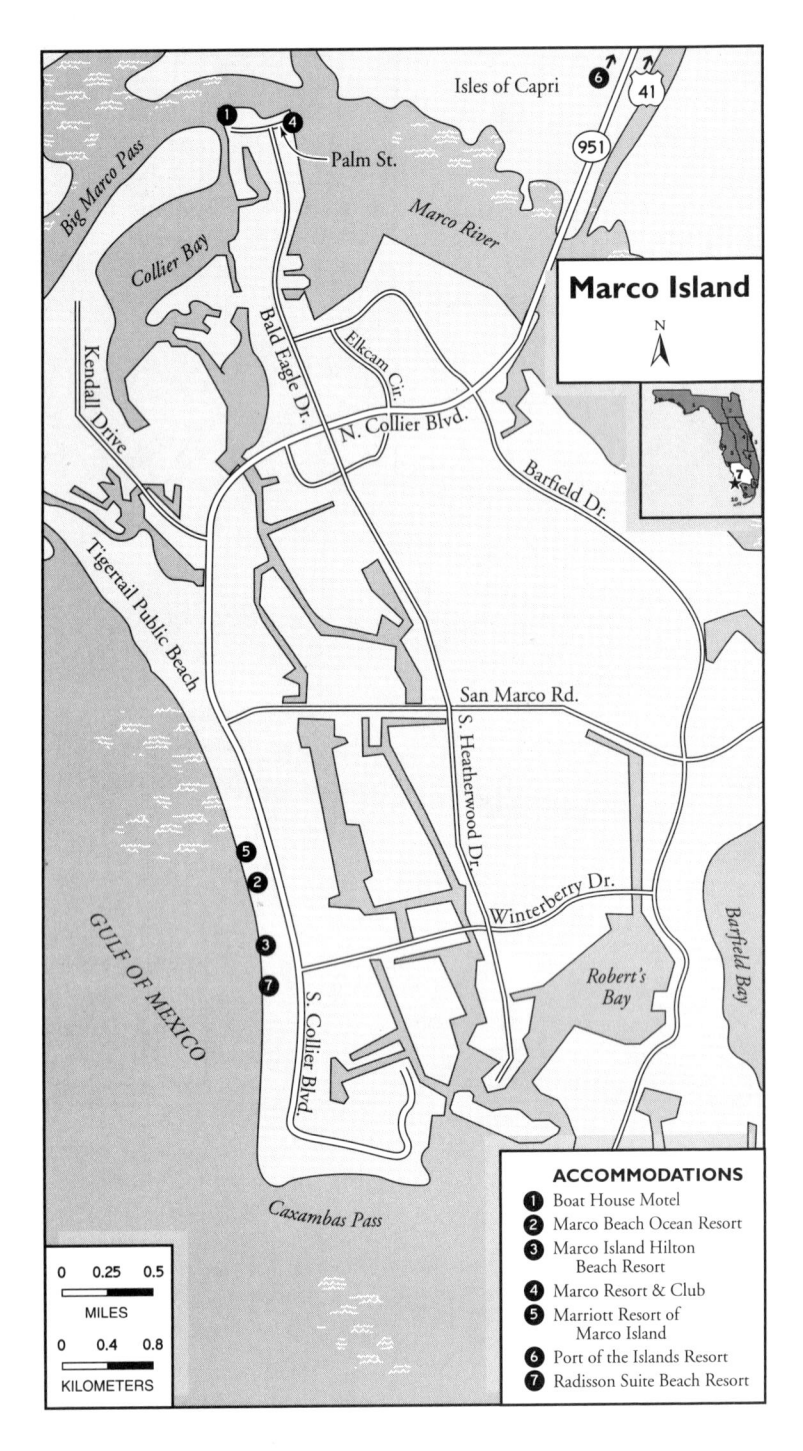

When wholesalers and consolidators deal directly with the public, they frequently represent themselves as "reservation services." When you call, you can ask for a rate quote for a particular hotel, or, alternatively, ask for their best available deal in the area where you prefer to stay. If there is a maximum amount you are willing to pay, say so. Chances are the service will find something to suit you. Sometimes you will have to pay for your room when you make your reservation using your credit card. Other times you will pay as usual, when you check out. Listed below are several services that frequently offer substantial discounts:

Budget Reservations (800) 681-1993
Central Reservation Service (800) 950-0232
Hotel Reservations Network (800) 964-6835
Florida Hotel Network (800) 538-3616

Exit Information Guide

A company called EIG (Exit Information Guide) publishes a book of discount coupons for bargain rates at hotels throughout the state of Florida. These books are available free of charge in many restaurants and motels along the main interstate highways leading to the Sunshine State. Because most folks make reservations prior to leaving home, picking up the coupon book en route does not help much. For $2 ($5 Canadian), however, EIG will mail you a copy (third class) before you make your reservations. If you call and use a credit card, EIG will send the guide first class for $3. Write or call:

Exit Information Guide
4205 Northwest Sixth Street
Gainesville, FL 32609
(352) 371-3948

Condominium Deals

There are a large number of condo resorts and timeshares in Florida that rent to vacationers for a week or even less. Bargains can be found, especially during off-peak periods. Reservations and information can be obtained from Condolink, (800) 733-4445.

The majority of area condos that rent to visitors also work with travel agents. In many cases the condo owners pay an enhanced commission to agents who rent the units for reduced consumer rates. It's worth a call to your travel agent.

Finding Deals on the Internet

Wholesalers, packagers, and many other travel and lodging players operate on the Internet, as do specialized web travel vendors. By far the easiest way to scout room deals on the Internet is through **www.travelaxe.com.** At Travelaxe, you can download free software (which only runs on PCs, not Macs) that scans the better Internet sites selling discounted rooms. Enter your proposed check-in and check-out dates (required) as well as preferences concerning location and price (optional), and click "Search." The program scans a dozen or more vendor sites and presents the discounted rates for all hotels in a chart for comparison. Note that the prices listed in the chart represent the total you'll pay for your entire stay, not the rate per night. If you decide to book, you deal directly with the site offering the best price. The software doesn't scan the individual hotel websites, so if you have a specific hotel in mind, you might want to check the hotel's site also.

Finally, for Internet shopping, consider **www.priceline.com** to bid for a room. You can't bid on a specific hotel but you can specify location ("Downtown Miami," "Miami Beach" etc.) and the quality rating expressed in stars. If your bid is accepted, you will be assigned to a hotel consistent with your location and quality requirements, and your credit card will be charged in a non-refundable transaction for your entire stay. Notification of acceptance usually takes less than an hour. We recommend bidding $30 to $45 per night for a three-star hotel and $60 to $85 per night for a four-star.

How to Evaluate a Travel Package

Hundreds of Florida package vacations are offered to the public each year. Packages should be a win-win proposition for both the buyer and the seller. The buyer only has to make one phone call and deal with a single salesperson to set up the whole vacation: transportation, rental car, lodging, meals, attraction admissions, and even golf and tennis. Because selling vacation packages is an efficient way of doing business, and because the packager can often buy individual package components (airfare, lodging, etc.) in bulk at a discount, savings in operating expenses realized by the seller are sometimes passed on to the buyer so that, in addition to convenience, the package is also an exceptional value. In any event, that is the way it is supposed to work.

All too often, in practice, the seller realizes all of the economies and passes on nothing in the way of savings to the buyer. In some instances, packages are loaded with extras that cost the packager next to nothing, but that run the retail price of the package sky-high. When considering a package, first choose one that includes features you are sure to use. Second, make a few phone calls and see what the package would cost if you booked its individual components (airfare, rental car, lodging, etc.) on your own. If the package price is less than or the same as the à la carte cost, the package is a good deal.

Helping Your Travel Agent Help You

When you call your travel agent, ask if he or she has been to your Florida destination. If the answer is no, do not accept recommendations at face value. Check out the location and rates of any suggested hotel and make certain that the hotel is suited to your itinerary. Travel agents unfamiliar with Florida may try to plug you into a tour operator's or wholesaler's preset package. This essentially allows the travel agent to set up your whole trip with a single phone call and still collect an 8%–10% commission. Often, travel agents will use wholesalers who run packages in conjunction with airlines. Because of the wholesaler's exclusive relationship with the carrier, these trips are often more expensive than packages offered by high-volume wholesalers who work with a number of airlines in the Florida market.

To help your travel agent get you the best possible deal, do the following:

1. Determine where you want to stay in Florida and, if possible, choose a specific hotel. This can be accomplished by reviewing the hotel information provided in this guide and by writing or calling hotels that interest you.
2. Check out the Florida travel ads in the Sunday travel section of your local newspaper and compare them to ads running in the newspapers of one of Florida's key markets, i.e., New York, Philadelphia, or Boston.
3. Call the wholesalers or tour operators whose ads you have collected. Ask any questions you might have concerning their products, but do not book your trip with them directly.
4. Tell your travel agent what you find and ask if he or she can get you something better.
5. Choose from among the options uncovered by you and your travel agent. No matter which option you select, have your travel agent book it. It will probably be commissionable (at no additional cost to you). Also, as a travel professional, your agent should be able to verify the quality and integrity of the package.

If You Make Your Own Reservation

As you poke around trying to find a good deal, there are several things you should know. First, always call the hotel in question as opposed to the hotel chain's national toll-free number. Quite often, the national call center is uninformed of local specials. Always ask about specials before you inquire about corporate rates. Do not be reluctant to bargain. If you are buying a hotel's weekend package, for example, and want to extend your stay into the following week, you can often obtain at least the corporate rate for the extra days. Do your bargaining, however, before you check in, preferably when you make your reservations.

Hotels and Motels: Rated and Ranked

Room Ratings

To separate properties according to the relative quality, tastefulness, state of repair, cleanliness, and size of their standard rooms, we have grouped hotels and motels into classifications denoted by stars. Star ratings in this guide apply to Florida properties only, and do not necessarily correspond to ratings awarded by Mobil, AAA, or other travel critics. Because stars have little relevance when awarded in the absence of commonly recognized standards of comparison, we have tied our ratings to expected levels of quality established by specific American hotel corporations.

Star ratings apply to room quality only, and describe the property's standard accommodations. For most hotels and motels a "standard accommodation" is a hotel room with either one king bed or two queen beds. In an all-suite property, the standard accommodation is either a one- or two-room suite. In addition to standard accommodations, many hotels offer luxury rooms and special suites, which are not rated in this guide. Star ratings for rooms are assigned without regard to whether a property has restaurant(s), recreational facilities, entertainment, or other extras.

	WHAT THE RATINGS MEAN	
★★★★★	Superior Rooms	Tasteful and luxurious by any standard
★★★★	Extremely Nice Rooms	What you would expect at a Hyatt Regency or Marriott
★★★	Nice Rooms	Holiday Inn or comparable quality
★★	Adequate Rooms	Clean, comfortable, and functional without frills—like a Motel 6
★	Super Budget	

In addition to stars (which delineate broad categories), we also employ a numerical rating system. Our rating scale is 0 to 100, with 100 as the best possible rating. Numerical ratings are presented to show the difference we perceive between one property and another. Rooms at the Four Points Sheraton, Essex House Hotel, and the Riande Contine ntal on Miami Beach are all rated as three stars. In the numerical ratings, the Four Points Sheraton is rated a 73, the Essex House Hotel a 72, and the Riande Continental a 67. This means that within the three-star category, the Sheraton and Essex House are comparable, and both have slightly nicer rooms than the Riande.

Cost estimates are based on the hotel's published rack rates for standard rooms. Each "$" represents $50. Thus a cost symbol of "$$$" means a room (or suite) at that hotel will be about $150 a night.

How the Hotels Compare

Here is a hit parade of the nicest rooms in Florida. We've focused strictly on room quality, and excluded any consideration of location, services, recreation, or amenities. (Although, as previously noted, we strongly recommend that your business or touring itinerary influence your lodging choice.)

With each edition of the *Unofficial Guide,* we include new properties and adjust ratings to reflect such positive developments as guest room renovation or improved maintenance and housekeeping in hotels already listed. A failure to properly maintain guest rooms or a lapse in housekeeping standards can negatively affect the ratings.

However, even with the best of intentions and the most conscientious research, we cannot inspect every room in every hotel. What we do, in statistical terms, is take a sample: we check out several rooms selected at random in each hotel and base our ratings on those rooms. The inspections are conducted anonymously and without the knowledge of the property's management. Our researchers strive for impartiality, but you will naturally apply your own prejudices when evaluating a hotel's decor and amenities. The key to avoiding a disappointing stay is to do some advance snooping around. We recommend that you ask to be sent a photo of a hotel's standard guest room before you book, or at least get a copy of the hotel's promotional brochure. Be forewarned, however, that some hotel chains use the same room photo in their promotional literature for all hotels in the chain, and that the rooms in a specific property may not resemble the brochure photo. When you or your travel agent call, ask how old the property is and when the guest room you are being assigned was last renovated. If you arrive and are assigned a room inferior to that which you had been led to expect, demand to be moved to another room.

HOW THE HOTELS COMPARE IN THE FLORIDA PANHANDLE

Hotel	Star Rating	Quality Rating	Cost ($=$50)	Phone
Apalachicola				
The Consulate	★★★★	89	$$$$–	(850) 653-1515
Apalachicola River Inn	★★★½	82	$$+	(850) 653-8139
Coombs House Inn	★★★½	82	$$$+	(850) 653-9199
Bryant House B&B	★★★½	80	$$+	(850) 653-3270
Gibson Inn	★★★	74	$$+	(850) 653-2191
Raney Guest Cottage	★★★	72	$$+	(850) 653-9749
House of Tartts	★★★	66	$$+	(850) 653-4687
Best Western Apalach Inn	★★½	64	$+	(850) 653-9131
Rancho Inn	★★½	60	$$+	(850) 653-9455
Carrabelle				
Old Carrabelle Hotel	★★★½	82	$$–	(850) 697-9010
Island View Inn	★★½	60	$$–	(850) 697-2050
Destin				
Hilton Sandestin Beach Resort & Spa	★★★★	89	$$$$$$$	(850) 267-9500
Sandestin Inn	★★★★	85	$$$+	(850) 267-6898
Silver Shells Beach Resort & Spa	★★★★	85	$$$$$	(850) 650-9999
Hidden Dunes Beach & Tennis Resort	★★★½	82	$$$$–	(850) 837-3521

HOW THE HOTELS COMPARE IN THE FLORIDA PANHANDLE (continued)

Hotel	Star Rating	Quality Rating	Cost ($=$50)	Phone
Destin (continued)				
Beach House	★★★½	75	$$$+	(850) 837-6161
Club Destin Resort	★★★½	75	$$	(850) 654-4700
Fairfield Inn Destin	★★★½	75	$$–	(850) 837-6361
Beachside Inn	★★★	73	$$$	(850) 650-6300
Surfside	★★★	72	$$$$+	(850) 837-4700
Hampton Inn	★★★	70	$$$$–	(850) 654-2677
Beach Street Cottages	★★★	69	$$–	(850) 650-9130
Best Western Summer Place Inn	★★★	69	$$$–	(850) 650-8003
Country Inn & Suites	★★★	67	$$+	(850) 650-9191
Sea Oats Motel	★★★	66	$$$–	(850) 837-6655
Comfort Inn	★★★	65	$$$	(850) 654-8611
Howard Johnson Express Inn	★★½	64	$+	(850) 650-2236
Old Pier Motel	★★½	64	$$	(850) 837-6442
Eastpoint				
Sportsman's Lodge Motel/ Marina/RV Park	★★½	64	$+	(850) 670-8423
Fort Walton Beach				
Radisson Beach Resort	★★★½	81	$$$$	(850) 243-9181
Ramada Plaza Beach Resort	★★★½	80	$$$$–	(850) 243-9161
Holiday Inn Sun Spree Resort	★★★	72	$$$	(850) 244-8686
Hampton Inn	★★★	70	$$$+	(850) 301-0906
Best Western Fort Walton Beachfront Hotel	★★★	69	$$$+	(850) 243-9444
Marina Bay Resort	★★½	64	$$–	(850) 244-5132
Regency Inn	★★½	62	$$$	(850) 302-0460
Gulf Breeze				
Bay Beach Inn	★★½	60	$$–	(850) 932-2214
Mexico Beach				
Driftwood Inn	★★★	72	$$+	(850) 648-5126
Gulf View Motel	★★½	64	$–	(850) 648-5955
Buena Vista	★★½	63	$+	(850) 648-5323
El Governor Motel	★★½	63	$$+	(850) 648-5757
Surfside Inn	★★½	60	$+	(850) 648-5771
Miramar Beach				
Embassy Suites Destin at Miramar Beach	★★★½	78	$$$$	(850) 337-7000
Ramada Limited	★★½	64	$$$+	(850) 837-2378

HOW THE HOTELS COMPARE IN THE FLORIDA PANHANDLE (continued)

Hotel	Star Rating	Quality Rating	Cost ($=$50)	Phone
Navarre				
Best Western Navarre	★★½	63	$$	(850) 939-9400
Holiday Inn Navarre	★★½	56	$$$	(850) 939-2321
Panama City				
Country Inn & Suites	★★★	68	$$–	(850) 913-0074
Comfort Inn	★★★	65	$+	(850) 763-0101
Best Western Suites Panama City	★★½	64	$$–	(850) 784-7700
Scottish Inns	★★½	63	$–	(850) 769-2432
Days Inn Bayside	★★½	60	$+	(850) 763-4622
Days Inn Panama City	★★½	56	$$	(850) 785-0001
Days Inn Tyndall AFB	★★	50	$$–	(850) 769-7400
Econo Lodge	★★	47	$–	(850) 785-2700
Howard Johnson Inn	★★	47	$+	(850) 785-0222
Panama City Beach				
Edgewater Beach Resort	★★★★	88	$$$$$–	(850) 235-4044
Southwind Condominiums	★★★½	80	$$+	(888) 496-0244
Holiday Inn Sun Spree Resort	★★★	73	$$$$–	(850) 234-1111
Panama City Resort & Club	★★★	73	$$+	(850) 235-2002
Fontainebleau Terrace	★★★	71	$$$–	(850) 234-6581
Beachcomber by the Sea	★★★	70	$$–	(850) 233-3600
Bikini Beach Resort	★★★	70	$	(850) 234-3392
Georgian Terrace Motel	★★★	70	$$–	(850) 234-2144
Landmark Holiday Beach Resort	★★★	70	$$$$	(850) 233-1500
Pier 99 Waterfront Motel	★★★	70	$+	(850) 234-2257
Flamingo Motel	★★★	69	$	(850) 234-2232
Gulf View Motel	★★★	69	$+	(850) 234-7131
Legacy by the Sea	★★★	69	$+	(850) 249-8601
Driftwood Lodge	★★★	66	$+	(850) 234-6601
Howard Johnson at the Boardwalk Resort	★★★	66	$$–	(850) 234-6521
Holiday Terrace	★★★	65	$$–	(850) 249-0111
Ambassador Beach Condominium	★★½	64	$+	(850) 234-2112
Beach Tower Resort Motel	★★½	64	$+	(850) 235-0089
Beachbreak by the Sea	★★½	64	$+	(850) 234-6644
Best Value Inn Beach Resort	★★½	64	$	(850) 234-8845
Best Western Casa Loma Motel	★★½	64	$+	(850) 234-1100
Best Western Del Coronado	★★½	64	$–	(850) 234-1600

HOW THE HOTELS COMPARE IN
THE FLORIDA PANHANDLE *(continued)*

Hotel	Star Rating	Quality Rating	Cost ($=$50)	Phone
Panama City Beach *(continued)*				
Island Breeze	★★½	64	$+	(850) 234-8841
Palmetto Motel	★★½	64	$+	(850) 234-2121
Peeks Beach Motel	★★½	64	$+	(850) 234-2257
Chateau Motel	★★½	63	$	(850) 234-2174
Days Inn Beach	★★½	63	$$$$	(850) 233-3333
Ramada Limited	★★½	63	$$$	(850) 234-1700
Fiesta Motel	★★½	62	$+	(850) 235-1000
Quality Inn Beach Front	★★½	62	$$$–	(850) 234-6636
Sandpiper Beacon Beach Resort	★★½	62	$$–	(850) 234-2154
Wind Drift Motel	★★½	60	$	(850) 234-2415
Pensacola				
Crowne Plaza Grand Hotel	★★★★	89	$$$–	(850) 433-3336
New World Inn at New World Landing	★★★½	82	$$–	(850) 432-4111
Residence Inn	★★★½	80	$$+	(850) 432-0202
Homewood Suites	★★★	74	$$+	(850) 474-3777
Residence Inn	★★★	70	$$$–	(850) 479-1000
Holiday Inn University Mall	★★★	68	$+	(850) 474-0100
Seville Inn & Suites	★★★	68	$	(850) 433-8331
Hampton Inn Airport/ Cordova Mall	★★★	67	$$$+	(850) 478-1123
La Quinta Inn	★★★	66	$+	(850) 474-0411
Days Inn Downtown	★★★	65	$$	(850) 438-4922
Fairfield Inn	★★★	65	$+	(850) 484-8001
Holiday Inn Express	★★½	64	$$–	(850) 477-3333
Red Roof Inn	★★½	64	$–	(850) 476-7960
Motel 6 Pensacola North	★★½	60	$	(850) 476-5386
Motel 6 Pensacola East	★★½	58	$+	(850) 474-1060
Shoney's Inn & Suites	★★	55	$+	(850) 484-8070
Civic Inn	★★	48	$–	(850) 432-3441
Super 8	★★	48	$–	(850) 476-8038
Pensacola Lodge	★½	40	$	(850) 477-2554
Pensacola Beach				
SpringHill Suites	★★★½	80	$$+	(850) 932-6000
Hilton Garden Inn Pensacola Beach	★★★½	77	$$+	(850) 916-2999
Clarion Suites Resort & Convention Center	★★★	73	$$$+	(850) 932-4300
The Dunes	★★★	73	$$+	(850) 932-3536
Hampton Inn Pensacola Beach	★★★	73	$$$+	(850) 932-6800

HOW THE HOTELS COMPARE IN THE FLORIDA PANHANDLE (continued)

Hotel	Star Rating	Quality Rating	Cost ($=$50)	Phone
Pensacola Beach (continued)				
Holiday Inn Express Pensacola Beach	★★★	72	$$–	(850) 932-5361
Best Western Resort	★★½	64	$$$+	(850) 934-3300
Beachside Resort & Conference Center	★★½	63	$$$$–	(850) 932-5331
Comfort Inn	★★½	58	$$$–	(850) 934-5400
Five Flags Inn	★★	48	$$	(850) 932-3586
Port St. Joe				
Port Inn	★★★	65	$$+	(850) 229-7678
Rosemary Beach				
Rosemary Beach Rentals	★★★½	82	$$$$	(850) 278-2100
Santa Rosa Beach				
Watercolor Inn	★★★★½	95	$$$$$$$	(850) 534-5000
Sugar Beach Inn B&B	★★★½	80	$$$	(850) 231-1577
Sea Breeze Resort	★★★½	77	$$$$$$–	(850) 231-5654
Seagrove Cottages	★★½	64	$$$+	(850) 231-4206
Seagrove Villa Motel	★★½	63	$$$$–	(850) 837-4853
Seaside				
Seaside Rentals	★★★★½	90	$$$$$$$–	(850) 231-4224
St. George Island				
St. George Inn	★★★	72	$$	(850) 927-2666
Buccaneer Inn	★★½	56	$$–	(850) 927-2585
Tallahassee				
Doubletree Hotel	★★★½	82	$$$$	(850) 224-5000
Governor's Inn	★★★½	82	$$$–	(850) 681-6855
Radisson Hotel Tallahassee	★★★½	81	$$+	(850) 224-6000
Fairfield Inn	★★★	70	$+	(850) 562-8766
La Quinta Inn	★★★	70	$+	(850) 385-7172
Ramada Inn	★★★	70	$+	(850) 386-1027
Holiday Inn Select	★★★	66	$$+	(850) 222-9555
Hampton Inn I-10	★★½	64	$$–	(850) 562-4300
Comfort Inn	★★½	63	$+	(850) 562-7200
Best Western Seminole Inn	★★½	62	$+	(850) 656-2938
Holiday Inn Northwest	★★½	62	$+	(850) 562-2000
Microtel Inn & Suites	★★½	60	$	(850) 562-3800
Howard Johnson Express Inn	★★	54	$+	(850) 386-5000
Days Inn North	★★	53	$	(850) 385-0136
Shoney's Inn	★½	38	$+	(850) 386-8286

HOW THE HOTELS COMPARE IN NORTHEAST FLORIDA

Hotel	Star Rating	Quality Rating	Cost ($=$50)	Phone
Amelia Island				
Ritz-Carlton Amelia Island	★★★★★	98	$$$$$$	(904) 277-1100
Amelia Island Plantation	★★★★½	95	$$$$	(904) 261-6161
Summer Beach Resort	★★★★½	92	$$$$$$-	(904) 277-0905
Elizabeth Pointe Lodge	★★★★	84	$$$	(904) 277-4851
Florida House Inn	★★★	70	$$$	(904) 261-3300
Fernandina Beach				
Fairbanks House	★★★★	88	$$$+	(904) 277-0500
Amelia Island Williams House	★★★★	86	$$$$-	(904) 277-2328
Ash Street Inn	★★★½	80	$$$+	(904) 277-4941
Bailey House	★★★½	80	$$$+	(904) 261-5390
Hoyt House	★★★½	80	$$$+	(904) 277-4300
Hampton Inn & Suites	★★★½	75	$$	(904) 491-4911
1735 House	★★★	74	$$$	(904) 261-4148
Amelia Hotel & Suites	★★★	70	$$-	(904) 261-5735
Hampton Inn Amelia Island	★★½	64	$$-	(904) 321-1111
Best Western Inn at Amelia Island	★★½	63	$$-	(904) 277-2300
Beachside Motel	★★½	62	$$$-	(904) 261-5735
The Surf	★★	55	$$-	(904) 261-5711
Ocean View Inn	★★	50	$+	(904) 261-0193
Gainesville				
Baymont Inn & Suites	★★★½	82	$+	(352) 376-0004
Paramount Resort & Conference Center	★★★½	80	$$	(352) 377-4000
Residence Inn	★★★½	76	$$$-	(352) 371-2101
Courtyard	★★★½	75	$$+	(352) 335-9100
Holiday Inn University Center	★★★½	75	$$-	(352) 376-1661
Hampton Inn	★★★	74	$$	(352) 371-4171
Cabot Lodge	★★★	73	$$-	(352) 375-2400
Comfort Inn West	★★★	73	$$-	(352) 264-1771
Holiday Inn West	★★★	70	$$-	(352) 332-7500
Red Roof Inn	★★★	70	$$+	(352) 336-3311
Howard Johnson Express Inn	★★★	68	$+	(352) 371-2500
Fairfield Inn	★★★	65	$+	(352) 332-8292
La Quinta Inn	★★★	65	$+	(352) 332-6466
Days Inn Gainesville I-75	★★½	64	$+	(352) 332-3033
Quality Inn	★★½	63	$+	(352) 378-2405
Econo Lodge West	★★½	62	$+	(352) 332-2346
Travelodge	★★½	60	$+	(352) 335-6355

HOW THE HOTELS COMPARE IN NORTHEAST FLORIDA *(continued)*

Hotel	Star Rating	Quality Rating	Cost ($=$50)	Phone
Gainesville *(continued)*				
Econo Lodge University	★★½	57	$+	(352) 373-7816
Ramada Limited	★★½	57	$+	(352) 373-0392
Comfort Inn University	★★	55	$+	(352) 373-6500
Gator Lodge	★★	50	$+	(352) 376-4667
Scottish Inns	★★	50	$$	(352) 376-4423
Super 8 Gainesville	★★	50	$+	(352) 378-3888
Days Inn University	★★	48	$	(352) 376-2222
Florida Motel	★★	48	$$-	(352) 376-3742
Motel 6	★★	48	$+	(352) 373-1604
Super 8 University Hospital	★★	47	$+	(352) 372-3654
Villager Lodge	★★	47	$	(352) 372-1880
Budget Inn	★	30	$-	(352) 371-3811
Bambi Motel	½	28	$+	(352) 376-2622
Sands Motel	½	28	$	(352) 372-2045
Jacksonville				
Omni Jacksonville Hotel	★★★★	88	$$+	(904) 355-6664
Adam's Mark Jacksonville Hotel	★★★★	84	$$$-	(904) 358-6800
Hilton Jacksonville Riverfront	★★★½	81	$$-	(904) 398-8800
Radisson Riverwalk Hotel & Conference Center	★★★½	81	$$-	(904) 396-5100
Residence Inn Airport	★★★½	78	$$	(904) 741-6550
Wingate Inn	★★★	74	$$	(904) 421-5000
Courtyard Airport	★★★	73	$$-	(904) 741-1122
Hilton Garden Inn	★★★	73	$+	(904) 421-2700
Extended Stay America	★★★	72	$+	(904) 396-1777
Courtyard	★★★	70	$$$-	(904) 296-2828
Hampton Inn Central	★★★	70	$$+	(904) 396-7770
Holiday Inn Airport	★★★	70	$$-	(904) 741-4404
Country Inn & Suites	★★★	68	$$-	(904) 772-7771
La Quinta Inn Baymeadows	★★★	68	$+	(904) 731-9940
Fairfield Inn Airport	★★★	67	$+	(904) 741-3500
Hampton Inn Airport	★★½	64	$$-	(904) 741-4980
La Quinta Inn Jacksonville Orange Park	★★½	64	$+	(904) 778-9539
Red Roof Inn Jacksonville Orange Park	★★½	64	$+	(904) 777-1000
Red Roof Inn Jacksonville Southpoint	★★½	63	$+	(904) 296-1006
Comfort Suites Airport	★★½	62	$$-	(904) 741-0505
Hampton Inn Jacksonville Orange Park	★★½	62	$$-	(904) 777-5313

HOW THE HOTELS COMPARE IN NORTHEAST FLORIDA *(continued)*

Hotel	Star Rating	Quality Rating	Cost ($=$50)	Phone
Jacksonville *(continued)*				
Motel 6	★½	43	$+	(904) 777-6100
Ramada Limited Suites	★½	39	$+	(904) 741-4600
Red Roof Inn Airport	★½	38	$+	(904) 741-4488
Jacksonville Beach				
Casa Marina Inn	★★★	72	$$$-	(904) 270-0025
Quality Suites	★★★	70	$$$$+	(904) 435-3535
Best Western Oceanfront	★★½	64	$$$+	(904) 249-4949
Surfside Inn	★★½	64	$$+	(904) 246-1583
Comfort Inn Oceanfront	★★½	62	$$$-	(904) 241-2311
Hillsmoore Oceanfront Inn	★★½	60	$$$-	(904) 246-2837
Beach Landing Motel	★★	50	$$-	(904) 249-9778
Orange Park				
Fairfield Inn Orange Park	★★★	72	$$-	(904) 278-7442
Holiday Inn Orange Park	★★½	64	$$-	(904) 264-9513
Comfort Inn Orange Park	★★½	62	$$-	(904) 269-7381
St. Augustine				
Casa de la Paz B&B	★★★½	80	$$$$-	(904) 829-2915
Casablanca Inn B&B	★★★½	80	$$$+	(904) 829-0928
Whale's Tale B&B	★★★	73	$$+	(904) 829-5901
Agustin Inn	★★★	70	$$+	(904) 823-9559
Holiday Inn & Suites St. Augustine	★★★	70	$$+	(904) 494-2100
Anastasia Inn B&B	★★½	64	$$-	(904) 825-2879
Edgewater Inn	★★½	64	$$	(904) 825-2697
Holiday Inn Express	★★½	64	$$-	(904) 823-8636
La Quinta Inn	★★½	64	$$	(904) 824-3383
Merida Motel	★★½	64	$-	(904) 825-2398
Comfort Inn	★★½	63	$$-	(904) 824-5554
Historic Inn	★★½	63	$+	(904) 826-1700
Sleep Inn	★★½	62	$$-	(904) 825-4535
Best Western Historical Inn	★★½	61	$$-	(904) 829-9088
Budget Inn	★★½	60	$+	(904) 824-1962
Hampton Inn Historic	★★½	60	$$-	(904) 829-1996
Ramada Inn St. Augustine	★★½	60	$+	(904) 824-4352
Anchorage Inn	★★½	58	$+	(904) 829-9041
Hampton Inn	★★½	56	$$+	(904) 824-4422
Pirate Haus Inn & Hostelodge	★★	55	$+	(904) 808-1999
Ramada Limited St. Augustine	★★	55	$+	(904) 829-5643
Best Western St. Augustine I-95	★★	53	$$-	(904) 829-1999

Hotels and Motels in the Space Coast

HOW THE HOTELS COMPARE IN NORTHEAST FLORIDA *(continued)*

Hotel	Star Rating	Quality Rating	Cost ($=$50)	Phone
St. Augustine *(continued)*				
Days Inn	★★	52	$+	(904) 824-4341
Lion Inn	★★	52	$	(904) 824-2831
Sunrise Inn	★★	52	$-	(904) 829-3888
Super 8	★★	52	$+	(904) 829-5686
Scottish Inns	★½	42	$	(904) 824-4436
St. Augustine Beach				
Beacher's Lodge Oceanfront Suites	★★★½	76	$$$+	(904) 471-8849
La Fiesta Ocean Inn & Suites	★★★	74	$$+	(904) 471-2220
Holiday Inn St. Augustine Beach	★★★	73	$$+	(904) 471-2555
St. Augustine Beach Front Resort	★★★	71	$$+	(904) 471-2575
Hilton Garden Inn	★★★	70	$$-	(904) 471-5559
Regency Inn & Suites	★★★	68	$$-	(904) 471-7700
Ramada Limited St. Augustine Beach	★★★	66	$+	(904) 471-1440
Hampton Inn St. Augustine Beach	★★★	65	$$$-	(904) 471-4000
Super 8 St. Augustine Beach	★★	54	$$-	(904) 471-2330

HOW THE HOTELS COMPARE IN THE SPACE COAST

Hotel	Star Rating	Quality Rating	Cost ($=$50)	Phone
Cape Canaveral				
Radisson Resort at the Port	★★★½	77	$$-	(321) 784-0000
Cocoa				
Econo Lodge	★★½	60	$$-	(321) 632-4561
Cocoa Beach				
Resort on Cocoa Beach	★★★★	83	$$$$+	(321) 783-4000
Inn at Cocoa Beach	★★★½	80	$$-	(321) 799-3460
Wakulla Motel	★★★½	80	$$+	(321) 783-2230
Doubletree Hotel	★★★½	79	$$	(321) 783-9222
Hilton Cocoa Beach Oceanfront	★★★½	77	$$$+	(321) 799-0003
Ocean Suite Hotel	★★★	72	$$	(321) 784-4343
Surf Studio Beach Resort	★★★	72	$$-	(321) 783-7100
Courtyard	★★★	71	$$$-	(321) 784-4800
Fawlty Towers	★★★	70	$+	(321) 784-3870

HOW THE HOTELS COMPARE IN THE SPACE COAST (continued)

Hotel	Star Rating	Quality Rating	Cost ($=$50)	Phone
Cocoa Beach (continued)				
Hampton Inn Cocoa Beach	★★★	69	$$+	(321) 799-4099
Holiday Inn Cocoa Beach Resort	★★★	68	$$-	(321) 783-2271
Best Western Oceanfront Resort	★★★	67	$$$-	(321) 783-7621
Holiday Inn Express	★★½	64	$$+	(321) 868-2525
Luna Sea B&B Motel	★★½	64	$$-	(321) 783-0500
Sea Aire Motel	★★½	64	$$-	(321) 783-2461
Cocoa Beach Oceanside Inn	★★½	61	$$$+	(321) 784-3126
Quality Inn	★★½	61	$$	(321) 783-6868
Days Inn Oceanside	★★½	60	$$-	(321) 784-2550
Howard Johnson Express Inn	★★½	57	$+	(321) 783-8855
Motel 6	★★	50	$+	(321) 783-3103
Daytona Beach				
Plaza Resort & Spa	★★★★	85	$$$+	(386) 255-4471
Daytona Beach Regency	★★★★	83	$$$$-	(386) 255-0251
Ocean Walk Resort	★★★★	83	$$$+	(386) 323-4800
Adam's Mark Daytona Beach Resort	★★★½	82	$$$-	(386) 254-8200
Grand Seas Resort	★★★½	81	$$$+	(386) 677-7880
Treasure Island Resort	★★★½	81	$$+	(386) 255-8371
Hilton Daytona Beach Oceanfront Resort	★★★½	80	$$$-	(386) 767-7350
Radisson Resort Daytona Beach	★★★½	79	$$-	(386) 239-9800
Americano Beach Resort	★★★½	77	$$+	(386) 253-7431
Desert Inn Resort	★★★½	77	$+	(386) 258-6555
Holiday Inn Hotel & Suites Daytona Beach	★★★½	76	$$+	(386) 255-5494
Harbour Beach Resort	★★★	73	$$	(386) 944-2100
Tropical Winds Oceanfront Hotel	★★★	73	$$$$$	(386) 258-1016
Beachcomer	★★★	70	$$+	(386) 252-8513
Boardwalk Inn & Suites	★★★	70	$$$$	(386) 253-8300
Cove Motel	★★★	69	$+	(386) 252-3678
Tropical Manor Motel	★★★	69	$$	(386) 252-4920
El Caribe Resort & Conference Center	★★★	68	$$	(386) 252-1558
Palm Plaza Oceanfront Resort	★★★	68	$$$+	(386) 767-1711
Seven Seas Resort	★★★	68	$$-	(386) 257-1180
Silver Beach Club	★★★	68	$$$-	(386) 252-9681

HOW THE HOTELS COMPARE IN THE SPACE COAST *(continued)*

Hotel	Star Rating	Quality Rating	Cost ($=$50)	Phone
Daytona Beach *(continued)*				
Best Western Mayan Inn	★★★	66	$$-	(386) 252-2378
Beachside Motel	★★½	64	$$$	(386) 788-5569
Breakers Beach Oceanfront Motel	★★½	64	$$-	(386) 252-0863
Cardinal Inn	★★½	64	$+	(386) 252-1035
Daytona Beach Ocean Jewels	★★½	64	$$	(386) 252-2581
Magic Carpet Motel	★★½	64	$+	(386) 767-7312
Comfort Inn & Suites	★★½	63	$$-	(386) 255-5491
Ocean Inn	★★½	63	$+	(386) 238-6440
Esquire Beach Motel	★★½	62	$+	(386) 255-3601
Red Carpet Inn	★★½	60	$$-	(386) 255-4588
Seagarden Inn	★★	54	$$-	(386) 761-2335
Melbourne				
Baymont Inn & Suites	★★★	73	$$-	(321) 242-9400
Imperial's Hotel & Conference Center	★★★	73	$$-	(321) 255-0077
Merritt Island				
Clarion Hotel	★★★	65	$$-	(321) 452-7711
New Smyrna Beach				
Coconut Palms Beach Resort	★★★½	81	$$$-	(386) 428-1874
Oceania Beach Club	★★★½	80	$$$-	(386) 423-8400
Holiday Inn Hotel & Suites New Smyrna Beach	★★★	70	$$+	(386) 426-0020
Surfside Resort & Suites	★★★	65	$$+	(386) 672-8510
Beachcomber Motel	★★½	62	$$-	(386) 427-3786
Ormond Beach				
Best Western Mainsail Inn & Suites	★★½	64	$$-	(386) 677-2131
Coral Beach Resort	★★½	64	$$-	(386) 677-4712
Ivanhoe Beach Resort	★★½	63	$+	(386) 672-6711
Maverick Resort	★★½	63	$$-	(386) 672-3550
Symphony Beach Club	★★½	63	$$-	(386) 672-7373
Comfort Inn Ormond Beach	★★½	62	$$	(386) 677-8550
Makai Beach Lodge	★★½	61	$+	(386) 677-8060
Scottish Inns	★★	53	$-	(386) 677-8860
Satellite Beach				
Ramada Inn Satellite Beach	★★★	65	$$-	(321) 777-7200

76 Part One **Accommodations**

HOW THE HOTELS COMPARE IN THE SPACE COAST *(continued)*

Hotel	Star Rating	Quality Rating	Cost ($=$50)	Phone
Titusville				
Ramada Inn Kennedy Space Center	★★★	68	$$-	(321) 269-5510
Holiday Inn Kennedy Space Center	★★★	66	$$	(321) 269-2121
Best Western Space Shuttle Inn	★★½	63	$+	(321) 269-9100
Randolph Inn	★★½	62	$+	(321) 269-5945
Comfort Inn	★★½	61	$+	(321) 269-7110
Days Inn Kennedy Space Center	★★½	60	$+	(321) 269-4480
Riverside Inn	★★	50	$	(321) 267-7900

HOW THE HOTELS COMPARE IN THE ORLANDO AREA

Hotel	Star Rating	Quality Rating	Cost ($=$50)	Phone
Downtown Orlando				
Westin Grand Bohemian Hotel	★★★★½	93	$$$$	(407) 313-9000
Marriott Hotel Orlando Downtown	★★★★	88	$$+	(407) 843-6664
Embassy Suites Orlando Downtown	★★★★	87	$$$+	(407) 841-1000
EO Inn Spa	★★★★	86	$$$−	(407) 481-8485
Courtyard at Lake Lucerne	★★★★	84	$$	(407) 648-5188
Holiday Inn Orlando Downtown	★★★	72	$$−	(407) 996-0100
Courtyard Orlando Downtown	★★★	70	$$−	(407) 996-1000
Travelodge	★★½	62	$+	(407) 423-1671
Orlando Airport Area				
Crowne Plaza	★★★★	85	$$+	(407) 856-0100
Marriott Hotels Resorts Suites	★★★★	84	$$$−	(407) 851-9000
Renaissance Orlando Hotel Airport	★★★½	80	$$+	(407) 240-1000
Hilton Garden Inn	★★★½	77	$$+	(407) 240-3725
Holiday Inn Select	★★★½	77	$$	(407) 851-6400
Baymont Inn & Suites	★★★	74	$+	(407) 240-0500
Clarion Hotel	★★★	70	$+	(407) 859-2711
Holiday Inn Express Florida Mall	★★★	67	$$−	(407) 851-8200
Comfort Suites	★★½	64	$+	(407) 581-7900
La Quinta Inn	★★½	64	$+	(407) 857-9215
Best Western Airport Inn	★★½	63	$+	(407) 581-2800
Quality Inn & Suites	★★½	63	$+	(407) 856-4663
Sleep Inn & Suites	★★½	63	$+	(407) 855-4447
AmeriSuites	★★½	62	$$	(407) 816-7800

HOW THE HOTELS COMPARE IN THE ORLANDO AREA *(continued)*

Hotel	Star Rating	Quality Rating	Cost ($=$50)	Phone
Orlando Airport Area (continued)				
Fairfield Inn	★★½	62	$+	(407) 240-8400
Countryside Lodge	★★½	60	$-	(407) 851-1050
Days Inn	★★	48	$	(407) 581-5000
International Drive Area				
Hard Rock Hotel	★★★★★	96	$$$$-	(407) 503-ROCK
Portofino Bay Hotel	★★★★½	94	$$$$$-	(407) 503-1000
Crowne Plaza Universal	★★★★	86	$$+	(407) 355-0550
Radisson Barcelo Inn International (Tower)	★★★★	85	$$-	(407) 345-0505
Hawthorn Suites Universal	★★★½	82	$$	(407) 581-2151
Holiday Inn Family Suites Resort	★★★½	82	$$$	(407) 387-5437
Renaissance Orlando Resort	★★★½	80	$$$	(407) 351-5555
Sheraton World Resort (Tower)	★★★½	79	$$$	(407) 352-1100
Residence Inn Convention Ctr.	★★★½	77	$$-	(407) 226-0288
Quality Suites International Drive	★★★½	75	$$-	(407) 363-0332
SpringHill Suites by Marriott	★★★	72	$$$-	(407) 345-9073
Comfort Suites Universal	★★★	66	$$-	(407) 363-1967
Country Inn & Suites	★★½	63	$+	(407) 313-4200
Microtel Inn & Suites	★★½	63	$	(407) 226-9887
Motel 6 International Drive	★★½	61	$	(407) 351-6500
Lake Buena Vista and the I-4 Corridor				
Hawthorn Suites Lake Buena Vista	★★★★	87	$$	(407) 597-5000
Sheraton Vistana Resort	★★★★	85	$$$-	(866) 208-0003
Sheraton Royal Safari	★★★½	82	$$+	(800) 423-3297
Marriott Village SpringHill Suites	★★★	74	$$$+	(407) 938-9001
Marriott Village Courtyard	★★★	71	$$$+	(407) 938-9001
Holiday Inn Sun Spree Resort	★★★	69	$$+	(407) 239-4500
Marriott Village Fairfield Inn	★★½	64	$$	(407) 938-9001
US 192				
Westgate Resorts (Town Center)	★★★★½	93	$$$-	(800) 925-9999
Radisson Resort Parkway	★★★★½	90	$$$-	(407) 396-7000
Westgate Resorts (Villas)	★★★★½	90	$$$-	(800) 925-9999
Hyatt Orlando	★★★★	84	$$+	(407) 396-1234
AmeriSuites Lake Buena Vista South	★★★½	82	$$	(407) 997-1300
Country Inn & Suites	★★★½	82	$+	(407) 997-1400
Holiday Inn Nikki Bird Resort	★★★½	80	$$+	(407) 396-7300
Westgate Resorts (Tower)	★★★½	78	$$$-	(800) 925-9999

HOW THE HOTELS COMPARE IN THE ORLANDO AREA *(continued)*

Hotel	Star Rating	Quality Rating	Cost ($=$50)	Phone
US 192 *(continued)*				
Westgate Towers	★★★½	76	$$$-	(407) 396-2500
Days Suites Maingate East	★★★	72	$+	(407) 396-7900
Clarion Maingate	★★★	71	$+	(407) 396-4000
Travelodge Suites Eastgate	★★★	67	$+	(407) 396-7666
Howard Johnson EnchantedLand Resort Hotel	★★★	66	$$-	(407) 396-4343
Super 8 Kissimmee Lakeside	★★½	58	$	(407) 396-1144
Super 8 Maingate	★★½	57	$	(407) 396-8883
Travelodge Suites Maingate	★★½	56	$+	(407) 396-1780
Walt Disney World Resort				
WDW Grand Floridian Resort	★★★★★	96	$$$$$	(407) 934-7639
WDW Animal Kingdom Lodge	★★★★½	95	$$$$$$$	(407) 934-7639
WDW Boardwalk Inn	★★★★½	93	$$$$$$-	(407) 934-7639
WDW Beach Club Resort	★★★★½	92	$$$$$$-	(407) 934-7639
WDW Old Key West Resort	★★★★½	92	$$$$$$-	(407) 934-7639
WDW Yacht Club Resort	★★★★½	92	$$$$$$-	(407) 934-7639
WDW Beach Club Villas	★★★★½	91	$$$$$$$$-	(407) 934-7639
WDW Boardwalk Villas	★★★★½	91	$$$$$$$$-	(407) 934-7639
WDW Wilderness Villas	★★★★½	91	$$$$$$-	(407) 934-7639
Celebration Hotel	★★★★½	90	$$$+	(407) 566-6000
WDW Polynesian Resort	★★★★½	90	$$$$$$	(407) 934-7639
WDW Contemporary Resort	★★★★	87	$$$$$+	(407) 934-7639
WDW Dolphin	★★★★	86	$$$$$$+	(407) 934-7639
WDW Swan	★★★★	86	$$$$$$+	(407) 934-7639
WDW Wilderness Lodge	★★★★	86	$$$$+	(407) 934-7639
Best Western Lake Buena Vista	★★★★	85	$$$	(407) 828-2424
Doubletree Guest Suites	★★★★	84	$$$	(407) 934-1000
WDW Coronado Springs Resort	★★★★	83	$$$	(407) 934-7639
WDW Port Orleans Resort	★★★½	81	$$$-	(407) 934-7639
Grosvenor Resort	★★★½	76	$$-	(407) 828-4444
WDW Caribbean Beach Resort	★★★½	76	$$$	(407) 934-7639
WDW Fort Wilderness Resort (Cabins)	★★★½	76	$$$$+	(407) 934-7639
Courtyard Disney Village	★★★½	75	$$+	(407) 828-8888
WDW All-Star Resort	★★★	73	$$-	(407) 934-7639

Hotels and Motels in the Central Gulf Coast

HOW THE HOTELS COMPARE IN THE CENTRAL GULF COAST

Hotel	Star Rating	Quality Rating	Cost ($=$50)	Phone
Anna Maria Island				
Sand Pebble Apartments & Motel	★★★	73	$-	(941) 778-3053
Bradenton Beach				
Tradewinds Resort	★★★★	86	$$+	(941) 779-0010
Brandon				
Holiday Inn Express Brandon	★★★	74	$$+	(813) 643-3800
La Quinta Inn & Suites	★★★	72	$+	(813) 643-0574
Homestead Studios	★★★	66	$+	(813) 643-5900
Hampton Inn	★★★	67	$+	(727) 797-8173
Quality Inn Clearwater	★★½	63	$+	(727) 799-6133
Clearwater Beach				
Sheraton Sand Key Resort	★★★★	85	$$$+	(727) 595-1611
Holiday Inn Sun Spree Resort Clearwater Beach	★★★★	83	$$$$-	(727) 447-9566
Radisson Suite Resort on Sand Key	★★★★	83	$$$$+	(727) 596-1100
Hilton Clearwater Beach Resort	★★★	74	$$$-	(727) 461-3222
Best Western Sea Wake Beach Resort	★★★	69	$$+	(727) 443-7652
Econo Lodge Clearwater Beach	★★½	60	$$-	(727) 446-3400
Quality Hotel on the Beach	★★½	60	$$$-	(727) 442-7171
Gulfport				
Peninsula Inn & Spa	★★★★	89	$$$-	(727) 346-9800
Sea Breeze Manor B&B Inn	★★★½	82	$$$+	(727) 343-4445
Holmes Beach				
Haley's Motel	★★★	74	$	(941) 778-5405
Indian Rocks Beach				
Anchor Court Apartments & Motel	★★½	63	$+	(727) 595-4449
Longboat Key				
Turtle Crawl Inn	★★★½	82	$	(941) 383-3788
Holiday Inn Hotel & Suites Longboat Key	★★★½	81	$$+	(941) 383-3771
Hilton Longboat Key Beach Resort	★★★½	80	$$-	(941) 383-2451

HOW THE HOTELS COMPARE IN THE CENTRAL GULF COAST *(continued)*

Hotel	Star Rating	Quality Rating	Cost ($=$50)	Phone
Longboat Key *(continued)*				
Holiday Beach Resort	★★★½	78	$$+	(941) 383-3704
Rolling Waves Cottages	★★★	74	$$$-	(941) 383-1323
Sea Horse Beach Resort	★★½	64	$$+	(941) 383-2417
Silver Beach Resort	★★½	64	$$+	(941) 383-2434
Madeira Beach				
Beach Suites Resort	★★★	66	$+	(727) 319-6393
N. Redington Beach				
Hilton Tampa Bay N. Redington Beach	★★★½	78	$$$	(727) 391-4000
Safety Harbor				
Safety Harbor Resort & Spa on Tampa Bay	★★★★	85	$$$-	(727) 726-1161
Ibis Bed & Breakfast	★★★	73	$$	(727) 723-9000
Sarasota				
Ritz-Carlton Sarasota	★★★★★	98	$$$	(941) 309-2000
Radisson Lido Beach Resort	★★★★	85	$$$-	(941) 388-2161
AmericInn Hotel & Suites	★★★½	82	$$-	(941) 342-8778
Siesta Sands on the Beach	★★★½	82	$$-	(941) 349-1929
Holiday Inn Lido Beach	★★★½	81	$$+	(941) 388-2181
Hyatt Sarasota	★★★½	81	$$	(941) 953-1234
Tropical Breeze Resort of Siesta Key	★★★½	76	$$-	(941) 349-1125
Siesta Key Suites	★★★	74	$$-	(941) 349-1236
Hampton Inn	★★★	70	$$-	(941) 371-1900
Siesta Holidays	★★★	68	$$$+	(941) 312-9882
Country Inn & Suites	★★★	67	$+	(941) 925-0631
Helmsley Sandcastle Hotel on the Beach	★★★	65	$$$-	(941) 388-2181
Gulf Beach Motel	★★½	64	$+	(941) 388-2127
Wellesley Inn & Suites	★★½	64	$+	(941) 366-5128
Quayside Inn	★★½	63	$+	(941) 366-0414
Beach Palms	★★½	58	$$$$-	(941) 349-9900
Oasis Resort Siesta Key	★★	55	$+	(941) 346-2525
Surfview Motel	★★	55	$	(941) 388-1818
Howard Johnson Express Inn	★★	54	$+	(941) 355-8867
Best Western Siesta Beach Resort	★★	47	$$$-	(941) 349-3211

HOW THE HOTELS COMPARE IN
THE CENTRAL GULF COAST *(continued)*

Hotel	Star Rating	Quality Rating	Cost ($=$50)	Phone
St. Petersburg				
Hilton St. Petersburg	★★★½	82	$$-	(727) 894-5000
Hampton Inn & Suites Downtown St. Petersburg	★★★½	81	$$$+	(727) 892-9900
Holiday Inn Sun Spree Resort St. Petersburg	★★★	65	$$-	(727) 867-1151
St. Petersburg Beach				
Don Cesar Beach Resort & Spa	★★★★½	93	$$$$+	(727) 360-1881
TradeWinds Island Resorts	★★★★	89	$$$-	(727) 562-1240
Holiday Inn Beachfront Resort	★★★½	80	$$$+	(727) 360-1811
Best Western Beachfront Resort	★★★	74	$$-	(727) 367-1902
Miramar Resort	★★★	69	$$-	(727) 367-2311
Gulf Strand Beach Front Resort	★★★	67	$$+	(727) 367-2878
Plaza Beach Resort Motel	★★★	66	$+	(727) 367-2791
Howard Johnson Resort Hotel	★★½	64	$$-	(727) 360-7041
Tampa				
Hyatt Regency Tampa	★★★★	88	$$$+	(813) 223-1351
Wyndham Westshore	★★★★	86	$$$-	(813) 286-4400
Hyatt Regency Westshore	★★★★	85	$$$+	(813) 874-1234
Crowne Plaza	★★★★	84	$$$-	(813) 623-6363
Doubletree Guest Suites Tampa Bay	★★★½	82	$$+	(813) 877-6181
Marriott Downtown Tampa	★★★½	82	$$-	(813) 229-1100
Chase Suites Hotel	★★★½	80	$$	(813) 281-5677
Radisson Bay Harbor Hotel	★★★½	80	$$$-	(813) 281-8900
Residence Inn	★★★½	80	$$-	(813) 627-8855
Radisson Riverwalk Hotel Tampa	★★★½	79	$$+	(813) 223-2222
Hilton Garden Inn Ybor City	★★★½	78	$$$+	(813) 769-9267
Baymont Tampa Brandon	★★★	74	$+	(813) 684-4007
Baymont Tampa Inn & Suites	★★★	74	$$-	(813) 930-6900
Hampton Inn Tampa Brandon	★★★	74	$$+	(813) 661-8888
Holiday Inn Express Tampa	★★★	74	$$+	(813) 287-8585
Oak Haven River Retreat	★★★	74	$$-	(813) 988-4580
Baymont Tampa Fairgrounds	★★★	73	$+	(813) 626-0885
Comfort Inn Suites & Tampa Brandon	★★★	72	$$-	(813) 630-4444

HOW THE HOTELS COMPARE IN THE CENTRAL GULF COAST *(continued)*

Hotel	Star Rating	Quality Rating	Cost ($=$50)	Phone
Tampa *(continued)*				
Days Inn Airport/Rocky Point Island	★★★	72	$+	(813) 281-0000
Red Roof Inn	★★★	68	$+	(813) 681-8484
La Quinta Inn	★★½	64	$$-	(813) 623-3591
Days Inn Fairgrounds	★★½	63	$+	(813) 623-5121
Howard Johnson Express Inn & Suites	★★½	63	$+	(813) 247-3300
Treasure Island				
Holiday Inn Treasure Island	★★★½	80	$$-	(727) 367-2761
Bilmar Beach Resort	★★★	74	$$+	(727) 360-5531
Seahorse Cottages	★★★	74	$$+	(727) 367-2291
Tahitian	★★★	73	$+	(727) 360-6264
Ramada Treasure Island	★★★	66	$$-	(727) 360-7051
Best Western Treasure Island	★★½	64	$+	(727) 360-6971
Jefferson Motel	★★½	64	$$-	(727) 360-5826
Fiesta Motel	★★½	63	$+	(727) 360-6737
Lorelei Resort	★★½	58	$$-	(727) 360-4351

HOW THE HOTELS COMPARE IN THE GOLD AND TREASURE COASTS

Hotel	Star Rating	Quality Rating	Cost ($=$50)	Phone
Boca Raton				
Embassy Suites Boca Raton	★★★★	85	$$	(561) 994-8200
Doubletree Guest Suites Boca Raton	★★★★	84	$+	(561) 997-9500
SpringHill Suites	★★★★	84	$$-	(561) 994-2107
Boca Raton Marriott	★★★½	80	$$$+	(561) 392-4600
Radisson Bridge Resort of Boca Raton	★★★½	80	$+	(561) 368-9500
Holiday Inn Boca Raton Town Center	★★★	74	$$-	(561) 368-5200
Boca Raton Plaza Hotel & Suites	★★★★	68	$$	(561) 395-6850
Holiday Inn Express Downtown Boca Raton	★★½	64	$+	(561) 395-7172
Best Western University Inn	★★½	60	$+	(561) 395-5225
Boynton Beach				
Holiday Inn Express	★★½	64	$$+	(561) 734-9100

HOW THE HOTELS COMPARE IN THE GOLD AND TREASURE COASTS (continued)

Hotel	Star Rating	Quality Rating	Cost ($=$50)	Phone
Dania Beach				
Sheraton Fort Lauderdale Airport	★★★★	85	$$+	(954) 920-3500
SpringHill Suites	★★★	74	$$−	(954) 920-9696
Sleep Inn & Suites Fort Lauderdale Airport	★★½	63	$$−	(954) 874-1800
Deerfield Beach				
Embassy Suites Deerfield Beach Resort	★★★★	85	$$$	(954) 426-0478
Howard Johnson Plaza Resort	★★½	64	$$−	(954) 428-2850
Comfort Inn Oceanside	★★½	56	$+	(954) 428-0650
Delray Beach Marriott	★★★★	89	$$$$$	(561) 274-3200
Sundy House	★★★★	89	$$$$−	(561) 272-5678
Colony Hotel & Cabana Club	★★★½	80	$$$+	(561) 276-4123
The Seagate	★★★½	78	$$$−	(561) 276-2421
Wright by the Sea	★★★	70	$$+	(561) 278-3355
Fort Lauderdale				
Hyatt Regency Pier Sixty-Six	★★★★½	90	$$$$	(954) 525-6666
Marriott's Harbor Beach Resort	★★★★½	90	$$$$−	(954) 525-4000
Embassy Suites Fort Lauderdale	★★★★	85	$$$−	(954) 527-2700
Marriott Fort Lauderdale Marina	★★★★	85	$$$$$	(954) 463-4000
Riverside Hotel	★★★★	85	$$$$	(954) 467-0671
Ireland's Inn Beach Resort	★★★★	83	$$	(954) 565-6661
Marriott BeachPlace Towers	★★★★	83	$$$$	(954) 525-4440
Doubletree Guest Suites	★★★½	82	$$+	(954) 565-3800
Wyndham Fort Lauderdale Airport	★★★½	77	$$+	(954) 969-0069
Radisson Bahia Mar Beach Resort	★★★½	76	$$+	(954) 764-2233
Sheraton Yankee Clipper	★★★½	75	$$+	(954) 524-5551
Sheraton Yankee Trader	★★★½	75	$$$$+	(954) 467-1111
Fort Lauderdale Beach Resort	★★★	68	$$+	(954) 566-8800
Best Western Pelican Beach Resort	★★★	65	$$$−	(954) 568-9431
Days Inn Bahia Cabana	★★½	63	$+	(954) 524-1555
Holiday Inn Fort Lauderdale Beach	★★½	60	$$+	(954) 563-5961
Best Western Oceanside Inn	★★½	56	$$−	(954) 525-8115
Ramada Sea Club Resort	★★	54	$+	(954) 564-3211
Howard Johnson Ocean's Edge Fort Lauderdale	★★	48	$$$−	(954) 563-2451

HOW THE HOTELS COMPARE IN THE GOLD AND TREASURE COASTS *(continued)*

Hotel	Star Rating	Quality Rating	Cost ($=$50)	Phone
Fort Pierce				
Radisson Beach Resort	★★★★	89	$$+	(772) 465-5544
Beachwood Motel on the Ocean	★★★	74	$$-	(772) 465-3157
Dockside Harborlight Resort	★★★	65	$+	(772) 468-3555
Days Inn Fort Pierce Beach	★★½	64	$	(772) 461-8737
Holiday Inn Express Fort Pierce	★★½	64	$+	(772) 464-5000
Days Inn Fort Pierce	★★	55	$+	(772) 466-4066
Oceanaire Lodge	★★	55	$+	(772) 466-5244
Econo Lodge Fort Pierce	★★	48	$+	(772) 461-2323
Farrell's Motel	★½	45	$-	(772) 464-1019
Days Inn & Suites	★½	40	$-	(772) 465-7000
Highland Beach				
Holiday Inn Highland Beach	★★★½	78	$$	(561) 278-6241
Jensen Beach				
Courtyard Jensen Beach	★★★★	89	$$$-	(772) 229-1000
Holiday Inn Jensen Beach	★★★½	82	$$	(772) 225-3000
River Palm Cottages	★★★	70	$$-	(772) 334-0401
Jensen's Waterfront Cottages	★★½	64	$$-	(772) 334-6607
Coral Reef Motel	★★	48	$+	(772) 334-1474
Jensen Beach Motel	★★	48	$	(772) 334-3331
Pelican Rest Motel	★★	47	$+	(772) 334-3676
Hollywood				
Westin Diplomat Resort & Spa	★★★★½	92	$$$$	(954) 602-6000
Hollywood Sands	★★★	73	$$$-	(954) 925-2285
Ramada Plaza Hotel	★★★	69	$+	(954) 620-7000
Comfort Inn Fort Lauderdale Airport	★★½	64	$+	(954) 922-1600
Hampton Inn & Suites	★★½	64	$$-	(954) 922-0011
Sheldon Ocean Resort	★★	48	$-	(954) 922-6020
Hollywood Beach				
Holiday Inn Hollywood Beach	★★★	72	$$	(954) 923-8700
Ramada Inn Hollywood Beach Resort Hotel	★½	42	$$-	(954) 921-0990
Hollywood Beach Inn	★½	38	$+	(954) 925-1411
Lauderdale-by-the-Sea				
Courtyard Villas on the Ocean	★★★½	78	$$$-	(954) 776-1164
High Noon Resort	★★★	74	$$-	(954) 776-1121
Windjammer Resort & Beach Club	★★½	64	$$$-	(954) 776-4232

HOW THE HOTELS COMPARE IN THE GOLD AND TREASURE COASTS (continued)

Hotel	Star Rating	Quality Rating	Cost ($=$50)	Phone
Manalapan				
Ritz-Carlton Palm Beach	★★★★★	99	$$$$$$$$$	(561) 533-6000
Palm Beach				
Breakers Palm Beach	★★★★★	97	$$$$$$$$$	(561) 655-6611
Four Seasons Resort Palm Beach	★★★★½	95	$$$$$$$$$	(561) 582-2800
Chesterfield Palm Beach	★★★★½	90	$$$$$$$	(561) 659-5800
PGA National Resort	★★★★	89	$$$–	(561) 627-2000
Colony Palm Beach	★★★★	85	$$$$+	(561) 655-5430
Embassy Suites Palm Beach Gardens	★★★½	82	$$$–	(561) 622-1000
Doubletree Hotel in the Gardens	★★★½	80	$$$–	(561) 622-2260
Heart of Palm Beach Hotel	★★★	68	$$$–	(561) 655-5600
Inns of America Palm Beach Gardens	★★½	64	$+	(561) 626-4918
Pompano Beach				
Holiday Inn Oceanside	★★★	74	$$	(954) 781-1300
Best Western Beachcomber	★★½	64	$$+	(954) 941-7830
Villamar Inn	★★½	64	$	(954) 941-3530
Quality Inn Pompano Beach	★★½	60	$$–	(954) 782-5300
Paradise Beach Resort	★★½	56	$$	(954) 785-3300
Ramada Ocean Beach Resort	★★½	56	$$$+	(954) 941-7300
Sea Castle Inn	★★½	56	$+	(954) 941-2570
Port St. Lucie				
Best Western All Suites	★★★	73	$+	(772) 878-7600
Singer Island				
Hilton Singer Island Oceanfront Resort	★★★★	83	$$$+	(561) 848-3888
Canopy Palms Resort	★★★½	82	$+	(561) 848-5502
Crowne Plaza Singer Island	★★★½	82	$$$$+	(561) 842-6171
Stuart				
Holiday Inn Stuart	★★★½	78	$$	(772) 287-6200
Ramada Inn	★★★	70	$$+	(772) 287-6900
Suburban Extended Stay Hotel	★★★	68	$+	(772) 286-1010
Palms Inn & Suites	★★	55	$+	(772) 546-6568
Howard Johnson	★½	46	$+	(772) 287-3171
Sunrise				
Crowne Plaza Sawgrass	★★★	70	$$+	(954) 851-1020
Baymont Inn & Suites Sunrise	★★★	68	$+	(954) 846-1200

HOW THE HOTELS COMPARE IN THE GOLD AND TREASURE COASTS *(continued)*

Hotel	Star Rating	Quality Rating	Cost ($=$50)	Phone
Vero Beach				
Jupiter Waterfront Inn	★★★½	82	$$+	(561) 747-9085
Vero Beach Inn	★★★½	78	$$-	(772) 231-1600
Holiday Inn Vero Beach	★★★½	75	$$-	(772) 231-2300
Best Western Vero	★★	55	$+	(772) 567-8321
West Palm Beach				
Sheraton West Palm Beach	★★★½	82	$$	(561) 833-1234
Crowne Plaza West Palm Beach	★★★½	78	$$$$$	(561) 689-6400
Hilton Palm Beach Airport	★★★½	78	$$+	(561) 684-9400
Hibiscus House B&B	★★★	74	$$	(561) 863-5633
Radisson Suite Inn Palm Beach Airport	★★★	68	$$+	(561) 689-6888
Hampton Inn West Palm Beach	★★½	64	$$-	(561) 471-8700
Holiday Inn Palm Beach Airport	★★½	62	$$-	(561) 659-3880
La Quinta Inn West Palm Beach	★★½	60	$	(561) 697-3388
Days Inn Turnpike/Airport West	★★	55	$+	(561) 686-6000

HOW THE HOTELS COMPARE IN SOUTHWEST FLORIDA

Hotel	Star Rating	Quality Rating	Cost ($=$50)	Phone
Boca Grande				
Boca Grande Club	★★★★	84	$$$-	(941) 964-2211
Bokeelia				
Bokeelia Tarpon Inn	★★★★	89	$$$$$$	(239) 283-8961
Beachouse Motel	★★★½	82	$$+	(239) 283-4303
Tropic Isles RV Park & Apartments	★★★	68	$-	(239) 283-4456
Jug Creek Cottages	★★½	59	$+	(239) 283-0015
Bonita Springs				
Trianon Bonita Bay	★★★★	88	$$-	(239) 948-4400
Bonita Beach Resort Motel	★★★½	80	$+	(239) 992-2137
Tradewinds	★★★½	80	$$+	(239) 992-2111
Baymont Inn	★★★	74	$+	(239) 949-9400
Comfort Inn Bonita Springs	★★★	74	$+	(239) 992-5001
Hampton Inn Bonita Springs	★★★	68	$$-	(239) 947-9393
Holiday Inn Express Hotel & Suites	★★★	68	$+	(239) 948-0699
Flamingo Motel	★★½	58	$	(239) 992-7566

HOW THE HOTELS COMPARE IN SOUTHWEST FLORIDA (continued)

Hotel	Star Rating	Quality Rating	Cost ($=$50)	Phone
Cape Coral				
Quality Inn Nautilus	★★★	65	$+	(239) 542-2121
Rainbow Motel Resort	★★½	64	$+	(239) 542-0061
Colonial Resort Motel & Apartments	★★½	60	$	(239) 542-2149
Casa Loma Motel	★★½	58	$	(239) 549-6000
Del Prado Inn	★★	50	$−	(239) 542-3151
Cape Haze				
Palm Island Resort	★★★★	84	$$$$$−	(941) 697-4800
Captiva				
Captiva Island Bed & Breakfast	★★★	73	$$+	(239) 395-0882
Tween Waters Inn	★★★	70	$$+	(239) 472-5161
Jensen's Twin Palm Cottages & Marina	★★★	69	$$+	(239) 472-5800
Everglades City				
Ivey House Inn	★★★	72	$$−	(239) 695-3299
Captain's Table Motel	★★★	65	$+	(239) 695-4211
Rod & Gun Club Lodge	★★½	64	$$−	(239) 695-2101
Barron River Motel & Villas	★★½	59	$$−	(239) 695-3591
Fort Myers				
Hilton Garden Inn	★★★½	82	$$$−	(239) 790-3500
Ramada Inn	★★★½	79	$+	(239) 337-0300
Courtyard	★★★½	78	$$	(239) 275-8600
Residence Inn	★★★½	76	$$	(239) 936-0110
Homewood Suites Hotel	★★★½	75	$$	(239) 275-6000
Country Inn & Suites	★★★	74	$$−	(239) 454-0040
Holiday Inn Riverwalk	★★★	74	$+	(239) 334-3434
Holiday Inn Select Airport	★★★	73	$$$$−	(239) 482-2900
Wellesley Inn & Suites	★★★	70	$+	(239) 278-3949
Comfort Inn (Boatways Rd.)	★★★	65	$+	(239) 694-9200
Radisson Inn	★★★	65	$+	(239) 936-4300
Suburban Lodge of Fort Myers	★★★	65	$+	(239) 938-0100
Howard Johnson Inn Edison Mall	★★½	64	$+	(239) 936-3229
La Quinta Inn	★★½	64	$+	(239) 275-3300
Old Florida River Tours Black Tie Yacht B&B	★★½	64	$$+	(239) 826-2457
Quality Hotel	★★½	64	$+	(239) 332-3232
Radisson Inn Sanibel Gateway	★★★	64	$+	(239) 466-1200
Super 8	★★½	60	$+	(239) 275-3500

HOW THE HOTELS COMPARE IN SOUTHWEST FLORIDA *(continued)*

Hotel	Star Rating	Quality Rating	Cost ($=$50)	Phone
Fort Myers *(continued)*				
Ramada Limited Fort Myers	★★½	59	$+	(239) 275-1111
Fort Myers Inn	★★½	56	$−	(239) 936-1959
Days Inn South	★★	55	$	(239) 936-1311
Comfort Inn (S. Cleveland Ave.)	★★	54	$+	(239) 936-3993
Fort Myers Beach				
Gullwing Beach Resort	★★★★½	91	$$$$	(239) 765-4300
Pointe Estero Resort	★★★★½	91	$$$+	(239) 765-1155
DiamondHead All Suite Beach Resort	★★★★	84	$$$+	(239) 765-7654
Edison Beach House	★★★½	82	$$+	(239) 463-1530
GrandView All Suite Resort	★★★½	80	$$$+	(239) 765-1155
Best Western Pink Shell Beach Resort	★★★½	78	$$$$−	(239) 463-6181
Casa Playa Beach Resort	★★★½	78	$+	(239) 765-0510
Days Inn Island Beach Resort	★★★	71	$$−	(239) 463-9759
Best Western Beach Resort	★★★	70	$$$+	(239) 463-6000
Lighthouse Island Resort	★★★	70	$+	(239) 463-9392
Ramada Inn Beachfront	★★★	70	$$−	(239) 463-6158
Sandpiper Gulf Resort	★★★	70	$$	(239) 463-5721
Ti Ki Resort	★★★	70	$$$	(239) 463-9547
Hidden Harbor Inn	★★★	68	$$−	(239) 463-9382
Holiday Inn Fort Myers Beach	★★★	68	$$	(239) 463-5711
Quality Inn & Suites at the Lani Kai	★★★	68	$$+	(239) 463-3111
Neptune Inn	★★½	64	$$	(239) 463-6141
Holiday Court Motel	★★½	63	$$−	(239) 463-2830
Howard Johnson Beachfront	★★½	63	$$−	(239) 463-9231
Island Motel	★★½	62	$+	(239) 463-2381
GuestHouse Inn Mariner's Lodge & Marina	★★½	61	$+	(239) 466-9700
Kahlua Beach Club	★★½	60	$+	(239) 463-5751
Outrigger Beach Resort	★★½	60	$$−	(239) 463-3131
Sandy Beach Hideaway	★★½	60	$+	(239) 463-1080
Tropical Inn Resort	★★½	60	$$−	(239) 463-3124
Dolphin Inn	★★	54	$	(239) 463-6049
Beacon Motel & Gift Shop	★★	53	$$−	(239) 463-5264
Marco Island				
Marco Beach Ocean Resort	★★★★★	99	$$$$$+	(239) 393-1400
Marriott Resort of Marco Island	★★★★	87	$$$+	(239) 394-2511
Marco Island Hilton	★★★½	82	$$$+	(239) 394-5000

Hotels and Motels in Southwest Florida

HOW THE HOTELS COMPARE IN SOUTHWEST FLORIDA (continued)

Hotel	Star Rating	Quality Rating	Cost ($=$50)	Phone
Marco Island (continued)				
Marco Resort & Club	★★★½	80	$$–	(239) 394-2777
Radisson Suite Beach Resort	★★★½	75	$$$–	(239) 394-4100
Boat House Motel	★★½	59	$$–	(239) 642-2400
Matlacha				
Bridge Water Inn	★★★	72	$+	(239) 283-2423
Bayview Bed & Breakfast	★★★	70	$$–	(239) 283-7510
Knoll's Court Motel	★★½	64	$–	(239) 283-0616
Naples				
Ritz-Carlton Naples	★★★★★	99	$$$$$	(239) 598-3300
Inn on Fifth	★★★★½	95	$$+	(239) 403-8777
Hotel Escalante	★★★★½	93	$$$$–	(239) 659-3466
Registry Resort	★★★★½	93	$$$	(239) 597-3232
La Playa Beach Resort	★★★★	88	$$$$+	(239) 597-3123
Doubletree Guest Suites Naples	★★★★	85	$+	(239) 593-8733
Inn at Pelican Bay	★★★★	85	$+	(239) 597-8777
Naples Beach Hotel & Golf Club	★★★★	85	$$$+	(239) 261-2222
Hilton Naples & Towers	★★★½	82	$$$–	(239) 430-4900
Port of the Islands Resort	★★★½	82	$$–	(239) 394-3101
Vanderbilt Beach Resort House	★★★½	82	$$	(239) 597-3144
Ramada Plaza Hotel	★★★½	80	$+	(239) 430-3500
Naples Courtyard	★★★½	78	$+	(239) 434-8700
Lighthouse Inn	★★★½	75	$$–	(239) 597-3345
Best Western Naples	★★★	74	$+	(239) 261-1148
Residence Inn	★★★	74	$$–	(239) 659-1300
Staybridge Suites by Holiday Inn	★★★	74	$$–	(239) 643-8002
Bel Mar Resort	★★★	73	$$+	(239) 403-4747
Holiday Inn Naples	★★★	73	$+	(239) 262-7146
Hawthorne Suites	★★★	70	$$–	(239) 593-1300
Hampton Inn Naples	★★★	69	$+	(239) 261-8000
White Sands Resort Club	★★★	69	$$–	(239) 261-4144
Clarion Inn & Suites	★★★	68	$+	(239) 649-5500
Quality Inn Gulfcoast	★★★	65	$+	(239) 261-6046
Lemon Tree Inn	★★½	64	$+	(239) 262-1414
Comfort Inn Downtown Naples	★★½	62	$+	(239) 649-5800
Sea Court Hotel	★★½	60	$	(239) 435-9700

HOW THE HOTELS COMPARE IN SOUTHWEST FLORIDA *(continued)*

Hotel	Star Rating	Quality Rating	Cost ($=$50)	Phone
North Fort Myers				
Best Western Waterfront Fort Myers	★★★	70	$+	(239) 997-5511
Howard Johnson Express Inn	★★½	57	$+	(239) 656-4000
Motel 6 North Fort Myers	★★	55	$	(239) 656-5544
Days Inn North	★★	50	$+	(239) 995-0535
Econo Lodge	★½	46	$	(239) 995-0571
Port Charlotte				
Hampton Inn Port Charlotte	★★★	67	$$–	(941) 627-5600
Holiday Inn Express Port Charlotte	★★★	67	$$–	(941) 764-0056
Punta Gorda				
Best Western Waterfront Punta Gorda	★★★	65	$$–	(941) 639-1165
Days Inn Punta Gorda	★½	46	$+	(941) 637-7200
Motel 6 Punta Gorda	★½	46	$+	(941) 639-9585
Sanibel				
Casa Ybel Resort	★★★★½	93	$$$$$$–	(239) 472-3145
Hurricane House	★★★★	86	$$$$$–	(239) 472-1696
West Wind Inn	★★★★	84	$$$	(239) 472-1541
Caribe Beach Resort	★★★	74	$$$–	(239) 472-1166
Sundial Beach Resort	★★★	74	$$$$+	(239) 472-4151
Waterside Inn on the Beach	★★★	73	$$$$–	(239) 472-1345
Beach View Cottages	★★★	70	$$$–	(239) 472-1202
Island Inn	★★★	70	$$+	(239) 472-1561
Tropical Winds Cottages	★★★	70	$$$+	(239) 472-1765
Palms of Sanibel	★★★	70	$$+	(239) 395-1775
Buttonwood Cottages	★★★	68	$$+	(239) 395-9061
Holiday Inn Beach Resort	★★★	68	$$$+	(239) 472-4123
Sanibel Inn	★★★	68	$$$$	(239) 472-3181
Seahorse Cottages on Sanibel	★★★	68	$$–	(239) 472-4262
Tarpon Tale Inn	★★★	68	$$$$+	(239) 472-0939
Best Western Sanibel Beach Resort	★★★	67	$$$–	(239) 472-1700
Palm View Motel	★★★	67	$+	(239) 472-1606
Sandpiper Inn Sanibel Island	★★★	67	$$+	(239) 472-1529
Shalimar Resort	★★★	65	$$$–	(239) 472-1353
Forty/Fifteen Resort	★★½	64	$$$–	(239) 472-1232
Mitchell's Sand Castles	★★½	64	$$$	(239) 472-1282
Sanibel's Seaside Inn	★★½	64	$$$$+	(239) 472-1400

HOW THE HOTELS COMPARE IN MIAMI AND MIAMI BEACH

Hotel	Star Rating	Quality Rating	Cost ($=$50)	Phone
Bal Harbour				
Sheraton Bal Harbour Resort	★★★★½	90	$$$$$+	(305) 865-7511
Sea View Hotel	★★★★	85	$$$$–	(305) 866-4441
Coconut Grove				
Grove Isle Club and Resort	★★★★★	98	$$$+	(305) 858-8300
Wyndham Grand Bay Hotel	★★★★½	93	$$$–	(305) 858-9600
Doubletree at Coconut Grove	★★★★	84	$$+	(305) 858-2500
Sonesta Hotel & Suites	★★★★	84	$$+	(305) 529-2828
Coral Gables				
Biltmore Hotel	★★★★½	95	$$$$$+	(305) 445-1926
Hotel Place St. Michel	★★★★½	92	$$+	(305) 444-1666
Omni Colonnade Hotel	★★★★½	92	$$$–	(305) 441-2600
Hyatt Regency Coral Gables	★★★★½	91	$$$$$$–	(305) 441-1234
David William Hotel	★★★★	89	$$$$	(305) 445-7821
Florida City				
Best Western Gateway to the Keys	★★½	64	$$–	(305) 246-5100
Hampton Inn Florida City	★★½	64	$$+	(305) 247-8833
Comfort Inn	★★½	62	$	(305) 248-4009
Fairway Inn	★★½	60	$–	(305) 248-4202
Travelodge	★★	55	$+	(305) 248-9777
Key Biscayne				
Sonesta Beach Resort	★★★★	83	$$$$–	(305) 361-2021
Miami				
Mandarin Oriental	★★★★★	99	$$$$$$$$$	(305) 913-8288
Ritz-Carlton Coconut Grove	★★★★★	99	$$$$$$	(305) 644-4680
Doral Golf Resort & Spa	★★★★½	93	$$$–	(305) 592-2000
JW Marriott Hotel Miami	★★★★½	92	$$$$$	(305) 374-1224
Hotel Intercontinental	★★★★½	91	$$$$$	(305) 577-1000
Doubletree Grand Hotel	★★★★	85	$$$$+	(305) 372-0313
Summerfield Suites	★★★★	85	$$+	(305) 269-1922
Embassy Suites Airport	★★★★	84	$$$–	(305) 634-5000
Marriott Biscayne Bay	★★★★	84	$$$–	(305) 374-3900
Hotel Sofitel	★★★★	83	$$+	(305) 264-4888
Miami Airport Marriott	★★★★	83	$$$–	(305) 649-5000
Wyndham Miami Airport	★★★★	83	$$+	(305) 871-3800
New Radisson Hotel Miami	★★★½	82	$$+	(305) 374-0000
Hilton Miami Airport	★★★½	80	$$–	(305) 262-1000
Sheraton Biscayne Bay Hotel	★★★½	80	$$+	(305) 373-6000

HOW THE HOTELS COMPARE IN MIAMI AND MIAMI BEACH (continued)

Hotel	Star Rating	Quality Rating	Cost ($=$50)	Phone
Miami (continued)				
Clarion Hotel & Suites	★★★½	78	$$–	(305) 374-5100
Crowne Plaza Hotel	★★★½	76	$$+	(305) 446-9000
Miami Airport Courtyard South	★★★½	76	$$$–	(305) 642-8200
Courtyard Downtown	★★★	73	$$–	(305) 374-3000
Baymont Inn & Suites	★★★	72	$$–	(305) 871-1777
Holiday Inn Marina Park	★★★	68	$$$–	(305) 371-4400
Doubletree Club Hotel	★★★	67	$+	(305) 266-0000
Sleep Inn	★★½	64	$$–	(305) 871-7553
Howard Johnson Miami Airport	★★	54	$$–	(305) 945-2621
Howard Johnson Port of Miami	★★	53	$$–	(305) 358-3080
Miami Beach				
Loews Miami Beach Hotel	★★★★½	95	$$$$$$$+	(305) 604-1601
The Tides	★★★★½	95	$$$$$$$–	(305) 604-5000
Hotel Delano	★★★★½	94	$$$$$$$$$$+	(305) 672-2000
Hotel Impala	★★★★½	93	$$$	(305) 673-2021
Hotel Ocean	★★★★½	93	$$$$$$–	(305) 672-2579
Bentley Hotel	★★★★½	92	$$$$$$–	(305) 938-4600
Hotel Astor	★★★★½	92	$$$–	(305) 531-8081
Wyndham Miami Beach Resort	★★★★½	91	$$$–	(305) 532-3600
Marlin	★★★★½	90	$$$$$$$–	(305) 673-8770
Alexander Hotel	★★★★	89	$$$+	(305) 865-6500
Blue Moon	★★★★	89	$$+	(305) 673-2262
Eden Roc Hotel	★★★★	89	$$$$$$	(305) 531-0000
The Hotel	★★★★	89	$$$+	(305) 531-2222
Casa Grande Suite Hotel	★★★★	87	$$$$$–	(305) 672-7003
Park Central Imperial Hotels	★★★★	87	$$$–	(305) 538-1611
Fontainebleau Hilton Resort & Spa	★★★★	83	$$$$–	(305) 538-2000
Doubletree Surfcomber	★★★½	82	$$$$	(305) 532-7715
Lily Guesthouse	★★★½	82	$$$–	(305) 535-9900
National Hotel	★★★½	81	$$$+	(305) 532-2311
The Palms	★★★½	81	$$$$–	(305) 534-0505
Cardozo Hotel	★★★½	80	$$$	(305) 535-6500
La Flora	★★★½	80	$$$	(305) 531-3406
Newport Beachside Resort	★★★½	80	$$–	(305) 949-1300
Ritz Plaza Hotel	★★★½	80	$$+	(305) 534-3500
Waldorf Towers Hotel	★★★½	80	$$$–	(305) 531-7684

HOW THE HOTELS COMPARE IN MIAMI AND MIAMI BEACH (continued)

Hotel	Star Rating	Quality Rating	Cost ($=$50)	Phone
Miami Beach (continued)				
Nassau Suite Hotel	★★★½	79	$$+	(305) 534-2354
Winterhaven	★★★½	79	$$$+	(305) 531-5571
Four Points Sheraton	★★★	73	$$	(305) 531-7494
Essex House Hotel	★★★	72	$$+	(305) 534-2700
Avalon Majestic Hotel	★★★	70	$$$−	(305) 538-0133
Indian Creek Hotel	★★★	69	$$	(305) 531-2727
Ramada Plaza Marco Polo	★★★	68	$$+	(305) 932-2233
Riande Continental	★★★	67	$$−	(305) 531-3503
Days Inn Oceanside	★★★	66	$$	(305) 673-1513
Brigham Gardens	★★★	65	$+	(305) 531-1331
Best Western Oceanfront Resort	★★½	64	$$−	(305) 864-2232
Clinton Hotel South Beach	★★½	64	$$$$$−	(305) 938-4040
Best Western Beach Resort	★★½	63	$$−	(305) 532-3311
Comfort Inn on the Beach	★★½	63	$$−	(305) 868-1200
Tudor Hotel	★★½	63	$$−	(305) 534-2934
Beach Plaza Hotel	★★½	60	$$−	(305) 531-6421
Seville Beach Hotel	★★½	60	$+	(305) 532-2511
The Creek South Beach	★★	55	$	(305) 538-1951
Ramada Resort Miami Beach	★★	52	$$−	(305) 531-5771
Miami Lakes				
Don Shula's Hotel & Golf Club	★★★★	84	$$$+	(305) 821-1150
Miami Springs				
Courtyard Airport West	★★★	74	$$$−	(305) 477-8118
Holiday Inn Airport North	★★★	65	$$−	(305) 885-1941
Homestead Studio Suites Hotel	★★★	65	$+	(305) 870-0448
Comfort Inn & Suites Airport	★★½	62	$$−	(305) 871-1000
Days Inn Miami Airport North	★★½	56	$$−	(305) 888-3661
Sunny Isles				
Trump International Sonesta Beach Resort	★★★★½	90	$$$$+	(305) 692-5600
Homewood Suites Sunny Isles	★★★½	80	$$$+	(305) 932-8900

HOW THE HOTELS COMPARE IN THE FLORIDA KEYS

Hotel	Star Rating	Quality Rating	Cost ($=$50)	Phone
Duck Key				
Hawk's Cay Resort	★★★★	83	$$$$	(305) 743-7000
Grassy Key				
Yellowtail Inn	★★★	65	$$$−	(305) 743-8400
Islamorada				
Cheeca Lodge	★★★★	85	$$$$$$$	(305) 664-4651
Pelican Cove Resort	★★★	68	$$$	(305) 664-4435
Chesapeake Resort	★★★	66	$$$+	(305) 664-4662
Hampton Inn & Suites	★★½	63	$$$+	(305) 664-0073
HoJo Holiday Isle Resort	★★	50	$$$	(305) 664-2711
Key Largo				
Kona Kai Resort & Gallery	★★★★★	96	$$$+	(305) 852-7200
Key Largo Marriott Beach Resort	★★★★	85	$$$$−	(305) 453-0000
Amy Slate's Dive Resort	★★★	74	$$$−	(305) 451-3595
Best Western Suites at Key Largo	★★★	70	$$$$−	(305) 451-5081
Ramada Limited	★★★	65	$$$	(305) 451-3939
Howard Johnson Resort Key Largo	★★½	62	$$−	(305) 451-1400
Gilbert's Resort	★★½	61	$$+	(305) 451-1133
Holiday Inn Key Largo Resort	★★½	60	$$$$−	(305) 451-2121
Key West				
Heron House	★★★★½	90	$$$$$−	(305) 294-9227
Gardens Hotel	★★★★½	90	$$$−	(305) 294-2661
Pier House	★★★★	87	$$$$	(305) 296-4600
Avalon Bed & Breakfast	★★★★	86	$$	(305) 294-8233
Dewey House	★★★★	85	$$$$+	(305) 296-5611
Hyatt Key West Resort	★★★★	85	$$$$$$−	(305) 296-9900
La Mer Hotel	★★★★	85	$$$$+	(305) 296-5611
Ambrosia House	★★★★	84	$$$+	(305) 294-5181
Ocean Key Resort & Marina	★★★★	83	$$$$$$+	(305) 296-7701
Wyndham Casa Marina Resort	★★★★	83	$$$$$$+	(305) 296-3535
Wyndham Reach Resort	★★★★	83	$$$−	(305) 296-5000
Island City House Hotel	★★★★	83	$$+	(305) 294-5702
Suite Dreams	★★★½	82	$+	(305) 292-4713
Sheraton Suites Key West	★★★½	80	$$$$+	(305) 292-9800
Southernmost on the Beach	★★★½	80	$$+	(305) 296-5611
Crowne Plaza La Concha	★★★½	79	$$$$$$ $$$+	(305) 296-2991

HOW THE HOTELS COMPARE IN THE FLORIDA KEYS (continued)

Hotel	Star Rating	Quality Rating	Cost ($=$50)	Phone
Key West (continued)				
Frances Street Bottle Inn	★★★½	75	$$	(305) 294-8530
Artist House	★★★	74	$$$$	(305) 296-3977
La Te Da Hotel	★★★	74	$$	(305) 296-6706
Courtyard	★★★	70	$$+	(305) 294-5541
Curry Mansion Inn	★★★	70	$$$$−	(305) 294-5349
Duval House	★★★	70	$$$−	(305) 294-1666
Garden House	★★★	70	$$+	(305) 296-5368
Eaton Lodge	★★★	69	$+	(305) 292-2170
Eden House	★★★	69	$$	(305) 296-6868
Hampton Inn	★★★	68	$$$−	(305) 294-2917
Southernmost Motel	★★★	67	$$+	(305) 296-6577
Holiday Inn Beachside	★★★	66	$$$$+	(305) 294-2571
Comfort Inn Key West	★★★	65	$$−	(305) 294-3773
Palms Hotel	★★★	65	$$+	(305) 294-3146
Quality Inn Key West	★★★	65	$$+	(305) 294-6681
Spanish Gardens	★★★	65	$$−	(305) 294-1051
Westwinds	★★★	65	$$	(305) 296-4440
Atlantic Shores Motel	★★½	64	$$	(305) 296-2491
Best Western Key Ambassador	★★½	64	$$−	(305) 296-3500
Radisson Hotel Key West	★★½	64	$$+	(305) 294-5511
Blue Marlin	★★½	63	$$	(305) 294-2585
Travelodge Key West	★★½	62	$$+	(305) 296-7593
Best Western Hibiscus Motel	★★½	60	$$+	(305) 296-6711
Days Inn Key West	★★½	60	$$+	(305) 294-3742
Eaton Manor Guesthouse	★★	51	$+	(305) 294-9870
Little Torch Key				
Parmer's Resort	★★★	70	$$−	(305) 872-2157
Marathon				
Best Western Marathon	★★★	65	$$$+	(305) 743-9009
Holiday Inn Marathon	★★★	65	$$	(305) 289-0222
Kingsail Resort Motel	★★½	64	$$$−	(305) 743-5246

The Best Deals

Having listed the nicest rooms in town, let's reorder the list to rank the best combinations of quality and value in a room. As before, the rankings are made without consideration of location or the availability of restaurant(s), recreational facilities, entertainment, or amenities. Once again, each lodging property is awarded a value rating on a 0 to 100 scale. The higher the number, the better the value.

We recently had a reader complain to us that he had booked one of our top-ranked rooms in terms of value and had been very disappointed in the room. We noticed that the room the reader occupied had a quality rating of ★★½. We would remind you that the value ratings are intended to give you some sense of value received for dollars spent. A ★★½ room at $50 may have the same value rating as a ★★★★ room at $100, but that does not mean the rooms will be of comparable quality. Regardless of whether it's a good deal or not, a ★★½ room is still a ★★½ room.

Listed below are the best room buys for the money, regardless of location or star classification, based on averaged rack rates. Note that sometimes a suite can cost less than a hotel room.

THE TOP 10 BEST DEALS IN THE FLORIDA PANHANDLE

Hotel/Rank	Star Rating	Quality Rating	Cost ($=$50)	Phone
1. Bikini Beach Resort	★★★	70	$	(850) 234-3392
2. Flamingo Motel	★★★	69	$	(850) 234-2232
3. Seville Inn & Suites	★★★	68	$	(850) 433-8331
4. Best Western Del Coronado	★★½	64	$–	(850) 234-1600
5. Gulf View Motel	★★½	64	$–	(850) 648-5955
6. Red Roof Inn Pensacola	★★½	64	$–	(850) 476-7960
7. Gulf View Motel	★★★	69	$+	(850) 234-7131
8. Legacy by the Sea	★★★	69	$+	(850) 249-8601
9. New World Inn at New World Landing	★★★½	82	$$–	(850) 432-4111
10. Old Carrabelle Hotel	★★★½	82	$$–	(850) 697-9010

THE TOP 10 BEST DEALS IN NORTHEAST FLORIDA

Hotel/Rank	Star Rating	Quality Rating	Cost ($=$50)	Phone
1. Baymont Inn & Suites Gainesville	★★★½	82	$+	(352) 376-0004
2. Merida Motel	★★½	64	$–	(904) 825-2398
3. Extended Stay America	★★★	72	$+	(904) 396-1777
4. Sunrise Inn	★★	52	$–	(904) 829-3888
5. Howard Johnson Express Inn Gainesville	★★★	68	$+	(352) 371-2500
6. La Quinta Inn Baymeadows	★★★	68	$+	(904) 731-9940
7. Omni Jacksonville Hotel	★★★★	88	$$+	(904) 355-6664
8. Ramada Limited St. Augustine Beach	★★★	66	$+	(904) 471-1440
9. Hilton Jacksonville Riverfront	★★★½	81	$$–	(904) 398-8800
10. Radisson Riverwalk Hotel & Conference Center	★★★½	81	$$–	(904) 396-5100

THE TOP 10 BEST DEALS IN THE SPACE COAST

Hotel/Rank	Star Rating	Quality Rating	Cost ($=$50)	Phone
1. Desert Inn Resort	★★★½	77	$+	(386) 258-6555
2. Fawlty Towers	★★★	70	$+	(321) 784-3870
3. Radisson Resort Daytona Beach	★★★½	79	$$-	(386) 239-9800
4. Cove Motel	★★★	69	$+	(386) 252-3678
5. Inn at Cocoa Beach	★★★½	80	$$-	(321) 799-3460
6. Best Western All Suites Port St. Lucie	★★★	73	$+	(772) 878-7600
7. Radisson Resort at the Port	★★★½	77	$$-	(321) 784-0000
8. Randolph Inn	★★½	62	$+	(321) 269-5945
9. Doubletree Hotel Cocoa Beach	★★★½	79	$$	(321) 783-9222
10. Baymont Inn & Suites Melbourne	★★★	73	$$-	(321) 242-9400

THE TOP 10 BEST DEALS IN THE ORLANDO AREA

Hotel/Rank	Star Rating	Quality Rating	Cost ($=$50)	Phone
1. Country Inn & Suites	★★★½	82	$+	(407) 997-1400
2. Radisson Barcelo Inn International (Tower)	★★★★	85	$$-	(407) 345-0505
3. Countryside Lodge	★★½	60	$-	(407) 851-1050
4. Courtyard at Lake Lucerne	★★★★	84	$$	(407) 648-5188
5. Grosvenor Resort	★★★½	76	$$-	(407) 828-4444
6. Westgate Resorts (Town Center)	★★★★½	93	$$$-	(800) 925-9999
7. Marriott Hotel Orlando Downtown	★★★★	88	$$+	(407) 843-6664
8. Hawthorn Suites Lake Buena Vista	★★★★	87	$$	(407) 597-5000
9. Microtel Inn & Suites	★★½	63	$	(407) 226-9887
10. Travelodge Suites Eastgate	★★★	67	$+	(407) 396-7666

THE TOP 10 BEST DEALS IN THE CENTRAL GULF COAST

Hotel/Rank	Star Rating	Quality Rating	Cost ($=$50)	Phone
1. Turtle Crawl Inn	★★★½	82	$	(941) 383-3788
2. Sand Pebble Apartments & Motel	★★★	73	$-	(941) 778-3053
3. Haley's Motel	★★★	74	$	(941) 778-5405
4. Siesta Sands on the Beach	★★★½	82	$$-	(941) 349-1929

THE TOP 10 BEST DEALS IN THE CENTRAL GULF COAST *(continued)*

Hotel/Rank	Star Rating	Quality Rating	Cost ($=$50)	Phone
5. Red Roof Inn Tampa	★★★	68	$+	(813) 681-8484
6. AmericInn Hotel & Suites Sarasota	★★★½	82	$$−	(941) 342-8778
7. La Quinta Inn & Suites Brandon	★★★	72	$+	(813) 643-0574
8. Days Inn Tampa Airport/Rocky Point Island	★★★	72	$+	(813) 281-0000
9. Ritz-Carlton Sarasota	★★★★★	98	$$$	(941) 309-2000
10. Marriott Downtown Tampa	★★★½	82	$$−	(813) 229-1100

THE TOP 10 BEST DEALS IN THE GOLD AND TREASURE COASTS

Hotel/Rank	Star Rating	Quality Rating	Cost ($=$50)	Phone
1. Doubletree Guest Suites Boca Raton	★★★★	84	$+	(561) 997-9500
2. Canopy Palms Resort Singer Island	★★★½	82	$+	(561) 848-5502
3. Radisson Bridge Resort of Boca Raton	★★★½	80	$+	(561) 368-9500
4. SpringHill Suites Boca Raton	★★★★	84	$$−	(561) 994-2107
5. Ramada Plaza Hotel Hollywood	★★★	69	$+	(954) 620-7000
6. Embassy Suites Boca Raton	★★★★	85	$$	(561) 994-8200
7. Suburban Extended Stay Hotel Stuart	★★★	68	$+	(772) 286-1010
8. Ireland's Inn Beach Resort Fort Lauderdale	★★★★	83	$$	(954) 565-6661
9. Radisson Beach Resort Fort Pierce	★★★★	89	$$+	(772) 465-5544
10. Dockside Harborlight Resort Fort Pierce Beach	★★★	65	$+	(772) 468-3555

THE TOP 10 BEST DEALS IN SOUTHWEST FLORIDA

Hotel/Rank	Star Rating	Quality Rating	Cost ($=$50)	Phone
1. Doubletree Guest Suites Naples	★★★★	85	$+	(239) 593-8733
2. Tropic Isles RV Park & Apartments	★★★	68	$−	(239) 283-4456
3. Bonita Beach Resort Motel	★★★½	80	$+	(239) 992-2137
4. Ramada Plaza Hotel Naples	★★★½	80	$+	(239) 430-3500
5. Ramada Inn Fort Myers	★★★½	79	$+	(239) 337-0300

THE TOP 10 BEST DEALS IN SOUTHWEST FLORIDA (continued)

Hotel/Rank	Star Rating	Quality Rating	Cost ($=$50)	Phone
6. Inn at Pelican Bay	★★★★	85	$+	(239) 597-8777
7. Naples Courtyard	★★★½	78	$+	(239) 434-8700
8. Trianon Bonita Bay	★★★★	88	$$−	(239) 948-4400
9. Casa Playa Beach Resort	★★★½	78	$+	(239) 765-0510
10. Inn on Fifth	★★★★½	95	$$+	(239) 403-8777

THE TOP 10 BEST DEALS IN MIAMI-DADE COUNTY

Hotel/Rank	Star Rating	Quality Rating	Cost ($=$50)	Phone
1. Fairway Inn Florida City	★★½	60	$−	(305) 248-4202
2. Hotel Place St. Michel	★★★★½	92	$$+	(305) 444-1666
3. Clarion Hotel & Suites Miami	★★★½	78	$$−	(305) 374-5100
4. Wyndham Grand Bay Hotel	★★★★½	93	$$$−	(305) 858-9600
5. Hotel Astor	★★★★½	92	$$$−	(305) 531-8081
6. Omni Colonnade Hotel	★★★★½	92	$$$−	(305) 441-2600
7. Hilton Miami Airport	★★★½	80	$$−	(305) 262-1000
8. Newport Beachside Resort	★★★½	80	$$−	(305) 949-1300
9. Comfort Inn Florida City	★★½	62	$	(305) 248-4009
10. Blue Moon	★★★★	89	$$+	(305) 673-2262

THE TOP 10 BEST DEALS IN THE FLORIDA KEYS

Hotel/Rank	Star Rating	Quality Rating	Cost ($=$50)	Phone
1. Suite Dreams	★★★½	82	$+	(305) 292-4713
2. Avalon Bed & Breakfast	★★★★	86	$$	(305) 294-8233
3. Kona Kai Resort & Gallery	★★★★★	96	$$$+	(305) 852-7200
4. Eaton Lodge	★★★	69	$+	(305) 292-2170
5. Gardens Hotel	★★★★½	90	$$$−	(305) 294-2661
6. Island City House Hotel	★★★★	83	$$+	(305) 294-5702
7. Frances Street Bottle Inn	★★★½	75	$$	(305) 294-8530
8. Southernmost on the Beach	★★★½	80	$$+	(305) 296-5611
9. Parmer's Resort	★★★	70	$$−	(305) 872-2157
10. Wyndham Reach Resort	★★★★	83	$$$−	(305) 296-5000

Part Two

The Florida Panhandle: Pensacola, Fort Walton, Destin, Panama City, and Tallahassee

Welcome to the Panhandle

There's a famous saying in the Panhandle, "Welcome to the western gate to the Sunshine State, where thousands live the way millions wish they could." Broad, white beaches, more than 50 miles of shoreline, and Gulf sunsets make the Panhandle one of Florida's most romantic destinations. Add the gentle lapping waves and you'll be reminded of the Caribbean—minus Customs and a long, expensive flight over the ocean.

The pace is slow in this part of Florida—perhaps because the Panhandle is in the central time zone, an hour behind the rest of the state. Sometimes called the Emerald Coast, it has some of the prettiest stretches of oceanfront in the United States, dotted with charming towns. You can drive from one end to the other in about four hours, but where there used to be long stretches of uninhabited coast and small seaside villages, new towns, like Watercolor and Rosemary Beach, are cropping up with multimillion-dollar homes.

Stretching from Navarre Beach, just east of the historic city of Pensacola on the state's western border, to the shores of the Suwannee River on the east, Northwest Florida has miles and miles of pristine beaches, much of it undeveloped and protected as the Gulf Islands National Seashore.

Panama City is still the mecca for Southerners in the summertime, with dozens of inexpensive beachside motels, tacky souvenir shops, fast-food joints, and colorful amusement parks. But just minutes to the east it gets quiet again, with pristine places like nearby St. Andrews State Recreation Area, one of the most beautiful beaches in the United States.

Head inland to the Blackwater, Escambia, and Yellow Rivers near Pensacola, and the Suwannee River near the eastern border for canoeing, kayaking, and boating. Stop for a walk through the eerie limestone caverns in Marianna or for a dip in Wakulla Springs. This part of the state is full of outdoor adventures.

Rich Southern History

The Apalachee Indians lived throughout the panhandle from A.D. 500 through the 1600s. In 1539, Hernando de Soto spent the first Christmas in the New World in the woods near the present State Capitol. As more Spanish colonists entered the panhandle, disease and fighting reduced the native population. The Apalachee abandoned the village that was later dubbed "Tallahassee," a Native American word meaning "old town" or "abandoned fields."

When Florida became a territory of the United States in 1822, both St. Augustine and Pensacola, the major cities in Florida at the time, competed to be the capital. Unable to come to an agreement, it was decided to locate the capital at a point between the two cities. Tallahassee's tall hills attracted the search party, and in 1824 the city of Tallahassee was created, with a log cabin for its capitol. Today it remains the center of state government, with handsome buildings and beautiful historic homes.

Another historic Panhandle town is Apalachicola, a major cotton-shipping port that boomed in the nineteenth century. The town turned to oystering and fishing in the 1920s, and today it's the oyster capital of Florida.

The Panhandle today defines "Southern" with a slower-paced lifestyle, stately homes and historic buildings, ancient oaks dripping with Spanish moss, and sweet tea served most everywhere.

Visiting the Panhandle

Gathering Information

Apalachicola Bay Chamber of Commerce, 99 Market Street, Suite 100, Apalachicola 32320; (850) 653-9419; **www.baynavigator.com.**

Emerald Coast Convention Center and Visitor Bureau, P.O. Box 609, Fort Walton Beach 32549; (800) 322-3319 (U.S. and Canada); **www.destinfwb.com.**

Hamilton County Tourist Development Council, 207 Northeast First Street, Room 106, Jasper 32052; (386) 792-1300.

Navarre Beach Tourist Information Center, P.O. Box 5337, Navarre 32566; (850) 939-3267 or (800) 480-SAND (U.S. only); **www.navarrefl.com.**

Panama City Beach Convention and Visitors Bureau, P.O. Box 9473, Panama City Beach 32417-9473; (800) 722-3224 (U.S. and Canada); **www.800pcbeach.com.**

Pensacola Convention and Visitor Center, 1401 East Gregory Street, Pensacola, 32501; (850) 434-1234, (800) 874-1234 (U.S. only); **www.visitpensacola.com.**

South Walton Tourist Development Council, P.O. Box 1248, Santa Rosa Beach 32459; (800) 822-6877; **www.beachesofsouthwalton.com.**

Tallahassee Area Convention and Visitors Bureau, 106 East Jefferson Street, Tallahassee, 32301; (800) 628-2866 (U.S. and Canada); **www.seetallahassee.com.**

Getting There

By Plane Oskaloosa County Air Terminal (phone (850) 651-7160), one mile east of Destin; Bay County International Airport (phone (850) 763-6751), four miles northwest of Panama City; Pensacola Regional Airport (phone (850) 436-5005), three miles northeast of Pensacola, **www.flypensacola.com**; Tallahassee Regional Airport (phone (850) 891-7800), five miles southwest of Tallahassee; and Williston Regional Airport (phone (352) 528-4900), one mile southwest of Williston.

By Train The Amtrak transcontinental Sunset Limited stops in Pensacola near the bayfront, at 980 East Heinberg Street, and at 918½ Railroad Avenue in Tallahassee; (800) USA-RAIL or **www.amtrak.com**.

By Car From the east or west take I-10, which runs between Mobile, Alabama and Jacksonville; US 90, connecting Mobile and Pensacola; or US 98, which follows the Panhandle coastline. Some major north-south routes into the panhandle include I-65, which intersects I-10 in Mobile; US 231, running north from Panama City; and US 19, which heading south from Georgia, intersects US 27 as it leaves Tallahassee and continues on to St. Petersburg/Tampa.

Getting Around

Major Roadways

As noted above, US 98 is the Panhandle's primary east-west thoroughfare. It runs close to the beach, and consequently passes most hotels and resorts. Of course, it can slow to a crawl during peak tourist seasons. You'll especially want to avoid Panama City's beachfront roads at night—unless you wish to join the throngs cruising along just for kicks. State Route 20/267 and I-10 are viable alternative north of the coastline. From either, you can access Fort Walton Beach via SR 85; Panama City Beach via SR 79; Panama City via SR 77 or US 231; Port St. Joe via SR 71; and Apalachicola via SR 65. From I-10, Pensacola is just south on I-110. From SR 20/267, Tallahassee is due north on US 319.

Driving in Pensacola isn't complicated, with the beaches about 20 minutes from downtown. Or you can rent a bike at **Key Sailing** on Pensacola Beach (500 Quietwater Beach Road; (850) 932-5520).

Tallahassee is equally navigable. The main north-south thoroughfare is Monroe Street, with downtown at the city's geographic center. The Florida State University campus is to the west.

HIGHLIGHTS

- Raw oysters on the back porch of Boss Oyster in Apalachicola
- Grayton Beach State Recreation Area
- Old-fashioned amusement park rides at Miracle Strip, Panama City Beach
- Glass bottom boats at Wakulla Springs
- St. George Island State Park

Public Transportation

In Panama City, the **Bay Town Trolley** (phone (850) 769-0557) travels up and down Beach Front Road five times a day. Cost is 50 cents. For scooters (the first choice of high-school and college kids), **California Cycle** (13416 Front Beach Road; (850) 233-1391) rents bicycles and scooters as well as motorcycles.

The Best Beaches

Dog Island, Carabelle   You can reach Dog Island only by private boat or ferry, but the sandy barrier island, just three-and-a-half miles offshore from Carrabelle, is worth the trip. There's just one small inn with eight efficiencies (Pelican Inn, (800) 451-5294) and no stores but six miles of powdery white-sand beach on the south side. To check ferry times, call the Carrabelle Area Chamber of Commerce, (850) 697-2585.

Grayton Beach State Recreation Area, Grayton Beach   Grayton, one of the oldest townships on the Gulf Coast, has 356 acres for camping (with just 37 campsites), easy-to-navigate nature trails with self-guided leaflets, and some of the best beaches around (rest rooms and showers; no lifeguards). Campfire interpretive programs are available to summer campers. Cost to camp is $15–$18, or $3.25 per vehicle for the day. Call (850) 231-4210 for more information.

Gulf Islands National Seashore/Fort Pickens   This stretch of undeveloped beaches, islands, and keys hopscotches along the coast between Gulfport, Mississippi, and Destin, Florida, protected as a National Seashore since 1971. There are historic forts and other structures and myriad wildlife—more than 280 species of birds have been spotted.

Though much of the protected seashore is not accessible by car, there are two easy entrances; one at Perdido Key (see below) and the other at Fort Pickens on Santa Rosa Island (both have additional information on the entire national seashore). On the way to Fort Pickens, you'll pass three public beaches; the first two offer parking only, and the third, called Langdon Beach, has rest rooms, outdoor showers, and a picnic area. There are lifeguards during the peak summer season.

Fort Pickens was a fortress that saw combat during the Civil War, but it's best remembered as the home of Geronimo, an Apache medicine man who was imprisoned there from 1886 to 1888. The fort and museum are open daily from 9:30 a.m. to 5 p.m, closed on Christmas Day. Seven-day admission permits are $8 per vehicle. Also popular is bicycling on the six-mile, round-trip, oyster-shell trail that begins and ends at the Fort Pickens Visitor Center. The fort is located at 1400 Fort Pickens Road, Santa Rosa Island; (850) 934-2635. Take US 98 and SR 399 to Pensacola Beach, then follow signs west. For Fort Pickens campground reservations, call (850) 934-2621 or (800) 365-2267. A campsite costs $20 per night.

Henderson Beach State Recreation Area   This beach is sugar white and home to gulls, brown pelicans, and the protected sea turtle. There are 208 acres, with several boardwalks for easy access to the beach. There are two pavilions with rest rooms and showers. Hours are 8 a.m.–sunset daily. Entrance fee is $2 per vehicle, per day. Entrance is just east of Destin on US 98; (850) 837-7550.

Perdido Key Fifteen miles southwest of Pensacola, Perdido Key is a barrier island with spectacular, powdery beaches. The eastern third of the island, known as Johnson Beach Area, is part of the Gulf Islands National Seashore, with great beachside hiking on seven clear miles of pristine sand and rolling dunes with boardwalks providing handicapped access. There are rest rooms and showers but no lifeguards. Hours are 7 a.m.–sunset daily. Seven-day admission permits are $8 per vehicle; (850) 492-7278.

St. Andrews State Recreation Area, Panama City This is one of the most popular parks in the state, with beautiful beaches (though it can get crowded in the summer, and there are no lifeguards), two fishing piers, and a boat ramp. A nature trail leads through habitats fragrant with wild rosemary that are home to wading birds, alligators, and many small animals—even a herd of deer. There are picnic areas, a playground, rest rooms, and open-air showers. Admission is $4 per car; open 8 a.m.–sunset. The campground has 176 tent sites, with picnic shelters, a playground, rest rooms, and showers. Cost to camp is $18–$23.

A ferry runs from St. Andrews a few hundred yards across the inlet to Shell Island, a seven-and-a-half-mile-long, ten-mile-wide barrier island where you can look for shells, swim, or just enjoy the solitude, peace, and quiet. The shuttle runs every 30 minutes during the summer between 9 a.m. and 5 p.m.; off-season, it runs 10 a.m.–3 p.m. Fare is $9.50 for adults, $5.50 for children ages 12 and under (4607 State Park Land, Panama City Beach; (850) 233-5140).

St. Joseph Peninsula State Park, Port St. Joe This isolated beach gets high ratings, and its towering dunes make it a hiker's paradise. There are rest rooms and showers but no lifeguards. The park encompasses 2,516 acres on a 14-mile-long island off the Gulf Coast, surrounded by the Gulf of Mexico and St. Joseph Bay. Camping, eight cabins, hiking trails, and miles of natural beach make this perfect for visitors looking for an active, but quiet, getaway. Bird-watching is excellent (more than 209 species have been noted), and shelling is good. An 18-mile round-trip trail starts at the state park and runs to the end of the preserve, and the island is never more than a mile wide so you're always within sight or earshot of the Gulf. Hikers need to register, because only 20 are allowed each day in the preserve. Entry is $3.25 per vehicle; camping is $16–$19. Eight cabins rent for $70 in the summer, $55 in the off-season (minimum stay two nights in summer and off-season). Campfire programs and guided walks are scheduled seasonally. Located near Port St. Joe off CR 30-E, off US 98; (850) 227-1327.

Topsail Hill State Preserve Located in Santa Rosa Beach ten miles east of Destin, this state park is one of Florida's most stunning coastal getaways, a 1,640-acre paradise with rare coastal dune lakes and white-sand beaches. It's tough to get there, but you'll find free parking and a rest room, 300 yards from the beach, and there are campsites one mile from the beach. Hours are 8 a.m.–sunset daily; (850) 267-0299.

Outdoor Adventures and Sports

Recommended Outings

Adventures Unlimited This 88-acre park at the confluence of the Coldwater River and Wolfe Creek, which is said to have the purest water of any in the state, is a great starting place to get your family out on Santa Rosa's streams. Santa Rosa County has been designated as the Canoe Capital of Florida by the state legislature.

If you want to stay overnight, Adventures Unlimited can outfit you with everything necessary except clothes and food: a canoe, tents, sleeping bags. At Tomahawk Landing, for a two-night minimum stay, they also have air-conditioned cabins with full kitchens, and the Old Schoolhouse Inn with eight bedrooms—but no phones, TVs, or clocks. Cabins start at $39; guest rooms in the inn start at $79. To get there, follow SR 6, 15 miles north of Milton; from US 90 in Milton, turn north on SR 87; go 12 miles and follow the signs on the right. Turn right and go 4 miles to Adventures Unlimited Tomahawk Landing; (850) 623-6197; (800) 239-6864; **www.adventures unlimited.com.**

Alfred B. Maclay State Gardens In the hills near Tallahassee, Maclay State Gardens are just too pretty to pass up when the azaleas and snowy dogwoods are in bloom from January through April (optimum time is mid-March). The ornamental gardens and a plantation home built in 1909 are open 8 a.m.–5 p.m., and it's a great place for a long, peaceful walk. You can also swim, canoe, and boat here. Admission year-round is $3.25 per vehicle. To visit the formal gardens from January through April, cost is an additional $3 for adults and $1.50 for children ages 6–11. The gardens are a half-mile north of I-10 in Tallahassee on US 310; (850) 487-4556.

Big Lagoon State Recreation Area With sandy beaches and salt marshes, Big Lagoon is home to myriad birds and animals—cardinals are common in the uplands, while great blue herons frequent the marshes and the lagoon. Elaborate boardwalks and a 40-foot observation tower at the east beach give a panoramic view of Big Lagoon and Gulf Island National Seashore across the Intracoastal Waterway. Activities include swimming, picnicking, and nature study. Camping on 75 sites is $16. Located on CR 292A, about ten miles west of Pensacola; (850) 492-1595.

Blackwater River State Park The Blackwater is considered one of the purest sand-bottom rivers in the world, and it is still in a natural state for most of it length. Canoes can be rented at the park, and the run is especially good for novice paddlers because of an easy current with no whitewater. Camping on 31 sites is around $8, $10 with electricity. There are easy nature trails and decent fishing here, too. Pets are permitted. The parks is located 15 miles northeast of Milton, off US 90; SR 1, Box 57-C, Holt; (850) 983-5363.

Falling Waters State Recreation Area, Chipley The name comes from a 67-foot waterfall (the only one in Florida) that tumbles into a 20-foot-wide cylindrical sinkhole. The water's unknown final destination remains mysterious. Nature trails guide you through primeval Florida. There's a nice picnic area near the falls. Camping on 24 sites runs $11–$13. The recreation area is located three miles south of Chipley off SR 77A; (850) 638-6130.

Florida Caverns State Park, Marianna A bizarre series of connecting caves containing limestone stalactites, stalagmites, columns, rimstone, flowstone, and draperies are found at Florida Caverns State Park. All the enchanting formations are composed of calcite, which is dissolved from the limestone when the surface water containing carbonic acid percolates through the rock and into the cave. Guided tours (45 minutes, with up to 25 per tour) are provided every day. You'll see the Waterfall Room, the Cathedral Room, and the Wedding Room—all impressive. The air is dry, there's no humidity, and it's always 65 degrees.

Picnicking, swimming on a man-made white-sand beach, fishing, and canoeing are available. There are two horse trails with rentals. Camping on 32 sites is $12–$14. Admission to the park is $3.25 per vehicle, with admission to the caves $5 for adults, $2.50 for children ages 2–12. Florida Caverns is located three miles north of Marianna on SR 167; (850) 482-1228.

Gulf Specimen Marine Laboratories Aquarium If you make the trip to Wakulla Springs, just a few miles south you'll find this quirky laboratory of sea life. Author-explorer Jack Rudloe and his wife own the place, and you'll be lucky if they're around and not out scouting for more Florida marine life to add to the living collection. Jack will take his time walking you through the gurgling lab, wall to wall with open tanks teeming with unusual seal life (he also conducts research and stocks biomedical labs around the world). Kids can touch sea cucumbers, blowfish, sea anemones, and more. The aquarium is located at 300 Clark Drive at Palm Street south of US 98, Panacea; (850) 984-5297; **www.gulfspeciman.org**. It's open Monday–Friday 9 a.m.–5 p.m., Saturday 10 a.m.–4 p.m., and Sunday noon–4 p.m. Admission is $5; $3 for children under age 12.

Jeanni's Journeys Owner Jeanni McMillan is a jack-of-all-trades, with a captain's license, a divemaster certificate, a lifeguard certificate, a Florida teaching certificate, and a certificate in first aid and CPR. She'll arrange family trips to the barrier island for snorkeling, shelling, and dolphin-watching kayak and canoe trips to neat places like undeveloped St. Vincent or Little St. George Island. Her kids-only trips include sand-sculpting on the beach, rainy-day art projects, night critter identification, and a three-hour fishing adventure in Apalachicola Bay (children must be at least nine years old for the fishing trip). Kids-only trips range from $25 to $60; others are based on the excursion. Jeanni's Journeys is open from

March 5 through December 31 at 240 East Third Street, St. George Island; (850) 927-3259; **www.sgislandjourneys.com**.

Stephen Foster State Folk Culture Center   This center is worth a stop to learn about the songwriter who penned "The Old Folks at Home." The 247-acre center honors the memory of Foster and serves as a gathering place for those who perpetuate the crafts, music, and legends of early and contemporary Floridians. The center is most enjoyable when there are special events, so check as you plan your trip.

It's fun to get out on the river made famous by the song, the beautiful Suwannee. It's a great biking spot, too, with an easy, four-mile ride that's part of the Florida National Scenic Trail. You may spot deer, turkey, gray foxes, or gopher tortoises. Camping on 32 sites is $12, $14 with electricity. Admission to the park is $3.25 per car, and there are additional fees for some events. Located in White Springs, on US 41 North (three miles from I-75 and nine miles from I-10); (386) 397-4331.

The little burg of White Springs is excellent bicycling territory, noted as headquarters of the Suwannee Bicycle Association. There are more than 700 miles of clearly marked trails, from short ones up to 100 miles. For information call (386) 397-2347 on weekends only.

St. George Island State Park   This little jewel on the northeast corner of St. George Island is a best-kept secret, where you can see Florida in its almost-natural state. With nine miles of sandy shores and grass flats, it's a bird-watcher's paradise, with trail boardwalks and observation platforms for an easy hike. Though the beach is outstanding, be sure to take a little time to explore the bay side of the island, alive with birds and other wildlife. Some of the best shelling on this part of the Gulf Coast is here, and you can even harvest your own oysters. There are picnic areas, rest rooms, showers, and a campground with 60 sites. The cost is $4 per vehicle; $10.60–$17 to camp. The park is located on St. George Island, ten miles southeast of the town Eastpoint, off US 98 and across a three-mile causeway; (850) 927-2111.

Suwannee River State Park, Live Oak   It's doubtful that Stephen Foster ever saw the river he made famous with "The Old Folks at Home," but it's a good spot for camping, fishing, picnicking, and canoeing; it also has five short nature trails (look for the amazing Balance Rock). The River Trail, part of the Florida National Scenic Trail, is a little over nine-miles long, beginning on the CR 141 bridge on the Withlacoochee River, half a mile from the state park, and continuing to the park's northern boundary. Admission is $3.25 per car and the park is open daily, 8 a.m.–sunset. The park is located 13 miles west of Live Oak, off US 90; (386) 362-2746. Camping is $8–$10 and $2 additional for pets. To rent a canoe, see **Suwannee Canoe Outpost** on SR 129; (386) 364-4991. The per-adult costs for guided trips are one hour, $9; two or three hours, $13; and four-and-a-half or six hours, $16. Children ages 3–12 pay half-price on all trips. You can rent just the canoe for $5 per hour or $20 per day. Reservations are recommended. No trips are offered on Wednesdays.

Tallahassee–St. Marks Historic Railroad State Trail   From 1837 until 1984 the Tallahassee–St. Marks Railroad was the oldest railroad in Florida; it transported cotton and other products to the port of St. Marks on the Gulf Coast. Now an easy, 16-mile trail starts at Tallahassee and ends at St. Marks, a wide, paved path with a parking lot on SR 363, just south of Tallahassee at the entrance to the trail; (850) 922-6007. You can rent bikes or in-line skates at **St. Marks Trail Bikes and Blades** at the north entrance; (850) 656-0001. Bikes rent for $9 for two hours or $16 for four hours, and they'll give you a good deal if you're renting bikes for the whole family. The shop is open Monday–Friday, noon–sunset, and Saturday and Sunday, 9 a.m.–6 p.m.

Torreya State Park, Bristol   High bluffs along the Apalachicola River are a rare sight in Florida—steep rises 150 feet above the river. A moderate, seven-mile loop trail takes you past hundreds of plants more common to the Appalachian mountains—mountain laurel, wild ginger, and wild hydrangea, for instance. Wildlife such as deer, beaver, bobcat, and gray fox live here, and more than 100 species of birds have been spotted. You'll also see plenty of torreya, a rare species of tree that grows only along the Apalachicola River bluffs. Camping on 35 sites costs $8–$10 per night. The park is located off SR 12 on CR 1641, 13 miles north of Bristol; (850) 643-2674.

Wakulla Springs State Park   This memorable state park is home of the world's largest and deepest freshwater springs—every minute 600,000 gallons of crystal-clear water bubble from a cave 185 feet below the surface. There's an abundance of wildlife—about 2,000 waterfowl make the park their migratory winter home, along with alligators, deer, bears, snakes, and bobcats.

Glass-bottom boat tours operate over the spring when the water is clear, and there are also 30-minute riverboat cruises on the spring run. The guides love to tell the stories about the old Tarzan movies that were filmed here and how the bones of Ice Age creatures have been recovered from the depths of the 35-million-year-old limestone caverns. Boats run daily from 9:45 a.m.–5 p.m. during daylight savings time; 11 a.m.–3 p.m. during the rest of the year. The cost is $4.50 for adults, half price for children ages 3–12, and free for those younger.

The park is also great for picnicking, nature walks, swimming, and snorkeling in a designated area near the head of the spring.

Bicycling, though a bit challenging, is a real treat on a ten-mile (round-trip) trail. Check in with the ranger before setting out, as the last three miles are a bit remote; ask for a map as you pay your user fee. The park is located 14 miles south of Tallahassee on SR 267 at SR 61; (850) 922-3632.

If you're in luck, you can book a room at the **Wakulla Springs Lodge.** This beautiful old lodge features rare Spanish tiles, marble floors, and paintings of old Florida on the ceiling beams. Rooms are simple and spacious. The dining room has a wood-burning fireplace, tall windows that overlook the springs, and food that is pure Southern. Phones are provided in each room, but not TVs. Rates run $89–$99 on the weekends and $79–$99 weekdays.

Located at 1 Springs Drive (14 miles south of Tallahassee via SR 61); (850) 224-5950; www.wakullacounty.com.

Canoeing and Kayaking

Santa Rosa County is home to more than 100 miles of famously clear streams with verdant banks clad in juniper, cypress, and oak. Beautiful, white sand bars are perfect for picnicking, and the average depth of two to three feet, coupled with high water clarity, make for an unintimidating experience for novices and children.

The town of Milton, the epicenter of area canoeing on the crystal-clear Blackwater River and nearby Coldwater River, Sweetwater Creek, and Juniper Creek, is just north of I-10 and south of Blackwater River State Forest. **Blackwater Canoe Rental** (10274 Pond Road, 32507; (800) 967-6789 or (850) 623-0235; www.blackwatercanoe.com) rents a wide variety of paddling boats and equipment. Guided trips, including overnight excursions, average $20–$30 per person. Nearby, the aforementioned **Adventures Unlimited** offers guided trips averaging $20–$25 per person, as well as a campground and cabins. Reservations are advised, especially on weekends. If possible, plan a trip in the spring or fall, when rain swells the rivers and tourists are fewer.

Suwanee River State Park (13 miles west of Live Oak, off US 90; (386) 362-2746), also noted above, is home to the nine-mile River Trail, part of the Florida National Scenic Trail. **Suwannee Canoe Outpost** (located on SR 129; (386) 364-4991) rents canoes for $20 per day and offers guided trips for $13–$16. Reservations are recommended; note that the outfitter is closed on Wednesday.

Scuba Diving and Snorkeling

Divers in the area can explore natural, historical, and artificial reefs. Get the scoop on the best sites at **Panama City Dive Center** (4823 Thomas Drive; (850) 235-3390), **Hydrospace Dive Shop** (Hathaway Marina, 6422 US 98 (850) 234-3063), and **Diver's Den** (3120 Thomas Drive; (850) 234-8717).

Also in Panama City, try **Island Time** (3605 Thomas Drive, Slip #22, next to The Treasure Ship Restaurant (850) 234-7377; www.islandtimesailing.com) for snorkeling trips, dolphin watches, and cruising.

Kokomo Snorkeling Headquarters at 500 US 98 East in Destin offers daily trips to two locations—one for shelling, one for feeding fish. An instructor gives how-to lessons for those ages four and older. The cost is $20 per person for a three-hour trip. Call (850) 837-9029 for more information.

Sailing and Boating

Cruises from Destin Harbor aboard a 72-foot schooner can be arranged with **Sailing South** (phone (850) 837-7245; www.sailingsouth.com) for $15 for adults and $13 for children ages 12 and under. The 90-minute morning cruises feature dolphin-spotting. Afternoon outings run an hour longer, include a stop for snorkeling, and cost $35 for adults, $18 for children.

Glass-bottom boats offer underwater viewing, dolphin encounters, crab trapping, bird feeding, and nature cruises from **Boogies Dock** at the foot of Destin Bridge (2 US 98 East, Destin; (850) 654-7787). Cruises cost $17 for adults and $7.50 for children; ages two and under are free.

Southern Star offers dolphin cruises all year from **Harbor Walk Marina** at the foot of Destin Bridge; (850) 837-7741. The cost is $17 for adults, $14 for seniors, and $7 for children.

In Panama City, the **Glass Bottom Boat** is a family-run charter out of Treasure Island Marina (3605 Thomas Drive; (850) 234-8944), an easy way to spot puffer fish, seahorses, and other exotic marine life. The guides even bring along a shrimp net to scoop out treasures for a closer look. The boat heads to Shell Island, where you get to spend about 45 minutes on shore, collecting shells. It's about three hours round-trip, and they advise you to call ahead for reservations, especially in the summertime. Prices are $15, $14 for seniors, and $8 for children.

Fishing

Freshwater fishing is available at numerous Panhandle state parks, including those mentioned above. Nonresidents over the age of 16 are required to procure a Florida fishing license before casting. You can purchase a license from the Fish and Wildlife Conservation Commission over the phone at (888) 347-4356.

Fishing in the Gulf of Mexico yields Panhandle red snapper, grouper, and tuna, among other species, and is a popular activity with locals and tourists alike. **Pensacola Beach Gulf Fishing Pier** is the longest fishing pier on the Gulf, at 1,471 feet (located on Fort Pickens Road; (850) 934-7200). **St. Andrews State Recreation Area** in Panama City can get crowded in the summer, but offers anglers two fishing piers and a boat ramp.

Party Boats

Party boats offer typically half-day deep-sea fishing trips for $30–$35. Equipment is provided, and crew members will help you land your catch. Try **Moody's** (phone (850) 837-1293) in Destin or **Capt. Anderson's Deep Sea Fishing** (phone (850) 234-5940) in Panama City.

Charter Boats

For a higher cost, you'll get smaller party sizes, a more personalized fishing experience, as well as scheduling convenience if you charter a boat. Tackle and licenses are supplied; costs vary depending on the size of the boat, how many people want to fish, and how long you'd like to spend on the water. Expect to spend between $400 and $900 depending on your party's size and the destination and length of your trip. Charter-boat fishing is particularly popular in Destin, where marinas line the north shore of Destin Harbor. In Panama City, North Lagoon Drive and Thomas Drive are home to several fleets.

NORTHWEST FLORIDA CHARTERS, CHARTER SERVICES, AND MARINAS

Charter Service	Phone
Pensacola	
Entertainer	(850) 932-0305
Lively One	(850) 932-5071
Rod and Reel Marina	(850) 492-0100
Destin	
Boardwalk Fishing Charters	(850) 837-2343
Fisherman's Charter Service	(850) 654-4665
Harbor Cove Charters	(850) 837-2222
Pelican Charters	(850) 837-2343
Panama City	
Lighthouse Marina	(850) 234-5609
Panama City Boat Yard	(850) 234-3386
Pirates Cover Marina	(850) 234-3839
Treasure Island Marina	(850) 234-6533

Biking

Cycling enthusiasts will find plenty of scenic and challenging bike trails in the Tallahassee area, including the **Tallahassee–St. Marks Historic Railroad State Trail,** the first designated bike trail in the state. It stretches 16 miles through pine forests and rural communities and ends up in the small coastal town of St. Marks. Branching off the St. Marks Trail is the 11-mile **Munson Hills Off-Road Bicycle Trail,** a real workout in the sugary Panhandle sand.

Pensacola and Pensacola Beach

Warm, Southern heritage and warmer Gulf beaches are the best drawing cards any tourist destination could dream up, and Pensacola has both. The city is in the heart of the Gulf Islands National Seashore, which flanks the city with a pair of barrier islands—Perdido Key to the west and Santa Rosa Island to the east.

Santa Rosa Island, five miles south of Pensacola via US 98, is home to Pensacola Beach, with eight miles of unspoiled white sand and a minimum of traffic. Much of Santa Rosa is protected from development but accessible to visitors. You'll find everything from tall condominiums to historic Fort Pickens, a Civil War fortress that is popular with campers (see Gulf Islands National Seashore above). One of the newest attractions is the Pensacola Beach Fishing Pier, the longest pier (1,471 feet) on the Gulf of Mexico, providing breathtaking views of the shoreline.

Pensacola

N

GOLF COURSES
1. The Club at Hidden Creek
2. Marcus Pointe
3. The Moors
4. Tiger Point Golf and Country Club

ATTRACTIONS
5. Fort Barrancas
6. National Museum of Naval Aviation
7. Sam's Fun World
8. The Zoo

RESTAURANTS
9. Dharma Blue
10. Flounder's Chowder House
11. Hopkins' House
12. Jackson's
13. Peg Leg Pete's Oyster Bar

NIGHTCLUBS
14. Bamboo Willie's
15. Capt'n Fun Beach Bar & Dance Club
16. Flora-Bama Lounge & Package Store
17. Seville Quarter

TO CENTURY

TO NEW ORLEANS

ALABAMA
FLORIDA
Perdido Bay
Bayou
PENSACOLA
Pensacola Bay
Big Lagoon
Fort Pickens National Park
Gulf Islands National Seaboard
PERDIDO KEY
PENSACOLA BEACH
GULF OF MEXICO

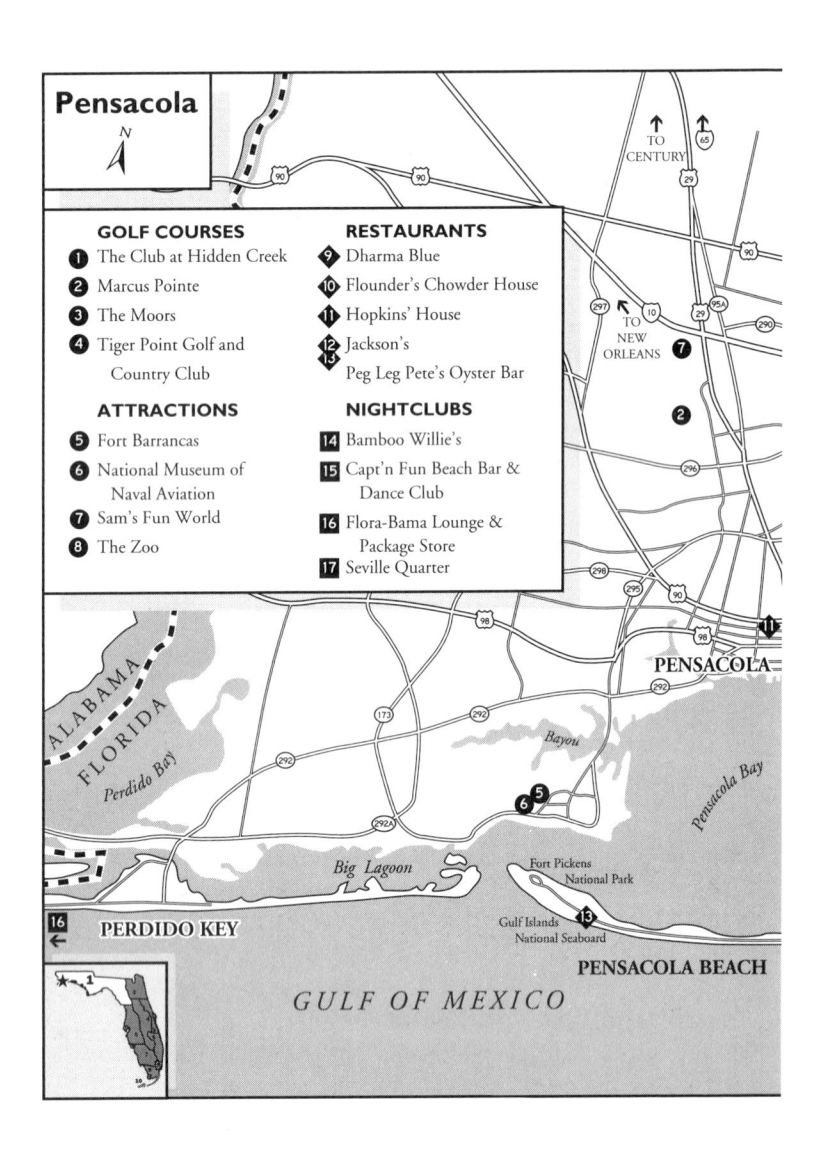

112

113

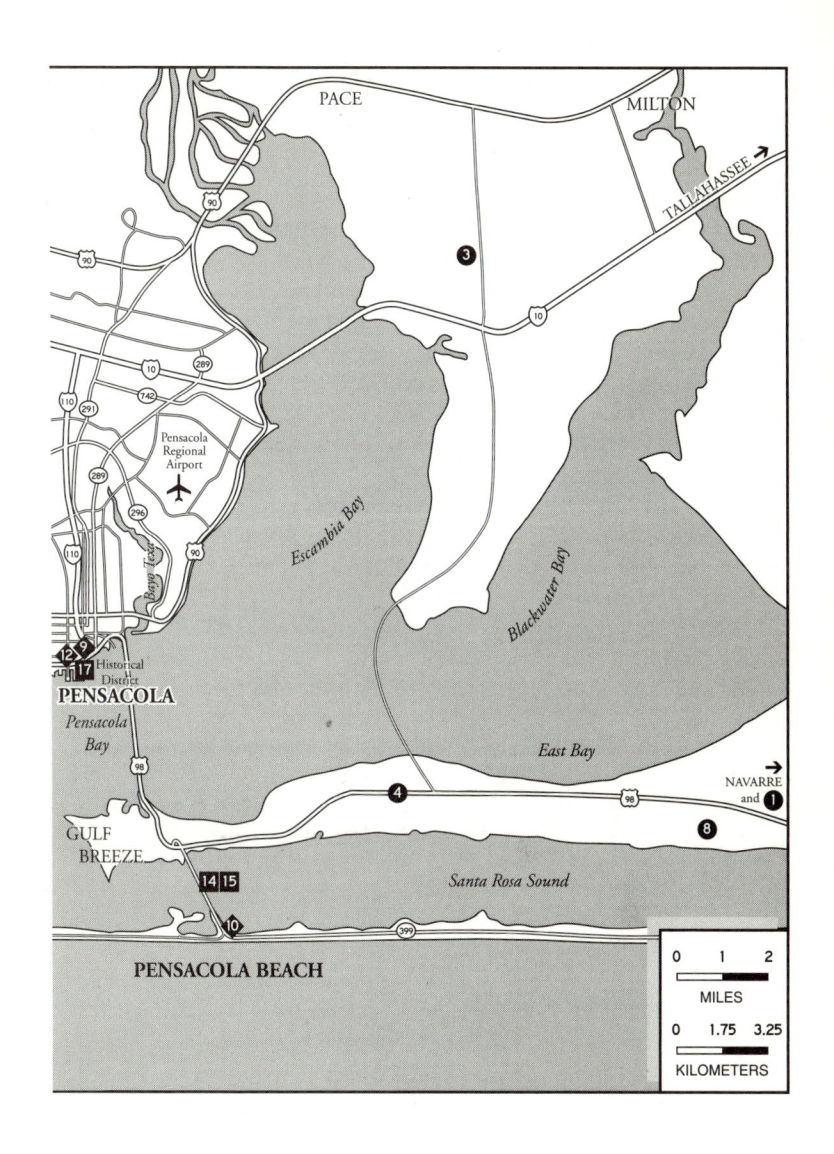

Pensacola's restored downtown reflects much of the 400-year-old city's history—a town that has changed hands more than a dozen times and flown five flags—Spain, France, England, the United States, and the Confederacy.

The city has three historic districts:

North Hill Preservation District is a downtown neighborhood occupying 50 blocks and containing more than 300 beautiful homes built primarily between 1895 and 1940. Of these homes, about 25% are 100 years or older, and a few are situated on historic brick streets.

Pensacola's **Seville Historic District** is one of the oldest and most intact in all of Florida. Within this small neighborhood are Florida's oldest church (1832) and St. Michael's Cemetery, deeded to Pensacola by the King of Spain in 1822. Houses date back to 1795, a mix of French Creole, Victorian, Gulf Coast, and Gothic Revival. Before that, a British fort encompassed the entire neighborhood.

Palafox Historic District was the commercial heart of Old Pensacola. Today, many of the older buildings have been restored to their original beauty, complete with New Orleans ironwork balconies and brick sidewalks lining the walkway.

Visitors enjoy the U.S. Museum of Naval Aviation at Pensacola Naval Air Station, known as the cradle of naval aviation. And you can see the Blue Angels soar skyward off Pensacola Beach during special events in July and November.

TAKE A FREE RIDE

At Pensacola Beach, a free island trolley runs May–September, Friday–Sunday, 10 a.m.–3 p.m. There are two routes: parallel to the beach on Via de Luna and Fort Pickens Road, and along Pensacola Beach Boulevard from the Bob Sikes Bridge to Casino Beach (phone (850) 595-3228).

Golf

The Club at Hidden Creek

3070 PGA Boulevard, Navarre; (850) 939-1939; www.hiddengolf.com
Established 1988 | **Designer** Ron Garl | **Holes** 18

Tees Gold, 6,844/Blue, 6,284/White, 5,722/Red, 5,213
Par 72/72/72/72 **Slope** 139/129/120/123
Fees $49 before noon; $39 noon–3 p.m.; $29 after 3 p.m. **Specials** Reduced fees weekdays, twilight, juniors; first-time Web visitors certificate $39 **Cart rental** Included **Club rental** $35 **Payment** V, MC, AmEx **Tee times** 7 days in advance **Facilities** Clubhouse, banquet facilities, restaurant, golf shop, range, sauna and steam rooms
Comments Hidden Creek is well known for its fast greens, lush landscaping, and scenic rolling terrain, and provides a golf experience challenging enough to serve as a former host site of the U.S. Open Qualifying Rounds.

Marcus Pointe

2500 Oak Pointe Drive, Pensacola; (800) 362-7287 or (850) 484-9770
Established 1990 | **Designer** Earl Stone | **Holes** 18

Tees Gold/Blue/White/Red
Par 72/72/72/72
Slope 129/125/120/119
Fees $49 **Specials** None **Cart rental** Included **Club rental** $12 per set **Payment** V, MC **Tee times** 3 days in advance **Facilities** Range, pro shop, restaurant

Comments Located on 600 acres of rolling terrain and cut through oak and pine trees, this beautiful course may just be the best bargain in town. Unlike many of its neighboring courses, Marcus has minimal water that comes into play. If you have limited funds and are looking for a course that will challenge but not break the bank, head to Marcus Pointe.

The Moors

3220 Avalon Boulevard, Milton; (850) 995-4653; www.moors.com
Established 1993 | **Designer** John LaFoy | **Holes** 18

Tees Gold, 6,841/Blue, 6,449/White, 6,003/Red, 5,263
Par 72/70/68/70 **Slope** 126/122/119/117
Fees $49 Monday–Thursday; Friday–Sunday $59 **Specials** None **Cart rental** Included **Club rental** $30 per set **Payments** All credit cards accepted **Tee times** 7 days in advance **Facilities** Clubhouse, restaurant, lodge

Comments If you want a little taste of what golf is like in Scotland, put The Moors on your "must-play" list. Just minutes from Pensacola, the Moors is a links-style course, complete with moguls, sand, and exotic grasses. Wide-open fairways invite you to really belt it, but the deep pot bunkers ensure that this course is no pushover. There is a definite dearth of trees. Wetlands remind you that yes, you still are in the Panhandle.

A SIDESHOW OF BEACH MANIA

Opened in 1950 in the heart of Gulf Breeze, **Allan Davis Seashells & Souvenirs** is no ordinary souvenir shop, but a well-preserved collection of shells under glass that represents a lifetime of collecting from all over the world. Lining the walls are marine specimens—giant loggerhead shells and skulls, a mummified devil ray, tiny squid, sharks, and other sea creatures. You can buy retro shell souvenirs to carry home. On East US 98, Gulf Breeze, 32561; (850) 932-2151; open 8 a.m.–5 p.m. daily.

Tiger Point Golf and Country Club, East Course

1255 Country Club Road, Gulf Breeze, 32561; (888) 218-8463 or (850) 932-1333; www.tigerpointclub.com

Established 1965 (renovated 2001) | **Designer** Jerry Pate | **Holes** 18
Tees Gold, 7,065/Blue, 6,603/White, 6,090/Red, 5,178
Par 72/72/72/72 **Slope** 143/133/127/115
Fees $65 weekdays before noon, $45 after noon; $59 weekends before noon, $45 after noon **Specials** Golf packages available **Cart rental** Included **Club rental** $20–$30 per set **Payments** V, MC, AmEx **Tee times** 14 days in advance **Facilities** Golf shop, driving range, putting green, chipping area, restaurant, pool, picnic facilities
Comments Tiger Point's East Course, located on Santa Rosa Sound, has strategically deployed water hazards on 14 holes that not only lend character to this links-style course but also add to its difficulty. Additional peril comes in the form of bunkers and breezes.

Attractions

Fort Barrancas

1801 Gulf Breeze Parkway, Gulf Breeze; (850) 455-5167
Hours 9:30 a.m.– 4:45 p.m. daily
Admission Free
Appeal by Age Group

Pre-school ★★★	Teens ★★★	Over 30 ★★★
Grade school ★★★★	Young Adults ★★★	Seniors ★★★

Touring Time *Average* 1 hour; *minimum* 45 minutes
Rainy-Day Touring Not recommended
Author's Rating ★★; interesting history lesson
Description and Comments Fort Barrancas was started by the Spanish in 1797 and finished by American troops between 1839 and 1844. The fort was restored by the National Park Service and is part of Gulf Island National Seashore. Kids enjoy exploring the old fort; guided tours are available.

HISTORIC PENSACOLA VILLAGE

More than 400 years of history are displayed in historic Pensacola Village, with ten restored buildings and museums in a four-block area. Now preserved by the state, the village hosts costumed characters, who demonstrate crafts and daily chores. Charming boutiques and restaurants are now part of the historic area, bounded by Government, Zaragoza, Adams, and Alcanz Streets. Start at the T. T. Wentworth Jr. Florida State Museum at 330 South Jefferson Street to purchase tour tickets. Two-hour walking tours run Monday to Friday in winter and Monday to Saturday in summer, leaving at 11 a.m. and 1:30 p.m. from the Tivoli House, 205 East Zaragoza Street.

Important landmarks include the Museum of Industry, the Museum of Commerce, the French Creole–style Charles Lavalle House, the Victoria Dorr House, the Quina House, and the Julee Cottage Black History Museum. Admission is $6 adults, $5 seniors and military, $2.50 children ages 4–16, $13 families. Open Memorial Day–Labor Day, daily, 10 a.m.–4 p.m.; closed Sundays, Mondays, and holidays the rest of the year; (850) 595-5985; www.historicpensacola.org.

National Museum of Naval Aviation

Radford Boulevard on the U.S. Naval Air Station; (850) 452-3604

Hours Daily, 9 a.m.–5 p.m.; closed New Year's Day, Thanksgiving, and Christmas

Admission Free, but donations are appreciated

Appeal by Age Group

Pre-school ★	Teens ★★★	Over 30 ★★★
Grade school ★★★	Young Adults ★★★	Seniors ★★★

Touring Time *Average* 4 hours; *minimum* 2 hours

Rainy-Day Touring Recommended

Author's Rating ★★; great for history buffs

Description and Comments This Naval Air Station has been used by the U.S. Navy and Marine Corps since the turn of the twentieth century, and the museum showcases more than 170 vintage aircraft from the first biplane to the Skylab Command Module. This is one of the world's largest air and space museums, with acres of aircraft parked outside. The IMAX theater, with a screen nearly seven stories tall and 80-feet wide, takes you along for a ride with the Pensacola-based Blue Angels. Call (850) 435-2024 for information. And if you're lucky, the Blue Angels might be practicing rolls, loops, and other precision maneuvers; check **www.blueangels.navy.mil** for the schedule.

Sam's Fun City

On US 29 near "W" Street, Pensacola; (850) 505-0800; www.samsfuncity.com

Hours 11 a.m.–10 p.m., Sunday–Thursday; Friday and Saturday, 10 a.m.–midnight

Admission Free; ticket books start at $6

Appeal by Age Group

Pre-school ★★★	Teens ★★★	Over 30 ★
Grade school ★★★	Young Adults ★★	Seniors ★

Touring Time Half a day on average

Rainy-Day Touring Not recommended

Author's Rating ★★; theme-park fun on a small scale

Description and Comments This new, 20-acre amusement park has something for everyone, including a go-cart track, mini-golf, bumper boats, and a game arcade, plus a new water park opening in 2004. Old-fashioned rides like the scrambler, the swinger, and a Ferris wheel are divided among the park's three "lands," which are Terry Town, Yesterville, and Westerville. Fun for the whole family.

The Zoo

On US 98 about 10 miles east of Gulf Breeze and 15 miles east of Pensacola; (850) 932-2229; www.thezoo.com

Hours 9 a.m.–5 p.m. daily
Admission $11 for adults, $10 for senior citizens ages 62 and older, $8 for children ages 3–11, free for those younger
Appeal by Age Group

Pre-school ★★★	Teens ★★★	Over 30 ★★
Grade school ★★★	Young Adults ★★	Seniors ★★

Touring Time *Average* half a day; *minimum* 2 hours
Rainy-Day Touring Not recommended
Author's Rating ★★★; fun family afternoon after a morning at the beach
Description and Comments This 50-acre park is home to more than 700 exotic animals—including white Bengal tigers, gorillas, bears, tigers, rhinos, and zebras—surrounded by botanical gardens. A Safari Line train takes you through a 30-acre wildlife preserve with free-roaming animals. Hand-feed a giraffe or ride Ellie the Elephant when she's not painting or playing music. The farm has a petting zoo and a nursery for newborn animals. Regularly scheduled shows feature birds of prey, elephants, reptiles, and other wildlife.

Shopping

Cordova Mall (5100 North Ninth Avenue; (850) 477-5563) is the area's largest shopping center, with a Parisian, Dillard's, and 140 specialty stores.

While you're sightseeing, you can shop in the Seville and Palafox historic districts, where there are shops like **Mole Hole** (425 East Zaragoza Street; (850) 434-7329) with gifts and art; and **Moon Dance** (423 East Government Street; (850) 436-2052) featuring gifts, home accessories, art, and beads for making jewelry. In Palafox Place, you'll find **Bayfront Gallery** (713 South Palafox Street; (850) 438-7556) with a large collection of art and fine crafts. Nearby, **Blue Morning Gallery** (112 Palafox Place; (850) 429-9100) showcases local artists with specialties in painting, collage, photography, ceramics, sculpture, and jewelry. **Grand Reserve** (210 South Palafox Street; (850) 429-0078) sells tobacco and smoking products. Other favorites include **Ginger Bender Stationery, Etc.** (8 Palafox Place; (850) 435-7797), **Quayside Thieves Market** (712 South Palafox Street; (850) 438-5399), and **This Ole House** (712 South Palafox Street; (850) 432-2577). Antiques are in abundance, with the best concentration on Antique Alley on North T Street between West Cervantes Street and West Fairfield Drive.

On Pensacola Beach, **Market on the Island** (655 Pensacola Beach Boulevard; (850) 916-7192) is a high-end grocery store with fine wines and gourmet groceries—and they'll pack a picnic lunch for fishing trips. Also check out **Island Style** (782 Quietwater Beach Road; (850) 934 3100) and a handful of shops—**Alvin's Island, Go Fish,** and **Nina Fritz Gallery**—along the Quietwater Beach Boardwalk.

Flea Market For weekend browsing, check out the Flea Market at Gulf Breeze (3760 Gulf Breeze Parkway; (850) 934-1971), open 9 a.m. to 5 p.m. every Saturday and Sunday with 500 dealers, rain or shine.

Dining

Dharma Blue
300 South Alcaniz Street, Pensacola; (850) 433-1275

Meals served Lunch and dinner (dinner only on Sunday) **Cuisine** Asian/American **Entree range** $8–$9, lunch; $15–$24, dinner **Reservations** No **Payment** V, MC, AmEx

Comments This charming restaurant—schoolhouse plank floors, plaster wall, and big-paned windows—occupies a corner just opposite Seville Square, with coveted outdoor tables. The delectable menu varies with the seasons, but you'll always find buttery filet mignon and vegetarian offerings. If you're a sushi fan, try the Dragon roll or any of the sushi or sashimi offerings.

Flounder's Chowder House
800 Quietwater Beach Road, Pensacola Beach; (850) 932-2003

Meals served Lunch and dinner **Cuisine** Seafood/American **Entree range** $6–$20, lunch; $8–$22, dinner **Reservations** No **Payment** All major credit cards accepted

Comments Right on the beach, Flounder's is another spot for local seafood, with an outside dining area with live entertainment, nightly volleyball tournaments, and a play area for kids.

Hopkins' House
900 North Spring Street, Pensacola; (850) 438-3979

Meals served Breakfast, lunch, and dinner, Monday–Friday; breakfast and lunch on Saturday and Sunday **Cuisine** Southern **Entree range** Full meals $8 (all you can eat) **Reservations** Not accepted **Payment** Cash and check only

Comments You might have to wait for a spot in the dining room, but the rocking chairs on the wraparound porch make it easy. Everyone gathers around the large tables to eat family style, with platters piled high with freshly cooked vegetables from area farms, hot biscuits, fried chicken (Tuesday and Friday), fried fish, or the special of the day. And everyone cleans up, just like at home, except here you pay in cash.

Jackson's
400 South Palafox Street, Pensacola; (850) 469-9898

Meals served Dinner, Monday–Saturday **Cuisine** Continental with Southern flair **Entree range** $22–$54 **Reservations** Yes **Payment** All major credit cards accepted

Comments Jackson's is on the ground floor of an 1860s-era building overlooking historic Plaza Ferdinand, where General Andrew Jackson accepted the transfer of Florida from Spain in 1821. The menu includes specials like hickory-grilled grouper and lump crab cakes with pecans. A solid wine selection enhances the "modern Southern Florida coastal cuisine."

McGuire's Irish Pub

600 East Gregory Street, Pensacola; (850) 433-6789

Meals served Lunch and dinner daily **Cuisine** American/seafood **Entree range** $7–$23 lunch; $13–$29 dinner **Reservations** No **Payment** All major credit cards accepted

Comments This award-winning restaurant has been around since 1977 and makes its present home in Pensacola's 1927 firehouse. Inside it's like a turn-of-the-century, New York Irish saloon, with $250,000 in autographed dollar bills pinned to the ceiling by diners. There are 11 themed rooms, with live Irish entertainment nightly in the Pub Room. The menu features steaks, seafood, and traditional Irish pub fare. Ales and stouts are brewed on the premises, and there are 450 selections—from an 8,000-bottle wine cellar.

Peg Leg Pete's Oyster Bar

1010 Fort Pickens Road, Pensacola Beach; (850) 932-4139

Meals served Lunch and dinner **Cuisine** American **Entree range** $8–$36 **Reservations** Not accepted **Payment** All major credit cards accepted

Comments This casual eatery is out toward Fort Pickens, with an outside deck and indoor dining rooms upstairs, with a bar downstairs. Cajun specialties are popular, as is the whopping seafood-for-two platter that includes lobster, shrimp, and snow crab. Steaks are also on the menu.

Arts and Culture

Pensacola Museum of Art (407 South Jefferson Street; (850) 432-6247) is housed in Pensacola's old jail, with about 20 traveling exhibitions a year. Admission is $2, $1 student or military, and it's free on Tuesdays. **Palafox Street** and **Seville Square** are the main thoroughfares for about a dozen art galleries downtown.

Nightlife

Bamboo Willie's

Who Goes There Locals and tourists

400 Quietwater Boardwalk, Pensacola Beach; (850) 916-9888; www.bamboowillies.com

Cover No **Miminum** No **Mixed drinks** $4 and up **Food available** Not available **Hours** Open 11 a.m.–1 a.m. (weekdays); until 2:30 a.m. (weekends)

What goes on Outdoor patio is packed on weekends, with live music, Fat Tuesday frozen drinks and the infamous "Bushwacker" mixed drink with rum that's Pensacola Beach's claim to fame.

Comments The crowd runs the gamut, from bronzed bodies to middle-aged couples sipping cocktails. On the boardwalk, Bamboo Willie's overlooks Quietwater Sound and is accessible by car or boat.

Capt'n Fun Beach Bar & Dance Club

Who goes there Locals and tourists

400 Quietwater Boardwalk, Pensacola Beach; (850) 934-3978; www.gotrealfun.com
Cover No **Miminum** No **Mixed drinks** $3.50 and up **Food available** None **Hours** Open 11 a.m. daily
What goes on With a two-level, open-air deck overlooking Quietwater Sound, Capt'n Fun is open every night, with ten TVs for sports viewing, and the Dance Club with laser lights and a super sound system.
Comments The best place to dance on the beach.

Flora-Bama Lounge and Package Store

Who goes there Locals and tourists

17401 Perdido Key Drive, Pensacola; (850) 492-0611; www.florabama.com

Cover No **Miminum** No **Mixed drinks** $4 and up **Food available** Yes. Oysters and other seafood, chicken fingers, sandwiches, salads, hamburgers **Hours** Open 11 a.m.
What goes on The quintessential roadside dive at the Florida-Alabama line features live entertainment—singer Keith Lambert has had a regular gig since 1978. The clientele crosses all generations, with special events from bikini contests to masquerade parties.
Comments Great gulf views from the Deck Bar. Since the 1960s, the Flora-Bama has been a gathering place for locals and anyone else who happens by. The owners say they're "intent on remaining an oasis of goodwill for generations to come."

Seville Quarter

Who goes there Vacationers of all ages looking for after-dark entertainment

130 Eat Government Street; (850) 434-6211; www.rosies.com

Cover Only after 8 p.m. ($3 until 10 p.m., $5 after 10 p.m.) **Miminum** 21 **Mixed drinks** $3.50 and up **Food available** Full-service restaurant **Hours** Open 11 a.m.–2:30 a.m. daily
What goes on Seville Quarter in the historic district features the Rosie O' Grady's Goodtime Emporium with seven rooms and two courtyards in a restored antique brick complex: Phineas Phogg Balloon Works for dancing; Palace Oyster Bar; Lili Marlene's for live entertainment; Fast Eddie's Billiard Parlor, Apple Annie's Courtyard for dining; and End O' the Alley Bar.
Comments After 30 years, this night spot is going strong. Whether you want to dance or just dine, there's something for everyone. It's touristy, but there are plenty of diversions.

Fort Walton, Destin, and the Beaches of South Walton

More fabulous sugary sand and emerald waters are the claim to fame for these Southern sea towns—24 miles of powdery beaches, with more than 60% protected by law from development. And if you see and hear military jets overhead, they're likely on a training run from one of the 21 runways at Eglin Air Force Base, the largest in the world, at more than 450,000 acres.

The beaches have been voted the safest in the country, with gentle waves and sloping, sandy shallows, and have consistently been named a "favorite family vacation spot" by readers of *Southern Living*. This part of the Panhandle is considered one of the top five shelling destinations in the world—but you have to snorkel (or dive) the off-coast sandbars to find them, spots like Sand Dollar City, a pure white sandbar 200 feet off Destin Beach that is rich with circular "sea money."

Destin has been called the "world's luckiest fishing village," with the "100 Fathom curve" drawing closer to Destin than to any other spot in Florida. The proximity of the curve creates the speediest deep-water access to the Gulf, and the town has the largest charter boat fleet in Florida.

"The beaches of South Walton" is the area between Destin and Panama City Beach that includes a string of seaside villages along Scenic 30-A, and US 98. Among the noted stops is Seaside, famed for its internationally acclaimed, award-winning pastel architecture. Over the past several years, two "new towns," WaterColor and Rosemary Beach, have sprung up near Seaside, with multimillion-dollar beachside homes. Grayton Beach is also here, the oldest community in the area, surrounded by Grayton Beach State Recreation Area, one of the prettiest beaches in Florida (see below).

For vacationers looking for a sophisticated-yet-comfortable place at the beach, Seaside is ideal. No two homes are alike, but there's a lovely visual harmony to Seaside, thanks to a building code that, among other stipulations, requires each home to have a picket fence (and no two identical fences on the same street). The result is a community of more than 200 tasteful residences in warm colors with the architectural details of the 1920s. Many are available for rent.

The creative new town spurred similar developments nearby, notably, WaterColor. Designed by leading architects, WaterColor includes an inn and restaurants and a variety of diversions, including beautiful beachfront, a 220-acre coastal dune lake bordered by pine forests, hiking and bike paths, and a small collection of retail shops.

For information on Seaside, call (800) 277-8696 or visit **www.seasidefl.com**. For information on WaterColor, call (866) 426-2656 or visit **www.watercolorflorida.com**.

Golf

Bluewater Bay Resort

1950 Bluewater Boulevard, Niceville; (850) 897-3241; www.bwbresort.com
Established 1981 | **Designer** Tom Fazio, Jerry Pate | **Holes** 36

Tees Bay and Magnolia/Lake and Marsh/Magnolia and Lake/Marsh and Bay
Par 72/72/72/72 **Slope** 135/128/133/128

Fort Walton Beach

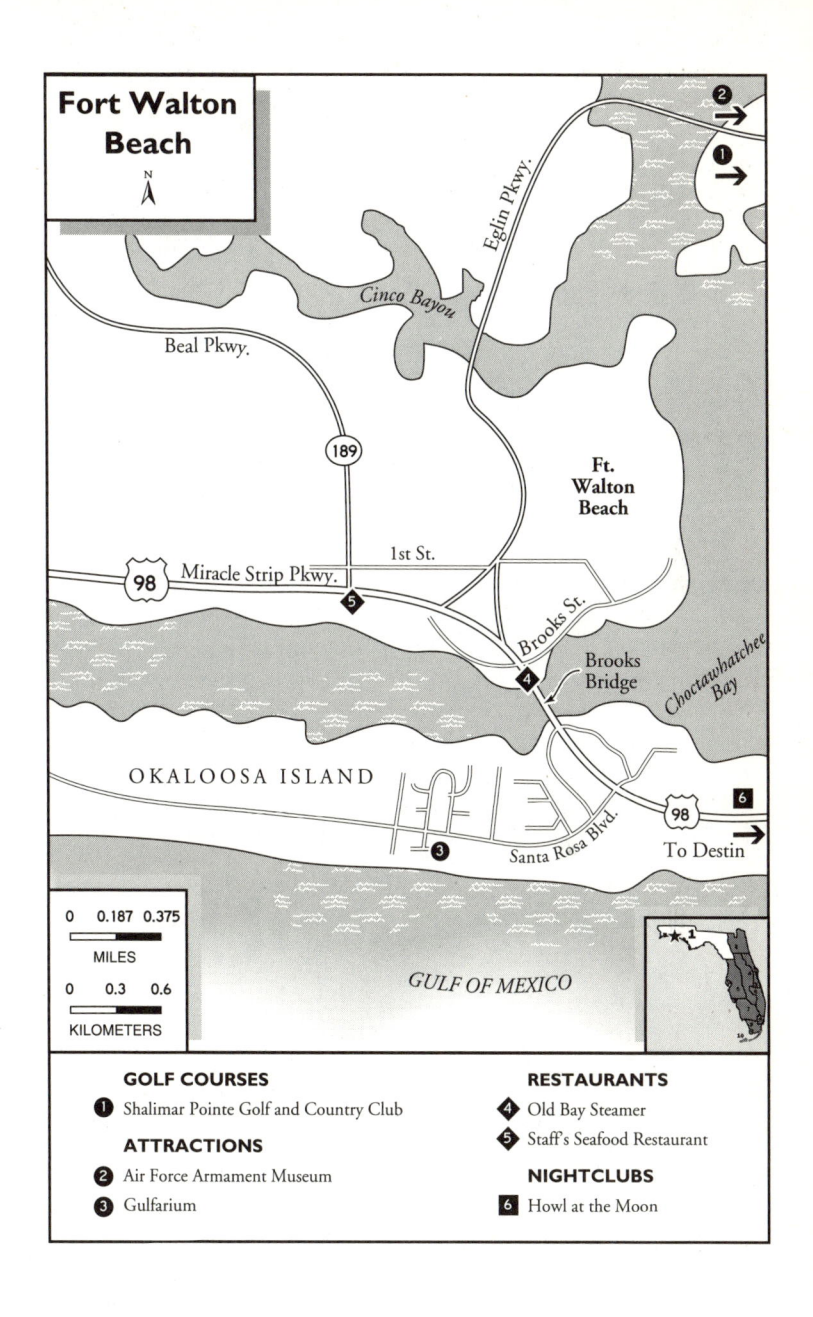

GOLF COURSES
1. Shalimar Pointe Golf and Country Club

ATTRACTIONS
2. Air Force Armament Museum
3. Gulfarium

RESTAURANTS
4. Old Bay Steamer
5. Staff's Seafood Restaurant

NIGHTCLUBS
6. Howl at the Moon

123

Destin Area

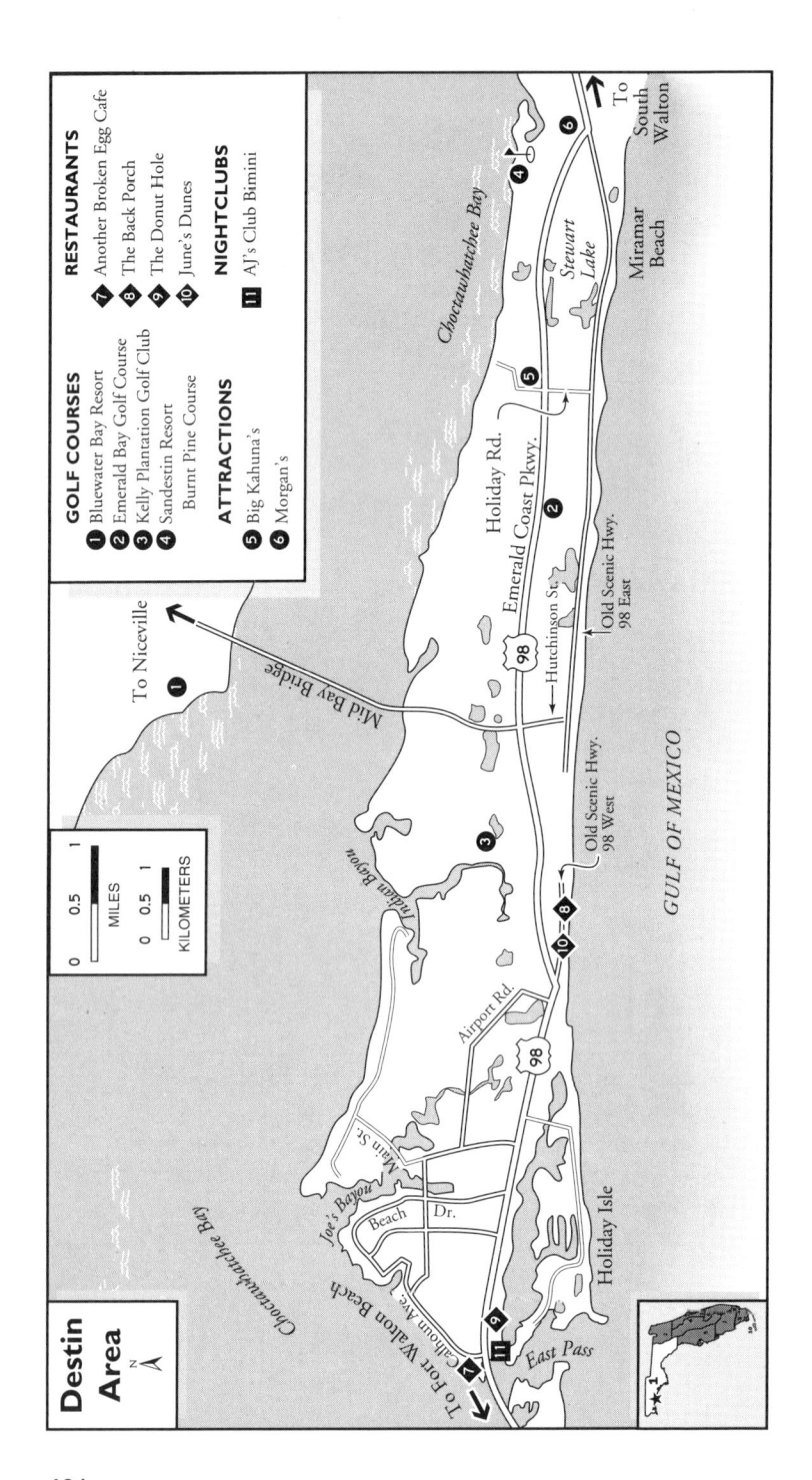

GOLF COURSES
1. Bluewater Bay Resort
2. Emerald Bay Golf Course
3. Kelly Plantation Golf Club
4. Sandestin Resort Burnt Pine Course

ATTRACTIONS
5. Big Kahuna's
6. Morgan's

RESTAURANTS
7. Another Broken Egg Cafe
8. The Back Porch
9. The Donut Hole
10. June's Dunes

NIGHTCLUBS
11. AJ's Club Bimini

125

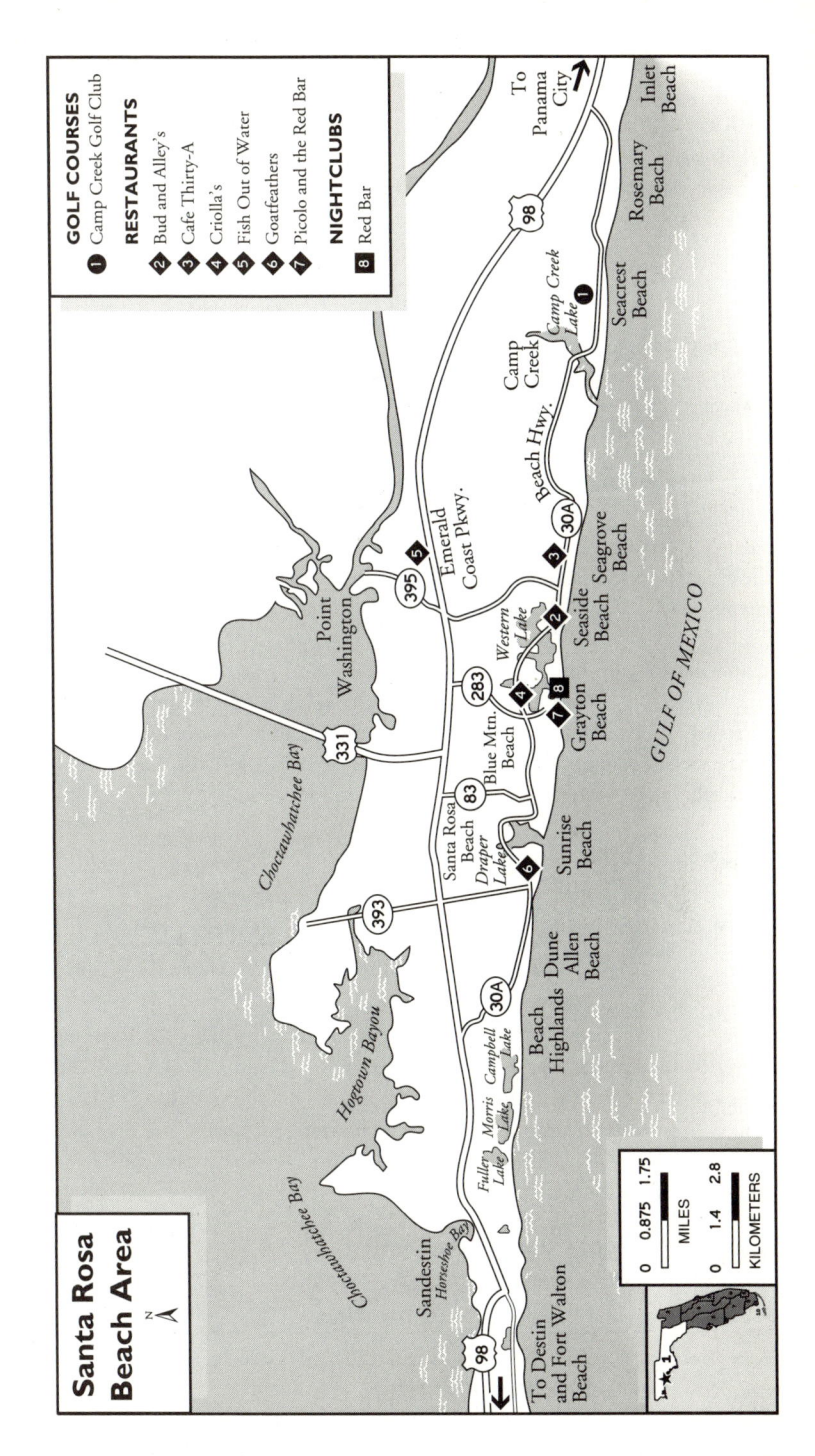

Fees $69 **Specials** $7 off coupon offered online **Cart rental** Included **Club rental** $25 per set **Payment** All major credit cards accepted **Tee times** Up to 2 weeks in advance **Facilities** Clubhouse, range, golf shop

Comments Fazio designed 27 of the 45 holes (the Bay, Lake, and Marsh nines); Jerry Pate added the Magnolia nine. Each of the courses has its own distinctive character, and places a premium on accuracy and shotmaking, as many of the holes travel through thick pine forests and marshland, creating a beautiful but treacherous jail if you stray off the recommended path.

Emerald Bay Golf Course

40001 Emerald Coast Parkway, Destin; (850) 837-5197;
www.emeraldbaydestin.com

Established 1991 | **Designer** Robert Cupp | **Holes** 18

Tees Gold, 6,802/Blue, 6,482/White, 5,967/Red, 5,184
Par 72/72/72/72 **Slope** 135/127/120/122
Fees $90 before 11 a.m.; $75 11 a.m.–3 p.m.; $50 after 3 p.m. **Specials** Golf packages available **Cart rental** Included **Club rental** $30 per set **Payments** V, MC, AmEx **Tee times** 14 days in advance **Facilities** Range, guesthouse, pro shop

Comments Cupp built a course that is a fun and enjoyable course for all skill levels. The course affords magnificent views of the beautiful green water of Choctaw Bay, but it also plays through an imposing forest. Both nines are appealing, but the back is the most amazing, with magnificent postcard views of the bay.

Kelly Plantation Golf Club

307 Kelly Plantations Drive, Destin; (850) 650-7600; www.kellyplantation.com
Established 1998 | **Designers** Fred Couples and Gene Bates | **Holes** 18

Tees Couples, 7,099/Plantation, 6,521/Palmetto, 6,118/Magnolia, 5,170
Par 72/72/72/72 **Slope** 146/138/128/124
Fees $118 morning, $59 twilight (fees vary day by day) **Cart rental** Included **Club rental** $30 per set **Payments** V, MC, AmEx, D **Tee times** 30 days in advance **Facilities** Golf shop, restaurant, clubhouse, putting greens

Comments Kelly Plantation is one of the newest additions to the Emerald Coast. It's layered on the southern shores of Choctawhatchee Bay, with fairways for both novice and master golfers.

Sandestin Resort, Burnt Pine Course

9300 US 98 West, Destin; (800) 277-0800 or (850) 267-8000
Established 1994 | **Designer** Rees Jones | **Holes** 18

Tees Gold, 6,996/Blue, 6,474/White, 5,950/Red 5,096
Par 72/72/72/72 **Slope** 135/130/124/122

Fort Walton, Destin, and the Beaches of South Walton

Fees $105–$149 **Specials** Daily golf packages, twilight rates **Cart rental** Included **Club rental** $40 per set **Payments** All major credit cards accepted **Tee times** 14 days in advance **Facilities** Golf shop, practice facilities, sports bar, golf learning and performance center

Comments Burnt Pine is arguably the best course in the Panhandle region and in the top 25 in the entire state. It's a solid golf course—no gimmicks to be found here. On its diverse terrain, golfers will be confronted by two separate settings: the front nine plays through a pine forest, and the back nine is bordered by the Choctawhatchee Bay. It is a private club, but non-members can golf before 8 a.m. or after 1 p.m.

Shalimar Pointe Golf and Country Club

302 Country Club Road, Shalimar; (800) 964-2833 or (850) 651-1416; www.shalimarpointe.com

Established 1968 | **Designer** Ken Dye and Joe Finger | **Holes** 18

Tees Gold, 6,765/Blue, 6,470/White, 6,137/Red, 5,427
Par 72/72/72/72 **Slope** 129/123/119/125
Fees $45 weekdays, $55 weekends **Specials** Twilight rates and weekly specials available **Cart rental** Included **Club rental** $20 per set **Payments** V, MC **Tee times** Electronically up to 60 days in advance **Facilities** Pro shop, putting and chipping green driving range

Comments Shalimar has been around since 1968, but it was really the touch-up job by Pete Dye in 1985 that put it on the map. Dye added a number of water bunkers and improved the water hazards. The result: a much more enjoyable and challenging layout. The course features rolling, tree-lined fairways and a backdrop of Choctawhatchee Bay.

Attractions

Air Force Armament Museum

Route 85, Eglin Air Force Base; (850) 882-4062

Hours 9:30 a.m.–4:30 p.m. daily
Admission Free
Appeal by Age Group

Pre-school ★★	Teens ★★	Over 30 ★★
Grade school ★★	Young Adults ★	Seniors ★★★

Touring Time Two hours, including a 32-minute film
Rainy-Day touring Recommended
Author's Rating ★★

Description and Comments Just outside the gates at Eglin Air Force Base is "the world's only facility dedicated to the display of Air Force armament." Start with the 32-minute film about the base's history, then check out uniforms, weapons, aircraft, and more from World Wars I and II and the

Korean and Vietnam wars. Outside, transport planes and other large craft are on the grounds.

Big Kahuna's

1007 US 98 East, Destin; (850) 837-4061

Hours 10 a.m.–6 p.m seven days a week, except in winter, when the park closes

Admission $30 adults; $28 under 48" tall, free for ages 2 and under

Appeal by Age Group

Pre-school ★★★	Teens ★★★	Over 30 ★
Grade school ★★★	Young Adults ★★	Seniors ★

Touring Time *Average* 5–6 hours; *minimum* 2 hours

Rainy-Day Touring Not recommended

Author's Rating ★★; something for everyone when you're bored with the beach

Description and Comments If your family wants action, there's plenty in this water park with more than 50 slides and attractions, including "the world's largest tube river" and Bombs Away Bay with a real B-25 bomber. Also miniature golf, arcade games, go-carts, dune buggies, and a Vertical Accelerator that drops ten stories—but they all cost extra and it adds up quickly.

Gulfarium

On US 98 just east of Fort Walton Beach; (850) 244-5169

Hours Daily, 9 a.m.–5 p.m.

Admission $16.99 for adults, $14 for senior citizens ages 55 and older, $10 for children ages 4–11

Appeal by Age Group

Pre-school ★★★	Teens ★★	Over 30 ★★
Grade school ★★★	Young Adults ★★	Seniors ★★

Touring Time *Average* 3–4 hours; *minimum* 2 hours

Rainy-Day Touring Not recommended

Author's Rating ★★; fun for a beach diversion

Description and Comments Opened in 1955, Gulfarium is one of America's original marine parks. The "Living Sea" exhibit is a panorama of undersea life, from a 600-pound gray seal to a two-ounce clownfish. There are also performances by trained dolphins; sea lion shows; marine life exhibits featuring seals, otters, penguins, and a host of other sea animals.

Morgan's

10676 Emerald Coast Parkway (Silver Sands Factory Stores), Destin; (850) 650-0041

Hours Different hours for market, bakery, entertainment center, and restaurant

Fort Walton, Destin, and the Beaches of South Walton

Admission Free

Appeal by Age Group

Pre-school ★★★	Teens ★★★	Over 30 ★★★
Grade school ★★★	Young Adults ★★★	Seniors ★★★

Touring Time *Average* 2–3 hours; *minimum* 1½ hours

Rainy-Day Touring Recommended

Author's Rating ★★★; perfect rainy-day option—parents get to shop, the kids get to play

Description and Comments The third-largest designer outlet center in the United States, this is a favorite place for local families. There are two levels of entertainment and eateries, with more than 160 video games, virtual sports, motion-simulation rides, and a "soft play" maze for little ones. Creehan's Market is an upscale food court with five quick-service restaurants offering everything from pizza to sushi. For sit-down service, Harbor Docks Seafood and Brewery gets rave reviews for its fresh fish and six different beers brewed on the premises.

Shopping

Thanks to upscale communities and multimillion-dollar homes under construction in Seaside, WaterColor, and Rosemary Beach, this stretch of Florida offers marvelous shopping. **Santa Rosa Mall** (Mary Esther Boulevard, Mary Esther; (850) 244-2172; **www.santarosamall.com**) is the only enclosed mall in the Fort Walton Beach–Destin area, with Dillard's, JCPenney, Sears, a ten-screen movie theater, and more than 100 specialty stores. Shoppers come for miles to **Silver Sands Factory Stores** (10562 Emerald Coast Parkway, Destin; (800) 510-6255; **www.silversandsoutlet.com**), one of the country's largest outlet malls with more than 100 designer-name shops, everything from Banana Republic to Baby Gap and Calvin Klein. It's fun to take an afternoon and drive along 18 miles of Scenic Highway 30-A in south Walton County, where small shops dot the string of seaside villages on the two-lane road. Heading east from Destin, favorites include quaint **Magnolia House** (2 Magnolia Street, Grayton Beach; (850) 231-5859; **www.magnoliahouse.com**) with everything from hand-tufted wool rugs to jewelry and chocolates. Also in Grayton Beach, **Tres Monet** (50 Uptown Grayton Circle; (850) 231-0092; **www.flowersbymonet.com**) sells flowers (dried and silk), candles, oil lamps, and other accessories. The town of Seaside has a collection of eclectic shops, including nearly a dozen art/gallery boutiques (**www.seasidefl.com**). Some favorites include **Catherine Dickson Fine Art** (phone (850) 231-3679), with works by regional artists, and **Keramikos** (phone (850) 231-5564), a ceramic art gallery with whimsical creations by more than 60 artists. On the beachside, **Perspicacity** is a small open-air market with women's clothing, accessories, and funky beach furniture. In Seagrove Beach, **Collaborations** (4721 Highway 30-A; (850) 231-0171; **www.collabart.com**) features mosaics, glassware, watercolors, furniture, and other original works of art. Nearby, a longtime favorite is **Gourd Garden & Curiosity Shop** (4808 Highway 30-A; (850) 231-2150; www.gourdgarden.com), which offers healthy herbs, a butterfly garden, and quirky folk art from around the globe. In the little community of Carillon, **108 Auction Company** (108 Market Street, Carillon; (850) 230-0414; www.108auction.com) carries antiques from around the world—sculpture, crystal, silver, rugs, and vintage fashions.

Dining

Another Broken Egg Cafe

US 98 East, Destin; (850) 650-0499

Meals served Breakfast, lunch, and dinner **Cuisine** American **Entree range** $7–$12 **Reservations** Yes **Payment** All major credit cards accepted
Comments This cozy little eatery specializes in omelets—you name it, they'll make it. Try the grits sweetened with blackberries.

The Back Porch

1740 Old US 98 East, Destin; (850) 837-2022

Meals served Lunch and dinner **Cuisine** Seafood **Entree range** $7–$24 **Reservations** Not accepted **Payment** All major credit cards accepted
Comments This quintessential seafood shack sits near the western boundary of Henderson Beach State Recreation Area, with lovely beach and Gulf views. Fish and burgers are grilled over coals—the local favorite, amberjack, is the house specialty.

Bud and Alley's

2236 East Highway 30-A, Santa Rosa Beach (Seaside); (850) 231-5900

Meals served Lunch and dinner **Cuisine** American/continental **Entree range** $8–$23 lunch; $8–$29 dinner **Reservations** Accepted **Payment** V, MC
Comments Go early, because this casual Seaside eatery, named after a dog and a cat, gets crowded. *Florida Trend* magazine calls it one of the best restaurants in Florida, and everything is fresh and creatively prepared, from tempura soft-shell blue crab to a blackened grouper.

Cafe Thirty-A

Located on Highway 30-A, between Destin and Panama City (near the town of Seaside); (850) 231-2166

Meals served Dinner, daily **Cuisine** Contemporary/eclectic **Entree range** $21–$34 **Reservations** Accepted **Payment** V, MC, AmEx, D
Comments Trendy Cafe Thirty-A makes a killer martini to go with the upscale menu. Try the rich, fried soft-shell crab if it's on the menu; otherwise, whether it's lamb, fish, or beef, Cafe Thirty-A does a splendid job.

Criolla's

170 East Highway 30-A, Grayton Beach, near Seaside; (850) 267-1267

Meals served Dinner **Cuisine** Gourmet/Creole-style **Entree range** $19–$34 **Reservations** Accepted **Payment** V, MC, AmEx, D

Comments This award-winning restaurant is pricey, but worth a special family night out. You won't be disappointed with any fish, and save room for the from-scratch desserts, like Aunt Irma's banana-and-pecan beignets. The upscale children's menu offers grilled beef tournedos ($13) and grilled fish or shrimp ($9).

The Donut Hole

635 US 98 East, Destin; (850) 837-8824

Meals served Open 24 hours **Cuisine** American **Entree range** $3.50–$10 **Reservations** No **Payment** Cash only

Comments Who needs a kid's menu when the menu has burgers, shakes, and 28 varieties of doughnuts. Breakfast is served all day. Omelet fans will love the Destin omelet, with fresh crabmeat, peppers, onions, and cheese.

Fish Out of Water

34 Goldenrod Circle, Seagrove Beach; (850) 534-5050

Meals served Dinner daily **Cuisine** Seafood/Southern **Entree range** $23–$35 **Reservations** Yes **Payment** All major credit cards accepted

Comments Fish out of Water artfully reflects its Gulf Coast setting in the "new town" of WaterColor. The chic dining room features an ice bar showcasing fresh seafood, and an exhibition grill. A private dining room is also available, lined with wine bottles from a collection of 3,000 selections, representing about 325 labels. Cuisine focuses on Gulf seafood, sushi, and upscale Southern cuisine.

Goatfeathers

3865 Highway 30-A, between Dune Allen and Blue Mountain Beach; (850) 267-3342

Meals served Lunch and dinner daily **Cuisine** Seafood **Entree range** Lunch, $12–$16; dinner, $16–$26 **Reservations** Accepted **Payment** All major credit cards accepted

Comments The food is hearty, Southern, fried—and fresh under that crunchy breading. Seafood po' boy sandwiches come with fries or steamed new potatoes; fried scallops, oysters, shrimp, and fish come with coleslaw, hush puppies, and potatoes or vegetables. OK, you can get fish or shrimp grilled, but go for the fried unless you're on fat patrol. The extensive kids menu offers a dozen entrees, from burgers to pizza.

June's Dunes

1780 Old US 98 East, Destin; (850) 650-0455

Meals served Breakfast and lunch **Cuisine** American **Entree range** $2–$7 **Reservations** Not accepted **Payment** No credit cards

Comments This is one of those "junk food" places the locals favor, where you eat beachside on picnic tables. The menu is on a chalkboard and includes hearty breakfast favorites like waffles and biscuits with sausage gravy. Good burgers for lunch. And, yes, June is usually there.

Old Bay Steamer

102 Santa Rosa Boulevard, Fort Walton; (850) 664-2795

Meals served Dinner **Cuisine** Seafood **Entree range** $14–$23 **Reservations** Not accepted **Payment** V, MC, AmEx, DC

Comments Locals don't go for the view (there isn't one), but for the enormous platters of steamed seafood. Old Bay's motto: "We don't do fried." Try the royal red shrimp fresh from the Gulf, mussels, crabs, or lobsters, and don't worry about making a mess—just toss your empty shells in a bucket on the table.

Picolo and the Red Bar

70 Hotz Avenue, Grayton Beach; (850) 231-1008

Meals served Lunch and dinner **Cuisine** Seafood **Entree range** $6.50–$10 lunch; $10–$17 dinner **Reservations** Not accepted **Payment** Cash only

Comments This casual eatery bustles with activity—a lively bar is just inside the front door, and most of the restaurant seating is on a big screened porch right on the beach. The locals love this place, and it's definitely a lively crowd on the weekends. Try the chicken with lemon caper sauce or the crab cakes.

Staff's Seafood Restaurant

24 Miracle Strip Parkway Southeast (US 98), Fort Walton Beach; (850) 243-3482

Meals served Dinner **Cuisine** Seafood **Entree range** $15–$51 **Reservations** Not accepted **Payment** All major credit cards accepted

Comments The Staff has been around since 1913, and its delicious homebaked wheat bread has been homemade with Pop Staff's recipe since the 1920s. The seafood gumbo is excellent; another house specialty is the Seafood Skillet, brimming with yellowfin tuna, shrimp, scallops, and crab cooked with plenty of butter and cheese.

Nightlife

AJ's Club Bimini

Who goes there Locals, tourists

168 US 98, Destin; (850) 837-1913

Mixed drinks $4 and up **Food available** Yes **Hours** 11 a.m.–11 p.m. (restaurant); 11 a.m.–4 a.m. (bar)

What goes on Live entertainment seven days a week and dancing on the open-air dance floor.

Comments Try the Bimini Bash, a delicious (and potent) mix of cranberry, orange, and pineapple juices with a "five-rum" kick. Boasting the largest tiki hut on the Emerald Coast, AJ's regularly gets the vote for best outdoor bar. Great sunset views, too.

Howl at the Moon

Who goes there Locals and tourists of all ages

1450 Miracle Strip Parkway, Fort Walton; (850) 301-0111; www.howlatthemoon.com

Mixed drinks $4 and up **Food available** Limited appetizers (chicken wings, shrimp, crab claws) **Hours** 7 p.m.–4 a.m., Wednesday–Sunday

What goes on Dueling pianos and singalongs. Ladies Night, Open Mic Night, Comedy Night

Comments The piano players and staff get the crowd going, and before long, they're part of the show. Hot spot for birthdays, anniversaries, and other celebrations.

Red Bar

Who goes there Eclectic crowd of locals, tourists

70 Hotz Avenue, Grayton Beach; (850) 231-1008

Mixed drinks $5 and up **Food available** In the adjacent Piccolo restaurant (pasta with crawfish and shrimp, chicken and mashed potatoes, stuffed eggplant, fish of the day, and rotating specials) **Hours** 11 a.m.–10:30 p.m. (open until 11:30 p.m. Friday and Saturday)

What goes on Laid-back evening with a house jazz band almost nightly, blues band, or good music on the CD player.

Comments Red Bar was around long before the chi-chi new towns, a ramshackle sort of place painted red, with European film posters, Christmas lights, and an assortment of curios on the walls. It may look like a local bar, but it's quite hip and cosmopolitan; Sheryl Crow and Jim Carrey have been spotted here.

Panama City Beach

If you're looking for nonstop entertainment and action, you can find plenty to do in this high-energy, affordable beach town. You name it, you'll probably find a place to do it here, from bungee jumping and parasailing to jet skiing, wind surfing, even oceanfront minigolf.

The locals boast that the sun shines about 320 days a year, and the "sand is like a bar of Ivory soap—99.44% pure quartz," according to Dr. Stephen P. Leatherman, a.k.a. "Dr. Beach," from the University of Maryland. The pretty beach is, however, lined with hotels, motels, and beach houses.

Be forewarned: This is the beach for high-school spring breakers from neighboring states, and it's also full of teenagers in the summertime. And as

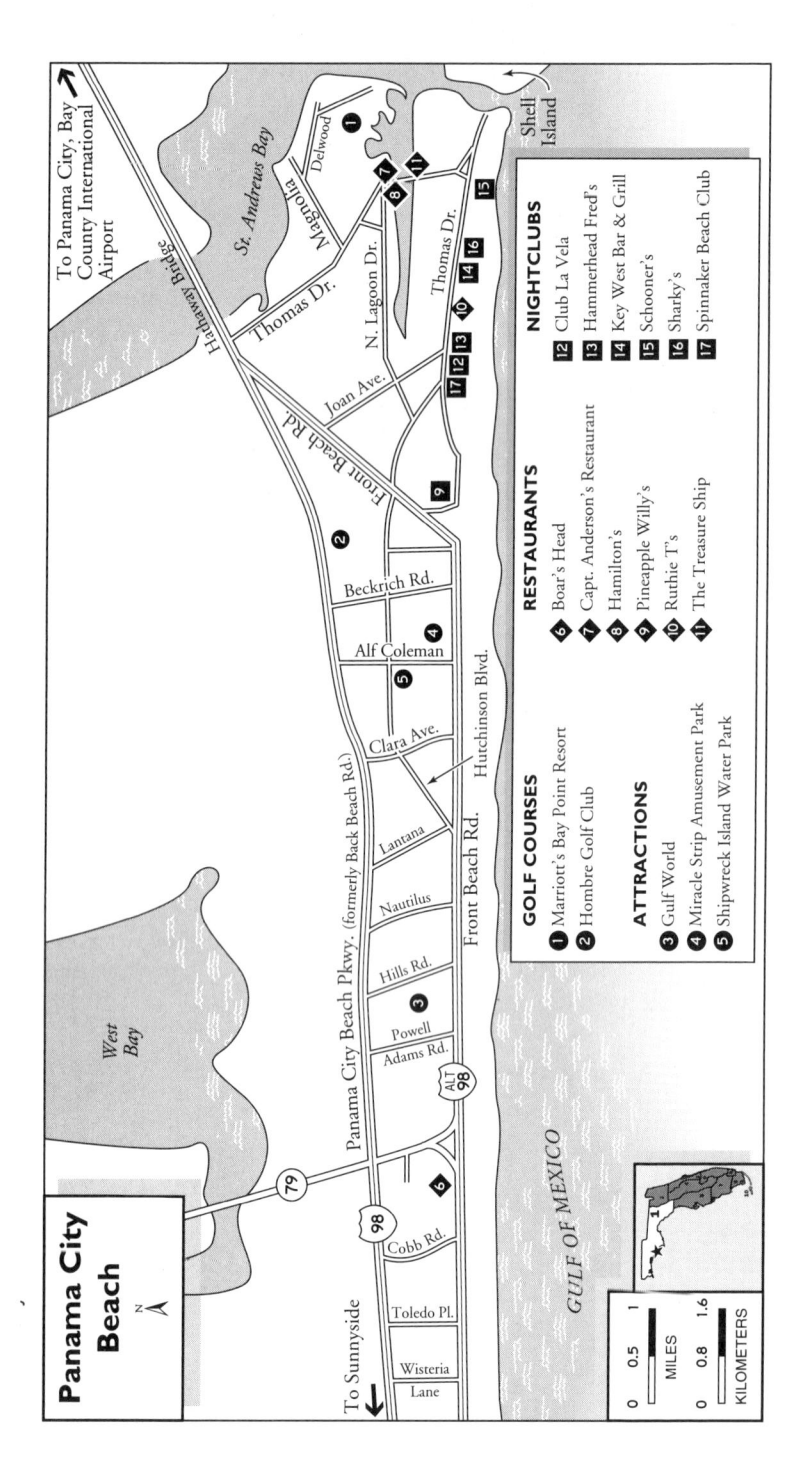

Panama City Beach

GOLF COURSES
1. Marriott's Bay Point Resort
2. Hombre Golf Club

ATTRACTIONS
3. Gulf World
4. Miracle Strip Amusement Park
5. Shipwreck Island Water Park

RESTAURANTS
6. Boar's Head
7. Capt. Anderson's Restaurant
8. Hamilton's
9. Pineapple Willy's
10. Ruthie T's
11. The Treasure Ship

NIGHTCLUBS
12. Club La Vela
13. Hammerhead Fred's
14. Key West Bar & Grill
15. Schooner's
16. Sharky's
17. Spinnaker Beach Club

Panama City beach has grown up, there has not been a lot of thoughtful planning—just more T-shirt shops, fast-food joints, and motels crowded along the oceanfront. Still, it's full of energy, and if you don't mind sharing your space with other revelers, this can be a pretty fun place. If you're looking for peace and quiet, head farther east.

Golf

Hombre Golf Club

120 Coyote Pass, Panama City Beach; (850) 234-3673; www.hombregolfclub.com

Established 1989 | **Designer** Wes Burnham | **Holes** 18

Tees Championship, 6,820/Members, 6,063/Seniors, 5,275/Ladies, 4,793
Par 72/72/72/72 **Slope** 137/131/125/132
Fees $75 before 11 a.m., $60 11 a.m.–2 p.m., $50 after 2 p.m. **Specials** Golf packages available **Cart rental** Included **Club rental** $20 per set **Payments** V, MC, D **Tee times** 7 days in advance **Facilities** Golf school, lodging, pro shop, full-service bar and grill
Comments Hombre offers golfers a challenging layout, particularly from the tips, and especially in the wind, as the course winds through 145 acres of lakes and dogwoods. Accuracy is paramount, as fairways are slender and water comes into play on 15 of the 18 holes. The 11th hole, a 166-yard, par-3, is the signature hole.

Marriott's Bay Point Resort

4200 Marriott Drive, Panama City; (800) 874-7105 or (850) 234-3307; www.baypointgolf.com

Lagoon Legend Course

(850) 235-6937 (direct)

Established 1986 | **Designers** Bruce Devlin and Robert von Hagge | **Holes** 18

Tees Orange, 6,885/Blue, 6,421/White, 6,066/Green, 5,559/Red, 4,942
Par 72/72/72/72/72
Slope 152/148/144/135/127

The Club Meadows Course

(850) 235-6950 (direct)

Established 1972 | **Designer** Willard Byrd | **Holes** 18

Tees Blue, 6,913/White, 6,372/Green, 5,919/Red, 5,634/Gold, 4,999
Par 72/72/72/72 **Slope** 126/120/116/124/118
Fees Lagoon Legend, $65–$85; The Club Meadows, $55-$75 (rates based on season) **Specials** Website specials and seasonal packages available **Cart rental** Included **Club rental** $25 per set **Payments** All major credit cards

accepted **Tee times** 60 days in advance **Facilities** Resort offers swimming pool, tennis courts, and picnic areas

Comments Only a handful of courses in the United States are sloped higher than Lagoon Legend, a whopping 152 from the tips. There's trouble awaiting you at every turn, from water on no fewer than 16 holes, blind shots, small landing areas, and bunkers. There are no easy holes. The fun factor comes from simply finding out how well you can cope with the course's relentless nature. The Club Meadows is one of Florida's most popular courses, long and narrow from the tips but forgiving from the forward tees.

Attractions

Gulf World

15412 Front Beach Road, Panama City Beach; (850) 234-5271

Hours Open 9 a.m.; last show starts at 4 p.m.

Admission $19.51 for adults, $13.47 for children ages 5–11

Appeal by Age Group

Pre-school ★★	Teens ★★	Over 30 ★★
Grade school ★★★	Young Adults ★★	Seniors ★★

Touring Time *Average* 3 hours; *minimum* 2 hours

Rainy-Day Touring Not recommended

Author's Rating ★★; entertaining and educational

Description and Comments This old-fashioned marine park features educational exhibits and 25 shows, including dolphin, sea lion, and tropical birds, as well as a nightly laser-light show. The dolphin educational program lets guests get in the water with dolphins (additional fee and reservations required). Kids can touch a stingray, see sharks, sea turtles, alligators, and other water creatures.

Miracle Strip Amusement Park

12001 Front Beach Road, Panama City Beach; (850) 234-5810; www.miraclestrippark.com

Hours April–June, open 6–11 p.m. Friday and Saturday evenings; June–Labor Day, 6–11 p.m. Sunday–Friday; 2–11 p.m. on Saturdays

Admission $18 per person, under 35" tall free admission; admission for both Miracle Strip and Shipwreck Island (following profile) is $33 (above 50"); $5.50 Gate Pass available for carousel and train only

Appeal by Age Group

Pre-school ★★★	Teens ★★★★	Over 30 ★★
Grade school ★★★★	Young Adults ★★	Seniors ★★

Touring Time *Average* 3–4 hours; *minimum* 2 hours

Rainy-Day Touring Not recommended

Author's Rating ★★; it will make your kids happy

Panama City Beach

Description and Comments Family owned and operated for more than 40 years, Miracle Strip features more than 25 rides and attractions with the 18-story O2 Tower (a three-second drop to earth), 105-foot-high roller coaster, the 40-foot swinging Sea Dragon, the stomach-turning Shock Wave, kiddie rides, live stage shows, an arcade, and food concessions.

Shipwreck Island Water Park

12000 West Front Beach Road, Panama City Beach; (850) 234-0368; www.miraclestrippark.com

Hours April–June, 10:30 a.m.–5 p.m.; June–Labor Day, until 5:30 p.m.
Admission $24 above 50" tall; $19 under 50" tall; under 35" tall, free; $14 for senior citizens ages 62 and older; admission for both Miracle Strip (preceding profile) and Shipwreck Island is $33 (above 50")

Appeal by Age Group

Pre-school ★★	Teens ★★★	Over 30 ★
Grade school ★★★	Young Adults ★★	Seniors ★

Touring Time *Average* 3–4 hours; *minimum* 2 hours
Rainy-Day Touring Not recommended
Author's Rating ★★; fun if the beach gets boring
Description and Comments Next door to Miracle Strip Amusement Park, this ever-expanding water park has six acres of rides and picnic areas. Water rides include the Rapid River Run, the Wave Pool, the Lazy River, and the awesome Tree Top Drop, a free-fall slide. The Tadpole Hole is exclusively for young visitors.

Shopping

Panama City Beach shops cater to tourists, with plenty of swimwear and sportswear. One of the most popular stores is **Alvin's Island,** with a dozen locations in the Panhandle. The flagship store is "Magic Mountain" (12010 Front Beach Road; (850) 234-3048; www.alvinsisland.com), with daily live shark and alligator feedings along with beachwear, sportswear, and souvenirs. You'll find more beachwear at **Shipwreck Ltd.** (10570 Front Beach Road; (850) 233-6750). **Florida Linen Outlet** (12011 Panama City Beach Parkway; (850) 230-4261) has a new 10,000-square-foot showroom with linens and accessories—more than 1,500 bedspreads. If you want national chains, head to **Panama City Mall** (US 98 east over the Hathaway Bridge, left on 23rd Street; (850) 785-9587; www.panamacity-mall.com) where JCPenney, Sears, Gap, American Eagle Outfitters, and Victoria's Secret are located.

Dining

Boar's Head

17290 Front Beach Road; (850) 234-6628

Meals served Dinner **Cuisine** American **Entree range** $14–$50 **Reservations** No **Payments** All major credit cards accepted

Comments A favorite with locals, who go to the casual restaurant for the prime rib, steaks, and baby-back ribs. There's plenty of seafood on the menu, too.

Capt. Anderson's Restaurant

5551 North Lagoon Drive at Thomas Drive, Panama City Beach; (850) 234-2225

Meals served Dinner, closed Sunday **Cuisine** Seafood **Entree range** $12–$39 **Reservations** Not accepted **Payment** All major credit cards accepted

Comments Try to snag a window table to watch fishers unload the catch of the day at the marina next door, but come early because this famous, award-winning restaurant gets crowded after the boats come in. Opt for whatever fish is freshest or the seafood platter and you can't go wrong—shrimp is the No. 1 seller.

Hamilton's

5711 North Lagoon Drive, Panama City Beach; (850) 234-1255

Meals served Dinner **Cuisine** Seafood **Entree range** $12–$24 **Reservations** Not accepted **Payment** V, MC, AmEx, D

Comments Dine right on the lagoon in the air-conditioned dining room. Locals recommend the Florida bay scallops and the Apalachicola oysters. All desserts, salad dressings, sauces, and soups are made fresh from original recipes.

Pineapple Willy's

9875 South Thomas Drive, Panama City Beach; (850) 235-0928

Meals served Lunch, dinner **Cuisine** American **Entree range** $11–$18 **Reservations** No **Payment** V, MC, D, DC

Comments Go for the ribs—slow-cooked with Jack Daniel's barbecue sauce. A versatile menu with seafood, prime rib, chicken, and salads.

Ruthie T's

8503 Thomas Drive, Panama City Beach; (850) 234-2111

Meals served Dinner **Cuisine** American **Entree range** $9–$27 **Reservations** Yes **Payment** All major credit cards accepted

Comments Casual setting where owner/chef Eric Hernandez turns out favorites like blackened prime rib, pan-seared grouper, and a honey-mustard salad dressing that everyone raves about. The menu changes with the seasons, and there's entertainment nightly in the dining room.

The Treasure Ship

3605 Thomas Drive, Panama City Beach; (850) 234-8881

Meals served Lunch and dinner, daily **Cuisine** American/Caribbean/seafood **Entree range** Lunch, $7–$20; dinner, $11–$20 **Reservations** Not accepted **Payment** All major credit cards accepted

Comments Hook's Grille is open for lunch, but go for dinner when the "pirates" invade the Treasure Ship dining room to entertain the kids. Try the Calypso Grouper, Cuban loin of pork, or pepper steak Port-au-Prince. Family-style, all-you-can-eat crab legs, $23; all-you-can-eat prime rib, $25.

Nightlife

Club La Vela

Who goes there Glamorous, young 20-something crowd

8813 Thomas Drive, Panama City Beach; (850) 235-1061; www.clublavela.com

Cover $15 **Minimum** 18 **Mixed drinks** $6 and up **Food available** No **Hours** 10 a.m.–5:30 p.m. and 7 p.m.–4 a.m.

What goes on Club La Vela is a sprawling nightclub with room for 6,000. There are nine DJs nightly with 15 themed rooms, spinning techno, rave, Top 40, hip-hop, and rock dance music. The largest is the MTV-endorsed Thunderdome with stainless-steel dance floors and a high-tech light show. Check out the Pussykat Lounge, the spot to see and be seen, or the Foam room, flooded with bubbles. Just for teens, the Darkroom is their own private, pre-18 club.

Comments Club La Vela continues to reinvent itself to keep the crowds coming, with nonstop action day and night—bikini contests, beach parties, and other crowd-pleasing special events guarantee a full house.

Hammerhead Fred's

Who goes there Locals, thirsty young vacationers

8752 Thomas Drive, Panama City Beach; (850) 233-3907; www.hammerheadfreds.com

Cover No **Miminum** None **Mixed drinks** $3.75 and up **Food available** Yes **Hours** 11 a.m.–midnight

What goes on With 12 big-screen TVs, all-you-can-eat wings and 64-ounce pitchers of draft, Fred's is like a college bar. There's a dance floor, rock music, and a DJ, but the crowd is fairly subdued until spring break fever hits and young revelers spill over to Fred's "party tent."

Comments Ambience is casual, the spot for a tropical drink and pub grub—fresh Apalachicola oysters, coconut shrimp, gator tail, and those wings.

Key West Bar and Grill

Who goes there A mix of tourists and locals, an older, friendly crowd

6804 Thomas Drive, Panama City Beach; (850) 230-9099; www.panamacitybeach.com/KeyWest

Cover No **Miminum** No **Mixed drinks** $3.50 and up **Food available** Shrimp, burgers, oysters **Hours** 11 a.m.–4 a.m.

What goes on Dancing (mostly rock music) with live bands, many of them local bands just getting started.

Comments Nothing fancy, but the friendly staff is a favorite with the locals, the kind of place that will cook the fish you caught that day. A simple menu with late-night service includes burgers, cinnamon shrimp, and grouper.

Schooners

Who goes there Beach lovers of all ages

5121 Gulf Drive, Panama City Beach; (850) 235-3555; www.schooners.com

Cover No **Miminum** No **Mixed drinks** $4 and up **Food available** Appetizers, salads, soups, sandwiches, baskets on a plate **Hours** Open 11 a.m. daily

What goes on The crowd starts wandering in from the beach around noon for frozen margaritas and lunch, but the fun really starts with the nightly blast from an old cannon as the sun dips into the horizon. Live bands and an annual Lobster Festival draw hefty crowds.

Comments Schooners opened in the 1960s as The Beach Party, and for more than 40 years the beachfront bar has survived hurricanes and numerous owners. Voted by the locals as "the best place for live music" and "the best place to take friends from out of town," tin-roofed Schooners is the quintessential Florida bar. A full menu includes fried Apalachicola oysters, a grilled grouper sandwich, and other local specialties.

Sharky's

Who goes there A mixed crowd of 20-somethings; couples out for a nice dinner

15201 Front Beach Road, Panama City Beach; (850) 235-2420; www.sharkysbeach.com

Cover No **Miminum** No **Mixed drinks** $5.25 and up **Food available** Yes (seafood, sandwiches, salads) **Hours** 11 a.m.–midnight

What goes on Known for having the "world's largest tiki hut," Sharky's is a nice place to dine on the beach or slurp raw oysters at Big Daddy's Oyster Bar. There's live, low-key music in the Tiki Bar nightly, and live bands Wednesday through Saturday. During spring break the place gets manic.

Comments A great beachfront setting for sunset-watching and dinner. The margaritas get high marks, as well as the local seafood specialties.

Spinnaker Beach Club

Who goes there Locals, tourists, teens

8795 Thomas Drive, Panama City Beach; (850) 234-7892; www.spinnakerbeachclub.com

Cover $5 after 11 p.m. if you're over 21 **Miminum** 18 **Mixed drinks** $3.50 and up **Food available** Appetizers only (chicken wings, shrimp, onion rings, oysters) **Hours** 10 p.m.–4 a.m.

What goes on Site of MTV's first spring-break broadcast, Spinnakers has 34 bars, three live-band stages, dance floors, and a few hideaway bars for taking a breather from the crowd. Beach-front amphitheater hosts top-name concerts year-round.

Comments Jam-packed Spinnaker sprawls along the beach with volleyball games during the day, dancing after dark with bars inside and out.

Tallahassee

This is a great little town for walking or a trolley ride, with lush rolling hills, fragrant magnolias in the springtime, ancient oaks, and lovely springs and lakes.

Visitors enjoy touring the seat of state government, including the **Old Capitol**, restored to its 1902 American Renaissance splendor with red-and-white striped awnings and stained-glass dome. Behind it is the **New Capitol**, where you can view from public galleries the legislature from March through May. The New Capitol's 22nd-floor observatory offers a breathtaking view—clear to the Gulf of Mexico, about 20 miles away, on a cloudless day.

The Old Capitol is open for self-guided tours Monday–Friday, 9 a.m.–4:30 p.m.; Saturday, 10 a.m.–4:30 p.m.; and Sunday, noon–4:30 p.m. The New Capitol is open Monday–Friday, 8 a.m.–5 p.m. Tour times vary. Call (850) 487-1902 for capitol tour reservations. Admission is free to both buildings.

Peek in the **Governor's Mansion** just north of the capitol, furnished with eighteenth- and nineteenth-century antiques; tours are given when the legislature is in session and at Christmas. For a tour of the Governor's Mansion, call (850) 488-4661.

The Old Town Trolley is free, and you can get on or off at any point between Adams Street Commons, at the corner of Jefferson and Adams Streets, and the Governor's Mansion. The trolley runs every 20 minutes Monday–Friday, 7 a.m–6:30 p.m. Or you can stroll the **Downtown Tallahassee Historic Trail** from the capitol complex through the city's historic district; starting point is the New Capitol, where you can get maps and brochures at the visitor center.

A beautiful driving tour is Tallahassee's five "official" **canopy roads**, lined with sprawling, moss-draped live oaks and historical homes, some for up to 20 miles. Ask for a free copy of the driving tour at the visitor center in the New Capitol building. Old Bainbridge is the most scenic, leading to the Lake Jackson Mounds State Archaeological Site.

A MOON PIE AND A COLA

In Tallahassee, take time for a break at Bradley's Country Store—now on the National Register of Historic Places—where you'll likely meet one of the Bradley clan, who have run the place since it opened in 1927. Along with Moon Pie and a cola, they also make world-famous sausage—they sell more than 80,000 pounds over the counter every year. Or ask for one of Grandma Mary's seasoned sausage biscuits hot off the griddle. Bradley's is open Monday–Friday, 8 a.m.–6 p.m. and Saturday, 8 a.m.–5 p.m. (closed Sunday). Located on Centerville Road 12 miles north of Tallahassee; (850) 893-1647.

GOLF COURSES
1. Hilaman Park Municipal Golf Course

ATTRACTIONS
2. Tallahassee Museum of History and Natural Science

RESTAURANTS
3. Boss Oyster
4. Kool Beanz
5. Mon Pere Et Moi
6. Mori
7. Nicholson's Farmhouse
8. Oyster Cove Seafood Bar & Grill
9. Posey's Oyster Bar

NIGHTCLUBS
10. Clyde & Costello's
11. Floyd's Music Store

Downtown Tallahassee

142

Golf

Hilaman Park Municipal Golf Course
2737 Blair Stone Road; (850) 891-3935
Established 1971 | **Designer** Lawrence Packard | **Holes** 18

Tees Mens, 6,333 **Par** 72 **Slope** 125
Fees Weekdays, $27, $24 after 2 p.m., $18 for 9 holes after 5 p.m.; weekends and holidays, $32, $28 after 2 p.m., $22 9 holes after 5 p.m. **Specials** Juniors and seniors pay the twilight rate; reduced fees for walkers **Cart rental** Included **Club rental** Available **Payments** V, MC **Tee times** Available in advance **Facilities** Driving range, raquetball and squash courts, swimming pool, adjacent 9-hole course.
Comments Hilaman is one of the best golf values in the Panhandle—and a boon to travellers who do not have reciprocal-membership privileges at Tallahassee's Killearn Country Club.

Attractions

Tallahassee Museum of History and Natural Science
3945 Museum Drive, Tallahassee; (850) 576-1636
Hours Monday–Saturday, 9 a.m.–5 p.m.; Sunday, 12:30–5 p.m.
Admission $7 for adults, $6.50 for seniors, $5 for children ages 4–15
Appeal by Age Group

Pre-school ★★	Teens ★★★	Over 30 ★★★
Grade school ★★★	Young Adults ★★★	Seniors ★★★

Touring Time *Average* 2 hours; *minimum* 1½ hours
Rainy-Day Touring Not recommended
Author's Rating ★★★; one of the few museums in the U.S. that combines historical buildings, displays of native wildlife, and a beautiful natural setting
Description and Comments History, nature, and wildlife are intertwined to tell about the culture and natural history of the Big Bend. Along a trail through 52 acres of woodlands, you can see alligators, red wolves, Florida panthers, and other animals—the state's only zoological collection solely devoted to native wildlife. A collection of historical buildings, including an original plantation house from the 1840s, a church, and a one-room schoolhouse, illustrate what life was like in a bygone era. The Big Bend Farm is a recreation of a farm typical of the region during the late nineteenth century, with volunteers spinning, weaving, and churning butter.

Shopping

Governor's Square (1500 Apalachee Parkway, one mile east of the Capitol; (850) 671-INFO; **www.governorssquare.com**) is an enclosed mall with four department stores and specialty shops including Ann Taylor, Banana Republic, Abercrombie & Fitch, Eddie Bauer, and other national retailers.

Betton Place (1950 Thomasville Road) is a charming collection of shops with stores like **My Favorite Things** (phone (850) 681-2824), which specializes in fine china, gifts, and home accessories; **The Strauss Gallery** (phone (850) 222-6983) features fine art; and **The Museum Shop** (phone (850) 681-8565) offers fun and interesting gifts—nature, the arts, science, and world cultures—for all ages from museums around the country.

Market Square shopping district (1355 Market Street) is home to a handful of specialty shops, but the best reason to check it out is the Farmer's Market in the center pavilion featuring fresh regional produce every Saturday.

Carriage Gate Shopping Center on Thomasville Road has favorites like **Bedfellows** (phone (850) 893-1713), which features bed, bath, and table accessories and Vera Bradley luggage and bags; **Trixi and Grace** (phone (850) 893-7074), which offers women's clothing from top designers; and **The Gem Collection** (phone (850) 893-4171), which specializes in fine jewelry and accessories.

Just northwest of Tallahassee, small-town **Havana** considers itself "the antiques capital of North Florida," a boon for bargain hunters who enjoy sifting through old treasures.

Dining

Boss Oyster

125 Water Street, Apalachicola; (850) 653-9364

Meals served Lunch and dinner **Cuisine** Seafood **Entree range** $18–$24 **Reservations** Not accepted **Payment** V, MC, AmEx, D
Comments Locals recommend Boss Oyster not just for the freshly shucked oysters with more than 30 creative toppings but also for their delicious burgers. It's the best spot on the water in Apalachicola.

Kool Beanz

921 Thomasville Road, Tallahassee; (850) 224-2466

Meals served Lunch and dinner, closed Sundays **Cuisine** American/ Southwestern/Creole **Entree range** $5–$9 lunch; $7–$17 dinner **Reservations** No **Payment** All major credit cards accepted
Comments Kool Beanz is a 48-seat diner where it's almost impossible to score a seat. But if you do, you won't be disappointed. Though the menu changes often, favorites like sublime crab cakes, cornmeal-fried oysters, and Creole-spiced chicken are usually on the eclectic menu. Choice seats include the counter in front of the open kitchen, where you can watch the chefs in action.

Mon Pere Et Moi

3534 Maclay Boulevard, Tallahassee; (850) 877-0343

Meals served Breakfast and lunch Tuesday–Saturday, dinner Saturday only
Cuisine French **Entree range** Breakfast $2–$6; lunch $6–$9.50; dinner

$16–$18 (changes weekly) **Reservations** Yes (dinner only) **Payment** V, MC, AmEx

Comments The Vivier family opened this inviting bistro to accompany Monsieur Vivier's stunning chocolate creations, a favorite of locals for years. Now his young daughter works in the restaurant that serves classic French creations like seared salmon with beurre blanc and roast leg of lamb with garlic and rosemary, with wines from $4 a glass. Save room for dessert: marzipans, ganaches, pralines, and more.

Mori

2810 Sharer Road, Tallahassee; (850) 386-8449

Meals served Lunch and dinner daily **Cuisine** Japanese **Entree range** $7–$13 lunch; $12–$40 dinner **Reservations** Yes **Payment** All major credit cards accepted

Comments Japanese chefs show off as they flip, slice, dice, and sizzle your food before your eyes, shoveling piles of steak, chicken, or shrimp and veggies onto the plates of communal diners gathered around the hibachi table. Skip the sushi unless you want it tempura style.

Nicholson's Farmhouse

Off SR 12 in Havana (small town located 30 minutes north of Tallahassee); (850) 539-5931; www.nicholsonfarmhouse.com

Meals served Dinner, Tuesday–Saturday **Cuisine** American **Entree range** $14–$33 **Reservations** Recommended **Payment** V, MC, AmEx, D

Comments Folks come for miles around to dine at this historic farmhouse on five acres, built in 1828. There are five homes in all, restored and converted to dining areas. A traditional Southern treat, boiled peanuts, begins your dining experience. The food is as old-fashioned as it gets, with buttery steaks as the specialty and fresh-baked bread. No alcohol is served, but if you bring your own, they'll provide the glassware.

Oyster Cove Seafood Bar and Grill

Corner of East Pine and East Second Streets, St. George Island; (850) 927-2600

Meals served Dinner **Cuisine** Seafood/American **Entree range** $12–$23 **Reservations** Not necessary **Payment** V, MC, AmEx

Comments Locals love the Oyster Cove for its consistently good seafood dishes, though they also go for their "famous" East Bay steak, a rib eye grilled with oysters and Spanish onions. And the Key lime pie is perfection. Ask for a window seat for a world-class view of Apalachicola Bay, especially at sunset.

Posey's Oyster Bar

55 Riverside Drive, St. Marks; (850) 925-6172

Meals served Lunch and dinner **Cuisine** Seafood **Entree range** $9–$11 **Reservations** Not accepted **Payment** V, MC

Comments Posey's is at the south end of the Tallahassee–St. Marks Historic Rail Trail, the perfect respite after a bicycle ride. The dilapidated eatery has for years served fresh Apalachicola oysters. If you don't like raw oysters, try them baked with cheddar cheese, butter, bacon bits, or garlic. Also on the menu are grouper, shrimp, scallops, and clams.

Nightlife

Clyde & Costello's

Who goes there Well-dressed, up-and-comers in their 20s and 30s

210 South Adams Street, Tallahassee; (850) 224-8885

Mixed drinks $3.75 and up **Food available** Only until 8 p.m. from the pizza place next door **Hours** 3:30 p.m.–2 a.m.

What goes on "It's a place you go to dance and hook up," says a 20-something recent college grad. Close to the state Capitol, this upscale pub gets rowdy on Friday nights when ties are loosened and there's a $5 all-you-can-drink frenzy.

Comments An interesting mix of college kids and politicos.

Floyd's Music Store

Who goes there Music fans who don't mind the bare bones ambience

666-1 West Tennessee Street, Tallahassee; (850) 222-3506

Mixed drinks $3.50 and up **Food available** Limited appetizers **Hours** From 8 p.m. (depending on the event)

What goes on A bar, a stage, live music—a perfect trio for dance fans.

Comments The place for live music. Lots of FSU freshmen head here to dance and look for dates.

Side Trips

Apalachicola In the 1860s Apalachicola was the third-largest town on the Gulf, when steamboats from Georgia and Alabama carried cotton down the river to the Gulf of Mexico. Sponge fishing also was big business, but by the 1920s shellfish reigned as the most prosperous way to make a living.

Today, 90% of all oysters eaten in Florida are harvested here, and fisherfolk still work the waters. But progress passed Apalachicola by, and today it's a sleepy little fishing town, where most visitors are stopping for the fresh fish or oysters at the little seafood eateries found all over town. We suggest a meal at **Boss Oyster** (see above), where you can sit right next to the docks and watch the oyster and shrimp boats unloading their day's catch. After a satisfying lunch or dinner, you can take a scenic walking tour of some of the more than 200 historic sites; Apalachicola has one of the largest collections of antebellum homes in the state. One of its most famous spots is the **Gibson Inn,** with outdoor rockers for catching the Gulf breeze and a wonderful little restaurant called **Nola's Grill** (**www.gibsoninn.com**). Browse in **Grady**

Market, a nineteenth-century warehouse that's now an upscale gift and gourmet shop, or stop on Market Street for a chocolate malt at the **Old Time Soda Fountain.** There's not a stop light in the entire town other than a blinking caution light at the intersection of Market Street and Avenue E downtown.

Cedar Key Just three miles from the mainland, Cedar Key is like a step back in time. Back in the mid-1800s it was the second-largest city in Florida, when the first major railroad in Florida ran from Fernandina Beach in the northeast to Cedar Key. After the Civil War, pencil making was big business—until the cedar forests were leveled. Today it's a haven for fishers, bird-watchers, and photographers.

Stop off at the **Cedar Key Historical Museum** for brochures that offer self-guided tours of the city. The museum is in an 1870s-era house on Second Street at SR 24; (352) 543-5549. Cycle past the picturesque city docks, one of the most-photographed sites on Florida's west coast, or stop for seafood at any of the Dock Street restaurants.

Part Three

Northeast Florida: Amelia Island, Jacksonville, St. Augustine, and Gainesville

Welcome to Northeast Florida

Authentic history lessons and the great outdoors are two of the best reasons to head to northeast Florida, a region alive with meticulously re-created historic districts, natural springs, lush inland forests, tree-lined rivers, and wide beaches.

Northeast Florida is the spot on the map where intrepid Spanish explorers, determined English settlers, and French homesteaders seeking religious freedom landed—and immediately began to battle over their respective claims. Today, St. Augustine, the oldest continuous European settlement in the United States, is a fascinating melting pot of cultures that influenced the formation of the New World. North of St. Augustine, tiny Amelia Island shows off blocks of old mansions, miles of beaches, and lots of seafood.

But Florida's "First Coast" is also home to Jacksonville, one of the most modern cities in Florida, which swiftly moved into the twenty-first century with a thriving seaport.

Heading southwest from Jacksonville, it looks as though time stood still in the 1930s in lovely old towns like Micanopy, Alachua, and Newberry, where freshwater springs, gentle hills, and forests dot the landscape. Gainesville, home of the very modern University of Florida, manages to retain its small-town charm with architecture dating back to the late 1800s. Just south of Gainesville is Cross Creek, hometown of Pulitzer Prize–winning author Marjorie Kinnan Rawlings, who was attracted to the timeless landscape in the 1920s.

A Brief History

Northeast Florida's history is a wild mix of pirates, invasions, and unconquerable fortresses. The European chapter of Florida's history began in the early 1500s, when Spanish explorer Juan Ponce de Leon began searching the area for the fountain of youth. A spring in St. Augustine is said to be the very fountain Ponce de Leon sought.

Pedro Menéndez de Avilés founded the city of St. Augustine in 1565, 55 years before the pilgrims landed at Plymouth Rock. In the years following, the city came under several attacks, including one by Sir Francis Drake, who plundered and burned the town in 1586. The Spanish built the Castillo de San Marcos fort in the late 1600s, and it was never conquered.

In the 1880s, Henry Flagler arrived in Florida and began developing the St. Augustine area as a tourist destination. The mild winter climate made the area ideal for affluent Northern travelers; thus began an industry that would become one of Florida's primary sources of income.

HIGHLIGHTS
- Castillo de San Marcos National Monument
- Cummer Museum of Art and Gardens
- Shopping along St. George Street in St. Augustine
- Amelia Island beaches
- Historic Haile Homestead at Kanapaha

Visiting Northeast Florida

Gathering Information

Amelia Island Tourist Development Council, 961687 Gateway Boulevard, Amelia Island 32034; (800) 226-3542; **www.islandchamber.com.**

Beaches Chamber and Visitors Center, 325 Jacksonville Drive, Jacksonville Beach 32250; (904) 249-3868.

Jacksonville and the Beaches Convention and Visitors Bureau, 550 Water Street, Suite 1000, Jacksonville 32202; (904) 798-9111, (800) 733-2668; **www.jaxcvb.com.**

St. Augustine–St. Johns County Chamber of Commerce, 1 Riberia Street, St. Augustine 32084; (904) 829-5681; **www.staugustinechamber.com.**

St. Augustine, Ponte Vedra, and the Beaches Visitors and Convention Bureau, 88 Riberia Street, Suite 400, St. Augustine 32084; (800) OLD-CITY; **www.visitoldcity.com.**

Alachua County Visitors and Convention Bureau, 30 East University Avenue, Gainesville 32601; (352) 374-5231; **www.visitgainesville.net.**

Getting There

By Plane Serving Jacksonville International Airport (phone (904) 741-4902; **www.jaxairports.org**) are Southwest, US Airways, Northwest, Continental, American Airlines, United Airlines, Delta, and Airtran. Rental-car companies at the airport include Thrifty, Budget, Avis, Hertz, Alamo, National, Enterprise, and Dollar, with Payless off the premises. You can also call for taxi, limo, or shuttle services. The airport is located just a mile from I-95, 18 miles north of downtown Jacksonville.

Gainesville Regional Airport (phone (352) 373-0249; **www.flygainesville.com**) offers flights from Delta and US Airways. The airport is a 15–20 minute drive from downtown; you can rent a car from Avis, Budget, Hertz, or National.

You can charter flights to the St. Augustine/St. Johns County Airport (phone (904) 825-6860) and to the Fernandina Beach Municipal Airport (phone (904) 261-7890).

Also close by is Daytona International Airport (phone (386) 248-8069; **www.flydaytonafirst.com**).

By Car Northeast Florida's major cities (Gainesville, Jacksonville, and St. Augustine) are located within an afternoon's drive from other popular Florida destinations, including Orlando, Daytona Beach, Cocoa Beach, and Tampa. Major roads include I-95, I-10, US 1, and I-75. I-95 runs north-south and is the major interstate in the St. Augustine and Jacksonville areas; I-75 runs through Gainesville. I-10, running east-west, ends at I-95 near Jacksonville. US 1 runs north-south on the mainland and travels through both Jacksonville and St. Augustine. SR A1A runs along the Atlantic with some beautiful ocean views.

By Train Amtrak stations are in Lake City, Waldo, Jacksonville, Palatka, and Gainesville; (800) USA-RAIL; **www.amtrak.com**.

Getting Around

Public transportation is an option, but as elsewhere in Florida, a car is the most efficient way to see the area. Traffic conditions in Northeast Florida range from busy city streets in Jacksonville to sleepy back roads in small towns such as Micanopy. You can get specific directions from hotels and rental-car companies. Keep in mind that road construction often clogs popular routes.

Speed limits vary from 30–35 mph in neighborhoods and near hotels and major attractions. Larger roads, such as US 1, typically run 45–55 mph, but speed limits change depending on the area. I-10 averages 65, I-95 is commonly 65–70 mph. Speeds on SR A1A range, but the average is 35–40 mph.

Major Roadways

The main roads in St. Augustine are SR A1A, which runs north-south on the coast, and US 1, which runs north-south on the mainland. You can reach St. Augustine attractions from roads off these two routes. During the summer, tourists flock to St. Augustine, which can make both driving and finding a place to park difficult. The Visitor Center offers $5-per-day parking.

Traffic conditions vary in Gainesville depending on the time of year: The University of Florida has a student body of 40,000-plus, so the roads are more congested during fall and spring semesters. University Avenue runs east-west, and Main Street runs north-south—streets downtown are numbered, starting in the middle of the city. The closer you are to downtown, the smaller the numbers get. The major interstate in Gainesville is I-75, which runs through the western part of the city.

The city of Jacksonville is located at the junction of I-10 west and I-95, with I-295 and 9A connecting to form a loop around the city. Butler, Beach, and Atlantic Boulevards all run east to the beaches; SR A1A runs north-south along the coast. I-75 is a 30-minute drive from the city.

The city is spread out, so the roads here aren't as congested as other large metro areas. Rush hour does pack the roads, though, so avoid driving around 5 p.m.

To reach Amelia Island, take I-95 to SR A1A, which crosses the Intracoastal Waterway onto the island via the Thomas Shave Bridge. From Jacksonville, take SR A1A and head south. Driving on tiny Amelia Island isn't difficult due to its size—SR A1A runs the length of the island. Traffic isn't a problem either; roads can get clogged during festivals or when Jacksonville hosts a large football game, but on most days the roads are easy to navigate.

The Best Beaches

Amelia Island   The island's 13 miles of white sandy beach are among the state's most scenic. A state park and state recreation area offer convenient access points.

Anastasia State Recreation Area   Anastasia Boulevard in St. Augustine is the perfect beach for those looking for lots of activity. There's a parking lot in front of the high dunes that's big enough to hold 500 cars. On the beach there are volleyball, tennis courts, and beach paraphernalia for rent, including bicycles, sailboards, paddleboats, beach chairs, and umbrellas. Admission is $3.25 per vehicle. You can also camp inland for $17.44, $19.56 with electricity; (904) 461-2033.

Jacksonville Beaches   Vacationers don't generally head to Jacksonville for a beach retreat, but there are several options about 12 miles from downtown via J. Turner Butler Boulevard. Bustling Jacksonville Beach, a favorite for teens and families, has lifeguards, an oceanfront pavilion with live entertainment, plenty of restaurants, and nearby hotels. Sleepy Mayport Beach is where you can watch the naval fleet come home to the Mayport Naval Station. The more secluded Atlantic and Neptune Beaches are where many Jacksonville residents head on the weekends. We recommend the Kathryn Abbey Hanna Park just south of Mayport on SR A1A at 500 Wonderwood Drive—450 acres on the ocean with a great beach, lifeguards, nature trails, picnicking, and freshwater fishing.

St. Augustine Beach   About a ten-minute drive from downtown St. Augustine, cross the Bridge of Lions to SR A1A and head south to Dondanville Road. You can park right on the beach. Cost is $5 per vehicle from Memorial Day to Labor Day at official access points. Driving is permitted on this beach. Lifeguards are on duty 8 a.m.–5 p.m. There are restaurants nearby, but no bathrooms on the beach; (904) 471-6616.

Washington Oaks State Gardens   About a 20-minute drive south of St. Augustine on SR A1A is a picturesque, boulder-strewn beach where shorebirds feed at low tide while brown pelicans soar overhead. It's not great for swimming because of the coquina rocks in the surf, but it's lovely for wading and walking or fishing for whiting and bluefish. There are no lifeguards. Admission is $3.25 per vehicle; (386) 446-6780.

Outdoor Adventures and Sports

Recommended Excursions

Amelia Island State Recreation Area If you want to take a horseback ride on the beach, this state recreation area has guided rides operated by Seahorse Stables. The hour-long, five-mile beach ride is $45. Reservations are a must. The state recreation area has pristine beaches, salt marshes, and coastal maritime forests that provide a glimpse of the original Florida. The 200-acre park also is great for bird watching, fishing, and hiking. For horseback riding reservations, call **Kelly Seahorse Ranch** at (904) 491-5166.

Anastasia State Recreation Area This popular beachfront recreation area stretches over 1,800 acres, and for outdoor enthusiasts it's a complete vacation destination with four-and-a-half miles of sandy beach, shaded picnic areas with grills, 139 campsites, nature trails, windsurfing, sailing, and canoeing on a saltwater lagoon. The odds are good that you'll hook pompano or whiting in the surf. In the summer there are chairs, beach umbrellas, and surfboards for rent. And bird-watching is good, too; ask for a free brochure as you enter. Campsites in a pretty wooded area are $18, $20 with electricity, and each has a picnic table and grill. The beach is the perfect place to watch the sunset. Admission is $3.25 per vehicle; open daily 8 a.m.–8:30 p.m. Located at St. Augustine Beach off SR A1A at SR 3; (904) 461-2033.

Big Talbot Island State Park This park is recommended for surf fishing for bluefish and whiting. Photographers also love Big Talbot, with its rock outcroppings and fallen tress that have become bleached and weathered with time. There aren't places to swim here, but the island's spectacular bluffs, two plantation ruins, and canoe routes through salt marshes add to the experience. Admission is $3.25 per vehicle. Located 20 miles east of downtown Jacksonville via SR A1A at 12157 Heckscher Drive; (904) 251-2320.

Bulow Plantation Ruins State Historic Site The Bulow Plantation was the largest sugar plantation on the East Coast (1,000 acres) and grew sugar cane, cotton, rice, and indigo in the early 1800s. John James Audubon noted the Bulows' hospitality after a stop here on a collecting and painting trip. The plantation was abandoned during the Second Seminole War as John Bulow followed the troops northward. The Seminoles burned "Bulowville" around 1836, along with other plantations in the area. All that is left today are the coquina ruins of the sugar mill, several wells, a springhouse, and the crumbling foundation of the mansion. A scenic, mile-long walking trail leads to the ruins. You can picnic, canoe, and fish at Bulow Creek. Admission is $2 per car. The site is 35 minutes from St. Augustine and three miles west of Flagler Beach (take SR 100 and head south on CR 2001); (386) 517-2084.

Gainesville-Hawthorne Rail Trail This flat, winding trail is perfect for cycling or walking; you can trek or bike as little or as long as you like, with 16 miles of asphalt along a scenic railway corridor. The trail extends from Gainesville's historic Boulware Springs Park at Paynes Prairie through Lochloosa Wildlife Management Area to the town of Hawthorne. You'll see sinkholes, abundant wildlife including alligators, and osprey nests. Head south on Southeast 15th Street from University Avenue in Gainesville; look for the Boulware Springs Park sign; (352) 466-3397.

Ginnie Springs Smaller and far less crowded than Ichetucknee Springs (see below), these springs are memorable and fun and perfect for tubing or snorkeling in crystal-clear water that stays 72° year-round. There are also picnic tables and a playground. Admission is $10 for adults and $3 for children ages 7–14. Located about 30 miles from Gainesville. Take I-75 to Exit 399 (Old 78); go north on US 441; turn left on Main Street; turn right on CR 340; and continue 6.5 miles to 7300 Northeast Ginnie Springs Road, High Springs; (386) 454-7182; www.ginniespringsoutdoors.com.

Guana River State Park This park provides guests a wilderness ambience, with 2,400 acres of hardwood hammock, marshes, pine forests, and beaches. If you want to fish, there are plenty of opportunities, with abundant catches in the Atlantic, Guana River, or Guana Lake. The beach is nice for swimming, but there are no lifeguards. There are nine miles of multipurpose trails, recommended for beginners, with wide paths marked by color codes that can easily be followed except on the north end where the trails leave the park and enter a wildlife management area. Admission is $2 per car. Located off SR A1A near Ponte Vedra Beach, nearly equidistant from Jacksonville and St. Augustine; (904) 825-5071.

Ichetucknee Springs State Park The three-and-a-half-hour innertube float down this crystal-clear spring has become so popular that park rangers now limit the number of tubers to 750 per day from the north entrance—it's best to arrive early. The least crowded days are Tuesday through Thursday, say the park rangers.

The Ichetucknee River is fed by a series of springs producing 233 million gallons of water daily, so the water is a constant and cool 73° year-round. The north entrance is open from Memorial Day through Labor Day, with a shuttle waiting at the end of the run to take you back to your car. Or if you prefer, it's a 20-minute hike.

The park is open year-round from 8 a.m. to sundown for hiking, picnicking, and swimming. All year round, you can tube from the south entrance. When the shuttle is running, the cost is $3.25 per person, free for children ages 5 and under. During the summer, tubing from the north entrance costs $4.25 per person.

You cannot rent innertubes in the park, but private roadside vendors rent them—or you can bring one from home. No food, drinks, or pets are allowed on the run. Take I-75 to SR 47 south 12 miles to CR 238 (Elim Church Road), then turn right on SR 238 and follow it to the park entrance; (386) 497-2511; www.ichetuckneeriver.com.

Kanapaha Botanical Gardens Sixty-two acres of woodlands, meadows, vineyards, and specialized gardens grow in Florida's most diverse and second-largest botanical gardens. Highlights are Florida's largest bamboo grove, the largest herb garden in the state, and the hummingbird and butterfly gardens. There's a shaded picnic area. Open Monday–Friday, 9 a.m.–5 p.m.; Saturday and Sunday, 9 a.m.–dusk; closed Thursday. Admission is $5 adults, $3 children ages 6–13, and free for ages 6 and under. Located at 4700 Southwest 58th Drive; (352) 372-4981; **www.kanapaha.org**.

Kathryn Abbey Hanna Park Just about a 20-minute drive from downtown Jacksonville, this 450-acre oceanfront park is a favorite of locals who take advantage of the beaches, freshwater lakes, and wooded campsites. It offers more than 15 miles of trails for bicycling, with trails for beginners, intermediates, and experts (though it can be sandy and hard to pedal if the weather has been particularly dry). The bicycling trail, also great for hiking, runs near the Atlantic for about a mile. The entry fee is $1 per person over age 6. The nearly 300 campsites are $18 per night. Exit onto Atlantic Boulevard from I-10 or take I-95 to SR A1A heading north to Mayport; continue right on CR 101 when SR A1A turns left to Mayport. Then turn right at the Hanna Park sign; 500 Wonderwood Drive; (904) 249-4700.

Little Talbot Island State Park You can hear the waves at night when you're camping here, near more than five miles of wide, unspoiled beaches. Bird-watchers love this park, with its vegetated dunes and undisturbed salt marshes, where river otters, marsh rabbits, and bobcats join the shorebirds. Fishing, too, is excellent—bluefish, striped bass, redfish, flounder, and mullet are often on the line. The beach has bathhouses, a picnic site, an observation deck, and campsites near a salt marsh (bring the mosquito repellent). Admission is $3.25 per vehicle; camping is $15, $18 with electricity. Open daily, 8 a.m.–sunset. Located at 12157 Heckscher Drive (15 miles south of Fernandina Beach via SR A1A); (904) 251-2320.

Morningside Nature Center Take a step back in time and experience the life of a farmer of 100 years ago. The 278-acre farm is run by the city of Gainesville, with seven miles of nature trails and boardwalks (more than 130 species of birds and 225 species of wildflowers have been counted). On the premises are a turn-of-the-twentieth-century schoolhouse, a Florida homestead garden, and a farmhouse built in 1840. Open daily, 9 a.m.–5 p.m. Admission is free. Saturday is Farm Day and costs $2 for adults, $1 for children. There's also an area for picnicking. Located at 3540 East University Avenue, Gainesville; (352) 334-2170; **www.natureoperations.org**.

O'Leno State Park Woods that are fun for exploring are the big draw at O'Leno—turkey, deer, even an occasional bobcat can be spotted on the hiking trails. There's also camping, mountain biking, fishing, swimming, canoeing, and horseback riding (no stables) in this 6,000-acre park. The Santa Fe River disappears and flows underground for more than three miles in the park before it again becomes a surface stream. There's a great view of the river from a suspension bridge that was built in the 1930s by the Conservation Corps. O'Leno started as a town in the mid-1800s named Keno (after a game of chance), and the name was changed to Leno in 1876. Like many early Florida towns, Leno became a ghost town, and after 1896 was referred to as O'Leno, a variation on the local name for "Old Leno." Admission is $3.25 per vehicle. Camping is $11, $13 with electricity. Take US 441 six miles north of High Springs; (386) 454-1853.

Paynes Prairie State Preserve A flat stretch of prairie that's home to wild horses and a herd of American bison makes this an unusual destination. You can boat, camp, hike, bird-watch, fish, and picnic on this 21,000-acre wildlife sanctuary. Named for a Seminole chief, Paynes Prairie is one of the most significant and historic areas in Florida, with more than 350 kinds of animals living in the freshwater marsh, lakes, pine flatwoods, hammock, scrub, and grasslands, including plenty of reptiles, fish, and amphibians. Six miles of trails are available for hiking. A 50-foot-high viewing tower with a telescope gives an awesome view of the prairie. If you fish, you'll need a license. Free ranger-led activities are held November–April. Admission is $3.25 per vehicle. Camping is $10, with $2 extra for electricity. Open daily 8 a.m.–sundown; visitors center open 9 a.m.–5 p.m. US 441, ten miles south of Gainesville, near Micanopy; (352) 466-3397.

Santa Fe River Pack your own picnic and rent canoes for day trips from 3 to 15 miles—you paddle downstream with the current, local outfitters pick you up in a van and bring you back. Florida wildlife is abundant—egrets, ibis, great blue herons, turtles, deer, fox, raccoons, possums, and more. There are no big boats, as the river is a no-wake zone; the Santa Fe River is also shallow. Real outdoor enthusiasts can also arrange one- to seven-night camping trips (all the gear will be provided). **Santa Fe Canoe Outpost** is located on US 441 at the Santa Fe River Bridge, 23 miles north of Gainesville in High Springs; (386) 454-2050; www.santaferiver.com.

Tree Hill Nature Center If you want to skip a day at the beach but still want to spend some time outdoors, this is a great place, with 50 acres of urban wilderness. There's a self-guided nature walk through wetland vegetation with all kinds of trees—even the woodpecker holes are clearly marked along the paths. A small natural history museum is open Monday–Friday, 8:00 a.m.– 4:30 p.m. Admission is $2 adults, $1 children ages 17 and under. Located at 7152 Lone Star Road (off Arlington Road in Jacksonville, less than ten minutes from downtown); (904) 724-4646; www.treehill.org.

Washington Oaks State Gardens This small state beach is distinguished by 400 acres of lovely gardens on property that extends from the Atlantic Ocean to the Matanzas River. The park is named after a relative of George Washington who worked the land in the years before the Civil War. The gardens were expanded with azaleas, camellias, and roses when the place was purchased in 1936 by the Young family (the father was chairman of the board of General Electric). The land was donated to the state in 1964 and has a small museum, which details the history of the site. It's a pleasant stop to stretch on the way north or south, with walking trails and good fishing, but swimming isn't recommended because of the rocky shoreline. At low tide shorebirds feed; limpets and mussels cling to the rocks; and anemones, starfish, and crabs are common in the tidal pools. Admission is $3.25 per vehicle. Located at 6400 North Ocean Boulevard (on both sides of SR A1A); (386) 446-6780.

Canoeing and Kayaking

The northeast region of Florida boasts plenty of excellent canoeing and kayaking opportunities. The Amelia Island, Big Talbot Island, and Little Talbot Island areas have some protected waterways, as well as some areas for experienced paddlers only. It can be easy to find yourself in over your head if you stray into the ocean.

Guana River State Park is teeming with wildlife, including waterfowl, birds of prey, otters, and alligators, just to name a few. The Guana River is dammed, which protects it from tidal flows, but also prevents dolphins and manatees from visiting the river. The Moses Creek Conservation Area also abounds with wildlife and is accessed by manatees and some marine animals such as dolphins and sea turtles.

Inland, you'll find canoeing and kayaking spots on the St. Johns River, the Santa Fe River in Gainesville, and the Silver and Oklawaha rivers in Ocala. For more information on canoeing or kayaking in northeast Florida, contact **Coastal Outdoors** at (904) 471-4144.

Scuba Diving and Snorkeling

Northeast Florida offers numerous offshore wreck sites and natural reefs to explore. Beach dives are not so popular, as the surf churns the water and greatly reduces visibility. Miles away from the surf and the crowds, however, you'll find dive sites such as St. Augustine's Intruder Reef and Jacksonville's Coppedge Reef.

Springs diving is a popular option—try **Ginnie Springs,** ten minutes outside of the city of High Springs. The area offers clear water and great views. Cave divers will also find plenty of diversions here. For more information, call (386) 454-7188 or visit **www.ginniespringsoutdoors.com.**

Surfing

Northeast Florida offers surfers great waves (on good days) and fairly clean beaches. Some of the best area surfing spots are near the St. Augustine pier and on the beaches near A Street. The surf at Jacksonville Beach is relatively calm, but on certain days the waves do kick up. In the summer, offshore tropical storms bring larger waves to the coast. Check with a local surf report for daily information on weather and wave conditions.

Sailing and Sailing Schools

The Intracoastal Waterway is popular for sailing in the northeast Florida region. In the summer, winds on the Intracoastal tend to be from the east, allowing you to sail both directions. Boaters also enjoy looking at historic districts from the waterway, but traffic here can be congested. For more information, contact the **Southern Sailing Academy** (phone (866) 252-SAIL; www.southernsailingacademy.com) or **St. Augustine Sailing** (phone (904) 829-0648; www.sta-sail.com), both in St. Augustine.

Fishing

Inshore, you'll find excellent salt flats fishing in the St. Augustine area. Fish for redfish, trout, and flounder, with tarpon making an appearance in the summer. Use light tackle and live shrimp, mullet, or mud minnows. On the St. Johns River, anglers hook black bass, bluegill, crappie, and catfish; you can even find shrimp in the river during certain times of the year. Fishing on feeder creeks off the Intracoastal Waterway, you might find red bass, trout, flounder, tarpon, shark, sheepshead, ladyfish, mangrove snapper, and jack crevalle. In the Gainesville area, cast your line in the Orange or Lochloosa lakes or the Santa Fe River; you can find brim, panfish, bluegill, speckled perch, and bass. Use light tackle and shiners, crickets, worms, or artificial baits for river and lake fishing.

Fishing on the beaches and from piers and jetties is a popular option. Most commonly caught are whiting, redfish, trout, and jacks, with sheepshead, black drum, and angelfish caught near pier pylons. Bottom rigs and surf rigs are recommended. You can also find anglers fishing from bridges along SR A1A.

Nonresidents over the age of 16 are required to procure a Florida Fishing license before casting. You can purchase a license from the Fish and Wildlife Conservation Commission over the phone, (888) 347-4356.

Party Boats

You don't need a license to fish from a party boat. Prices average about $55 for a full day of fishing. A half-day of fishing usually costs $35 and is available south of Jacksonville. Bait and tackle are included, and anglers of all ages are welcome. Offshore fishing often yields tuna, sailfish, wahoo, bonita, sea bass, barracudas, sharks, dolphin fish, snapper, grouper, and king mackerel.

Charter Boats

Chartering a boat is a more expensive, but also more private option. Enjoy smaller party sizes (averaging 1–6 people) and a more personalized fishing experience, compared to large party boats. Tackle and licenses are supplied; costs range depending on the size of the boat, how many people want to fish, and how long you'd like to spend on the water. Prices start around $400 and can go up to as much as $1,200 for off-shore fishing. You can also charter an inland fishing trip at around $300–$600. For more information about chartering a boat, or for northeast Florida fishing information, contact **Captain Jim Hammond** (phone (904) 757-7550; **www.hammondfishing.com**).

NORTHEAST FLORIDA MARINAS

Marina	Location	Phone
Amelia Island		
Amelia Island Yacht Basin	251 Creekside Drive	(904) 277-4615
Fernandina Harbor Marina	1 Front Street	(904) 261-0355
Jacksonville		
Arlington Marina	5137 Arlington Road	(904) 743-2628
Beach Marine	2315 Beach Boulevard	(904) 249-8200
Edward's Marina	451-B Trout River Drive	(904) 764-7022
Julington Creek Marina	12807 San Jose Boulevard	(904) 268-0098
Main Street Marine	9211 N. Main Street	(904) 757-3100
Ortega River Boat Yard	4451 Herschel Street	(904) 387-5538
Ortega Yacht Club Marina	4585 Lakeside Drive	(904) 389-1199
Pier 17 Marina	4619 Roosevelt Road	(904) 387-4669
Saint Augustine		
Camachee Cove Yacht Harbor	3070 Harbor Drive	(904) 829-5676
Conch House Marina	57 Comares Avenue	(904) 824-4347
Hidden Harbor	10 Prawn Street	(904) 829-0750
High Tide Boat Yard	164 Nix Boat Yard Road	(904) 826-3591
Sebastian Harbor Marina	975 S. Ponce de Leon Blvd.	(904) 825-4666
St. Augustine Municipal Marina	111 Avenue Menendez	(904) 825-1026

Spectator Sports

Football

The **Jacksonville Jaguars (www.jaguars.com)** joined the National Football League in 1995 and became a smash hit—they have already been in the playoffs numerous times and have won two AFC Central Division championships. The Jags play their home games in Jacksonville's ALLTEL Stadium, which can seat up to 80,000. For tickets, call (877) 4-JAGS-TIX.

The University of Florida boasts one of the best college football teams in the country—the **Florida Gators.** The team has many SEC Championships to its name, as well as a National Championship title. The Gators play at the Ben Hill Griffin Stadium at Florida Field, which can seat over 80,000. For tickets and information, call (352) 375-4683 or visit **www.gatorzone.com.**

Baseball

The **Jacksonville Suns** play about 70 home games per season. The Southern League, Eastern Division, team plays its games at the Baseball Grounds of Jacksonville, which can seat up to 11,000 people. For more information, call (904) 358-2846 or visit **www.jacksonvillesuns.com.**

Hockey

The **Jacksonville Barracudas** are part of the newly formed World Hockey Association 2 (WHA2) and play their games in the 16,000-seat Jacksonville Arena. For more information, call (904) 367-1423 or visit the team's website: **www.jacksonvillebarracudas.com**.

Amelia Island and Fernandina Beach

Beautiful beaches and an unhurried atmosphere are the best reasons to head to this quiet little island, just 2.5 miles wide, located 30 miles northeast of Jacksonville. Though small, the island has 13 miles of scenic beaches and is home to one of the most varied populations of wildlife on the East Coast.

There's plenty of history, too. Though Amelia Island's first inhabitants, the Timucuan Indians, arrived as early as 2000 B.C., it's nicknamed the "Isle of Eight Flags" because it's the only site in the United States that's been controlled by eight different governments in its 400 years: France, Spain, England, the Patriots of Amelia Island, the Green Cross of Florida, Mexico, the Confederacy, and the United States.

Despite the military influences, the most lasting impact on the island was made by the railroad industry. In the late 1800s, Fernandina was developed as a stop to accommodate passengers traveling to Florida for the winter. The island enjoyed its glory days, building grand Victorian summer homes and a luxurious resort on the ocean.

When the rails expanded, Fernandina Beach was bypassed as travelers hurried to Miami. As a result, Amelia Island and the city of Fernandina Beach still retain the charm and graciousness of the Victorian era, leaving many historical landmarks, such as the Silk Stocking District, a collection of sherbet-hued mansions, and one of the state's oldest saloons. There are 50 blocks in all on the National Register of Historic Places. The focal point is Centre Street, with its boutiques and art galleries, outdoor cafés, and waterfront restaurants.

Amelia Island also is the birthplace of the modern-day shrimping industry. Local shrimpers invented a method to preserve the freshness of the shrimp for shipping around the turn of the twentieth century. You can watch as shrimp boats unload their bounty, then try the sweet-tasting fresh seafood in local eateries—nearly one million tons of shrimp are caught off Amelia Island every year.

Golf

Fernandina Beach Municipal Golf Club
2800 Bill Melton Road; (904) 277-7370
Established 1956 | **Designer** Ed Matteson | **Holes** 27

Tees Blue/White/Gold/Red **Par** 71–73, depending on which 9 you play **Slope** North/West 124/120/115/118; West/South 128/125/113/115; South/North 124/122/112/116

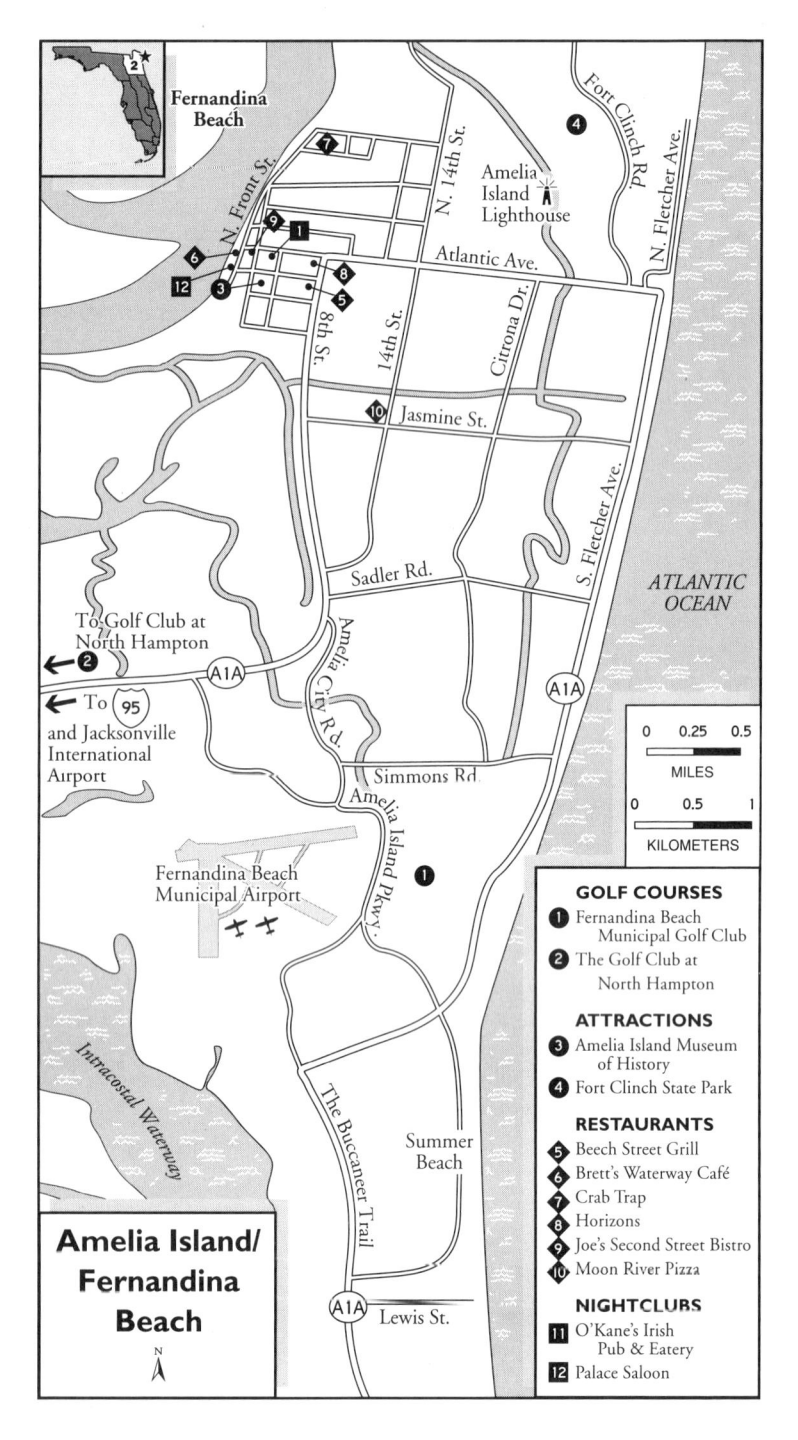

Amelia Island/Fernandina Beach

GOLF COURSES
1. Fernandina Beach Municipal Golf Club
2. The Golf Club at North Hampton

ATTRACTIONS
3. Amelia Island Museum of History
4. Fort Clinch State Park

RESTAURANTS
5. Beech Street Grill
6. Brett's Waterway Café
7. Crab Trap
8. Horizons
9. Joe's Second Street Bistro
10. Moon River Pizza

NIGHTCLUBS
11. O'Kane's Irish Pub & Eatery
12. Palace Saloon

Fees $37 weekdays, $41 weekends and holidays **Specials** After 4 p.m., $24 weekdays, $29 weekends **Cart rental** Included **Club rental** $25 **Payment** V, MC **Tee times** Up to 5 days in advance **Facilities** Pro shop, driving range, restaurant, putting green

Comments Each 9 is different at this public course—the North 9 is tree-lined but open, with plenty of doglegs. The West 9 is longer. The South 9 is the tightest of the three; trees drape their branches over the greens on the South 9, so the feeling is much more close and contained.

The Golf Club at North Hampton

22680 North Hampton Club Way; (904) 548-0000; www.hamptongolfclubs.com
Established 2000 | **Designer** Arnold Palmer | **Holes** 18

Tees Gold/Black/Blue/White/Green/Burgundy (Family)
Par 72/72/72/72/72/72 **Slope** 143/140/134/121/128/N/A
Fees Average $65 in summer and $100 in winter **Specials** Summer-twilight, $25 after 4 p.m. **Cart rental** Included **Club rental** $25 **Payment** V, MC, AmEx **Tee times** Up to 7 days in advance **Facilities** Pro shop, clubhouse, dining room, bar, locker rooms with showers, putting green, chipping green, driving range

Comments This challenging, Scottish links-style course (Palmer's first Scottish links design) is located on 70 acres of land and has over 40 feet of elevation. Watch out for number 16, a par 4 with water all the way on the left, lateral hazards on the right, water in front, and traps guarding the green.

Attractions

Amelia Island Museum of History

233 South Third Street, Fernandina Beach; (904) 261-7378
Hours Monday–Saturday, 10 a.m.–4 p.m.
Admission $5 adults, $3 students, children under age 5 free
Appeal by Age Group

Pre-school ★★	Teens ★★★	Over 30 ★★★
Grade school ★★★★	Young Adults ★★★	Seniors ★★★

Touring Time *Minimum* 1 hour without tour, 2 hours with
Rainy-Day Touring Recommended
Author's Rating ★★★

Description and Comments This fascinating museum, housed in the former Nassau County jailhouse, recently reopened with half a million dollars' worth of new exhibits. Eight rooms feature displays chronicling Amelia Island's history, ranging from Native American civilizations to modern-day tourism. The second floor is home to a research library.

Perhaps the most noteworthy aspect of this museum is its commitment to continuing a tradition of oral history. Volunteers who live in the area give presentations, telling stories about the island's fascinating history. In the cooler months, take a guided walking tour of the island. You may be able to join a tour with a costumed docent—they've done pirate tours, ghost tours, and more. Another interesting option is a Step-On tour: you provide the vehicle, and the museum provides the tour guide.

Fort Clinch State Park

2601 Atlantic Avenue, Fernandina Beach; (904) 277-7274

Hours Park, 8 a.m.–sundown daily; fort, 9 a.m.–5 p.m.

Admission $3.25 per vehicle (up to 8 people) to enter state park; 50 cents per person (more than 8 people); $2 per person age 6 and older to enter the fort

Appeal by Age Group

Pre-school ★★★	Teens ★★★	Over 30 ★★★
Grade school ★★★★★	Young Adults ★★★	Seniors ★★★

Touring Time *Average* 3–4 hours; *minimum* 2 hours

Rainy-Day Touring Not recommended

Author's Rating ★★★

Description and Comments Amelia Island's most famous historical site is a must-see for history buffs. Park rangers act as living historians as they reenact the daily life of Civil War–era soldiers. You can even sit on a bunk covered with a straw-filled mattress and imagine what it was like for young recruits. Climb the ramparts and look across the sound to Georgia.

There's also fishing from a jetty, the pier, or in the surf—trout, redfish, and sheepshead are abundant. Camping, picnicking, and other activities are available.

Shopping

In **Historic Downtown Fernandina Beach,** on the brick-lined Centre Street, you can find an abundance of excellent antique shops, quirky art galleries, and quaint sidewalk cafés. The street is lined with Victorian residences and buildings constructed in the 1800s, now homes to charming shops such as the **Art and Antiques Centre of Amelia Island, Susan's Slightly Off-Centre Gallery,** and **Ribault's Gallery.**

Another shopping hotspot is the upscale, sophisticated **Village Spa and Shops** at the entrance to Amelia Plantation. Shop for clothing, gifts, home decor, and more.

Farmers' Markets The Fernandina **Farmers' Market** is located at 11th Street and Atlantic Avenue and offers fresh produce and flowers, as well as cheesecakes, nuts, and occasionally barbecue. The market is open on Saturdays from 9 a.m. to 1 p.m. For more information, contact Eileen Shannon Moore at (904) 261-9679.

Dining

Beech Street Grill

801 Beech Street; (904) 277-3662

Meals served Dinner **Cuisine** Eclectic **Entree range** $22–$35 **Reservations** Recommended **Payment** All major credit cards accepted

Description and Comments "Eclectic" may be the best word to describe the Beech Street Grill. Housed in a Victorian home built in 1889, the restaurant has a fun, yet classical atmosphere, with Mediterranean accents and wine memorabilia. The house specialty is the Parmesan Crusted Snapper, with a mustard basil cream sauce and a tomato-caper confetti. The restaurant has won numerous awards, including a *Wine Spectator* Award of Excellence.

Brett's Waterway Café

1 South Front Street; (904) 261-2660

Meals served Lunch, dinner **Cuisine** Continental **Entree range** Lunch, $6–$15; dinner, $18–$27 **Reservations** For parties of six or more **Payment** V, MC, AmEx

Comments A local favorite, Brett's offers continental dining with a great view—eating here at sunset is particularly nice. Brett's is also known for its martinis; favorites include the cosmopolitan, the appletini, and the chocolate martini.

Crab Trap

31 North Second Street, Fernandina Beach; (904) 261-4749

Meals served Dinner **Cuisine** American/seafood **Entree range** $12–$24 **Reservations** Not accepted **Payment** V, MC, AmEx

Comments This is one of the best-known restaurants on the island. Ask for seafood blackened, broiled, or fried, and try the fresh oysters. The Crab Trap also serves up classics like steak and chicken dinners, as well as hamburgers.

Horizons

802 Ash Street; (904) 321-2430

Meals served Dinner **Cuisine** Continental **Entree range** $16–$19 **Reservations** Accepted **Payment** All major credit cards accepted

Comments Horizons offers upscale, fine dining in a relaxed atmosphere. They're known for fresh seafood, as well as steaks and rack of lamb.

Joe's Second Street Bistro

14 South Second Street; (904) 321-2558

Meals served Dinner **Cuisine** New American **Entree range** $15–$26 **Reservations** Recommended **Payment** All major credit cards accepted

Comments Joe's is known for its excellent desserts—try the apple bread pudding or the Key lime pie. You can choose to eat outdoors on the patio. The atmosphere is "resort casual," and men should wear collared shirts.

Moon River Pizza

925 South 14th Street, Fernandina Beach; (904) 321-3400

Meals served Lunch and dinner **Cuisine** Pizzas and salads **Entree range** Pizzas start at $8 and up **Reservations** No **Payment** Cash only
Comments If you're craving pizza, this family-owned shop is the place. Calzones, pizzas, and salads comprise the menu, with dough and sauce made fresh daily. They offer 20 different toppings, but we recommend their simple white pizza.

Nightlife

Palace Saloon

Who goes there Tourists and locals; a younger crowd on Monday and Thursday

117 Centre Street; (904) 491-3332

Cover $5 on Saturday for the comedy show; $3 Saturday for the bands **Minimum** 21 and up after 9 p.m. during the week, 10 p.m. on weekends; 18 and up for comedy night **Mixed drinks** $4 and up **Food available** Full menu until 9 p.m. during the week and 10 p.m. on weekends **Hours** 11:30 a.m.–2 a.m. daily (closes at midnight some Sundays)
What goes on The Saloon features live bands on Friday and Saturday, 10 p.m. to closing. On Friday nights, a jazz trio performs during dinner (6–10 p.m.), and Saturday is comedy night from 8 p.m. to 10 p.m. Tuesday is karaoke night.
Comments The Palace Saloon is the oldest saloon in Florida, and if a bar can be a tourist attraction, this would be it. Try their famous rum drink, Pirate's Punch, and ask about the resident ghost, Charlie.

O'Kane's Irish Pub & Eatery

Who goes there A healthy mix of locals and tourists

318 Centre Street; (904) 261-1000; www.okanes.com

Cover None **Minimum** None, but after 10 p.m. expect an over-21 crowd **Mixed drinks** $3.75 and up **Food available** Yes, full-service restaurant **Hours** Monday–Thursday, 11:30 a.m.–midnight or later; Friday and Saturday, 11:30 a.m.–2 a.m.; Sunday, noon to midnight
What goes on On Monday and Tuesday nights, enjoy live acoustic guitar. Wednesday through Sunday nights feature a local band that has been playing at the pub since it opened over ten years ago—hear a variety of music, from Jimmy Buffet to Irish jigs.
Comments The award-winning O'Kane's offers small-town comfort combined with a large bar and plenty of food choices. Most people who come here know each other, and that atmosphere is evident whether you're from the area or just visiting.

Jacksonville

One of Florida's major urban areas with miles of Atlantic beaches on its eastern border (and the largest city in land area in the lower 48), busy, sprawling

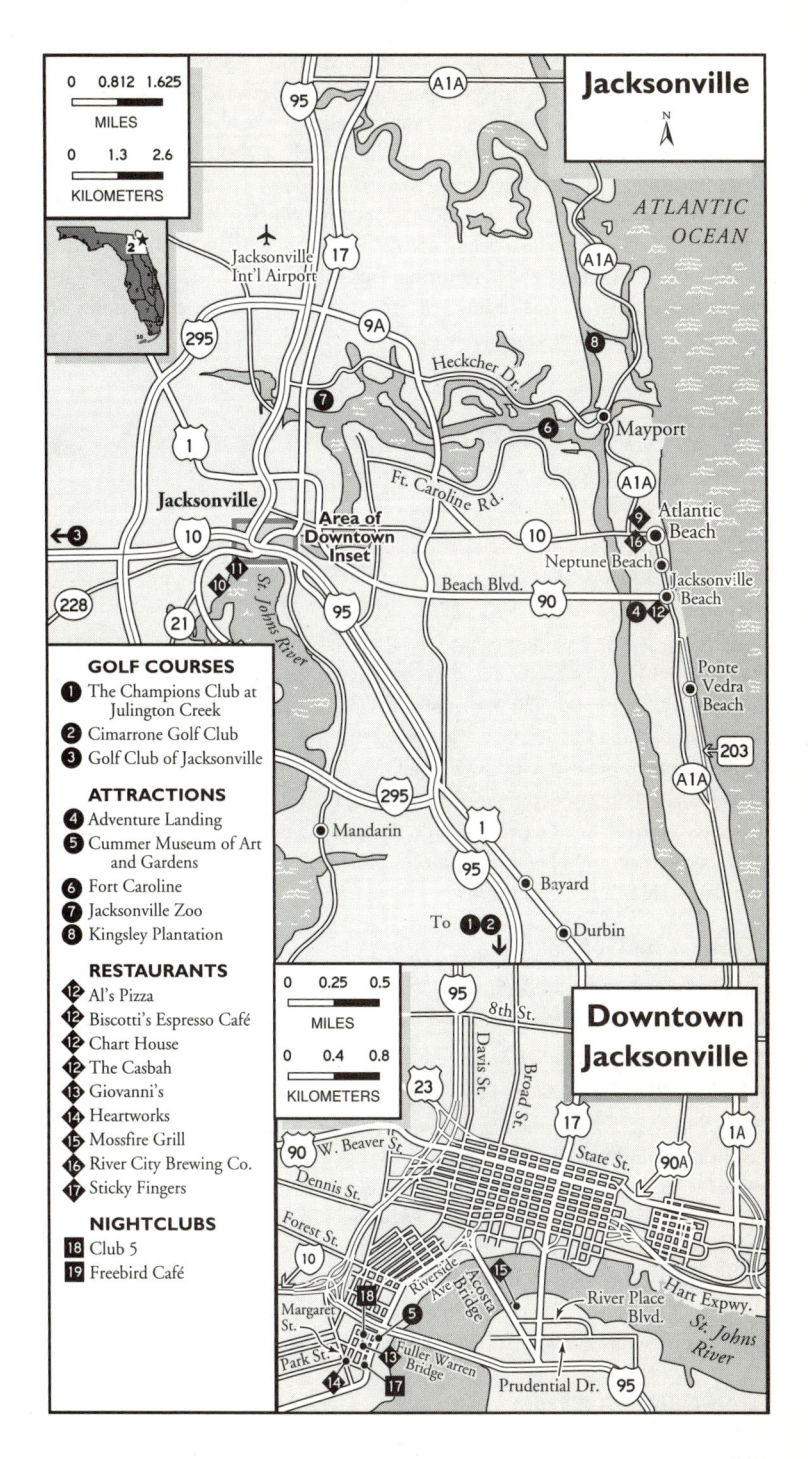

Jacksonville

Downtown Jacksonville

GOLF COURSES
1. The Champions Club at Julington Creek
2. Cimarrone Golf Club
3. Golf Club of Jacksonville

ATTRACTIONS
4. Adventure Landing
5. Cummer Museum of Art and Gardens
6. Fort Caroline
7. Jacksonville Zoo
8. Kingsley Plantation

RESTAURANTS
12. Al's Pizza
12. Biscotti's Espresso Café
12. Chart House
12. The Casbah
13. Giovanni's
14. Heartworks
15. Mossfire Grill
16. River City Brewing Co.
17. Sticky Fingers

NIGHTCLUBS
18. Club 5
19. Freebird Café

165

Jacksonville is centered around the waterfront. The St. Johns River divides the city, with water taxis to carry passengers to Riverwalk and Jacksonville Landing. A Skyway monorail gives riders an elevated view of the city.

Though urban Jacksonville may not be your first choice for a Sunshine State vacation, beyond downtown is another side of Jacksonville, offering hours of exploration and close encounters with Mother Nature. Just a few miles east is Little Talbot Island State Park, one of the few remaining undeveloped barrier islands in Florida. Big Talbot Island, just north of Little Talbot, offers magnificent views from towering dunes, three miles of undeveloped beaches, salt marshes, and a scenic driftwood forest.

Golf

The Champions Club at Julington Creek

1111 Durbin Creek Boulevard; (904) 287-GOLF; www.championsclubgolf.com
Established 1987 (first 9), 1992 (back 9) | **Designer** Steve Melnyk | **Holes** 18

Tees Gold/Blue/White/Green
Par 72/72/72/72 **Slope** 132/127/121/112
Fees Summer, $45 weekdays, $55 weekends; call for winter rates **Specials** Summer twilight, $29 after 2 p.m. weekdays, $35 weekends **Cart rental** Included **Club rental** $20 **Payment** All major credit cards accepted **Tee times** Up to 7 days in advance **Facilities** Pro shop, restaurant, driving range, bunkers, putting green, chipping green
Comments This course is located in the beautiful woodlands of St. Johns County, with plenty of trees and pretty lakes. The course accommodates players of all skill levels—the back tees present quite a challenge, while the front tees are fun for beginners.

Cimarrone Golf Club

2800 Cimarrone Boulevard; (904) 287-2000; www.cimarronegolf.com
Established 1988 | **Designer** David Postlethwait | **Holes** 18

Tees Gold/Black/Blue/White/Red
Par 72/72/72/72/72 **Slope** 132/129/124/120/115
Fees Summer, $50 weekdays, $60 weekends; call for winter rates **Specials** Summer twilight, $28 after 2 p.m. weekdays, after 3 p.m. weekends **Cart rental** Included **Club rental** $15 **Payment** All major credit cards accepted **Tee times** Up to 7 days in advance **Facilities** Driving range, putting green, chipping green, pro shop, restaurant/snack bar
Comments This course has water on every hole, forcing players to hit straight. The most challenging hole is number 18; a par 4 with a 230-yard carry over water, this hole is surrounded by bunkers.

Golf Club of Jacksonville

10440 Tournament Lane; (904) 779-0800; www.golfclubofjacksonville.com

Established 1989 | **Designers** Bobby Weed and Mark McCumber | **Holes** 18

Tees Blue/White/Red **Par** 71/71/71 **Slope** 133/132/120
Fees Weekends, $48 before 12 p.m., $39 after 12 p.m., $29 after 3 p.m.; weekdays, $38 before 12 p.m., $31 after 12 p.m., $26 after 3 p.m **Specials** See above **Cart rental** Included **Club rental** $40 **Payment** V, MC, AmEx
Tee times Up to 14 days in advance **Facilities** Pro shop, restaurant, practice facilities (lighted until 9 p.m.) including putting green, chipping green, driving range, and sand practice areas
Comments The Golf Club of Jacksonville, managed by the PGA Tour, meanders through Florida wetlands. Watch out for number 11—you've got to clear two large wetland areas on this par 4 hole, 459 yards from the back tees.

Attractions

Adventure Landing

1944 Beach Boulevard, Jacksonville Beach; (904) 246-4386; www.adventurelanding.com

Hours Waterpark, 10 a.m.–8 p.m. daily (limited hours off-season); dry park open until 1 a.m.
Admission Waterpark, $22; 42" and under, $19; a $32 ticket includes unlimited go-carts, miniature golf, and laser tag

Appeal by Age Group

Pre-school ★★★	Teens ★★★★★	Over 30 ★★
Grade school ★★★★	Young Adults ★★	Seniors ★

Touring Time *Average* full afternoon or evening; *minimum* 2 hours
Rainy-Day Touring Not recommended
Author's Rating ★★
Description and Comments Jacksonville's largest amusement park and only water park, Adventure Landing features two miniature golf courses, batting cages, go-cart racing, laser tag, and Shipwreck Island, an interactive water park complete with a wave pool, 65-foot-tall Pirate Village with 12 slides, and more than 200 water nozzles. The adventurous will enjoy the Hydro Half Pipe, a U-shaped ride that drops you 40 feet and brings you up again. Note that there are two locations in the Jacksonville area, but only the one in Jacksonville Beach has the water park.

Cummer Museum of Art and Gardens

829 Riverside Avenue, Jacksonville; (904) 356-6857; www.cummer.org

Hours Tuesday and Thursday, 10 a.m.–9 p.m.; Wednesday, Friday, Saturday, 10 a.m.–5 p.m.; Sunday, noon–5 p.m.; closed Monday
Admission $6 for adults, $4 for seniors over age 62 and military personnel, $3 for students and children over age 5, $1 for ages 5 and under; students get in free Tuesday–Friday, 1:30–4:30 p.m.; Tuesday free general admission 4–9 p.m.

Appeal by Age Group

Pre-school ★★	Teens ★★	Over 30 ★★★
Grade school ★★★	Young Adults ★★★	Seniors ★★★

Touring Time *Average* a half-day; *minimum* 2 hours
Rainy-Day Touring Recommended
Author's Rating ★★★; beautiful man-made art combined with splendid natural art
Description and Comments The museum has a beautiful permanent collection with works from the Renaissance, Baroque, Rococo, Impressionist, and Modern periods. And the gardens are amazing—stroll through spectacular displays of flora, divided into three separate sections (the upper, the English, and the Italian gardens). Azaleas are brilliant in the spring, and jasmine and camellias flourish in the cooler months.

Fort Caroline

12713 Fort Caroline Road (off Monument Road), Jacksonville; (904) 641-7155; www.nps.gov/foca

Hours Daily, 9 a.m.–5 p.m.; closed Thanksgiving, Christmas, and New Year's
Admission Free
Appeal by Age Group

Pre-school ★	Teens ★★	Over 30 ★★
Grade school ★★	Young Adults ★★	Seniors ★★

Touring Time *Average* 2–3 hours (1 hour for fort, several hours on trails); *minimum* 45 minutes
Rainy-Day Touring Not recommended
Author's Rating ★★; a chance to get outdoors and see places where history happened
Description and Comments Explore the area's colonial past at this national memorial, where guided tours of the replica sixteenth-century French fort explain the struggle between European colonial powers for control of Florida. Thirty-minute ranger tours are available, followed by fascinating one-hour guided nature walks through the Theodore Roosevelt Area. The two-mile hike along the trail goes into Native American country, inhabited as far back as 500 B.C. For more information and a schedule, call (904) 641-7155.

Jacksonville Zoo

8605 Zoo Parkway, Jacksonville; (904) 757-4462; www.jaxzoo.org

Hours Monday–Friday, 9 a.m.–5 p.m.; Saturday and Sunday, 9 a.m.–6 p.m.; closed Thanksgiving and Christmas
Admission $10 for adults, $8 for seniors ages 65 and older, $5 for children ages 3–12

Appeal by Age Group

Pre-school ★★★	Teens ★★★	Over 30 ★★
Grade school ★★★	Young Adults ★★	Seniors ★★

Touring Time *Average* half a day; *minimum* 2 hours
Rainy-Day Touring Not recommended
Author's Rating ★★
Description and Comments The Jacksonville Zoo borders the Trout River and features over 1,000 animals in habitats designed to imitate their native environments. Two popular exhibits are the Wild Florida area with black bears, bald eagles, river otters, and other native species, and the Outback Australian Adventure, which displays koalas, kangaroos, wallabies, and more. From the Seronera Overlook, get a unique view of elephants and Cape buffalo. Other zoo favorites include cheetahs, Nile crocodiles, antelope, lions, giraffes, birds, and primates.

Kingsley Plantation

11676 Palmetto Avenue, Jacksonville; (904) 251-3537; www.nps.gov/timu

Hours Daily, 9 a.m.–5 p.m.; closed Thanksgiving, Christmas, and New Year's
Admission Free, but donations are appreciated
Appeal by Age Group

Pre-school ★	Teens ★★★	Over 30 ★★★
Grade school ★★	Young Adults ★★★	Seniors ★★★

Touring Time *Average* 1–2 hours; *minimum* 1 hour
Rainy-Day Touring Not recommended
Author's Rating ★★★; fascinating peek into history; the natural scenery is right out of a picture book, with spectacular views of barrier islands and savannahs
Description and Comments The plantation is the oldest in Florida, built in 1798 on Fort George Island near Jacksonville. Cotton and other crops were cultivated here in the eighteenth and nineteenth centuries, and it is now a State Historic Site preserved by the National Park Service as part of the Timucuan Ecological and Historic Preserve. You can tour the kitchen house, a barn/carriage house, and the remains of 23 slave cabins.

Between 1814 and 1839, British merchant Zephaniah Kingsley purchased about 32,000 acres of land in northeast Florida, including the 1,000-acre Fort George Island that houses the plantation. Kingsley and his wife, an African slave he purchased and then freed, managed the plantation and slaves together.

Shopping

For posh boutiques and classy sidewalk cafés, head to **Avondale,** an upscale strip of historic buildings and tree-lined streets home to numerous sophisticated shops and eateries. The nearby Five Points shopping district, where five streets intersect, offers shopping in a hip, energetic atmosphere known for its people-watching. Here, you'll find artsy coffeehouses, vintage clothing stores, shoe shops, and stylish boutiques, as well as several restaurants. Avondale and Five Points are located on the northwest bank.

At **San Marco Square,** on the south bank, you'll find classy shops selling everything, from home decor to ice cream, clothing to kitchen supplies. Unwind at the little park here, where you can relax on a bench and listen to gurgling fountains next to a pretty gazebo.

The **Avenues Mall** is located at 10300 Southside Boulevard (phone (904) 363-3060) and features mall regulars including the Gap, Abercrombie and Fitch, and Express, as well as department stores JCPenney, Sears, Belk, and Dillard's. The clean, well-maintained mall is two-stories tall, and if food court fare doesn't suit you, you'll find several restaurants close by.

Farmers' Markets The Jacksonville **Farmers' Market** is open all day, every day, selling fresh produce. The market is located at 1780 West Beaver Street (phone (904) 354-2821).

Pecan Park Flea and Farmers' Market (614 Pecan Park Road; (904) 751-6770) offers goods from about 450 vendors on Saturday and Sunday from 8 a.m. to 5 p.m. Find fresh produce, fruits, and flowers in the farmers' market section.

Dining

Al's Pizza

303 Atlantic Boulevard, Atlantic Beach; (904) 249-0002

Meals served Lunch, dinner **Cuisine** Italian **Entree range** $6–$21 **Reservations** Not accepted **Payment** V, MC, AmEx

Comments A Jacksonville favorite, Al's serves up great pizza, as well as calzones, pastas, subs, and more.

Biscotti's Espresso Café

3556 St. Johns Avenue, Jacksonville; (904) 387-2060

Meals served Lunch, dinner, breakfast (closed Monday) **Cuisine** Mediterranean **Entree range** $11–$21 **Reservations** Not accepted **Payment** All major credit cards accepted

Comments This bistro-style neighborhood café sports a great atmosphere, accentuated with exposed beam ceilings and brick walls displaying local art. You'll find fresh fish, a wide range of pastas, salads, pizzas, and more, but be sure to save room for the café's popular desserts. Try the Oreo mousse cake or the cappuccino torte.

The Casbah

3628 St. Johns Avenue (in Avondale); (904) 981-9966

Meals served Lunch, dinner **Cuisine** Middle Eastern **Entree range** $14–$22 **Reservations** Not accepted **Payment** V, MC, AmEx

Comments You can choose to sit at a table, at the bar, or on the floor at this unique, Middle Eastern restaurant where bellydancers entertain diners Thursday through Saturday on the hour, 7–11 p.m. With swords on the wall and fresh flowers on each table, The Casbah serves healthy portions of lavish atmosphere in a small and intimate setting.

Giovanni's

1161 Beach Boulevard, Jacksonville Beach; (904) 249-7787

Meals served Dinner **Cuisine** Continental, with an Italian flair **Entree range** $18–$36 **Reservations** Recommended **Payment** V, MC, AmEx

Comments Giovanni's offers creative dishes with an Italian influence in a contemporary atmosphere. For example, the pan-seared snapper with black olives, pine nuts, tomatoes, and capers, served atop fresh arugula, with a warm lump crab and shrimp salad. Upstairs you'll find a piano bar.

Heartworks

820 Lomax Street; (904) 355-6210

Meals served Lunch, Monday–Saturday; dinner, Thursday and Friday, 6–9 p.m.; brunch, Sunday 10 a.m.–2 p.m. **Cuisine** Vegetarian **Entree range** $3–$11 **Reservations** Not recommended **Payment** V, MC

Comments This eclectic little café offers a vegetarian and vegan menu that features more than just salads; even nonvegetarians are sure to find something appetizing. Two popular entrees are the carrot dogs and the black-bean burrito. Local artwork is displayed in this part-gallery, part-café.

Mossfire Grill

1537 Margaret Street; (904) 355-4434

Meals served Lunch, dinner **Cuisine** Southwestern **Entree range** $8–$16 **Reservations** Not accepted; preferred seating available **Payment** V, MC, AmEx

Comments This comfortable, family-friendly restaurant sports a Southwestern motif and excellent food that keeps locals and tourists coming back for seconds. Ample servings, tasty burritos, and a good martini menu are all reasons to try this Jacksonville favorite.

Sticky Fingers

363 Atlantic Boulevard, Atlantic Beach; (904) 241-7427

Meals served Lunch, dinner **Cuisine** Barbecue **Entree range** $6–$19 **Reservations** Not accepted **Payment** All major credit cards accepted

Comments Pictures of jazz musicians adorn the walls and blues music plays in the background of this popular barbecue restaurant known for its ribs.

Arts and Culture

The **Alexander Brest Museum** (2800 North University Boulevard; (904) 256-7371) is located on the Jacksonville University campus and displays a collection of pre-Columbian art; one of the highlights is the room full of ivory pieces—ranging from statues, Oriental figures, and headwear to cabinets inlaid with ivory. Admission is free, as is parking in visitor lots.

The **Museum of Southern History** (4304 Herschel Street; (904) 388-3574) displays a collection of exhibits detailing the Civil War; see wax sculptures of famous war figures, as well as other exhibits and artifacts pertaining to the South's antebellum period.

Nightlife

Club 5

Who goes there Young partiers; crowd depends on the show

1028 Park Street; (904) 356-5555

Cover $5 over 21; $10 18–20; prices vary depending on the band **Minimum** None **Mixed drinks** $3.75 and up **Food available** No **Hours** Thursday–Saturday, opens at 9 p.m. but closing depends on the crowd and band (it can be as late as 4 a.m.); Sunday, 6 p.m.–2 a.m.

What goes on Club 5 attracts a wide range of bands, both local and nationally touring, representing all styles of music, from bluegrass to heavy metal. Friday and Saturday nights feature DJs, while the shows are mostly on Thursday nights.

Comments Club 5 is located in a historic building built in the 1920s, which served as Jacksonville's first movie theater. The crowd, atmosphere, and cover charge change with the bands.

Freebird Café

Who goes there Anyone and everyone, ranging from hippies to punks, depending on the band playing

200 North First Street; (904) 246-2473

Cover $5–$50, depending on the band **Minimum** None **Mixed drinks** $3.25 and up **Food available** Full menu until the band starts (about 8:30 or 9 p.m.) **Hours** Wednesday–Sunday, 5 p.m.–2 a .m.

What goes on The main focus here is the music—see live bands every night they're open, with styles ranging from hard rock to blues, punk to jazz, with occasional jam nights.

Comments This two-story restaurant and music venue features an open-air wraparound porch upstairs and Lynyrd Skynyrd memorabilia, including gold and platinum records.

River City Brewing Co.

Who goes there Workers for happy hour, upper class, professionals

835 Museum Circle; (904) 398-2299

Cover None **Minimum** None **Mixed drinks** $5 and up **Food available** Menu available until 10 p.m. during the week, 11 p.m. on weekends **Hours** Monday–Thursday, 3–10 p.m.; weekends, noon–midnight

What goes on Live music and DJs on the weekend; happy hour every day. Listen to music and sip a drink outside on the deck, weather permitting.

Comments This upscale restaurant also includes a bar that is popular with professionals winding down after work. The bar takes on a club-like atmosphere at night, with DJs and occasional live music.

Side Trips

Ponte Vedra Inn and Club This seaside retreat dates back to 1928, and generations of fiercely loyal visitors have been returning for decades. The impeccable service, gently sloped white beaches, oversized rooms, luxurious amenities—including two 18-hole golf courses, notable tennis courts, and an award-winning spa—keep pampered guests coming back. Add to that four pools, fishing, and sailing.

Gear and bait are available for fishing in Lake Vedra. Trail rides and lessons are available at nearby Sawgrass Stables. For a day at the beach, bicycles, boogie boards, surfboards, paddleball equipment, volleyballs, Frisbees, ocean kayaks, and even sand buckets are for rent.

Most rooms have refrigerators; some have kitchenettes. Rates are seasonal and start at $200, with children ages 18 and under free in parents' room. Located at 200 Ponte Vedra Boulevard, Ponte Vedra Beach (20 minutes southeast of Jacksonville); (800) 234-7842; **www.pvresorts.com**.

St. Augustine

St. Augustine is not only the oldest city in the United States, but probably the oldest Florida vacation stopover.

We recommend spending a day or two in St. Augustine—longer if you also want to spend some time at the beach, just minutes from the heart of town and less crowded than those farther south. To get the most out of your stay, settle into one of the local bed-and-breakfasts.

The city of St. Augustine is a tourist attraction in itself, an amazing composite of the lavish splendor of Florida's early boom years and the honest simplicity of the city's ancient heritage. Narrow streets, warm and intimate, fronted with the worn but enduring homes and courtyards of long-departed garrison populations, blend almost effortlessly with the embellished Spanish Renaissance design of Flagler College, formerly the Ponce de Leon Hotel; the former Alcazar Hotel, now city hall; and modern downtown St. Augustine.

Much of St. Augustine can be enjoyed without admission charges; the city's lovely thoroughfares and aged streets are treasures.

The city is busiest in summer, on weekends, and during holiday periods. At many other times of the year, you can almost have the place to yourself. Getting oriented is not difficult; stop at the official information center at the corner of San Marco Avenue, SR A1A, and Castillo Drive as you enter the city from the north. The information center has plenty of free maps, brochures, and hotel and restaurant information.

It's best to take a drive around St. Augustine and get a feel for the city. Be sure to drive up and down the small side streets on both the north and south

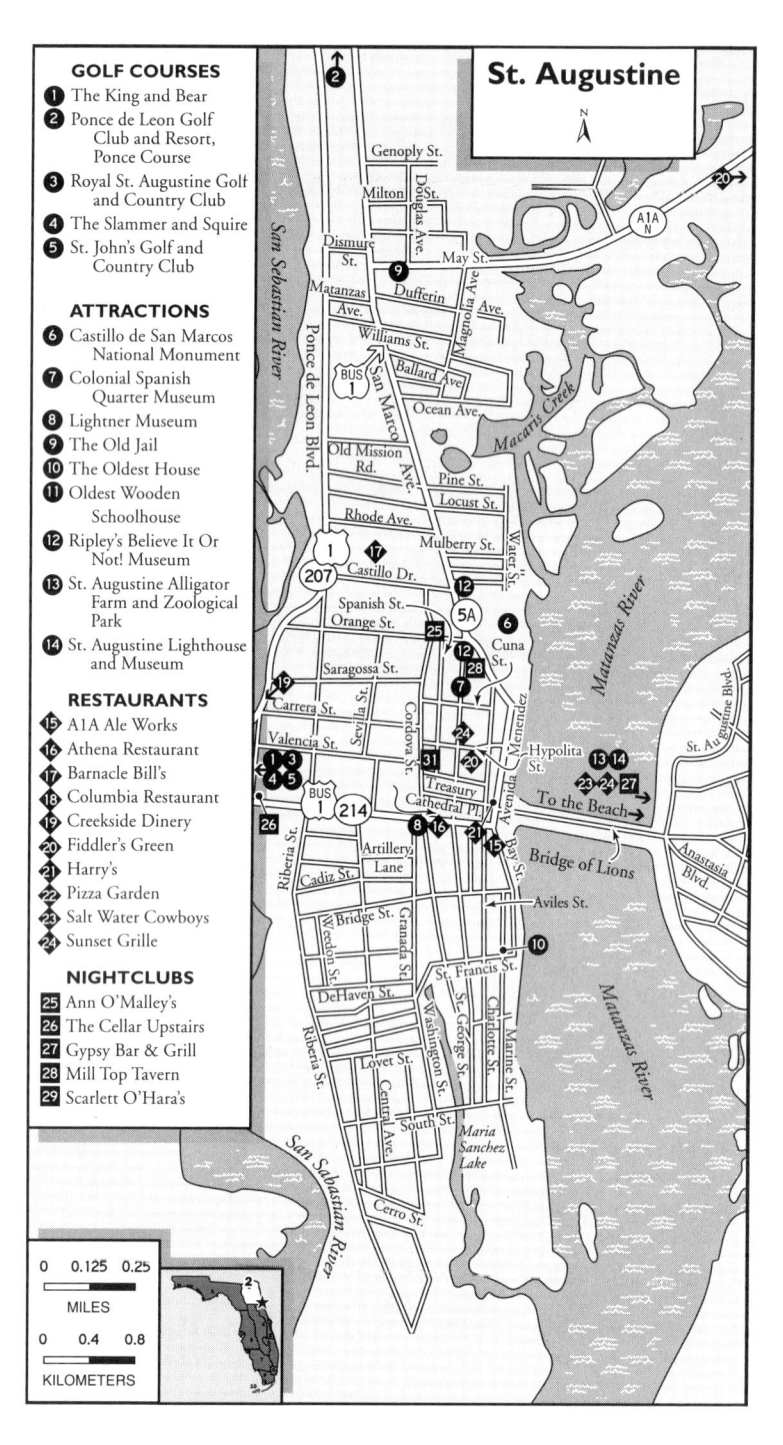

St. Augustine

GOLF COURSES
1. The King and Bear
2. Ponce de Leon Golf Club and Resort, Ponce Course
3. Royal St. Augustine Golf and Country Club
4. The Slammer and Squire
5. St. John's Golf and Country Club

ATTRACTIONS
6. Castillo de San Marcos National Monument
7. Colonial Spanish Quarter Museum
8. Lightner Museum
9. The Old Jail
10. The Oldest House
11. Oldest Wooden Schoolhouse
12. Ripley's Believe It Or Not! Museum
13. St. Augustine Alligator Farm and Zoological Park
14. St. Augustine Lighthouse and Museum

RESTAURANTS
15. A1A Ale Works
16. Athena Restaurant
17. Barnacle Bill's
18. Columbia Restaurant
19. Creekside Dinery
20. Fiddler's Green
21. Harry's
22. Pizza Garden
23. Salt Water Cowboys
24. Sunset Grille

NIGHTCLUBS
25. Ann O'Malley's
26. The Cellar Upstairs
27. Gypsy Bar & Grill
28. Mill Top Tavern
29. Scarlett O'Hara's

174

sides of the plaza (central square). Next take a walking tour that includes the restoration area, much of which is limited exclusively to pedestrian traffic. Don't rush your visit; we recommend short walking tours punctuated with meals, a few hours at the beaches, or maybe a nap at the hotel. The sightseeing trains are a good alternative to walking, stopping at several points along the way (you can disembark and jump back on later, as the tours run throughout the day) and giving a good narrated orientation to the city.

Golf

The King and Bear

1 King and Bear Drive; (904) 940-6200

Established 2000 | **Designers** Jack Nicklaus and Arnold Palmer | **Holes** 18

Tees Stone/Black/Blue/White/Green
Par 72/72/72/72/72 **Slope** 141/139/135/128 (men)/137 (women)/123
Fees $79–$200, depending on season **Specials** Call for current specials **Cart rental** Included **Club rental** $40 **Payment** All major credit cards accepted **Tee times** Up to a year in advance **Facilities** Pro shop, restaurant and bar, driving range, putting green, chipping green, showers, dressing room **Comments** Two of the biggest names in golf, Arnold Palmer and Jack Nicklaus, paired to create this challenging course. You'll have to navigate water on 17 holes; much of the course's challenge is off the tee. The front is links style and has an open feel, while the back winds through clusters of oak trees—some of which are over 100 years old.

Ponce de Leon Golf Club and Resort, Ponce Course

4000 US 1 North; (904) 829-5314 or (888) 829-5314; www.theponce.com

Established 1916 | **Designer** Donald Ross | **Holes** 18

Tees Stone/Gold/White/Red
Par 72/72/72/72 **Slope** 131/127/123 (men)/133 (women)/121
Fees Average summer $35, winter $60 **Specials** Twilight specials available after 11 a.m. and 3 p.m. in summer; one rate change available in winter **Cart rental** Included **Club rental** $20 **Payment** All major credit cards accepted **Tee times** No limit on reservations **Facilities** Pro Shop, snack bar, putting green, practice bunker, driving range, chipping green, par 3 course **Comments** Coastal breezes off the Intracoastal Waterway add an interesting dynamic to this Donald Ross course (they also help keep players cool in the summer). The front 9 is links style, while the back 9 sports a more traditional, wooded style.

Royal St. Augustine Golf and Country Club

301 Royal St. Augustine Boulevard; (904) 824-4653

Established 2000 | **Designer** Christopher Commins | **Holes** 18

Tees Gold/Blue/White/Red **Par** 71/71/71/71 **Slope** 137/131/121/123

Fees Summer, $31 weekdays, $36 weekends; winter average, $36 weekdays, $40 weekends **Specials** Summer-twilight special, $25 after 2 p.m. weekdays, $29 weekends **Cart rental** Included **Club rental** $15 **Payment** V, MC, AmEx **Tee times** Up to 7 days in advance **Facilities** Pro shop, restaurant, bar, driving range, putting green

Comments This par-71, rolling course has plenty of moguls, lakes, and waste bunkers to spice up the game. You'll find the biggest challenge on hole 12; this par 5 has out-of-bounds on the right and water on the left, putting a premium on driving.

St. John's Golf and Country Club

4900 Cypress Links Boulevard; (904) 825-4900

Established 1989 | **Designer** Bob Walker | **Holes** 27

Tees Gold/Blue/White/Red

Par North/East 72; East/South 71; South/North 71

Slope North/East 136/128/124/117; East/South 136/126/121/117; South/North 130/124/118/115

Fees Summer, $31 weekdays, $36 weekends; winter, $40 **Specials** Summer after 1 p.m., $22 **Cart rental** Not required in summer (walking rate, $19 weekdays); required in winter **Club rental** $25 **Payment** All major credit cards accepted **Tee times** Up to 7 days in advance **Facilities** Pro shop, restaurant, driving range, chipping green, putting green

Comments Each 9 has a slightly different feel to it, but any way you play it, the course is fair yet challenging.

The Slammer and Squire

2 World Golf Place; (904) 940-6100

Established 1998 | **Designer** Bobby Weed (with Gene Sarazen and Sam Snead as consultants) | **Holes** 18

Tees Stone/Black/Blue/White/Green **Par** 72/72/72/72/72

Slope 135/128/123 (men)/131 (women)/119 (men)/124 (women)/116

Fees $49–$175, depending on season **Specials** Call for current specials **Cart rental** Included **Club rental** $40 **Payment** All major credit cards accepted **Tee times** Up to a year in advance **Facilities** Pro shop, restaurant and bar, driving range, putting green, chipping green, showers, dressing room

Comments The Slammer and Squire, always well maintained, offers challenges galore, especially around the greens. The front is open, while the back has plenty of loblolly pines.

St. Augustine

Attractions

Castillo de San Marcos National Monument
1 South Castillo Drive; (904) 829-6506; www.nps.gov/casa

Hours Daily, 8:45 a.m.– 4:45 p.m.; closed Christmas
Admission $5 for adults, $2 children ages 6–16, under age 6 free
Appeal by Age Group

Pre-school ★★	Teens ★★★	Over 30 ★★★
Grade school ★★★	Young Adults ★★★	Seniors ★★★

Touring Time *Average* 1–3 hours; *minimum* 45 minutes
Rainy-Day Touring Not recommended
Author's Rating ★★★

Description and Comments The oldest masonry fort in the continental United States, this monument was constructed of native shell stone (coquina) between 1672 and 1695 by the Spanish to guard St. Augustine from pirate raids and from Great Britain during a time when this coastline was an explosive international battleground.

A double drawbridge over a 40-foot moat makes an impressive entrance for this massive coquina fort. You can tour prison cells, the chapel, guardrooms, and more with a self-guided tour map. The staff is quite helpful, and rangers give 15-minute talks every hour, on the hour. During certain months, witness the cannon being fired by costumed soldiers.

Colonial Spanish Quarter Museum
53 St. George Street; (904) 825-6830

Hours Daily, 9 a.m.–5:30 p.m. (last ticket sold at 4:45 p.m.)
Admission $7 for adults, $6 for seniors, $4 for children ages 6–18, free for children ages 5 and under
Appeal by Age Group

Pre-school ★★	Teens ★★★	Over 30 ★★★
Grade school ★★★	Young Adults ★★★	Seniors ★★★

Touring Time *Average* 2–3 hours; *minimum* 1.5 hours
Rainy-Day Touring Not recommended
Author's Rating ★★★; this little area really brings history to life

Description and Comments This restored part of old St. Augustine, operated by the state of Florida, shows how life was lived in the 1740s. If you're interested in the old city you won't want to miss this part of St. Augustine. This living history museum has demonstrations by candlemakers, leather workers, blacksmiths, carpenters, cooks, seamstresses, and herbalists, all showing how the work was done in the eighteenth century. Today there are six restored and reconstructed houses and a blacksmith shop.

Lightner Museum

75 King Street; (904) 824-2874; www.lightnermuseum.org
Hours Daily, 9 a.m.–5 p.m.; closed Christmas
Admission $6 for adults, $2 ages 12–18, free for children ages 12 and under
Appeal by Age Group

Pre-school ★	Teens ★★	Over 30 ★★★
Grade school ★	Young Adults ★★★	Seniors ★★★

Touring Time *Average* 2–3 hours; *minimum* 2 hours
Rainy-Day Touring Recommended
Author's Rating ★★★

Description and Comments Ask the locals about what not to miss in St. Augustine, and the Lightner Museum is mentioned time after time. There's a well-justified sense of civic pride in this not-for-profit museum.

The museum is housed in what once was the 300-room Alcazar hotel, constructed in 1888 by railway magnate Henry Flagler. Closed in 1930, the hotel was bought in 1947 by Otto C. Lightner of Chicago. Lightner, who died in 1950, donated the building and his collection to the citizens of St. Augustine.

The museum has been called the "Little Smithsonian of Florida." The vast collection includes Tiffany glass, extraordinary music boxes, beautiful furnishings, and other artifacts of the nineteenth century. The hotel's swimming pool, known as the world's largest in 1888, now houses a café and shops.

The Old Jail

167 San Marco Avenue; (904) 829-3800
Hours Daily, 8:30 a.m.–4:30 p.m.; closed Christmas Eve day, Christmas, and Easter
Admission $5 for adults, $4 for children ages 6–12 (Note: Special tickets can be purchased at the Old Jail for admission into St. Augustine Historical Tours, the Old Jail, and the Florida Heritage Museum all located at 167 San Marco Avenue. Tickets are $25 for adults and $19 for children ages 6–12.)
Appeal by Age Group

Pre-school ★	Teens ★★	Over 30 ★
Grade school ★★	Young Adults ★	Seniors ★

Touring Time *Minimum* 30 minutes
Rainy-Day Touring Recommended
Author's Rating ★★

Description and Comments Fun tours are given by costumed guides playing different roles (such as the sheriff, his wife, or an inmate) in this attraction that epitomizes small-town jails of the Deep South in the late 1800s through about 1940. Spartan, austere, cramped, and hot pretty well sum up the centerpiece of the attraction, but there's a neat collection of manacles, knives, small arms, and other weapons and memorabilia. You get to clamber up and down the stairs and gawk at the cellblocks, bunks, steel tables, and other trappings of prisoner life.

The Oldest House

14 St. Francis Street; (904) 824-2872; www.oldcity.com/oldhouse

Hours Daily, 9 a.m.–5 p.m.; closed Thanksgiving, Christmas, and Easter. Tours depart on the hour and half-hour, with the last tour leaving at 4:30 p.m.

Admission $6 for adults, $6 for seniors, $4 for students, free for children ages 6 and under, $14 for families

Appeal by Age Group

Pre-school ★	Teens ★★	Over 30 ★★★
Grade school ★★	Young Adults ★★★	Seniors ★★★

Touring Time *Average* 1–2 hours; *minimum* 1 hour
Rainy-Day Touring Recommended
Author's Rating ★★★

Description and Comments The Oldest House is one of the "must" stops for history buffs. There's been a house on this site since the seventeenth century, but the first one probably was burned by the British in 1702. Today, the Gonzales-Alvarez House is there, where Tomas Gonzales lived from about 1727 to 1763. The Alvarez family bought the house at an auction in 1790. The downstairs furniture is Spanish; most of it is more than 200 years old. The oldest piece—a credenza—dates back more than 500 years. Only the first floor is wheelchair accessible, but nonambulatory guests are admitted free, and a video of the second floor is available.

Oldest Wooden Schoolhouse

14 St. George Street; (904) 824-0192, (888) 653-7245; www.oldestschoolhouse.com

Hours Daily, 9 a.m.–5 p.m.

Admission $3 for adults, $3 for seniors (ages 55 and older) and military, $2 for children ages 6–12, free for children under age 6

Appeal by Age Group

Pre-school ★	Teens ★★	Over 30 ★★
Grade school ★★	Young Adults ★★	Seniors ★★

Touring Time *Average* 15 minutes; *minimum* 10 minutes
Rainy-Day Touring Recommended
Author's Rating ★

Description and Comments Unless you're a real student of this sort of thing, so to speak, a stroll through the Oldest Wooden Schoolhouse will take less than 15 minutes. This schoolhouse, constructed of red cedar and cypress joined by wooden pegs and handmade nails, was built before the American Revolution. A backyard kitchen contains cooking utensils used during colonial times. It is the oldest wooden structure in St. Augustine and is entirely original.

The classroom is re-created today using animatronics of pupils and a teacher. The last class attended school here in 1864.

Ripley's Believe It Or Not! Museum

19 San Marco Avenue, just north of the fort; (904) 824-1606; www.staugustine-ripleys.com

Hours Monday–Friday, 9 a.m.–7 p.m.; Saturday and Sunday, 9 a.m.–8 p.m.
Admission $11 for adults, $7 for children ages 5–12, $8 for seniors
Appeal by Age Group

Pre-school ★★★	Teens ★★★	Over 30 ★★
Grade school ★★★	Young Adults ★★★	Seniors ★★

Touring Time *Average* 2–3 hours; *minimum* 1 hour
Rainy-Day Touring Recommended
Author's Rating ★★★; full of fun, fascinating stuff
Description and Comments People are fascinated by weird things, and the Ripley's Believe It or Not! Museum is the height of weirdness.

Where else can you find paintings on ordinary potato chips, a genuine shrunken head from Ecuador, or the disciples at the Last Supper sculpted of pecans? There are plenty of exhibits like those representing genuine oddities produced by man or natural mishap, all of them fascinating.

The museum building is interesting in its own right. It's the old Castle Warden, built in 1888 by an associate of Henry Flagler, the railroad company official who was so influential in Florida's development.

St. Augustine Alligator Farm and Zoological Park

999 Anastasia Boulevard; (904) 824-3337; www.alligatorfarm.com

Hours Daily, 9 a.m.–6 p.m.; 9 a.m.–5 p.m. after Labor Day
Admission $15 for adults, $9 for children ages 5–11, under age 5 free
Appeal by Age Group

Pre-school ★★★	Teens ★★★	Over 30 ★★★
Grade school ★★★	Young Adults ★★★	Seniors ★★★

Touring Time *Average* 2–4 hours; *minimum* 2 hours
Rainy-Day Touring Not recommended
Author's Rating ★★★; the way attractions used to be—low key, clean, fun, and uncrowded
Description and Comments Founded in 1893, this attraction really is a piece of old Florida that has aged gracefully. There is cool shade everywhere and beautiful boardwalks through the wetlands. The park's rookery is especially neat in the spring, when you can see the newborns in their nests. The presence of the alligators keeps out such predators as raccoons and snakes, so birds find the swampy lagoon an ideal nesting place.

Be sure to check out the rare albino alligators: Only 30 of these creatures are estimated living in the world. The Alligator Farm is the only attraction in the world where you can see a complete collection of crocodilians—all 23 species—in one place.

The 20-minute-long alligator and reptile shows throughout the day are educational and quite entertaining in an old-fashioned sort of way.

St. Augustine Lighthouse and Museum

81 Lighthouse Avenue; (904) 829-0745; www.staugustinelighthouse.com

Hours Daily, 9 a.m.–7 p.m.; 9 a.m.–6 p.m. in the winter

Admission $7 for adults, $6 for seniors over age 55, $5 for children ages 7–11, free for children under age 7

Appeal by Age Group

Pre-school ★★★	Teens ★★	Over 30 ★★
Grade school ★★★★	Young Adults ★★★	Seniors ★★

Children must be 7 years old and 48" to climb tower.

Touring Time *Average* 1–2 hours; *minimum* 1 hour

Rainy-Day Touring Recommended

Author's Rating ★★; it's fun to climb the winding stairs, and the view is definitely worth the climb.

Description and Comments This is the site of Florida's first lighthouse, and today's lighthouse is an active aid to navigation, with a beam that can be seen for 19 nautical miles. The tower is 165 feet tall with 219 steps that can be climbed for a panoramic view of St. Augustine and the beaches.

The Spanish erected a wooden watchtower here in 1565, and in 1824 it officially became Florida's first lighthouse. By 1870 erosion threatened the tower, and the current light tower replaced the original in 1875. A lightkeeper's house was added, and lightkeepers and their families lived and worked on the site until 1955.

FREE OR ALMOST FREE

Chocolate lovers, head to Whetstone Chocolates (2 Coke Road; (904) 825-1700) for a tour of the chocolate factory and some yummy free samples. Self-guided tours are available from 10 a.m. to 5 p.m., Monday through Saturday. A video steps you through the production of chocolate. A walking tour gives you views of the machines and workers producing the candies.

Tours

Ghost Tours of St. Augustine

Meets every night at the city gate; (888) 461-1009; www.ghosttoursofstaugustine.com

Hours Nightly walks begin at 8 p.m., 9:30 p.m. Friday and Saturday

Admission $8 per person, free for children under age 5

Appeal by Age Group

Pre-school ★★★	Teens ★★★	Over 30 ★★★
Grade school ★★★	Young Adults ★★★	Seniors ★★★

Touring Time *Average* 1½ hour; *minimum* 1 hour
Rainy-Day Touring Not recommended
Author's Rating ★★★
Description and Comments Does Henry Flagler really haunt the hallways of Flagler College? Does a lone soldier still guard a home on St. George Street? Tour through the streets by lantern light and enjoy spooky tales of centuries past, legendary stories, and folklore.

Old Town Trolley Tours

167 San Marco Avenue; (904) 829-3800
Hours 8:30 a.m.–4:30 p.m. daily
Admission $15 per person, $5 for children ages 6–12, free for children ages 5 and under (Note: Special tickets can be purchased at the Old Jail for admission into St. Augustine Historical Tours, the Old Jail, and the Florida Heritage Museum all located at 167 San Marco Avenue. Tickets are $25 for adults and $19 for children ages 6–12.)

Appeal by Age Group

Pre-school ★★	Teens ★★★	Over 30 ★★★
Grade school ★★	Young Adults ★★★	Seniors ★★★

Touring Time 1 hour
Rainy-Day Touring OK; ponchos are available
Author's Rating ★★★
Description and Comments The trolleys stop at several points throughout the city, and riders can disembark, visit an attraction, then catch the next trolley about 15 minutes later. The narrated tour is an interesting overview of the city.

St. Augustine Scenic Cruises

Depart from Municipal Marina, just south of the Bridge of Lions; (800) 542-8316; www.scenic-cruise.com
Hours Schedules change, so call for hours; in the summer, tours run 11 a.m.–8:30 p.m.; Labor Day through October, the last tour is at 6:15 p.m.; October through March, tours end at 4:30 p.m.
Admission $12 for adults, $9 for seniors over age 60, $8 for children ages 13–18, $6 for children ages 5–12, free for children ages 4 and under

Appeal by Age Group

Pre-school ★★	Teens ★★	Over 30 ★★
Grade school ★★	Young Adults ★★	Seniors ★★★

Touring Time 75 minutes
Rainy-Day Touring Not recommended

Author's Rating ★★

Description and Comments Owned by the Usina family since the turn of the century, this is a great way to get out on the beautiful bay without piloting your own craft. Watch for frolicking dolphins and shorebirds. Rest rooms on board.

SAN SEBASTIAN WINERY

It's been said that St. Augustine is the birthplace of American wine. Wine connoisseurs and non-drinkers alike will enjoy a tour of the San Sebastian Winery (157 King Street; (888) 352-9463; www.sansebastianwinery.com). This classy winery offers fascinating tours and tastings every day of the week. Your guide will walk you through the winemaking process while touring the 18,000-square-foot facility. After the tour, you'll get to taste the product for yourself. There's also a gift shop and an upstairs wine and jazz club, The Cellar Upstairs.

St. Augustine Sightseeing Trains

170 San Marco Avenue; (904) 829-6545, (800) 226-6545; www.redtrains.com

Hours Daily, 8:30 a.m.–5 p.m., with departures every 15–20 minutes

Admission $15 for adults, $5 for children ages 6–12, free for ages under 6

Appeal by Age Group

Pre-school ★★	Teens ★★	Over 30 ★★★
Grade school ★★	Young Adults ★★	Seniors ★★

Touring Time Tour runs 1 hour long; visiting attractions adds extra time

Rainy-Day Touring Yes (trains are covered to protect from rain)

Author's Rating ★★★

Description and Comments A great way to relax and avoid the traffic on the narrow streets of St. Augustine—plus get a quick and fairly interesting history lesson that covers 500 years. Tickets include stop-off privileges at attractions.

St. Augustine Transfer Co.

Bayfront near entrance to Fort Castillo de San Marcos; (904) 829-2818; www.staugustinetransfer.com

Hours Daily, 9:30 a.m.–11 p.m.

Admission $20 for adults, $10 for children ages 5–11, free for children ages 4 and under (call for private tour prices)

Appeal by Age Group

Pre-school ★★	Teens ★★	Over 30 ★★
Grade school ★★	Young Adults ★★	Seniors ★★

Touring Time *Average* 1 hour; *minimum* 45 minutes

Rainy-Day Touring OK, because carriage is covered

Author's Rating ★★; good way to get acclimated; especially nice at sunset

Description and Comments This family-owned business has been showing visitors around town since 1877. The quaint carriages are a pleasant, relaxing way to see the sights, especially if your driver knows a little history and likes to chat.

Shopping

St. Augustine is an antiquer's paradise. The city itself is so infused with history, is it any wonder that some of the best antiques can be found within city limits? The best places to find that special something are the **Lightner Museum Courtyard** and the antique district on San Marco Avenue. The antique district is located a block north of the visitor center and just north of Ripley's Believe It or Not.

The Oldest City is also home to two outlet malls. **Belz Factory Outlet World,** an enclosed outlet mall, is located off of I-95 (500 Belz Outlet Boulevard; (904) 826-1311; **www.belz.com**) and features almost 70 name-brand merchants, including Nike, Liz Claiborne, Guess, and Tommy Hilfiger. The **St. Augustine Premium Outlet Center** (2700 SR 16; (904) 825-1555; **www.premiumoutlets.com**) features close to 90 outlets; star players include Gap, Mikasa, Movado, and Brooks Brothers.

Another great shopping district is the four-block walking-only section of **St. George Street.** You'll find dozens of quaint shops selling everything from glass and pottery to leather goods, shells, and unique gifts. It's best to park at the visitor center ($5 per day), which is in walking distance of both St. George Street and the antique district on San Marco Avenue.

Farmers' Markets You can find two farmers' markets in St. Augustine: The **St. Augustine Beach Farmers' and Crafts Market** is held on Wednesdays, from 7 a.m. to 12:30 p.m., at the St. Johns County Pier (phone (904) 471-1686). The market features fresh produce and seafood, as well as a wide range of arts and crafts, including fine arts, jewelry, woodwork, pottery, soaps, and custom teas. It's run by the St. Augustine Beach Civic Association, and proceeds go to sponsoring free concerts at the Pier Pavilion.

The second, **Old City Farmers' Market,** is on Saturdays from 8:30 a.m.–12:30 p.m., year-round, at the St. Augustine Ampitheater (1340 A1A South). The market features fresh produce, organic produce, plants, baked goods, nuts, and herbs, as well as crafts such as pottery and soap. For more information, call Lynn Whettach at (904) 824-8247.

Dining

A1A Ale Works

1 King Street; (904) 829-2977

Meals served Lunch and dinner **Cuisine** New world (described as a "fusion of culinary influences that includes the regional dishes of Florida, Cuba, the Caribbean, and Latin America") and microbrewery **Entree range** $10–$20 **Reservations** Not accepted, but priority seating is available **Payment** All major credit cards accepted (no checks)

Comments Try the snapper burger with mango ketchup, or the Key lime shrimp and lobster. Great microbrewed beers and homemade root beer. You have the option of outdoor seating on a balcony overlooking the bay.

Athena Restaurant

14 Cathedral Place; (904) 823-9076

Meals served Breakfast, lunch, and dinner **Cuisine** Greek/American **Entree range** $6–$19 **Reservations** Recommended **Payment** V, MC, AmEx, D

Comments Breakfast (except waffles) is served anytime at this wonderful little diner right in the middle of historic St. Augustine. There's something for everyone, including traditional Greek souvlaki, moussaka, and lamb kebabs, and they also have gourmet burgers.

Barnacle Bill's

14 Castillo Drive; (904) 824-3663

Meals served Lunch and dinner (just dinner on Sundays) **Cuisine** Seafood, chicken, and steaks **Entree range** $11–$17 **Reservations** Not accepted **Payment** V, MC, AmEx, D

Comments Barnacle Bill's serves traditional seafood in a casual atmosphere, and locals recommend the fried shrimp.

Columbia Restaurant

98 St. George Street; (904) 824-3341; www.columbiarestaurant.com

Meals served Lunch and dinner **Cuisine** Spanish/Columbian **Entree range** Lunch, $10–$15; dinner, $15–$20 **Reservations** Highly recommended **Payment** All major credit cards accepted

Comments This boisterous and beautiful Spanish restaurant is an integral part of the St. Augustine experience. Try arroz con pollo (yellow rice and chicken), black-bean soup, or their authentic paella. Sunday brunch is especially crowded.

Creekside Dinery

160 Nix Boat Yard Road (off US 1); (904) 829-6113

Meals served Dinner **Cuisine** Old-fashioned Florida **Entree range** $8–$17 **Reservations** Not accepted **Payment** All major credit cards accepted

Comments You may have a wait for a table, but even that is pleasant on the vine-covered front porch. Fresh fish baked on an oak plank and pan-broiled shrimp are favorites. Also barbecue and Aunt Ada's Florida-style fried chicken.

Fiddler's Green

2750 Anahma Boulevard, Vilano Beach; (904) 824-8897

Meals served Dinner **Cuisine** Traditional seafood **Entree range** $10–$25 **Reservations** Recommended for certain times (starting around 7 p.m.); not accepted on Saturday **Payment** All major credit cards accepted
Comments This popular eatery is right on the ocean and serves fresh fish and shellfish, but you'll find steaks and chicken, too. The specialty is crispy fried coconut shrimp.

Harry's

46 Avenida Menendez; (904) 824-7765

Meals served Lunch and dinner **Cuisine** New Orleans–inspired seafood, pastas, steak, and chicken **Entree range** $8–$24 **Reservations** Not accepted; call-aheads available **Payment** All major credit cards accepted
Comments A favorite of the locals, with dining al fresco in the lovely garden. Jambalaya, etouffée, and red beans and rice are on the menu.

Pizza Garden

21 Hypolita Street; (904) 825-4877

Meals served Lunch and dinner **Cuisine** Pizza, salads, and sandwiches **Entree range** $1.75–$19 **Reservations** Not accepted **Payment** All major credit cards accepted
Comments Great pizza, just $1.75 a slice—a whole vegetarian pie is $16. Calzones are tasty, and the salads are ample. Located in the heart of old St. Augustine, with outdoor tables in a fenced courtyard.

Salt Water Cowboys

299 Dondanville Road; (904) 471-2332

Meals served Dinner **Cuisine** Seafood **Entree range** $9–$22 **Reservations** Not accepted **Payment** All major credit cards accepted
Comments Lines get long in the summer at this rustic, tin-roofed eatery built out over a saltwater marsh. The atmosphere is casual and family-oriented. The house specialty is the blackened fish over grits.

Sunset Grille

421 A1A Beach Boulevard, St. Augustine Beach; (904) 471-5555

Meals served Lunch and dinner **Cuisine** American **Entree range** $10–$24 **Reservations** Not accepted **Payment** All major credit cards
Comments Seafood and steaks are served at this little restaurant across the street from the beach, but locals go for the cheeseburgers. You can even order from the walk-up window and dine at window counters or in the air-conditioned dining room.

Arts and Culture

St. Augustine is a museum-lover's paradise. Historical attractions abound in this city, from the oldest house to the oldest masonry fort in the United States, the fountain of youth, and Florida's first lighthouse. If you haven't had enough history, consider a trip to the **Florida Heritage Museum** (phone (904) 829-3800), which covers Florida history from Native American civilizations to the Flagler railroad era. See a shipwreck exhibit, a re-created Timucuan Indian village, and a model of the Flagler railroad.

Two more options are the **Government House Museum** (phone (904) 825-5079), which chronicles the history of St. Augustine from 1500 to 1900, and the **Old Florida Museum** (SR 16 and San Marco Avenue; (800) 813-3208; **www.oldfloridamuseum.com**), which offers hands-on exhibits at three different stations. The first demonstrates how the Timucuan Indians lived in the area; the second focuses on the Spanish; and the third highlights the Florida pioneers. You can try your hand at milling corn, plowing ground, planting beans, and writing with a quill pen.

Nightlife

Ann O'Malley's

Who goes there Mostly locals

23 Orange Street (near the Old City Gate); (904) 825-4040

Cover None **Minimum** None (21 and up to drink) **Mixed drinks** Beer, wine, and soft drinks only **Food available** Full menu until midnight **Hours** 11 a.m.–midnight

What goes on Locals love this little pub, which offers a "home away from home" atmosphere. There's no live music, but expect loads of conversation.

Comments Smoking is only outside on the porch, and tourists provide the entertainment—if you're not a local, you can expect to be "interviewed" at this friendly, welcoming Irish pub.

The Cellar Upstairs

Who goes there Couples enjoying a romantic evening, groups of singles, families

157 King Street; (888) 352-9463

Cover None **Minimum** None **Mixed drinks** Beer, wine, and soft drinks only **Food available** Yes, appetizers **Hours** Opens Thursday and Friday at 4:30 p.m., Saturday and Sunday at noon; closing time depends on the crowd, usually about midnight (weather permitting)

What goes on You'll find live music by performers from the area and around the state every night this jazz and wine bar is open.

Comments Relax as you sip wine and enjoy the live jazz in this classy venue located on the top floor of the San Sebastian Winery. The "Cellar" is actually on the roof, so keep in mind that the weather dictates the schedule of events.

Gypsy Bar & Grill

Who goes there A mixed crowd of locals and tourists, mostly ages 30 and up; Wednesday draws more singles

830 Anastasia Boulevard; (904) 824-8244 (comedy club, (904) 461-8843)

Cover $11 for comedy club; no cover on Tuesday and Wednesday **Minimum** 18 (teens allowed with parental permission) **Mixed drinks** $4 and up **Food available** Full menu until 10 p.m. **Hours** Tuesday and Wednesday, 4–10 p.m.; Thursday–Saturday, 4–11 p.m. (comedy club hours differ—see below)

What goes on There's live music every Wednesday, which attracts more singles; you'll find couples out on dates on Tuesdays, and a wide range of people, from teens to seniors, in for the comedy club on the weekends.

Comments Thursday through Saturday nights, the bar transforms into a comedy club, with nationally touring comedians entertaining guests. On Thursday night, the show starts at 8 p.m.; on Friday, it's 9 p.m.; and Saturday shows are at 8:30 p.m. and 10:30 p.m.

Mill Top Tavern

Who goes there A wide range of tourists and locals, ages 21–71

19½ St. George Street, at the Fort; (904) 829-2329

Cover Friday and Saturday $1, Tuesday $2 **Minimum** 21 after 10 p.m. on weeknights, 11 p.m. weekends **Mixed drinks** $3.75 and up **Food available** Full menu until 10 p.m. on weeknights, 11 p.m. weekends **Hours** 11 a.m.–1 a.m.

What goes on Live music is played here from 1 p.m. until closing, seven days a week. From 1 p.m. to 9 p.m., hear acoustic music, and after 9 p.m., enjoy live bands playing a variety of music, ranging from Southern rock to folk. Tuesdays feature younger, up-and-coming local bands, while Friday and Saturday nights often host out-of-town bands.

Comments The Mill Top Tavern is proof that the city of St. Augustine can find a way to inject history into everything, including the nightlife. The front room of the tavern dates back to 1869, when it was used as a gristmill. A two-story mill wheel still turns at the tavern, said to be the second most photographed place in St. Augustine, next to the fort.

Scarlett O'Hara's

Who goes there Variety of tourists, locals, couples, and singles

70 Hypolita Street; (904) 824-6535

Cover None **Minimum** None **Mixed drinks** $3.50 and up **Food available** Full menu available until 10 p.m. **Hours** 11 a.m.–1 a.m., last call at 12:30 a.m.

What goes on Live music or karaoke happens every night they're open.

Comments In the late 1800s, this bar was a Florida Cracker home, and the place has still retained its Southern charm. Scarlett O'Hara's is divided into several rooms, with a front porch complete with rockers, as well as downstairs and upstairs areas.

Side Trips

Fort Matanzas Built by the Spanish between 1740 and 1742 to protect St. Augustine, Fort Matanzas is now part of a 298-acre park. A free ferry (donations are accepted) takes you to the fort on Rattlesnake Island in the Matanzas River. (Matanzas means "slaughter" in Spanish, so named for a battle that took place in 1565 near here.) Park rangers give free tours, and you can explore the living quarters and observation deck, hiking trails, and beach. Browse the visitor center, and enjoy a picnic lunch at the park. Open seven days a week, 9 a.m. to 5:30 p.m.; closed Christmas. About 14 miles south of St. Augustine on SR A1A; (904) 471-0116.

Gainesville and Environs

Heading southwest from Jacksonville, you'll discover off-the-beaten path adventures along the quiet rural routes leading to Gainesville, home of the University of Florida. Unless you're visiting the college campus or have a special interest in history or architecture, you might bypass this quaint little town. The town's Northeast Historic District, listed on the National Register of Historic Places, is a 63-block area of 290 buildings that reflect Florida architectural styles from 1880 through the 1920s, worth a stroll if you enjoy historic architecture. Step back in time and see what Florida was like in the 1800s with a visit to nearby Micanopy, 13 miles south of Gainesville, or High Springs, an old railroad town to the north. Though there are no beaches or theme parks, this part of the Sunshine State is for those who love to be outdoors. There are excellent camping, canoeing, fishing, hiking, and bicycling opportunities, including sections of the Florida Trail, which links one end of Florida to the other.

Golf

Gainesville Golf and Country Club

3700 Southwest 35th Way; (352) 372-0961; www.gainesvillegolf.com
Established 1963 | **Designer** George Cobb | **Holes** 18

Tees Blue/White/Green/Red **Par** 72/72/72/72 **Slope** 135/129/126/119
Fees Winter, $50 weekends, $40 Wednesday and Thursday, $30 Tuesday; call for summer rates **Specials** Weekday discounts **Cart rental** $16, optional **Club rental** $10 **Payment** V, MC, AmEx **Tee times** Up to 4 days in advance **Facilities** Pro shop, driving range, restaurant, pool, snack bar, putting green, chipping green
Comments A member of the Audubon Cooperative Sanctuary System, this environmentally friendly course is home to lots of protected wildlife,

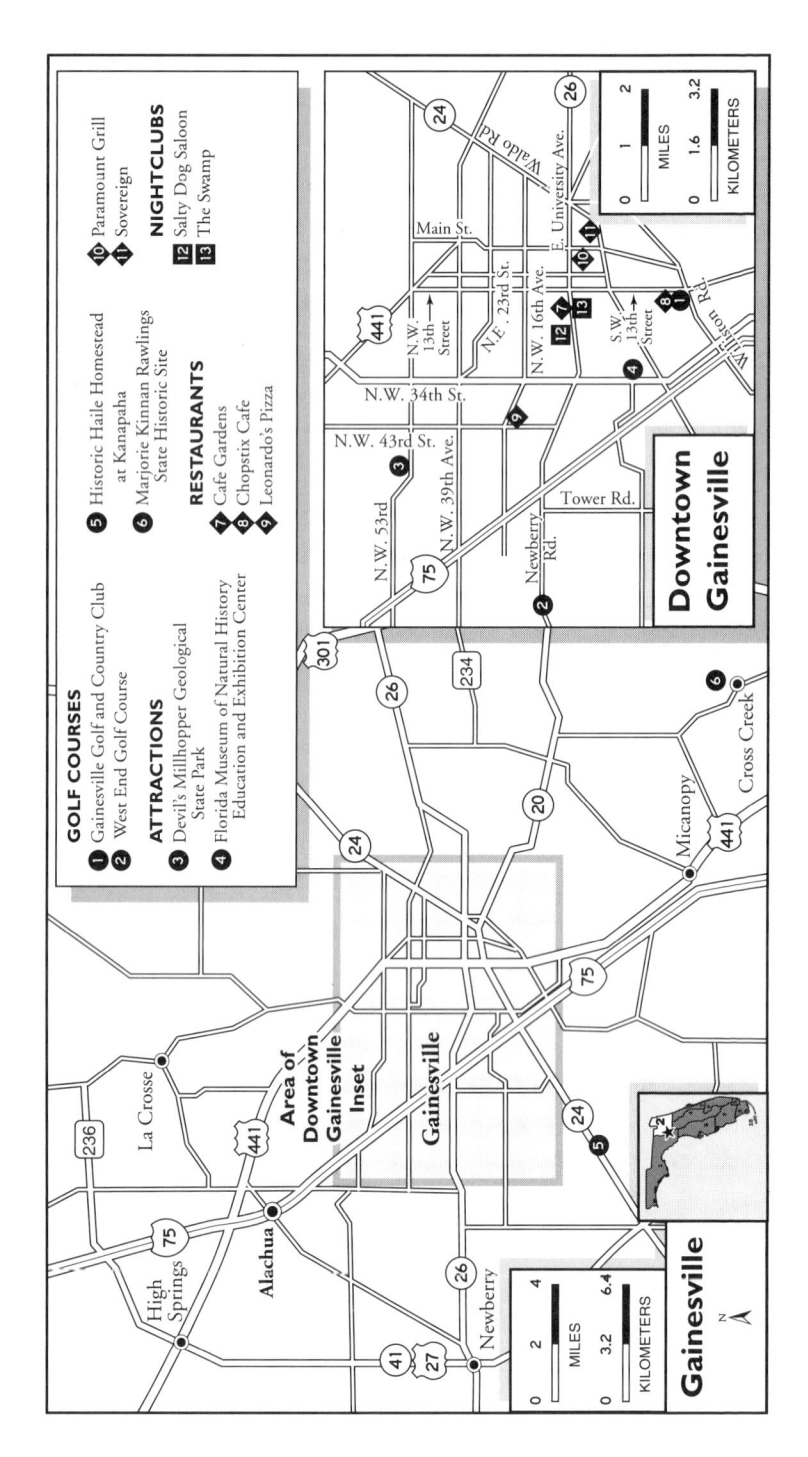

Gainesville

GOLF COURSES
1. Gainesville Golf and Country Club
2. West End Golf Course

ATTRACTIONS
3. Devil's Millhopper Geological State Park
4. Florida Museum of Natural History Education and Exhibition Center
5. Historic Haile Homestead at Kanapaha
6. Marjorie Kinnan Rawlings State Historic Site

RESTAURANTS
7. Cafe Gardens
8. Chopstix Cafe
9. Leonardo's Pizza
10. Paramount Grill
11. Sovereign

NIGHTCLUBS
12. Salty Dog Saloon
13. The Swamp

including alligators and coyotes. The course's abundance of pine trees and absence of marshes give it a Northern feel. After rainy days, the course can be quite wet.

West End Golf Course

12830 West Newberry, Newberry; (352) 332-2721; www.westendgolf.com
Established 1968 | **Designer** John O'Connor | **Holes** 18

Tees Blue/Red **Par** 60/60 **Slope** 87/87
Fees $13 nights and weekends, $12 weekdays **Specials** $17 cart and greens fees **Cart rental** $16 **Club rental** $10 **Payment** V, MC **Tee times** Up to 3 days in advance **Facilities** Pro shop, snack bar, driving range, putting green, chipping green
Comments West End boasts the world's largest and longest night-lighted course. The course has plenty of trees and very little water. The most challenging hole is number 4, a 421-yard par 4.

Attractions

Devil's Millhopper Geological State Park

4732 Millhopper Road; (352) 955-2008; (386) 462-7905 for San Felasco Hammock Preserve State Park
Hours 9 a.m.–5 p.m.; closed Monday and Tuesday
Admission $2 per vehicle

Appeal by Age Group

Pre-school ★	Teens ★★★	Over 30 ★★★
Grade school ★★	Young Adults ★★★	Seniors ★★

Touring Time *Average* 1 hour
Rainy-Day Touring Not recommended
Author's Rating ★★★
Description and Comments If you're up for a hike, this giant sinkhole—120 feet deep and 500 feet across—is worth about an hour's visit, with nature trails around its rim, a dozen waterfalls tumbling down its steep slopes, and 232 steps leading to its foundation. Fossilized sharks' teeth, marine shells, and fossilized remains of extinct land animals have been found at the bottom, evidence that the sea once covered the state. It was once said that the millhopper fed bodies to the devil. (A millhopper is the container that fed grain into gristmill grinders in the 1800s.) There's also a nice shady area for picnicking.

Florida Museum of Natural History Education and Exhibition Center

Southwest 34th Street and Hull Road (Powell Hall), Gainesville; (352) 846-2000; www.flmnh.ufl.edu

Hours Monday–Saturday, 10 a.m.–5 p.m.; Sunday, 1–5 p.m.; closed Thanksgiving and Christmas
Admission Free
Appeal by Age Group

Pre-school ★	Teens ★★★	Over 30 ★★★
Grade school ★★★	Young Adults ★★★	Seniors ★★★

Touring Time *Average* 2 hours; *minimum* 1 hour
Rainy-Day Touring Recommended
Author's Rating ★★★
Description and Comments Rated among the top ten natural history museums in the United States, the Florida Museum of Natural History features exhibit subjects from paleontology and animal life to cultural diversity and computers. You can venture into a man-made cave populated by rattlesnakes, opossum, bats, barn owls, wood rats, raccoons, and other Florida wildlife as well as learn more about the Native American tribes that have populated Florida since years before the first European explorers arrived on these shores.

Historic Haile Homestead at Kanapaha

8500 Southwest Archer Road, Gainesville; (352) 372-2633; www.hailehomestead.org
Hours Sundays, noon–4 p.m.
Admission $7 adults, children ages 12 and under free
Appeal by Age Group

Pre-school ★	Teens ★★★	Over 30 ★★★
Grade school ★	Young Adults ★★★	Seniors ★★★

Touring Time *Average* 45 minutes–1 hour
Rainy-Day Touring Recommended
Author's Rating ★★★
Description and Comments Built between 1884 and 1886, this 7,000-square-foot plantation home is still owned by descendants of the original family and has never been modernized. By far, the most distinctive feature of this traditional, South Carolina–style home is that every wall has been written on—the family covered their wall space with writing of all kinds, from grocery lists and silverware inventories, to weather observations and poems. Over 12,000 words adorn the walls.

Marjorie Kinnan Rawlings State Historic Site

On CR 325, in Cross Creek, 21 miles southeast of Gainesville; (352) 466-3672
Hours Guided tours Thursday–Sunday, 10 a.m., 11 a.m., and every hour from 1 to 4 p.m. on a first-come, first-served basis; tours are not available in August and September; closed Thanksgiving and Christmas
Admission $3 for adults, $2 for children ages 6–12, free for children ages 5 and under

Appeal by Age Group

Pre-school ★	Teens ★★★	Over 30 ★★★
Grade school ★★	Young Adults ★★★	Seniors ★★★

Touring Time *Average* 2 hours; *minimum* 1 hour

Rainy-Day Touring Not recommended

Author's Rating ★★★; we love this old farmhouse nestled in the shade of an orange grove and the nostalgic ambience that lingers

Description and Comments This is truly a step back in time. Rawlings' turn-of-the-century home is on a country road, still far from civilization, and the gardens and house look much the same today as they did in the 1920s when she recorded her impressions in the award-winning Cross Creek—even her table, chair, and typewriter are still there on the screened porch. There's also a quarter-mile hammock trail, as well as picnic tables.

Shopping

The **Oaks Mall** (6419 West Newberry Road; (352) 331-4411; www.theoaksmall.com) is home to 140 stores, including department stores such as Dillard's, Burdines, JCPenney, Belk, and Sears as well as other shops such as Bath and Body Works, and Victoria's Secret.

At nearly a mile long and known as The Miracle Mile, **Butler Plaza** (I-75 and Archer Road; (352) 376-5225; www.butlerplaza.com) spans 1.2 million square feet. With movie theaters, two supermarkets, numerous restaurants, and just about everything else, Butler Plaza is an established Gainesville shopping destination.

For an entirely different shopping experience, try **Angel Gardens** (10100 Northwest 13th Street; (386) 462-7722; www.angelgardens.com). The shop is located in a restored farmhouse, and the atmosphere created by the gardens surrounding the house, as well as the charming decor inside, is said to leave shoppers feeling more relaxed than when they first arrived. Waterfalls and ponds surround this shop, and some shoppers visit the gardens just to soak up the place's healing atmosphere. Shop for angel figurines and statues, garden accessories, live plants, antiques, Victorian gifts, and more. The gardens are also home to one of the nation's largest live oaks.

For antiques, visit the two-story **Waldo's Antique Village** (17805 Northeast US 301, Waldo; (352) 468-3111). You'll find an eclectic mix of styles and time periods at this 24,000 square feet shop, which sells antiques ranging from glass and china to primitives and plowing equipment.

Flea Markets **Waldo Farmers' and Flea Market** (17805 Northeast US 301; (352) 468-2255) is open Saturdays and Sundays from 7:30 a.m. to 4:30 p.m., but you'll find most of the vendors there after 9 a.m. (the best times to visit are between 9 a.m. and 2 p.m.). The market hosts vendors selling an assorted mix of antiques, collectibles, clothing, and more. From Gainesville, take University Avenue to Waldo Road and turn left; turn right onto US 301 and look for the signs.

Farmers' Markets Alachua County is a highly agricultural area, and you'll find several farmers' markets here, overflowing with fresh vegetables, fruits, plants, and herbs. For a listing of markets and restaurants offering produce grown in north Florida, visit the North Florida Local Food Partnership's site, **www.buylocalflorida.org**.

In downtown Gainesville, the **Union Street Market** meets at the Sun Center on Wednesdays from 4–7 p.m., every week of the year (for more information, contact Charlie Lybrand, (386) 462-3192). Located near the Hippodrome, the growers-only market offers fresh vegetables, fruits, and bakery goods, as well as bath products and crafts. In the south section of Gainesville, you can visit the small market that meets at Butler Plaza during some summer months (call Sharon Yeago, (386) 454-3950, for more information on availability). The **Haile Plantation Farmers' Market** (phone (352) 331-1804) offers mostly edibles, including produce, fruits, plants, herbs, and honey; the market meets on Saturdays, 8:30 a.m.–noon, from October 15 to July 15, in the upscale, sophisticated Haile Village Center. The **Alachua County Farmers' Market** (5920 Northwest 13th Street, at the intersection of US 441 and SR 121; (386) 454-3950) is the area's first and largest market, selling fruits, plants, vegetables, jams and jellies, and more all year long, on Saturdays from 8:30 a.m. to 1 p.m. In beautiful historic downtown High Springs, the **High Springs Farmers' Market** meets year-round on Thursdays from 4 to 7 p.m. Each market features special events such as food tastings, entertainment, and more; call for details and schedules.

Dining

Cafe Gardens

1643 Northwest First Avenue; (352) 376-2233

Meals served Lunch, dinner **Cuisine** American **Entree range** $7–$16 **Reservations** Not accepted **Payment** All major credit cards

Description and Comments With a casual, romantic atmosphere, this quaint outdoor café has a good-sized vegetarian menu and is known for their sweet-potato fries. You'll also find live music there almost every night of the week.

Chopstix Cafe

3500 Southwest 13th Street; (352) 367-0003

Meals served Breakfast, lunch, dinner **Cuisine** Pan Asian **Entree range** $6–$14 **Reservations** Not accepted **Payment** All major credit cards accepted

Description and Comments Chopstix, which overlooks a pretty lake, is a local Pan Asian favorite, serving up good food that is fairly inexpensive.

Leonardo's Pizza

4131 Northwest 16th Boulevard; (352) 376-2001

Meals served Lunch and dinner **Cuisine** Italian **Entree range** $6–$25 **Reservations** Not accepted **Payment** All major credit cards accepted

Description and Comments A "Gainesville classic," Leonardo's serves delicious pizza, great salads, and more at reasonable prices. The house specialty is the Big Leo, a 14" deep-dish, Chicago-style pizza that weighs "at least five pounds." Also, try the garlic rolls.

Paramount Grill

12 Southwest First Avenue; (352) 378-3398

Meals served Lunch (Monday–Friday), dinner (Monday–Saturday), Sunday brunch **Cuisine** Eclectic **Entree range** $13–$30 **Reservations** Recommended **Payment** V, MC, AmEx

Description and Comments One of Gainesville's best, this small restaurant offers original dishes in a classy, intimate atmosphere. The menu changes often and draws from a wide range of culinary influences.

Satchel's Pizza

1800 Northeast 23rd Avenue; (352) 335-7272

Meals served Lunch, dinner **Cuisine** Italian **Entree range** $6–$15 **Reservations** Not accepted **Payment** Cash only

Description and Comments This family-owned pizza parlor serves up the basics (pizza, calzones, and salads), fresh and homemade.

Sovereign

12 Southeast Second Avenue; (352) 378-6307

Meals served Dinner (Monday–Saturday) **Cuisine** American **Entree range** $22–$24 **Reservations** Recommended, especially on weekends **Payment** All major credit cards accepted

Description and Comments This restaurant is housed in a building over 110 years old—the romantic atmosphere is accented with stained glass, wooden floors, and high ceilings.

Arts and Culture

Art enthusiasts will enjoy a trip to the **Harn Museum of Art,** located on the University of Florida campus next to the Museum of Natural History (phone (352) 392-9826; **www.harnmuseum.org**). The museum's collections and rotating exhibits range in styles and time periods and include paintings, photography, and sculpture from the Americas, Europe, Africa, and Asia.

Nightlife

Salty Dog

Who goes there A mix of ages—plenty of singles

1712 West University Avenue; (352) 376-5153

Cover None **Minimum** 21 **Mixed drinks** $2.75 and up (drink specials vary) **Food available** Full menu until midnight **Hours** Noon–2 a.m.

What goes on Play pool or just grab a booth with some friends and enjoy drinks and conversation.

Comments "The Dog" draws a largely single crowd; there's no live music, but you will find plenty of chatting and laughter. Salty Dog is a smoking bar, but there is decent ventilation, and the drink specials are good.

The Swamp

Who goes there College fraternities and sororities; Gators fans watching away games on TV

1642 West University Avenue; (352) 377-9267

Cover Monday, Wednesday, and Friday, $5 men, $3 women **Minimum** Men 21, women 18 **Mixed drinks** $3 and up **Food available** Full menu available until closing **Hours** Monday–Saturday, 11 a.m.–2 a.m.; Sunday, 11 a.m.–11 p.m.

What goes on On Wednesday and Friday nights, there's live local music on the front lawn and patio area.

Comments This bar is one of the most popular in Gainesville, especially with University of Florida students. During the day, it's a sports bar and restaurant, and at night students and other partiers arrive for drinks and food—the full menu is available all night, until closing.

FREE OR ALMOST FREE

Few people would plan a trip to a retirement home as part of a Florida vacation, but Mill Creek Farm is not your ordinary adult community. It is a kind of retirement home—but for horses. On Saturdays, between 11 a.m. and 3 p.m., you can visit the farm and its inhabitants: about 120 horses, as well as dogs, pigs, and goats. The horses have been rescued or retired and happily live the rest of their lives at the farm without being worked or ridden. Admission is two carrots; you can also bring sliced apples for toothless horses. Located at 20307 Northwest 235 A, Alachua. For more information, call (386) 462-1001 or visit **www.millcreekfarm.org**.

Part Four

The Space Coast: Daytona Beach, New Smyrna Beach, and Cocoa Beach

Welcome to the Space Coast

Sand, surf, space shuttles, the Speedway—and don't forget the seafood. The Space Coast, stretching down the Atlantic from the tiny resort town of Ormond Beach to Palm Bay, has plenty to satisfy travelers.

When most vacationers think of this area, they think of Daytona Beach. More than eight million worldwide visitors come to the area each year, mainly because of the location. The beaches are the closest to Walt Disney World and other Central Florida attractions, but the area has some star attractions of its own, including wide, sweeping beaches and the Daytona International Speedway, known as the world center of car racing.

Early automotive pioneers once raced horseless carriages on the hard-packed sands of Daytona-area beaches, and today vacationers still drive along most of the 23-mile-long shore from Ormond Beach to Ponce Inlet.

The beach and the Speedway may lure first-time visitors to the area, but hidden treasures keep them coming back, such as Blue Spring State Park, with a natural spring that's a winter home for manatees and Ponce de Leon Lighthouse, still a beacon in the night.

Drive south from Daytona to the Cocoa Beach area, and the biggest draw is the Kennedy Space Center (KSC) Visitor Complex. You can look at rockets and see the launch pads for the space shuttle. Real space hardware, combined with hands-on exhibits, make this a fun lesson in science and U.S. history.

The Kennedy Space Center is located adjacent to the Merritt Island National Wildlife Refuge. The refuge is a very different experience, where giant sea turtles lay their eggs in the sand in the summer, and gators bask in the sun (sometimes in the middle of the road).

Hands down, the prettiest beach on the Space Coast is Canaveral National Seashore, where there are no miniature-golf courses, no bikes or boogie boards for rent—nothing but sand and sea.

A Brief History

Pirates, shipwrecks, colonization, Native American settlements, racing, and space exploration—the Space Coast's history is an eclectic mix of exploration, tension, and technology.

Before the Spanish occupation of Florida, the Timucua tribe inhabited the Daytona Beach and New Smyrna areas, and the Ais people populated the Cocoa and Titusville areas. However, the Timucuan and Ais numbers were almost completely depleted within 250 years of the arrival of Juan Ponce de Leon in 1513.

The Spanish controlled the area until 1763, when the British assumed authority. In 1767, Dr. Andrew Turnbull, a Scottish physician, came to the New Smyrna area with over 1,200 settlers. The colony was almost three times larger than Jamestown, but it failed a mere ten years later due to illness, political skirmishes, and financial difficulties.

In the early 1900s, the sport of auto racing began in Florida; the Ormond and Daytona beaches were used as natural racetracks for roadsters, and drivers raced for prizes such as motor oil, cigars, and alcohol. The 1940s and 1950s saw the birth of NASCAR and the construction of the Daytona International Speedway.

That time also brought about great changes south of Daytona to Cape Canaveral. In the 1940s, the federal government selected Cape Canaveral as a long-range testing site. Cape Canaveral had "the right stuff": sparsely populated land, a climate conducive to year-round launches, and proximity to the ocean, allowing over-the-water launches. Cape Canaveral boomed in the 1950s, as missile contractors moved to the area. In 1958, NASA began operations at Cape Canaveral, and three years later it launched the first American, Alan Shepherd, into space.

HIGHLIGHTS

- Kennedy Space Center Visitor Complex
- Canaveral National Seashore
- Daytona International Speedway/Daytona USA
- Ponce de Leon Inlet Lighthouse
- Brevard Zoo

Visiting the Space Coast

Gathering Information

Daytona Beach Area Convention and Visitors Bureau, 126 East Orange Avenue, Daytona Beach, 32114; (800) 854-1234; **www.daytonabeach. com.**

Cocoa Beach Area Chamber of Commerce, 400 Fortenberry Road, Merritt Island, 32952; (321) 459-2200; **www.cocoabeachchamber.com.**

New Smyrna Beach Area Visitors Bureau, 2242 SR 44, New Smyrna Beach, 32168; (386) 428-1600; (800) 541-9621; www.newsmyrna beachonline.com.

Florida's Space Coast Office of Tourism, 8810 Astronaut Boulevard, Suite 102, Cape Canaveral, 32920; (800) USA-1969; www.space-coast.com.

Getting There

By Plane Daytona Beach International Airport (phone (386) 248-8069; www.flydaytonafirst.com) is located off of I-95 on US 92 (International Speedway Boulevard), one of Daytona Beach's main drags. From I-95, take Exit 261, heading east. From I-4 east, follow the signs to International Speedway Boulevard. DBIA is located near the International Speedway, and is also close to the beaches. To get to the beach from the airport, take US 92 to SR A1A, which runs north-south along the coast. Flying to DBIA are Delta, ASA, ComAir, Continental, and commuter flights from Vintage Props and Jets (phone (800) 852-0275; www.flyvpj.com).

The Orlando Sanford International Airport is located 18 miles northeast of Orlando, 28 miles southwest of New Smyrna Beach, in the city of Sanford (phone (407) 585-4000; www.orlandosanfordairport.com). The airport offers flights from Pan American, Southeast, and TransMeridian. To Daytona Beach, take I-4 east to International Speedway Boulevard. To New Smyrna Beach, take SR 415 to SR 44 east. To Cocoa Beach, take SR 46 to I-95 south.

Melbourne International Airport (phone (321) 723-6227; **www.mlb air.com**) offers flights from Delta and Vintage Props and Jets. Take US 192 to I-95 north from the airport to reach Cocoa Beach, New Smyrna Beach, and Daytona Beach.

Shuttle, taxi, limo, and bus services are available from the airports. Taxi fares from Daytona Beach International Airport to the beach resorts run $12–$20. No reservations are required, but some companies allow you to call ahead and arrange for a car to be waiting at the airport when you arrive. From the Orlando Sanford International Airport, a taxi to Daytona Beach will run about $100, and reservations are recommended. Rental-car companies from both airports include Avis, Alamo, National, Dollar, Hertz, Budget, and Enterprise.

By Car The Space Coast is conveniently located within driving distance of many major Florida cities. Orlando is under two hours from both Daytona and Cocoa Beach; Jacksonville and Miami are both within a day's drive away. The Bee Line Expressway (528), which runs east-west, connects Orlando with I-95, US 1, and SR A1A. I-4 (east-west) also runs from Orlando to I-95, close to the Daytona Beach area. I-95 (north-south) is a major road in this area, running the length of Florida's east coast and ending near Miami—take I-95 north to Jacksonville or south to Miami. SR 40 connects to I-75, US 1, US 92, and SR A1A.

By Train Amtrak services the town of Deland; (800) USA-RAIL, www.amtrak.com.

Getting Around

Traffic conditions vary widely depending on the dates and times you're traveling. Each city has certain attractions and events that drastically change the traffic conditions—Daytona Beach has races; Cocoa Beach has launches. Be sure to check your travel dates against local events.

Speed limits range from 30–35 mph in neighborhoods and heavily congested areas. Larger roads, such as US 92 and US 1, typically run 45–55 mph, but speed limits change depending on the area. I-95 is commonly 70 mph, but be on the lookout for construction zones.

Major Roadways

I-95, running north-south, is the major connecting road on the Space Coast. Daytona Beach, New Smyrna Beach, Cocoa Beach, and Melbourne are all accessible from the interstate. While the drive is not particularly scenic (you'll see plenty of pine trees, but not much else), it is direct and has fairly consistent speed limits with no stops except for construction. SR A1A runs north-south along parts of the coastline; it travels through Daytona Beach, New Smyrna Beach, Port Canaveral, and Cocoa Beach, but it isn't a straight shot down the coast. Traffic on SR A1A can be heavy, but in some places the drive is scenic, and the route takes you by the beaches.

Major roads in Daytona Beach and New Smyrna Beach are US 92 (International Speedway Boulevard) and SR A1A. US 92 runs east-west and connects I-95 to SR A1A, taking you past the International Speedway and Historic Beach Street. SR A1A, known as Atlantic Avenue in the area, stretches north-south along the coastline. Due to heavy traffic and attractions in certain areas, SR A1A stays fairly congested.

During races, expect bumper-to-bumper traffic on US 92 and congested traffic on I-95 near Daytona Beach. Check race dates and times by calling (386) 254-2700 or visiting **www.daytonaintlspeedway.com**.

Spring Break brings crowds and heavy traffic to the area in March, filling the hotels, beaches, and roadways with college students from around the country. Bike Week (late February/early March) and Biketoberfest (mid October) both fill the streets with motorcycles and tourists. Black College Reunion (spring) is another event that draws a crowd to the area. For more information, check with the Daytona Beach Chamber of Commerce (phone (386) 255-0981; **www.daytonachamber.com**).

Major roads in the Cocoa Beach area are SR 528 (the Bee Line), SR A1A, SR 520, and US 1. The Bee Line (528) runs east-west between Orlando and the beaches and merges with SR A1A (north-south, also known as Atlantic Avenue on the Space Coast) near the beaches. SR 520 (known as the Cocoa Beach Causeway in the area) runs east-west through Merritt Island and intersects with SR A1A at Cocoa Beach.

Expect considerable traffic delays during launches, especially on US 1 in Titusville and anywhere near the coast. Visit **www.ksc.nasa.gov** or call (800) KSC-INFO or (321) 867-4636 for more information.

The Best Beaches

Canaveral National Seashore No driving on the beach, no condos, no high-rise hotels, no neon—this beach is deliberately undeveloped. But what this area north of the Kennedy Space Center does have is more than 25 miles of beautiful beaches where more than 310 species of birds and 1,045 species of plants make their home. Apollo Beach is at the north end of the seashore, and Playalinda Beach is at the south end. Both have lifeguards on duty from Memorial Day to Labor Day. Klondike Beach, in the middle, is accessible only by foot, bicycle, or horseback; it's worth the walk to Klondike just for the seashells. You can obtain the proper permits at the park entrance. The north end of the beach offers some great trails; check out Castle Windy. Turtle Mound at the north end is also a must: the 50-foot-tall mound of shells offers a great view of the ocean and nearby lagoon. The south end of the beach is great for birdwatching. In the midst of all this wilderness, civilization is not far away: space shuttle launch pads also are in full view from the south end of the beach.

Both Apollo and Playalinda beaches have parking areas and rest rooms (although no running water), but there are no snack-bar areas so take water and food. The seashore is open daylight hours, except when the road is closed because of NASA activities. For more information on the seashore, call the district ranger's office at (321) 267-1110.

Daytona Beach Look both ways before you cross the ... beach? Cars can cruise on most of this wide—500 feet at low tide—beach of firmly packed sand from an hour before sunrise to an hour after sundown, at a cost of $5 per vehicle (February–November). A welcome change is a one-mile, vehicle-free beach area in front of Daytona Beach's Boardwalk and the Pier. This area begins at Seabreeze Boulevard and ends at US 92 (International Speedway Boulevard). Day guests can park in a garage ($1 per half-hour, $6 per day) at the Ocean Center arena. From this parking garage, you can take a tram to several stops along the beach. The parking garage is located at 701 Earl Street, off Atlantic Avenue.

At the beach you'll find floats, umbrellas, beach cruiser bicycles, and motorbikes available for rent, and vendors sell everything from hot dogs to beach towels and T-shirts. Lifeguards regularly patrol the beach. For entertainment, the Bandshell, constructed of coquina rock in 1937, offers free weekly concerts in the summer.

Lighthouse Point Park To escape Daytona's packed beaches around the pier, travel south to this park, named for the nearby lighthouse still in use. The park features a picnic area, nature trails, and a marina. To the south, the beach is especially beautiful and peaceful and the waves are gentle; however, there are no lifeguards. Admission is $3.50 per vehicle, up to eight people per vehicle. Hours are 7 a.m.–9 p.m. daily. The park is located at the south end of Atlantic Avenue in Daytona Beach; call (386) 756-7488 for more information.

New Smyrna Beach This is actually 13 miles of beach and a small town just south of Daytona where Central Floridians often escape. A wooden walkway stretches more than a mile over the dunes at Smyrna Dunes Park at the north end of Peninsula Avenue. Canaveral National Seashore marks the southern tip. It's a little less hectic and less developed than nearby Daytona. The ocean is considered extra safe here because of rock ledges offshore that protect against undercurrents. Vehicles are permitted on New Smyrna Beach between Flagler Avenue and 27th Avenue ($5 per vehicle, February 1– November 30). There are lifeguards and rest rooms.

Ormond Beach Three miles of beach adjoin Daytona's north end, with concessions, lifeguards, rest rooms, picnic tables, and showers. The sand is different here, with a reddish-brown hue thanks to an offshore coquina reef.

Sebastian Inlet State Recreation Area This popular park is a favorite with surfers and is a premier saltwater fishing location. The beach has lifeguards and a decent, protected snorkeling area (you can rent gear there). Many anglers bunk down at the 51 campsites that overlook the inlet; the nightly rate is $19, $21 with electricity. For reservations, call (800) 326-3521. The fee to enter the recreation area is $3.25 per vehicle. If you need to rent fishing gear, call (321) 984-4852; rates are $3 per hour, $9.50 for four hours, $12 all day.

Special activities include nighttime walks to see loggerhead turtles in the summer. The McLarty Treasure Museum (phone (772) 589-2147), showcasing treasures from a 1715 shipwreck, is two miles south of the Sebastian Inlet Bridge.

NO DRIVING ZONES

Daytona Beach has been given the title World's Most Famous Beach, but infamous may be more like it. Why? The beach and its related activities attract auto enthusiasts, motorcyclists, and spring breakers. This is especially true in the early spring when many of the special events are held.

In addition to the one-mile zone of vehicle-free beach in front of the Pier, there is a small piece of Daytona Beach oceanfront that does not allow traffic—south of the pier between Emilia Avenue and Beach Street is considered a "natural conservation zone" with no cars. At New Smyrna Beach, vehicles are permitted on about half the beach, from Smyrna Dunes Park on the north to 27th Avenue on the south. South of 27th Avenue is considered a natural conservation zone.

Outdoor Adventures and Sports

Recommended Outings

Ecotourism One of the fastest growing tourist attractions on the space coast isn't a theme park or a man-made attraction, but it can be a thrill ride. Called "Ecotourism," this type of attraction puts the spotlight on nature, usually in the form of a guided tour. A vacation to the Space Coast isn't

Outdoor Adventures and Sports 203

quite complete without an excursion through one of the coast's most precious resources: its natural habitats.

You can speed through the St. Johns area on an airboat with **Grasshopper Airboat Ecotours** (phone (321) 631-2990; www.airboatecotours.com) or **Twister Airboat Rides** at Lone Cabbage Fish Camp (phone (321) 632-4199; www.twisterairboatrides.com).

For a slower-paced tour, try a **Space Coast Nature Tour** (phone (321) 267-4551; www.spacecoastnaturetours.com) on the Indian River Lagoon. Or look for manatees and dolphins on a **Wildside Tour** (phone (800) 695-1770; www.wildsidetours.com). In New Smyrna, board the *Manatee* (phone (386) 428-0201; www.manateecruise.com) for cruises on the Intracoastal Waterway; see waterfront homes, the Ponce de Leon lighthouse, and, of course, plenty of wildlife.

Some tours take a different approach to ecotourism—**Flying Boat Adventures** (phone (321) 267-4551; www.spacecoastnaturetours.com/flyingboat) lets you soar above the Merritt Island or St. Johns River areas . . . in a boat. The vehicle looks like an inflatable dinghy from a yacht, with a hang glider-style wing on top. Once you're airborne, you can see the Space Center and wildlife such as dolphins and manatees. If it's clear, you might see as far north as New Smyrna or as far west as Orlando (on the Merritt Island flight).

For the ultimate off-road experience, try **Trolley Boats** (phone (386) 238-3499), which tours both land and water in the same vehicle—an "amphibious trolley," or a bus that becomes a boat. See the Halifax River, Daytona's historic district, the oldest house in Volusia County, and the beach, as you learn about the area's history and ecology.

Other tours include the **Island Boat Lines** Water Taxi tour, which offers sunset cruises (phone (321) 794-7717; www.islandboatlines.com). Daytona Beach's **A Tiny Cruise Line** offers several tours, including wildlife tours, history tours, and a "Rivertown Treasures" tour, which combines the two (phone (386) 226-2343; www.visitdaytona.com/tinycruise).

Merritt Island Wildlife Refuge This 40-mile-long, 7-mile-wide stretch of land was set aside in the 1950s as a buffer zone for the nearby NASA facility. Since 1963, the U.S. Fish and Wildlife Service, in cooperation with NASA, has managed the refuge, a safe haven for more endangered or threatened animals than in any other area of the continental United States. The animals include sea turtles, West Indian manatees, southern bald eagles, wood storks, peregrine falcons, eastern indigo snakes, and Florida scrub jays. Some of the more commonly seen wildlife are laughing gulls, royal terns, snowy egrets, great blue herons, and turkey vultures. Year-round residents include 310 species of birds, 25 species of mammals, 117 species of fish, and 65 species of amphibians and reptiles.

Admission to the refuge is free; it is open daily, dawn to dusk. The visitor center on SR 402 provides great brochures to help you find your way around, with many pamphlets available on spotting animals. The center is open Monday–Friday, 8 a.m.–4:30 p.m., and Saturday and Sunday, 9 a.m.–5 p.m.; closed on federal holidays and on Sundays from April through October. From I-95, take Exit 220 east; cross over US 1, and the refuge is five miles ahead on the right; call (321) 861-0667.

CANAVERAL AND MERRITT TRAIL TIPS

Canaveral National Seashore Rangers offer ranger walks to teach about beach vegetation, sand dunes, and marine life. Call (386) 428-3384 for more information on these one- to two-hour hikes.

The cool-weather months, October–April, are usually the best times of year for bird-watching. The best times of day are early morning and late afternoon.

Don't forget insect repellent!

Scenic Drives and Hikes at Canaveral and Merritt Island Canaveral National Seashore and its neighbor to the south, Merritt Island National Wildlife Refuge, are accessible by car and on foot. If your schedule allows, hike the trails to get closer to the marsh habitat of area birds. For more information on Canaveral trails, call (386) 428-3384 or visit **www.nps.gov/cana;** for Merritt Island call (321) 861-0667 or visit **www.merrittisland.fws.gov.**

Canaveral National Seashore

Castle Windy Beginning at Parking Area 3 in the North District, this one-mile round-trip trail crosses the island from the beach to Mosquito Lagoon. Don't attempt to hike here during the summer; there's a reason this pool of water is called Mosquito Lagoon.

Eldora This driving loop has four different parking lots. At Parking Area 8, take a short walk through a coastal hammock to the banks of the Mosquito Lagoon. The trail ends at the Eldora State House.

Merritt Island National Wildlife Refuge

Black Point Wildlife Drive A seven-mile self-guided auto tour that takes motorists on a sand-and-shell road through pine woods and marshlands This drive is located off SR 406 north of Titusville. Estimated time: 30–60 minutes.

Cruickshank Trail Named after famous wildlife photographer, writer, and naturalist Allan Cruickshank, this trail begins at stop Number 8 along Black Point Wildlife Drive. Closed to vehicles, this five-mile trail circles a water marsh and is a great place to bird-watch; a trip averages two or three hours.

Oak Hammock This half-mile trail through the trees, with a portion of the trail on a boardwalk, is located three-quarters of a mile west of the visitor center. Estimated time: 20 minutes.

Tomoka State Park Tomoka State Park was once the site of a Timucuan Indian village, at the junction of the Tomoka and Halifax rivers. After Florida was acquired from Spain by the British in 1763, the area was used to plant indigo, rice, and sugarcane in what became the Mount Oswald

Plantation. Today, Tomoka is back to its original condition. This 1,540-acre park is filled with beautiful oaks and offers camping, fishing, canoeing, nature trails, and picnic areas to its visitors. There are 100 campsites; cost with electricity is $14. Canoe rentals are available for a 13-mile trip down the beautiful Tomoka River. (The canoe trail starts at SR 40, a mile west of I-95.) Also on the property is the Fred Dana Marsh Museum and Visitor Center. The park is open daily, 8 a.m.–sundown. The museum is open 8 a.m.–4:30 p.m. Tomoka State Park is located at 2099 North Beach Street, Ormond Beach; (386) 676-4050.

SEA TURTLES

Endangered sea turtles are often spotted along this part of the East Coast; in fact, the area is the largest sea turtle nesting area in the United States.

From May through August, the giants lumber ashore to lay their eggs—about 100 round, white, leathery eggs per nest. If the eggs survive, they begin to hatch in about 60 days, and the tiny turtles try to make it to the ocean (though raccoons, ghost crabs, and birds create quite an obstacle course).

If they make it past the surf, they swim to a region of the Atlantic Ocean known as the Sargassum Sea, a large area of seaweed that drifts with the ocean currents. Here the hatchlings feed on seaweed and tiny animals. When they reach adolescence, many turtles return to the inshore waters of the Florida coastline.

It's important never to disturb a turtle nest, and if you encounter turtles on a beach, turn off flashlights and car lights and don't interfere with the turtle's activities—if a sea turtle is disturbed, it will not nest.

Canoeing and Kayaking

The Space Coast provides plenty of water environments (from open rivers to streams running between mangrove islands) perfect for canoeing and kayaking. The **Canaveral National Seashore** offers excellent kayaking and canoeing opportunities. There are two ways to paddle the Mosquito Lagoon—access the lagoon from either the north or south ends of the park and explore the waters at your own discretion, or take a self-guided tour on a trail. Try the Shipyard Island Canoe Trail, located at the north district of the park. The **Indian River Lagoon** also provides visitors with hours of paddling; canoe or kayak in waters teeming with wildlife such as manatees, osprey and other birds, and dolphins.

For a more structured experience, take a kayak tour. **Blue Heron Adventures** provides two- to three-hour tours of the Thousand Island mangrove estuary on the Banana River in Cocoa Beach. Call (321) 799-3740, or visit **www.blueheronadventures.com.**

Parasailing and Hot Air Ballooning

For a bird's-eye view of the Space Coast, try parasailing. **Daytona Beach Parasailing** has been thrilling tourists and locals alike for four-and-a-half years now. They are open daily, 9 a.m.–6 p.m. Call (386) 547-6067 or visit **www.daytonaparasailing.com** for more information.

Another way to experience the Space Coast from above is a ride in a hot-air balloon. In Brevard County, contact **Balloons Over Florida** at (321) 956-1148. In Volusia, try **Fantasy Ballooning** (phone (386) 736-1010; www.fantasyballooning.com).

Scuba Diving and Snorkeling

The waters off the Space Coast offer diving and snorkeling buffs plenty of territory to explore. Check out one of the many artificial reefs off the coast of Daytona Beach or Port Canaveral. About 10–15 miles offshore, you will find numerous wreck sites; farther out, there are miles of natural reefs to explore. Blue Spring State Park and De Leon Springs State Park offer snorkeling. You can also snorkel in the Banana and Indian Rivers. The rivers, which are clearer in the winter months, aren't extremely popular snorkeling destinations, but you may see brackish water fish and even seahorses (look for those in patches of seagrass). For more information about diving on the Space Coast, check with local dive shops and charters, such as **Sea Dog Divers** (phone (386) 424-1644; www.seadogdiver.com) and **Discover Diving** (phone (386) 760-3483; www.divefl.com) in Daytona Beach or **Adventure Diving Florida** (phone (321) 452-3737; www.adventurediving florida.com) in Merritt Island.

FUN AT SEA: GAMBLING CRUISES

Have some leftover vacation money? Port Canaveral offers two gambling ships—Sterling Casino and SunCruz Casino. There is no sailing fee and both offer both slot machines and table games.

Sterling Casino sails on a 440-foot vessel and offers a free deli buffet; gaming participants drink free. In addition to the casinos, the ship boasts a lounge and an onboard massage therapist. For more information, visit the website (**www.sterlingcasinolines.com**) or call (800) 765-5711.

SunCruz provides passengers with buffet and a la carte menus; drinks are free while gaming. The ship is 205 feet long and sports 31 table games as well as a private poker room. Call (321) 799-3511 or visit **www.suncruzcasino.com**.

Surfing and Surfing Schools

Surfing is a popular pastime, enjoyed by visitors and locals alike. Cocoa Beach, home of World Champion Kelly Slater, boasts both the atmosphere and the waves that make for a great surfing location. Surf shops, such as Ron Jon's and the Cocoa Beach Surf Company, are in abundance on SR A1A. Numerous additional surfing beaches can be found on the coast—some offer nearly complete isolation, while others provide audiences.

If you've never surfed, but have dreamed of catching the perfect wave, it may be time for a surfing lesson. Contact the Cocoa Beach Surfing School for private lessons at hourly rates (phone (321) 868-1980;

Outdoor Adventures and Sports 207

www.cocoabeachsurfingschool.com). The surfing school also offers a summer camp for kids.

Fishing

Fishing options abound on the Space Coast. You can cast your line in lakes and sleepy rivers, the pounding surf of the Atlantic Ocean, or go even deeper on a chartered boat.

River fishing on the Space Coast can yield redfish, snook, black drum, flounder, sheephead, and spotted sea trout year-round, with tarpon available in the summer. Known as the most diverse estuary in North America, the Indian River is home to about 700 species of saltwater and freshwater fish. The Cocoa and Titusville area of the Space Coast is known as the "Redfish Capital of the World"; use shrimp, mullet, top water plugs, and spoons to catch redfish, as well as trout.

Surf fishing is another popular option in the area. Enjoy fishing while listening to waves crash against the shoreline or a rock jetty—in the spring and summer, ocean breezes offer sweet relief from the Florida heat. Year-round, catch flounder, whiting, and Spanish mackerel. In the summer, you may catch tarpon and tripletail; pompano are found in the area in winter. Try your luck on one of several jetties on the Space Coast, including the Ponce Inlet Jetty, near New Smyrna Beach, and Jetty Park near Cocoa Beach. Baits for saltwater fishing include shrimp, clams, cut bait, mullet, and squid, as well as others.

At Canaveral National Seashore, enjoy fishing for trout and redfish on the shallow Mosquito Lagoon, or test the waters off the Eldora fishing pier. Try Playalinda Beach, on the south end of the park, near Titusville, where you may catch trout, redfish, or pompano.

You can fish from beaches, piers, bridges, or docks with a proper license. A freshwater, saltwater, or combination license is required for nonresidents over the age of 16. See the Florida Fish and Wildlife Conservation Commission's website for more information (phone (352) 732-1230; **www.floridafisheries.com**).

Party Boats

Fishing licenses are supplied on party boats, and fishers of any age can go out. Tackle is also provided, and boats are usually 60–100 feet with a rest room and a small galley. Average cost per person is $25 for half a day and $40 for a full day.

Charter Boats

Charter boats offer smaller party sizes (averaging 1–6 people) and a more personalized fishing experience, compared to large party boats. You can charter a captain and boat for a half-day or full day. Tackle and licenses are supplied; costs range from $150 for half-day to $650 for a full day.

SPACE COAST MARINAS

Marina	Location	Phone
Merritt Island		
Banana River Marine Service	1360 S. Banana River Drive	(321) 452-8622
Indian Cove Marina	14 Myrtice Avenue	(321) 452-8540
Jay's Harbor Light Marina	2705 S. Tropical Trail	(321) 453-6354
Tingley's Marina/Fishing Camp	SR 3 and Barge Canal	(321) 452-0504
Titusville		
Titusville Municipal Marina	451 Marina Road	(321) 383-5600
Loughman Lake Lodge	1955 Hatbill Road	(321) 268-2277
Westland Marina	419 N. Washington Avenue	(321) 267-1667
Cocoa Beach and Cape Canaveral		
Cape Marina	800 Scallop Drive	(321) 783-8410
Lake Poinsett Lodge/Fishing Camp	5665 Lake Poinsett Road	(321) 636-0045
New Port Marina	960 Mullet Drive	(321) 799-9411
Orange Cove Marina	400 Cocoa Beach Causeway	(321) 783-8349
Sunrise Marina	505 Glen Cheek Drive	(321) 783-9535
Whitley Marina	96 Willard Street	(321) 632-5445
Daytona Beach and New Smyrna Beach		
Adventure Yacht Harbor	3948 S. Peninsula Drive	(386) 756-2180
Caribbean Jack's Marina	741 Ballough Road	(386) 253-5647
Daytona Marina and Boat Works	645 S. Beach Street	(386) 252-6421
Fishing Cove Marina	111 N. Riverside Drive	(386) 428-7827
Halifax Harbor Marina	450 Basin Street	(386) 253-0575
Inlet Harbor Marina	133 Inlet Harbor Road	(386) 767-3266
Seven Seas Marina	3300 S. Peninsula Drive	(386) 761-3221

Spectator Sports

Racing

Daytona Beach is home to the International Speedway, a world-famous racing destination. Racing is one of the fastest-growing sports in the nation, and the sport draws race fans to this area in droves. In the early 1900s, drivers raced the Daytona and Ormond Beaches for such prizes as alcohol, cigars, and motor oil. John D. Rockefeller was a fan, and he enjoyed watching the beach races during his winter stays in Ormond Beach. NASCAR was formed in Daytona by William H. G. France in 1947. France opened the Daytona International Speedway in 1959; today the track is known as the "World Center of Racing."

And there's a reason the Speedway has acquired that nickname. The track is famous for its "Speedweeks," which includes races from series such as

Busch, Craftsman Truck, True Value IROC, Goody's Dash, and ARCA RE/MAX. The event ends with the Daytona 500, known as "The Great American Race."

Other notable races are the Pepsi 400 (July), which features one of the largest fireworks displays in the state after the race, and the Daytona 200. Coinciding with Daytona Beach's Bike Week, the Speedway hosts Daytona 200 Week, more than a week of motorcycle racing, with the Daytona 200 race ending the festivities.

In addition to NASCAR and motorcycle races, the Speedway hosts Historic Sportscar Racing (HSR) and go-kart racing; the track is also used for community activities such as car shows and police motorcycle training, as well as civic and social gatherings. For more information about the Speedway, call (386) 254-2700 or visit **www.daytonaintlspeedway.com**.

Daytona Beach

Although most people want to leave traffic behind on a vacation, many vacationers flock to Daytona Beach to be in the heart of auto action. Today, vehicles are still allowed to cruise the sand (at a law-abiding speed of 10 mph), but the real racing takes places just miles away from the beach at the Daytona International Speedway. In mid-February race enthusiasts take over the beach for the Daytona 500, followed by leather-clad cyclists for Bike Week. And finally, college students eager to release midterm-exam stresses pile in their cars and head to Daytona's beaches in March for spring break.

Daytona Beach has tried to change its raucous image, but for visitors looking for a quiet vacation, we suggest checking out the areas north and south of Daytona Beach, such as Ormond Beach, Ponce Inlet, or Daytona Beach Shores. Or visit the Daytona area during the winter months when it's relatively quiet. If, however, you're looking for an action-packed vacation, rev up your motor and head to Daytona Beach.

Golf

Daytona Beach Golf Club, South Course

600 Wilder Boulevard, Daytona Beach; (386) 671-3500; www.ci.daytona-beach.fl.us/golfcourse

Established 1922 | **Designer** Donald Ross | **Holes** 18

Tees Blue/White/Red **Par** 71/71/71 **Slope** 118/116/123

Fees January–March, $30; April–December, $18 **Specials** After noon, $18 summer, $25 winter **Cart rental** Included **Club rental** $12 **Payment** V, MC, D **Tee times** Up to 3 days in advance **Facilities** Pro shop, restaurant, driving range, putting green, chipping green, PGA pro instruction

Comments An oldie, but a goodie, this course has generous fairways and small, heavily bunkered greens. Look out for hole 12—this par 3 features a pond in front of the small green, plus trees and bunkers to account for ... and it usually plays into the wind.

Daytona

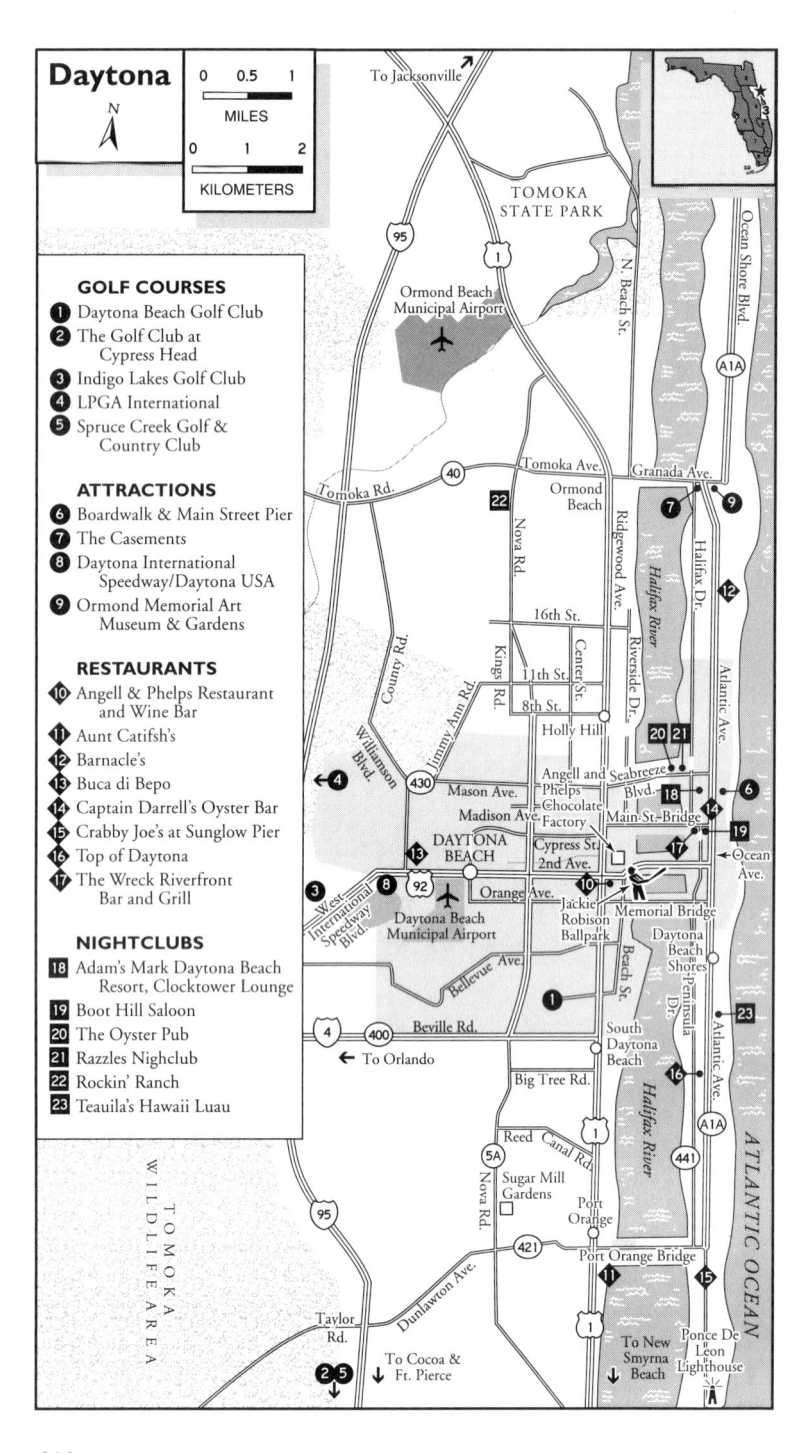

N

GOLF COURSES
1. Daytona Beach Golf Club
2. The Golf Club at Cypress Head
3. Indigo Lakes Golf Club
4. LPGA International
5. Spruce Creek Golf & Country Club

ATTRACTIONS
6. Boardwalk & Main Street Pier
7. The Casements
8. Daytona International Speedway/Daytona USA
9. Ormond Memorial Art Museum & Gardens

RESTAURANTS
10. Angell & Phelps Restaurant and Wine Bar
11. Aunt Catifsh's
12. Barnacle's
13. Buca di Bepo
14. Captain Darrell's Oyster Bar
15. Crabby Joe's at Sunglow Pier
16. Top of Daytona
17. The Wreck Riverfront Bar and Grill

NIGHTCLUBS
18. Adam's Mark Daytona Beach Resort, Clocktower Lounge
19. Boot Hill Saloon
20. The Oyster Pub
21. Razzles Nighclub
22. Rockin' Ranch
23. Teauila's Hawaii Luau

210

The Golf Club at Cypress Head

6231 Palm Vista Street, Port Orange; (386) 756-5449; www.cypressheadgolf.com

Established 1992 | **Designer** Arthur Hills/Mike Dasher | **Holes** 18

Tees Black/Blue/White (men)/White (ladies)/Red
Par 72/72/72/72/72 **Slope** 139/130/119/137/123
Fees January 15–April 15, $45; April 15–June 15, $40; June 15–Oct. 15, $33; Fall Oct. 15–January 15, $40; special prices available for residents **Specials** Summer, $18 10 a.m.–1 p.m., league rate $11 after 5 p.m.; winter, $35 after 2 p.m. **Cart rental** Included in green fees **Club rental** $15 **Payment** V, MC, AmEx **Tee times** Up to 7 days in advance **Facilities** Pro shop, restaurant, putting green, chipping green, driving range

Comments Cypress Head prides itself on its well-manicured, undulating greens. This challenging course can be fun for golfers at any skill level. The course allows for a high level of diversity in game play; it's rarely the same from day to day, depending on how you play it.

Indigo Lakes Golf Club

312 Indigo Drive, Daytona Beach; (386) 254-3607; www.indigolakesgolf.com

Established 1976 | **Designer** Lloyd Clifton | **Holes** 18

Tees Black/Light Blue/White/Green
Par 72/72/72/72/72 **Slope** 132/128/124/117
Fees June–December, $30 before 9 a.m.; January–May, $45–65 **Specials** 9 a.m.–2 p.m., $27; after 2 p.m., $20 **Cart rental** Included **Club rental** $10 **Payment** V, MC, AmEx **Tee times** Up to 7 days in advance **Facilities** Pro shop, bar/restaurant, locker room with showers, driving range, putting green, chipping green, sand trap

Comments *Golfweek* magazine rated Indigo Lakes "One of the top ten golf courses in Florida." Its unique design sets this course apart—expect a tight, tree-lined course with water on half the holes. The most challenging is hole 6, a 600-yard, par 5, dogleg left with strategically placed bunkers.

LPGA International, Champions Course

1000 Champions Drive, Daytona Beach; (386) 274-LPGA; www.lpgainternational.com

Established 1994 | **Designer** Rees Jones | **Holes** 18

Tees Black/Blue/White/Gold/Red
Par 72/72/72/72/72 **Slope** 137/132/124/117/125
Fees Seasonal, call for prices **Specials** Call for specials **Cart rental** Included **Club rental** $30 premium, $20 standard **Payment** V, MC, AmEx **Tee times** Up to 30 days in advance **Facilities** Restaurant, snack bar, driving range, putting green, chipping green, bunkers, pro shop

Comments This is one of the first courses built in the country specifically for women, but what awaits you here is a formidable test, no matter what your gender. The course is links-style with only a minimal number of trees. This contributes to the biggest challenge—the wind. There's nothing to deflect it as it blows off the nearby (but unseen) ocean. You also have to negotiate a profusion of wetlands and water hazards on every hole, as well as numerous gaping sand and grass bunkers.

Spruce Creek Golf and Country Club

1900 Country Club Drive, Daytona Beach; (386) 756-6114
Established 1972 | **Designer** Bill Amick | **Holes** 18

Tees Gold/Blue/White/Red **Par** 72/72/72/72 **Slope** 128/126/120/123 **Fees** May–December, $35; January–April, $55 **Specials** Twilight, $20 after 4 p.m. in summer, $40 after 2 p.m. in winter **Cart rental** Included **Club rental** $20 **Payment** V, MC **Tee times** 4 days in advance **Facilities** Restaurant, pro shop, banquet hall, locker room, driving range, putting green, chipping green

Comments The Spruce Creek course has somewhat of a split personality—the front 9 is tree lined, while the back 9 has lots of water, producing a course with two distinct feels to it. The most challenging hole is number 16. This 448-yard par 4 sports bunkers on the corner of a dogleg right.

MOTORCYCLE MANIA

Daytona driving isn't just for NASCAR fans—this popular beach destination is also known to many as "Hog Heaven." Since 1924, bikers have been flocking to Daytona Beach for **Bike Week**, a ten-day festival in March that includes bike-themed activities and events. In October, bikers make another pilgrimage to Daytona for **Biketoberfest**, a half week of events, races, and concerts.

Daytona Beach is also home to the world's largest Harley-Davidson dealer, **Daytona Harley-Davidson**, located at 290 North Beach Street (call (800) 307-4HOG or visit www.daytonaharleydavidson.com). For the ultimate biking experience, rent a Harley-Davidson and ride in style; the store will even arrange to pick you up or drop you off at the Daytona Beach International Airport, except during major event weeks.

Attractions

Boardwalk & Main Street Pier

Ocean Avenue (off SR A1A), Daytona Beach; (386) 253-1212
Hours Daily, 6 a.m.–11 p.m. (extended hours in summer)
Admission To fishing end of pier, $3.50 for adults, $2.50 for children ages 12 and under; $1 for adult spectators, 50 cents for children

Appeal by Age Group

Pre-school ★★	Teens ★★	Over 30 ★★
Grade school ★★	Young Adults ★★	Seniors ★★

Touring Time *Minimum* 30 minutes
Rainy-Day Touring Not recommended
Author's Rating ★; old Florida kitsch
Description and Comments This low-tech boardwalk and pier looks like a movie set from the '60s, a bit worn on the edges. After dark the crowd is often raucous, but in the daytime, try fishing off the pier. No cars are allowed on the beach in this area, so you can stroll and play arcade games, munch on junk food, and re-live another era.

The Casements

25 Riverside Drive, Ormond Beach; (386) 676-3216

Hours Monday–Thursday, 9 a.m.–9 p.m.; Friday, 9 a.m.–5 p.m.; Saturday, 9 a.m.–noon
Admission Free
Appeal by Age Group

Pre-school ★	Teens ★★	Over 30 ★★★
Grade school ★★	Young Adults ★★★	Seniors ★★★

Touring Time At least 45 minutes
Rainy-Day Touring Recommended
Author's Rating ★★★
Description and Comments In 1918, John D. Rockefeller, once the wealthiest man in the country, purchased the Ormond Beach estate called the Casements. Drawn to Florida because of its idyllic winter weather and superb golfing, Rockefeller lived in the large home each winter until his death at the house in 1937. Since that time, the estate has served as a women's junior college, a retirement home, and an apartment building. In the '60s, the house fell into severe disrepair and was left vacant until the City of Ormond Beach purchased it in 1973. Be sure to take a guided tour of the estate, and check out the Boy Scout Historical Exhibit and the Hungarian Folk Art Museum.

Daytona International Speedway/Daytona USA

1801 West International Speedway Boulevard, Daytona Beach; (386) 253-7223 for tickets; (386) 254-2700 for general information; (386) 947-6530 for Daytona USA; www.daytonaintlspeedway.com

Hours Daily, 9 a.m.–7 p.m., with extended hours during certain race events
Admission Tram only is $7 per person, children ages 5 and under get in free with a paying adult; Daytona USA, with tram, is $20 for adults, $17 for seniors ages 60 and older, $8 for children ages 6–12, free under age 6
Appeal by Age Group

Pre-school ★★	Teens ★★★	Over 30 ★★★
Grade school ★★★	Young Adults ★★★	Seniors ★★

Touring Time *Average* 2 hours; *minimum* 1 hour
Rainy-Day Touring Recommended
Author's Rating ★★★; live vicariously—simulators allow you to race on a virtual Speedway
Description and Comments The Speedway hosts ten weekends of racing a year, including NASCAR, stock car, sports car, and motorcycle races, plus vehicle testing throughout the year. But for racecar enthusiasts, the only time to visit is during Speedweeks, a two-week-long event at the Daytona International Speedway that begins the first weekend in February. Each year, more than 160,000 people attend the Daytona 500, the culmination of Speedweeks. Racing is one of the country's fastest-growing spectator sports, and its fans are a faithful bunch.

If you don't plan your vacation around a race, there are still ways to get your motor fix at the Speedway. A 30-minute tram tour, takes you on the Speedway's high-banked, 2.5-mile tri-oval course and 3.5-mile road course. You'll also see the infield, pit, and garage areas. These tours depart daily, every half-hour, 9:30 a.m.–4 p.m., weather and track schedule permitting.

Interactive **Daytona USA** is the other big draw at the Speedway. Called "The Ultimate Motorsports Attraction," Daytona USA has an admittance fee separate from the tram. Guests enter the building through a replica of the raceway's famous twin tunnels. Visitors can change tires in a timed pit stop competition, broadcast a race, talk to drivers through video monitors, and test their knowledge in an auto trivia game. Playing in the attraction's Pepsi Theater is *The Daytona 500,* a film that gives fans a behind-the-scenes glimpse at the famous race. Victory Lane displays the winning car from the latest Daytona 500. Included in admission is the motion simulator ride Daytona Dream Laps. For an extra fee ($5 per driver, with complementary passenger), compete against your peers on Acceleration Alley, a simulated racing game featuring an 80-percent scale stock car.

For those who can't get enough speed, there's the **Richard Petty Driving Experience** ticket for $134 (which includes admission to Daytona USA). Climb into the front seat of a stock car with a professional instructor at the wheel for three laps on the 2.5-mile track. You must be at least 16 years old. This experience is not always available, so call ahead.

Ormond Memorial Art Museum and Gardens

78 East Granada Boulevard, Ormond Beach; (386) 676-3347
Hours Monday–Friday, 10 a.m.–4 p.m.; Saturday and Sunday, noon–4 p.m.; gardens close at sundown; museum closed periodically due to changing exhibits
Admission $2 per person donation requested
Appeal by Age Group

Pre-school ★	Teens ★★	Over 30 ★★★
Grade school ★★	Young Adults ★★★	Seniors ★★★★

Touring Time At least 30 minutes

Rainy-Day Touring Not recommended

Author's Rating ★★½

Description and Comments Located on busy Granada Boulevard, the gardens provide visitors the opportunity to forget the hustle of nearby Daytona Beach. Follow the twisting paths through the gardens and relax, taking time to watch a turtle sun itself on the bank of a small pond. The Ormond Memorial Gardens are kept in a more natural, wild state, and are not as manicured and manipulated as other gardens.

FREE OR ALMOST FREE

Take a guided tour of Angell & Phelps Chocolate Factory, a Daytona Beach original established in 1924, and watch as more than 100 kinds of candies are made. Of course, there are free samples. Open Monday–Friday, 9:30 a.m.–5:30 p.m.; Saturday, 9 a.m.–5 p.m. Thirty-minute tours available at 10 and 11 a.m. and 1, 2, 3, and 4 p.m., Monday–Friday. Located at 154 South Beach Street; (386) 252-6531 or (800) 969-2634.

Shopping

Riverfront Marketplace is one of the area's most popular shopping districts. Located on historic Beach Street, the marketplace is home to an impressive number of antique dealers, cafés, boutiques, and other shops. Star players are Angell & Phelps Chocolate Factory and the **Beach Street Antique Mall & Emporium** (166 South Beach Street, (386) 258-5990). You'll also find the Halifax Historic Museum in this charming area.

The **Volusia Mall** (1700 West International Speedway Boulevard, (386) 253-6783) offers department stores such as Sears, JC Penney, Dillard's, and Burdine's, as well as a food court and over 100 specialty shops.

For Florida souvenirs (shells, T-shirts, etc.) try one of the many souvenir shops along the beach on SR A1A. Bikers will enjoy the expansive **Daytona Harley-Davidson** at 290 North Beach Street. Several other bike shops are located in the same area—drive north on Beach Street and find stores both selling and repairing motorcycles.

Flea Market The **Daytona Flea and Farmers' Market** (2987 Bellevue Avenue; (386) 253-3330) offers selections ranging from jewelry to clothing and gift items. The market has a focus on fresh fruits and vegetables.

Fruit

Pell's Citrus and Nursery (phone (800) 459-8897; www.pellcitrus.com) has a booth at the Daytona Flea and Farmers' Market and offers fresh Florida citrus, including oranges, tangerines, grapefruits, and more. The fruit comes from their own groves and is washed and prepared in their own facilities.

Dining

Angell & Phelps Restaurant and Wine Bar

156 South Beach Street, Daytona Beach; (386) 257-2677;
www.angellandphelps.com/cafe

Meals served Lunch, Monday–Saturday, 11 a.m.–3 p.m.; dinner, Tuesday–Thursday, 4:30–9 p.m., and Friday and Saturday, 4:30–10 p.m. **Cuisine** American **Entree range** Lunch $3.50–$8.50, dinner $14–$21 **Reservations** Recommended on weekends **Payment** V, MC, D, AmEx

Comments This charming café by day, sassy restaurant and bar by night, is located next door to the Angell & Phelps Chocolate Factory in one of Daytona's best shopping districts—Riverfront Marketplace on historic Beach Street. If you're there for lunch, try the deli sandwiches. On Thursday, Friday, and Saturday nights, enjoy live jazz.

Aunt Catfish's

4009 Halifax Drive (west end of Port Orange Bridge), Port Orange; (386) 767-4768

Meals served Lunch and dinner **Cuisine** "Down South River Cookin'" **Entree range** Lunch $5–$7, dinner $10–$27 **Reservations** Priority seating and call-ahead seating **Payment** V, MC, AmEx, D

Comments Seafood, anything you could want: shrimp, lobster, crabs, scallops, oysters, and fish, and any way you want it: Cajun, fried, broiled, grilled, or baked. Wash it down with an ice-cold glass of sweet tea or freshly squeezed lemonade. With special menus for early birds, seniors, and children, this restaurant aims to please. In the summer, lounge on the dock and listen to the bands.

Barnacle's

869 South Atlantic Avenue, Ormond Beach; (386) 673-1070;
www.barnaclesrestaurant.com

Meals served Dinner **Cuisine** Seafood **Entree range** $10–$28 **Reservations** Accepted for parties of more than six, call-ahead available for smaller parties **Payment** Major credit cards accepted

Comments Barnacle's offers plenty of seafood options, as well as an extensive "For Ye Landlubbers" section, which includes their popular baby-back ribs.

Buca di Bepo

2514 West International Speedway Boulevard, Daytona; (386) 253-6523

Meals served Dinner daily, lunch on Saturday, Sunday **Cuisine** Italian **Entree range** Lunch $6–$10, dinner $18–$30 **Reservations** Accepted **Payment** All major credit cards accepted

Comments When you're hungry after a day at the beach, this is the place to bring a crowd for gargantuan servings of pasta, pizza, and more. Save room for tiramisu, but keep in mind that it's enough to share.

Captain Darrell's Oyster Bar

13 Boardwalk, Daytona Beach; (386) 255-5822

Meals served Lunch and dinner **Cuisine** Seafood **Entree range** $4–$15 **Reservations** Not accepted **Payment** Cash only

Comments Seafood is plentiful, but Darrell's also pleases the picky with staples such as hamburgers and chicken. The highlight—a go-cart track on the roof.

Crabby Joe's at Sunglow Pier

3701 South Atlantic Avenue, Daytona Beach Shores; (386) 788-3364; www.sunglowpier.com

Meals served Breakfast, lunch, and dinner **Cuisine** Seafood **Entree range** $9–$17 **Reservations** Only for large groups **Payment** V, MC, AmEx

Comments Enjoy Florida seafood with the ocean directly underneath your seat. Weather permitting, opt for a seat outside and enjoy the sights and sounds of the Atlantic. On Wednesday and Thursday nights, enjoy live entertainment, and unleash your inner performer during karaoke on Friday and Saturday nights.

Top of Daytona

2625 South Atlantic Avenue, Daytona Beach Shores; (386) 767-5791; www.topofdaytona.com

Meals served Dinner **Cuisine** Continental/American **Entree range** $14–$24 **Reservations** Recommended **Payment** V, MC, AmEx, D

Comments Top of Daytona offers the ultimate "dinner with a view." Located on the 29th floor of the Peck Plaza in Daytona Beach Shores, this restaurant offers a 360º view of the beach and the city.

The Wreck Riverfront Bar and Grill

115 Main Street, Daytona Beach; (386) 226-3000; www.wreckbar.com

Meals served Lunch and dinner **Cuisine** American/seafood **Entree range** $7–$20 **Reservations** Accepted **Payment** V, MC, AmEx, D

Comments Overlooking the Halifax River, this restaurant's atmosphere is an eclectic "nautical motorcycle theme," complete with Harley memorabilia and mounted fish. There is live entertainment at night. The specialty is the Wreck Pasta, with shrimp and scallops in a tomato basil garlic sauce.

Arts and Culture

For a treat, plan to see a concert at the **Bandshell**—an open-air amphitheater that looks somewhat like a large sandcastle (phone (386) 673-2080; **www.bandshell.org**). The 48-foot by 114-foot coquina structure enjoyed its first performance on July 4, 1937. The Bandshell seats 4,500 and provides spectacular ocean views and convenient access to local attractions and shopping (a short walk south takes you to the Boardwalk and Main Street Pier).

Nightlife

Adam's Mark Daytona Beach Resort, Clocktower Lounge

Who goes there Tourists, convention-goers, vacationers

100 North Atlantic Avenue, Daytona Beach; (386) 254-8200

Cover None **Minimum** None **Mixed drinks** $3.50 and up **Food available** Dinner and appetizers are available **Hours** 11 a.m.–1 a.m.

What goes on Wednesdays through Sundays, enjoy live, "easy-listening" music (piano, acoustic guitar, vocals).

Comments This lobby bar offers fabulous views of the Atlantic Ocean and the historic clocktower through its large bay windows. The atmosphere is classy and sophisticated, with soft candlelight and generous chairs and loveseats.

Boot Hill Saloon

Who goes there Bikers, bikers, and more bikers

310 Main Street, Daytona Beach; (386) 258-9506; www.boothillsaloon.com

Cover None **Minimum** 21 **Mixed drinks** $1.25 and up **Food available** No **Hours** 11 a.m.–3 a.m.

What goes on Somewhat seedy, but there's plenty of conversation and good times as bikers reminisce about days gone by and discuss upcoming rides. Live music on Friday and Saturday nights.

Comments When the Boot Hill Saloon building was constructed in the 1800s, it was one-third barbershop, one-third bar, and one-third church. Today, the saloon is a biker icon and boasts memorabilia from decades of partying. The crowd gets huge during Bike Week and Biketoberfest.

The Oyster Pub

Who goes there Locals, tourists, businesspeople at lunch and after work, couples, singles

555 Seabreeze Boulevard; (386) 255-6348; www.oysterpub.com

Cover None **Minimum** None **Mixed drinks** $3.50 and up **Food available** Full menu, including plenty of oysters **Hours** 11:30 a.m.–3 a.m. daily

What goes on Visitors watch satellite TV on 34 screens, play pool and games in the game room, and enjoy plenty of the pub's famous oysters.

Comments For over 20 years, the Oyster Pub has been providing the Daytona Beach area with oysters and entertainment. But, hands down, the oysters are the main attraction here—you can have them steamed, raw, or fried, or try one of the pub's specialty oysters.

Razzles Nightclub

Who goes there Singles looking to see and be seen, people-watchers, young partiers

611 Seabreeze Boulevard, Daytona Beach; (386) 257-6236; www.razzlesnightclub.com

Cover $5 for ages 21 and up, $10 under 21 **Minimum** 18 **Mixed drinks** $3.50 and up (two-for-one drink specials nightly) **Food available** No **Hours** Nightly, 8 p.m.–3 a.m.

What goes on Lots of dancing and drinking—Razzles sports a large dance floor, a 40,000-watt sound system, 6 bars, several pool tables, and plenty of televisions.

Comments This flashy, 14,000-square-foot dance club has a VIP lounge and a dress code; no shorts and sandals here. Leave baggy clothing, tank tops, and headbands at home or at the hotel. Bandanas are prohibited, except during bike events.

Rockin' Ranch

Who goes there Locals, cowboys, and cowgirls

801 South Nova Road, Ormond Beach; (386) 673-0904

Cover Wednesday, Friday, and Saturday, no cover for ages 21 and up (ladies 18–20, $5) **Minimum** Monday, Tuesday, and Thursday, 2 drinks **Mixed drinks** $3.50–$7 **Food available** Appetizers (pizza, wings, etc.); free popcorn and nachos **Hours** Monday–Saturday, 6 p.m.–2:30 a.m.

What goes on The Rockin' Ranch is half bar, half dance hall; try a free country dance lesson, available six nights a week.

Comments This local hangout attracts mostly an older crowd, except on weekends when 20-somethings come for drinks and dancing. The Rockin' Ranch offers a fairly clean and friendly atmosphere.

Teauila's Hawaii-Luau

Who goes there Tourists, locals celebrating special events

2301 South Atlantic Avenue, Daytona Beach; (386) 255-5411; www.teauilashawaii.com

Cover $28 for dinner and show; $16 for children ages 5–10; free for children under age 5 **Minimum** None **Mixed drinks** $2.50 and up **Food available** Dinner options include American, Seafood, and Hawaiian fare **Hours** Open Wednesday–Sunday, September–January; daily in December; and Tuesday–Sunday, February–August. Happy hour at 5:30 p.m., dinner seating at 6:30 p.m.

What goes on The longest-running dinner theater in Daytona, the Teauila's Hawaii Luau features women in grass skirts and men with flaming swords in a 250-seat auditorium. Guests enjoy having their picture taken next to the ten-foot active indoor volcano.

Comments The atmosphere is very retro; neon lights, black lights, and tiki masks are everywhere.

Side Trips

Blue Spring State Park Every January or February lumbering manatees take refuge in the 72° water of Blue Spring, one of the few places you can observe them in their native habitat, and it's not unusual to see 25 or more on a January morning. About 121 million gallons of water flow from Blue

Spring, making snorkeling fun in the summertime, when you'll see lots of catfish, gar, tilapia, and largemouth bass. A frame house built in the 1800s is now the visitor center, restored to look as it did back when farmers sent their crops to Jacksonville by steamboat. There's also picnicking, camping on 51 sites ($15 plus tax, $17 plus tax with electricity) and canoe rentals. The park opens daily at 8 a.m. and closes at sunset year-round. The vehicle entry fee is $4. Located two miles west of Orange City off I-4 and US 17/92; (386) 775-3663.

DeLeon Springs State Recreation Area   This beautiful spring feeds into a swimming pool with concrete sides. Canoes and kayaks are for rent, and a nearby nature trail helps you work up an appetite. Plan your visit around breakfast at the **Old Spanish Mill and Griddle House** (phone (386) 985-5644), once an old stone waterhouse and now a restaurant with specially built tables with big griddles in the middle. You order pitchers of batter and little bowls of nuts, fresh fruit, chocolate chips, or peanut butter and make your own all-you-can-eat flapjacks for $4 a person (extras cost $1 and up). If it's cool outdoors, ask for a seat on the screened porch. Go early; the lines get long; reservations are accepted for parties of ten or more. Open daily, weekends at 8 a.m., weekdays at 9 a.m. Cost is $4 per carload (up to eight people) to enter the park at 601 Ponce de Leon Boulevard, DeLeon Springs Park, (386) 985-4212.

Hontoon Island State Park   You can only get there by boat, and a daily ferry will take you across the St. Johns River to this little island. There's great fishing, and you can camp in primitive cabins (shared bathhouses) for $20–$35, or in tents for $8. Open daily, 8 a.m.–an hour before sunset year-round. Southwest of DeLand six miles, off SR 44; (386) 736-5309.

New Smyrna Beach

New Smyrna Beach is rich in history and natural treasures and has become a popular destination for visitors looking for a Florida beach vacation with less glitz and more R&R.

The area is known for its peaceful, underdeveloped beaches. Compared to Daytona Beach, its sister just to the north, New Smyrna Beach is a slower, less commercialized beach town. Underwater rock ledges protect the beach from dangerous rip currents, and New Smyrna Beach has been called the "World's Safest Bathing Beach."

The Ponce de Leon Inlet Lighthouse is tallest in Florida. Climb to the top for unbeatable views of the Inlet.

Surfing is a popular pastime here, and national surfing championships have been held at the beach. For fun inland, enjoy shopping in one of New Smyrna Beach's charming, idyllic historic areas, or visit one of the historic ruins in the area.

If you're looking for a Florida destination where nature and history are the main attractions, schedule a visit to sleepy New Smyrna Beach.

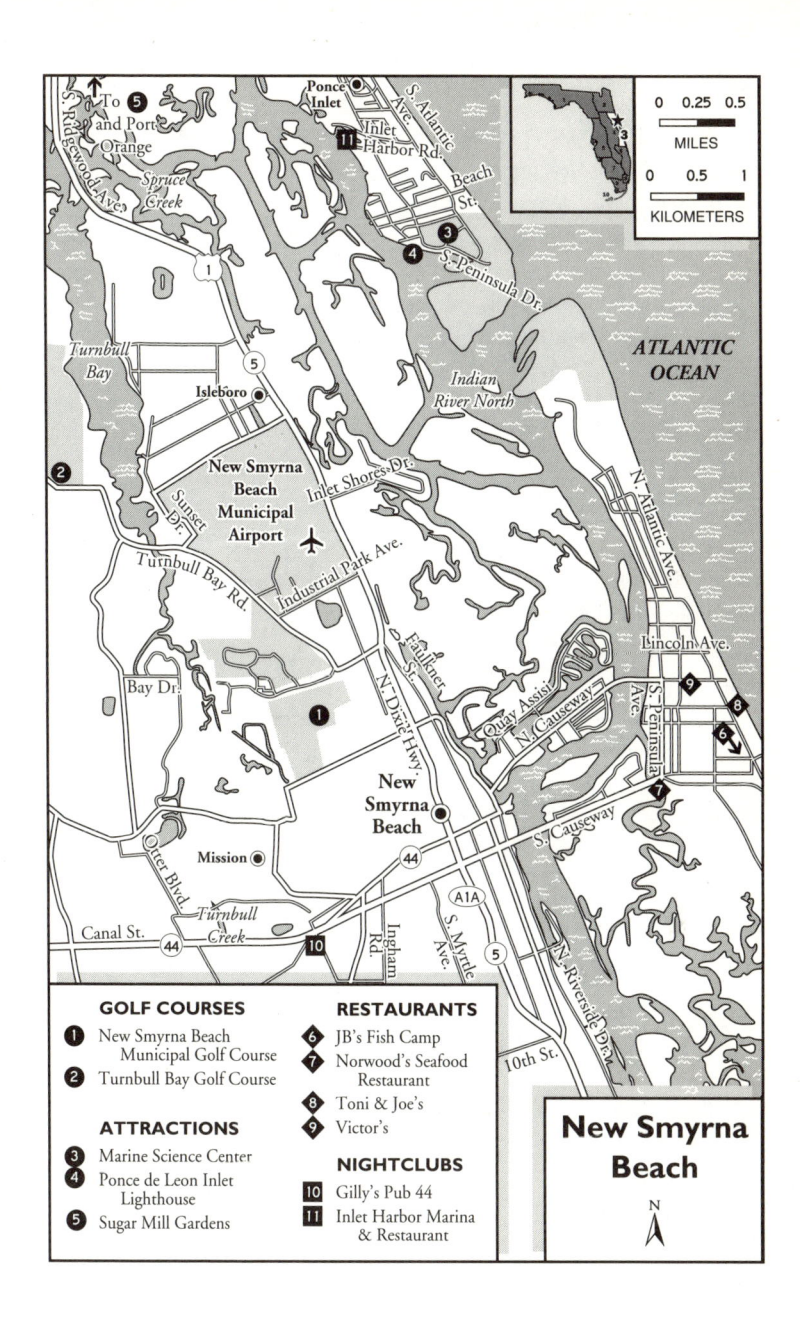

GOLF COURSES

1. New Smyrna Beach Municipal Golf Course
2. Turnbull Bay Golf Course

ATTRACTIONS

3. Marine Science Center
4. Ponce de Leon Inlet Lighthouse
5. Sugar Mill Gardens

RESTAURANTS

6. JB's Fish Camp
7. Norwood's Seafood Restaurant
8. Toni & Joe's
9. Victor's

NIGHTCLUBS

10. Gilly's Pub 44
11. Inlet Harbor Marina & Restaurant

New Smyrna Beach

Golf

New Smyrna Beach Municipal Golf Course

1000 Wayne Avenue, New Smyrna Beach; (386) 424-2192
Established 1950 | **Designer** Donald Ross | **Holes** 18

Tees Blue/White/Gold/Red **Par** 72/72/72/72 **Slope** 124/122/115/116
Fees April 15–October, $26; call for winter rates **Specials** Summer afternoon, $20 with cart **Cart rental** $11, not required **Club rental** $7 **Payment** V, MC, D **Tee times** Up to 2 days in advance **Facilities** Pro shop, restaurant, driving range
Comments This municipal golf course is one of Donald Ross's last designs—well balanced without an overabundance of either trees or water. Carts are not required, so you can enjoy walking the course.

Turnbull Bay Golf Course

2600 Turnbull Estates Drive, New Smyrna Beach; (386) 427-8727; www.turnbullbaygolfcourse.com
Established 1995 | **Designer** Gary Wintz | **Holes** 18

Tees Blue/White/Gold/Red **Par** 72/72/72/72 **Slope** 129/124/116/119
Fees Summer $32, winter $48 **Specials** Call for specials **Cart rental** Included **Club rental** $15 **Payment** V, MC **Tee times** Available 4 days in advance **Facilities** Pro shop, concession, driving range, putting green
Comments Turnbull Bay Golf Course, located near Turnbull Bay and the Atlantic Ocean, prides itself on the natural setting it offers players. The course has been called an "Environmental Masterpiece" and sports 21 lakes, plenty of large trees, and plant life including azaleas and ferns.

Attractions

Marine Science Center

100 Lighthouse Drive; (386) 304-5545; www.marinesciencecenter.com
Hours Tuesday–Saturday, 10 a.m.–4 p.m.; Sunday, noon–4 p.m.; closed Monday
Admission Adults, $3; children, $1 (ages 5–12); under age 5 free
Appeal by Age Group

Pre-school ★★★	Teens ★★	Over 30 ★★½
Grade school ★★★	Young Adults ★★½	Seniors ★★½

Touring Time *Minimum* 45 minutes
Rainy-Day Touring Recommended
Author's Rating ★★½
Description and Comments Highlights of the Marine Science Center include the 5,000-gallon artificial reef aquarium and the sea turtle rehabilitation laboratory. From Turtle Terrace, you can observe the rehab facility, and at certain times of the day you can watch turtles being tube-fed.

Ponce de Leon Inlet Lighthouse

4931 South Peninsula Drive, Ponce Inlet; (386) 761-1821; www.ponceinlet.org
Hours Daily, 10 a.m.–5 p.m. (extended hours in summer)
Admission $5 adults, $1.50 children ages 11 and under
Appeal by Age Group

Pre-school ★★	Teens ★★	Over 30 ★★★
Grade school ★★★	Young Adults ★★★	Seniors ★★★

Touring Time *Minimum* 1 hour
Rainy-Day Touring Not recommended (lighthouse closes if it is lightning)
Author's Rating ★★★; spectacular view
Description and Comments It's a challenge to climb all 203 spiraling steps, but the sweeping view of Daytona and New Smyrna Beach is worth the trek. Built in 1887, this 175-foot-high working lighthouse is Florida's tallest (the second tallest in the United States) and is designated a National Historic Landmark. And the lighthouse itself isn't the only attraction: all seven original buildings still stand, including the lightkeeper's restored house.

Sugar Mill Gardens

950 Old Sugar Mill Road, Port Orange; (386) 767-1735
Hours November–March, 8 a.m.–6 p.m. daily; April 1–Oct. 31 8 a.m.–7 p.m. daily
Admission Free; donations appreciated
Appeal by Age Group

Pre-school ★	Teens ★★	Over 30 ★★★
Grade school ★★	Young Adults ★★	Seniors ★★★

Touring Time *Minimum* 45 minutes
Rainy-Day Touring Not recommended
Author's Rating ★★
Description and Comments Sugar Mill Gardens is located on what was once a thriving, 995-acre sugar plantation. The first mill was built in 1804 and was operated until the Civil War, when the plantation was used for salt production for the Confederate army. In the 1940s, 12 acres of the plantation were converted into an amusement park called Bongoland, which contributed five large concrete dinosaur statues that still stand today. The botanical gardens were established in 1988 and feature magnolias, camellias, ginger, native holly, and many more varieties of plants.

Shopping

Old-fashioned charm abounds in New Smyrna Beach shopping districts. The two most notable historic shopping areas are **Canal Street** and **Flagler Avenue.** On the mainland, Canal Street is built over an actual canal used by early settlers in the area and is home to a variety of merchants, from antiques and jewelry stores to clothing and home decor shops. Flagler Avenue is located within walking distance of the beach; its merchants (more than 50) offer goods ranging from handmade pottery to beach souvenirs.

Flea Market The **New Smyrna Flea Market** is held on Canal Street every Saturday morning and showcases gifts, collectibles, and fresh fruits and vegetables.

Dining

JB's Fish Camp

859 Pompano Avenue, New Smyrna Beach; (386) 427-5747; www.jbsfishcamp.com

Meals served Lunch, dinner **Cuisine** Seafood **Entree range** $13–$21 **Reservations** Not suggested **Payment** All major credit cards accepted
Comments This waterfront restaurant has been serving fresh seafood in a casual atmosphere for over 24 years. If the weather's nice, ask for a table outside and enjoy the cool river breeze while you eat. The restaurant is so close to the water that some diners arrive on boats.

Norwood's Seafood Restaurant

400 Second Avenue, New Smyrna Beach; (386) 428-4621; www.norwoods.com

Meals served Lunch, dinner **Cuisine** Seafood/American **Entree range** $7–$25 **Reservations** Recommended **Payment** Major credit cards
Comments Since its opening in 1946, Norwood's has won a slew of awards, for everything from catering to chowder cook-offs. The menu offers a wide selection of both surf and turf; a crowd favorite is Norwood's chicken, charbroiled and topped with turkey, teriyaki, and Swiss.

Norwood's prides itself on its enormous selection of wines. There's a complimentary wine tasting every Friday, 5–7 p.m.

Toni & Joe's

309 Buenos Aires, New Smyrna Beach; (386) 427-6850

Meals served Lunch **Cuisine** American **Entree range** $3–$13 **Reservations** Not necessary **Payment** No credit cards accepted
Comments It doesn't get any more casual than Toni & Joe's. Shirts and shoes are not required at this beachfront restaurant, and there isn't even a set closing time, just 11 a.m. to "sunset," or when customers wander off. Their cheese steaks are a popular favorite with beachgoers.

Victor's Backstreet Cuisine

103 South Pine Street, New Smyrna Beach; (386) 426-5000

Meals served Dinner **Cuisine** American **Entree range** $8.50–$23 **Reservations** Recommended **Payment** Cash, check
Comments The dining room is small (only eight tables), but the personality and charm of this restaurant are enormous. Owner and chef Victor Detec is proud of the unique combinations on the menu. Star players are

the Apple Brandy Pork Loin, Teriyaki Tuna, and the baby-back ribs. The atmosphere is casual, and the only thing dressed up is the food.

Nightlife

Gilly's Pub 44

Who goes there All ages during the day, at night mix of locals and out-of-towners
1889 State Road 44, New Smyrna; (386) 428-6523; www.gillyspub44.com
Cover None **Minimum** None **Mixed drinks** $2 and up **Food available** Full menu, 11 a.m.–10 p.m. (until midnight Friday and Saturday); limited menu, 10 p.m.–1 a.m. **Hours** Daily, 11 a.m.–2 a.m.
What goes on Gilly's Pub features live entertainment on the weekends and a comedy club on Wednesdays. There's something for everyone here—they've got arcade games, a tiki bar, TVs, and pool tables.
Comments Gilly's has been in New Smyrna for over 20 years and remains one of the most popular pubs in the area.

Inlet Harbor Marina and Restaurant

Who goes there Tourists, locals, singles, families
133 Inlet Harbor Road, Ponce Inlet; (386) 767-5590; www.inletharbor.com
Cover None **Minimum** None **Mixed drinks** $3.75 and up **Food available** Full dinner menu, seafood **Hours** Sunday–Thursday, 11 a.m.–10 p.m.; Friday and Saturday, 11 a.m.–11 p.m.
What goes on Live music every night, ranging from Caribbean to R&B.
Comments Enjoy torch-lit dancing and dining in a family-friendly, Caribbean setting.

Cocoa Beach and Surrounding Areas

Since NASA began its operations in Cape Canaveral in 1958, the Cocoa Beach area has grown from a mostly rural area to the busy vacation destination it is today. The Kennedy Space Center Visitor Complex is a major attraction that combines hands-on exhibits, IMAX films, a bus tour of restricted areas, a full-scale model of the shuttle, and more for a fun and interactive look into the space program. The Valiant Air Command Warbird Air Museum displays planes from World War I to the present.

Not only does the Space Coast have command of the air, but it also dominates the sea. Cape Canaveral is home to Florida's fastest-growing cruise port served by Carnival, Disney, and Royal Caribbean Cruise Lines. Natural coral and artificial reefs attract numerous fish, and trawlers supply Central Florida with hours-old seafood. Mackerel, sailfish, wahoo, tuna, and more can be found in these waters.

Cocoa Beach is one of Florida's most popular beaches. The closest beach to Orlando, its location has made a visit to the beach a popular addition to

Cocoa Beach and Surrounding Area

N

GOLF COURSES
1. Baytree National Golf Club
2. Cocoa Beach Country Club
3. The Habitat at Valkaria
4. The Majors
5. Spessard Holland
6. Turtle Creek Golf Club
7. Viera East Golf Club

ATTRACTIONS
8. Astronaut Memorial Planetarium and Observatory
9. Brevard Zoo
10. Cocoa Beach Pier
11. Kennedy Space Center Visitor Complex
12. Vallant Air Command Warbird Air Museum

RESTAURANTS
13. Alma's
14. Bernard's Surf
15. The Black Tulip
16. Café Margaux
17. Coconuts on the Beach
18. Dixie Crossroads
19. Jack Baker's Lobster Shanty
20. The Mango Tree

NIGHTCLUBS
21. The Beach Shack
22. Big Daddy Dave's Jazz & Blue's Club
23. Dino's Supper Club
24. Heidi's Jazz Club

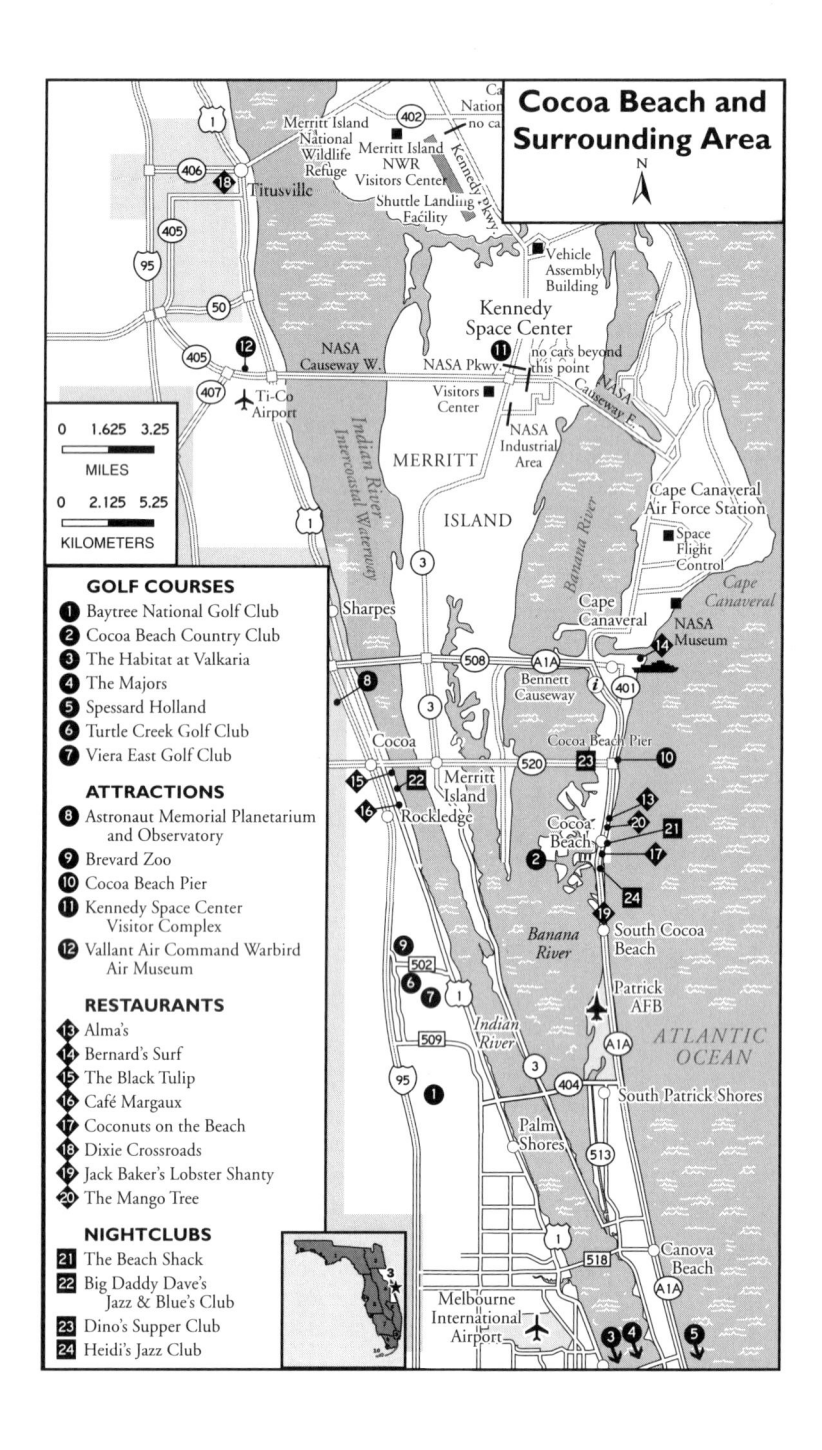

Central Florida vacations. Ron Jon's Surf Shop, a local landmark, sells anything from surfboards to the famous Ron Jon T-shirts.

Offering a more natural beach experience, Merritt Island Wildlife Refuge is home to over 500 species of animals, many of them endangered or threatened. You can take a self-guided driving tour through the refuge, or hike along one of the nature paths.

Golf

Baytree National Golf Club

8207 National Drive, Melbourne; (321) 259-9060; www.golfbaytree.com

Established 1994 | **Designer** Gary Player | **Holes** 18

Tees Black/Gold/Blue/White/Red

Par 72/72/72/72/72 **Slope** 135/129/123/114/121

Fees Monday–Thursday, $39 before noon, $33 after; Friday–Sunday (and holidays), $49 before noon, $39 after **Specials** Twilight, $26 after 4 p.m. **Cart rental** Included **Club rental** $30 **Payment** V, MC, AmEx **Tee times** 6 days in advance **Facilities** Pro shop, restaurant, banquet room, locker room, putting green, chipping green, driving range

Comments A "golfer's golf course," Baytree has a well-manicured layout, lots of variety, and plenty of challenge. There's a hazard on every hole, and the course requires that you hit the ball straight on most holes. Baytree's signature hole is 18, with its intimidating semi-island layout.

Cocoa Beach Country Club

5000 Tom Warriner Boulevard, Cocoa Beach; (321) 868-3351; www.ci.cocoa-beach.fl.us/recreation/golf

Established 1991 | **Designer** Charles Ankrom | **Holes** 27

Tees Gold/Blue/White/Red **Par** 72 (River), 71 (Dolphin and Lakes)

Slope Lakes and River, 119/114/110/113; Lakes and Dolphin, 115/110/105/109; River and Dolphin, 116/111/106/108

Fees Summer, $40 nonresidents, $33 Brevard County residents, $31 Cocoa Beach residents; winter, $46 nonresidents, $35 Brevard County residents, $33 Cocoa Beach residents **Specials** Twilight, $22 summer after 1 p.m., $27 winter; unlimited walking, $13 summer, $18 winter **Cart rental** Included **Club rental** $20 **Payment** V, MC, AmEx **Tee times** Up to 28 days in advance **Facilities** Pro shop, snack bar/lounge, auditorium, putting greens, chipping green, driving range

Comments This course is literally one of the coolest in the area—1.4 miles of its course runs right along the edge of the Banana River, providing cool breezes on hot summer days. The club's three courses (River, Dolphin, and Lakes) aren't as challenging as some others in the area, but it's hard to beat the course's great views and plenty of wildlife.

The Habitat at Valkaria

3591 Fairgreen Street, Valkaria; (321) 952-4588;
www.golfspacecoast.com/brevard/habitat

Established 1991 | **Designer** Charles Ankrom | **Holes** 18

Tees Black/Gold/Blue/White/Green
Par 72/72/72/72/72 **Slope** 141/137/133/132/119
Fees Nonresidents, $24 with cart, $12 without; Brevard County residents, $20 with cart, $8 without **Specials** 18 holes and cart after 1 p.m., $12 **Cart rental** No required **Club rental** $15 **Payment** V, MC **Tee times** Up to 3 days in advance **Facilities** Pro shop, snack bar, putting green, chipping green, driving range
Comments The Habitat boasts a course with plenty of variety and no houses. Its natural setting includes wetlands and pine forest areas. The course sports plenty of bunkers and a variety of water and tree obstacles; the back 9 is tighter and more tree-lined than the front.

The Majors

3775 Bayside Lakes Boulevard Southeast, Palm Bay; (321) 952-8617;
www.majorsgolfclub.com

Established 1999 | **Designer** Arnold Palmer | **Holes** 18

Tees Black/Blue/White/Gold/Red
Par 72/72/72/72/72 **Slope** 140/136/129/125/128
Fees Summer, $25–$30; winter, $50–$55 **Specials** Summer twilight, $20; winter, $30–$35 **Cart rental** Included **Club rental** $20 **Payment** V, MC, D **Tee times** Up to 5 days in advance **Facilities** Clubhouse, pro shop, conference room, restaurant, bar, locker room with showers, driving range, putting green, chipping green
Comments This Palm Bay course may be somewhat hard to find, but it is well worth the drive. It prides itself on being a "public course with private amenities." The playtime is long if you play from the back tees—the course can take over five hours. This difficult course has a "Carolina feel," with plenty of hazards.

Spessard Holland (Executive Course)

2374 Oak Street, Melbourne Beach; (321) 952-4530;
www.golfspacecoast.com/brevard/spessardholland

Established 1977 | **Designer** Arnold Palmer Enterprises | **Holes** 18

Tees Black/Gold/Blue/Green
Par 67/67/67/67 **Slope** 119/117/109/101
Fees $29 nonresidents, $25 Brevard County residents **Specials** After 1 p.m., $19 **Cart rental** Included **Club rental** $15 **Payment** V, MC **Tee times** Up to 3 days in advance **Facilities** Pro shop, restaurant, chipping green, driving range, putting green

Comments Spessard Holland prides itself on its prime location—the course is located on the Indian River and is only about 25 yards from the ocean. Sea breezes add dynamic challenges to this course. Spessard Holland gives you the choice of walking the course or renting a cart. And after finishing your game, head to the beach to relax.

Turtle Creek Golf Club

1279 Admiralty Boulevard, Rockledge; (321) 632-2520; www.turtlecreekgolfclub.com
Established 1973 | **Designer** Robert Renaud | **Holes** 18

Tees Gold/Blue/White/Red **Par** 72/72/72/72 **Slope** 130/125/116/113
Fees $25 until 1 p.m., $20 after 1 p.m. (June and July) **Specials** 9-hole special $15 after 4 p.m. (June and July) **Cart rental** Included in greens fee; walking restricted to members only **Club rental** $20 **Payment** V, MC, AmEx, D **Tee times** 7 days in advance **Facilities** Full-service pub and grill, pro shop, putting and chipping greens, driving range
Comments Turtle Creek offers a course that winds through natural vegetation and has homes on only two holes. The course is the only one in Brevard County to offer the Pro Link GPS Yardage System, which gives players the exact yardage from a computer screen mounted in their carts.

Viera East Golf Club

2300 Clubhouse Drive, Viera; (321) 639-6500; www.vieragolf.com
Established 1994 | **Designer** Joe Lee | **Holes** 18

Tees Men: Gold/Blue/White/Silver; Women: Silver/Orange/Red
Par 72/72/72/72; 72/72/72
Slope 139/136/134/126; 126/122/116
Fees Weekdays, $29–$59 (depending on season); weekends, $35–$59
Specials Call for special rates after noon and 3 p.m.; summer 5-round special, $99; back 9 special, morning back 9 play, $17 **Cart rental** Included
Club rental $15 **Payment** V, MC, AmEx, D **Tee times** Reservations up to 7 days in advance by phone, up to 60 days for online reservations **Facilities** Pro shop, restaurant, driving range, putting green, chipping green
Comments The course has a four-star rating given by *Golf Digest* (2000–2003) and the "Best in Brevard" (2001–2003) title by the *Florida Today* newspaper. Nearly every hole has a lake or a wetland area to negotiate, and number 14 is a peninsula green that requires an accurate tee shot. The course sports Joe Lee trademark bunkers that are well placed and challenging.

Attractions

Astronaut Memorial Planetarium and Observatory

1519 Clearlake Road, Cocoa; (321) 634-3732; www.brevard.cc.fl.us/~planet
Hours Wednesday, 1:30–4:30 p.m.; Friday and Saturday, 6:30–10:30 p.m. Observatory open Friday and Saturday, 7:30–10 p.m.

Admission Observatory and exhibits, free; single show (planetarium or movie), $6 adults, $5 seniors and students, $4 children ages 12 and under; combination (planetarium and movie), $10 adults, $8 seniors/students, $6 children; triple combination (planetarium, movie, and laser), $14 adults, seniors/students, and children.

Appeal by Age Group

Pre-school ★★	Teens ★★	Over 30 ★★★
Grade school ★★★	Young Adults ★★★	Seniors ★★

Touring Time *Minimum* 1 hour
Rainy-Day Touring Recommended
Author's Rating ★★★

Description and Comments For views that are literally out of this world, head to the Astronaut Memorial Planetarium and Observatory. Its 24-inch telescope is available for free public viewings. You can also peruse exhibits with mission badges, photographs, and flags. In the Science Quest Exhibit Hall, find out what you would weigh on Mars and look at a real-time image of the sun. Take time to see a film in their 170-seat IWerks Motion Picture Theater, or watch a planetarium program or laser show on the 70-foot dome projection screen.

Brevard Zoo

8225 North Wickham Road, Melbourne; (321) 254-9453; www.brevardzoo.org

Hours Daily, 10 a.m.–5 p.m.; closed Christmas and Thanksgiving.
Admission Adults, $7; seniors ages 60 and older, $6; children ages 2–12, $5

Appeal by Age Group

Pre-school ★★★	Teens ★★★	Over 30 ★★★
Grade school ★★★	Young Adults ★★★	Seniors ★★★

Touring Time *Average* half a day; *minimum* 3 hours
Rainy-Day Touring Not recommended
Author's Rating ★★★

Description and Comments The Brevard Zoo is more than just a zoo—it's a wildlife experience. The zoo highlights four areas—Latin America, Native Florida, Australia, and Africa—providing glimpses of the native ecologies, including, of course, plenty of animals. The zoo showcases a Florida panther, exotic birds, giant anteaters, crocodiles and alligators, kangaroos, giraffes, gazelles, ostriches, and a pair of rhinos. Watch alligators and crocodiles being fed every Wednesday, Friday, and Sunday at 3:30 p.m.

For an extra fee, the Wetlands Outpost allows you to kayak through 22 acres of natural Florida wetlands. You can also schedule a kayak safari on the Nyami Nyami River, which runs through Expedition Africa. For a "behind-the-scenes" experience, try a guided tour with a zookeeper (called a Wildside Tour).

Cocoa Beach Pier

401 Meade Avenue, Cocoa Beach; (321) 783-7549; www.cocoabeachpier.com

Hours Weekdays, 10 a.m.–10 p.m.; weekends, 10 a.m.–11 p.m.; hours vary with the weather

Admission Free admission onto the pier; $5 for pole rental

Appeal by Age Group

Pre-school ★	Teens ★★	Over 30 ★★
Grade school ★★	Young Adults ★★	Seniors ★★★

Touring Time Maximum 45 minutes

Rainy-Day Touring Not recommended

Author's Rating ★★

Description and Comments Established in 1962, the Cocoa Beach Pier stretches 800 feet over the Atlantic Ocean. Feast on fresh seafood from one of the casual restaurants overlooking the beach and ocean, and shop for a Florida souvenir from one of the gift shops that dot the pier. Enjoy fishing, or just gaze out over the ocean. On some days, you can watch dolphins playing just beyond the pier.

Kennedy Space Center Visitor Complex

Off SR 405; (321) 449-4444 or (800) ksc-info; www.kennedyspacecenter.com

Hours Monday–Friday, 9 a.m.–5:30 p.m.; closed Christmas and certain launch dates. Last tour leaves 2:15 p.m.

Admission Maximum Access Admission Badge (includes a tour into restricted areas, all shows and movies, and the Astronaut Hall of Fame): $33 for adults, $23 for children ages 3–11. Standard Admission Badge (includes a tour into restricted areas and all shows and movies): $28 for adults and $18 for children ages 3–11. Ticket add-ons include Dine with an Astronaut, which combines the Maximum Access Admission Badge with the chance to have lunch with an astronaut. Two additional tours are also available: Cape Canaveral: Then and Now and NASA Up Close. Both include a Maximum Access Admission Badge and cost $50 for adults and $40 for children.

Appeal by Age Group

Pre-school ★★★	Teens ★★★★	Over 30 ★★★★
Grade school ★★★★	Young Adults ★★★★	Seniors ★★★★

Touring Time *Minimum* 2 hours; *Average* half day to full day

Rainy-Day Touring Recommended

Author's Rating ★★★★; a "must-see" attraction

Description and Comments As you approach the Visitor Complex, you'll see the Astronaut Memorial, a stunning, $6.4-million monument to the astronauts who have died during missions. Their names are etched in black granite panels that rotate above a mirrored steel structure. A computer controls the granite so that it rises and sets with the sun. And you can't miss the full-scale model of the space shuttle *Explorer* that you can actually board. Nearby, the Rocket Garden displays rockets from each stage of the U.S. exploration program.

In the Exploration in the New Millennium exhibit, you'll have the opportunity to touch a piece of Mars, and in the Early Space Exploration Museum, you'll see artifacts from the Gemini and Mercury programs.

As part of the bus tour into the restricted areas of KSC, you'll visit the Launch Complex 39 Observation Gantry, a 60-foot tower less than half a mile away from space shuttle launch pad 39A; the Apollo/Saturn V Center where you can participate in hands-on displays and see a real Saturn V rocket—one of the most powerful rockets ever built; the Vehicle Assembly Building, one of the largest buildings in the world; and the Crawler, which transports space shuttles to the launch pad.

The Visitor Complex offers back-to-back IMAX theaters, each with 70-foot-wide screens that put you in space with an extraordinary sound system. There are two films, each about 40 minutes long—*Space Station* and *The Dream Is Alive*.

The **U.S. Astronaut Hall of Fame,** newly renovated, is also included in the Maximum Access Admission Badge. The Hall of Fame takes guests back to the early days of the U.S. space program, featuring Mercury and Gemini astronauts. The memorabilia include artifacts, rare video, and personal mementos. Guests can board a full-scale space shuttle orbiter mock up for an interactive trip to the future, land the space shuttle Columbia, take a virtual moon walk, or board the G-Force Simulator. Hours are 10 a.m.–6:30 p.m. daily.

If your schedule is flexible, plan your visit around a launch date. Call (800) KSC-INFO or (321) 867-4636 for current shuttle launch information, which is always subject to change. And on the day of a launch, allow plenty of time for bumper-to-bumper traffic.

MORE FOR SPACE BUFFS

If you just can't get enough of space, try the KSC Visitor Complex's newest attraction—**Astronaut Training Experience.** Spend a day receiving hands-on training and flight preparation; you'll get to try out training simulators and even a full-scale space shuttle mission simulation. The program cost is $200 and includes a mission polo shirt and a VIP tour of the Kennedy Space Center. You must be age 14 or over to participate. For more information, call (321) 449-4400 or visit www.ksctickets.com/atx.html.

Valiant Air Command Warbird Air Museum

6600 Tico Road, Titusville; (321) 268-1941; www.vacwarbirds.org

Hours Daily, 10 a.m.–6 p.m.; closed Thanksgiving, Christmas, and New Year's

Admission Adults $9, seniors/military $8, children ages 4–12 $5; tour rates are $6 for adults, $4 children

Appeal by Age Group

Pre-school ★★	Teens ★★½	Over 30 ★★★
Grade school ★★	Young Adults ★★½	Seniors ★★★★

Touring Time *Minimum* 2 hours

Rainy-Day Touring Recommended

Author's Rating ★★★

Description and Comments The Valiant Air Command Warbird Museum is located at the Space Center Executive Airport. The museum has two main parts; one is the memorabilia hall, which showcases artifacts from before World War II to the present, including a Pearl Harbor tribute. The other is a 30,000-square-foot hangar that displays aircraft from WWI to present. The collection includes an F-14, which is still flight-ready, and a Wildcat that spent 50 years on the bottom of the ocean before it was restored. There is also a restoration hangar, where planes are being repaired and rebuilt.

TAKE A WEEKEND CRUISE

Port Canaveral is the second-largest multiday cruise port in the world, with many cruise ships that depart every day. Take a weekend trip to the Bahamas, or spend a week touring the Caribbean. For more information, visit Port Canaveral's website (**www.portcanaveral.org**) or call (888) PORTCAN.

Shopping

Sophisticated coffee shops, stylish boutiques, and picturesque scenery await you in **Historic Cocoa Village** (**www.cocoavillage.com**). Located off of SR 520, between US 1 and the Indian River, Cocoa Village offers window shoppers and buyers alike a charming, old-world shopping experience with an artistic twist. Walk along the tree-lined streets and shop for almost anything, from antiques and collectibles to books and gourmet kitchen supplies.

It's impossible to miss the 52,000-square-foot pastel-and-neon castle that is **Ron Jon Surf Shop** on the corner of SR 520 and SR A1A (4151 North Atlantic Avenue; (321) 799-8888; **www.ronjons.com**). A Cocoa Beach icon, this surfer's paradise sells a wide selection of beach gear and surf-themed home accessories. And the store's interior is almost as grandiose as its exterior—with a glass elevator and a waterfall. Open 24 hours a day, 7 days a week, Ron Jon's also rents beach equipment, including, of course, surfboards. You can also find other surf shops on SR A1A, including the **Cocoa Beach Surf Company** (4001 North Atlantic Avenue; (321) 799-9930) and the **Natural Art Surf Shop** (2370 South Atlantic Avenue; (321) 783-0764; **www.naturalart.com**), which also houses a surf museum.

Stores selling beach merchandise—shells, bathing suits, T-shirts—abound along SR A1A in Cocoa Beach, but for a different kind of souvenir, check out **The Dinosaur Store** (299 SR 520, just before the intersection of 520 and SR A1A; (877) 560-DINO; www.dinosaurstore.com). The owners have handpicked the store's items, and the selection is amazing. Browse the shop's assortment of castings, authentic fossils, and meteorites (and much more), and go home with a truly unique keepsake.

Flea Markets

Visit **Frontenac Flea Market** in Cocoa (5605 North US 1; (321) 631-0241) for anything from tools to T-shirts. This traditional-style flea market (parts of it are not air conditioned) showcases merchandise from several hundred vendors; some have been with the market for 20 years.

The **SuperFlea and Farmers' Market** in Melbourne (4835 West Eau Gallie Boulevard; (321) 242-9124) attracts up to 30,000 shoppers each week and sells T-shirts, produce, antiques, jewelry, and more.

Fruit

Indian River Gift Fruit (1885 North US 1 in Titusville; (888) FRUIT-2-U; www.indianriver.com) sells fresh Florida citrus. They offer gift baskets (which can also include nuts and noncitrus fruits) and will ship them to your home or to friends and family.

Dining

Alma's

306 North Orlando Avenue, Cocoa Beach; (321) 783-1981

Meals served Dinner **Cuisine** Italian **Entree range** $9–$22 **Reservations** Accepted **Payment** All major credit cards accepted

Comments We have friends who dined at this mom-and-pop eatery back in the 1960s and recently returned to find the same friendly service and hearty portions of authentic Italian cuisine. It's been around for generations for a good reason—service with a smile, fair prices, and comfort food.

Bernard's Surf

2 South Atlantic Avenue, Cocoa Beach; (321) 783-2401

Meals served Dinner **Cuisine** American/seafood **Entree range** $5–$11 raw bar; $10–$16 bar and grill; $15–$25 fine dining area **Reservations** Recommended for dinner **Payment** All major credit cards accepted

Comments This longtime favorite is divided into three parts: a raw bar (Rusty's), a bar and grill (Fischer's), and a formal dining room (Bernard's). The restaurant opened in 1948 with Bernard Fischer serving fish caught by his fleet of boats. His nephew now runs the restaurant, and they still use their own fleet.

The Black Tulip

207 Brevard Avenue, Cocoa (in Historic Cocoa Village); (321) 631-1133; www.blacktulip.com

Meals served Lunch and dinner **Cuisine** Continental **Entree range** Lunch $7–$10, dinner $6–$24 **Reservations** Suggested for dinner **Payment** All major credit cards accepted

Comments The Black Tulip has been serving the Cocoa area for over 20 years. The restaurant is known for its romantic, European atmosphere. Their signature item is the roast duck, double roasted and with a sauce made of apples, cashews, and red wine.

Café Margaux

220 Brevard Avenue, Cocoa (in Historic Cocoa Village); (321) 639-8343; www.cafemargaux.com

Meals served Lunch and dinner (closed Sunday and Tuesday) **Cuisine** French/European **Entree range** Lunch $6–$13, dinner $18–$25 **Reservations** Suggested **Payment** All major credit cards accepted

Comments Café Margaux prides itself on its service—each table sees an average of six servers during the course of a meal. The goal is to anticipate a customer's needs, instead of having the customer ask. The atmosphere is quaint and romantic, with an eclectic decor.

Coconuts on the Beach

2 Minutemen Causeway, Cocoa Beach; (321) 784-1422; www.coconutsonthebeach.com

Meals served Lunch and dinner **Cuisine** American/seafood **Entree range** Lunch $5–$10, dinner $11–$19 **Reservations** Only for large groups **Payment** V, MC, D

Comments A beach bar during the day and nightclub at night, Coconuts serves seafood (they recommend the coconut-crusted mahimahi or the almond grouper) and more in an ultra-casual party atmosphere.

Dixie Crossroads

1475 Garden Street, Titusville; (321) 268-5000; www.dixiecrossroads.com

Meals served Lunch and dinner **Cuisine** Seafood **Entree range** $6–$30 **Reservations** A limited number are accepted **Payment** All major credit cards accepted; no checks

Comments Although this is a large restaurant (with a seating capacity of more than 400), they don't compromise on quality. Dixie Crossroads will offer seafood only from local waters; their policy guarantees freshness. Usually, about six seafood items are offered—by fishermen in the area fishing exclusively for the restaurant. One of the most popular items is the rock shrimp, and the restaurant goes through about 1,000 pounds a day. Entrees are served with all the fixin's, including shrimp or vegetable soup, salad or starch, and their famous corn fritters.

Jack Baker's Lobster Shanty

2200 South Orlando Avenue, Cocoa Beach; (321) 783-1350

Meals served Lunch and dinner **Cuisine** Seafood **Entree range** Lunch $5–$9, dinner $9–$27 **Reservations** Accepted **Payment** All major credit cards accepted

Comments This "shanty" promises fresh seafood with a great view. The atmosphere is casual and comfortable, and the seafood is caught fresh by local fishermen. The restaurant looks out onto the Banana River; keep an eye on the water—you might see manatees or dolphins playing.

The Mango Tree

118 North Atlantic Avenue, Cocoa Beach; (321) 799-0513; www.themangotreerestaurant.com

Meals served Dinner **Cuisine** Continental **Entree range** $15–$39 **Reservations** Suggested **Payment** V, MC, AmEx

Comments Mango Tree offers fine dining in a tropical atmosphere, with gardens and a waterfall, and a saltwater aquarium in the dining room. Appetizers range from classic escargot to rare-seared tuna, and entrees include Indian River crab cakes, scallops in puff pastry, and rack of lamb.

Arts and Culture

If you're planning a museum day, check out the **Brevard Museum of History and Natural Science** (phone (321) 632-1830; **www.brevardmuseum.com**), a Cocoa museum that chronicles life in early Brevard County. Learn more about the Windover archaeological site, located near Titusville.

Located in a Melbourne historic district, the **Brevard Museum of Art and Science** (phone (321) 242-0737; **www.artandscience.org**) displays an impressive collection of art in rotating exhibits. The permanent collection ranges in styles from Southeast Asian objects and contemporary art to Pre-Columbian pieces and American Art Deco. The Science Center has over 30 hands-on exhibits.

Nightlife

The Beach Shack

Who goes there Locals, tourists visiting the beach

1 Minutemen Causeway, Cocoa Beach; (321) 783-2250

Cover None **Minimum** 21 after 8 p.m. **Mixed drinks** $3.25 and up **Food available** No **Hours** 10 a.m.–2 a.m.

What goes on The 30+ crowd enjoys live blues and classic rock music here every Thursday–Sunday.

Comments This oceanfront bar is popular with locals; a beach landmark, it's been in the area for over 40 years now, and its no-frills charm keeps people coming back. The bar area is open air, so the atmosphere isn't as smoky as in other bars. They also have a deck area outside.

Big Daddy Dave's Jazz & Blues Club

Who goes there Tourists, locals, jazz connoisseurs, businesspeople, socialites

105 Harrison Street, Cocoa Village; (321) 638-1370; www.bigdaddydaves.com

Cover No cover charge (two drink minimum per person during entertainment hours) **Minimum** 21 **Mixed drinks** $2.50 and up **Food available** No **Hours** Tuesday–Saturday, 5 p.m.–2 a.m.

What goes on Live jazz entertainment every night. The club prides itself on the diversity of its patrons: people ages 21 to 80 enjoy the great drinks, ambience, and music of Big Daddy Dave's.

Comments A local nightlife staple located in Historic Cocoa Village, the club attracts a slightly more upscale crowd. The low light and deep, rich colors, coupled with the original 115-year-old exposed brick, create a classy, dark atmosphere.

Dino's Supper Club

Who goes there Locals, KSC workers winding down

315 West Cocoa Beach Causeway, Cocoa Beach; (321) 799-4677; www.dinossupperclub.com

Cover None **Minimum** 21 **Mixed drinks** $4 and up **Food available** Appetizers; dinner and lunch are also available, American cuisine **Hours** Sunday–Thursday, 11 a.m.–midnight; Friday and Saturday, 11 a.m.–2 a.m.

What goes on The weekends see live entertainment; pianists and a band perform in the lounge on Friday and Saturday nights.

Comments Dino's attracts an older crowd (35+) and is especially popular with Kennedy Space Center workers winding down after work. The supper club also boasts a large dance floor.

Heidi's Jazz Club

Who goes there Jazz lovers, artists, musicians

7 North Orlando Avenue, Cocoa Beach; (321) 783-4559; www.heidisjazzclub.com

Cover $5 and up, depending on featured artist **Minimum** 21 **Mixed drinks** $3.75 and up ($2.75 and up during happy hour) **Food available** Full dinner menu, European cuisine **Hours** Vary, usually Tuesday–Sunday, 5 p.m.–1 a.m.

What goes on Heidi's offers live jazz every night the club is open. On Friday and Saturday nights, a wide range of featured performers from around the country play at the club. Open jam sessions are held Sunday nights, starting at 7 p.m.

Comments The atmosphere is artsy and intimate, and the jazz is well respected in the area.

Side Trips

Sebastian Inlet   Plan a day trip to Sebastian Inlet, located south of Melbourne and Cocoa Beach. Work on your tan or catch the perfect wave on one of the Inlet's pristine beaches. If you plan to be there on a weekday, you may find yourself one of only a handful of beachgoers in the area.

While you're on the beach, keep your eyes peeled—you could find some treasure! Beachcombers hunt these shores for gold and jewels (especially after a storm), and treasure is still being discovered every year. Visit the **McLarty Treasure Museum** (13180 North A1A, Vero Beach; (772) 589-2147) and learn about ships destroyed off the coast. The small museum is open daily from 10 a.m. to 4:30 p.m. and filled with treasure and artifacts. Admission is $1 for adults and free for kids ages 6 and under. Be sure to watch the video about the 1715 Spanish Plate Fleet destroyed by a hurricane off the coast of Sebastian Inlet; the last video showing is at 3:15 p.m.

Head to the **Sebastian Inlet State Recreation Area** and browse through the **Sebastian Fishing Museum.** Learn how early fishermen made their living on Florida waters—and how they battled mosquitoes without the help of spray-on bug repellent.

Just south of the inlet is the **Pelican Island National Wildlife Refuge** (phone (772) 562-3909, ext. 275; **www.pelicanisland.fws.gov**), the first United States wildlife refuge, established in 1903. The "main attraction" is a small island accessible by boat or a short hike to a viewing area. Pelican Island provides over 30 species of birds a rookery, roost, loafing area, and/or feeding ground. Observe dozens of brown pelicans, along with egrets, herons, and other birds on the island; the wildlife refuge is also home to several endangered species, including wood storks, manatees, and green sea turtles, among others.

Part Five

Orlando: Walt Disney World, Universal, and Beyond

Introduction

When Walt Disney flew over the Orlando area and selected 28,000 acres on which to build his theme park, he jump-started a multibillion-dollar tourism industry and forever changed the face of sleepy Central Florida. Truth is, the attractions got their start way before Walt, back in the 1930s when Richard Pope bought 200 acres along the shores of Lake Eloise near Winter Haven and created a water-themed park called Cypress Gardens, with daily ski shows (the park closed in 2003). Today, Walt Disney World Resort, Universal Orlando, SeaWorld Orlando, and other attractions vie for the time (and dollars) of millions of vacationers.

There are now more than 110,000 hotel rooms and dozens of man-made attractions that lure vacationers from around the world.

Beyond the glitz of the themed attractions, there are little towns such as Winter Park, where you can wander amid the world's most extensive collection of Tiffany glass in the Morse Museum of American Art; and Kissimmee, where camping, horseback riding, bass fishing, and the rodeo take precedence. The ocean may be miles away, but the lakes in Central Florida offer adventures from canoe rides to airboat treks through alligator country. Or you can traverse the St. John's River, the state's longest navigable waterway, by pontoon or on guided boat tours.

Covering 378,178 acres, Ocala National Forest is divided into three recreation areas linked by a 65-mile-long trail. You can hike, fish, camp, snorkel, swim, and canoe.

A Brief History

Long before Walt Disney World forever changed the sleepy Central Florida landscape from cattle and citrus, Orlando was an army post, Fort Gatlin. The name Orlando most likely came from a soldier, Orlando Reeves, who was injured by Seminole Indians on the shores of Lake Eola in 1835.

Cuba's demand for beef cattle created a major industry in Orlando in the mid-1800s, and people began to plant orange seeds in the 1870s. At the industry's peak in the 1950s, more than 80,000 acres of citrus trees thrived in Central Florida.

That same decade, nearby Cape Canaveral brought a technology boom, overshadowed in the 1960s when Walt Disney started buying up land to build his theme park. Since the opening of the Magic Kingdom at Walt Disney World in 1971, nearly 100 theme parks and attractions have opened, and most of those orange groves have been replaced by new developments. Today, there are more than 110,000 hotel rooms and 4,500 restaurants catering to more than 43 million visitors annually.

Visiting the Orlando Area

Gathering Information

Kissimmee–St. Cloud Convention and Visitors Bureau, 1925 East Irlo Bronson Highway, Kissimmee 34744; (800) 327-9159 (U.S. and Canada); (800) 333-5477 (worldwide); **www.floridakiss.com.**

Lake County Convention and Visitors Bureau, 20763 US 27, Groveland 34736; (352) 429-3673 or (800) 798-1071 (U.S. only); **www.lakecountyfl.com.**

Orlando-Orange County Convention and Visitors Bureau, 8123 International Drive, open daily 8 a.m.–7 p.m.); (800) 551-0181 (U.S. and Canada) or (407) 363-5871; **www.orlandoinfo.com.**

The Walt Disney Travel Company, Walt Disney World Vacations Brochure, Walt Disney World, P.O. Box 10,000, Lake Buena Vista 32830-1000; (407) 934-7639 or (800) 327-2996; **www.disneyworld.com.**

Seminole County Convention and Visitors Bureau, Tourist Development Council, 105 International Parkway, Heathrow 32746; (407) 665-2900 or (800) 800-7832 (U.S. and Canada); **www.visitseminole.com.**

Getting There

By Plane Two airports service Central Florida. Orlando International Airport is seven miles south of Orlando; (407) 825-2001. Orlando-Sanford Airport is two miles east of Sanford; (407) 322-7771. More than 49 scheduled airlines and 41 charters provide nonstop service from 69 U.S. destinations and 17 international cities.

By Train Amtrak (phone (800) USA-RAIL; www.amtrak.com) serves Orlando with four daily trains originating from New York and Miami with stops in downtown Orlando, Winter Park, Sanford, and Kissimmee, as well as with a tri-weekly train originating from Los Angeles. Amtrak also offers the Auto Train, which transports passengers and their vehicles, running daily between Lorton, Virginia, and Sanford, leaving each town at 4 p.m. and arriving at the destination at 9 a.m. the next morning

By Car Orlando is approximately in the center of the state, midway between Jacksonville and Miami. Major interstates include I-4, which runs from Daytona Beach in the east to St. Petersburg on the west coast, through downtown Orlando and past the attractions; I-10, which enters the state at the southwest tip in Pensacola and extends to Jacksonville in the northeast; I-75, which enters Florida just south of Valdosta, Georgia, and runs south to Naples and then east to Fort Lauderdale; I-95, which enters the state just north of Jacksonville and extends south to Miami; and Florida's Turnpike, which connects with I-75 south of Ocala, extending southeast through Orlando and continuing to Miami.

HIGHLIGHTS

- Magic Kingdom at Walt Disney World Resort
- Islands of Adventure at Universal Orlando
- Discovery Cove at SeaWorld Orlando
- A canoe trip down Wekiva Springs
- Snorkeling, swimming, or canoeing in Ocala National Forest

Getting Around

Should You Rent a Car?

If you're here to see the big three—Disney, Universal, SeaWorld—many hotels offer a bus to the major attractions, so you can save on car rental. Transportation across Disney property is free if you're a Disney resort guest. International Drive offers an efficient trolley system, I-Ride, to carry you from one end of that street to the other (phone (407) 248-9590). **Mears Motor Transportation Service** (phone (407) 423-5566 or 422-4561; **www.mearstransportation.com**) operates handicapped-accessible, air-conditioned shuttles that run from the baggage-claim level at Orlando International Airport to area hotels, and they operate around the clock. Round-trip cost is about $28 per adult to hotels near the theme parks, $24 to downtown. Children ages 5–11 ride for $20, $14 to downtown; children age 4 and under ride free. If you have small children, however, it's often convenient to have a car so you can return to your hotel on your own schedule. More than a dozen rental-car companies have fleets in Orlando, so shop around for the best rates if you decide to rent.

Interstate 4 is the main thoroughfare, linking the Atlantic Coast to the Gulf of Mexico—but it runs north-south through Orlando, so don't get confused. I-4 East (to Daytona) is generally northbound, and I-4 West (to Tampa) is generally southbound. Highway 528 (also know as the Beeline Expressway) links Orlando to the Space Coast and Interstate 95.

International Drive, or I-Drive, is another busy tourist area, with exits clearly marked off I-4. South of Disney World, US 192 is home to another concentration of hotels and restaurants that runs from Kissimmee and crosses Disney property, with exits to the Disney parks.

The Florida Turnpike runs south to Miami and northeast to join Interstate 75.

Outdoor Adventures and Sports

Recommended Excursions

Boggy Creek Airboat Rides These half-hour rides cover ten miles of wetlands and creeks with plenty of wildlife. The U.S. Coast Guard–approved outfit is open daily, 9 a.m.–dusk. Rides are $18, $13 for children ages 12 and under. Nightly gator tours, held 9–10 p.m., cost $30, $25 for children ages 12 and under. Located at 3702 Big Bass Road, Kissimmee; (407) 344-9550.

Forever Florida Just minutes from Disney World, experience a wilderness adventure that combines a two-hour tour of the 1,500-acre working Crescent J. Ranch and a 3,200-acre nature preserve with nine Florida ecosystems. It's Florida *au naturel,* with deer, alligators, herds of cattle, and flocks of sandhill cranes, and the best way to take it all in is the guided Cracker Coach Tour in an elevated swamp buggy. The first tour of the morning leaves at 9 a.m., and we recommend this one to both avoid the heat and to improve your odds for sighting wildlife. After the tour, kids can feed calves and goats at the petting zoo or take a pony ride. The attraction is open daily and costs $28, $18 for ages 5–12. Trips for groups of 12 or more can be arranged anytime during the week with reservations. Located at 4755 North Kenansville Road, St. Cloud. (866) 854-3837; www.foreverflorida.com.

Florida Audubon Society's Center for Birds of Prey Located just north of Orlando, the Center for Birds of Prey is noted as the leading raptor rehabilitation center on the Eastern Seaboard. Thousands of birds—bald eagles and other raptors—have been released since 1979 after rehabilitation at the center. Birds that can't be released are housed at a lakeside aviary. Requested entry donations are $5 for adults, $4 for children ages 6–15. Located at 1101 Maitland Way, Maitland; (407) 644-0190.

Florida Pack and Paddle Outdoor Adventure Tours This full-service outdoor tour company offers canoeing, camping, and hiking to some of the best natural attractions in the area, including Wekiva River, Ichetucknee Springs, Suwannee River, and Peace River. They provide everything, including food, camping equipment, and guides. Trips can be as short as half a day or as long as six days; one-day trips start with a continental breakfast and include lunch as well as "farewell toast" at 4 p.m. The best time to go is spring or fall when there's a nice breeze. Located at 11025 Southeast US 192, Summerfield. Call (800) 297-8811 for rental rates and reservations.

Harry P. Leu Gardens Camellias, palms, roses, and orchids are showcased in these magnificent gardens surrounding the Leu House Museum, a turn-of-the-century Florida farmhouse that's open for tours daily, 9 a.m.–6 p.m. (closed Christmas). Admission is $4, $1 for students. Located at 1920 North Forest Avenue, Orlando; (407) 246-2620; www.leugardens.org.

Historic Bok Sanctuary This is an incredibly beautiful setting, with a 57-bell carillon tower as its centerpiece, surrounded by 157 acres of gardens and nature trails. Bok Tower is listed in the National Register of Historic Places, dedicated to the American people by Edward Bok, a Dutch immigrant. There are daily bell serenades from the 205-foot "singing tower," which has been called one of the world's great carillons. The gardens are located on Iron Mountain, the Florida peninsula's highest point at 295 feet. Open daily, 8 a.m.–5 p.m. Admission is $8, $3 for ages 5–12, and free for those younger. Located north of Lake Wales three miles, off CR 17A (Burns Avenue) and Tower Boulevard; (863) 676-1408; **www.boksanctuary.org.**

Houseboat on the St. John's Adventurous families can cruise the scenic St. John's River on a houseboat, for rent from the **Hontoon Landing Marina.** The boats sleep six to ten and are furnished with gas grills, cooking and eating utensils, linens, and a microwave. Rentals start at $360 a day or $975 for a weekend (Friday–Sunday), and you're free to cruise as far south as Lake Monroe or as far north as Palatka. If you're planning a day or two on the boat, we recommend heading to Silver Glen Spring, about a five-and-a-half-hour ride, where you can anchor overnight and swim in the crystal-clear water. There's plenty of great fishing along the way. It takes no special training to operate a houseboat; most renters have never driven a houseboat, say the folks at Hontoon Landing. Just be sure to bring along mosquito repellent, especially in the summertime. Hontoon Landing Resort and Marina is located at 2317 River Ridge Road, DeLand 32720; (904) 734-2474 or (800) 248-2474; **www.hontoon.com.**

Kelly Park–Rock Springs Run This old park just north of Orlando has been a favorite of Central Floridians for generations. Bring an inner tube or snorkel and while away the day in the icy (72° year-round) water. Tubers, by the way, have right of way, but it's great fun and easy to snorkel along the one-and-a-half-mile-long spring run with a sandy bottom and plenty of fish and turtles for viewing (no fishing allowed). Snorkeling is best in early morning, late afternoon, and on weekdays, when the crowds haven't scared away the fish. Camping is available, with a two-night minimum (sites are $15, $18 with electricity; Orange County residents get a $5 discount). Admission is $1 per person. Take I-4 to Exit 51, then west on Highway 46 and follow the signs to Kelly Park—Rock Springs Run; (407) 889-4179.

Ocala National Forest This 400,000-acre refuge for wildlife has a quartet of untamed springs, winding streams, and natural lakes that brighten one of the oldest national forests east of the Mississippi. There are also numerous hiking and horseback trails; perfect for families is the Juniper Nature Trail, complete with signs describing the fauna and ecology. Some other highlights:

1. **Alexander Springs** is the place for excellent swimming and snorkeling—the springs pumps out 76 million gallons of 72° water each day. There are also picnicking, canoe rentals, and camping ($17 per site). Take US 441 to the intersection of SR 19 at Eustis; turn right at the overpass and follow SR 19 to SR 445. Turn right and follow the signs to the recreation area; (352) 669-3522.

2. **Silver Glen Springs** is known for its thick grass beds, white-sand bottom, and plenty of fish, like largemouth bass and striped bass in the spring. Beware, boat traffic on the half-mile spring run is especially heavy on the weekends. No fishing rentals. Located on SR 19 about six miles north of the SR 19–SR 40 intersection; (352) 685-2799.

3. **Salt Springs** has three spring boils to snorkel around and a five-mile run that leads to Lake George. There are gators along the way, so be especially careful during springtime mating season—and always leave the water if you spot one. Located on SR 19 in the town of Salt Springs; (352) 685-2048.

4. **Juniper Springs** has a popular campground ($17 for tent and RV camping, no electricity) where you can't make reservations—it's first-come, first-served. The springs pump out 20 million gallons every day, ideal for swimming. There's also excellent canoeing on the seven-mile spring run. Located on SR 40 just west of SR 19; (352) 625-3147.

Wekiva Springs State Park The Wekiva River meanders 25 miles north of Orlando, a gin-clear ribbon of water fed by springs. Flat and gentle currents make it perfect for novice canoers. There are eight miles of trail intended for horseback riding and mountain biking, and the rolling terrain is prime habitat for black bears. This lush park contains almost 6,900 acres of wild scenery, with a main spring that pumps out 42 million gallons of water each day into a near-perfect "swimmin' hole." Canoe rentals, walking trails, and camping are available. Admission is $4 per car. Located 15 miles northwest of Orlando (take I-4 to Exit 49 and follow the signs); (407) 884-2009; **www.floridastateparks.org**.

ORLANDO'S LAKE EOLA PARK

Right in the middle of downtown, Lake Eola Park (195 North Rosalind Avenue; (407) 246-2827) is the largest and most-visited park in Orlando. A majority of the 43 acres are covered by the lake, with its distinctive "spaceship fountain" and a 0.9-mile sidewalk around the waterfront. There are swan-shaped paddle boats, a well-equipped playground, a small café, rest rooms, and plenty of benches. Year-round festivals are scheduled, and the Walt Disney amphitheater hosts outdoor theatrical and musical performances.

Snorkeling

Unlike the rest of the Florida regions, Orlando and Central Florida lack coastline. Scuba diving opportunities are consequently lacking. Snorkeling however, requires only a short trip to one of the area's natural springs. **Kelly Park, Alexander Springs,** and **Wekiva Springs** (all noted above) each offer the chance to snorkel in crystal-clear freshwater springs and creeks. Seasoned snorkelers and divers can explore an underwater world altogether different from their saltwater haunts, and many novice snorkelers find the shallow rivers less intimidating that the ocean.

Fishing

Deep-sea fishing is a non-option in Central Florida, but the lakes make it a bass-fishing haven. Some of Central Florida's easiest bass fishing is in the stocked lakes at **Walt Disney World**, where trophy-sized largemouth bass in the 14-pound range sometimes lurk in lakes and canals. During construction of the Magic Kingdom in the late 1960s, more than 70,000 bass fingerlings were released into Bay Lake and Seven Seas Lagoon, and organized fishing tours didn't start until 1977, leaving the bass to grow and breed undisturbed for years. Two-hour tours for up to five are $180–$210; call (407) W-DISNEY.

Other top bass guides offering full- and half-day trips on Central Florida lakes include **A#1 Bass Guide Service** (15712 Bay Lake Trail, Clermont; (352) 394-3660; www.a1bassguideservice.com); **Bass Anglers Guide Service** (6526 SR 535, Windermere; (407) 257-2241; **www.tyree.net/bassanglers.com**); and **A Pro Bass Guide Service Inc.** (398 Grove Court, Winter Garden; (407) 877-9676; **www.probassguideservice.com**).

ORLANDO MAGICARD

A free Orlando Magicard, good for up to six people, can mean savings on attractions, rooms, dining, and more. More than 100 area businesses will give you a break on everything from theme park tickets to dinner theaters. You can get it ahead of your trip by calling (800) 551-0181 or at www.orlandoinfo.com. Or if you don't get one ahead of time, they're at the Official Visitor Center, 8723 International Drive, Orlando, open 8 a.m.–7 p.m. every day except Christmas.

Bicycling Central Florida

Rail Trails

General James A. Van Fleet Trail in the Green Swamp, Clermont   Travel 29 miles from Mabel to Polk City on this rail-trail through the Green Swamp, which is home to many varieties of wildlife and plant life. Trailheads are located at Green Pond and Mabel; (352) 394-2280.

West Orange Trail, Orlando   This paved trail traverses 19 miles from the Lake County line into Apopka. You can rent bikes and Rollerblades from West Orange Trail Bikes & Blades Co. at 17914 SR 438 in Winter Garden, at the very western end of the West Orange Trail; (407) 877-0600.

Withlacoochee State Trail, Clermont   With trailheads at Citrus Springs and SR 50, this 46-mile paved trail from Dunellon to Trilby passes through the Withlacoochee State Forest, Fort Cooper State Park, and neighboring rural areas. Forest, sandhill, and wetland climates play host to gopher tortoises, bobcats, deer, and turkeys; (352) 394-2280.

Mountain Biking

Orlando Wilderness Park   This park offers 15–20 miles of easy, scenic riding, with spectacular bird life (especially in winter). The park is open from February 1 to September 30, dawn to dusk; (407) 568-1706.

Santos Trailhead The Santos Trailhead system, built by the Ocala Mountain Bike Association, is one of the Southeast's premier mountain bike destinations. The system, located on 80th Street in south Ocala just west of the intersection of US 441, offers over 50 miles of prime singletrack with trails color-coded according to level of difficulty. Most of the riding is fast and mellow through some of central Florida's most scenic pine and live oak forests. Two large rock quarries, however, are integrated into the system, and though avoidable, serve up healthy doses of advanced and expert riding accompanied by not a little blood letting. For more information, visit **www.omba.org**.

Tosohatchee State Reserve Near Christmas, Florida, in East Orange County, this preserve welcomes bikers on all roads in the park and on the orange-blazed trail (the white-blazed trails are for hikers only). There's plenty of wildlife, but hunting is allowed in the fall, so call first; (407) 568-5893.

Spectator Sports

Baseball

You can watch four teams get ready for the season in Orlando-area spring-training camps: **The Atlanta Braves** play at Disney's Wide World of Sports (710 South Victory Way, Kissimmee; (407) 939-1500); the **Cleveland Indians** train at Chain of Lakes Park in Winter Haven (Cypress Gardens Boulevard; (941) 293-3900); the **Detroit Tigers** practice in Lakeland (2125 North Lake Avenue; (863) 686-8075); and the **Kansas City Royals** train in Davenport (300 Stadium Way; (941) 424-2500). The **Orlando Rays**, the AA Minor League affiliate of the Tampa Bay Devil Rays, also plays each spring at Disney's Wide World of Sports (phone (407) 939-4263).

Basketball and Football

The NBA's **Orlando Magic** (**www.nba.com/magic**) play at the T. D. Waterhouse Centre (600 West Amelia Street, Orlando; (407) 849-2020) in downtown Orlando, along with the **Orlando Predators** (**www.orlando predators.net**) arena football team.

Walt Disney World

Walt Disney World encompasses 43 square miles, an area twice as large as Manhattan Island or roughly the size of Boston. There are four theme parks, three water theme parks, a shopping, dining, and entertainment district, a competitive sports complex, several golf courses, hotels and campgrounds, more than 400 places to eat, four large interconnected lakes, and a complete transportation system consisting of four-lane highways, elevated monorails, and a network of canals.

If you are selecting among the tourist attractions in Central Florida, the question is not whether to visit Walt Disney World but how you can see the best of the various Disney offerings with some economy of time, effort, and money.

Walt Disney World

Make no mistake, there is nothing on earth quite like Walt Disney World. Incredible in its scope, genius, beauty, and imagination, it is a joy and wonder for people of all ages. Infused with the wonder of childhood, the best Disney attractions transcend simple entertainment, freeing us for an hour or a day to live the dreams of our past, present, and future.

> **DISNEY ON THE INTERNET**
>
> Disney's official Internet address is **www.disney.com;** the company also maintains **www.disneyworld.com.** The official website offers much of the same information as the Walt Disney Travel Company's vacation guidebook, but the guidebook has better pictures. However, you can now purchase theme-park admissions and make resort and dining reservations on the Internet. The website also offers online shopping, weather forecasts, and information on renovations and special events. There is a vast array of websites devoted to Disney World that are not affiliated with Disney. Among the best are **www.wdig.com, www.mousesavers.com,** and **www.wdwmagic.com.** Universal Studios Florida also offers a home page at **www.universalorlando.com.**

Selecting the Time of Year for Your Visit

Peak times at Walt Disney World are the Fourth of July, Christmas Day through New Year's Day, Thanksgiving weekend, the week of Washington's birthday, Martin Luther King holiday weekend, spring break for colleges, and the two weeks around Easter. Only those who absolutely cannot go at any other time should challenge the Disney parks at their peak periods.

The least busy time is from mid-January through the first week of February, the week after Labor Day until Thanksgiving, and the week after Thanksgiving through the week before Christmas. Crowds ebb and flow according to spring-break schedules and the timing of Presidents' Day weekend. Though crowds have grown markedly in September and October as a result of special promotions aimed at locals and the international market, these months continue to be good for weekday touring at the Magic Kingdom, Disney-MGM Studios, and the Animal Kingdom, and for weekend visits to Epcot.

10 Tips for an Optimum Disney Visit

1. Do your homework before you go. Our annually revised *Unofficial Guide to Walt Disney World* offers much more in-depth information and flexible touring plans.
2. Let the whole family help with the planning—everyone can choose favorites that can be worked into the itinerary.
3. In spite of all your planning, be flexible once you arrive.
4. If intend to spend more than a couple of days at Disney, spring for a multiday pass. You'll save a few bucks and have the flexibility to move between the theme parks. Some passes even include admission to the water parks.

248

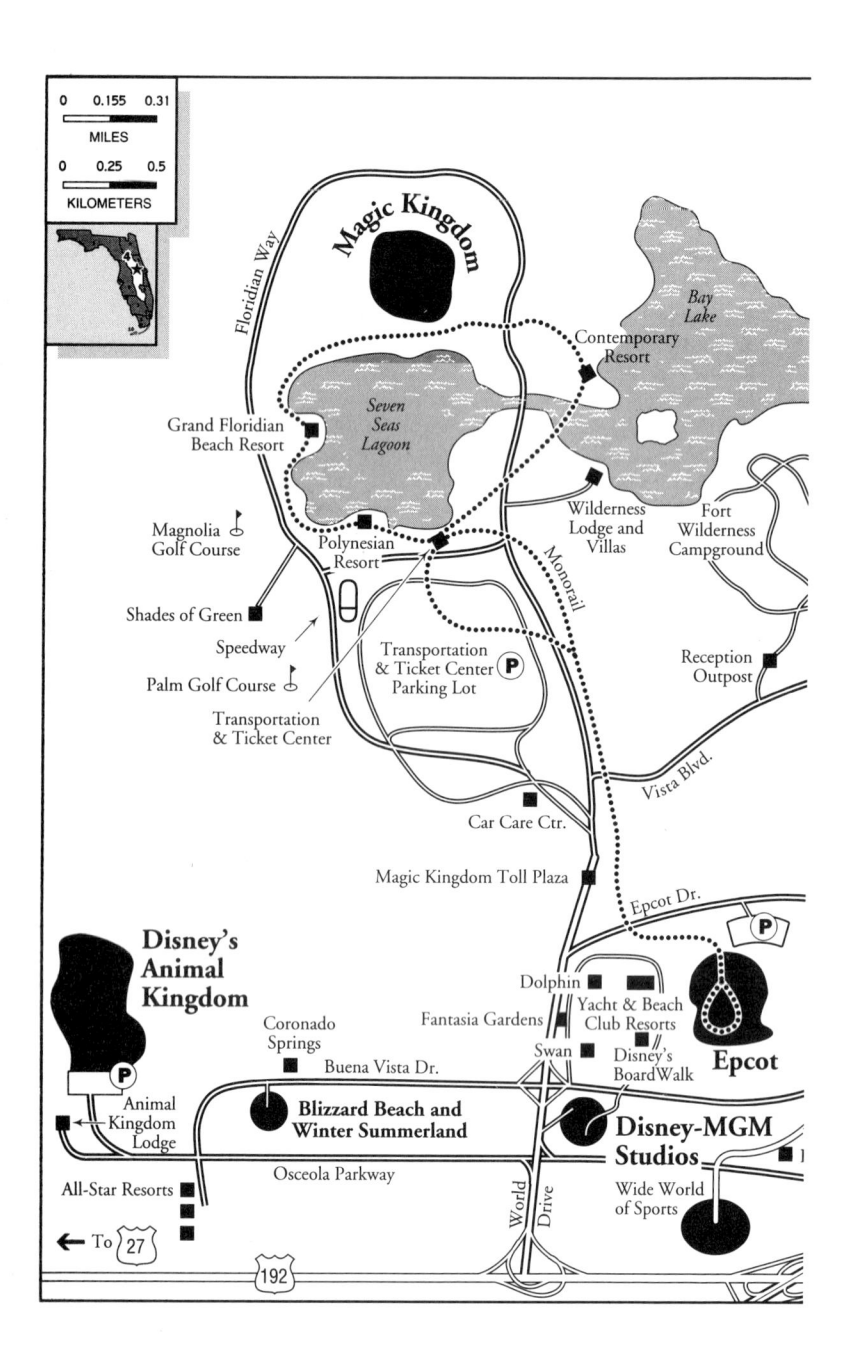

249

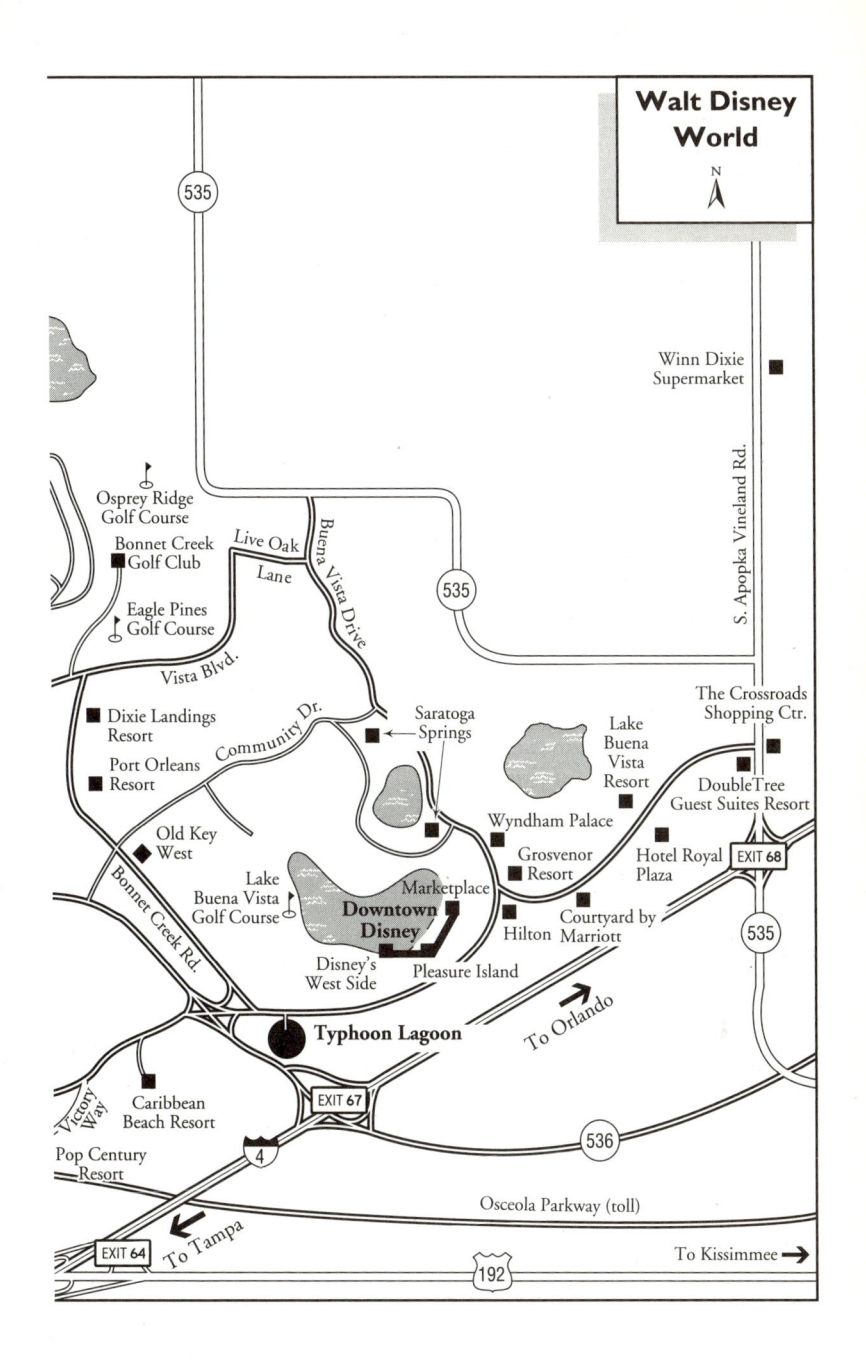

5. Start your day early—arrive at the parks at least 30 minutes before the scheduled opening and plan a break in the middle of the day, returning to your hotel for a swim or a nap, then back to the theme parks for the evening. Also, mix and match parks if you have a multiday pass; if you spent the morning in the Magic Kingdom, head to Epcot for dinner and fireworks.
6. Families with kids of various ages should plan to split up—let dad do the thrill rides with an older child while mom spends time in Fantasyland with younger siblings. If you have at least two teenagers, they can take off on their own, as the parks are very safe. Just be sure to pick a meeting place, and advise them not to lose track of time.
7. If your budget is tight but you don't want to miss out on the themed restaurants, book lunch instead of dinner. Portions are generally huge, so you also can share meals. The top choices in each park: Crystal Palace in the Magic Kingdom, Hollywood Brown Derby or 50's Prime Time Café at the Disney-MGM Studios, Coral Reef at Epcot, and Tusker House in Disney's Animal Kingdom.
8. Don't try to see it all. Enjoy what you can, and save some attractions for another visit.
9. Take a break from the theme parks. Even if you don't leave Disney property, you can play at one of the water parks or take an afternoon to visit Downtown Disney.
10. Wait until it's time to go home to buy souvenirs. You'll see plenty of things you want to buy, but you won't waste money if you wait and anticipate buying one really special keepsake.

Admission Options

Prices quoted below are those prevailing at press time. Please note that the prices below include sales tax, and are gate prices—you can save around ten percent if you purchase in advance.

Type of Pass	Adult Price w/ Tax	Child Price w/ Tax
1-Day/One-Park-Only Pass	$55	$45
4-Day Park-Hopper Pass	$222	$178
5-Day Park-Hopper Pass	$255	$204
5-Day Park-Hopper Plus Pass	$287	$230
6-Day Park-Hopper Plus Pass	$318	$256
7-Day Park-Hopper Plus Pass	$350	$281
Annual Passports	$393	$314
Annual Premium Passports	$521	$443

The 1-Day/One-Park-Only Pass is good for admission and unlimited access to "attractions and experiences" at the Magic Kingdom, Epcot, Disney's Animal Kingdom, or Disney-MGM Studios.

The 5-, 6-, and 7-Day Park-Hopper Plus Passes provide admission to all four theme parks plus two visits to a choice of Blizzard Beach, Typhoon Lagoon, Pleasure Island, or Disney's Wide World of Sports.

The Annual Premium Passport provides unlimited theme-park admission plus Pleasure Island, water parks, Disney's Wide World of Sports, and DisneyQuest.

Also available are Ultimate Park Hopper tickets, based on the length of stay in a Disney resort (from two to ten days). These are available through the Walt Disney Travel Company exclusively to guests as Disney-owned properties.

Unused days on any multiday ticket except the Ultimate Park Hopper never expire and can be used for a future visit.

EXTRA HELP NAVIGATING THE THEME PARKS

Disney launched a free service to provide synchronized narration in five languages for popular theme-park attractions. The personal translation devices, available at Guest Relations in each of the theme parks, are in French, German, Japanese, Portuguese, and Spanish, and feature lightweight headphones that automatically receive digital-quality audio, triggered by infrared signals throughout the attractions.

Another new "park guide" is Pal Mickey, a ten-inch plush Mickey Mouse programmed with hundreds of messages, from show details to Disney trivia to height requirements for all four Walt Disney World theme parks. He even tells jokes and plays games. You can rent the high-tech toy for $8 a day or keep him and take him home for $50.

Should You Book a Room at Disney?

Luxury accommodations can be found both in and out of Walt Disney World. Budget lodging, however, is another story. Room rates start at about $90 in Walt Disney World and range to more than $500. Outside Walt Disney World, rooms go for as low as $45.

There are specific privileges and amenities available to guests staying at a Walt Disney World resort:

Convenience   Decreased commuting time made possible by proximity to the theme parks and easy access to the Walt Disney World bus, boat, and monorail transportation system is especially advantageous if you stay in one of the hotels connected by the monorail or by boat service.

Baby-sitting and Childcare Alternatives   Several of the resort hotels offer themed child-care centers where potty-trained children ages 3–12 can be dropped off during the evening while adults go out. In-room baby-sitting is offered by Kinder-Care, (407) 827-5444.

Guaranteed and Early Admission   Regardless of crowds, guests staying at Disney properties are guaranteed admission and are eligible for "Extra Magic Hour," which allows admission to one of the four theme parks an hour before opening to the general public. On days of unusually heavy attendance, "E-Ride Night" allows resort guests with multiday passes (for an extra $12, $10 ages 3–9) to remain in the Magic Kingdom after official closing time and ride all the biggies with little or no waiting.

Children Sharing a Room with Their Parents   There is no extra charge per night for children under age 18 sharing a room with their parents (but that's also the case in many non-Disney hotels).

Free Parking   Walt Disney World resort guests with cars do not have to pay for parking in the theme park lots ($8 a day).

DISNEY'S FASTPASS

At Walt Disney World's most popular attractions, guests can choose the regular wait line or opt to use FASTPASS. After inserting a valid theme park ticket into the special FASTPASS machines at these attractions, guests receive a ticket denoting a one-hour window of time when they can return and enter the attraction with little or no wait. There is no extra charge to use FASTPASS.

Always check the sign near the FASTPASS machines that indicates the return time; if it is hours away, you might want to forgo the option. Try to obtain a FASTPASS before 11 a.m. for blockbuster attractions.

You are able to get as many FASTPASS tickets in a day as you want, but you have to use a current FASTPASS ticket or wait two hours before getting another.

Magic Kingdom

The Magic Kingdom/Transportation and Ticket Center parking lot opens about two hours before the park's official opening time for the general public. After paying the parking fee, you board a tram for the Transportation and Ticket Center, where you can take either a monorail or a ferry to the entrance of the Magic Kingdom.

Entering **Main Street, U.S.A.,** be sure to pick up a guide map at City Hall; it lists all attractions, shops, and eating places, as well as information about first aid, baby care, and entertainment for the day.

Main Street, U.S.A., ends at a central hub, from which branch the entrances to five other sections of the Magic Kingdom: **Adventureland, Frontierland, Liberty Square, Fantasyland,** and **Tomorrowland,** in clockwise order. **Mickey's Toontown Fair** is wedged between Fantasyland and Tomorrowland and does not connect to the central hub.

Cinderella Castle is the entrance to Fantasyland and the focal landmark and visual center of the Magic Kingdom. It's a great place to meet if your family decides to split up or if you are accidentally separated.

Only five rides in the Magic Kingdom have age or height requirements: Splash Mountain, Space Mountain, Alien Encounter, Tomorrowland Speedway, and Big Thunder Mountain Railroad.

Avoid lines by taking advantage of FASTPASS at Big Thunder Mountain Railroad, Buzz Lightyear's Space Ranger Spin, The Haunted Mansion, Jungle Cruise, The Many Adventures of Winnie the Pooh, Peter Pan's Flight, Space Mountain, Splash Mountain. To get a FASTPASS, insert your park ticket in the turnstile for a free FASTPASS ticket with your designated ride time.

Top 10 Attractions

Big Thunder Mountain Railroad (Frontierland)   On this roller coaster through and around a Disney "mountain," the idea is that you're on a runaway mine train during the Gold Rush. A superb Disney experience, but not a wild roller coaster. Emphasis is much more on the sights than on the thrill of the ride. You must be at least 40 inches tall to ride. FASTPASS available.

Alien Encounter (Tomorrowland)   The scariest attraction in any of the Disney parks features an angry alien and an experiment that goes awry. Mayhem ensues. A departure from typical Disney theme-park entertainment, so be forewarned. You must be at least 44 inches tall to ride.

Haunted Mansion (Liberty Square)   More fun than scary, with some of the Magic Kingdom's best special effects, the Haunted Mansion is a masterpiece of detail. "Doom Buggies" on a conveyor belt transport you throughout the house from parlor to attic, and then through a graveyard. FASTPASS available.

Jungle Cruise (Adventureland)   A cruise through jungle waterways with animatronic elephants, lions, hostile natives, and a menacing hippo. Since the advent of the Animal Kingdom, the attraction's appeal has diminished, but you can always depend on the Jungle Cruise's robotic critters being present as you motor past. FASTPASS available.

The Many Adventures of Winnie the Pooh (Fantasyland)   Hop in a "hunny pot" for a four-minute tour of Pooh's Hundred Acre Wood. For little ones, this is Nirvana with a happily-ever-after storybook ending that features a hero's party, a colorful rainbow, and all the gang safe in the Hundred Acre Wood ready for another escapade. FASTPASS available.

Mickey's Philharmagic (Fantasyland)   This new, ten-minute special-effects laden film stars classic Disney characters—Donald Duck, Mickey Mouse, with computer-generated 3-D graphics on a 150-foot-wide screen and in-theater sounds, smells, and other effects that put you in the middle of the action. FASTPASS available.

Parades and Fireworks   Magic Kingdom parades are full-fledged spectaculars with every Disney character imaginable and amazing special effects.

SpectroMagic is the nighttime parade, an extravaganza of more than 600,000 lights that are synchronized to sound effects and a musical score—Goofy's xylophone keys dance with light at his touch and Mickey's cape transforms in a 24-step cascade of color sweeping from the base of his float upward to 17 feet above his head.

Wishes is the stellar new fireworks display, unleashed after dark on nights the park is open late. For an uncluttered view and lighter crowds, watch from the terrace of The Plaza Pavilion restaurant in Tomorrowland.

Pirates of the Caribbean (Adventureland)   Disney Audio-Animatronics at its best, this indoor cruise depicts a pirate raid on an island settlement. Undoubtedly one of the park's most elaborate, imaginative, and longest-running attractions.

Space Mountain (Tomorrowland)   Space Mountain has long been the Magic Kingdom's most popular attraction, a space flight through dark recesses of the galaxy. The effects are superb, and the ride is the fastest and wildest in the park. Children must be 44 inches tall to ride; those younger than age 7 must be accompanied by an adult. FASTPASS available.

Splash Mountain (Frontierland)   This water-flume ride combines steep chutes with excellent special effects. The ride covers more than half a mile, splashing through swamps, caves, and backwood bayous before climaxing in a five-story plunge. More than 100 audio-animatronic characters, including Brer Rabbit, Brer Bear, and Brer Fox, regale riders with songs, including "Zip-a-Dee-Doo-Dah." Children must be 40 inches tall to ride; those younger than age 7 must ride with an adult. FASTPASS available.

FANTASY IN THE SKY CRUISE

For a different view, you can watch the fireworks from the Seven Seas Lagoon aboard a chartered pontoon boat. The charter costs $120 and accommodates up to 12 persons. Your Disney cast member captain will take you for a little cruise and then position the boat in a perfect place to watch the fireworks.

For an additional $80 per four persons, the captain will provide deli sandwiches, snacks, and beverages. A major indirect benefit of the charter is that you can enjoy the fireworks without fighting the mob afterwards.

To reserve, call (407) WDW-PLAY at exactly 7 a.m. 90 days before the day you want the charter. Similar charters are available to watch *IllumiNations* at Epcot.

Epcot

With Epcot, the second theme park to open at Walt Disney World, Disney combined two different areas—Future World and World Showcase—into a one-of-a-kind theme park, with all the attractions oriented toward education. Epcot is more than twice the physical size of the Magic Kingdom or Disney-MGM Studios, and it requires a considerable amount of walking from attraction to attraction. One can't really see the whole place in a day without skipping an attraction or two and giving other areas a cursory glance.

As in the other theme parks, we have identified several attractions in Epcot as "not to be missed." However, part of the enjoyment of a place like Epcot is that there is something for everyone; let your interests shape your touring.

There are height restrictions for Mission: Space and Test Track. Disney FASTPASSes are available to cut time waiting in line at Mission: Space, Honey I Shrunk the Audience, Living with the Land, Maelstrom, and Test Track.

Note that Future World and World Showcase have separate operating hours. Though schedules change throughout the year, Future World always opens before World Showcase in the morning and usually closes before World Showcase in the evening. Most of the year, World Showcase opens two hours later than Future World. For exact hours during your visit, call (407) 824-4321.

Plan to arrive at the turnstiles 30–40 minutes prior to official opening time. Give yourself an extra ten minutes or so to park and make your way to the entrance. If you are a guest at one of the nearby Disney resorts, it will take you about 20–30 minutes to walk from your hotel to the Future World section of Epcot.

DINING AT EPCOT

Some of the best Walt Disney World restaurants are in the World Showcase countries, where you can sample *queso fundido* in Mexico, slow-roasted lamb in Morocco, and bouillabaisse in France. Each pavilion has a restaurant, and priority seating can be made through (407) WDW-DINE. If you haven't made reservations, sidewalk cafés offer delicious (and less expensive) fare. Another favorite is the Matsunoma Lounge, where you can have sushi and drinks with no reservations.

Future World

This is the first area you encounter, and everything, including the bountiful landscaping, is clean and sparkling to the point of asepsis and seemingly bigger than life. Seven pavilions dedicated to man's past, present, and future technological accomplishments form the perimeter of the Future World area, with Spaceship Earth and its flanking Innoventions East and West standing prominently front and center.

World Showcase

This is the second theme area of Epcot, situated around picturesque World Showcase Lagoon. It is an ongoing World's Fair, with the cuisine, culture, history, and architecture of almost a dozen countries permanently on display in individual national pavilions. The pavilions are spaced along a promenade a little more than a mile long, which circles the impressive 40-acre lagoon. Countries include **Mexico, Norway, China, Germany, Italy, American Adventure, Japan, Morocco, France, United Kingdom,** and **Canada.**

Though many guests fail to notice, World Showcase features some of the loveliest gardens in Florida. Located in Germany, France, England, Canada, and to a lesser extent, China, they are sometimes tucked away and out of sight of pedestrian traffic on the World Showcase promenade.

While most adults enjoy World Showcase, some children find it boring. Disney has added a craft booth at each country, called Kidcot, with hands-on activities, such as painting with watercolors in Paris or learning Arabic lettering in Morocco. And there's also live entertainment to keep kids amused, from colorful dancing dragons in China to participatory street theater in Italy.

Passport Kits are available for about $10 in most Epcot retail shops. Each kit contains a blank passport and stamps for all the World Showcase countries. As kids accompany their folks to each country, they tear out the appropriate stamp and stick it on the passport. The kit also contains some information on the respective countries, as well as a Mickey Mouse button.

Top 10 Attractions

American Adventure (World Showcase)   This theater is a composite of everything Disney does best. Located in an imposing brick structure reminiscent of colonial Philadelphia, the production is a stirring, 29-minute sanitized rendition of American history narrated by an audio-animatronic Mark Twain and Ben Franklin. Behind a stage almost half the size of a football field is a 28 x 55–foot rear-projection screen on which motion picture images are interwoven with action on stage.

Body Wars (Future World)   On this thrill ride through the human body in a flight simulator, the story is that you're a passenger in a miniature capsule injected into a human body, on a mission to rescue a scientist who's been sucked into the circulatory system. The simulator creates a visually graphic experience, seeming to hurtle at fantastic speeds through human organs. You must be 40 inches tall to ride.

France (World Showcase)   *Impressions de France* is an exceedingly beautiful, 18-minute movie projected over 200° onto five screens. The film takes the audience to the Eiffel Tower, Versailles, the French Alps, Cannes, and other beautiful locations. The soundtrack in the music of French classical composers.

Honey I Shrunk the Audience (Future World)   This 3-D offshoot of Disney's feature film, *Honey, I Shrunk the Kids* features an array of special effects, including simulated explosions, smoke, fiber optics, lights, water spray, and moving seats. This attraction is played strictly for laughs, a commodity in short supply in Epcot entertainment. The sound level is earsplitting, frightening some young children. FASTPASS available.

IllumiNations (World Showcase)   This 13-minute, after-dark show consists of lasers, water, fire, and fireworks (2,800 shells are exploded during the nightly display), all set to a symphonic score. In the center of the lagoon is an "Earth Globe," a 28-foot diameter sphere that becomes a three-story video screen to tell the story of planet Earth. In the show finale, the Earth Globe opens with a fire torch rising 40 feet into the air. Viewing is excellent all around World Showcase Lagoon.

The Living Seas (Future World)   Among Future World's most ambitious offerings, scientists and divers conduct actual marine experiments in this 200-foot-diameter, 27-foot-deep tank containing fish, mammals, and crustaceans. Visitors can watch the activity through eight-inch-thick windows below the surface (including some in the Coral Reef restaurant) and aboard a three-part adventure ride consisting of a movie dramatizing the link between the ocean and man's survival, a simulated elevator descent to the bottom of the tank, and a three-minute gondola voyage through an underwater viewing tunnel.

Living with the Land (Future World)   This boat ride takes visitors through swamps, past inhospitable farm environments, and through a futuristic, innovative greenhouse where real crops are grown using the latest agricultural technologies. Inspiring and educational, with excellent effects and a good narrative. FASTPASS available.

Mission: Space (Future World) This simulated space adventure combines Disney storytelling with NASA technology. A powerful launch literally pushes you back into your seat. After you "slingshot" around the moon, you continue on to Mars where you land at a very high rate of speed. The attraction left one rider feeling "like socks in a dryer." Skip it if you are prone to motion sickness or are claustrophobic, and head for the post show video game Space Race, where up to 60 visitors can compete against each other in a race to send their rocket from Mars back to Earth. Guests must be 44 inches tall to ride. FASTPASS available.

Test Track (Future World) Visitors test a futuristic car at high speeds through hairpin turns, up and down steep hills, and over rough terrain. The six-guest vehicle is a motion simulator that rocks and pitches. Unlike simulators at Star Tours, Body Wars, and Back to the Future (at Universal Studios), however, the Test Track model is affixed to a track and actually travels. Guests must be 40 inches tall to ride. FASTPASS available.

Reflections of China (World Showcase) The new Circle-Vision 360° film in the China pavilion reflects the dramatic changes in that nation during the past 20 years. A crew of American and Chinese filmmakers worked together to capture fresh views of Hong Kong, Macau, and Shanghai.

DIVE QUEST

The soggiest behind-the-scenes experience available anywhere is Epcot's Dive Quest, where open-water scuba-certified divers can swim around with the fish at The Living Seas. Offered twice daily, each tour lasts three-and-a-half hours, including a 30–40-minute dive. The cost is about $140 per diver and includes all gear, a souvenir T-shirt, a dive log stamp, and refreshments. A video of your dive is $30. Reservations are required and can be made with a credit card by calling (407) WDW-TOUR. For recorded information, call (407) 560-5590. The experience is for adults only: no junior certifications are accepted and divers must be 15 or older.

Disney's Animal Kingdom

With its lush flora, winding streams, meandering paths, and re-created exotic villages, the Animal Kingdom is a stunningly beautiful theme park. The landscaping alone conjures images of rain forest, veldt, and even formal gardens. Add to this loveliness a population of more than 1,000 animals, replicas of Africa's and Asia's most intriguing architecture, and a diverse array of singularly original attractions, and you have the most unique of all Disney theme parks. And though you will encounter the typical long lines, pricey food, and shops full of Disney merchandise, you will also (with a little effort) experience a day of stimulating private discoveries.

At 500 acres, Disney's Animal Kingdom is five times the size of the Magic Kingdom and more than twice the size of Epcot. But like Disney-MGM Studios, most of the Animal Kingdom's vast geography is only accessible on guided tours or as part of attractions. The Animal Kingdom features six sections, or "lands": The Oasis, Discovery Island, DinoLand U.S.A., Camp Minnie-Mickey, Africa, and Asia.

Its size notwithstanding, the Animal Kingdom features a limited number of attractions. However, two of the attractions—Dinosaur and Kilimanjaro Safaris—are among the best in the Disney repertoire.

You must park your car and board a tram to reach the entrance. Be sure to pick up a guide map and entertainment schedule upon entering; this is also the place for package pick-up, Guest Services, lockers, rest rooms, and kennels. There is an ATM, and wheelchairs and strollers can be rented in Garden Gate Gifts shop.

Immediately past The Oasis is Safari Village, the park's "hub" to the other lands. The buildings are covered in brilliantly colored animal designs. But most visitors are more amazed by the giant Tree of Life, more than 14 stories high, with nearly 350 animal forms hand-carved into its massive trunk. Live animals, too, live at the base, like otters, ring-tailed lemurs, and red kangaroos.

From Safari Village, you can choose from six "lands": Africa; Chester and Hester's Dino-Rama, a new mini-land; DinoLand, USA; Asia; Conservation Station; or Camp Minnie-Mickey if your kids need a dose of Disney characters. You may use FASTPASS on Dinosaur, *It's Tough to Be a Bug!*, Kali River Rapids, Kilimanjaro Safaris, and Primeval Whirl. Height restrictions apply to Kali River Rapids, Primeval Whirl, and Dinosaur.

Top 10 Attractions

Dinosaur (Dinoland, U.S.A.) Dinosaur serves up nonstop action from beginning to end with brilliant visual effects, a combination track ride and motion simulator. The plot has you traveling back in time on a mission of rescue and conservation. Your objective is to haul back a living dinosaur before the species becomes extinct. However, you arrive on the prehistoric scene just as a giant asteroid is hurling toward Earth. Mayhem ensues. May be too intense for young children. FASTPASS available.

Festival of the Lion King **(Camp Minnie-Mickey)** This energetic production, inspired by Disney's *Lion King* film, is part stage show, part parade, and part circus. Guests are seated in four sets of bleachers surrounding the stage and organized into separate cheering sections, which are called on to make elephant, warthog, giraffe, and lion noises. There is a great deal of parading around, some acrobatics, and a lot of singing and dancing. By our count, every tune from *The Lion King* (plus a couple of others) is belted out and reprised several times.

Flights of Wonder **(Asia)** Both interesting and fun, Flights of Wonder is well paced and showcases a surprising number of different bird species. The focus is on the natural talents and characteristics of the various species, so don't expect any bicycle-riding parrots.

***It's Tough to Be a Bug!* and the Tree of Life** The Tree of Life, apart from its size, is quite a work of art. Although from afar it is certainly magnificent and imposing, it is not until you examine the tree at close range that you see that what appears to be ancient gnarled bark is in fact hundreds of carvings depicting all manner of wildlife, each integrated seamlessly into the trunk, roots, and limbs of the tree.

In sharp contrast to the grandeur of the tree is the subject of the attraction housed within its trunk. Called *It's Tough to Be a Bug!*, this humorous 3-D film is about the difficulties of being very small. Combining a 3-D film with an arsenal of tactile and visual special effects, the production is very intense and will do a number on young children and those who squeamish about insects. FASTPASS available.

Kali River Rapids (Asia) The ride consists of an unguided trip down a man-made river in a circular rubber raft with 12 persons. Because the river is fairly wide, with numerous currents, eddies, and obstacles, there is no telling exactly where the raft will go. Kali River Rapids flows through a dense rain forest, past waterfalls, temple ruins, and bamboo thickets, emerging into a cleared area where greedy loggers have ravaged the forest, and finally drifting back under the tropical canopy. Along the way, your raft runs a gauntlet of raging cataracts, log jams, and other dangers. Guests must be 38 inches tall to ride. FASTPASS available.

Kilimanjaro Safaris (Africa) Kilimanjaro Safaris offers an exceptionally realistic, albeit brief, imitation of an actual African photo safari in a simulated veldt habitat. Animals such as zebra, wildebeest, impala, Thomson's gazelle, giraffe, and even rhinoceros roam apparently free, while lions and potentially dangerous large animals like hippos, are separated from both prey and guests by all-but-invisible, natural-appearing barriers. Although the animals have more than 100 acres of savanna, woodland, streams, and rocky hills to call home, careful placement of water holes, forage, and salt licks ensure that the critters are hanging out by the road when safari vehicles roll by. FASTPASS available.

Maharajah Jungle Trek (Asia) This walk-through exhibit features an Asian setting and Asian animals, including Komodo dragons, Malayan tapirs, fruit bats, Bengal tigers, and an aviary. From the top of a parapet in the palace, you can view a herd of blackbuck antelope and Asian deer.

Pangani Forest Exploration Trail (Africa) Winding between the domain of two troops of lowland gorillas on this route, it's hard to see what, if anything, separates you from the primates. Also on the lush trail are a hippo pool with an underwater viewing area, hyenas, a beautiful bird aviary, and a naked mole rat exhibit.

Primeval Whirl (Dinoland, U.S.A.) A small coaster with short drops, curves, and spins—and you can't control the spinning, so don't try. It may look like a kiddie coaster, but it delivers quite a jolt when the spin is braked

260 Part Five Orlando: Walt Disney World and Beyond

to a jarring halt after half a revolution, or you're twirled two complete spins. It's silly fun. Guests must be 48 inches tall to ride. FASTPASS available.

Tarzan Rocks! (Dinoland, U.S.A.)   In the 1,500-seat Theater in the Wild, this 30-minute show features aerial acts as well as acrobatic stunts, including extreme skating. The musical score is by Phil Collins and drawn from the soundtrack of the eponymous film.

Disney-MGM Studios

Disney-MGM Studios is about the same size as the Magic Kingdom. Unlike the other parks, however, Disney-MGM Studios is a working motion picture and television production facility. This means that some of the studio area is controlled access, with guests permitted only on tours accompanied by guides. It's easy to see the park in a single day.

Guest Relations, on your left as you enter, serves as the park headquarters and information center, similar to City Hall in the Magic Kingdom. Go there for a schedule of live performances, maps, lost persons, package pickup, lost and found (on the right side of the entrance), general information, or in an emergency. To the right of the entrance are locker, stroller, and wheelchair rentals.

There are height restrictions for Rock 'n' Roller Coaster Starring Aerosmith, Star Tours, and The Twilight Zone Tower of Terror.

The FASTPASS system is available for *Indiana Jones Epic Stunt Spectacular, Jim Henson's Muppet Vision 3-D,* Rock 'n' Roller Coaster Starring Aerosmith, Star Tours, Twilight Zone Tower of Terror, Who Wants to Be a Millionaire—Play It!, and *Voyage of the Little Mermaid.*

Top 10 Attractions

Beauty and the Beast—Live on Stage   This 25-minute musical in the park's Theater of the Stars uses elaborate props, extravagant costumes, colorful production numbers, and special effects to tell the love story of Belle and the Beast in the Theater of the Stars. Credit for the collection of toe-tapping tunes belongs to Academy Award-winning composers Howard Ashman and Alan Menken.

Indiana Jones Epic Stunt Spectacular   Coherent and educational, though somewhat unevenly paced, this popular production showcases professional stunt men and women, who demonstrate dangerous stunts with a behind-the-scenes look at how it's done. Sets, props, and special effects are very elaborate. FASTPASS available.

Disney-MGM Studios Backlot Tour   This 35-minute tour begins in a special-effects water tank where you see how rain effects and a storm at sea are staged. From there, board trams with stops in wardrobe and craft shops and through the backlot to Catastrophe Canyon, an elaborate special-effects movie set where a thunderstorm, earthquake, oil-field fire, and flash flood are simulated. It's education and fun.

Jim Henson's Muppet Vision 3-D This movie provides a total sensory experience, with wild 3-D action augmented by auditory, visual, and tactile special effects. If you're tired and hot, this zany presentation will make you feel brand new. It's a little loud at end for toddlers. FASTPASS available.

Rock 'n' Roller Coaster Starring Aerosmith Although the rock icons and synchronized music add measurably to the experience, the ride itself, as opposed to sights and sounds along the way, is the focus here. The Rock 'n' Roller Coaster offers loops, corkscrews, and drops. What really makes this metal coaster unusual, however, is that it's in the dark (like Space Mountain) and launches you up the first hill like a jet off a carrier deck. By the time you crest the hill, you'll have gone from 0 to 57 mph in less than three seconds. When you enter the first loop, you'll be pulling five Gs. By comparison, that's two more Gs than astronauts experience at lift-off on a space shuttle. Guests must be at least 48 inches tall to ride. FASTPASS available.

Star Tours Based on the *Star Wars* movie series, this ride uses flight simulators modeled after those used to train pilots and astronauts. You're supposedly on an outing in space, piloted by a robot on his first flight with real passengers. This attraction is not for anyone prone to motion sickness; guests must be 40 inches tall to ride. FASTPASS available.

The Twilight Zone Tower of Terror The new version of this attraction multiplies the thrills inside the 13-story haunted hotel with a faster ride and more drops. In addition, visual, audio, and olfactory special effects were added. Though the final plunges are calculated to thrill, the meat of the attraction is its extraordinary visual and audio effects. There's richness and subtlety here, enough to keep the ride fresh and stimulating after many repetitions. Guests must be 40 inches tall to ride. FASTPASS available.

Who Wants to Be a Millionaire—Play It! This version of the TV game show is played on a replica of the real set; contestants are selected from among the audience and play for points and prizes (but not a million bucks). FASTPASS available.

Fantasmic! Far and away the most extraordinary and ambitious outdoor spectacle ever attempted in a theme park, *Fantasmic!* stars Mickey Mouse in his role as the Sorcerer's Apprentice from *Fantasia*. The production uses lasers, images projected on a shroud of mist, fireworks, lighting effects, and music in combinations so stunning you can scarcely believe what you have seen. It could be argued, with some validity, that *Fantasmic!* alone is worth the price of the Disney-MGM Studios admission. The program is staged in a 6,900-seat amphitheater, which can accommodate an additional 3,000 standing guests.

Voyage of the Little Mermaid Romantic, lovable and humorous, this stage show is a winner, appealing to every age. The story is simple and engaging, the special effects impressive, and the Disney characters memorable. FASTPASS available.

> **EASY WAY TO CHECK WAITING TIMES**
>
> At the corner of Hollywood and Sunset boulevards is a large display listing current waiting times for all Disney-MGM Studios attractions. It's updated continuously throughout the day. We've found the waiting times listed to be slightly overstated. If the display says the wait for Star Tours is 45 minutes, for example, you probably will have to wait about 35–40 minutes.

The Disney Water Theme Parks

There are two water theme parks to choose from at Walt Disney World. Before you go, call (407) 824-4321 the night before you go for opening times. For a day at the water parks consider the following:

- Visit on weekdays, when the parks are less crowded. We recommend Monday or Tuesday, when most tourists are visiting the theme parks; Fridays are also a good bet, because people traveling by car often use this day to start home.

- Go early in the morning or late in the afternoon. Don't wait for the Disney bus if you have your own car, and arrive 30 minutes before park opening. The parks often close by 11 a.m. when they are filled to capacity, and they don't open again until guests pack up in the afternoon. There can be long waits—up to 30 minutes—for some slides.

- The perfect time to go is after an afternoon storm, when the park has been closed due to bad weather. When the parks reopen after the inclement weather has passed, you can almost have a whole park to yourself. Evenings are great, too, when special lighting after dusk makes Typhoon Lagoon and Blizzard Beach enchanting places, and crowds are definitely lighter.

- Wear your bathing suit under your clothes, and wear shoes. Take your own towel and sunscreen.

- Since wallets and purses just get in the way, lock them in the trunk or leave them in the hotel. Carry enough cash for the day and a Disney resort ID (if you have one) in a plastic bag. It's relatively safe to leave stuff at your chair instead of renting a locker—just be sure it's well concealed.

- Don't bring personal gear (fins, masks, rafts, etc.)—it's not allowed. You can rent towels, or buy bathing suits or sunscreen. Tubes and personal flotation devices are free (you need a credit card or driver's license as a deposit, held until the equipment is returned).

- Head straight for the most popular slides and ride them first thing in the morning, before the crowd has time to build up.

- You can take a picnic, but no glass containers or alcoholic beverages.

- If your children are young, choose a base spot near the children's swimming area in all three parks. There are shelters for those who prefer shade and even a few hammocks. There are also picnic tables.

Blizzard Beach

This is Disney's newest and most exotic water adventure park, and like Typhoon Lagoon, it arrived with its own legend. This time, as the story goes, an optimistic entrepreneur tried to open a ski resort in Florida during a particularly savage winter. But alas, the snow melted, the palm trees grew back, and all that remained of the ski resort was its Alpine lodge, the ski lift, and of course, the mountain. Plunging off the mountain are ski slopes and bobsled runs transformed into water slides. Visitors to Blizzard Beach catch the thaw in midcycle—with dripping icicles and patches of snow here and there. The melting snow has formed a large lagoon (the wave pool), fed by gushing mountain streams.

Blizzard Beach is distinguished by its landscaping and detailed theme. There are 17 slides in all, among them Summit Plummet, the world's longest, fastest-speed slide, which begins with a 120-foot free fall, and the Teamboat Springs bobsled run, 1,200 feet long. If you are going primarily for the slides, you will have about two hours in the early morning to enjoy them before the waiting becomes intolerable during busy times of the year.

A ski lift carries guests to the top of the mountain where they choose from three rides—Summit Plummet, the Slush Gusher, and Teamboat Springs. If you are among the first in the park, the ski lift is fun and provides a bird's-eye view of the park. After riding it once, however, you are better off taking the stairs to the top of the mountain.

A wave pool and a float creek circle the park. The children's areas, Tike's Peak and Ski Patrol Training Camp, are creatively designed, nicely isolated from the rest of the park, and visually interesting, with attractions like Frozen Pipe Springs, where your kids can take a trip through a frozen pipe and drop down into eight feet of water.

Quick-service restaurants, rest rooms, shops, as well as tube, towel, and locker rentals are located in the ski resort's now-converted base area.

Admission is about $31 a day for adults, $25 for children ages 3–9, and free for children under age 3.

Typhoon Lagoon

Typhoon Lagoon is comparable in size to Blizzard Beach. Nine water slides and streams, some as long as 400 feet, drop from the top of a 100-foot-high man-made mountain. An "aftermath of a typhoon" theme imparts an added adventure touch to the wet rides.

Beautifully landscaped, Typhoon Lagoon is entered through a misty rain forest that emerges in a ramshackle tropical town, where concessions and services are located. Disney special effects make every ride an odyssey, as swimmers encounter bat caves, spinning rocks, dinosaur bone formations, and other imponderables.

Like Blizzard Beach, Typhoon Lagoon is costly: $31 a day for adults and $25 for children ages 3–9; free for children under age 3. If you are going primarily for the slides, you will have only two early morning hours to enjoy the slides before the wait becomes prohibitive during busy seasons.

Ketchakiddee Creek, for those under four feet tall, features geysers, tame slides, bubble jets, and fountains. For the older and more adventurous there are two speed slides, three corkscrew body slides, and three tube rapids rides (plus one children's rapids ride) plopping off Mount Mayday.

Two attractions, the surf pool and Shark Reef, are unique. The wave pool is the world's largest inland surf facility, with waves up to six feet. Shark Reef is a saltwater snorkeling pool, where guests can swim around with a multitude of real fish.

Shark Reef is a great opportunity for youngsters to try snorkeling in a controlled environment. Guests are grouped into impromptu classes for a briefing, then launched together. You're not allowed to paddle about aimlessly, but must swim more or less directly across the reef.

If you don't want to swim with fish, you can avail yourself of an underwater viewing chamber, accessible any time.

Elsewhere in the World

Downtown Disney

Encompassing three areas—the Marketplace, Pleasure Island, and West Side—Downtown Disney is the place to shop, dine, and play away from the theme parks—nearly a dozen restaurants, 24 movie-theater screens, and more than 50 shops and stores. The world's largest Disney character shop, World of Disney, is one-stop shopping for souvenirs. There are plenty of restaurants to choose from—Rainforest Cafe, Planet Hollywood, House of Blues, Wolfgang Puck, to name a few. During the winter holidays, from late November to early January, Disney builds an outdoor ice-skating rink, a real novelty in 80° weather.

DisneyQuest

DisneyQuest is a five-story, indoor interactive theme park at Downtown Disney's West Side that combines Disney creativity with technology, including virtual reality and real-time 3-D. There are activities for every age group in four zones: Explore Zone with virtual reality attractions; Score Zone that tests game-playing skills; Create Zone, a studio for artistic self-expression and invention; and Replay Zone, a favorite for youngsters with retro midway games and high-tech bumper cars.

DisneyQuest is open daily from 10:30 a.m. until midnight. Admission is $31, $25 for children ages 3–9, and free for children under age 3. All children ages 9 and under must be accompanied by an adult.

Cirque du Soleil

Recognized throughout the world for its astounding shows, Cirque du Soleil has a permanent home at Downtown Disney's West Side for the theatrical, spellbinding *La Nouba,* presented twice nightly Wednesday through Sunday. This extraordinary show wows audiences with surreal sets, theatrical lighting, and high-energy choreography. More than 60 artists from around the world, including gymnasts, acrobats, dancers, and clowns, weave a story of life and high drama during each 90-minute performance. It's definitely worth the ticket ($72–$82; $44–$49 ages 3–9).

Walt Disney Speedway

Adjacent to the Transportation and Ticket Center parking lot, this one-mile tri-oval course is host to several races each year. Between competitions, it's home to the **Richard Petty Driving Experience,** where you can ride in a two-seater stock car for $89 or learn to drive one. Courses are by reservation only and rides start at $89. You must be age 18 or older (16 for the Ride-Along Program), have a valid driver's license, and know how to drive a stick shift to take a course. For information, call (800) 237-3889.

Miniature Golf

First, **Fantasia Gardens:** We actually found it a little frustrating and too difficult for amateur golfers. But then we discovered there are two courses, and we were on the tougher approach-and-putt course with serious sand traps and water hazards. The other course is easier, themed after Disney's animated film *Fantasia,* and kids (and nongolfing parents) actually have a chance to reach the hole without picking up the ball. So pick the one that suits your game. The two, 18-hole courses are on Epcot Resorts Boulevard, directly across from the Walt Disney World Dolphin hotel.

Disney's **Winter Summerland** offers two 18-hole courses near Blizzard Beach water park. Both courses are loaded with interactive gadgets, like the snowman who squirts you with water when a golf ball passes beneath him. Fun for families ready for a break from the theme parks. A round at either course runs $9.25 for adults and $7.50 for children; phone (407) WDW-GOLF for more information.

Disney Cruise Line

You can combine a Disney World vacation with a cruise, or just sail on one of two ships, the *Disney Magic* and the *Disney Wonder.*

The ships are designed to offer activities and areas for all ages, including an adults-only spa, a sports club, four restaurants, a movie theater and a theater for Broadway-style shows, a nightclub for families, and a nighttime entertainment district for adults.

If your cruise starts at Disney World, one key will open both your hotel room and your onboard stateroom. Three- and four-day cruises sail to Nassau in the Bahamas; seven-day cruises offer ports in the Caribbean. Both ships stop at Castaway Cay, Disney's private Bahamian Island. For information, call (407) 566-7000.

Disney's Wide World of Sports

This 200-acre, multimillion-dollar sports complex hosts more than 30 types of sporting events, from baseball and basketball to tennis and aerobics. It's the home of the Amateur Athletic Union, the spring training home of the **Atlanta Braves,** and the training site of the **Tampa Bay Buccaneers** football team, and hosts the **Harlem Globetrotters** basketball showteam.

When at Disney, check to see if there's an event you might like to watch; tickets to premium events like an Atlanta Braves game can be purchased through TicketMaster at (407) 839-3900. If you want to take a chance and see what's going on or take a self-guided tour through the complex, tickets are $10 for adults and $9 for children ages 3–9.

Disney Dining

Reservations in World Disney World are known as "Priority Seating," a term that suggests you may still encounter a brief wait. When you call to make a priority seating, a Disney representative takes your name and essential information, then explains that you will be seated ahead of walk-ins, i.e., those without priority seating. Whether you reserve early or make arrangements once you're there, the number to call is (407) WDW-DINE.

For most full-service restaurants, buffets, and character meals, you can make priority seatings 120 days in advance. Exceptions include the character breakfast at Cinderella's Royal Table, where priority seating arrangement can be made 60 days in advance, and Disney dinner shows such as the Polynesian Luau and the Hoop-Dee-Doo Revue, where priority seatings can be scheduled two years in advance.

FAVORITE DISNEY EATS

Best seafood Flying Fish Café at Disney's BoardWalk, Coral Reef at Epcot

Best steak Yachtsman's Steakhouse, Disney's Yacht Club Resort

Best sushi Disney's California Grill

Best upscale theme-park dining Hollywood Brown Derby at Disney-MGM Studios

Best pasta Alfredo's at Italy in World Showcase, Epcot

Best quick service in the Magic Kingdom Cosmic Ray's Starlight Café in New Tomorrowland

Best all-you-can-eat Boma at Disney's Animal Kingdom Lodge, Whispering Canyon Café at Disney's Wilderness Lodge, or 'Ohana at Polynesian Resort

Most entertaining A seat next to the aquarium at Coral Reef in the Living Seas pavilion in Future World, Epcot; or a Disney character meal

Best family fun Hoop-Dee-Doo Musical Revue at Fort Wilderness Resort and Campground

World's best milk shakes The peanut-butter-and-jelly shake at 50's Prime Time at the Disney-MGM Studios

Most fun for kids Chef Mickey's at Disney's Contemporary Resort

Best splurge for grown-ups Victoria & Albert's or Cítricos at Disney's Grand Floridian

---

If you fail to make priority seating before you leave home, or if you want to make your dining decisions spontaneously while at Walt Disney World, your chances of getting a table at the restaurant of your choice are pretty good, but not a slam dunk. The Hoop-Dee-Doo Revue and Cinderella's Royal Table breakfast will most certainly be sold out, as will several of the other more popular character meals and Boma, a buffet at the Animal Kingdom Lodge. Other restaurants will still have priority seatings available if you call at least a day in advance.

Once in the theme parks, you can make priority seatings in person at the door of the restaurant, at Guest Services at Epcot, or at the kiosk at the intersection of Hollywood and Sunset Boulevards at the Disney-MGM Studios. With a few exceptions, you'll have no problem getting your priority seating at the park. If you fail to make priority seatings, most full-service theme park restaurants will take you as a walk-in between 2:30 and 4:30 p.m.

Walt Disney World Shopping

Downtown Disney

Downtown Disney has three shopping areas: the Marketplace, Pleasure Island, and the West Side. If you have time constraints and need to limit your Disney shopping spree to a single stop, this is it.

Downtown Disney stretches along the shore of Buena Vista Lagoon at the intersection of Buena Vista Drive and Hotel Plaza Boulevard. It's a pleasant walk from the Marketplace on the east end to the West Side, with Pleasure Island situated between the two areas. The West Side has smaller shops with trendy merchandise; the Marketplace is loaded with Disney merchandise and a smattering of non-Disney products; Pleasure Island is really a nighttime entertainment district, but there are a few shops worth considering. So, what you're shopping for determines the best place to park—free parking on a surface lot spreads from one end to the other.

DISNEY SHOPPING TIPS

If you are staying in a Disney hotel, you can have all of your packages delivered to the front entrance of any of the four Disney parks to avoid carrying them around. For a nominal charge, you can ship them by FedEx to your home.

If you remember on your flight home that you forgot to buy mouse ears for your nephew, call the Walt Disney Attractions Mail Order Department on weekdays at (407) 363-6200 or the catalog department at (800) 237-5751. Most trademark merchandise sold at Walt Disney World is available.

The Marketplace

The Marketplace is open Sunday–Thursday, 9:30 a.m.–11 p.m.; Friday and Saturday, 9:30 a.m.–11:30 p.m. There are more than 20 shops and seven eateries, including Rainforest Cafe. Top shops include: **Art of Disney** with limited-edition animation cels and pricey Disney creations; **World of Disney**, the Disney superstore with 12 rooms—50,000 square feet—stacked with Disney merchandise, from underwear to clocks to Cinderella dresses; Disney's **Days of Christmas** with hundreds of holiday decorations and a two-story tree decorated with Disney characters; **Disney at Home** with something Disneyesque for every room in the house; **LEGO Imagination Center** with all the latest LEGO paraphernalia, and **Once Upon a Toy** with five rooms of toys, from choose-your-own Mr. Potato Head parts and Lincoln Logs to popular board games.

Pleasure Island

It's best known for its nightclubs, but Pleasure Island's shops are open daily from 10:30 a.m. to 2 a.m. The newest Pleasure Island addition is **Zen Zone,** where shoppers can purchase sessions in massage chairs or aqua massage beds—long tubes that massage with 36 powerful jets of water (you stay dry). Anti-stress and massage products are for sale.

West Side

The West Side is open every day, 11 a.m.–11 p.m. This is the hip new extension of the Marketplace and Pleasure Island, with shops that are full of fun tchotchkes for compulsive buyers. Top shops include **Virgin Megastore** with more than 150,000 music titles on CD and cassette and 300 listening stations for previewing CDs; **Guitar Gallery,** offering more than 150 custom, collector, and rare guitars and accessories; and **Hoypoloi,** with one-of-a-kind pieces of art from various regions of the United States—Zen water fountains, contemporary art glass, and wooden boxes.

Epcot

It's one of the treats of Epcot to wander in and out of the shops in the 11 World Showcase pavilions, looking for unusual finds and bargains. Often you will see sale items, especially in the shops in France and Italy, but most of the imported merchandise is relatively expensive. However, the Epcot shops may be the only place in the United States that carries some lines of merchandise.

Walking clockwise around the World Showcase, here's what you'll find:

Mexico Carts are piled with blankets, sombreros, paper flowers, tambourines, and straw bags. Sure, the merchandise may be cheaper south of the border, but these prices aren't bad, with piñatas at $5–$11, kids' straw hats at $4.50, and straw bags for $12.

Norway The Puffin's Roost is a series of small shopping galleries with popular imports such as an entire room of trolls and wooden Christmas ornaments. Other hard-to-find imports include Laila perfume and body lotion and Helly Hansen outerwear.

China Yong Feng Shangdian department store features real silk kimonos, cloisonné, and thick silk rugs. Kids love rummaging through the toy bins in the covered outdoor area.

Germany Eight small shops interconnect on both sides of the cobblestone central plaza and provide an impressive collection of imports: cuckoo clocks, dolls, crystal, wine, and sweets are among the treasures.

Italy Il Bel Cristallo showcases Venetian glass, porcelain figurines and Giuseppe Armani figurines from Florence, along with handbags, ties, and scarves.

Japan A U.S. branch of Japan's 300-year-old Mitsukoshi Department Store stretches along one entire side of the pavilion. A recent renovation expands the culinary display and adds a sake-tasting bar.

Morocco Three shops offer everything from leather sandals, purses, and fezzes to brass and inexpensive kitchenware.

France Plume et Palette, a perfume shop, carries more than 100 imports, among them Chanel, Christian Dior, Jean Patou, and Cabotine de Grès. Other merchandise includes French wines, dishes, cookbooks, and finds from Provence.

United Kingdom/Canada The popular Roots boutique has a wide selection of merchandise, including caps, jackets, T-shirts, boots, clogs, and backpacks.

The Other Parks

Beyond Epcot, shopping is hit-or-miss in the other three theme parks. You'll find the same basic Disney merchandise everywhere, with specialty items for each park tossed in. However, there are still some unusual shops amid all the Disney goods. At **Disney-MGM Studios,** Sid Cahuenga's One-of-a-Kind, loosely inspired by junk shops in southern California, carries autographed photos of film and TV stars, and old movie posters. The park's Animation Gallery in the Animation Building has an impressive collection of cels and other collectibles.

Mombasa Marketplace at **Disney's Animal Kingdom** showcases reasonably priced African-themed pottery, musical instruments, and masks. Often you'll find an artisan from Kenya carving walking sticks on the front porch.

In the **Magic Kingdom,** if you want a monogrammed mouse-ears hat, The Chapeau on Main Street is the only place at Walt Disney World to purchase it (there is a hat shop at the Studios, but there you pay extra for the monogramming).

Universal Orlando

Universal Orlando (1000 Universal Studios Plaza, Orlando; (407) 363-8000 or (800) U-ESCAPE; **www.universalorlando.com**) is spacious, beautifully landscaped, meticulously clean, and delightfully varied in its entertainment offerings.

UNIVERSAL EXPRESS PASS

A great advantage for resort guests is the new Universal Express Pass. If you're staying in a Universal hotel, you simply show your room keycard to be directed to an "express line" for almost every ride and attraction in the two parks. The system is also available to nonresort guests who buy theme park tickets—but they must receive an Express Pass for a single ride or attraction, and can only get another Express Pass after visiting the attraction or after two hours have passed.

The two Universal parks—Universal Studios and Islands of Adventure—have lots of exciting, innovative rides, and individual shows on movie making. Both open daily at 9 a.m., with closing times that vary seasonally. Stretching between the two theme parks is Universal CityWalk, a 30-acre entertainment district.

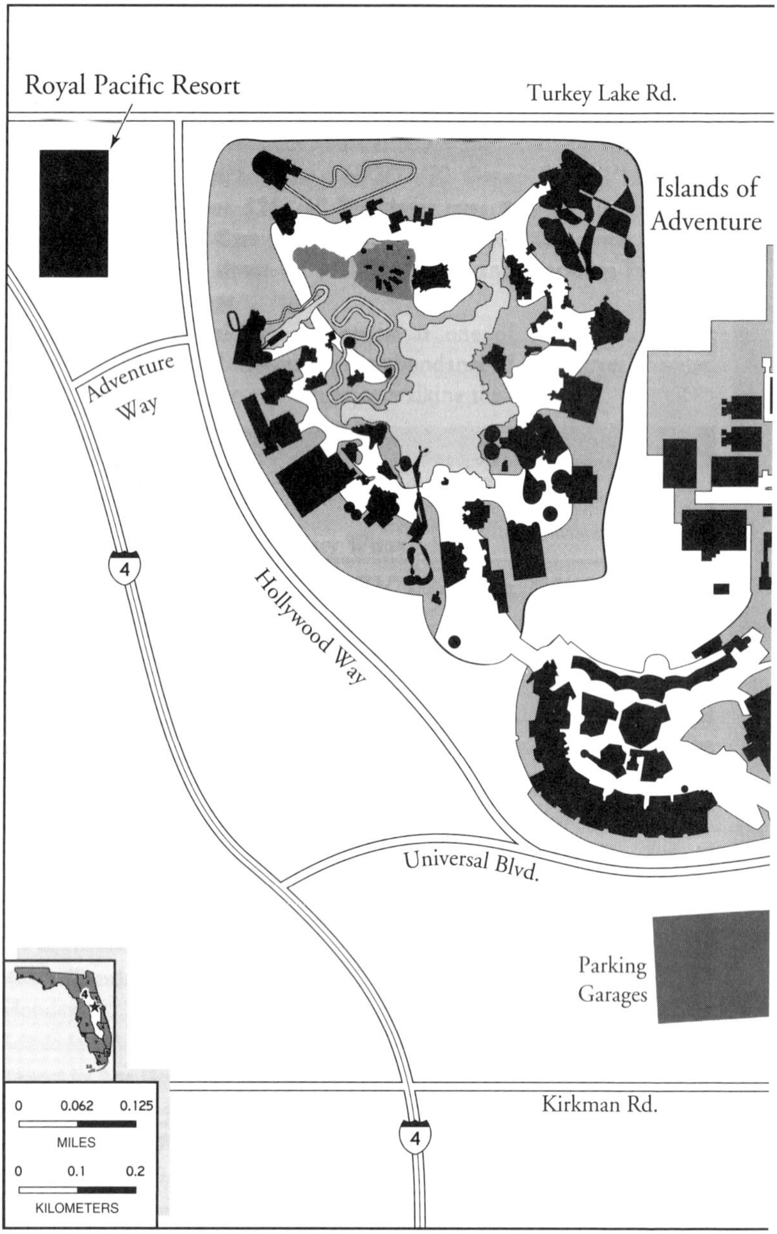

Royal Pacific Resort
Turkey Lake Rd.
Islands of Adventure
Adventure Way
Hollywood Way
4
Universal Blvd.
Parking Garages
Kirkman Rd.
4
0 0.062 0.125
MILES
0 0.1 0.2
KILOMETERS

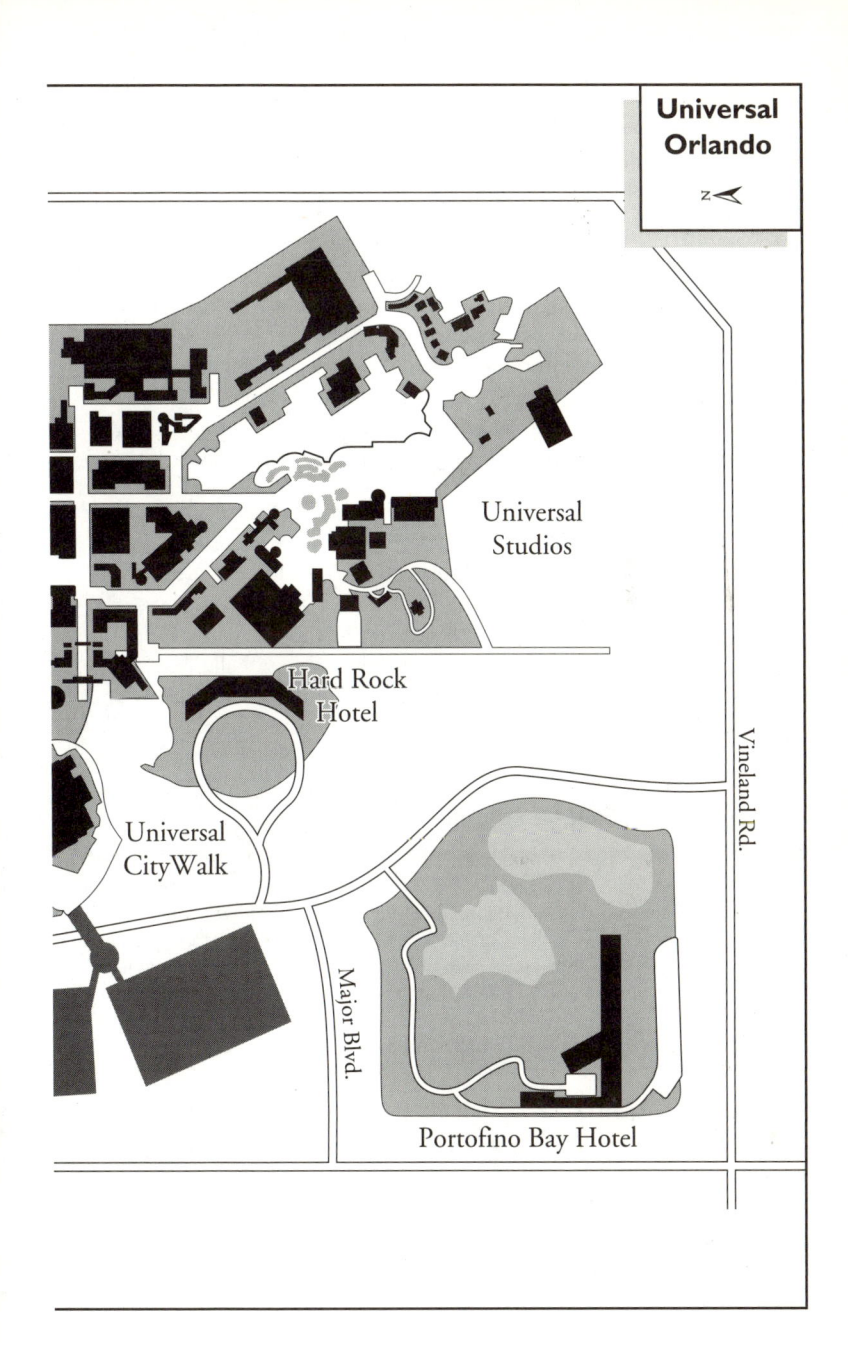

Universal Orlando

N

Universal Studios

Hard Rock Hotel

Universal CityWalk

Vineland Rd.

Major Blvd.

Portofino Bay Hotel

Universal Orlando features three hotels: Portofino Bay Hotel, with a Mediterranean theme; Hard Rock Hotel, with a cache of cool rock 'n' roll memorabilia; and the Royal Pacific Resort. All are just a short (and free) boat taxi ride from CityWalk and the theme parks.

Admission Options

A one-day, one-park pass is $55, $46 for children ages 3–9; those under age 3 are admitted free of charge. A two-day, two-park pass costs $104, $90 for children. A three-day, two-park pass runs $120, $104 for children.

Several multiday ticket options are available, including annual passes and a flex ticket that includes SeaWorld, Wet 'n Wild, and Busch Gardens in Tampa. The website **www.universalorlando.com** has a list of options, with some tickets only available online. Most multiday tickets must be used within 14 days.

Arriving, Parking, and Transportation

Universal Orlando can be accessed directly from I-4. Once on-site, you will be directed to park in one of two multi-tiered parking garages. Be sure to write down the location of your car before heading for the parks. From the garages, moving sidewalks deliver you to Universal CityWalk; from CityWalk you can access the main entrances of both Universal Studios and Islands of Adventure theme parks. Even with the moving walkways it takes about 10–12 minutes to commute from the garages to the entrances of the theme parks. Parking is $8 for cars, $9 for RVs, and it's free after 6 p.m. Valet parking is available for $16; follow the signs.

UNIVERSAL THEME PARK DINING

CityWalk and the Universal hotels have a handful of good restaurants, but inside the theme parks, if you're looking for more than quick-service fare, there are just two recommendations: **Mythos** (phone (407) 224-4533) at Islands of Adventure, and **Lombard's** (phone (407) 224-6400) at Universal Studios. Lombard's does a nice job with seafood, while Mythos's pricier offerings are more eclectic, from wood-fired pizzas to pork tenderloin. You'll need reservations for both.

Universal Studios

Universal's first Central Florida theme park is all about "living the movies," with stage sets, soundstages, and backlots—the "lands" are loosely delineated as you wander from **Production Central** to **New York, San Francisco/Amity, World Expo, Woody Woodpecker's Kidzone,** and **Hollywood**.

Universal Studios is laid out in an upside-down L configuration. Beyond the main entrance, a wide boulevard stretches past several shows and rides to a New Your City backlot. Branching off this pedestrian thoroughfare to the right are five streets that access other areas of the studios and intersect a promenade circling a large lake.

Universal Orlando

Top Attractions

Animal Planet Live! Too cute—live animals, from pigs and dogs to horses, parrots and a baby chimpanzee—take center stage to show off. Some audience members get to participate. Universal Express Pass available.

Back to the Future ... The Ride A seven-story Omnimax screen and a flight simulator disguised as a time-traveling DeLorean take you on a jarring, jolting high-speed chase from the Ice Age to the year 2015. Thought the story line doesn't make much sense, the visual effects are wild and powerful. Not for anyone with motion sickness. Guests must be 40 inches tall to ride. Universal Express Pass available.

Earthquake—The Big One Remember this movie? This attraction puts you on a San Francisco subway train before the big one hits (8.3 on the Reichter), creating fires, crashes, tumbling walls, and a tidal wave. You have to be 40 inches tall to ride. Universal Express Pass available.

Jaws The thriller that kept hordes from the beaches is brought to life with a three-ton shark that menaces your little boat. Jaws builds an amazing degree of suspense, with nonstop action leading up to the moment the Great White makes his appearance. Universal Express Pass available.

Jimmy Neutron's Nicktoon Blast A kid-pleaser from the minute you're buckled in your "rocket," the lights go down, and you "lift off" for a bumpy ride through the animated world of Nickelodeon characters. By the final moments, kids are squealing with delight and most grown-ups look relieved that the jostling rockets have settled back to earth. Universal Express Pass available.

Men in Black Alien Attack This supercharged video game lets you chase aliens with your on-board laser gun. And these bad guys shoot back, sending your car spinning out of control. You rack up points and depart a winner or loser. You must be 42 inches tall to ride. Universal Express Pass available.

Nickelodeon Studios Fans of the Nickelodeon network line up for "Nick Slime Time," live from the studios on select weekday afternoons. Head over to the Nick Studios to pick up a ticket for one of the coveted seats. Throughout the day, tours show set construction, soundstages wardrobe, props, lighting, video production, and special effects.

Shrek 4-D Universal Studios' newest attraction picks up where the Oscar-winning *Shrek* left off, with Shrek, Princess Fiona, and their chatterbox Donkey setting off for a honeymoon. Within seconds after putting on OgreVision glasses, the audience gets startling proof that 4-D means there are cutting-edge special effects in the theater as well as on-screen. In-your-face spiders, a fire-breathing dragon, and a wild plunge down a waterfall (your seats bob and bounce, too) make for a spectacular, fast-paced attraction. Universal Express Pass available.

Terminator 2: 3-D The attraction, like the *Terminator* films, is all action, and you don't really need to understand much. Ah-nold wants you out of the building in this battle to prevent mankind's extinction at the cold, steel hands of futuristic cyborgs. You're immersed in the battle with live action stunts, special effects, and 3-D . . . it's "hasta la vista, baby." Universal Express Pass available.

Twister: Ride It Out Based on the hit movie *Twister,* but this time you're on the set with a screaming, five-story tornado with wind, pounding rain, and a flying cow just 20 feet from where you are standing. The ominous funnel even has the terrifying "freight train" sound, created by circulating more then two million cubic feet of air per minute. Universal Express Pass available.

COMING SOON: REVENGE OF THE MUMMY

At press time, construction was under way on Universal Studios' next blockbuster, "Revenge of the Mummy," scheduled to open in April 2004. Ten years in development, Universal says it's the first indoor ride to fuse roller-coaster technology, robotics, and pyrotechnic special effects, including a "ceiling of flame" inches overhead. Guests will hurtle through Egyptian sets in this psychological thrill ride based on the popular *Mummy* films.

Islands of Adventure

This theme park expanded Universal's offerings, and features the best collection of roller coasters and thrill rides of any Central Florida attraction. Many of the rides have characters for inspiration—The Cat in the Hat, Spider-Man, Popeye, The Incredible Hulk, and the dinosaurs of Jurassic Park.

The park is configured with five islands, each with rides, attractions, shows, and restaurants: **Seuss Landing, Toon Lagoon, Marvel Super Hero Island, The Lost Continent,** and **Jurassic Park.**

Islands of Adventure is arranged much like the World Showcase section of Epcot, in a large circle surrounding a lake. Each island is self-contained and visually consistent in its theme.

Top Attractions

The Amazing Adventures of Spider-Man Spider-Man is frenetic, fluid, and astounding. The visuals are rich and wild, but not jerky, as you're immersed in a 3-D world to help Spider-Man retrieve the Statue of Liberty from the bad guys. It's a high-tech battle from start to finish, including a 400-foot drop that leaves you wondering just how they did that. A little too intense for some kids. Universal Express Pass available.

Caro-Seuss-el Totally outrageous, everyone can be a kid again when they pick their personal favorite Seuss character for a spin on the elaborate carousel, from the Dog-a-lopes and Mulligatawnies from "If I Ran the Zoo" to the Elephant-birds from "Horton Hatches an Egg." Universal Express Pass available.

The Cat in the Hat Chaotic fun for all ages, this ride brings the famous Seuss book to life with Thing 1 and Thing 2, and the goldfish who tries to maintain order in the house as you ride by on "couches" through 18 different sets. Universal Express Pass available.

> ### BREEZE PAST THE LONG LINES
>
> If you can afford it, Universal Studios offers a guided tour of the top attractions for $100 per person. An employee meets your family and escorts you to the front of the line at major attractions. Theme park tickets are $55 and $46 for ages 3–9, so you're spending about $45 not to stand in interminably long lines, but you also get free valet parking, a DVD (we got *The Mummy Returns*), and a collectible pin. It's a great way to experience the best of the park in a few hours. Just be aware that many of the attractions on the tour are not suitable for children under age 6.

Dudley Do-Right's Ripsaw Falls Wet, wet, wet, so don't even consider this flume ride unless getting soaked is an option. Dudley Do-Right has to save Nell from the evil Snidely Whiplash, and just like an episode of *Rocky and Bullwinkle,* there's an inescapable waterfall. Riders must be at least 48 inches tall. Universal Express Pass available.

Dueling Dragons Hulk may look scarier, but these inverted coasters get high marks from daredevils who love the two intertwined tracks that whiz over, under, and around each other at speed up to 60 mph—at one point a mere 12 inches apart. It's the park's highest coaster and also claims the longest drop—115 feet. Guests must be 54 inches tall to ride. Universal Express Pass available.

The Incredible Hulk Coaster There's nothing quite like blastoff from 0 to 40 mph in two seconds, then an inversion, seven rollovers, and two dips underground. It's over in two minutes and 15 seconds—before you know it, you're lining up again. Guests must be 54 inches tall to ride. Universal Express Pass available.

Jurassic Park River Adventure You drift pleasantly along until, of course, something goes awry. Before you know it, you're prey for a Tyrannosaurus rex who descends on your ride car just before an eight-story plunge—the longest, fastest, steepest water descent in a theme park. Riders must be at least 42 inches tall. Universal Express Pass available.

Popeye & Bluto's Bilge-Rat Barges Water again, and most of the riders looked like drowned rats as they exit the white-water raft ride—not only from the churning waters, but thanks to overzealous (and dry) park guests who take aim at riders with water cannons along the way. Be a good sport, or skip this one. Riders must be at least 48 inches tall. Universal Express Pass available.

Poseidon's Fury: Escape from the Lost City You've a front-row seat for the battle between Poseidon and Zeus—water and fire—in this dramatic theatrical performance that includes more than 350,000 gallons of water and 200 fiery effects. It wraps with quite an impressive flourish. Universal Express Pass available.

Universal Studios CityWalk

CityWalk, a 30-acre entertainment district, stretches between the two theme parks. After parking in the garage, you must walk through CityWalk to reach either of the two Universal theme parks.

Perhaps CityWalk's biggest claims to fame are **Emeril's Restaurant Orlando** by famed Chef Emeril Lagasse, and **Jimmy Buffett's Margaritaville,** where the musician has been know to drop by for an impromptu concert. Other eateries include **Hard Rock Café** (next door is a Hard Rock Live concert venue), **NBA City, Bob Marley—A Tribute to Freedom, Motown Café, NASCAR Café, Pat O'Brien's,** and **Latin Quarter.**

A 20-screen, **Universal Cineplex** draws crowds on weekends and rainy days. Shopping is limited but fun, with about a dozen specialty shops carrying everything from cigars to surf and beach wear.

Children are welcome in most of the restaurants. Shops open at 10 a.m. daily, and many are open until midnight. A CityWalk Party Pass costs $9, $12 with a movie pass.

Greater Orlando Area

It is true that but for Walt Disney, Orlando might remain a sleepy central-Florida hamlet to this day. However, it is equally correct that the thousands of tourists who see no more of Greater Orlando that the Disney and Universal parks bypass a wealth of recreation, shopping, and entertainment in Orlando and nearby towns. Besides lavish theme parks like SeaWorld and Wet 'n Wild (see Attractions below), which pale only in comparison to their gargantuan neighbors, Orlando is home to peculiar roadside attractions, themed hotels and eateries, and, thankfully, tasteful respites from the outlandish. And although most of them subsist on residual Disney-vacation dollars, tourists can easily spend a week or two in Orlando without setting foot in a Disney or Universal theme park.

Golf

ChampionsGate, International Course

1400 Masters Boulevard, Championsgate
(888) 558-9301 or (407) 787-4653; www.championsgategolf.com

Established 2001 | **Designer** Greg Norman | **Holes** 18

Tees Trophy/Legends/Champions/Heritage
Par 72/72/72/72 **Slope** 143/137/132/117

Fees $50 before 3 p.m. (Florida residents); $68 (non-Florida residents), $48 after 3 p.m. **Cart rental** Included **Club rental** $40 per set **Payment** V, MC, AmEx **Tee times** 60 days in advance **Facilities** Pro shop, driving range, practice greens, locker rooms, restaurant, beverage cart, and club and shoe rentals.

Comments The tougher and more highly ranked of the two layouts at Champions Gate, the International lives up to its name by re-creating the feel of the championship courses of the British Isles. Laid out in a links style, the course has carpet-like fairways framed by the stark unfinished look of brown dunes, mounds, and severe pot bunkers. From the tips, it is one of the state's most challenging courses.

Grand Cypress, New Course

1 North Jacaranda, Orlando
(800) 835-7377, (407) 239-4700; www.grandcypress.com/golf/golfclub.htm
Established 1988 | **Designer** Jack Nicklaus | **Holes** 18

Tees Black/White/Red **Par** 72/72/72 **Slope** 126/117/117
Fees Seasonal from $115–$175 **Specials** Golf packages available **Cart rental** Included in green fees **Club rental** $60 per set **Payment** V, MC, AmEx, D **Tee times** 60 days in advance **Facilities** Pro shop, driving range, practice greens, locker rooms, restaurant, beverage cart, carts equipped with Global Positioning Systems, and club and shoe rentals.
Comments The New Course is Jack Nicklaus' homage to the famous Old Course at St. Andrews, Scotland, the birthplace of golf. The first and last two holes are replicas of those at the Old Course, and other features such as the famous Swilcan Bridge and some of the huge bunkers are recreated here.

In between are Nicklaus's original holes, done in a links style, with double greens, pot bunkers, tall rough, and wide, hard fairways.

Grenelefe Golf and Tennis, West Course

3200 FL 546, Haines City
(800) 237-9549; (863) 422-7511; www.westgateresorts.com
Established 1971 | **Designers** Robert Trent Jones Sr. and David Wallace | **Holes** 18

Tees Dark Green/Light Green/White/Yellow
Par 72/72/72/72 **Slope** 130/126/122/118
Fees $45 **Specials** $25 unlimited golf **Cart rental** Included in green fees **Club rental** $20 per set **Payment** V, MC, AmEx, D **Tee times** 10 days in advance **Facilities** Pro shop, driving range, putting green, restaurant
Comments Grenelefe has three courses, but the main attraction is the West course—stretching more than 7,300 yards from the tips. In fact, six of the ten par-4s on the course are over 400 yards and most of the par-3s over 200 yards. But the real beauty of Grenelefe is that it tests your touch as well as your strength. The greens tend to be small and well bunkered; your approach shots are as important as your drives.

Mission Inn Golf and Tennis Resort, El Campeon Course

10400 CR 48, Howey-In-The-Hills
(352) 324-3885; www.missioninnresort.com
Established 1926 | **Designer** Charles Clark | **Holes** 18

Tees Blue/White/Gold/Red **Par** 72/72/72/72 **Slope** 133/128/119/118

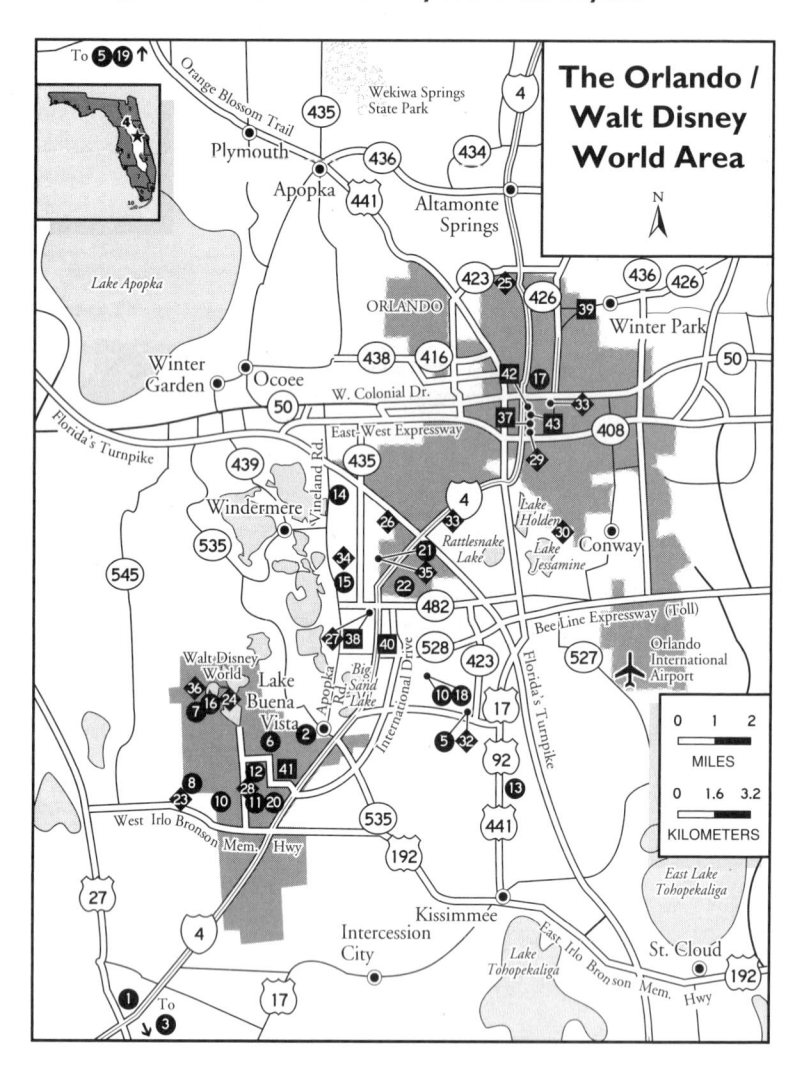

Fees $50 **Specials** Call in inquire **Cart rental** Included **Club rental** $50 per set **Payment** V, MC, AmEx, DC **Tee times** 7 days in advance **Facilities** Driving range, putting green, pro shop, restaurant

Comments El Campeon plays through 625 acres of isolated, rolling terrain featuring a number of lakes, elevation changes up to 85 feet, sculpted bunkers, and tight fairways lined with mature oaks. The back 9 has a series of difficult and intriguing holes. Known as the "Devil's Delight," the 17th is a 538-yard par-5 that easily lives up to its moniker.

GOLF COURSES
1. Champions Gate
2. Grand Cypress
3. Grenelefe Golf & Tennis, West Course
4. Mission Inn Golf & Tennis Resort
5. Ritz-Carlton Golf Club
6. Walt Disney World Resort- Eagle Pines/Osprey Ridge
7. Walt Disney World Resort- Magnolia/Palm

ATTRACTIONS
8. Animal Kingdom
9. Blizzard Beach
10. Discovery Cove
11. Disney-MGM Studios
12. Epcot
13. Gatorland Zoo
14. Holy Land Experience
15. Islands of Adventure
16. Magic Kingdom
17. Orlando Science Center
18. SeaWorld Orlando
19. Silver Springs
20. Typhoon Lagoon
21. Universal Studios Orlando
22. Wet 'n' Wild

RESTAURANTS
23. Boma
24. California Grill
25. Del Frisco's
26. Delfino Riviera
27. Emeril's Restaurant Orlando
28. Flying Fish
29. Hue
30. Le Coq Au Vin
31. McCormick & Schmick's
32. Norman's at the Ritz-Carlton
33. Pho 88
34. Seasons 52
35. Tchoup Chop
36. Victoria & Albert's

NIGHTCLUBS
37. Bösendorfer Lounge
38. CityWalk
39. Fiddler's Green
40. Matrix/Metropolis
41. Pleasure Island
42. Sky60
43. Tabu

Ritz-Carlton Golf Club

4012 Central Florid Parkway, Orlando; (407) 393-4900; www.grandelakes.com

Established 2003 **Designer** Greg Norman **Holes** 18

Tees Black/Gold/Blue/White/Green
Par 72/72/72/72/72 **Slope** 139/135/127/121/115

Fees $85 for hotel guests, $95 for nonguests **Cart rental** Included **Club rental** $20 per set **Payment** All major credit cards accepted **Tee times** 14 days in advance **Facilities** Very large driving range, pro shop, showers, Fairway Pub & Grill

Comments This new course is promoted as "enjoyable for golfers of every skill level." A Golf Caddie-Concierge Program, the first of its kind at a U.S. golf resort, offers a professional attendant to accompany each twosome or foursome. Along with traditional caddie services, the concierge caddies provide other services, including food and beverage orders and dinner reservations. The club also has a "Golf FORE Kids Etiquette Class" for kids 5–12.

Walt Disney World Resort, Eagle Pines, and Osprey Ridge

3451 GolfView Drive, Lake Buena Vista;
(407) WDW-GOLF; www.disneyworld.com

Eagle Pines Course

Established 1992 | **Designer** Pet Dye | **Holes** 18

Tees Talon/Crest/Wings/Feathers
Par 72/72/72/72 **Slope** 131/125/115/116

Osprey Ridge Course

Established 1992 | **Designer** Tom Fazio | **Holes** 18

Tees Talon/Crest/Wings/Feathers
Par 72/72/72/72 **Slope** 135/128/121/122

Fees Seasonal, $105–$170; call for current rates **Specials** Twilight rates; replay rates are 50% of applicable full rate on the same day, on a space-available basis, and may not be reserved in advance. **Cart rental** Included **Club rental** $45 per set **Payment** All major credit cards accepted **Tee times** Resort guests can reserve tee times up to 90 days in advance, and day guests can reserve up to 30 days in advance by calling (407) WDW-GOLF. All reservations must be guaranteed with a credit card. **Facilities** Pro shop, driving range, practice green, locker rooms, club and shoe rentals, snack bar, beverage cart, and Sand Trap Bar & Grill (Osprey Ridge).

Comments At **Eagle Pines,** in contrast to neighboring Osprey Ridge, Pete Dye crafted a course reminiscent of the Carolina Sandhills, with fairways lined with native grasses and flanked by waste areas of straw and sand. Dish-shaped greens are at or below the levels of the fairway, emphasizing approach shots. Water is in play on nearly every hole, and aesthetically, this is the most impressive of the Disney courses.

The Tom Fazio layout at **Osprey Ridge** is a thoroughly modern course, the construction of which required much earth moving. Its main characteristics are large rolling mounds and elevated tees and greens. The greens are huge, which makes them easy to hit but leaves long approach shots.

Walt Disney World Resort, Magnolia and Palm

1950 West Magnolia/Palm Drive, Lake Buena Vista;
(407) WDW-GOLF; www.disneyworld.com

Magnolia Course

Established 1971 | **Designer** Joe Lee | **Holes** 18

Tees Blue/White/Gold/Red **Par** 72/72/72/72 **Slope** 128/128/123/123

Palm Course

Established 1971 | **Designer** Joe Lee | **Holes** 18

Tees Blue/White/Gold/Red **Par** 72/72/72/72 **Slope** 133/128/124/123

Fees Seasonal, $105–$170; call for current rates **Specials** Twilight rates; replay rates are 50% of the applicable full rate on same day, on a space-available basis, and may not be reserved in advance. **Cart rental** Included **Club rental** $45 per set **Payment** All major credit cards accepted **Tee times** Resort guests can reserve tee times up to 90 days in advance, and day guests can reserve up to 30 days in advance by calling (407) WDW-GOLF. All reservations must be guaranteed with a credit card. **Facilities** Pro shop, driving range, practice green, locker rooms, sports bar, beverage cart, and club and shoe rentals

Comments A fine Joe Lee creation, **Magnolia** shares its best traits with the Palm, including excellent greens, practice facilities, a dramatic finishing sequence, and plenty of water. From the back tees it is Disney's longest course and features a whopping 97 bunkers, including the famous one in the shape of Mickey Mouse's head. But the layout is slightly less challenging than the Palm, with no water on most of the par-3s.

The Palm is Disney's best course, with lesser-known architect Joe Lee showing up the marquee designers that headline the Bonnet Creek Golf Club. The defining characteristic is a set of holes where water separates tees from landing areas and landing areas from greens, a wet take on desert-style target golf. The signature 18th, with its island green, caps a fine set of finishing holes and has been ranked as high as fourth in difficulty among all holes on the PGA Tour's many venues. But four sets of well-spaced tees make the course playable for all abilities.

Attractions

International Drive

International Drive, or "I-Drive," is the epicenter of Central Florida's tourism business. This is where you'll find most of the factory outlet stores, many hotel chains, and just about any fast food restaurant you can dream up.

If you're staying on I-Drive, there are myriad small attractions that are great for rainy days, or if you're short on time or have overspent the budget for the premier parks. The **I-Ride Trolley** (phone (407) 248-9590; www.iridetrolley.com) is a fun way to get around International Drive. A single fare is 75 cents; kids under 12 ride free. Hours are 8 a.m.–10:30 p.m. daily.

Along with Wet 'n Wild water park (profiled below), here are a few top attractions:

WonderWorks (9067 International Drive; (407) 351-8800; wonderworksonline.com), in the distinctive "upside-down" building, is an interactive playground where you can experience earthquakes and hurricanes, swim with sharks, put yourself inside a huge bubble, design and ride a roller coaster, or play in the world's largest laser-tag arena. The owners visited science centers all over the world, then re-created the best of the best. Hours are 9 a.m.–midnight daily; the cost is $17, $13 ages 4–12.

Ripley's Believe It or Not (8201 International Drive; (407) 363-4418; www.ripleysorlando.com) is just plain fun, filled to the rafters with oddities like shrunken heads, unusual animals, and animals made of matchsticks. Hours are 9 a.m.–1 a.m. daily; cost is $16, $11 ages 4–12.

Vans Skateboard Park (5220 International Drive; (407) 351-3881; www.vans.com) is the place to go if you've got a kid who's jonesin' for a little skateboard time. The skatepark features 61,000 square feet of indoor and outdoor skating with riding areas and obstacles. Highlights include the "Dough Boy," an above-ground bowl, and a 40-foot competition-size vertical ramp. Grown-ups can hang out on the mezzanine viewing area.

The **Hard Rock Vault** (8437 International Drive; (407) 445-7625; www.hardrock.com) showcases about 1,000 artifacts from more than 200 artists, from blues pioneers to heavy metal and punk stars—from an Elvis jumpsuit to Michael Jackson's red jacket. Pieces have been chosen from memorabilia displayed at the more than 100 Hard Rock Cafés around the world. Also a music listening room.

Gatorland Zoo

14501 South Orange Blossom Trail, Kissimmee; (407) 855-5496; www.gatorland.com

Hours Daily, 9 a.m.–dusk

Admission $20 for adults, $10 for children ages 3–12, free for ages 2 and under

Appeal by Age Group

Pre-school ★★★	Teens ★★★★	Over 30 ★★★
Grade school ★★★★	Young Adults ★★★★	Seniors ★★★

Touring Time *Average* 3 hours; *minimum* 1½ hour

Rainy-Day Touring Some of the exhibit is under cover

Author's Rating ★★★; a unique Florida experience

Description and Comments A kitschy roadside attraction, but the kids really love to see the alligators leap as high as five feet from the water and snatch the whole chickens in *Gator Jumparoo,* one of three daily shows at this old-fashioned attraction.

The 70-acre park opened in 1949, and the trademark gaping gator jaws at the entrance were put in place back in 1962. The jaws lead to a boardwalk spanning a seven-acre lake filled with dozens of the critters.

Gator Wrestlin' Cracker-Style demonstrates how Florida cowboys used to go one-on-one with the reptiles.

Covered walkways lead past monkeys, goats, deer, bears, and wild birds. At the far end of the park is an ancient cypress swamp with a three-level observation tower that offers a great view of gators and thousands of birds nests.

Holy Land Experience

4655 Vineland Road, Orlando; (866) 872-4659

Hours 9 a.m.–5 p.m. Monday–Thursday; 9 a.m.–6 p.m. Friday and Saturday; noon–6 p.m. Sunday; closed Thanksgiving and Christmas Day

Admission $30, $20 ages 6–12

Appeal by Age Group

Pre-school ★	Teens ★★	Over 30 ★★★
Grade school ★★	Young Adults ★★	Seniors ★★★

Touring Time *Average* 3 hours

Rainy-Day Touring Not recommended

Author's Rating ★★

Description and Comments The Holy Land Experience is a peaceful retreat and a fascinating look at places recorded in the Bible. From the moment you pass through the gates of the "Walled City," the architecture transports you to Jerusalem, circa 1450 B.C. to A.D. 66, with replicas of Calvary's garden tomb, the Qumran Caves (where the Dead Sea Scrolls were found in 1947), the Wilderness Tabernacle, the Temple of the Great King, and the Plaza of the Nations. The newest addition is the Scriptorium, which houses one of the world's finest private collections of biblical artifacts—cuneiform, scrolls, codices, manuscripts, and Bibles. Throughout the day, live shows are staged, showing, for instance, ancient Jewish rituals in the Wilderness Tabernacle or the resurrection of Jesus. The park's Christian message is obvious.

Orlando Science Center

777 East Princeton Street, Orlando; (407) 514-2000; www.osc.org

Hours Tuesday–Thursday, 9 a.m.–5 p.m.; Friday and Saturday, 9 a.m.–9 p.m.; Sunday, noon–5 p.m.; closed Monday

Admission $10 for adults, $9 for senior citizens; $7.50 for children ages 3–11; $7 for adults, $6 for senior citizens, $5 for children ages 3–11 additional for films, and combo tickets are available for $13 adults, $12 senior citizens and $10.50 children ages 3–11.

Appeal by Age Group

Pre-school ★★★	Teens ★★★	Over 30 ★★
Grade school ★★★★	Young Adults ★★★	Seniors ★★

Touring Time *Average* 4 hours; *minimum* 2 hours

Rainy-Day Touring Recommended

Author's Rating ★★★★; this new science center keeps kids entertained for hours, and there's plenty for adults to do, too

Description and Comments A good place to start is on the ground floor (one story down from the entrance), where children ages 8 and under—no parents allowed—let their imaginations run free in Kids Town. They can explore the root system of a tree by crawling though an underground tunnel, build with blocks at the construction site, and shop in the miniature stores.

The number of exhibits can be overwhelming—there are ten interactive exhibition halls on four floors, so take a few moments to study a guide map.

Make time during your visit to experience a show in the CineDome (separate admission), with an eight-story domed screen that immerses you in the image—traveling to the depths of a live volcano, swimming with a great white shark, racing through the human blood stream.

The Orlando Science Center is a perfect rainy-day solution. Even parking is covered, with a new 600-space garage that's connected to the building by a glass walkway.

SeaWorld Orlando

7007 SeaWorld Drive, Orlando; (407) 351-3600; www.seaworld.com

Hours Open daily at 9 a.m., closing time varies by season

Admission $52 for adults, $43 for children ages 3–9, free for ages 2 and under; $7 for parking

Appeal by Age Group

Pre-school ★★★★★	Teens ★★★★	Over 30 ★★★★★
Grade school ★★★★★	Young Adults ★★★★	Seniors ★★★★★

Touring Time *Average* 6 hours; *minimum* 4 hours

Rainy-Day Touring Not recommended

Author's Rating ★★★★★

Description and Comments SeaWorld is a world-class marine-life theme park that admirably combines entertainment, education, research, and conservation to create a fascinating experience. And it's got Kraken, Orlando's longest, fastest, steepest roller coaster. The newest addition is the WaterFront, a five-acre area with live entertainment, themed restaurants, and shops and boutiques.

The park is open every day of the year, and you should allow at least six hours to see the shows and exhibits—a great plan is to arrive at midday and stay later into the evening when temperatures are cooler and there are nighttime fireworks and laser shows.

Make a left when you enter the park and start your day in Key West at SeaWorld, where the kids can pet the dolphins or stingrays while you strategize a game plan for the day.

Unless you want to head straight for the two thrill rides—Kraken or Journey to Atlantis—the *Dolphin Fest* in the Key West area is as good a place as any to start the day. While you're waiting for the show to start, you can observe (and sometimes feed) the dolphins, turtles, stingrays, and other species indigenous to the Florida Keys.

SeaWorld primarily features open-air theater shows or walk-through exhibits, so you will spend a lot less time waiting in line at SeaWorld than you would at a Disney park. Just check show times and be at the theater about 15 minutes early—there's plenty of seating, and even if you're a few minutes late you won't miss much (with one exception, the sea lion and otter show).

The park is big enough to recommend seeing shows in some order. Rent strollers for little ones since there's quite a bit of walking. Wheelchairs can move around easily.

Aside from *Key West Dolphin Fest,* there are three other big daytime shows: the *Shamu Adventure, Clyde and Seamore Take Pirate Island,* and *Pets Ahoy!.* When you arrive, develop your touring itinerary around these four shows. New WaterFront shows worth checking out if time allows include *Kat 'n' Kaboodle,* a street show with 16 exotic breeds of cats; and *Rico & Roza's Musical Feast,* a 25-minute musical revue.

If you're visiting on a tight schedule, the only "don't miss" is the *Shamu Adventure.* Where else can you sit inches away from Shamu, the 8,000-pound killer whale, and be splashed by his wake? Keep in mind that Shamu's antics can really soak your clothes, so if it's chilly, you may want to sit a few rows back from the splash zone. There's also a nighttime Shamu show—definitely worth staying past sunset.

The only consistent waits are for the Kraken roller coaster, Journey to Atlantis water-coaster thrill ride, and Wild Arctic, a fast-paced flight simulator. For Wild Arctic, you can bypass the ride and walk into a superb exhibit of live beluga whales, walruses, harbor seals, and polar bears.

Animal attractions include sea lions, harbor seals, sharks, penguins manatees, dolphins, stingrays, pelicans, spoonbills, flamingos, and the Anheuser-Busch Clydesdale horses, plus a tidal pool and tropical reef.

CLOSE ENCOUNTERS OF THE WET KIND

SeaWorld's Sharks Deep Dive lets you go underwater in a sturdy metal cage with more than 50 sharks in a 660,000-gallon saltwater tank. You can snorkel or scuba, and up to two at a time can occupy the cage for about 30 minutes. The cost is $125 or $150 depending on whether you snorkel or use scuba gear.

If you prefer whales, another program lets you interact one-on-one with a false killer whale, and help out with a SeaWorld training session. The cost is $200 for the two-hour program.

To make reservations for either program, call (800) 432-1178 or book online at www.seaworld.com.

Sea World's Discovery Cove

6000 Discovery Cove Way, Orlando; (877) 4-DISCOVERY

Hours Open daily from 9 a.m.–5:30 p.m.

Admission All-inclusive, $229; without dolphin swim, $129; trainer for a day, $399. Includes a seven-day pass to SeaWorld Orlando.

Appeal by Age Group

Pre-school ★★★★	Teens ★★★★★	Over 30 ★★★★★
Grade school ★★★★★	Young Adults ★★★★★	Seniors ★★★★★

Touring Time *Average* 7 hours; *minimum* 5 hours

Rainy-Day Touring Not recommended

Author's Rating ★★★★

Description and Comments A welcome departure from the hustle and bustle of other Orlando parks, Discovery Cove lets you swim with dolphins, snorkel with tropical fish, and just plain relax on a sandy beach without driving 50 miles to the Atlantic Ocean. The park requires reservations and is limited to 1,000 guests a day. You pay for that privilege, but the experience is worth it.

The park is a managable 30 acres and beautifully landscaped, with four main attractions: the Dolphin Lagoon, swimming with stingrays, snorkeling with 4,000 tropical fish, and a 100-foot-long aviary filled with birds.

Visitors check in at a concierge desk and a personal guide takes them for a walking tour and overview of the park. Dolphin Lagoon is the only timed part of the day. Otherwise, you're free to swim, sleep, eat, and play on the sandy beaches. A word of caution: bring water socks or rubber pool shoes, as the sand gets scorching hot in the middle of the day.

The highlight, of course, is the bottlenose dolphins, and children must be age 6 or older to get in the water with the mammals. The program starts with a 30-minute orientation for groups up of to eight swimmers, then swimmers wade into Dolphin Lagoon for a shallow water introduction. Next, three guests at a time go with the trainer into deeper water to swim, snorkel, or hang onto a dorsal fin for a high-speed ride.

The Ray Lagoon inhabitants are harmless (no barbs), and it's a startling experience to snorkel amidst dozens of sleek southern and cownose rays, some up to four feet in diameter. If you hold out a hand, they will take a finger in their mouths (they have no teeth).

The Coral Reef is designed with underwater shipwrecks and grottos and more than 75 species of tropical fish. Barracudas and sharks are just inches from snorkelers, separated by acrylic glass.

The free-flight aviary is a treat for tropical-bird lovers with more than 30 species and hundreds of birds, from tiny thrushes and starlings to big, brightly colored parrots—they're friendly enough to perch on heads, arms, and hands.

You need to be comfortable in the water, but not an exceptional swimmer to enjoy Discovery Cove, as everyone must wear a personal flotation device in the Dolphin Lagoon, the Coral Reef, and Tropical River. There also is an abundance of lifeguards. If you wear sunscreen, Discovery Cove offers one that is safe for the animal habitats, and it is the only sunscreen you can wear there. Wetsuits also are offered, but the water temperature is 78°–85° year-round.

Silver Springs

5656 East Silver Springs Boulevard, Silver Springs; (352) 236-2121; www.silversprings.com

Hours Daily, 10 a.m.–5 p.m., with longer hours during summer and select holidays

Admission $33 for adults, $30 seniors 55 and older, $24 for children ages 3–10, free for ages 2 and under

Appeal by Age Group

Pre-school ★★★	Teens ★★	Over 30 ★★★★
Grade school ★★★★	Young Adults ★★★	Seniors ★★★★

Touring Time *Average* 5 hours; *minimum* 3 hours

Rainy-Day Touring Not recommended

Author's Rating ★★★

Description and Comments Billed as "Florida's Original Attraction," Silver Springs is a 350-acre nature park surrounding the headwaters of the beautiful Silver River.

The attraction, celebrating 125 years, is a Florida tradition. Chances are if you enjoyed it as a kid, you'll enjoy watching your own children experience this piece of old Florida. If you've never been before, be forewarned—the animals are real; there are no nifty mechanical fish; and the boats are not on a track.

The hallmark of Silver Springs is a tour of the natural springs in the glass-bottom boats. More than half a billion gallons of water bubble out of the ground each day, forming a crystal-clear lagoon in the midst of a luxurious tropical jungle. Wildlife abounds both above and below the water, but it is the diverse aquatic life seen through the glass that captivates most visitors. The boat ride, relaxed and unhurried, is informatively narrated by the driver of the boat. The boats are covered top and side, providing protection from sun and rain. Boats depart every few minutes.

Also at Silver Springs are a Jeep Safari through 35 acres of Florida backwoods, lots of live animal shows, reptile shows, and a kids' playground.

Wet 'n Wild

6200 International Drive, Orlando; (407) 351-1800; www.wetnwild.com

Hours Daily, 10 a.m.–5 p.m., with extended hours in peak seasons

Admission $32 for adults, $16 for seniors ages 55 and older, $26 for children ages 3–9, free for children ages 2 and under (admission does not include tube or towel rentals)

Appeal by Age Group

Pre-school ★★★★	Teens ★★★★★	Over 30 ★★★★
Grade school ★★★★	Young Adults ★★★★★	Seniors ★★

Touring Time *Average* 5 hours; *minimum* 3 hours

Rainy-Day Touring Not recommended

Author's Rating ★★★★; it's not themed or as aesthetically pleasing as the Disney water parks, but the rides are awesome, and there are more than you'll find anywhere else. Just be prepared for the crowds.

Description and Comments Before Disney started building water parks, this was the place to cool off in Central Florida. Universal Orlando acquired the park, so it's been spiffed up substantially. Conveniently located on 25 acres on International Drive, Wet 'n Wild still offers more rides than any other water park, and teenagers in particular can make a day of it.

Wet 'n Wild doesn't offer the themed ambience of the Disney water parks, but in over 20 years the rides have gotten higher, faster, and more popular—waits for a 60-second splashdown can be up to 20 minutes. But thrill-ride enthusiasts swear that patience pays off for rides like the new Blast that propels riders down a 390-foot slide with powerful jets and rushing water; Fuji Flyer, which sends four passengers plunging down six stories through 450 feet of banked curves; and the Black Hole, which propels riders through 600 feet of twisting, turning, watery darkness.

Of course, there are tamer rides, like the Bubba Tub or Raging Rapids that the whole family can experience together. And for children under 48 inches tall (or under age ten), Kids Park features miniature versions of the park's most popular attractions along with water-oriented playground equipment.

Though the park employs an army of certified lifeguards, we recommend constant vigil for children under age ten and non-swimmers. The park gets quite crowded during peak seasons, and it can be a major headache just keeping up with little ones.

Pools are heated on chillier days. The fast food is mediocre, but you're allowed to bring along a picnic (but no alcoholic beverages). And don't forget the sunscreen.

Shopping

Central Florida is a shopper's mecca. With more than 52 million square feet of retail space, Orlando is the fastest growing retail market in the United States, according to the Orlando–Orange County Convention and Visitors Bureau. Beyond the ubiquitous mouse ears and T-shirts, avid shoppers can find a wide array of items, from hard-to-find imports from Epcot's World Showcase (see page 255) to bargains at hundreds of off-price outlets.

DISNEY OUTLET STORES

At **Belz Factory Outlet Mall** (5401 Oakridge Road, Orlando; (407) 352-9611) and in the **Lake Buena Vista Factory Stores** (15591 SR 535, Orlando; (407) 238-9301), you can find marked-down Disney goods, but the selection is limited. And in between the markdowns was full-priced merchandise, so beware. If you're not picky, you can round up a fair number of souvenirs. Both stores are owned by one company, so stock is comparable. The Belz store is slightly larger, but when we visited the shop at the Lake Buena Vista Factory Stores had supplemented space with a giant outdoor tent sale, which they often do.

Outlets

Like every major tourist destination in the United States, central Florida has hundreds of factory outlets, and most are near major attractions. The granddaddy of outlet shopping in Orlando is still one of the best: Belz Factory Outlet World and Belz Designer Outlet Centre, both just off the north end of International Drive. The two comprise the largest of the outlet centers—160 name-brand stores. This is where the locals head for bargains.

Belz Factory Outlet Mall (5401 West Oakridge Road; (407) 352-9611; www.belz.com), the largest center of its kind in the United States, includes 185 stores in two separate malls and four annexes. Hours are Monday–Saturday, 10 a.m.–9 p.m.; Sunday, 10 a.m.–6 p.m. Major stores include Anne Klein, Bugle Boy, Danskin, Etienne Aigner, The Gap, Guess, Jockey, Levi's, Mikasa, Nike, Oneida, Olga Warner, and Reebok.

Just around the corner is **Belz Designer Outlet Center** (5211 International Drive; (407) 352-3632; www.belz.com). Hours are Monday–

Saturday, 10 a.m.–9 p.m.; Sunday, 11 a.m.–6 p.m. If you only have time to shop one outlet center, this is the one, mainly for the great buys at Off 5th—the Saks Fifth Avenue outlet. If you're lucky enough to be in town during a sale, the overstuffed racks in the big store offer some great bargains, with designer togs and shoes for up to 75% off. Also in this center are Coach, Donna Karan, Jones New York, Ann Taylor Loft, Cole Haan, Kenneth Cole, and Waterford/Wedgwood.

Belz also operates the nearby **Festival Bay** (5250 International Drive; (407) 351-7718; **www.belz.com**), featuring Bass Pro Shops Outdoor World, Ron Jon Surf Shop, Shepler's Western Wear, Steve & Barry's University Sportswear, Hilo Hattie Hawaiian-themed shop and 30 smaller shops. A 20-screen Cinemark Theaters and Van's Skatepark are also part of the center.

Orlando Premium Outlets (8200 Vineland Avenue; (407) 238-7787; **www.premiumoutlets.com**) is setting new standards for Orlando outlet shopping, with 110 shops, open Monday–Saturday, 10 a.m.–10 p.m.; Sunday, 10 a.m.–9 p.m. An array of shops includes Banana Republic, Barneys New York, Brooks Brothers, DKNY, Escada, Fubu, Giorgio Armani, Louis Feraud, Nautica, Nike, Polo Ralph Lauren, TSE, and Versace. You'll also find Disney's Character Premiere, with plenty of Disney merchandise, and a food court with numerous fast-food options.

Traditional Shopping

Orlando recently welcomed the long-awaited **Mall at Millennia** (4200 Conroy Road, Orlando; (407) 363-3555; **www.mallatmillenia.com**), anchored by Bloomingdale's, Macy's, and Neiman Marcus. Of about 150 stores, nearly half are new to the Orlando market, including Cartier, Burberry, Crate & Barrel, Tiffany & Co., Gucci, and Louis Vuitton. The two-level mall has seven full-service restaurants, a full-service concierge, and a U.S. post office.

We're told that next to Disney World, more tourists visit **Florida Mall** (8001 South Orange Blossom Trail, Orlando; (407) 851-6255; **www.simon.com**) than any other central Florida destination—one of the reasons it offers currency exchange and foreign-language assistance. It's the biggest mall in the area, with about 200 shops, including Saks Fifth Avenue, Nordstrom's, Lord & Taylor, Brooks Brothers, Pottery Barn, and Restoration Hardware. Hours are Monday–Saturday, 10 a.m.–9:30 p.m.; Sunday, 11 a.m.–6 p.m.

Another not-to-be-missed shopping destination in central Florida is **Park Avenue** in Winter Park, a small town just north of Orlando. The street, anchored by Rollins College on the south end, is lovely for strolling, window-shopping, and dining, and has a mix of high-end shops. Favorites include Restoration Hardware, Pottery Barn, Tuni's (women's chic apparel), Bebe's (trendy children's wear), Williams-Sonoma, Gap, Talbot's, Caswell-Massey, Crabtree & Evelyn, Timothy's Gallery (exquisite one-of-a-kind jewelry), and Birkenstock. Prices are high, but there are terrific sidewalk sales a few times a year.

Most stores open at 10 a.m. but close early, generally by 6 p.m., including weekends. Traffic on the two-lane brick street can be a bear, so avoid driving down Park Avenue; instead, take a side street and search for on-street parking a block or two off the main drag. Or use the new parking garage on the south end of the street.

To get to Park Avenue from the International Drive–Disney World–Universal area, take Interstate 4 north, exit at Fairbanks Avenue, and head east. Park Avenue is approximately five miles from the exit.

Dining

Central Florida, though not a culinary capital, has more than 2,000 restaurants, many of them familiar chains geared to serving tourists who patronize the attractions. If you're looking for ethnic cuisine, dozens of Asian restaurants are clustered around Mills Avenue at Colonial Drive in Orlando, where Korean, Vietnamese, and Chinese cuisines have turned storefronts into a culinary tour of the Far East. And the new "Restaurant Row" on Sand Lake Road just west of International Drive, offers 11 dining options, all opened in the last two years, with cuisine ranging from seafood to steak, Japanese, Pan-Asian, and Thai.

There are more than 200 Walt Disney World restaurants. In addition to the profiles later in this section, some favorite are listed on page 266.

Boma

Disney's Animal Kingdom Lodge, Walt Disney World Resort; (407) WDW-DINE

Meals served Breakfast, dinner **Cuisine** South-African–inspired cuisine **Entree range** $15 breakfast buffet; $24 dinner buffet **Reservations** Accepted **Payment** All major credit cards

Comments This is one of Central Florida's most recommended "all-you-care-to-eat" experiences, with cooking stations featuring grilled meats, fish, and vegetables, with curries, chutneys, and other interesting sauces. Soups and stews get high marks. Cultural representatives from South Africa serve as hosts.

California Grill

Disney's Contemporary Resort, Walt Disney World Resort; (407) WDW-DINE

Meals served Dinner **Cuisine** New American **Entree range** $18–$32 **Reservations** Accepted **Payment** All major credit cards

Comments This award-winning restaurant atop the Contemporary is one of Orlando's best dining experiences. It's hard to decide which is more fun: watching the energetic chefs in the open kitchen or a sunset over Disney World. And they dim the lights and pipe in music for the Magic Kingdom fireworks, so ask for a window seat. From starters to desserts, Chef John State's creations are extraordinary—salmon with lobster mashed potatoes and pork tenderloin with creamy polenta are two classics. And the sushi chef is a standout.

Delfino Riviera

Portofino Bay Hotel, Universal Orlando; (407) 503-3463

Meals served Dinner **Cuisine** Italian **Entree range** $16–$42 **Reservations** Accepted **Payment** All major credit cards

Comments Elegant dining here features traditional cuisine from the Ligurian region of Italy—authentic flavor combinations of shellfish, pasta, and other favorites, deftly orchestrated by Chef Massimo Fedozzi. There's a solid wine list with more than 200 vintages from Italy and France. Flawless service and a strolling guitarist add to the romance.

Del Frisco's

729 Lee Road, Orlando; (407) 645-4443

Meals served Dinner **Cuisine** Steakhouse **Entree range** $20–$36 **Reservations** Accepted **Payment** All major credit cards

Comments The quintessential steakhouse, Del Frisco's decor is dark woods and soft lighting, with the retro feel of supper clubs of days gone by. Efficient servers balance tray of martinis, succulent prime steaks, Australian lobster tails, and other hefty entrees—so loosen your belt.

Emeril's Restaurant Orlando

Universal Studios CityWalk; (407) 224-2424

Meals served Lunch and dinner **Cuisine** New Orleans contemporary **Entree range** Lunch $19–$25; dinner $20–$40 **Reservations** Yes **Payment** All major credit cards

Comments Emeril's Restaurant Orlando is a mecca for fans of the flamboyant chef and his high-calorie, New Orleans–style cooking—giant plates heaped with fish and meats. Entrees are big enough to share. Much of the food is heavily sauced; we love the simple grilled rib eye steak with garlic mashed potatoes. Save room for the banana-cream pie.

Flying Fish

Disney's BoardWalk Resort, Walt Disney World Resort; (407) WDW-DINE

Meals served Dinner **Cuisine** Seafood/New American **Entree range** $20–$34 **Reservations** Accepted **Payment** All major credit cards

Comments Another favorite of locals. You can bet on the freshest seafood at Flying Fish (the potato-wrapped snapper is sensational), but the New York strip is also a winner. Chef Robert Curry changes his menu to reflect seasonal fruits and vegetables. If the restaurant is crowded and you can't get a seat, ask for a spot at the bar in front of the exhibition kitchen.

Hue

629 East Central Boulevard, Orlando; (407) 849-1800

Meals served Lunch, dinner **Cuisine** American **Entree range** $13–$32

Reservations Accepted **Payment** All major credit cards

Comments The kitchen turns out cool, creative fare in this chic downtown spot, like a tender, tamari-roasted duck breast with stir-fried veggies and pearl pasta or wood-grilled ahi tuna with a sesame glaze. If you just want to nibble, the grilled flat breads or a half-dozen fresh oysters do the trick. Prices are steep and service is so-so, but no one seems to mind.

Le Coq Au Vin

4800 South Orange Avenue, Orlando; (407) 851-6980

Meals served Lunch, dinner **Cuisine** French **Entree range** $12–$27 **Reservations** Accepted **Payment** All major credit cards

Comments If you want to eat where the chefs eat on their night off, this is the place. Chef Louis Perrotte's humble little restaurant serves simple French fare, from the classic coq au vin to seafood, steak, and veal dishes. The sweetbreads with morel mushrooms is a favorite of regulars. And Perrotte's crème brûlèe and soufflé are divine.

McCormick & Schmick's

4200 Conroy Road, Orlando; (407) 226-6515

Meals served Lunch, dinner **Cuisine** Seafood **Entree range** $12–$20 **Reservations** Accepted **Payment** All major credit cards

Comments The menu changes daily according to what's freshest from waters around the globe. You might find Albacore tuna from Hawaii, Mako shark from Costa Rica, Alabama catfish, cod from Massachusetts and Florida rock shrimp. On the half shell—six kinds of oysters, including Malpeques from Prince Edward Island in Canada, Blue Points from New York and Olympias from Washington State. Meat lovers will find filet, sirloin, and New York strip on a corner of the menu. More than a dozen wines are offered by the glass, with a list that's mostly Californian.

Norman's at the Ritz-Carlton

4012 Central Florida Parkway, Orlando; (407) 393-4333

Meals served Dinner **Cuisine** Latin/Caribbean/Asian **Entree range** $55–$79 (3- and 5-course meals) **Reservations** Accepted **Payment** All major credit cards

Comments Just debuting at press time, this chic new restaurant introduces Norman Van Aken's cuisine to Orlando, an interesting blend of Latin, Caribbean, and Asian styles. For fans of the chef's Coral Gables restaurant, this promises to be a culinary bright spot.

Pho 88

730 North Mills Avenue, Orlando; (407) 897-3488

Meals served Lunch, dinner **Cuisine** Vietnamese **Entree range** $5–$19 **Reservations** Not necessary **Payment** All major credit cards

Comments Vietnamese families fill many of the tables in this spacious and spotless dining room that once was a grocery store. The chicken noodle soup arrives with a side dish piled high with fresh basil, jalapeños, and lime to toss in at your will. Shrimp and pork with egg noodles offers the hot broth on the side to add as desired. Every dish is fresh and delicious, and most of the ingredients are familiar, though the adventuresome will find elaborate combinations. Order a lychee juice or fresh lemon drink instead of dessert.

Seasons 52

7700 Sand Lake Road, Orlando; (407) 354-5212

Meals served Dinner **Cuisine** American **Entree range** $10–$20 **Reservations** Accepted **Payment** All major credit cards

Comments The novel concept behind this "casually sophisticated" grill and wine bar is that seasonally inspired menus change every week. The biggest buzz, however, is that none of the entrees is more than 450 calories, none of the desserts more than 250 calories. Delicious entrees like spicy rare tuna with stir-fried bok choy and a melt-in-your-mouth filet mignon are generous and satisfying, but save room for the brilliant "mini indulgences" at meal's end: each dessert arrives in a shot glass, just three or so bites. Options include tiramisu, Key lime pie, and strawberry shortcake. You might be tempted to order two. More than 65 wines are offered by the glass, with more than 100 by the bottle.

Tchoup Chop

Royal Pacific Resort at Universal Orlando; (407) 503-CHOP

Meals served Dinner **Cuisine** Pan Asian **Entree range** $18–$32 **Reservations** Accepted **Payment** All major credit cards

Comments Chef Emeril Lagasse's new restaurant takes Asian cuisine and "kicks it up a notch" with his unique style. Tchoup Chop (pronounced chop-chop) has a gorgeous "tiki bar" decor complete with bamboo, waterfalls, sculpted gardens, and giant woks in full view. Favorite main dishes include Kona-coffee-glazed duck breast served with vegetable chow mein, Kahlua slow-roasted pork and noodle sauté, and banana leaf–steamed fish with chile-onion salsa and sake-soy glaze. The restaurant also features specialty drinks (try the Pago Pago, tropical mint-flavored rum with lime juice and fresh mint leaves) and a tea menu.

Victoria & Albert's

Disney's Grand Floridian Resort & Spa, Walt Disney World Resort; (407) WDW-DINE

Meals served Dinner **Cuisine** Continental **Entree range** $90 per person, with wine pairing add $45 **Reservations** Accepted **Payment** All major credit cards

Comments This is Central Florida's only five-Diamond restaurant, a delightful experience from start to finish. There are just 65 seats in the intimate dining room, or try for the coveted Chef's Table in the kitchen. Creations change daily, and Chef Scott Hunnel pays special attention to every guest with his six-course, prix-fixe menu. From vegetarian to wild game, the menu is always exciting.

Dinner Shows

If you're looking for after-dark entertainment, consider a dinner show. The food isn't memorable, but there's plenty of it, and the entertainment is wholesome fun.

Arabian Nights Dinner Attraction   Equestrian performance featuring more than 60 horses, including white Lipizzans, and great riders. The highlight is a high-speed chariot race re-created from the film *Ben Hur.* Dine on prime rib or vegetable lasagna; for children, it's chicken fingers and mashed potatoes. Adults, $44; children ages 3–11, $27. Showtimes: Sunday–Thursday 6 p.m., Friday–Saturday 8:30 p.m. Located at 6225 West Irlo Bronson Highway (US 192); (407) 239-9223.

Dolly Parton's Dixie Stampede   It's a friendly rivalry between the North and the South, with 32 horses, ostrich racing, singing, dancing, and four courses of messy finger food (you have to request utensils)—vegetable soup (sipped from your own ladle), chicken, barbecued pork, potatoes, corn on the cob, and apple turnovers. The show finale is a patriotic tribute written by Dolly Parton. Adults, $44; children ages 3–11, $29. Shows nightly at 6:30 and 8:30 p.m. Located at 8251 Vineland Avenue, Orlando; (407) 238-4455; **www.dixiestampede.com.**

Hoop-de-Doo Revue   Even sophisticated New Yorkers end up hooping and hollering at this long-running show in Pioneer Hall. The revue plays three times nightly (5, 7:15, and 9:30 p.m.) with all-you-can-eat ribs and fried chicken. Adults, $49; children ages 3–11, $25. This one books up fast, so call early for reservations. Located at Disney's Fort Wilderness Campground and Resort; (407) 939-3463.

Makahiki Luau   This luau offers two hours of authentic island entertainment and a four-course meal, including teriyaki chicken, grilled mahimahi, Kahlua pork with orange sauce, and coconut muffins. Adults, $38; children ages 3–9, $28. Showtimes are 5:30 and 8:15 p.m. Held at SeaWorld; (407) 363-2200.

Medieval Times Dinner and Tournament   This cavernous dining hall takes you back to the days of knights, chivalry, and regal feasts with a banquet in an eleventh-century-style castle—and a show about a Princess's love for a handsome knight and a confrontation between a turncoat warrior and a defender of the crown. The four-course meal—chicken, ribs, bread, potatoes, soup, and dessert—isn't served with silverware; you dine just like in the olden days—eating with your hands. Adults, $46; children ages 3–11, $30. Shows nightly at 6:15 and 8:30 p.m. Located at 4510 North Irlo Bronson Highway (US 192), Kissimmee; (800) 229-8300.

Spirit of Aloha This new show replaces Disney's longstanding luau, with comedy, dancing, familiar Hawaiian songs and music from the Disney film *Lilo & Stitch*. Dine on roasted chicken, wild rice, vegetables, and dessert. Seatings nightly at 5:15 and 8 p.m. Adults, $49; children ages 3–11, $25. Held at Disney's Polynesian Resort; (407) 939-3463.

Arts and Culture

The world's finest collection of Tiffany glass is part of the collection at the **Charles Hosmer Morse Museum of American Art** in Winter Park (445 North Park Avenue, Winter Park; (407) 645-5311; **www.morsemuseum.org**), a jewel of a museum that also includes elements of Tiffany's 1893 chapel for the World's Columbian Exposition, completely reassembled and on exhibit.

The **Orlando Museum of Art** (2416 North Mills Avenue; (407) 896-4231; **www.omart.org**) offers permanent and traveling exhibitions, and the nearby **Mennello Museum of American Folk Art** (900 East Princeton Street; (407) 246-4278; **www.mennellomuseum.com**) showcases the work of Earl Cunningham and other American folk artists. In downtown Orlando, the **Orange Country Regional History Center** (65 East Central Boulevard; (407) 836-8500; **www.thehistorycenter.org**) offers a snapshot of Central Florida pre-Disney, in the days of cowboys and orange groves.

Nightlife

Bösendorfer Lounge

Who Goes There Well-dressed professional crowd

Westin Grand Bohemian, 325 South Orange Avenue, Orlando; (407) 313-9000; www.grandbohemianhotel.com

Cover No **Minimum** No **Mixed drinks** $7 **Food available** Yes **Hours** 11 a.m.–midnight Sunday–Thursday, 11 a.m.–1 p.m. Friday–Saturday

What goes on The posh Bösendorfer Lounge, named after the rare $250,000 Imperial Grand Bösendorfer Piano in the adjacent Klimt Rotunda (named for the collection of artwork in the room by Gustav Klimt), brings a new level of chic to downtown Orlando. You'll find attractively dressed men and women sipping martinis and chatting quietly at the round bar decorated in black marble with red stones and mirror pieces. Long red sconces hang from the gold-leafed ceiling for soft, sensual lighting. Sofas and chairs in soft red velvet decorate the rest of the room.

Comments This is a slightly older crowd than most of the downtown clubs. The adjacent dining room makes the Grand Bohemian a perfect (though expensive) spot for drinks and dinner.

CityWalk

Who Goes There A mix of locals and tourists, all ages

Universal Orlando; (407) 363-8000; www.citywalkorlando.com

Cover $9 **Minimum** No **Food available** Yes **Hours** Club opening times vary from late afternoon to early evening, restaurants are open beginning at 11:30 a.m.

What goes on Along with shopping and dining, there are live music venues and dance clubs:

Bob Marley—A Tribute to Freedom A small courtyard features live reggae. $5 cover charge after 8 p.m.

CityJazz Live jazz and martinis draw an upscale crowd. $5 cover charge after 7 p.m.

The Groove Dance club with special effects, three themed VIP lounges, and loud music—all more appealing to a 20-something crowd. Opens at 9 p.m. with $5 cover charge.

Hard Rock Live Orlando This concert venue draws top performers; check www.hardrocklive.com or call (407) 351-LIVE for upcoming bands.

Jimmy Buffet's Margaritaville Live music for Parrotheads, $5 cover charge after 10 p.m.

Latin Quarter Live entertainment draws a lively crowd to dine and dance to Latino music.

Motown Restaurant DJs and dancing start around 8 p.m. in this restaurant with a cool collection of Motown memorabilia. $5 cover after 10 p.m.

Pat O'Brien's Orlando Dueling pianos and a "flaming fountain" patio—and don't forget the infamous Hurricane drink. $5 cover charge after 9 p.m.

Comments Because cover charges aren't in effect until late evening, arrive early, check out the clubs, and if you like, settle into one for the rest of the night—many are both restaurants and clubs, so you can have dinner and dance the night away under the same roof.

Fiddler's Green

Who Goes There All ages and bank accounts

544 West Fairbanks Avenue, Winter Park; (407) 645-2050

Cover No **Minimum** After 10 p.m. you must be 21 or older **Mixed drinks** $4.25 **Food available** Yes **Hours** 11:30 a.m.–2 a.m. Monday–Saturday, 11 a.m.–midnight Sunday

What goes on The parking lot is packed by 6 p.m. on Thursday and Friday nights, when the regulars crowd in for pint of lager or stout, a game of darts, and camaraderie. You'll often hear a British, Irish, or Scottish accent, patrons who miss the UK and feel right at home in the dark and cozy bar, with framed drawings of pub life and carved woodwork. Irish folksingers often entertain.

Comments The quintessential Irish pub with friendly service, and ambience to spare. If you're hungry, the adjacent dining room serves delicious fish and chips and shepherd's pie.

Matrix/Metropolis

Who Goes There Tourists, conventioneers, and a few locals

9101 International Drive (Pointe Orlando); (407) 370-3700; www.pointeorlando.com

Cover Depends on night and event **Minimum** 18 (depends on night) **Mixed drinks** $5 **Food available** No **Hours** 8 p.m.–3 a.m.

What goes on The two clubs, side by side on the second floor or Pointe Orlando retail center, draw mostly a 20-something crowd, but conventioneers of all ages show up to party. The two clubs have different themes. Metropolis features a Moulin Rouge-inspired decor, with dark woods and crushed velvet lounge areas. Music is 1980s, 1990s, and Top 40, with a separate room for billiards. Across the walkway, the industrial decor at Matrix—cobalt blue and stainless steel, with funky furniture like lip-styled loveseats—draws a crowd to dance to techno, Eurotrance, and Top 40 on one of Orlando's largest dance floors. Together the clubs have about 30,000 square feet, with room for 3,000 patrons.

Comments Dress for success: no tennis shoes, no baseball caps or jerseys, and they frown on jeans.

Pleasure Island

Who Goes There Locals, but mostly tourists, a mix of ages

Walt Disney World Resort; (407) 934-7781; www.disneyworld.com

Cover $21 **Minimum** No **Mixed drinks** Cost varies in each club **Food available** Yes **Hours** 8 p.m.–2 a.m.

What goes on There are restaurants, shops, and eight clubs:

Adventurers Club Patterened after a stuffy English gentlemen's club, the Adventurer's Club is a two-story, turn-of-the-century affair with big armchairs, walls covered with animal heads (some of which talk), and other artifacts. The club's library downstairs in the main attraction, with a cabaret-inspired show every hour or so.

BET SoundStage Club Opened in partnership with Black Entertainment Television, this club features hip-hop, soul, and R&B. The dance floor is cool and showy, and the club gets packed as bands finish up at the West End Stage directly outside. Restricted to ages 21 and up.

The Comedy Warehouse Normally five shows nightly, including up-and-coming comedians and the "Who, What & Warehouse" Improv Company players.

8Trax A 1970s disco with lava lamps, mirror balls, and the sound from disco to recorded music from groups and artists like the Village People, Donna Summer, Bee Gees, Doobie Brothers, Tavares, and many others.

The Jazz Company The place for live jazz in Central Florida. The crowd, more diverse in age and appearance than at other clubs, sits at tables flanking the stage on three sides.

Mannequins Dance Palace A ritzy, techno-pop rock dance club with a revolving dance floor, incredible lighting, wild special effects, and the Island Explosion Dancers. The music is all DJ, but the sound system is superb. There is often a line waiting to enter. Patrons must be at least 21.

Motion A DJ spins the hottest chart hits nightly, backed by a huge video screen, pulsing speakers and swirling lights.

Rock 'n' Roll Beach Club Oldies and current rock, with first-rate bands. Electronic games and pool are available for those who don't wish to dance.

Comments Guests younger than 18 must be accompanied by a parent after 7 p.m. Guests who are 18, 19, and 20 will be admitted to clubs (except Mannequins and BET SoundStage Club) but will not be served alcohol. And parking can be a hassle, as the lot often fills up—it's easier to find a spot on the back side of Downtown Disney West Side and enter via the bridge connecting West Side to Pleasure Island.

Sky60

Who Goes There The South Beach crowd—chic, sexy, and expensive, mostly in their 20s and 30s

64 North Orange Avenue, Orlando; (407) 425-7588

Cover Weekends **Minimum** No **Mixed drinks** Expensive **Food available** No **Hours** From happy hour until 2 a.m.

What goes on Sky60's opening was a turning point for downtown Orlando, with its super-chic, all-white decor and an elite clientele who prefer to keep the place a secret. A rooftop terrace features private cabanas where you can hang out with friends or share drinks with strangers. DJs spin dance music, but it's a mellow crowd.

Comments If you love the Delano on Miami Beach, you'll love Sky60 and the cool confines of the rooftop—where you can actually hear what the person next to you is saying.

Tabu

Who Goes There 20-somethings dominate, but celebrities of all ages have been spotted in the private VIP lounge.

46 North Orange Avenue, Orlando; (407) 648-8363; www.tabunightclub.com

Cover $7 women, $10 men **Minimum** 18 **Mixed drinks** $4 **Food available** No **Hours** 9 p.m.–3 a.m.

What goes on Located in the historic Beacham Theatre downtown, Tabu looks pretty nondescript from the sidewalk, but inside Art Deco decor and three dance floors with hip-hop DJs or live bands keep the upscale crowd pumped. Dress for success, or you may be turned away at the door. The crème de la crème hurry to the upstairs VIP lounge, where stars from Britney Spears to Michael Jordan have been spotted.

Comments Themed events, from catwalk fashion shows, to live-comedy acts and concerts are a big draw for locals; check the website for upcoming events.

Greater Orlando Area 299

Side Trips

Kissimmee/Osceola County   Walt Disney World dramatically changed this quiet burg that's home to cattle farmers and real-life cowboys. Kissimmee is the town closest to the front door of Walt Disney World, just ten miles to the east, and today it's most noted for dozens of big hotels, tiny motels, souvenir shops, fast-food restaurants, and more that are packed side by side on US 192, a road that stretches from downtown Kissimmee through the main entrance to Walt Disney World.

But there's much more to Kissimmee and Osceola County, and for visitors who want to step outside the man-made attractions and connect with nature, the area is known for fishing, canoeing, boating, and airboating (see Outdoor Adventures, page 242). Lake Tohopekaliga near downtown Kissimmee has a waterfront park with a three-mile stretch that's perfect for strolling or bike riding. And for the real thing, visit the Silver Spurs Arena in February or October for one of the top rodeos in the nation, with bull and bronco riding, steer wrestling, and barrel racing. For tickets, call (407) 67-RODEO two months before the event.

Winter Park   This charming town just north of Orlando on I-4 has great shopping on Park Avenue and two offbeat recommendations: the Scenic Boat Tour (at the dock at East Morse Boulevard at Interlachen Avenue; (407) 644-4056; www.scenicboattours.com), a relaxing, one-hour cruise through the lakes and canals of this historic little burg, and the Morse Museum of American Art (445 Park Avenue North, (407) 645-5311), showcasing the rarest collection of Tiffany glass in the world. The boat tour leaves the dock daily (except Christmas) from 10 a.m.–4 p.m. Cost is $6, $3 ages 2–11. (407) 644-4056. The Morse Museum is open 9:30 a.m.–4 p.m. Tuesday–Saturday, 1–4 p.m. Sunday. Cost is $3, $1 ages 12 and under. (407) 645-5311.

Mount Dora   Antique fans might enjoy a trek to this small town 25 miles northwest of Orlando, where Renningers Antique Center (20651 US 441, Mount Dora; (352) 383-8393; www.renningers.com) draws crowds of antique collectors on the weekends. Named for its 184-foot elevation, Mount Dora has a quaint downtown with antique and gift shops, galleries, bookstores, restaurants, the historic Lakeside Inn and small bed-and-breakfast lodgings. The historic Cannonball steam train (phone (352) 735-4667; www.mtdoratrain.com) makes an hour-long run between Mount Dora and downtown Orlando.

Cassadaga   People come from all over the world to visit this curious little town, designated as a Historic District on the National Register of Historic Places. Located midway between Daytona and Orlando off I-4 (at Exit 114), Cassadaga is home to the Southern Cassadaga Spiritualist Camp Meeting Association, with about 25 spiritualist mediums—counselors who communicate with spirits—who offer their services to visitors. For more information, visit www.cassadaga.org.

Part Six

The Central Gulf Coast: Tampa, St. Petersburg, and Sarasota

Welcome to the Central Gulf Coast

Beautiful beaches, man-made attractions, sports, and history make the Central Gulf Coast a choice Florida destination.

For oceanfront fun, head to Clearwater Beach or St. Petersburg, with miles of beaches on the peninsula across the bay from Tampa. Added bonuses are glorious sunsets, which you miss on the Atlantic coast of Florida. These beaches, including Fort DeSoto, Clearwater Beach, Treasure Island, and Caladesi Island, boast an annual average of 361 days of sunshine and an average water temperature of 75°, making nearly every day a good one for shelling, sunning, and swimming.

Away from the ocean, there's more Florida wilderness. And small towns like Dunedin, with its Scottish heritage, and the Greek community of Tarpon Springs afford glimpses of the area's history.

HIGHLIGHTS

- Salvador Dali Museum in St. Petersburg
- Your favorite baseball team at spring training
- Ringling Museum Complex in Sarasota
- Roller coasters at Busch Gardens Tampa Bay
- Anna Maria Island

This also is a sports fan's mecca, with pro football, baseball, arena football, and hockey teams in Tampa (see page 311). Because of the beautiful weather, many baseball teams conduct their spring training camps in this region, a real treat for fans; the players are more relaxed, and the ballfields are often small and intimate. The Yankees venue is particularly special, a miniature replica of Yankee Stadium in the Bronx.

A little farther south along the coast is Sarasota, where the pace slows down a notch. A fine arts community thrives here. The city once was the home of John Ringling and his world-famous Ringling Bros. Circus; today, the legacy is on display at the John and Mable Ringling Museum of Art.

A Brief History

An Indian fishing village named Tanpa (meaning "sticks of fire") marks the beginning of Tampa's recorded history. Early European explores, including Ponce de Leon, explored here, but the area was largely untouched until 1885, when Henry B. Plant extended his railroad to Florida's west coast, built a world-renowned hotel, and started a steamship line from Tampa to Key West to Havana, Cuba. Around that same time, Don Vicente Martinez Ybor, an influential cigar manufacturer and Cuban exile, moved his cigar business from Key West to an area just east of Tampa, encouraging more Spanish cigar manufacturers to move their factories and workers here. The Spanish, Italian, German, and Cuban workers who settled in Tampa to work in the cigar industry created a strong, predominantly Latin community known as Ybor City (pronounced EE-bore), also known as the "Cigar Capital of the World." Fidel Castro's embargo on Cuban tobacco ended the glory days for Ybor City, now designated as one of three National Historic Landmark districts in Florida.

The Scottish settled in Sarasota at about the same time, but because the town was little more than a frontier camp, most of the pioneers left. Among those who stayed was John Hamilton Gillespie, a Scottish aristocrat, lawyer, and member of the Queen's Bodyguard for Scotland. It's believed he built America's first golf course in Sarasota. He was followed by John and Mable Ringling, who built a magnificent Venetian-style mansion on Sarasota Bay, named Cà d'Zan (house of John), the beginnings of Sarasota's burgeoning cultural scene, still vibrant today.

Visiting the Central Gulf Coast

Gathering Information

St. Petersburg–Clearwater Area Convention and Visitors Bureau, 14450 46th Street, North Clearwater 34622; (727) 464-7200; **www.floridasbeach.com.**

Sarasota Convention and Visitors Bureau, 655 North Tamiami Trail, Sarasota 34236; (941) 957-1877 or (800) 522-9799; **www.sarasotafl.org.**

Longboat Key Chamber of Commerce; (941) 383-2466; **www.longboatkeychamber.com.**

Tampa-Hillsborough Convention and Visitors Association, 400 North Tampa Street, Suite 1010, Tampa 33602; (800) 44 TAMPA or (813) 223-2752; **www.gotampa.com.**

Getting There

By Plane Hernando County Airport (phone (352) 754-4061) is 40 miles north of Tampa; St. Petersburg–Clearwater International Airport (phone

(727) 453-7800) is seven miles southeast of Clearwater; Sarasota-Bradenton International Airport (phone (941) 359-5200) is three miles north of Sarasota; Tampa International Airport (phone (813) 870-8700) is five miles west of downtown Tampa; and Venice Municipal Airport (phone (941) 486-2711) is half a mile south of Venice.

By Train Amtrak offers services to Tampa, St. Petersburg, and Sarasota; (800) USA-RAIL; **www.amtrak.com.**

By Car St. Petersburg–Clearwater is accessible from I-75, I-275, I-4, US 19, and SR 60.

Getting Around

Major Roadways

I-75 runs north to south, the quickest way to get from Tampa to Saraosta and points in between. I-4 connects to I-75 if you are driving from Central Florida. US 41 also runs north-south, but traffic is heavy because the road is lined with businesses. I-275 runs from Tampa across to Tampa Bay and St. Petersburg.

John F. Kennedy Boulevard cuts across Tampa driving east-west. I-275 is on the northern edge of the city, the Crosstown Expressway on the southern edge. East of downtown is Ybor City, Tampa's historic Latin Quarter; west of downtown is Hyde Park, a tony neighborhood with shops and trendy restaurants.

In St. Petersburg, Central Avenue divides the town into north and south addresses. Downtown is situated between Tampa Bay and Boca Ciega Bay, with most of the action along the Bayfront in Tampa Bay. St. Pete Beach is west of downtown, where Gulf Boulevard is the main north-south road.

Sarasota's downtown, on the mainland, sits along the bayfront, with US 41 running north-south through downtown. Across Sarasota Bay, four islands compose the beaches: Siesta Key, linked to the mainland by Siesta Drive Causeway and the Stickney Point Road Causeway; Lido Key, St. Armands Key, and Longboat Key, all accessed by the John Ringling Causeway.

Public Transportation

In Tampa, a fleet of bright yellow **TECO Line** trolleys (phone (813) 254-4278; **www.tecolinestreetcar.org**) travels a 2.3-mile route that links downtown hotels to attractions in the Channel District and Ybor City. Stops include the Florida Aquarium, Tampa Bay History Center, the St. Pete Times Forum Arena, the Garrison Seaport Center, and Centro Ybor. Fare is $1.25, and the service runs seven days a week. The **Tampa Town Water Taxi** connects downtown locations along the Hillsborough River—Harbour Island, the Tampa Convention Center, the Tampa Performing Arts Center, and the University of Tampa. The taxi operates at half-hour intervals beginning at 2 p.m. on weekdays, noon on weekends, and runs until 11 p.m. weekdays and Sundays, and 1 a.m. on Fridays and Saturdays.

The bright pink **Looper** trolley (phone (727) 821-5166) stops at a dozen different museums, hotels, and shops in St. Petersburg. It's $1 and runs 10 a.m.–5 p.m. Monday through Friday and 11 a.m.–5 p.m. Saturday and Sunday. You can board at any of the stops, including The Pier, Renaissance Vinoy Resort, BayWalk, Florida International Museum, Salvador Dali Museum, and the Bayfront Hilton.

The **Sarasota Trolley** (phone (941) 316-1234) operates a red route to the Ringling Estates, Marie Selby Botanical Gardens, Mote Marine Laboratory, St. Armand's Circle, and Lido Beach.

The Best Beaches

Caladesi Island State Park This undeveloped, 600-acre barrier reef lies off the coast of Dunedin north of Clearwater Beach. After a 15-minute ferry ride from Honeymoon Island to uninhabited Caladesi, you'll find three miles of beautiful beaches edged in sea grass and palmettos. A self-guided nature trail winds through the interior of the island, thick with live oak hammocks and a ridge of virgin pine flatwood. The beach side of Caladesi is on the Gulf of Mexico, and the bay side of Caladesi is a mangrove swamp, home to many wading birds and shorebirds. Boardwalks provide access from the beaches (no lifeguards) to the concession stand, playground, bathhouses, and picnic areas while protecting the dunes and sea oats. Ferry service runs every hour from 10 a.m. to 5:30 p.m. The cost is $7 for adults, $3.50 for children ages 4–12. Call the ferry at (727) 734-5263 for more information.

Clearwater Beach Known for its wide and long beaches, this is one of the most popular west coast beaches. The more populated areas of this three-mile beach are in the south end where there are many hotels; families visiting for the day may like the quieter north end. There are lifeguards all along the beach. At sunset, Pier 60, at the intersection of Causeway and Gulfview Boulevards, offers a sunset celebration patterned after Key West's popular Mallory Square, with craftspeople, artists, and entertainers performing nightly two hours before and after sunset.

Ample parking for the beach can be found off Gulfview Avenue, on the street from 15th to 27th Avenues, and on First and Eighth Avenues. For those with disabilities, Clearwater offers two beach wheelchairs that feature all-terrain-type tires. Call (727) 462-6466 for details.

Coquina Beach Powdery sand dunes and Australian pines frame the Gulf on this mile-long beach on the south end of laid-back Anna Maria Island four miles west of Bradenton. A playground, lifeguards, concessions, free parking, and a little café make this an ideal spot to spend the day. Call (941) 742-5923 for details.

Egmont Key State Park Accessible only by boat, this 400-acre island in the mouth of Tampa Bay has a one-and-a-half-mile beach for swimming and shelling, a fort from the Spanish American War, an 1858 lighthouse, and nature trails. Several boats offer snorkeling excursions to this island—the fort is sliding into the ocean, providing a new reef. Take sunscreen, water, and a picnic if you plan to stay, because there are no facilities here except a rest room, and there are no lifeguards. Egmont is located at the mouth of Tampa Bay, southwest of Fort DeSoto Beach, and is only accessible by boat. **Hubbard's Sea Adventures** (phone (727) 398-6577) offers trips out of St. Pete; the cost is $35 for adults, $25 for children ages 12 and under.

Fort DeSoto Beach   Five small islands create the 900 acres of Fort DeSoto Park, home to seven miles of picturesque, undeveloped beaches. Mullet Key is the largest island and the site of Fort DeSoto, an artillery installation built in 1898 to protect Tampa Bay during the Spanish American War. The war ended before construction was finished, and the fort's cannons were never fired. Hiking trails take you to the fort, now listed in the National Register of Historic Places.

Fort DeSoto has 235 campsites on the water, surrounded by giant oaks, palms, cactus, sea grape shrubs, and sea oats. The prettiest, most secluded areas are on the north and east ends of the park. Facilities include beaches with lifeguards, a boat ramp, a large playground, a concession stand, rest rooms, showers, picnic areas, and four miles of bicycle and in-line skating trails. There are also two piers, where the fishing is terrific. Call (727) 864-3345 for rod rentals, which cost $8 for four hours or $15 for eight hours, with a $30 refundable deposit. Entrance to the park is free; it is open sunrise to sunset, and the sunsets are spectacular. Camping is $27.75 per night (with or without electricity). Fort DeSoto Park is located six miles southwest of St. Petersburg at 3500 Pinellas Bayway South, Tierra Verde; (727) 582-2267.

Honeymoon Island State Recreation Area   Once named Hog Island, this island was renamed in 1939 when a developer constructed 50 palm-thatched honeymoon bungalows for use by couples chosen through a contest sponsored by Northern department stores. The developer's dream was interrupted by history—Pearl Harbor—and the site was recommissioned as a rest and recreation site during World War II. Today there's a cluster of retirement condos on the island's east end, but just beyond that is a beautiful stretch of beachfront, home to more than 208 species of plants and many shorebirds. The beaches aren't the greatest for swimming, but shelling is good, and the ocean here has a bounty of fish.

Facilities include picnic pavilions, bathhouses, and a park concession building. Not only is this beach family friendly, with lifeguards patrolling on weekends, but four-legged friends are welcome, too, with an area of the beach designated for pets. Admission is $4 per carload (two to eight people), $2 for a single person and vehicle, and $1 for walk-ins or bicyclists. The park is open 8 a.m.–sunset. Accessible by Dunedin Causeway, Honeymoon Island State Recreation Area is at the west end of SR 586, north of Dunedin; (727) 469-5942.

Lido Beach   This three-mile-long key just west of Sarasota has a trio of county beach parks. At the north end, you'll discover a pristine strip of white sand, accented by towering Australian pines—but currents can be dangerous, so beware. In the middle of Lido is a public beach with a swimming pool, a playground, and shops. Nature trails wind through the south end of the key in South Lido Park, where there are volleyball courts and picnic areas. Lifeguards are on duty year-round, and the beach can get crowded at times because parking is plentiful.

Pass-a-Grille Beach   This comfortable little town in the shadow of the palatial Don CeSar Beach Resort on the southern tip of Long Key has a wide, sandy beach running from 21st to 1st Avenues. Facilities include showers, dressing rooms, a snack bar, and a picnic area, but no lifeguards. Take the bridge spanning the opening of Boca Ciega Bay to get here. Day visitors can park on Eighth Avenue; (727) 367-2735.

Sand Key County Park   A beautifully landscaped park with sand dunes and a mile-long beach great for swimming, with lifeguards on duty. Facilities include showers, picnic areas, grills, and playground equipment. The park is located at the northern end of Belleair Beach on Gulf Boulevard. Drive to the southernmost tip of Clearwater Beach, then over the Clearwater Pass Bridge to get to here. Entrance is free, but parking is metered. Open 7 a.m.–sunset; (727) 588-4852.

Shell Island   Hunt for seashells or observe rare and endangered shorebirds on Shell Island. Remember to take water and snacks; there are no facilities here. Many boats offer sight-seeing packages that take you out to the island for sunbathing; the packages often include dolphin-watching. Shell Island is located just south of St. Petersburg. You must catch a ferry (there are no bridges to the island) at Merry Pier to Shell Island. One service, **Shell Island Shuttle,** provides ferry shuttles from Merry Pier at Pass-a-Grille to Shell Island. The cost is $9.50 for adults, $5.50 for ages 12 and under. Call (800) 227-0132 for more information.

Siesta Key   Siesta Key, southwest of Sarasota, is said to have some of the whitest, finest sand in the world. Not only is the eight-mile-long beach beautiful, but there's plenty of activities—playgrounds, volleyball nets, tennis courts, showers, rest rooms, concession stands, and picnic areas. Though there are several beach access points, a favorite is Siesta Key Public Beach on the north end, with lifeguards year-round. All these features, in addition to ample parking, make Siesta Key one of the most popular (and populated) beaches in Sarasota County, so be prepared for heavy traffic. Siesta Key is connected to the mainland by two bridges: SR 72 in the middle of the island, and SR 758 on the north end. Parking is free; (941) 316-1172.

Venice Beach   South of Sarasota, known as the "Fossilized Shark Tooth Capital of the World," Venice sands have lots of fossilized remnants from an off-shore burial ground where sharks mysteriously go to die. Brohard Park near the Venice Fishing Pier is a lively spot, with lifeguards, concessions, rest rooms, and picnic tables. Cast your line at the pier, or look for Grinder, the resident dolphin, in the Venice jetties. Venice, bordered by the

Intracoastal Waterway, is laced with canals and natural waterways—bearing a slight resemblance to its Italian counterpart. Plenty of public parking; (941) 316-1172.

Outdoor Adventures and Sports

Recommended Excursions

Boyd Hill Nature Park   Ask for a butterfly checklist when you enter the park to help you spot the 22 different kinds of butterflies that have been identified here. In addition to these beautiful creatures, you'll experience Florida's diverse ecosystem in this 245-acre park that has three miles of boardwalks and nature trails. On a small nearby island, you'll find the gopher tortoise; in the willow marsh, look for lizards on the trees; in the swamp woodlands, box turtles will be hiding on the forest floor; and in the pine flatwoods, the trees provide a canopy for blue jays and cardinals. You'll also find flying squirrels, possums, raccoons, snakes, and gators. More than three miles of trails and boardwalks lead visitors through these areas. There are also picnic areas and a playground. Admission is $2 for adults and $1 for children ages 3–17. Open daily, 9 a.m.–5 p.m.; closed on Thanksgiving and Christmas. Located at 1101 Country Club Way South, St. Petersburg; (727) 893-7326.

Hillsborough River State Park   History blends with nature in this 3,000-acre park, home of Fort Foster, built on the banks of the Hillsborough River during the Second Seminole War. The fort and the bridge it protected have been reconstructed on the original site. Park Service volunteers, often dressed in replica outfits, greet visitors. Call ahead for dates of monthly tours. Admission is $2 for adults, $1 for children ages 7–12.

You can also hike along eight miles of nature trails through live oaks, sabal palms, hickory, and magnolias bordering the scenic Hillsborough River. There are 106 sites for camping; cost is $16.70 with electric and $14.56 without electric. The park is open daily, 8 a.m.–sunset; $3.25 per car. Located six miles southwest of Zephyrhills at 15402 US 301 North; (813) 987-6771.

Homosassa Springs State Wildlife Park   The centerpiece of this 166-acre park is a huge spring from which millions of gallons of fresh, clear water bubble every hour. You can walk through an underwater observatory to view manatees and fish in this spring that's home to 10,000 fish (someone must be counting). Wildlife you'll see includes a Florida black bear, bobcats, alligators, and wild birds. Educational programs are offered on West Indian manatees, alligators, crocodiles, Florida snakes, and other wildlife. Boat tours are provided daily. The park is open daily 9 a.m.–5:30 p.m. (the ticket counter closes at 4 p.m.). Admission is $8 for adults, $5 ages 3–12. Homosassa Springs is 75 miles north of Tampa on US 19; call (352) 628-5343 or 628-2311 for recorded information.

Little Manatee River State Recreation Area   The Little Manatee has been designated an Outstanding Florida Water, and it flows for four-and-a-half miles through this 1,638-acre recreation area. Canoeing is especially popular, with a rich river hammock along the banks and many birds that make their permanent or migratory homes here. A six-and-a-half-mile hiking trail meanders through the north side of the area. There are 30 campsites for $13 ($2 more for electric). Little Manatee is located four miles south of Sun City in Hillsborough County, off US 301 on Lightfoot Road, Wimauma; (813) 671-5005.

Moccasin Lake Nature Park   This park is an odd combination, part nature park and part energy education center. The grounds include more than 51 acres of laurel, live oaks, and wildflowers. Alligators, bald eagles, barn owls, flying squirrels, and snapping turtles live here, and chances are you'll spot some on the mile-long nature trail that winds through forests and wetlands to five-acre Moccasin Lake. Once you reach the lake, you can climb the 30-foot observation pier for a better view of marine life. Often, you'll see the eyes of an alligator peering from the water. At the Interpretive Center, you'll find wildlife exhibits, live native reptiles and fish, and solar and wind power exhibits. The energy exhibits show how the park produces a portion of its energy, and the building itself is an example of energy conservation with its passive cooling design and wood stove heating system. Open Tuesday–Friday, 9 a.m.–5 p.m.; Saturday and Sunday, 10 a.m.–6 p.m. Admission is $2 for adults, $1 ages 3–12. Located at 2750 Park Trail Lane, Clearwater; (727) 462-6024.

Myakka Wildlife and Nature Tours   Board the "World's Largest Airboat," the 70-passenger *Gator Gal,* for a wild ride on Myakka Lake. Your guide will describe the lake and wildlife, and point out the alligators. Trips are at 10 a.m., 11:30 a.m., 1 p.m., and 2:30 p.m. daily.

If you'd rather see the wildlife by land, take the Tram Safari Land Tour that travels off paved roads into remote areas of subtropical forests and marshlands. Your guide explains the plants, animals, and birds, along with the history of area. The tram runs sporadically, so call ahead for schedules; (941) 365-0100.

Boat and tram tours leave from the Boat Basin located three miles inside main entrance of Myakka River State Park; bear left at the Y in the road. Fare for each tour is $8 per adult, $4 for ages 6–12, age 5 and under free.

The best way to experience Myakka River State Park is to camp. Cabins, constructed with the trunks of cabbage palms and chinked with tar and sawdust, were built in the 1930s by the Civilian Conservation Corps. A few modern conveniences have been added over the years. Each cabin now has air conditioning and heat, an electric stove, a refrigerator, and a bathroom with a shower. They are furnished with two double beds, a sofa bed, a dining area, linens, and kitchen utensils. Cost is $60.50 a night. You can also camp in tents here for $16.44 or $19.74 depending on the season. Reservations are needed. Myakka is just north of Sarasota on SR 72. Admission is $4 per vehicle or $1 per person (bike- or walk-in). Call (941) 361-6511 for more information.

Pinellas Trail This trail is part of the Rails-to-Trails Conservancy program that converts abandoned railroad tracks into recreation trails, and it's one of the most popular urban trails in the United States. This 34-mile paved trail begins (or ends) in the south end of St. Petersburg and meanders to the north at the sponge docks in Tarpon Springs, passing many coastal towns and cities along the way. Near the trail, you'll also find restaurants, campgrounds, and motels. Park in downtown Tarpon Springs, near the trail north of Curlew Road, or at Azalea Park in St. Petersburg below 22nd Avenue North. There is also on-street and lot parking near the trail for its entire length. Open during daylight hours. Pinellas County Parks; (727) 464-3347.

Sea Life Safari Join a Clearwater Marine Aquarium biologist for two hours aboard the *Island Explorer* for an excursion into one of the most diverse estuary systems on the Gulf Coast. The 46-foot catamaran takes you to a bird sanctuary, to an island for shelling, and into grass flats where you can spot starfish, seahorses, and puffer fish. Open Monday–Friday, 9 a.m.–5 p.m.; Saturday, 9 a.m.–4 p.m.; and Sunday, 11 a.m.–4 p.m. The cost is $8.75 for adults, $6.25 for children ages 3–12. Located at 249 Windward Passage, Clearwater; (727) 441-1790; **www.cmaquarium.org**.

Suncoast Seabird Sanctuary Suncoast is an unusual site—cages cover an acre site along the beach at one of the largest wild-bird hospitals in the United States, devoted to the rescue, repair, and release of sick or injured birds. You'll find 500 land and seabirds at the sanctuary compound at any one time; about 20 arrive daily. The sanctuary also breeds permanently disabled birds and releases the offspring into the wild. Educational programs are presented monthly, and guided tours and lectures are offered every Wednesday and Sunday at 2 p.m. Open daily, 9 a.m.–dusk. Donations requested. Located at 18328 Gulf Boulevard, Indian Shores Beach, just north of St. Petersburg Beach; (727) 391-6211; **www.seabirdsanctuary.org**.

Canoeing and Kayaking

As noted above, the four-and-a-half miles of flatwater at **Little Manatee River State Recreation Area** (Lightfoot Road, Wimauma; (813) 671-5005) are an excellent start for visitors looking to explore the Central Gulf Coast by canoe. Abundant riparian wildlife, including the many birds that make their permanent or migratory homes along Little Manatee, ensures a scenic trip. The **Canoe Outpost** south of Tampa rents paddling equipment and provides guided trips, but is closed on Wednesday (18001 US 301 South, Wimauma; (813) 634-228). **Myakka River State Park** (see above) also rents canoes (Highway 72; (941) 361-6511). Sea Kayakers interested in exploring a mangrove estuary should contact Sarasota Bay Explorers (Mote Aquarium; (941) 388-4200; **www.sarasotabayexplorers.com**) to schedule a naturalist-guided tour. Three-hour trips require reservations and cost $50 for adults, $40 for ages 4–17; experience is not required.

Scuba Diving and Snorkeling

Egmont Key State Park (see above) is a 400-acre island in the mouth of Tampa Bay accessible only by boat. Several boats offer snorkeling excursions to the island, where the Spanish American War–era fort is sliding into the ocean, providing a new reef. There is a one-and-a-half-mile beach, but there are no lifeguards. **Hubbard's Sea Adventures** (phone (727) 398-6577) offers trips out of St. Pete; $35 for adults, $25 for children ages 12 and under.

Sailing and Boating

The Clearwater Beach Marina (25 Causeway Boulevard, Clearwater Beach) is home to the largest commercial fleet on the West Coast of Florida. Directly across from the Pier 60 parking area, there's access to boating activities and fishing. Try the 72-foot *Sea Screamer* (phone (727) 447-7200; **www.sea screamer.com**) that races up to 40 mph. The dolphins love to dive in the wake created by the boat. Cruises are about an hour long, and admission is $13.50 for adults, $9 for children ages 5–12, free for children ages 4 and under. Also, **Dolphin Encounter** (phone (727) 442-7433; **www.dolphin encounter.org**), with sighting guaranteed ($15 adults, $7.50 children ages 4–12) and **Sea Life Safari Cruises** (phone (727) 462-2628) for a trip to a bird sanctuary and shell hunting on a barrier island ($15, $11 ages 3–12).

For families, **Captain Memo's Pirate Cruise** is an interactive adventure aboard a full-size reproduction of a 70-foot buccaneer pirate ship. The crew insists that everyone participate in dancing, treasure hunts, dolphin sightings, and water-pistol battles. Admission is $30 for adults, $20 for children ages 3–12; $25 for children ages 13–17 and seniors over age 65 (phone (727) 446-2587; **www.pirateflorida.com**).

Sarasota visitors looking to rent watercraft, from jet skis to pontoon boats, should try **All Watersports** (Boatyard Shopping Village, Stickney Point Bridge; (941) 921-2754) and **Siesta Key Boat Rentals** (1265 Old Stickney Point Road; (941) 349-8880). Those looking for a sailing cruise can arrange a voyage aboard the 41-foot *Enterprise* (Siesta Key Sailing, 1219 Southport Drive; (941) 346-7245; **www.siestakeysailing.com**) for $35 for two hours or $55 for four hours. Reservations are required.

Fishing

Tampa was originally settled by Native American fishermen, though today most area anglers prefer to try their luck outside the growing city. Along Florida's Central Gulf Coast, you can wet a line in lakes and rivers, from piers along the coast, or deep in the Gulf of Mexico from aboard a chartered boat. You can fish from beaches, piers, bridges, or docks with a proper license.

Fort DeSoto State Park (3500 Pinellas Bayway South, Tierra Verde; (727) 864-3345) south of St. Petersburg, as noted above, has two excellent fishing piers and even rents tackle ($8 for four hours or $15 for eight hours with a $30 deposit). **Honeymood Island State Recreation Area** (phone (727) 469-5942) north of Clearwater also offers great coastal fishing. The **Venice Beach Fishing Pier** (phone (941) 316-1172) south of Sarasota is a great place for morning fishing followed by afternoon sight-seeing. The Sarasota area is also home to the area's best charter fleet.

A freshwater, saltwater, or combination license is required for nonresidents over the age of 16. You can obtain licenses at local bait-and-tackle shops; through the Florida Marine Patrol (phone (321) 383-2740), which also provides information about fishing regulations; or from the Fish and Wildlife Conservation Commission (phone (352) 732-1230; **www.florida fisheries.com**).

Party Boats

Fishing licenses are supplied on party boats, and fishers of any age can go out. Tackle is also provided, and boats are usually 60–100 feet with a rest room and a small galley. Try **The Flying Fish Fleet** (phone (941) 366-3373) at Marina Jack's Marina in Sarasota. Half-day excursions cost $30 for adults, $25 for seniors, and $20 for children ages 4–12; for all-day trips, add $10.

Charter Boats

Charter boats offer smaller party sizes (averaging 1–6 people) and a more personalized fishing experience relative to party boats. You can charter a captain and boat for a half-day or full day. Tackle and licenses are supplied; costs vary widely, from $400 to $900 dollars. See **www.sarasotaboating.com** for information on area charters.

CENTRAL GULF COAST MARINAS AND CHARTER SERVICES		
Marina	Location	Phone
Tampa		
Light Tackle Fishing Expeditions	6015 Memorial Hwy., Suite 4 St. Petersburg	(813) 963-1930
Hubbard's Marina	John's Pass Village and Boardwalk, Madiera Beach	(727) 393-1947
Clearwater		
Clearwater Beach Marina	25 Causeway Boulevard	(727) 461-3133
Sarasota		
Angling Adventure	6691 Meandering Way, Bradenton	(941) 920-4891
Captain Action Charters	1727 Joyce Street	(941) 955-4524
Landing Marina	5353 South Tamiami Trail	(941) 922-0668
Marina Jack's Marina	US 41 at Island Park Circle	(941) 365-4232
Siesta Key Marina	7660 South Tamiami Trail	(941) 349-8880

Biking

The flat terrain of the Central Gulf Coast is immanently bike-friendly. The seven-mile Bayshore Boulevard abutting Hillsborough Bay in Tampa is a favorite for walkers and joggers, but is too congested for serious cycling. The Friendship Trail Bridge (phone (812) 289-4400) in St. Petersburg—formerly Gandy Bridge, which runs alongside its replacement of the same name—is a mere two-and-a-half miles long, but offers a steep climb to tire your legs. The Pineallas Trail is the area's premier trail, however, stretching 47 miles between Tampa and St. Petersburg along a former railroad bed. From Sarasota a walkway and bike path parallels the John Ringling Causeway and extends onto Longboat Key. Bike rentals are available from **Siesta Sports Rentals** (6551 Midnight Pass Road; (941) 346-1797; **www.siestasportsrentals.com**) for approximately $15 per day and $50 per week.

Spectator Sports

If you'd like to catch a game while you're vacationing, Tampa and St. Petersburg are great places to do it, with professional play in numerous sports happening year-round.

Baseball

Multiple professional baseball teams conduct spring training in the area, and in the summer, minor-league action abound. The **New York Yankees** make their spring-training home in Tampa at Legends Field (phone (813) 875-7753; **www.yankees.mlb.com**). The 10,000-seat replica of Yankee Stadium (the state's largest spring-training facility) is summer home for the team's eponymous Tampa minor-league outfit. The **Cincinnati Reds** train at Ed Smith Stadium in Sarasota (2700 12th Street; (941) 954-4464; **www.cincinatireds.com**), where the **Class-A Sarasota Red Sox** play during the summer (phone (941) 365-4460; **www.sarasox.com**). The **Philadelphia Phillies** conduct spring training in the area, at Jack Russell Stadium in Clearwater (800 Phillies Drive; (727) 442-8496), which hosts their minor-league affiliate, the **Clearwater Phillies** in the summer (phone (727) 441-8638). The **Toronto Blue Jays** train at Grant Field in Dunedin (373 Douglas Avenue; (813) 733-9302; **www.bluejays.mlb.com**), home to their minor-league **Dunedin Blue Jays** (phone (727) 733-9302; **www.dunedinbluejays.com**). And lastly, the Pittsburgh Pirates train at McKechnie Field in Bradenton (phone (941) 748-4610 or off-season, 747-3031).

The area's premier baseball venue, however, is 45,000-seat Tropicana Field in St. Petersburg, home to the American League's **Tampa Bay Devil Rays** (between 9th and 16th Streets; (727) 825-3137; **www.stpete.org/dome.htm**). The Rays' regular season runs from April through September. The team also trains in town, at Al Lang Field at Second Avenue and First Street.

Football

Tampa football fanatics are fiendishly devoted to the **Tampa Bay Buccaneers,** who play at the 66,000-seat Raymond James Stadium from August through December (4201 North Dale Mabry Highway; (813) 879-2827; www.buccaneers.com). The **Tampa Bay Storm** round out the area's football offerings with arena action (phone (813) 301-6500).

Hockey

The **Tampa Bay Lighting** brings National Hockey League competition to Tampa's waterside Ice Palace each winter (401 Channelside Drive; (813) 301-6500; www.tampabaylightening.com).

Tampa

A lot has changed since the days of Tampa's cigar factories and fishing villages. Cigars are still produced in Tampa—about 500 million a year, but machines have taken over what was once done by hand. Now, many of Ybor City's vacant cigar factories are transformed into shops and restaurants, but the strong Latin community created in the late 1800s still is present.

Today tourism is king, with the city's ideal port for the cruise industry. But there's also Busch Gardens Tampa Bay, rated tops by roller-coaster enthusiasts and animal lovers, and an abundance of recreational activities.

HISTORIC YBOR CITY

Tampa's historic Cuban enclave in the northeast section of the city was once known as the "Cigar Capital of the World" with more than 200 factories and 12,000 Spanish, Italian, German, and Cuban workers. Today Ybor City is one of Florida's three National Historic Landmark districts, with cobblestone streets and Spanish-tiled buildings remaining from the early 1900s. The heart of the district is La Septima (Seventh Avenue), a raucous spot after dark.

Though it's best known for bars and clubs, Ybor City has the Ybor City State Museum (1818 East Ninth Avenue; (813) 247-6323) for a quick history lesson. It is open 9 a.m.–5 p.m. daily, and the cost is $2. You can also stop by the Ybor City Chamber of Commerce at 1800 East Ninth Avenue (call (813) 248-3712) for a self-guided walking tour map. Ybor Square at Eighth Avenue and 13th Street showcases arts and crafts and specialty shops; you can still watch cigars being rolled here at Tampa Rico Cigars.

To get there, take Exit 1 on I-4 and drive south on 21st Street for three blocks.

Golf

Saddlebrook Resort

5700 Saddlebrook Way (30 miles north of Tampa), Wesley Chapel; (800) 729-8383; www.saddlebrookresort.com

Palmer Course

Established 1985 | **Designer** Arnold Palmer | **Holes** 18

Tees Blue/White/Red **Par** 71/71/71 **Slope** 134/129/127

Saddlebrook Course

Established 1983 | **Designer** Dean Refram | **Holes** 18

Tees Blue/White/Red **Par** 70/70/70 **Slope** 127/122/126
Fees $145 January 15–May 9; $70 May 10–September 30; $105 October 1–January 14
Specials Call for twilight rates **Cart rental** Included **Club rental** $35 per set **Payment** All major credit cards **Tee times** 48 hours in advance **Facilities** Pro shop, restaurant, world-class practice facility, European-style spa, 56 world class tennis courts with different surfaces
Comments The **Palmer Course** has quite a different look from its sister course: elevated tees, rolling terrain, and wider fairways. On both, you will find many bunkers and lakes guarding fairways and greens.

The resort's original course, **Saddlebrook**, is a tight layout with water on 17 of the 18 holes. This is the better of the two courses at the resort, where flat terrain prevails. Many pine and cypress trees line the fairways and surround the greens, placing a premium on accuracy.

Tournament Players Club of Tampa Bay

5300 West Lutz Lake Fern Road, Lutz; (813) 949-0090; www.tpc.com
Established 1991 | **Designer** Bobby Weed | **Holes** 18

Tees TPC/Blue/White/Red **Par** 71/71/71/71 **Slope** 131/128/118/109
Fees Monday–Thursday, $79 before noon, $59 noon–3 p.m., $49 after 3 p.m.; Friday–Sunday, $92 before noon, $69 noon–3 p.m., $55 after 3 p.m.
Specials Discounts available for groups of 12 or more players **Cart rental** Included in green fees **Club rental** $55 per set **Payment** V, MC, AmEx, DC **Tee times** 60 days in advance **Facilities** Practice facility, chipping/putting green, lockers, restaurant, clubhouse, pro shop
Comments The area's only PGA Tour facility and home of the Senior PGA Tour's Verizon Classic each February. Also a *Golf Digest* Four-Star Award Winner for Places to Play.

World Woods Golf Club, Pine Barrens Course

17590 Ponce De Leon Boulevard, Brooksville; (352) 796-5500; www.worldwoods.com
Established 1993 | **Designer** Tom Fazio | **Holes** 18

Tees Tournament/Back/Middle/Forward
Par 71/71/71/71 **Slope** 140/134/129/132
Fees Monday–Thursday, $40; Friday–Sunday, $50
Specials Twilight rates all week, $30 after 3 p.m. **Cart rental** Included in green fees **Club rental** $25 per set **Payment** All major credit cards accepted **Tee times** 30 days in advance **Facilities** Driving range, pro shop restaurant
Comments World Woods is off the beaten path—way off. It is located over and hour's drive from Tampa in an isolated location. But this course is more than enough reason to make the drive. Pine Barrens is the marquee course at World Woods, cutting through a tall pine forest.

Make sure you arrive early to avail yourself of the amazing practice facilities. World Woods might very well claim the finest practice facility on

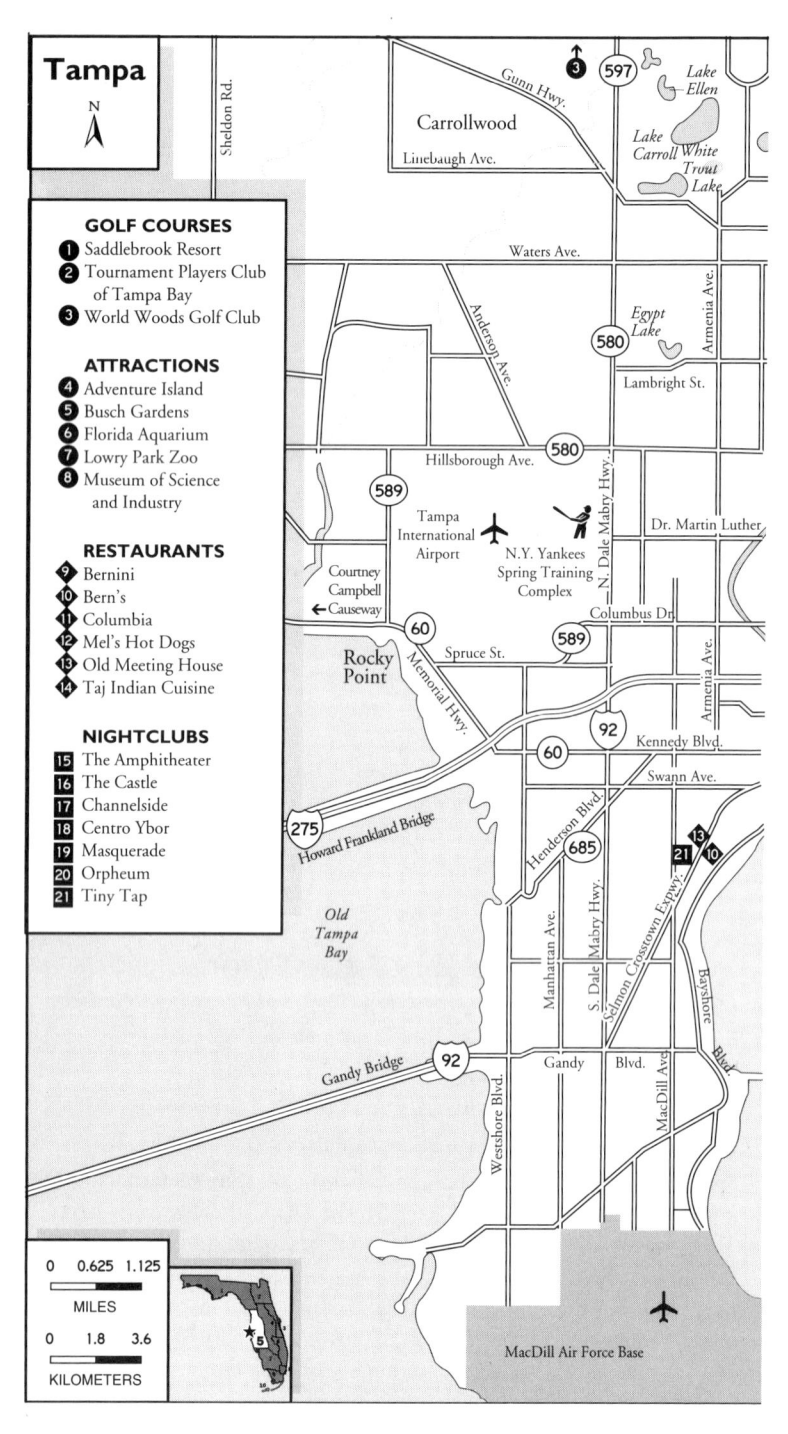

Tampa

N

GOLF COURSES
1. Saddlebrook Resort
2. Tournament Players Club of Tampa Bay
3. World Woods Golf Club

ATTRACTIONS
4. Adventure Island
5. Busch Gardens
6. Florida Aquarium
7. Lowry Park Zoo
8. Museum of Science and Industry

RESTAURANTS
9. Bernini
10. Bern's
11. Columbia
12. Mel's Hot Dogs
13. Old Meeting House
14. Taj Indian Cuisine

NIGHTCLUBS
15. The Amphitheater
16. The Castle
17. Channelside
18. Centro Ybor
19. Masquerade
20. Orpheum
21. Tiny Tap

315

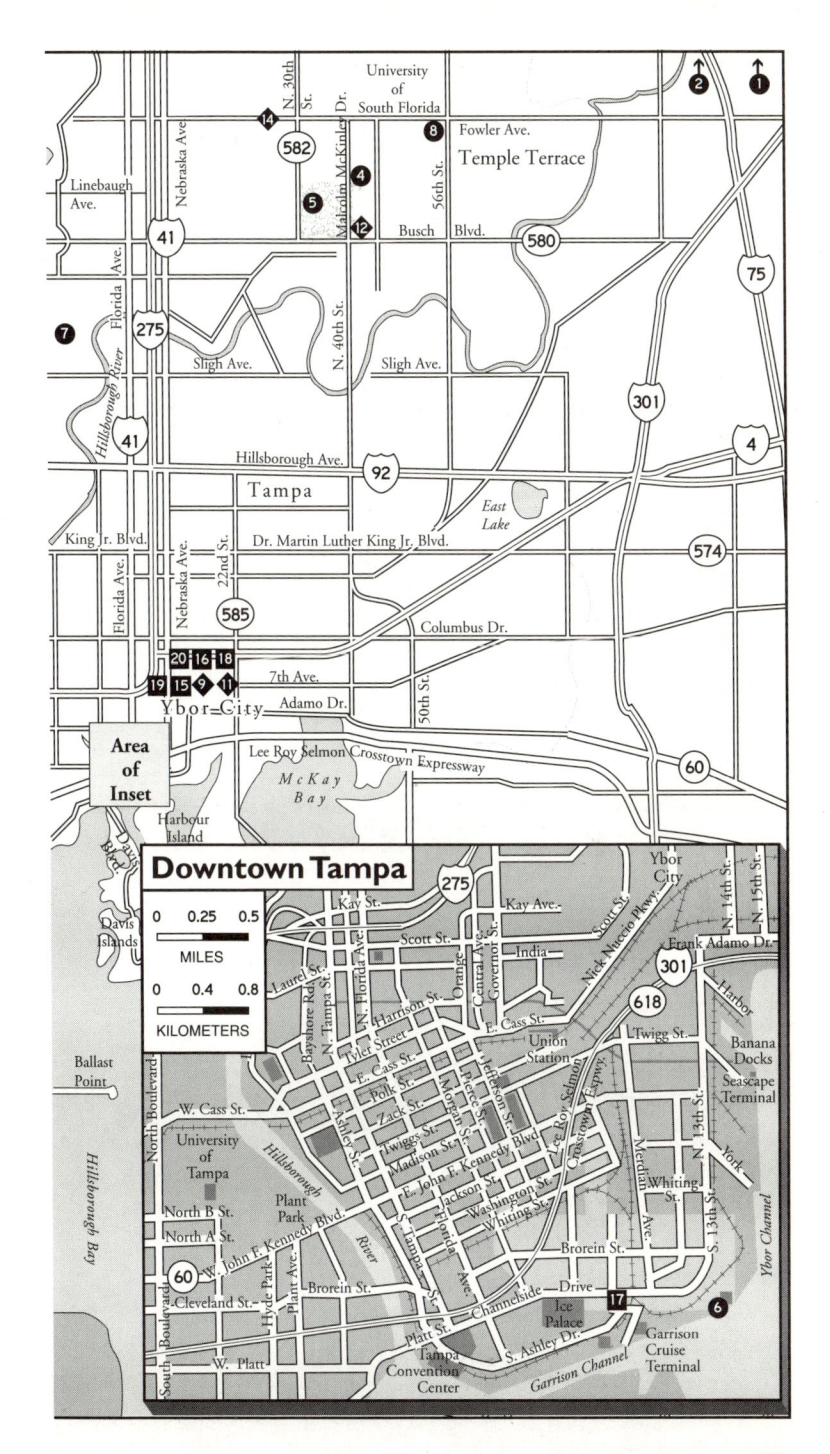

earth, public or private. The 22-acre driving range is shaped like a square so you can hit shots into all wind directions. The putting green covers two acres; there is a three-hole warmup course and a nine-hole par-3 course.

Attractions

Adventure Island

1001 McKinley Drive, Tampa, adjacent to Busch Gardens; (813) 987-5660

Hours 10 a.m.–5 p.m., varies seasonally (February 26–March 31, Saturday and Sunday; April 1–September 4, daily; September 9–October 29, Saturday and Sunday)

Admission $30 for adults, $28 for children ages 3–9; parking $5

Appeal by Age Group

Pre-school ★★	Teens ★★★	Over 30 ★★
Grade school ★★★★	Young Adults ★★	Seniors ★

Touring Time *Average* a whole day (6–8 hours); *minimum* half a day

Rainy-Day Touring Not recommended

Author's Rating ★★; works well with any vacation plan: a day at Busch, and a day at the water park

Description and Comments Water slides are plentiful, and everything is supervised—they generally have 50 lifeguards watching the pools at all times. There are also a championship volleyball complex, a game arcade, and outdoor cafes. Lockers, showers, and changing areas are located near the park's entrance. Adventure Island offers something for all ages, from a kid's area to daring slides like the Tampa Typhoon, a seven-story, near-free-fall drop.

Picnicking is permitted in the park, and there are tables throughout.

Busch Gardens Tampa Bay

Busch Boulevard, Tampa; (800) 4-ADVENTURE or (813) 987-5082 or 987-5171; www.buschgardens.com

Hours Open 365 days a year, hours vary daily; call ahead

Admission $52 for adults, $43 for children ages 3–9; parking $7

Appeal by Age Group

Pre-school ★★	Teens ★★★★★	Over 30 ★★★
Grade school ★★★★★	Young Adults ★★★★	Seniors ★★

Touring Time *Average* a whole day (6–8 hours); *minimum* a half-day

Rainy-Day Touring Not recommended

Author's Rating ★★★★; does anyone have some Pepto-Bismol?

Description and Comments One of the top theme parks in Florida, Busch Gardens features gravity-defying roller coasters that coexist with beautiful zoo animals. More than 2,700 animals representing more than 320 species make it one of the nation's top zoos.

The park covers 335 acres, so take it easy and board the sky ride, the monorail (that goes in a circle and will end where you started), or the Trans-Veldt Railroad for an informative overview of the theme park. Theming is turn-of-the-century Africa, with 11 separate regions in the park.

Morocco This is the first area guests encounter and consists mostly of shops and eateries, with snake charmers and roving sheiks performing in the streets. There are three theaters with impressive live shows: the Moroccan Palace Theater, the Marrakesh Theater, and the Tangiers Theater, but we recommend saving the shows for later in the day when the hot sun and lines for attractions can be unbearable.

In Morocco you'll find bank machines, bathrooms, a lost and found, and lockers. It's a great place to pick up your souvenirs and your last snack as you head for home. The most important thing about Morocco is that it can lead you to **Gwazi**, Busch Garden's newest coaster.

Nairobi Adjacent to Morocco is Nairobi, featuring an ample variety of small animal exhibits in an African, thatched-hut village setting. The walkways are a bit of a maze, making it difficult to see the exhibits systematically without backtracking.

Nairobi includes **Myombe Reserve: The Great Ape Domain,** a sophisticated three-acre habitat housing western lowland gorillas and chimpanzees. Nairobi's animal nursery, petting zoo, elephant habitat, and Aldabra tortoise habitat offer up-close encounters. Reptilian environments for crocodiles, alligators, and turtles for daily presentations. Nocturnal Mountain illustrates the behaviors of nighttime creatures.

Serengeti Plain Bordering Nairobi is the Serengeti Plain, an ideal place to start in the early morning when the animals are most active. Nearly 800 free-roaming African animals, including hippos, giraffes, antelopes, camels, Nile crocodiles, flamingos, and ostriches wander in 80 lushly landscaped acres.

You can see this area from the **Rhino Rally** attraction, or take a slower look via monorail, steam locomotive, Sky Ride, or promenade. The monorail allows the most unhindered view but is slow loading. The Sky Ride passes over the Serengeti, but it's a one-way trip to the Congo and also may have long lines. The steam train connects Nairobi with the Congo and Stanleyville, and it's a nice way to get a closer ground-view perspective of the Serengeti wildlife.

The highlight in this area is the animal exhibit **Edge of Africa,** which puts you in the heart of the veldt. The barriers between guests and the animals are natural and mostly hidden. The Edge of Africa begins at a welcome center that posts daily recordings of animal sightings and their diets. Close to the entrance, you'll spot a meerkat habitat. As you move on, you'll discover a "Masai village" that a nomadic African tribe has vacated—once you see the lions and hyenas, you'll know why. You are just inches away from these animals.

Farther into the exhibit, you'll see a crocodile nest and a hippopotamus pool from an underwater viewing area. Next, step into a vulture habitat, a giraffe feeding area, and a spring that is home to flamingos, turtles, and fish.

Roaming safari guides offer guests talks about the animals and the ecosystem. Guidebooks are also available to help with animal identification.

To get a special look at Edge of Africa, try the Serengeti Safari (separate fee). Board a safari-themed flatbed truck that puts guests even closer to giraffes, zebras, ostriches, and rhinos. This tour lasts about a half-hour and is offered several times throughout the day.

Crown Colony Overlooking the Serengeti, this is the place to get a bite to eat at the park's only table-service restaurant, the Crown Colony. There's also the Clydesdale Hamlet, home to the massive Clydesdale horses that Busch Garden's parent company, Anheuser-Busch, owns.

Egypt Egypt is the newest area of Busch Gardens, on seven acres tucked behind the Crown Colony. The highlight is **Montu**, the Southeast's longest (4,000 feet) and tallest inverted roller coaster, with speeds that exceed 60 miles per hour. This three-minute ride features a dropout platform that leaves your feet dangling, and the ride turns you upside down a total of seven times. Egypt also offers a tour through a replica of King Tut's Tomb as it appeared during the actual excavation in the 1920s and the Egypt Sand Dig area for young archaeologists.

Timbuktu Timbuktu is sandwiched between the Serengeti Plain and the Congo with a walkway connecting it to Nairobi. Arranged in a large square reminiscent of an African market or bazaar, Timbuktu offers the Scorpion, a small roller coaster that's a good "beginner coaster" with one inversion. The Dolphins of the Deep show is here, as well as the new 4-D theater attraction, R. L. Stine's Haunted Lighthouse.

Congo If your heart can take it, head over to the Congo for another roller coaster. **Kumba,** the Southeast's largest and fastest steel roller coaster, features a camelback weightless maneuver, a spiraling cobra roll, and a 135-foot drop. Nearby is the Congo River Rapids, complete with rapids, standing waves, geysers, caverns, and waterfalls—fun for the whole family (and refreshing on a hot day). Don't miss the Python corkscrew roller coaster, old-fashioned by today's standards, with a short, twisting-turning ride featuring a corkscrewing double helix.

For those who don't meet the height requirements for the wild rides, try the Ubanga-Banga Bumper Cars.

Claw Island is a beautifully executed exhibition of Bengal tigers, the perfect showcase for the big cats. The exhibit can be viewed from all sides as well as from a bridge passing over the tigers' lagoon. The cats, large, sleek, and ample in number, are usually on the move, providing a colorful spectacle for visitors.

Stanleyville Moving out of the Congo past the terminus of the Sky Ride, a trail leads to Stanleyville. The two water rides in Stanleyville—the Stanley Falls Log Flume and the Tanganyika Tidal Wave—are guaranteed to cool you off on a hot summer afternoon. Beware, many bystanders on a bridge near the tidal wave get drenched as the boats splash down into the pool.

You'll also find a habitat for warthogs and orangutans, and see snakes, insects, and reptiles in Stanleyville. Orchid Canyon provides a boardwalk tour of numerous species of these flowers.

Bird Gardens Across the bridge from Stanleyville is Bird Gardens, a nice place to take a breather from the long lines and hustle of the park, with exotic birds and birds of prey—and complimentary beer samplings from parent company Anheuser-Busch for guests 21 and older. Lory Landing allows bird lovers to feed nectar to colorful lorikeets (a type of parakeet). The *Birds of Prey* show is here, as well as a koala habitat that draws big crowds. Guests also can see the television production of *Jack Hanna's Animal Adventures*.

Land of the Dragons This adventure play area lets kids spend some energy while parents take a break. Dumphrey, a friendly, costumed dragon, makes appearances, and youngsters are invited to climb a three-story treehouse with towers and stairways that create a maze. Other activities include a rope climb, a ball crawl, an outdoor theater showing *A Dragon's Tale,* and various children's rides. Real dragons are here, too—a Komodo dragon and rhino iguana, for example.

Touring Tips It requires hustle to see Busch Gardens Florida in one day. Personal taste and family ages will serve to eliminate some exhibits or rides. Our recommendation is to plan your tour in advance and work out some objectives and compromises that will keep everybody reasonably happy. Alternatively, split your family (let teenagers take off, for example) and gather everyone back together at an appointed time for a show or to share a meal.

The single most effective strategy for efficient touring and avoiding long waits in line is to arrive at the park a little before 9 a.m. (gates usually open by 9:30 a.m.). Park, then purchase your admission pass and be at the turnstile ready to roll when the attraction opens. The same four rides you can experience in a single hour in the early morning will require more than three hours after 11:30 a.m.

Most of the live shows play in large amphitheaters, so save shows and walk-through zoological exhibits for after 11:30 a.m., when the lines for rides grow long.

BUSCH GARDENS BASICS

Roller Coasters: *Number of Inversions*

| Montu: 7 | Kumba: 6 | Python: 2 | Scorpion: 1 |

Water Rides: *Level of Wetness, 3 Meaning "Soaked"*

| Stanley Falls: 1 | Congo River Rapids: 2 | Tidal Wave: 3 |

Longest Lines

Montu, Congo River Rapids, Gwazi, and Kumba

Florida Aquarium

701 Channelside Drive, Tampa; (813) 273-4000; www.flaquarium.net
Hours Daily, 9:30 a.m.–5 p.m.
Admission $16 for adults, $11 for children ages 3–12, $14 seniors ages 60 and over
Appeal by Age Group

Pre-school ★★★	Teens ★★★	Over 30 ★★★★
Grade school ★★★★	Young Adults ★★★★	Seniors ★★★★

Touring Time *Average* 3 hours; *minimum* 2 hours
Rainy-Day Touring Perfect
Author's Rating ★★★★

Description and Comments You don't want to miss this beautiful glass-domed attraction on Tampa's downtown waterfront. The three-story aquarium features five galleries on three floors: Florida Bays and Beaches, Florida Coral Reefs, Florida Sea Hunt, No Bone Zone, and the Wetlands Gallery. In all, nearly 5,000 fish, plants, and animals representing 550 species native to Florida are represented.

Explore the museum on your own, or rent audio wands ($2) for a one-and-a-half-hour tour. Special tours include a 20-minute behind-the-scenes tour, offered three times a day. The tours are free; the information desk on the main level can give you details.

You can also get out on the water in the aquarium's 64-foot catamaran for a tour to see dolphins, manatees, and other wildlife. Cost is $19 for adults, $18 for seniors ages 60 and over, and $14 for children ages 3–11. Tours leave at 2 and 4 p.m. Monday–Friday and 12, 2, and 4 p.m. Saturday and Sunday. No reservations required; first come, first served.

Lowry Park Zoo

7530 North Boulevard, Tampa; (813) 932-0245 or 935-8552; www.lowryparkzoo.com
Hours Daily, 9:30 a.m.–5 p.m.
Admission $11.50 for adults, $8 for children ages 3–11, $10.50 for seniors ages 50 and older
Appeal by Age Group

Pre-school ★★★★	Teens ★★	Over 30 ★★★
Grade school ★★★★	Young Adults ★★	Seniors ★★★

Touring Time *Average* 3½ hours; *minimum* 2 hours
Rainy-Day Touring Not recommended
Author's Rating ★★½

Description and Comments Lowry Park Zoo is rated as one of the top three midsize zoos in the United States. Animals roam freely across much of the zoo's 41 acres, controlled by natural barriers. The zoo features more than 1,500 animals of 375 different species and includes a manatee hospital. When you arrive, check the show schedule for special attractions, such as the "Meet a Keeper" experience, to learn more about care and feeding for these animals.

Museum of Science and Industry (MOSI)

4801 East Fowler Avenue, Tampa; (813) 987-6100 or (800) 995-MOSI; www.mosi.org

Hours 9 a.m.–5 p.m. Monday–Friday; 9 a.m.–7 p.m. Saturday and Sunday
Admission $15 for adults, $13 for seniors, $11 for children ages 2–13, free for ages 2 and under. MOSIMAX movie is additional, but combination tickets can be purchased. Free parking. Visit the website for an online coupon.
Appeal by Age Group

Pre-school ★★★	Teens ★★★	Over 30 ★★★★
Grade school ★★★★	Young Adults ★★★	Seniors ★★★★

Touring Time *Average* 4–5 hours; *minimum* 3 hours
Rainy-Day Touring Recommended
Author's Rating ★★★★; an incredible museum, great for rainy days
Description and Comments MOSI's (rhymes with Rosie's) philosophy is "hands-on, minds-on." It's the largest science center (254,000 square feet on a 65-acre campus) in the southeastern United States, with three floors and more than 450 hands-on displays.

Schedule your visit around a film in MOSIMAX, a 353-seat IMAX theater that projects movies with a 180° fisheye lens onto an 82-foot-high curved dome screen. Different films are featured, often nature-based.

The Back Woods lets you head outdoors and showcases conservation efforts on several miles of trails. Signs identify plant life, and cassette players are available for an audio tour. There is also the BioWorks Butterfly Garden with 175 butterflies representing nine species. There may also be special traveling exhibits on hand during your visit.

Shopping

Genteel Old Hyde Park Village, one of the oldest neighborhoods in Tampa, located at Swan and Dakota just south of downtown, has about 50 shops including Ann Taylor, Banana Republic, Anthropologie, MAC Cosmetics, Pottery Barn Kids, Restoration Hardware, and Sharper Image. There's also an AMC theater with seven screens and restaurants with tables along the sidewalks. Parking is free in three garages on Swann and Rome avenues. Shop hours are daily 10 a.m.–7 p.m. and noon–5 p.m. Sunday.

The best mall shopping is at **International Plaza** (West Shore and Boy Scout Boulevard; (813) 342-3790) adjacent to the Tampa International Airport. Department stores include Neiman Marcus and Nordstrom, and there are 200 specialty shops, a dozen restaurants, and a hotel. **Westshore Plaza** (intersection of Westshore and Kennedy Boulevards) has a Saks Fifth Avenue, Burdines, Old Navy, and other national retailers, as well as a 14-screen movie theater and restaurants.

Flea Market Flea market fans will want to check out **Oldsmar Flea Market** (180 Race Track Road; (813) 855-5306) and the **Big Top** (9250 Fowler Avenue) with more than 1,000 booths.

Dining

Bernini

1702 East Seventh Avenue, Ybor City; (813) 248-0099

Meals served Lunch and dinner **Cuisine** Italian **Entree range** $8–$12 lunch, $16–$25 dinner **Reservations** Recommended **Payment** All major credit cards accepted

Comments Rated tops in Ybor City, this sophisticated Italian restaurant is in the historic Bank of Ybor City building, with a beautiful dining room that shows off the old-fashioned vaulted ceilings and marble floors. The gourmet menu changes often, but you'll usually find the award-winning lobster and shrimp cassoulet and lobster ravioli, along with steaks, duck, and fresh seafood. Save room for the crème brûlée.

Bern's

1208 South Howard Avenue, Tampa; (813) 251-2421

Meals served Dinner daily **Cuisine** Steakhouse **Entree range** $20–$207 (for a 60-oz. strip sirloin) **Reservations** Necessary **Payment** V, MC, D, AmEx, DC

Comments Bern's is a mecca for steak lovers. Owned and operated by the same family for more than 40 years, the interior looks like a turn-of-the-century brothel with gilded plaster columns and red wallpaper. The fabulous steaks are aged in specially built lockers controlled for humidity and temperature. The wine list is phenomenal, and when it's time for dessert you move upstairs to private dessert rooms. Ask for a tour of the kitchen, it runs like clockwork.

Columbia

2117 East Seventh Avenue, Ybor City; (813) 248-4961

Meals served Lunch and dinner daily **Cuisine** Spanish **Entree range** $5–$25 lunch, $15–$25 dinner **Reservations** Recommended **Payment** All major credit cards accepted

Comments Columbia is the largest and oldest Spanish restaurant in the United States, founded in 1905 in historic Ybor City, and operated by the same family for four generations. Classic Spanish cuisine, including paella and La Completa Cubana, a feast of roast pork, plantains, empanada de picadillo, black beans, and yellow rice, is served with flair. Flamenco and classical dance are performed Monday through Saturday nights.

Mel's Hot Dogs

4136 East Busch Boulevard, Tampa; (813) 985-8000

Meals served Lunch and dinner **Cuisine** American **Entree range** $3–$8
Reservations Not accepted **Payment** No credit cards (ATM machine on site)
Comments Try the special, an all-beef hot dog served on a poppy-seed bun with mustard, onions, sauerkraut, relish, and a pickle. The Chicago is another favorite, with mustard, onions, relish, pickle, tomatoes, celery salt, and hot peppers. Other items on the menu include veggie burgers, chicken sandwiches, bratwurst, and corn dogs.

Old Meeting House

901 South Howard Avenue, Tampa's Hyde Park district; (813) 251-1754

Meals served Breakfast, lunch, and dinner **Cuisine** American diner **Entree range** $4.50–$10 **Reservations** No **Payment** V, MC
Comments While everyone's going retro, the Old Meeting House has kept hungry guests coming back by staying exactly the same as when it opened in 1947. They create more than 45 flavors including brownie ice cream, Cherry Seinfeld, and more. After you fill up, visit nearby Hyde Park Village for shopping and strolling.

Taj Indian Cuisine

2734 East Fowler Avenue, Tampa; (813) 971-8483

Meals served Lunch and dinner **Cuisine** Indian **Entree range** $8–$16
Reservations Accepted **Payment** All major credit cards accepted
Comments Locals recommend this 126-seat Indian restaurant where specialties include chicken tikka, butter chicken, tandoori chicken, and rice pudding.

Arts and Culture

Tampa Museum of Art (600 North Ashley Drive; (813) 274-8130; **www.tampamuseum.com**) features a permanent collection of Greek and Roman Classical antiquities, contemporary art, photography, and nineteenth- and twentieth-century American sculpture.

The **Henry B. Plant Museum** (401 West Kennedy Boulevard, downtown Tampa; (813) 254-1891; **www.plantmuseum.com**) is the old Tampa Bay Hotel, with European furniture and original art treasures of the Gilded Age. Plant was a railroad magnate who helped develop Florida, and the museum transports you to turn-of-the-twentieth-century Florida.

Nightlife

The Amphitheater

Who goes there Chic 20-somethings; must be 18 to enter

1609 East Seventh Avenue, Ybor City; (813) 248-2331

Cover For some special events **Minimum** No **Mixed drinks** $3 and up
Food available Limited menu

Hours 9 or 10 p.m.–3 a.m.

What goes on Ybor City's nod to South Beach, the Amphitheater hosts concerts, fashion shows, and comedy acts. Most nights it's all about dancing, with master-mixed techno and house tunes and a revolving floor with special effects.

Comments There's also a VIP lounge and oxygen bar for a toke of pure air. A second-floor balcony overlooks Ybor City's busy Seventh Street.

The Castle

Who goes there A little older, martini-drinking crowd (that means 30s, not 20s)

2004 North 16th Street, Ybor City; (813) 247-7547; www.castle-ybor.com

Cover $2–$5 **Minimum** Must be 18 **Mixed drinks** $2 and up **Food available** Limited menu

Hours 9 p.m.–3 a.m.

What goes on The Castle is a more sophisticated than most of the Ybor City bars, and you'll feel out of place unless you're dressed in black. Even the bar is black granite.

Comments The dance floor is upstairs, with a DJ spinning new wave, house, and industrial music.

Channelside

Who goes there Tourists, some locals

615 Channelside Drive, downtown Tampa; (813) 223-4250; www.channelside.com

Cover No **Minimum** No **Mixed drinks** $4 and up **Food available** Several restaurants with full menus

Hours 10 a.m.–2 a.m.

What goes on Channelside is a huge entertainment complex next to the Florida Aquarium and within walking distance of the Ice Palace. There are clubs—Banana Joe's Island Party, Margarita Mamas, Stumps Supper Club, Howl at the Moon, Cigars by Antonio—a nine-screen movie theater with 3-D IMAX, and professional hockey games at the Ice Palace.

Comments Plenty of mainstream restaurants and open-air shops round out the action in this retail-entertainment complex.

Centro Ybor

Who goes there Rowdy 20-something tourists and locals in the bars; families and teenagers in GameWorks

1600 East Eighth Avenue, Ybor City; (813) 242-4660; www.centroybor.com

Cover No **Minimum** No **Mixed drinks** $4 and up **Food available** Several restaurants with full menus

Hours 10 a.m.–2 a.m.

What goes on This entertainment/shopping/dining complex has bars and clubs, including Adobe Gilas, Barley Hopper's, Big City Tavern, Game-

Works, and the Improv Comedy Club. Enjoy Apollo Sundays at The Improv or a film at the area's coolest theater, MUVICO.
Comments Purchase a movie ticket or $25 or more at any merchant and receive free valet parking Sunday–Thursday and $3 off parking Friday and Saturday.

Masquerade

Who goes there 20-somethings looking for cheap drinks, dancing, live music

1503 East Seventh Avenue, Ybor City; (813) 247-3319

Cover Varies for special events **Minimum** Must be 18 **Mixed drinks** $4 and up **Food available** Limited menu
Hours 9 p.m.–2 a.m.
What goes on Masquerade is in the historic Ritz Theatre, and has three areas: one for dancing, a pub, and one with a gothic/industrial buzz.
Comments Drinks are cheap—some nights it's all you can guzzle for one price. Local bands get their start here.

Orpheum

Who goes there 20- and 30-somethings looking for the best live music

1902 Avenida Republica de Cuba, Ybor City; (813) 248-9500

Cover Varies for special events **Minimum** Must be 18 **Mixed drinks** $3 and up **Food available** Limited menu
Hours 9 p.m.–2 a.m.
What goes on Orpheum hosts some of the best live music in Tampa Bay.
Comments Partly because the club shares ownership with the State Theater, it has a fabulous sound system and often gets major headliners as well as the best local bands.

Tiny Tap

Who goes there Locals and a few college kids

2105 West Morrison Avenue, Hyde Park; (813) 258-5212

Cover No **Minimum** No **Mixed drinks** Beer and wine only **Food available** Limited snacks
Hours 7 p.m.–3 a.m.
What goes on Tiny Tap has been offering cheap beer for more than 40 years for the pool, foozball, and darts crowd.
Comments If rowdiness and dancing are not your idea of after-dark fun, skip Ybor City and hang out here. It's casual and cash only

St. Petersburg and Clearwater

Bordered on the east by Tampa Bay and on the west by the Gulf of Mexico, the St. Petersburg and Clearwater area has 35 miles of white sand, with a

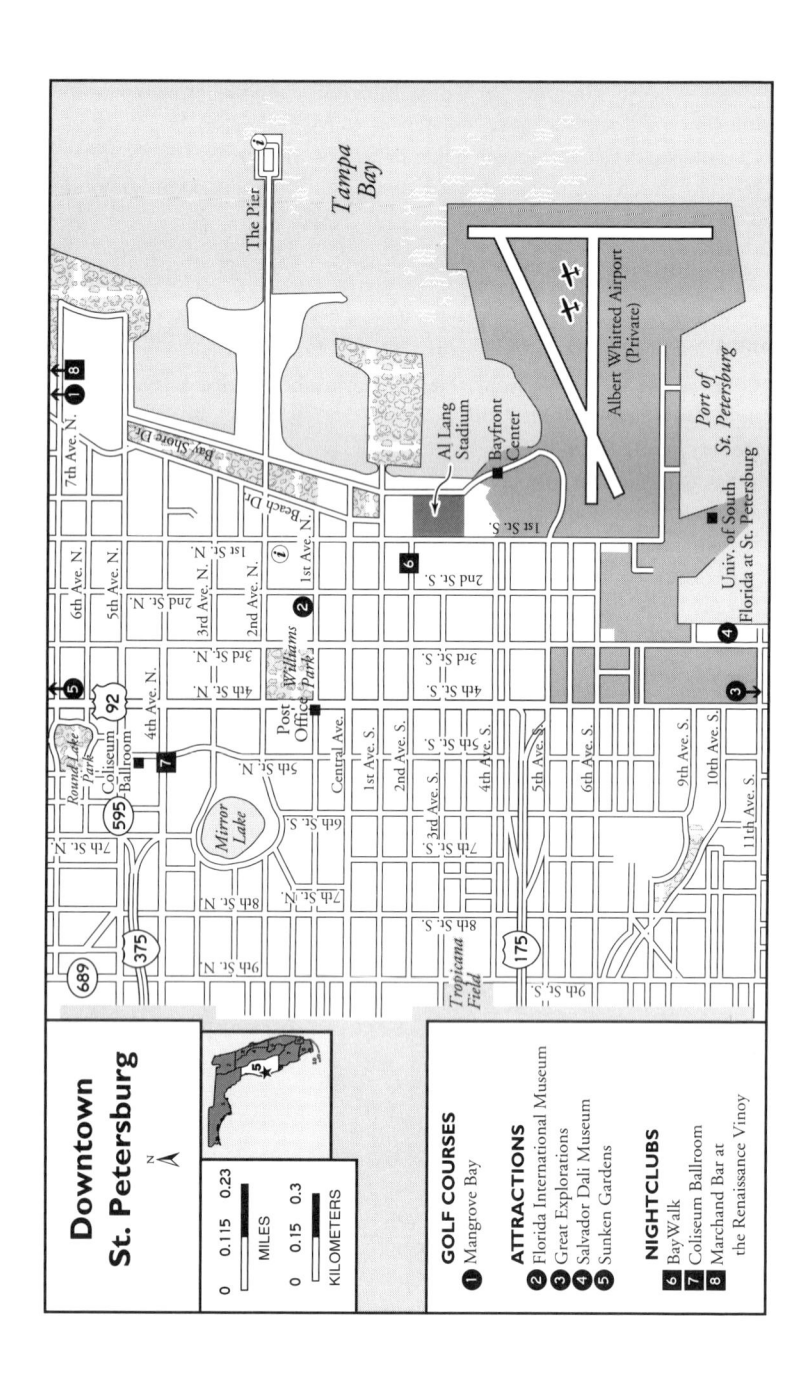

Downtown St. Petersburg

0   0.115   0.23
MILES

0   0.15   0.3
KILOMETERS

GOLF COURSES
1. Mangrove Bay

ATTRACTIONS
2. Florida International Museum
3. Great Explorations
4. Salvador Dali Museum
5. Sunken Gardens

NIGHTCLUBS
6. BayWalk
7. Coliseum Ballroom
8. Marchand Bar at the Renaissance Vinoy

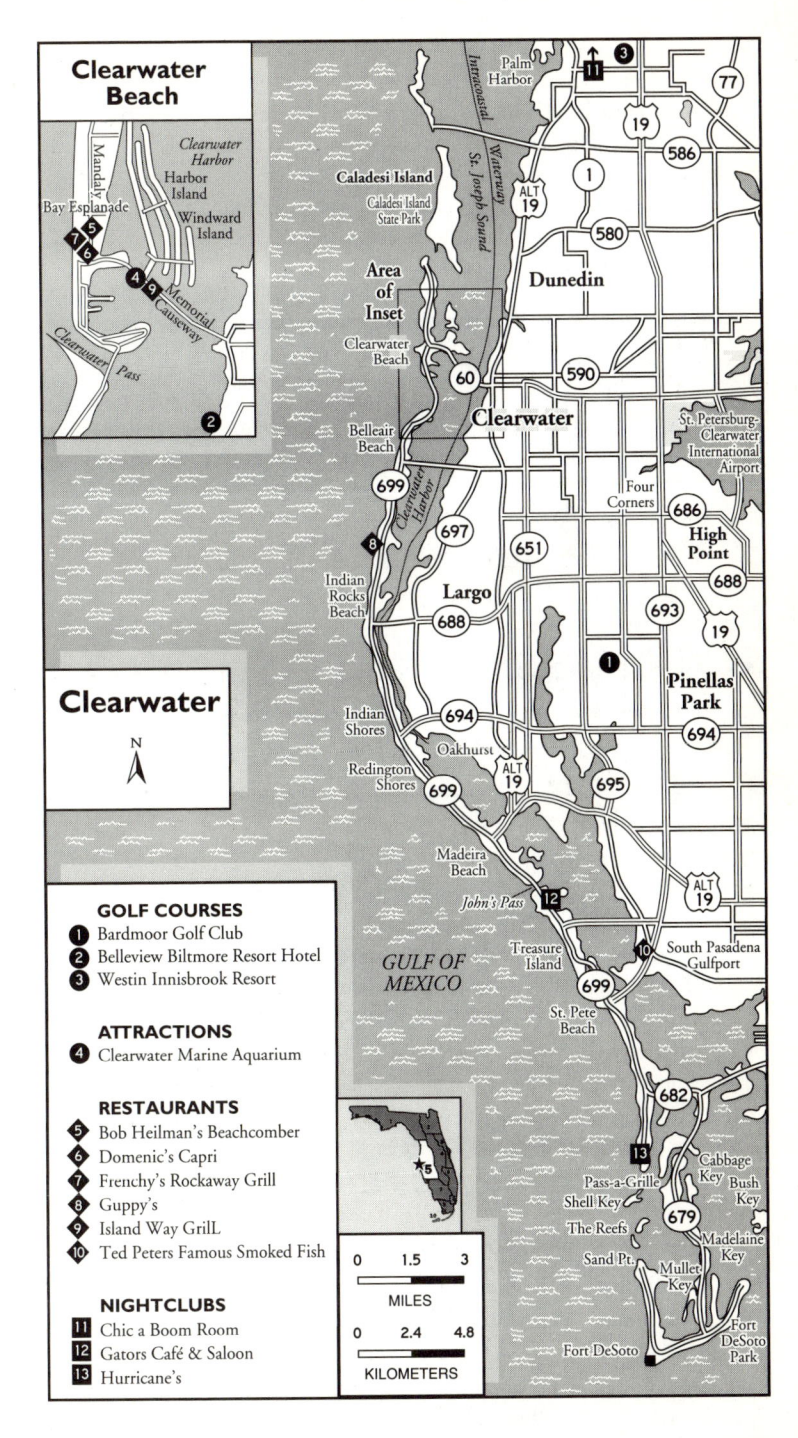

Clearwater Beach

Clearwater

N

GOLF COURSES
1. Bardmoor Golf Club
2. Belleview Biltmore Resort Hotel
3. Westin Innisbrook Resort

ATTRACTIONS
4. Clearwater Marine Aquarium

RESTAURANTS
5. Bob Heilman's Beachcomber
6. Domenic's Capri
7. Frenchy's Rockaway Grill
8. Guppy's
9. Island Way Grill
10. Ted Peters Famous Smoked Fish

NIGHTCLUBS
11. Chic a Boom Room
12. Gators Café & Saloon
13. Hurricane's

diverse ecosystem that includes amber sea oats, stands of pine, cypress, and mangrove hammocks.

St. Petersburg is 21 miles west of Tampa, home to a museum district which includes Florida International Museum, Salvador Dali Museum, Museum of Fine Arts, Museum of History, Great Explorations, and the Pier.

Twelve miles north of St. Petersburg is Clearwater and Clearwater Beach. The beach is on a peninsula between the Gulf of Mexico and Tampa Bay, with three miles of sand and calm waters.

HASLAM'S BOOK STORE

Before you head to the beach, hit Haslam's Book Store for some great summer reads. Haslam's, located near Tropicana Field and the downtown museums, opened in 1933 and has become the largest independently owned bookstore in the Southeast. Browse the new, used, and unusual books—there are more than 300,000 in every category imaginable. Located at 2025 Central Avenue; (727) 822-8616; www.haslams.com.

Golf

Bardmoor Golf Club

8001 Cumberland Road, Largo; (727) 392-1234; www.bardmoorgolf.com

Established 1971 | **Designer** William Diddle (renovated in 2001 by Gary Koch) | **Holes** 18

Tees Black/Gold/Silver/Copper
Par 71/71/71/71 **Slope** 131/127/117/120
Fees $45 before noon; $35 noon–4 p.m.; $25 after 4 p.m.
Specials Twilight rate **Cart rental** Included in green fees **Club rental** $30 per set **Payment** V, MC, AmEx, D **Tee times** 30 days in advance **Facilities** A Tom Fazio-designed practice facility, restaurant and lounge, clubhouse.
Comments This public course is the former site of the JC Penney Classic, reopened after a $2 million renovation in 2001. The 7,000-yard layout is challenging, and beautifully maintained. Caddie program allows you to walk.

Belleview Biltmore Resort Hotel

25 Belleview Boulevard, Clearwater; (800) 237-8947 ext. 800, or (727) 373-3000; www.belleviewbiltmore.com

Established 1925 | **Designer** Donald Ross | **Holes** 18

Tees Blue/White/Yellow/Red **Par** 71/71/71/71 **Slope** 124/120/118/115
Fees $30 Monday–Thursday; $40 Friday–Sunday
Specials Twilight rate, $25 after 3 p.m. **Cart rental** Included in green fees **Club rental** $30 per set **Payment** All major credit cards accepted **Tee times** 7 days in advance **Facilities** Full practice facility, restaurant, pro shop

Mangrove Bay

875 62nd Avenue Northeast, St. Petersburg; (727) 893-7800;
www.stpete.org/mangrove.htm

Established 1977 | **Designer** Bill Amick | **Holes** 18

Tees Red/Yellow/White/Black **Par** 72/72/72/72 **Slope** 115/110/114/119
Fees $26 before 3 p.m.; $23 after 3 p.m.
Specials Twilight rates **Cart rental** Included in green fees **Club rental** $15 per set **Payment** V, MC, AmEx, D **Tee times** 7 days in advance **Facilities** Practice facility with driving range, clubhouse with pro shop and snack bar, professional lessons.
Comments The city of St. Pete owns and operates the course, and many amateur tournaments are held here. Named one of the Top 100 Most Women Friendly Golf Courses by *Golf for Women* magazine in 1999.

Westin Innisbrook Resort

US 19 North, Palm Harbor (near Tarpon Springs); (727) 942-2000;
www.westin-innisbrook.com

Copperhead Course

Established 1972 | **Designer** Lawrence Packard | **Holes** 18

Tees Black/Gold/Silver/Jade **Par** 71/71/71/71 **Slope** 134/131/128/130

Island Course

Established 1970 | **Designer** Lawrence Packard | **Holes** 18

Tees Black/Gold/Silver/Jade **Par** 72/72/72/72 **Slope** 132/128/121/129
Fees Fees vary seasonally; Copperhead Course, $100–$180; Island Course, $80–$140
Specials Twilight rate (after 3 p.m.) is $60 Copperhead, $40 Island; based on availability **Cart rental** Included **Club rental** $50 per set **Payment** All major credit cards accepted **Tee times** As soon as you have a booking at the resort **Facilities** Troon Golf Institute, full practice facility, restaurant, pro shop
Comments You must be a guest of the resort to play here. **Copperhead** is one of Florida's premier courses, you will find tight fairways lined by Spanish moss-draped trees, numerous bunkers (73 to be exact), a handful of water hazards, and swift greens to contend with. The course demands both strength and finesse; this is just sensational Florida golf.

If you are looking for a "resort course," then consider playing **Island**, which tends to be a more user-friendly layout (though not by much). Island is a fun course to play for all skill levels; however, as is the case with Copperhead, you need to have both your long as well as your short games working to score well here. The numerous hazards and dogleg holes require that you play very strategically.

Attractions

Clearwater Marine Aquarium

249 Windward Passage, Clearwater; (727) 447-0980; www.cmaquarium.org

Hours Monday–Friday, 9 a.m.–5 p.m.; Saturday, 9 a.m.–4 p.m.; Sunday, 11 a.m.–4 p.m.

Admission $8.75 for adults, $6.25 for children ages 3–11, free for children under age 3

Appeal by Age Group

Pre-school ★★★	Teens ★★★	Over 30 ★★★
Grade school ★★★★	Young Adults ★★★	Seniors ★★★★

Touring Time *Average* 2 hours; *minimum* 1 hour

Rainy-Day Touring Recommended

Author's Rating ★★★; a chance to see some serious work with marine life

Description and Comments This nonprofit center rescues, rehabilitates, and releases injured and sick marine mammals, including whales, dolphins, otters, and sea turtles. Handicapped animals are given a permanent home here.

Part of the aquarium's mission is to educate the public and foster conservation, so there are interactive displays like Stingray Beach, where you can touch stingrays, hermit crabs, snails, and starfish. There is also the Mangrove Seagrass Tank, a 55,000-gallon aquarium with a fish-eye view of more than 100 species of Florida fish and invertebrates, including trout, grouper, snook, snapper, and sharks.

The aquarium is on an island in Clearwater Bay, accessible by the Memorial Causeway.

Florida International Museum

261 Second Avenue North, St. Petersburg; (727) 822-3693 or (800) 777-9882; www.floridamuseum.org

Hours Monday–Saturday, 10 a.m. to 5 p.m.; Sunday, noon–5 p.m.; last tour starts at 4 p.m.

Admission $12 for adults, $11 for seniors ages 65 and older, $6 for students. Admission includes an audio-guided tour, two theater presentations, and access to the galleries.

Appeal by Age Group

Pre-school ★	Teens ★★★★	Over 30 ★★★★
Grade school ★★★	Young Adults ★★★★★	Seniors ★★★★

Touring Time *Average* 2 hours; *minimum* 1 hour

Rainy-Day Touring Recommended

Author's Rating ★★★★

Description and Comments Florida International Museum is home to the largest collection of private Kennedy artifacts in the world and is an affiliate of the Smithsonian museum. The many galleries re-create times and places lodged in our minds—from Kennedy's PT109 days to the Oval Office.

You'll see china from Air Force One, Kennedy's rocking chair, an Oleg Cassini dress of Jaqueline Kennedy's, and much more. There's also an interactive walk-through exhibit on the Cuban Missile Crisis, and traveling exhibits in conjunction with the Smithsonian.

> **A MUSEUM ROUTE**
>
> If you want to make a day of the wonderful museums in St. Petersburg, jump on the teal-colored trolley that runs through downtown St. Petersburg and includes stops at the Pier, Museum of History, Museum of Fine Arts, the Renaissance Vinoy Resort, Florida International Museum, Salvadore Dali Museum, Great Explorations Museum, Bayfront Hilton Hotel, and Beach Drive. Stops are marked by special pink Looper signs. The cost is a reasonable $1. The trolley runs daily, 11 a.m.–4:30 p.m., every half-hour on the hour; (727) 821-6164.

Great Explorations: The Hands-On Museum

1925 Fourth Street North, St. Petersburg; or The Pier, 800 Second Avenue Northeast, third floor, St. Petersburg; (727) 821-8992; www.greatexplorations.org

Hours Monday–Saturday, 10 a.m.–8 p.m.; Sunday, 11 a.m.–6 p.m.

Admission $4, ages 3 and under free

Appeal by Age Group

Pre-school ★★★★	Teens ★	Over 30 ★
Grade school ★★★	Young Adults ★	Seniors ★

Touring Time *Average* 2 hours; *minimum* 1½ hours

Rainy-Day Touring Recommended

Author's Rating ★★; make a pit stop here if you have little ones

Description and Comments Museum focuses on art, science, and health, with exhibits like a climbing wall, a raceway where you can build a tabletop race car, and a sailboat exhibit to learn about direction and air pressure.

Salvador Dali Museum

1000 Third Street, St. Petersburg; (727) 823-3767; www.salvadordalimuseum.org

Hours Monday–Saturday, 9:30 a.m.–5:30 p.m. (open until 8 p.m. Thursday); Sunday, noon–5:30 p.m.; closed Thanksgiving and Christmas

Admission $10 for adults, $7 for seniors, $5 for students with college ID, free for children ages 10 and under; free parking; Thursday 5–8 p.m. admission is $5 adults, $3.50 seniors, $2.50 students

Appeal by Age Group

Pre-school ★	Teens ★★	Over 30 ★★★★
Grade school ★★	Young Adults ★★★★★	Seniors ★★★★

Touring Time *Average* 2 hours; *minimum* 1 hour

Rainy-Day Touring Recommended

Author's Rating ★★★★; incredible, pack a lunch to enjoy near the harbor after your visit

Description and Comments Dali is more than melting clocks. True, his Persistence of Memory (1931) is still one of the best-known surrealist works. But although Dali is best known for his Surrealist period (1929–1940), this collection spanning 1914–1970 affords guests the opportunity to view the scope of his artistic ability and style. It's the world's largest collection of his work, valued at more than $125 million, housed in a renovated waterfront warehouse situated on Bayboro Harbor.

The collection includes 95 oils, 100 watercolors and drawings, nearly 1,300 graphics, plus sculptures, objets d'art, photographs, documents, and an extensive archival library.

Of the 18 of his "master works," six are in this museum. They include Hallucinogenic Toreador and Discovery of America by Christopher Columbus, and they are stunning. The docent tours are recommended.

Sunken Gardens

1825 Fourth Street North, St. Petersburg; (727) 551-3100; www.stpete.org/sunken.htm

Hours Wednesday–Sunday, 10 a.m.–4 p.m; closed Monday and Tuesday
Admission $7 for adults, $3 for children ages 3–12, $5 for seniors
Appeal by Age Group

Pre-school ★★	Teens ★★	Over 30 ★★★
Grade school ★★★	Young Adults ★★	Seniors ★★★

Touring Time *Average* 2 hours; *minimum* 2 hours
Rainy-Day Touring Not recommended
Author's Rating ★; the orchids here are phenomenal

Description and Comments An original roadside attraction in the 1930s that once boasted of its alligator wrestling show, Sunken Gardens has now become a true botanical garden after being purchased by the city of St. Petersburg.

Change is good—the acquisition resulted in an addition of 6,000 plants and a butterfly garden, as well as greatly reduced ticket prices. You'll also find more then 50,000 tropical plants and flowers, including more than 200 species blooming year-round at the six-acre garden. A walk-through aviary features tropical birds of all types, and thousands of rare, fragrant orchids are found in the Orchid Arbor.

ST. PETERSBURG PIER

The quarter-mile-long St. Petersburg Pier in Tampa Bay features an inverted five-story pyramid housing a festival marketplace with shops, restaurants, and a large observation area. On the second floor there is an aquarium, and on the fifth floor an observation deck. Rentals include skates, boats, and bikes. Family-oriented cruises and Duck Tours of Tampa bay (aboard a WWII amphibious vessel) depart from here as well. The Pier shops and restaurants are open daily, 10 a.m.–9 p.m. The pier is located at 800 Second Avenue, St. Petersburg; (727) 821-6164; **www.stpete-pier.com.**

Shopping

For mainstream shopping and dining, **BayWalk Entertainment Center** (153 Second Avenue North, St. Petersburg; (727) 895-9277; **www.stpete.org/baywalk.htm**) is a downtown hot spot. There are 15 shops, including Ann Taylor, Mephisto, Cricket Shop swimwear, seven restaurants, and a 20-screen Muvico theater.

Antique shoppers recommend **Gas Plant Antique Arcade** (1246 Central Avenue, St. Petersburg), the largest antiques mall on the west coast with more than 150 dealers. And they ship anywhere in the world. Nearby **Belleair Bluffs** (562–596 Indian Rocks Road; (727) 785-7242) is also known for antiques, with a cluster of 18 shops.

Tiny Gulfport has **Art Village** (Beach Boulevard South; (727) 321-7741), which has more than 40 galleries, studios, boutiques, and restaurants all within walking distance in a pedestrian-friendly historic district. Other off-the-beaten-path shopping districts are in historic **downtown Dunedin,** and **John's Pass Village** and **Boardwalk** in Madeira Beach.

Flea Market **Wagon Wheel Flea Market** (7801 74th Street, Pinellas Park; (727) 544-5319) has more than 2,000 vendors on more than 125 acres in the middle of the St. Petersburg/Clearwater area.

Further afield is the **Webster Flea Market,** one of the largest flea markets in the Southeast. Central Floridians take off Mondays to spend the day here. Started in 1937 as a one-shed farmer's produce, it now includes nearly 2,000 vendors with everything from produce and homemade sausage to antiques. The market is open Mondays only, 6 a.m.–1:30 p.m., and is located at Route 478 and Northwest Third Street in Webster; (352) 793-9877.

HOME SHOPPING NETWORK STUDIO TOURS

Fans of this cultural phenomenon line up for tours of the worldwide headquarters and studio. Forty-five minute tours are Tuesday through Friday starting at 2 p.m. You must have a reservation; call (727) 872-1000.

Dining

Bob Heilman's Beachcomber

447 Mandalay Avenue, Clearwater Beach; (727) 442-4144

Meals served Lunch and dinner **Cuisine** American **Entree range** Lunch, $7–$13; dinner, $12–$26 **Reservations** Recommended **Payment** All major credit cards accepted

Comments In business since 1948, the Beachcomber serves freshly caught seafood; but for a down-home dinner, try their Back-to-the-Farm chicken, sautéed in a Dutch oven skillet and served with potatoes, gravy, vegetable, soup, coleslaw, and fresh bread. The wine list is named one of Florida's Top 10 by *Wine Spectator* magazine.

Domenic's Capri

411 Mandalay Avenue, Clearwater Beach; (727) 441-1111

Meals served Dinner nightly except Tuesday **Cuisine** Italian **Entree range** $15–$28 **Reservations** Accepted **Payment** V, MC, AmEx, DC
Comments Chef/owner Domenic Forlini welcomes his guests like family. Cuisine is classic Italian, from osso buco to homemade ravioli and linguine with clam sauce. And there's a solid wine list to match the cuisine.

Frenchy's Rockaway Grill

7 Rockaway Street, Clearwater Beach; (727) 446-4844; frenchysonline.com

Meals served Lunch and dinner **Cuisine** American, seafood **Entree range** $11–$14 **Reservations** Not accepted **Payment** V, MC, AmEx
Comments Frenchy's is an institution in Clearwater Beach, with its own fleet of boats and a to-die-for grouper sandwich that covers a plate (fried is best, but you can order it blackened or grilled). Dine inside or out.

Guppy's

1701 Gulf Boulevard, Indian Rocks Beach; (727) 593-2032

Meals served Lunch and dinner **Cuisine** Seafood **Entree range** $7–$22 **Reservations** Only for parties of six or more **Payment** All major credit cards accepted
Comments This casual oceanfront is often crowded and noisy, but there's a great view of the sunset restaurant and you can dine indoors or on the patio. Try the potato-crusted salmon in leek-and-garlic sauce.

Island Way Grill

20 Island Way, Clearwater Beach; (727) 461-6617

Meals served Dinner daily, lunch on Sunday **Cuisine** Seafood, steaks **Entree range** $9–$36 **Reservations** Accepted **Payment** All credit cards accepted
Comments Though this seafood and steakhouse on Mandalay Bay Lagoon has close to 500 seats and includes a large deck next to the water, it's often tough to get a table, so call ahead for reservations. Delicious creations include wok-fried soft-shell crabs, meatloaf and wasabi mashed potatoes, and tataki filet drizzled with chimichurri sauce. Save room for the chocolate lava cake. A beautiful setting and the artwork of Tampa artist Duncan McClellan create a casual-yet-upscale dining experience.

Ted Peters Famous Smoked Fish

1350 Pasadena Avenue, Pasadena (adjacent to St. Petersburg Beach); (727) 381-7931

Meals served Lunch and dinner daily except Tuesday **Cuisine** Seafood, steaks **Entree range** $7–$16 lunch, $11–$16 dinner **Reservations** No **Payment** Cash only
Comments For more than half a century, this laid-back, open-air eatery has been cooking fresh catches for fishermen (and women). The restaurant

St. Petersburg and Clearwater 335

uses red oak to smoke mullet and other fish in a smoker—a true taste of Florida cracker cuisine.

Arts and Culture

Along with the Salvador Dali Museum (page 331), St. Petersburg is home to **Florida International Museum** (100 Second Street North, St. Petersburg; (727) 822-3693), an affiliate of the Smithsonian Institution, with two permanent exhibitions: The Kennedy Collection and The Cuban Missile Crisis. Also in St. Pete are the **Florida Holocaust Museum** (55 Fifth Street South, St. Petersburg; (727) 820-0100; www.flholocaustmuseum.org); the **Museum of Fine Arts** (255 Beach Drive Northeast; (727) 896-2667; www.fine-arts.org), with pieces by Monet, Renoir, and O'Keeffe; and the **St. Petersburg Museum of History** (335 Second Avenue Northeast, St. Petersburg; (727) 894-1052; www.museumofhistoryonline.org), with a permanent exhibition of St. Petersburg's history.

Nightlife

BayWalk

Who goes there mainstream tourists of all ages, some locals

Second Avenue North between First and Second Streets North, St. Petersburg; (727) 384-6000

Cover No **Minimum** No **Mixed drinks** $3 and up **Food available** Full menus in several restaurants **Hours** 10 a.m.–2 a.m.

What goes on Shopping, dining, and movies, day and night.

Comments Clubs at Baywalk include Wet Willie's, an open-air daiquiri bar specializing in frozen drinks with a dance floor, and The Martini Bar, a sophisticated club with live music and a variety of martinis and other drinks.

Chic a Boom Room

Who goes there 30-something crowd, from sports fans to martini drinkers

319 Main Street, Dunedin; (727) 736-0206; www.thechicaboomroom.com

Cover No, except for big events about four times a year **Minimum** 21 and older **Mixed drinks** $3.75 and up **Food available** Limited menu, free buffet from 5–8 p.m. **Hours** 11 a.m.–midnight

What goes on Chic a Boom Room features music and occasional concerts. Big events include wide-screen TV parties to cheer the Tampa Bay Bucs.

Comments The specialty is martinis, with more than 20 varieties. The bar also has a *Wine Spectator* award for its solid wine list.

Coliseum Ballroom

Who goes there Serious dancers, mostly the over-50 crowd

534 Fourth Avenue North, St. Petersburg; (727) 892-5202

Cover Varies with special events **Minimum** No **Mixed drinks** No, some events are BYOB **Food available** No **Hours** Varies with special events

What goes on Highlights include a bi-weekly Big Band Ballroom Series held January through March, and tributes to the Andrews Sisters. Other popular dance events include the Summer Swing Series, the '50s Sock Hop, and country-and-western theme nights.
Comments Since the 1920s the beautiful Coliseum has hosted big bands, classical orchestras, and rock bands—and it was in the ballroom scene in the movie "Cocoon."

Gators Café & Saloon

Who goes there Sports and music fans

12754 Kingfish Drive, Treasure Island; (727) 367-8951

Cover No **Minimum** No **Mixed drinks** $4 and up **Food available** Full menu **Hours** 8 a.m–2 a.m.
What goes on There's live entertainment seven days a week, and 35 TVs for sports fans.
Comments Home of the "World's Longest Waterfront Bar," Gators has seven different rooms: the nonsmoking Mahogany Sports Bar, the Saloon overlooking John's Pass, the downstairs Main Bar, the Tiki Deck, the Swamp Restaurant & Sports Bar, the Bungalow Room, and the Gator Tower.

Hurricane's

Who goes there Anyone who wants to watch the sunset

807 Gulf Way, Pass-A-Grille; (727) 360-9558; www.thehurricane.com

Cover No **Minimum** No **Mixed drinks** $2.75 and up **Food available** Full menu **Hours** 8 a.m–1:30 a.m.
What goes on With seating for more than 400, this casual seafood restaurant is one of the best places to sip a drink and catch the sunset from the top floor's open deck overlooking the Gulf.
Comments Bruno, one of the owners, is a local sea turtle expert who regales guests with stories during cocktail hour. And they serve a fine grouper sandwich.

Marchand Bar at the Renaissance Vinoy

Who goes there Older, well-dressed crowd

501 Fifth Avenue Northeast, St. Petersburg; (727) 894-1000

Cover No **Minimum** No **Mixed drinks** $4 and up **Food available** Limited menu; full menu in the adjoining restaurant **Hours** 4 p.m.–midnight
What goes on A sophisticated crowd congregates at this beautiful old bar in a showplace hotel, the polished glamour of another era.
Comments This is great place to meet for drinks and quiet conversation.

Side Trips

Tarpon Springs About eight miles north of Clearwater, the music, sights, and sounds of Tarpon Springs recall a village on the Mediterranean. The heritage is Greek, and the language is still spoken here by many of the residents.

Tarpon Springs was known as "America's Sponge Capital" at the turn of the century, after a man named John Cocoris brought Greek sponge divers from Key West to settle this area because of the rich and sizable sponge beds in the Gulf of Mexico. In the 1930s and 1940s the industry prospered, until bacteria destroyed most of the sponge beds in the 1940s.

Today tourism and fishing are the major industries. The historic downtown of six waterfront blocks and alleys along the Anclote River includes Dodecanese Boulevard, where you can stroll among the heaps of harvested sponges (you can still buy them in local shops) and sample authentic Greek cuisine at one of the many restaurants—we recommend the family-run **Louis Pappas' Riverside Restaurant,** at 10 West Dodecanese Boulevard since 1925. The old Sponge Exchange has been converted into a shopping and dining district featuring Greek foods and handicrafts. And for antiques, locals head to Tarpon Avenue to browse the shops.

To learn more about the sponge diving and the Greek community, visit the free **Spongeorama** museum housed in an old sponge factory. A half-hour film is shown, and many tools, diving suits, and other equipment used by early divers are on display. Located at 510 Dodecanese Boulevard, Tarpon Springs; (727) 938-5366.

Weeki Wachee We imagine that most parents who visited Florida when they were young have fond memories of the amazing mermaids at Weeki Wachee. Today, children are still amazed by their ability to perform 12 feet under water.

The mermaid show has been a Weeki Wachee trademark of long-running distinction. You watch from a spacious theater facing a bank of large plate glass windows. As the show begins, visitors find themselves peering into the depths of the dazzling Weeki Wachee Spring, alive with verdant flora and brimming with marine life. Against the incomparable background a graceful and lively water ballet is performed. The performance is well paced, combining music, elaborate props, imaginative costuming, and a little melodrama for a visually rich experience.

Outdoor attractions include a narrated Wilderness River Cruise to a refuge where injured birds are nursed back to health. Young children will enjoy the Animal Forest Petting Zoo, where they can touch the llamas, goats, and other small animals.

Weeki Wachee is about a three-hour experience. And it's fun even in the rain. Admission is $19 for adults, $15 for children ages 3–10. Weeki Wachee is open year-round 10 a.m.–4 p.m. The park is located at US 19 and SR 50, 27 miles north of Tarpon Springs; (352) 596-2062.

Sarasota and Longboat Key

After you've conquered all the museums and roller coasters, expect the pace to slow down some here. Many families come here to relax on the beautiful barrier islands, with white sand, blue-green ocean, and 35 miles of beaches. About 65 miles south of Tampa, Sarasota is arguably the most cultured city on the Gulf, home to artists and artisans of every stripe.

The area is refined and sophisticated, with upscale shopping and gourmet restaurants on St. Armands Circle, as well as high-priced oceanfront resorts.

Golf

Longboat Key Club Islandside Course

301 Gulf of Mexico Drive, Longboat Key; (941) 387-1632; www.longboatkeyclub.com

Established Early 1960s | **Holes** 18 (two 9-hole combos)

Tees Back/Red and White/White and Blue /Blue and Red
Par 72/72/72/72 **Slope** 132/131/132/130
Fees $140 January–April; $78 May–December
Specials Call for afternoon rates **Cart rental** Included in green fees **Club rental** $55 per set January–April; $35 per set May–December **Payment** Greens fees and club rentals must be billed to room (other purchases in Pro Shop can be made using credit cards) **Tee times** 48 hours in advance **Facilities** Full practice facilities, pro shop, restaurant

Comments This course, located near the Gulf of Mexico, features magnificent views of Sarasota Bay. Situated in a spectacular tropical setting, this course boasts a superb combination of visual appeal and physical challenge. The most pervasive hazards come in the form of water, a lot of water. In fact, water comes into play on every single hole.

Attractions

Marie Selby Botanical Gardens

811 South Palm Avenue, Sarasota; (941) 366-5731 or 366-5730; www.selby.org

Hours Daily, 10 a.m.–5 p.m., except Christmas
Admission $10 for adults, $5 for children ages 6–11
Appeal by Age Group

Pre-school ★	Teens ★	Over 30 ★★★
Grade school ★★	Young Adults ★★	Seniors ★★★★

Touring Time *Average* 3 hours; *minimum* 1½ hour
Rainy-Day Touring Not recommended
Author's Rating ★★★★; beautiful orchids
Description and Comments What began as a pastime for amateur horticulturist Marie Selby has grown into a luxurious tropical garden—an open-air and under-glass museum of more than 20,000 colorful plants.

Sarasota

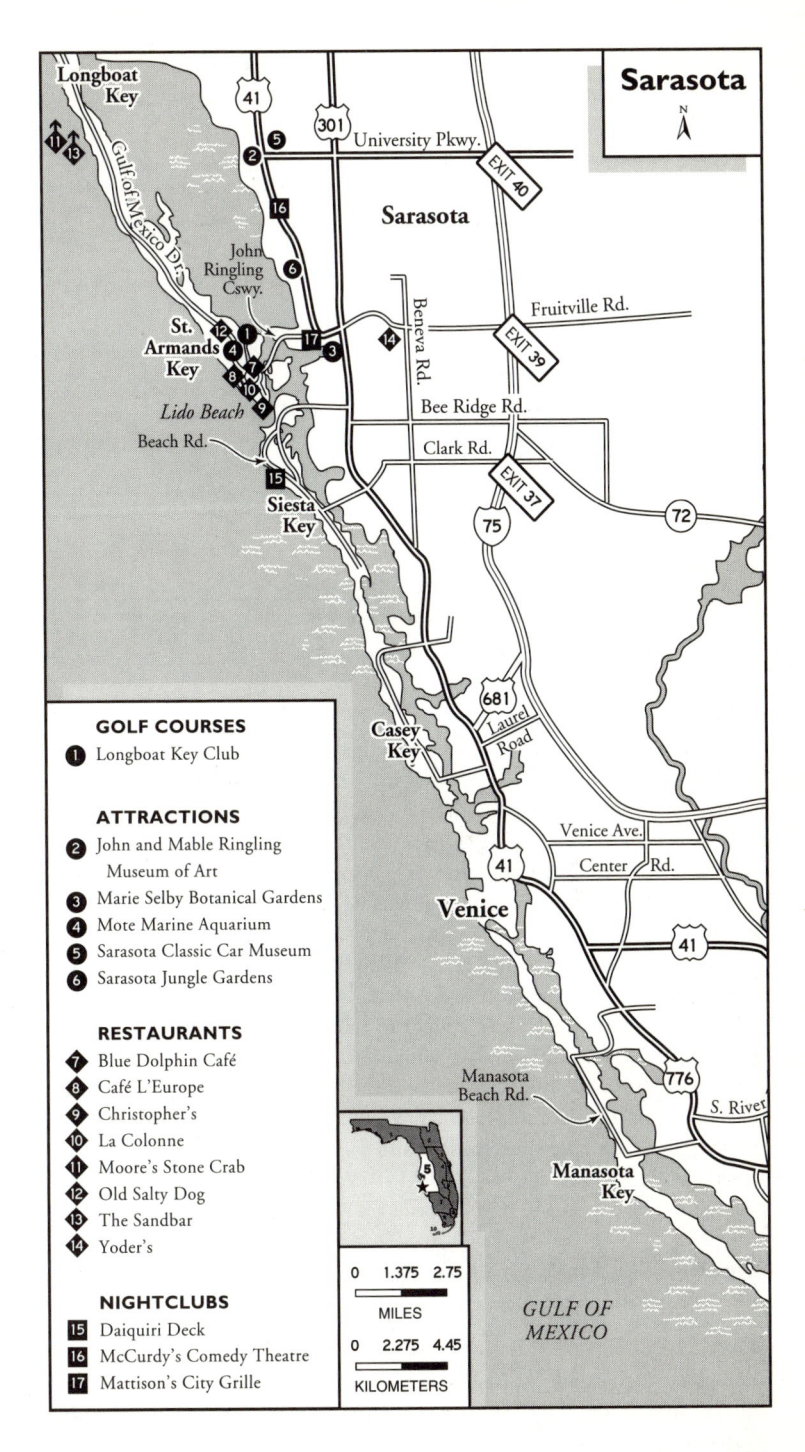

N

GOLF COURSES
1. Longboat Key Club

ATTRACTIONS
2. John and Mable Ringling Museum of Art
3. Marie Selby Botanical Gardens
4. Mote Marine Aquarium
5. Sarasota Classic Car Museum
6. Sarasota Jungle Gardens

RESTAURANTS
7. Blue Dolphin Café
8. Café L'Europe
9. Christopher's
10. La Colonne
11. Moore's Stone Crab
12. Old Salty Dog
13. The Sandbar
14. Yoder's

NIGHTCLUBS
15. Daiquiri Deck
16. McCurdy's Comedy Theatre
17. Mattison's City Grille

339

The focus is on tropical plants, with an emphasis on epiphytic plants, commonly known as "air plants," like delicate orchids, pineapples, and ferns. The garden's 6,000 orchids are stunning.

The Tropical Display House has the most concentrated collection of epiphytic plants in the United States in a rainforest setting. Torch ginger from Indonesia, colorful bromeliads from the Amazon, the vanilla orchid from Mexico, and others thrive in this fragrant greenhouse.

In all, there are 14 garden areas along Sarasota Bay, as well as a historic mansion that showcases art and photography.

Mote Marine Aquarium

600 Ken Thompson Parkway, Sarasota (between Lido and Longboat Keys); (800) 691-MOTE or (941) 388-2451; www.mote.org

Hours Daily, 10 a.m.–5 p.m.
Admission $12 for adults, $8 for children ages 4–12
Appeal by Age Group

Pre-school ★★★	Teens ★★★	Over 30 ★★★
Grade school ★★★	Young Adults ★★★	Seniors ★★★

Touring Time *Average* 2 hours; *minimum* 1½ hours
Rainy-Day Touring Recommended
Author's Rating ★★★; just the right size to be fun
Description and Comments As you wander through the aquarium, photos and text explain the serious research happening here every day, and now guests can peek into the aquarium's research labs to find more scientists hard at work, studying the sharks, sea turtles, seahorses, and more.

A short walk from the aquarium is the Marine Mammal Visitor Center, home to the manatees born in captivity at the Miami Seaquarium, now permanent residents at Mote. Sick and injured marine mammals recover here, and you can view their 52,000-gallon home through windows and on TV monitors. Injured sea turtles are rehabilitated nearby.

If your children really want a night to remember, plan your trip so they participate in the Mote overnight programs. They'll learn about shark tagging, shark teeth, and more. When bedtime arrives, they snuggle up next to the shark tank. There's also Moonlight with the Manatees, an overnight with resident manatees Hugh and Buffett, and Twilight with the Turtles. Contact the education division at (941) 388-4441 ext. 229 for information on these programs. The cost is $40 for children ages 7–12.

The Ringling Museum of Sarasota

5401 Bayshore Drive, Sarasota; (941) 359-5700; www.ringling.org

Hours Daily, 10 a.m.–5:30 p.m., except holidays
Admission $15 for adults, $12 for senior citizens age 55 and older, free for children under age 12. The art museum is free on Saturdays except the weekend of the Medieval Fair.

Appeal by Age Group

Pre-school ★	Teens ★★★	Over 30 ★★★
Grade school ★★★	Young Adults ★★★	Seniors ★★★★

Touring Time *Average* 3 hours; *minimum* 1½ hours

Rainy-Day Touring Recommended

Author's Rating ★★; great for rainy days; kids especially enjoy the circus museum

Description and Comments The Ringling Museums of Sarasota consist of John and Mable Ringling Museum of Art, John Ringling Ca' d'Zan mansion, the Museum of the Circus, the Asolo Theater, and 86 acres of grounds, all owned and operated by the state of Florida.

The building that houses the celebrated Ringling Museum of Art is as grand as the priceless art that graces its walls. An enormous, detailed duplication of a classic Italian villa of the fifteenth century, the museum's external facade is plain and inauspicious. Stepping through the entrance into the internal courtyard with its reflection pool, graceful statuary, and manicured formal gardens, you're launched on an odyssey in time and beauty. The gardens are surrounded on three sides by long rows of the delicately rounded arches of the museum's colonnades and on the fourth side by a Roman bridge from which a gigantic bronze cast of Michelangelo's David surveys a profusion of columns, sculptures, fountains, pools, and Italian oil pots.

The Museum of Art consists of 20 galleries in the original building plus a contemporary art gallery that is an extension of the museum's south wing. The Ringling art collection, with more than 250 paintings and other objects of art on display, is one of the world's largest collections of Baroque, Italian, and Flemish Renaissance and Old Master paintings.

Several hundred yards west of the museum, on Sarasota Bay, is Cà d'Zan (House of John in the Venetian dialect), the Ringling mansion that dazzles after a six-year, $15-million restoration. Patterned after the Doge's Palace in Venice, the 32-room mansion was built at a cost of $1.5 million in the 1920s. You can tour the residence on your own or take a 40-minute narrated tour.

The Museum of the Circus is a short walk north of the art museum and houses a fantastic collection of circus memorabilia. Most of the museum is devoted to the American circus with emphasis on The Greatest Show on Earth. The crown jewel is the "backyard," a full-scale re-creation of the circus back lot in the heyday of The Greatest Show on Earth.

The Asolo Theater is a 200-seat, horseshoe-shaped playhouse for opera, classical, and modern plays, and a year-round program of films, lectures, concerts, and recitals.

Sarasota Classic Car Museum

5500 North Tamiami Trail, Sarasota; (941) 355-6228

Hours Daily, 9 a.m.–6 p.m.

Admission $8.50 for adults, $7.65 for seniors ages 65 and older, $4 for ages 6–12, free for ages 6 and under

Appeal by Age Group

Pre-school ★★	Teens ★★	Over 30 ★★★
Grade school ★★	Young Adults ★★★	Seniors ★★★★

Touring Time *Average* 1½ hours; *minimum* 1 hour
Rainy-Day Touring Recommended
Author's Rating ★★; car buffs will enjoy the museum; kids love the music room and arcade
Description and Comments In the late 1990s, this museum was totally overhauled and dozens of cars were added to the collection of classic and antique cars. The collection includes several celebrated vintage models of Rolls-Royce and Pierce Arrows, rare antiques such as the 1930 Ruxton and the 1948 Tucker, and, wonderfully, the cars of almost everyone's youth, from Model A's to '57 Fords to '63 VWs.

A second room of football-field dimensions displays one of the world's largest collection of mechanical musical devices, everything from hurdy-gurdies to player pianos to calliopes. Access is by guided tour only, and the guide demonstrates many of the fascinating devices. The size of the collection is mind boggling, but not more so than the inventiveness of the antique machines.

Supplementing the two main museums is an extensive collection of antique penny arcade pieces that you can play.

Sarasota Jungle Gardens

3701 Bayshore Road, Sarasota; (941) 355-5305; www.sarasotajunglegardens.com
Hours Daily, 9 a.m.–5 p.m.
Admission $10 for adults, $9 for seniors ages 62 and older, $6 for children ages 3–12

Appeal by Age Group

Pre-school ★★★	Teens ★★	Over 30 ★★
Grade school ★★★	Young Adults ★★	Seniors ★★

Touring Time *Average* 2 hours; *minimum* 1 hour
Rainy-Day Touring Not recommended
Author's Rating ★★; old-fashioned fun

Description and Comments Tucked away in a Sarasota residential area, Sarasota Jungle Gardens is an artful blend of beauty, education, and showmanship. Central to the attraction is the Jungle Garden, a series of beautiful winding trails spread over ten acres of sparkling lakes and sunny greens. Manicured, planned landscapes and naturally occurring tropical hammock are integrated so skillfully that you can pass from one to the other and never sense the transition. Macaws, cockatoos, flamingos, and peacocks lend living color to the garden while leopards, monkeys, and otters add a touch of excitement. Shady resting spots are plentiful along the trails.

Two shows are offered several times each day in a roofed amphitheater. A colorful platoon of feathery performers work through a well-paced and imaginative routine in the bird show. And snakes and alligators are the stars in the reptile show, a straightforward and understandable presentation. Each show lasts about 25 minutes.

Smaller exhibits consist of a nice petting zoo and playground, and a sculptural oddity called the Gardens of Christ. This latter, tucked away next to the reptile show, consists of eight hand-carved religious dioramas depicting the life of Christ.

Shopping

Tops for shopping is **St. Armands Circle,** a busy, upscale retail roundabout with more than 150 shops, galleries, and restaurants just minutes from the beach—much more appealing than a trip to the mall. The circle is divided into four quadrants, identified by color banners—purple, pink, aqua, and gold—on the lamp posts.

There are more than two dozen clothing shops, everything from national retailers like Tommy Bahama and Chico's to small boutiques. Shoe stores, galleries, more than a dozen jewelers and two dozen gift shops make this a full-day excursion for shopaholics. Some favorites: **Chappy** for Lily Pulitzer designs, **Yves Delorme** for divine linens, **Global Navigator** for Tilley hats, and **Wet Noses** for pampered pooch accessories. Galleries range from **Sage Spirit** with handmade Native American creations to contemporary art at **Perry Sherwood Gallery** and marine sculptures at **Wyland Gallery.**

Restaurants dot the circle, along with four ice-cream shops; and for to-die-for fudge (made right in the window), stop in **Kilwin's.** If street parking is hard to find, there are some off-the-circle lot (one is behind The Met at 35 South Boulevard of the Presidents). Shop hours are 9:30 a.m.–5:30 p.m. Monday through Saturday.

Between Tampa and Sarasota in Ellenton, **Prime Outlets** (5461 Factory Shops Boulevard; (941) 723-1150; **www.primeoutlets.com**) draws a crowd with off-price shops for Coach, Movado, Bombay Company, Banana Republic, Brooks Brothers, Nike, Versace, and other high-end retailers.

Downtown Sarasota (**www.downtownsarasota.com**) offers a compact shopping district at historic Palm Avenue and Main Street, with sidewalk cafés and stores for about ten blocks from the bayfront to the county courthouse. Favorites include **Toy Lab** (1529 Main Street), **Gallerie des Artes** (1516 Main Street), **Main Bookshop** (1962 Main Street), **Living Walls Furniture and Design** (1311 Main Street) and **Ma Petite Amie** (1505 Main Street). **The Gourmet Market** (1469 Main Street) is a great place to pick up food for an impromptu picnic in Bayfront Park.

If you need a conventional mall, **Sarasota Square Mall** (8201 South Tamiami Trail; (941) 922-9600) has Burdines, Dillard's, JC Penney, Sears, and Gap.

ALBRITTON FRUIT COMPANY TROLLEY TOUR

Get to know Florida's history by touring 1,000 acres of citrus groves, plus fruit-packing and juicing facilities. You'll even see how the juice is squeezed and bottled. After the tour, stop by the original grove store, which opened in 1948. Tours are available at 10 a.m. and 3 p.m. on Thursdays only; call for reservations. Located at 5947 Clark Center Avenue; (941) 923-2573.

Dining

Blue Dolphin Café

312 John Ringling Boulevard, St. Armands Circle, Sarasota; (941) 388-3566

Cuisine American **Meals served** Breakfast and Lunch only (until 3 p.m.) **Entree range** $7–$8 **Reservations** Only for large groups **Payment** All major credit cards accepted

Comments A hot spot for breakfast. Their most popular creation is the spinach and feta omelette, but they'll make an egg sandwich on any type of bread or bagel. For lunch, it's sandwiches, burgers and wraps, including "The Surfer," a gargantuan burger.

Café L'Europe

431 St. Armands Circle, Sarasota; (941) 388-4415

Cuisine New European **Entree range** $19–$37 **Reservations** Accepted **Payment** All major credit cards accepted

Comments This elegant restaurant has been a mainstay on St. Armands Circle for decades, with gracious, formal service and delicious creations from a simple Dover sole with tarragon butter, to a rich veal Oscar with jumbo lump crab.

Christopher's

700 Ben Franklin Drive, Lido Key; (941) 388-5608

Meals served Dinner **Cuisine** Continental **Entree range** $16–$24 **Reservations** Recommended **Payment** All credit cards

Comments High atop the Radisson, Christopher's has great views of the Gulf and Sarasota's skyline. The eclectic menu ranges from Chateaubriand to seared tuna in tomato and ancho chili puree.

La Colonne

22 South Boulevard of the Presidents, St. Armands Circle, Sarasota; (941) 388-4348

Meals served Lunch and dinner **Cuisine** Italian **Entree range** $18–$21 **Reservations** Accepted **Payment** All major credit cards accepted

Commentos All pastas are handmade here. Osso buco is the specialty, and other favorites are Lobster stuffed ravioli, Grilled veal chop in Bordeaux wine with Portobello mushrooms and tomatoes, Sea Bass with ginger lemon sauce. Tiramisu, Canneloni, and cheesecake are popular desserts.

Moore's Stone Crab

800 Broadway, Long Boat Key; (941) 383-1748

Meals served Lunch and dinner **Cuisine** Seafood, American **Entree range** $6–$42 **Reservations** Not accepted **Payment** V, MC, AmEx, D

Comments Moore's boats work the traps from October to May to bring in the freshest crabs around. A day's catch runs from 500 to 600 pounds of claws. During stone crab season, close to 50,000 pounds of claws are served. Owned by the same family since the 1960s, this casual waterfront eatery is popular with the locals.

Old Salty Dog

1601 Ken Thompson Parkway, Sarasota; (941) 388-4311;
5023 Ocean Boulevard; Siesta Key Village (941) 349-0158

Meals served Lunch and dinner **Cuisine** American, seafood **Entree range** $4–$10 **Reservations** Not accepted **Payment** V, MC

Comments Service is fast, it's casual, and you can sit outside on the waterfront at both locations. Everyone goes for the fried grouper sandwich, the famous "Salty Dog" hot dogs, and British ales.

The Sandbar

100 Spring Avenue, Ana Maria; (941) 778-0444

Meals served Lunch and dinner **Cuisine** American, seafood **Entree range** $7–$20 **Reservations** Preferred seating available **Payment** All major credit cards accepted

Comments The menu is diverse, and you can't beat the oceanfront setting. Regulars recommend the pasta specialties and giant salads. Try the fresh fish, conch fritters, and conch chowder.

Yoder's

3434 Bahia Vista, Sarasota; (941) 955-7771

Meals served Breakfast, lunch, and dinner **Cuisine** Amish **Entree range** $6–$12 **Reservations** Not accepted **Payment** No credit cards (ATM available in dining room)

Comments Stop here for breakfast, lunch, or dinner—you can't go wrong with Yoder's Amish home cooking. It's the type of place that serves the daily specials locals look forward to—especially Thursday's scalloped potatoes with ham and Friday's cabbage rolls. Don't leave without trying the pie, made fresh every morning. Choose from chocolate peanut butter, coconut cream, strawberry, Key lime, pumpkin, blueberry, and more. On Thanksgiving Day, they sell close to 2,000 pies.

Nightlife

Daiquiri Deck

Who goes there Mostly tourists, but locals also

Siesta Key Village, 5250 Ocean Boulevard; (941) 349-8697; www.daiquirideckgrill.com

Cover No **Minimum** No **Mixed drinks** $4 and up, daiquiris are the specialty **Food available** Full menu **Hours** 11 a.m.–2 a.m.

What goes on This tourist-friendly bar specializes in daiquiris, with 15 flavors. Happy hour runs 3–7 p.m., and sports dominate the big-screen TVs.

Comments Lunch, dinner, late-night food are served.

McCurdy's Comedy Theatre

Who goes there Over-18 crowd, all ages who want to be entertained

3333 North Tamiami Trail; (941) 925-3869; www.mccurdyscomedy.com

Cover Varies with entertainment, $6–$12 **Minimum** Must be 18 **Mixed drinks** $4 and up **Food available** Light snack menu **Hours** Shows 7:30 p.m. and 9:45 p.m. Wednesday through Sunday nights

What goes on This cozy venue has hosted nationally known comedians like Richard Lewis, Jeff Foxworthy, Judy Tenuda, Chris Rock, and others.

Comments Larry the Cable Guy is a popular regular.

Mattison's City Grille

Who goes there 30-something and older, jazz aficionados

1 North Lemon Avenue, Sarasota; (941) 330-0440; www.mattisons.com

Cover No **Minimum** No **Mixed drinks** Beer and wine only **Food available** Light fare, tapas, pizza, burgers **Hours** 11 a.m.–11 p.m. Monday through Thursday, open until midnight on Friday and Saturday

What goes on Live jazz is performed nightly after 6 p.m. in the lounge.

Comments You can sit outside or in the lounge at this bar and grill.

Part Seven

The Gold and Treasure Coasts: Vero Beach, Palm Beach, and Greater Fort Lauderdale

Welcome to the Gold and Treasure Coasts

Originally dubbed the Gold and Treasure Coasts for tales of sunken treasure from shipwrecks along the rocky shore, today wealthy, cosmopolitan cities like Palm Beach, Boca Raton and Fort Lauderdale give a whole new meaning to the region's monikers. The Treasure Coasts stretches from Sebastian Inlet south to Jupiter Inlet; the Gold Coast, extends from north of West Palm Beach south to Miami. Traveling south, major stops in the region include Vero Beach, Fort Pierce, Boca Raton, and Fort Lauderdale.

Sebastian Inlet straddles Brevard and Indian River Counties and is a favorite with surfers, as well as a haven for saltwater-fishing enthusiast, where lucky anglers hook snook, redfish, bluefish, and Spanish mackerel from the jetties and bridge catwalks.

Fort Pierce, named for a military post built during the Second Seminole War, offers little to do on the mainland but beautiful barrier islands reached via two causeways across the Intracoastal Waterway.

Orlando may have the theme parks, and Miami the club scene, but this stretch of beach is famous for what it doesn't have: smog, traffic, congestion, and long lines. Indian River County is known for its oranges and grapefruit. The beaches are beautiful, and Vero Beach itself is known as a charming resort community with shopping, restaurants, and Dodgertown, spring training home of the Los Angeles Dodgers.

Affluent Palm Beach County has close to 150 golf courses as well as the Palm Beach Polo & Country Club, where Princes Charles has played. In the resort town of Boca Raton, polo and tennis are the favorite ways to while away the time. Much of Boca's handsome, 1920s Spanish-style architecture is the work of noted architect Addison Mizner.

Palm Beach's Trendy Worth Avenue, is a delightful corridor of tiles, staircases, sculptures, archways and hidden lanes lined with some 200 boutiques and charming, intimate restaurants. Cultural attractions include the Kravis Center, the Norton Museum, and the original mansion of Henry Flagler.

If you want to live in the same high style for a while, The Breakers in Palm Beach and the Boca Raton Hotel and Resort are two elegant old hotels, each redone at a tremendous cost. If you just want to look the part, Palm Beach thrift shops are the way to go, offering last year's designer outfits are at garage-sale prices.

Fort Lauderdale is glam in a more sedate way than nearby Miami, with trendy hotels, a thriving art scene and multi-million dollar mansions along the waterways. Broward County—now often synonymous with "Greater Fort Lauderdale"—stretches 23 miles along the Atlantic Ocean between Palm Beach County and Miami-Dade County. Broward's western boundary is 505,600 acres of the Everglades (occupying about two-thirds of the county). In all, the county encompasses 1,197 square miles.

The Fort Lauderdale area is also a haven for golfers, with more than 50 affordable courses, including municipal, public, semi-private, and private, and various nighttime driving ranges. Boaters enjoy the criss-crossed canals of the Intracoastal Waterway.

HIGHLIGHTS

- Arriving via water taxi to Fort Lauderdale's Riverwalk area for dinner and a performance at the Broward Center for the Performing Arts.
- Morikami Museum and Japanese Gardens west of Delray Beach.
- Sunday brunch at The Breakers in Palm Beach, followed by a drive past the oceanside mansions, then window shopping along Worth Avenue.
- John D. MacArthur Beach State Park on the north end of Singer Island in Palm Beach County.
- A turtle walk on Hutchison Island (May through August).

A Brief History

The earliest settlers in Southeast Florida were migratory Native Americans drawn to the region 10,000 years ago, like many since, by warm weather and good fishing. From hunter-gather tribes, there developed towns and, ultimately, societies, the remnants of which—pottery, burial mounds—await curious contemporary visitors.

The demographic mix and cultural identity of South Florida was changed forever with the arrival of one sixteenth-century Spanish immigrant. Ponce de Leon never found the Fountain of Youth, but he did claim what is now South Florida for Spain, in 1521 (on his second voyage to Florida). Wounded by Native Americans shortly after arriving, he and his expedition withdrew and sailed for Cuba (where he died shortly after landing).

Spanish settlement and political rule continued in Florida for 300 years, until the young United States bought the territory of Florida from Spain in 1821. The First Seminole War (1816–1818) prompted the acquisition. The Seminoles (literally "separatists") retreated from Georgia to the wilds of Florida in the eighteenth century. Two more wars followed, fought largely in South Florida and the Everglades, before most remaining Seminoles were resettled in the West.

Palm Beach County's high-brow image got its start in the late 1800s when Henry Morrison Flagler built the legendary Breakers and Royal Poinciana hotels. Today, you still can visit his lavish home and hop aboard his rail car at the Flagler Museum (see page 369).

Visiting the Gold and Treasure Coasts

Gathering Information

Indian River County Chamber of Commerce, 1216 21st Street, Vero Beach 32960; (772) 567-3491; www.indianriverchamber.com.

Palm Beach County Convention and Visitors Bureau, 1555 Palm Beach Lakes Boulevard, Suite 204, West Palm Beach 33401; (561) 233-3000; fax (561) 471-3900; www.palmbeachfl.com (request the coupon book "$1,000 Worth of the Palm Beaches for Free" to save on many dining, shopping, sight-seeing, and sports attractions).

Greater Fort Lauderdale Convention & Visitors Bureau, 19850 Eller Drive, Suite 303, Fort Lauderdale 33316; (800) 22-SUNNY ext. 711 (in U.S. and Canada); www.sunny.org (available information includes a free CD-ROM about local dive sites).

Getting There

By Plane Palm Beach International Airport (PBI) is a three-level modern facility three miles west of West Palm Beach with all the amenities of other large city airports, and it's serviced by most major airlines. The international status is primarily because of flights to the Bahamas, but the newest landing strip expansion and new direct highway connections from I-95 should lure more international airlines. Southwest Airlines, JetBlue, and Delta Express offer service. Rental car agencies have desks conveniently located in the luggage retrieval area. For more information, call (561) 471-7400.

The Fort Lauderdale/Hollywood International Airport (phone (954) 359-6100) is located between I-95 on the east and US 1 on the west, and between Griffin Road on the south and SR 84 on the north.

The airport is served by most major airlines, including the following domestic carriers: Air Canada, AirTran, America West, American, American Trans Air, Continental, Delta, Delta Express, JetBlue, MetroJet, Midway, Midwest Express, Northwest, Southwest, Spirit, TWA, United, USAirways, and USAirways Express.

It is undergoing an expansion project that is estimated to cost about $1 billion by the year 2012, more than doubling the airport's passenger capacity from 11 million in 1996 to 25 million by 2015. It is a comfortable, easy-to-use airport, well marked and well lighted.

By Car The area's main north-south arteries are Florida's Turnpike and I-95. Although the turnpike usually provides smoother sailing, it's several miles west of coastal destinations. And the cost of using the turnpike is considerable, especially in the county's northern reaches. I-95 generally has more traffic, particularly trucks. And when an accident occurs (which happens daily), there's often a traffic jam and start-and-stop movement in the opposite direction, as myriad rubber-neckers brake to see the carnage.

State Road A1A (Alternate 1A) offers a delightful, leisurely ride along the ocean, providing glimpses here and there of gorgeous beach vistas and millionaires' mansions. In some spots it narrows considerably, so visitors may watch the boat action on the Intracoastal Waterway and the seaside.

Avoid US1 if possible, as it moves slowly through outlying business districts with too much local traffic (and too many stoplights) to make it feasible for fast travel.

Speed limits vary throughout South Florida: 30 mph is common in congested areas, around hotels, or heavily populated neighborhoods; 40 or 45 mph in others; and 65 or 70 mph on the Turnpike. Remember, Florida has a seat-belt law requiring everyone to buckle up.

By Bus and Train   Greyhound Bus Lines and TriRail service Fort Lauderdale and Hollywood. Greyhound provides inter-city bus service. The main station is located at 515 Northeast Third Street, Fort Lauderdale; (954) 763-6551. More than 15 buses a day travel between Fort Lauderdale and Miami-Dade (many stop in Hollywood). Service starts at 7:50 a.m., and the last bus runs at 11:30 p.m.

Greyhound has terminals in West Palm Beach (205 South Tamarind Avenue; (561) 833-8536) and Lake Worth (929 North Dixie Highway; (561) 588-5002).

TriRail offers train service from Palm Beach County through Broward County and into Miami-Dade to Miami International Airport. Its main station is located at 205 South Andrews Avenue, Fort Lauderdale; (954) 357-8400 or (800) TRI-RAIL. The train service runs frequently throughout the day but less often on weekends. Both the Greyhound and TriRail stations are in marginal areas of town but are patrolled regularly.

Amtrak makes several stops in southeast Florida, including West Palm Beach and Fort Lauderdale; (800) USA-RAIL; **www.amtrak.com**.

Getting Around

Vero Beach   Traveling on I-95, take Exit 147 to reach downtown. The main street is US 1. You also can drive A1A up the coast or Old Dixie Highway (Route 605) on the mainland.

Fort Pierce   If you are traveling north on I-95, to get downtown take the Orange Avenue exit east. The main street is Second Avenue; to get to Hutchinson Island, travel north on Second Street, then east on Seaway Drive. You'll end up on A1A.

Palm Beach County   The main north-south arteries within Palm Beach County are Florida's Turnpike and I-95. Although the turnpike usually provides smoother sailing, it's several miles west of the county's major destinations. And the toll costs for using the turnpike add up, especially in the county's northern reaches (it costs $2.20 to drive a car from Boca Raton to Jupiter). I-95 generally has more traffic, particularly trucks. Although its road network is relatively simple in comparison to southern neighbors Broward and Miami-Dade, construction is endemic in growing Palm Beach County. By all means, avoid rush hours and use parallel roads such as Congress Avenue, Military Trail, and Jog Road/Powerline Road—the latter is inconsistently named in different sections. State Road A1A despite the stops and the slow traffic, offers a delightful, leisurely ride along the ocean, providing glimpses here and there of gorgeous beach vistas and millionaires' mansions.

Greater Fort Lauderdale and Broward County Broward County's major north-south arteries are: A1A, also called Ocean Drive because it runs along the Atlantic Ocean (except for a short run in Fort Lauderdale and Dania Beach where John U. Lloyd Beach State Recreation Area extends inland from the beach); US 1; I-95, a classic interstate with on-off ramps and the requisite fast-food outlets, gas stations, and strip malls; US 441 (SR 7), a slow-going road lined with auto showrooms, garages, chain restaurants, and seemingly perpetual construction; Florida's Turnpike, also called the Ronald Reagan Expressway; and University Drive, the major roadway toward suburbs and towns west of Fort Lauderdale and Hollywood.

Several area cities, Fort Lauderdale, Dania Beach, Hallandale Beach, and Pembroke Pines, for example, use a NW, NE, SW, SE pattern of street numbers from a core point in the city. Consider Fort Lauderdale: The intersection of Broward Boulevard and Andrews Avenue is effectively ground zero. North of Broward, addresses include "N" followed by an "E" or "W" denoting the direction east or west of Andrews. Streets, terraces, and courts generally run east-west. Avenues run north-south. Some streets run on an angle, however, starting out east and west then turning north or south. We suggest a good map as a traveling companion.

Public Transportation

Palm Beach Water Taxi (98 Lake Drive, Palm Beach Shores; (561) 683-8294 or (800) 446-4577) is the latest—and probably most pleasant—way to get around near the Intracoastal Waterway. Choose among guided tours or shuttle service to Clematis Street and waterfront restaurants.

Fort Lauderdale's water taxis crisscross the Intracoastal Waterway and the city's canals (phone (954) 728-8417), which have earned it the nickname, "Venice of America." You can take the enjoyable water taxi almost anywhere you want to go in Fort Lauderdale, gliding along the New River and the Intracoastal Waterway in an open-sided, canopied boat. Trips start daily at 10 a.m. and run until late night, with at least 70 stops along the Intracoastal. The cost is $4 one way, or you can buy a pass for $5 to ride all day; (954) 467-6677; www.watertaxi.com.

The Best Beaches

Bathtub Reef Park Along the southern tip of Hutchinson Island, this 1,000-foot-long beach has an area between an offshore reef and the sand that makes a "bathtub"— great for little ones and novice snorkelers. A boardwalk, showers, rest rooms, and lifeguards during peak season. Located off MacArthur Boulevard just south of Stuart Beach on Highway A1A.

Delray Beach Public Beach There's easy access and ample parking for this small beach with lifeguards, concession, rest rooms and showers. The beach is along Ocean Boulevard (A1A); (561) 272-3224.

Fort Lauderdale City Beach Long and crowded, with images from *Where the Boys Are* are still around, but it's also another popular family favorite with plenty of lifeguard stations. Across the road are dozens of watering holes, popular after hours, where you can watch the waves. Call (954) 468-1595.

Fort Pierce Inlet State Recreation Area Two pretty beaches and a coastal hammock at the southernmost end of North Hutchinson Island have a picnic area, rest rooms, and playground. We don't recommend swimming at Inlet Beach because the waters are swift, and that means unsafe swimming. But the ocean side, known as North Beach or Jetty Park, is protected from waves by its jetty, so it's safe for even small children, and lifeguards are on duty. Adjacent Jack Island on the Intracoastal Waterway is open to foot traffic only. You can take a footbridge from the recreation area over to the island and explore several miles of nature trails, where you can expect to see plenty of birds and butterflies. Open daily, 8 a.m.–sunset; admission is $3.25 per car. Located four miles east of Fort Pierce via the North Causeway; (561) 468-3985.

Golden Sands County Park This small park and nearby Treasure Shores Beach Park are excellent: both have well-maintained playgrounds, picnic shelters with grills, and lifeguards on the beach. The two parks are in Indian River Shores, just north of Vero Beach; (772) 388-5483.

Hollywood Beach Popular because of its wide Boardwalk running parallel mid-beach to the ocean for two miles, and dozens of little restaurants, many French in origin and geared to the French-Canadian tourists who winter in the area. It's a good family beach with many lifeguard stations. Call (954) 921-3423.

Hutchinson Island Located on the south side of Fort Pierce Inlet, this 16-mile barrier island has about 20 public beaches. Two favorites include **Frederick Douglass Memorial Beach** (four miles south of Fort Pierce Inlet on A1A; (561) 462-1521), with great shelling, lifeguards, picnic areas, volleyball courts and rest rooms, and secluded (i.e., no lifeguards or facilities) **Blind Creek Beach** (eight miles south of Fort Pierce Inlet on A1A).

John D. MacArthur Beach This state park covers much of Singer Island, a barrier island just north of Palm Beach. A two-mile stretch of white sand is great for walking and swimming; shell collecting and snorkeling are popular. There are no lifeguards. William T. Kirby Nature Center is open Wednesday–Sunday, 9 a.m.–5 p.m; $3.25 admission per car. Located just under three miles south of the intersection of US 1 and PGA Boulevard on A1A; (561) 624-6950.

Pepper Park   Spreading from the bayfront to the ocean, the park has a nice beach with lifeguards, bathhouses, and tennis and basketball courts (though they're getting a bit worn). On the bay, you can fish, hike, canoe, and picnic—there are two boat docks and six fishing piers. The park is open daily from dawn to dusk. In the park is the Navy Frogman Museum (phone (561) 595-5845) that tells about the Underwater Demolition Teams (UDT) and the navy's Sea Air and Land (SEAL) program. Admission is $4 adults, $1.50 children ages 5–12, free for preschoolers. The museum is open Tuesday–Saturday, 10 a.m.–4 p.m.; Sunday, noon–4 p.m.; and January–April, Monday, 10 a.m.–4 p.m. Located on A1A in north Fort Pierce.

South Beach Park   Just south of Vero Beach, this wide stretch of sand attracts families, retirees, and anyone looking for a wide beach and emerald surf. Parking is free, and there are lifeguards on duty, as well as picnic tables, showers, and rest rooms. Call (772) 231-4700.

Spanish River Park   This is the pride of Boca Raton and a great spot on the ocean—there's even a grassy area for picnics (with five covered shelters) that includes grills, rest rooms, and a 40-foot observation tower. Lifeguards are on duty. Tunnels under A1A lead to nature trails. Located off North Ocean Boulevard (A1A), two miles north of Palmetto Park Road in Boca Raton; (561) 393-7811.

Wabasso Beach Park   six miles north of Vero Beach, is wide and pretty, with covered picnic areas and plenty of action—boogie boarders, divers, and families share the space. There are lifeguards on duty. Call (772) 589-6411.

DO YOU WANNA SURF?

Surfer Lou Maresca swears he can have your kid surfing in just four short lessons. Maresca runs his Surf School in the Fort Pierce Inlet area, where waves are easy for beginners, and starts with children as young as 8. If you want to try surfing on your own, he rents equipment. Cost is $60 for a 1½-hour lesson, $100 for a full day, or $180 for two days. All you need are a bathing suit, towel, and sunscreen. His weeklong summer camps are popular, too. You can reach Lou at (772) 231-1044 or at his website: **www.surfschoolcamp.com**.

Outdoor Adventures and Sports

Recommended Excursions

Anne Kolb Nature Center   The center encompasses more than 1,500 acres of mangrove wetlands and forest habitat, minutes from the beach. You can take narrated boat tours, climb a five-story observation tower for a spectacular view of Southern Broward County, view wildlife, or bike, hike, or canoe through the wild. There's also a fishing pier nearby. Admission $2; under age 6 free. Open daily, 9 a.m.–5 p.m. 751 Sheridan Street, Hollywood; (954) 926-2410.

Fort Pierce Inlet State Recreation Area   There's an interesting variety of natural Florida in this 340-acre park on the north shore of Fort Pierce inlet: Atlantic beach, dunes, and coastal hammock, and adjacent Jack Island on the Intracoastal Waterway is a bird-watcher's paradise. You can swim, surf, picnic, and hike on Jack Island trails. Admission is $3.25 per vehicle, and the park is open dawn to dusk. Located four miles east of Fort Pierce via North Causeway; (561) 468-3985.

Gibert's Bar House of Refuge   Built in 1875 as a haven for shipwrecked sailors, the refuge is the last remaining in a chain of rescue stations established by the Coast Guard in the nineteenth century. Today, the site includes a boathouse, early life-saving equipment, model ships, and an aquarium. The family can enjoy an easy bicycle ride from the refuge to Elliott Museum (825 Northeast Ocean Boulevard, Stuart; (561) 225-1961). Built by inventor Harmon Parker, the museum features American memorabilia and an assortment of strange inventions, like the knot-tying machine and the quadricycle, a forerunner of the automobile. Kids will especially enjoy the scale model of an old-fashioned circus and the baseball memorabilia from Ty Cobb, Babe Ruth, and many others. Open Tuesday–Saturday, 10 a.m.–4 p.m. Admission is $6 for adults (Elliot Museum); (refuge) $4 adults, $2 for children ages 7–13. Located at 301 Southwest MacArthur Boulevard, Stuart; (561) 225-1875.

Gumbo Limbo Nature Center   This 20-acre outdoor nature preserve and indoor learning center (named for an indigenous hardwood tree) is one of the few surviving coastal hammocks in South Florida. You can walk through on a ⅓-mile boardwalk that ends at a 40-foot observation tower for pretty views of the Atlantic Ocean and much of Boca Raton. Another trail leads to the oceanside dunes where sea turtles nest from mid-April to September and the center conducts turtle-watching tours. Admission is free. Open Monday–Saturday, 9 a.m.–4 p.m., and Sunday, noon–4 p.m. 1801 North Ocean Boulevard, Boca Raton; (561) 338-1473.

Jonathan Dickinson State Park   This popular camping park covers 12,000 acres, including the Loxahatchee River. Bald eagles, scrub jays, and sandhill cranes are among the birds thriving amid the park's native plant life, including red mangroves, sabal palms, and gumbo limbo trees. Several walking trails include 18 miles of the Florida Trail.

Guided tours depart to Trapper Nelson's station, started in 1936 on the Loxahatchee River, accessible only by 40-passenger pontoon boat (no reservations taken). Nelson made scads of money trapping beavers and other animals, and bought land encompassing the park's present territory with more than $1 million remaining to leave to his heirs. Visitors may join a ranger-led tour through the log- and tin-roofed original buildings. You can roam on your own or take ranger-led trips. During rainy periods, three types of mosquitoes can make visitors miserable, especially at sunrise and sunset and in shady areas. Come prepared with insect repellent. Open daily, 8 a.m.–dusk. Admission is $3.25 per car (maximum eight people), $1 per person on bicycle, bus, or foot. The river tour fare is $12 adults, $7 children ages 6–12, children under age 6 free. Located on US 1 two miles south of Stuart; (561) 746-1466.

Jupiter Inlet Lighthouse   Guests here may visit the museum in The Oil House, a building harboring artifacts such as musket balls and old photos of ships and lighthouse keepers. They can also climb inside the 105-foot-tall red brick lighthouse for excellent views. To ascend the lighthouse, visitors must be at least four feet tall and in good health; they must also wear closed-back shoes. Admission is $5, $4 for seniors, $3 for children ages 6–18, and free for those younger. Open Tuesday–Friday, 10 a.m.–5 p.m.; Saturday and Sunday, noon–5 p.m.; closed Monday. Lighthouse tours are conducted Sunday, Tuesday, and Wednesday, 10 a.m.–5 p.m. Located at 805 North US 1, Jupiter; (561) 747-6639.

Loxahatchee National Wildlife Refuge   This federal preserve has great hiking trails and some of the state's best bird-watching plus a wide variety of reptiles, mammals, and waterfowl. An easy, half-mile boardwalk is near the visitors center; just beyond the boardwalk is a series of loops that let you choose a hike from one to ten miles. Admission is $5 per vehicle. Open daily, 6 a.m.–6 p.m; visitor center open 9 a.m.–4 p.m., closed Monday and Tuesday in summer. Located on US 441 and Lee Road in West Palm Beach, between SR 804 (Boynton Beach Boulevard) and SR 806 (Atlantic Avenue); (561) 734-8303.

Morikami Museum and Japanese Gardens   This serene spot dates back to 1905 and was once one of the most successful pineapple plantations in South Florida; it was owned by George Sukeji Morikami. Morikami gave the 200-acre gardens, dedicated to the preservation of Japanese culture, to Palm Beach County in 1977. It's a living history as you stroll through tranquil pine forests, past Japanese-style gardens, bonsai collections, reflective lakes, and waterfalls. There's a nice spot for picnics and a museum celebrating traditional and modern Japanese culture. Tea ceremonies are held in the Seishin-An Teahouse on the second Saturday of each month. Entrance to the gardens is always free; museum admission is $7 for adults, $6 for seniors ages 65 and older, $4 for students and children ages 6–18, free to those younger. The museum is open 10 a.m.–5 p.m., but is closed Monday and major holidays. Located at 4000 Morikami Park Road, Delray Beach; (561) 495-0233; www.morikami.org.

Canoeing and Kayaking

A world of coastal wildlife opens when you rent canoes and kayaks, which take you into shallow areas inaccessible to big boats. Check conditions before arriving, however, since droughts force some enterprises to temporarily cease operations.

Loxahatchee Canoe Rentals (10216 Lee Road, Boynton Beach; (561) 733-0192) rents canoes and kayaks at the Arthur R. Marshall Loxahatchee National Wildlife Refuge (see above). Paddle past sawgrass, swamp hibiscus, and arrowroot, and if you're lucky, you may spot otters, storks, and white-tailed deer. Boat rentals are $20 each; three- to four-hour guided tours cost $32 per canoe and $30 per two-person kayak.

Canoes and kayaks are available for rent at the **Jupiter Outdoor Center** on the Intracoastal Waterway (18090 North SR A1A, Jupiter; (561) 747-9666). Paddlers pass mangroves and may spot great blue herons and resident Smoky the dolphin. Rates for singles run $25 per day. For doubles it's $35 per person. The center also offers 50 guided tours. The most popular is the Saturday night tour, which focuses on stargazing and ends with a campfire. The cost is $35 per person.

Jonathan Dickinson State Park (US 1, Jupiter; (561) 546-2771), noted above, also rents canoes and kayaks on the northwest fork of the Loxahatchee River. You may see little blue herons, greenback herons, osprey, and manatees (which are usually more plentiful in winter). Loxahatchee means river of turtles, and you're very likely to see some of the local variety, peninsular cooters. Canoes cost $10 for the first two hours and $4 each additional hour. Kayaks rent for $15 for the first two hours ($20 doubles) and $6 each additional hour.

Closer to Fort Lauderdale, canoeing is offered at **Hugh Taylor Birch State Park** (3109 East Sunrise Boulevard, Fort Lauderdale; (954) 564-4521) and **Tree Tops Park** (3900 Southwest 100th Avenue, Davie; (954) 370-3750). Both canoeing and kayaking are available at **West Lake Park/Anne Kolb Nature Center** (751 Sheridan Street, Hollywood; (954) 926-2410).

Scuba Diving and Snorkeling

When the *Mercedes*, a 197-foot German freighter, was tossed upon a Palm Beach pool terrace in 1985, it was big news, and a nuisance to Palm Beach.

Today it is submerged in 97 feet of water, just a mile from the Fort Lauderdale beach, a habitat for myriad coral and other marine life. Legend tells that it is home to a barracuda so accustomed to divers, it can be hand-fed—if you dare. On clear days, the *Mercedes* can be seen from the dive boat on the surface.

The *Mercedes* helped position the Greater Fort Lauderdale area as one of the best wreck diving destinations in either the United States or the Caribbean. Other wrecks include the *Atria*, a 240-foot freighter lying in 112 feet of water, and the *Marriot*, a DC-4 airplane in 71 feet.

Divers in the area use more than 80 different sites between artificial reefs and the 23-mile-long, 1½–2-mile wide Fort Lauderdale Reef, which marks the northern end of the ancient living coral formation that runs from Palm Beach down past the Florida Keys.

In Palm Beach County, try **Scuba Club** (4708 North Flagler Drive, West Palm Beach; (561) 844-2466 or (800) 835-2466), which offers two-hour trips aboard a 40-foot boat Tuesday–Friday at 10 a.m. and 2:30 p.m.; Saturday and Sunday at 9 a.m. and 2 p.m. The cost is $23 per person. Another option is **Force-E Dive Centers,** family-owned since 1976 and with several locations: 2181 North Federal Highway, Boca Raton, (561) 365-0555; 7166 Beracassa Way, Boca Raton, (561) 395-4407; 660 Linton Boulevard, Delray Beach, (561) 276-0666; 11911 US 1, North Palm Beach, (561) 624-7136; and 155 East Blue Heron Boulevard, Riviera Beach, (561) 845-2333. Each center uses ten boats and operates daily. Two-tank dives cost $40–$45.

Force-E also offer snorkeling. The average price is $30 for four hours, depending on which boats are used and whether equipment is included or not. **American Dive Center** (1888 Northwest Second Avenue, Boca Raton; (561) 393-0621) is another option; they usually offer snorkeling trips on weekends. A four-hour trip costs $35.

In Broward County, contact **Brownie's Third Lung** (1530 Cordova Road, Fort Lauderdale; (954) 524-2112). Fees are $40 for a four-hour, two-tank dive from a boat. Brownie's offers rental, air fills, and lessons. Similar prices prevail at **Scuba Network** (199 North Federal Highway, Deerfield Beach; (954) 422-9982) and at **South Florida Diving "Aquanaut"** (101 North Riverside Drive, Pompano Beach; (954) 783-2299).

SAMPLE REEFS AND DEPTHS

Suzannes Ledges	13–16 feet	Curry Reef	70–75 feet
Twin Ledges	30–45 feet	Osborne Reef	60–75 feet
Copenhagen Wreck	15–30 feet	Dania EroJacks Reef	10–20 feet
Tenneco Platforms	105–190 feet	Fishamerica	110–115 feet

Sailing and Boating

Sailing seems a natural pastime in upscale Palm Beach, but rentals are limited because the Boca Inlet is rather difficult to navigate. **Fast Break Sailing Charters** (400-A North Flagler Drive, West Palm Beach; (561) 659-4472) heads down through the Hillsboro Inlet. Its 41-foot-long classic boat has been in the Palm Beach area for almost 20 years. They schedule only private charters for groups of one to six. A three-and-a-half-hour trip costs $300; a seven-hour trip costs $600 and includes lunch.

Glass-bottom boat cruises by **A Admiral's Cruse Line** (801 Seabreeze Boulevard, Bahia Mar; (954) 522-2220), sail boat rentals from **Palm Breeze Charter** (Hillsboro Boulevard at the Intracoastal; (561) 368-3566), and even gambling cruises aboard **SunCruz Casinos** (6024 North Ocean Drive, Hollywood; (954) 929-3800) are a few means of shipping out.

For a water-and-land experience, try the popular **Diva Duck** (phone (561) 844-4188; www.divaduck.com), an amphibian craft that takes you from the streets of Palm Beach and West Palm to the waters of the

Intracoastal. Along the way, you'll enjoy the gawkers from your high perch, make duck noises with your special whistle, and even get an aria or two from the guide.

Fort Lauderdale's *Jungle Queen* is a double-decker sternwheeler that has been cruising the Intracoastal and New River for more than 60 years. The narrated, three-hour cruises depart daily at 10 a.m. and 2 p.m. with a stop at Jungle Queen Indian Village to watch alligator wrestling and meet Seminole Indians. Cost is $13 for adults, $9 for children ages 2–10. Evenings, there's an all-you-can eat barbecue dinner cruise, with sing-alongs of family favorites. The fare is $30 for adults, $16 for ages 10 and under. Located at 801 Seabreeze Boulevard (Bahia Mar Yachting Center); (954) 462-5596; www.junglequeen.com.

Deep-Sea Fishing

Party Boats

Drift, or party, boats are popular with families looking to try deep-sea fishing. Usually the boat goes out for four hours at a time—generally in early morning, at noon, and occasionally at night. Hooks are baited, fish are cleaned, and all the gear you need (poles, reels, tackle, and bait) is supplied and covered in the cost.

Area operators include **Helen S. Drift Fishing** (101 North Riverside Drive, #107, Pompano Beach; (954) 941-3209); **Sea Legs III** (5400 North Ocean Drive, Hollywood; (954) 923-2109); and **Flamingo Fishing** (801 Seabreeze Boulevard, in Bahia Mar Marina; (954) 462-9194). Rates average $25 for adults and $15 for children.

Charter Boats

Chartering a boat is more costly, but a popular option with serious anglers and those looking to spend longer at sea. Local marinas are home to large charter fleets. A good way to find a captain or a boat is to hang out at a marina around 5 or 5:30 p.m. and see what the boats are bringing back from their all-day or afternoon runs.

| GOLD AND TREASURE COAST MARINAS |||
Marina	Location	Phone
Vero Beach		
Vero Beach Municipal Marina	3611 Rio Vista Boulevard	(561) 978-4960
Fort Pierce		
Ft. Pierce City Marina	1 Avenue A	(561) 464-1245
Harbortown Marina	1936 Harbortown Drive	(561) 466-0947
Riverside Marina	2350 Old Dixie Highway	(561) 464-5720
Taylor Creek Marina	1600 North Second Street	(561) 465-2663

Outdoor Adventures and Sports 359

GOLD AND TREASURE COAST MARINAS *(continued)*		
Marina	Location	Phone
Palm Beach		
Frenchman's Marina	2700 Donald Ross Road	(561) 627-6358
North Palm Beach Marina	1037 Marina Drive	(561) 626-4919
Palm Harbor Marina	400-A North Flagler Drive	(561) 655-4757
Fort Lauderdale		
City of Ft. Lauderdale, Cooley's Landing	450 SW Seventh Avenue	(954) 828-4626
City of Ft. Lauderdale, New River	2 S. New River Drive East	(954) 828-5423
Hall of Fame Marina	435 Seabreeze Boulevard	(954) 764-3975
Lauderdale Marina	1900 SE 15th Street	(954) 523-8507
Pier 66 Yacht Harbor	2301 SE 17th Causeway	(954) 525-6666

Bicycling

The **Palm Beach Bicycle Trail Shop** (223 Sunrise Avenue, in the Palm Beach Hotel; (561) 659-4583) rents bikes for $7 per hour, $18 per day. The shop is open Monday–Saturday, 9 a.m.–5:30 p.m., and Sunday, 10 a.m.–5 p.m. The business started here 28 years ago.

Bikers can cycle along the paved Lake Trail between millionaires' homes and the Intracoastal Waterway, spotting boats and dog-walkers along the way. The trail's south end starts at the Flagler Museum and continues for about one mile. Then, near the rental shop, it continues northward from Sunrise Avenue for another nine miles to Palm Beach Inlet. Guided tours, pointing out famous residents' homes, are available by reservation only.

An extremely popular trail parallels SR A1A (Ocean Boulevard) in Boca Raton and Highland Beach; bikers sometimes glimpse the ocean or Intracoastal. **Richwagen's Cycle Center** (217 East Atlantic Avenue, Delray Beach; (561) 243-2453) rents a variety of bikes, from single speeds and hybrids to tandem bikes and children's bikes. A seven-speed cruiser costs $8 per hour, $25 per day, or $45 per week. Open Monday–Friday, 9 a.m.–6 p.m., and Saturday, 9 a.m.–5 p.m.

Paralleling the ocean in Hollywood is the Boardwalk, where **Bike Shack** (101 North Ocean Drive/A1A, Hollywood; (954) 925-2453) rents equipment starting at $5, and bikers must be 18 with a valid driver's license.

There are bicycle paths at **Carlin Park** in Jupiter (south of Indiantown Road on SR A1A; (561) 746-5134); **John Prince Park** (2700 Sixth Avenue South, Lake Worth; (561) 966-6600), which offers a 1.2-mile fitness trail; and **Okeeheelee Park** (7715 Forest Hill Boulevard, West Palm Beach; (561) 966-6600); **Jonathan Dickinson State Park** (see above); and **Quiet Waters Park** in Pompano Beach (401 South Powerline Road; (954) 360-1315).

Spectator Sports

Baseball

Dodgertown is the **Los Angeles Dodgers'** spring-training headquarters, where you can watch your favorite players in the intimate setting of Holman Stadium. Exhibition games are from March to early April; the Vero Beach Dodgers regular season games are from mid-April to early September. Located at 3901 26th Street (take I-95 to SR 60; go east to Vero Beach; turn left on 43rd Avenue and follow the signs); (772) 569-4900. For ticket information, call (772) 569-6858. Fort Lauderdale Stadium hosts the **Baltimore Orioles** for spring training.

Hockey and Soccer

The state-of-the-art National Car Rental Center in Sunrise is home to the National Hockey League's **Florida Panthers** (2555 Southwest 137th Way). Individual tickets are available only through TicketMaster (phone (954) 835-8326). Ticket prices range from $14 to $110.

The **Fusion** major league soccer team plays at Lockhart Stadium (2200 West Commercial Boulevard, Fort Lauderdale; (954) 717-2200).

The Betting Sports: Horse Races, Greyhounds, Harness Racing, and Jai Alai

Pari-mutuel wagering, which enables winners to divide a pot after taking off a fee for management expenses, is a big-bucks business in Florida. Winter horse racing is on tap at **Gulfstream Park** (at US 1 and Hallandale Beach Boulevard, Hallandale; (954) 454-7000). At **Hollywood Greyhound Track** (it's actually at 831 North Federal Highway in Hallandale; (954) 924-3200), the sleek animals race at speeds of more than 40 miles an hour. The season runs November through May.

Pompano Park Harness Racing (1800 Race Trace Road, Pompano Beach; (954) 972-2000) offers races November through mid-April on Monday, Wednesday, Friday, and Saturday evenings.

Jai Alai is a speed game combining elements of lacrosse, tennis, and racquetball, played with a hard ball called a pelota, and a cesta, a long, curved wicker basket. The local venue is **Dania Jai Alai** (301 East Dania Beach Boulevard; (954) 920-1511). Admission is free until 6 p.m. for simulcast games and horse races as well as poker; the box office is open Wednesday–Friday, 4–10 p.m.; Saturday, 11 a.m.–4 p.m.; and Tuesday, 11 a.m.–1 p.m.

Golf and Tennis

The **PGA Resort,** of course, is almost synonymous with golf. It's host to several national tours and the Optimist International Junior Golf Championships. Also at the PGA Resort, March sees the annual five-day PGA National Invitational Croquet Tournament, luring players from throughout the country. It's open to the public with free admission. Call (561) 627-2000 for more information.

The **Boca Raton Resort and Club** (call (561) 395-3000) hosts the EMC² Skills Challenge on alternate years; past participants included Jack Nicklaus and Arnold Palmer.

At the **Delray Beach Tennis Center** (201 West Atlantic Avenue, Delray Beach; (561) 243-7360) you can watch such exciting matches as the Citrix Tennis Championships and the Chris Evert Pro-Celebrity in the top-notch facilities at the center stadium court.

Vero Beach

Vero Beach is the ideal spot for a quiet getaway. The resort community is home to excellent shops and eateries, but not the ostentatious sort—at least relative to the Treasure Coast. The soft Atlantic beaches here are less crowded, and shielded by barrier islands. Indian River County is widely renowned for it's citrus groves, and doubles as a saltwater angler's mecca. Floridians know the area as a nature-lover's respite from the tourist throngs of Daytona and Orlando to the north and the cosmopolitan cities and suburbs to the south.

Golf

Sandridge Golf Club, Lakes Course

5300 73rd Street, Vero Beach; (772) 770-5000; www.sandridgegc.com
Established 1992 | **Designer** Ron Garl | **Holes** 36

Tees Gold/Blue/White/Red **Par** 72/72/72/72 **Slope** 128/126/118/112
Fees $24
Specials Reduced fees weekdays, twilight, juniors **Cart rental** Included
Club rental $15 per set **Payment** Major credit cards **Tee times** Call up to two days in advance **Facilities** Driving range, Pro Shop, snack bar
Comments This modest course is a favorite with locals. With 36 holes, it offers visitors the chance to play multiple rounds with minimal repetition.

Attractions

Environmental Learning Center

255 Live Oak Drive, Vero Beach; (772) 589-5050; www.elcweb.org
Hours Weekdays, 9 a.m.–4 p.m.; Saturday 9 a.m.–4 p.m.; closed Sunday
Admission Free
Appeal by Age Group

Pre-school ★★	Teens ★★★	Over 30 ★★★★
Grade school ★★★★	Young Adults ★★★	Seniors ★★★★

Touring Time *Average* 2 hours; *minimum* 1½ hours
Rainy-Day Touring OK for indoors but not for outdoor part
Author's Rating ★★★; lots of first-person learning
Description and Comments Wet labs and dry labs? Bring back bad memories of chemistry class? Don't be alarmed, you and your kids will get a huge

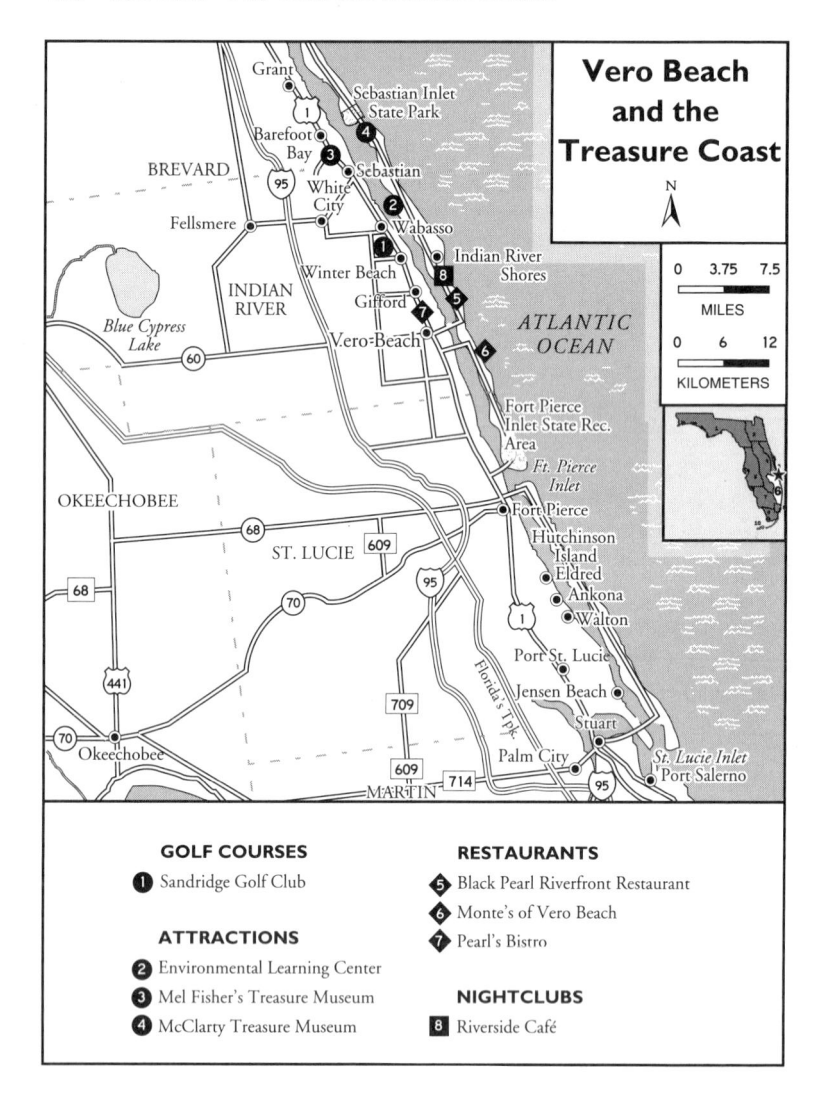

Vero Beach and the Treasure Coast

GOLF COURSES
1. Sandridge Golf Club

ATTRACTIONS
2. Environmental Learning Center
3. Mel Fisher's Treasure Museum
4. McClarty Treasure Museum

RESTAURANTS
5. Black Pearl Riverfront Restaurant
6. Monte's of Vero Beach
7. Pearl's Bistro

NIGHTCLUBS
8. Riverside Café

kick out of the Environmental Learning Center (ELC) located on Wabasso Island in Indian River County. The center encourages guests to become familiar with their surroundings and teaches visitors to respect and appreciate nature.

Visit the wet lab, home of the fish and snakes. In the dry lab, you'll find computers that take you through the center's grounds. Hands-on exhibit areas let you pick up skeletons, shells, and other remnants of marine life. You can even slide them under a microscope for a closer look. The outdoor laboratory is just as impressive. Visit the butterfly gazebo or stroll the grounds to look at the trees and flowers—everything is labeled.

Special programs let you talk to a "sharkologist" or track dolphins in the Indian River Lagoon. The cost of the programs is usually $3–$4. Guests must preregister for these programs.

> **MCKEE BOTANICAL GARDEN'S COMEBACK**
> Once a blooming beauty, this botanical garden was neglected in the 1970s after theme parks entered the tourism scene. The competition forced McKee to close its doors in 1976, despite the historical significance of the site. Landscape architect William Lyman Phillips, of the esteemed firm of Frederick Law Olmsted, designed the garden in 1932, and it became home to an amazing collection of water lilies and orchids. In 1995, the Indian River Land Trust purchased the property and began the garden's revival. It's now on the National Register of Historic Places and features ponds filled with water lilies, along with palms, ferns, and more. $6 admission; $5 seniors; $3.50 children ages 5–12. Located at 350 US 1, (772) 794-0601; www.mckeegarden.org.

Mel Fisher's Treasure Museum

1322 US 1, Sebastian; (772) 589-9875; www.melfisher.com

Hours Monday–Saturday, 10 a.m.–5 p.m.; Sunday, noon–5 p.m. (closed the month of September)

Admission $6.50 for adults, $5 for seniors ages 55 and older, $2 for children ages 6–12, free for children ages 5 and under

Appeal by Age Group

Pre-school ★★	Teens ★★★	Over 30 ★★★
Grade school ★★★★	Young Adults ★★★	Seniors ★★★★

Touring Time *Average* 1½ hours; *minimum* 1 hour
Rainy-Day Touring Recommended
Author's Rating ★★★; great fun to see all the stuff Mel dredged up
Description and Comments Visitors can actually pick up a $250,000 gold bar from the ship Atocha, found off of Key West by Fisher in 1985.

McClarty Treasure Museum

13180 North Route A1A; (772) 589-2147

Hours 10 a.m.–4:30 p.m. daily
Admission $1, under 6 free
Appeal by Age Group

Pre-school ★★	Teens ★★	Over 30 ★★★
Grade school ★★	Young Adults ★★★	Seniors ★★★

Touring Time *Average* 1½ hours; *minimum* 1 hour
Rainy-Day Touring Recommended
Author's Rating ★★★; comprehensive collection
Description and Comments You'll understand why this piece of the Atlantic shore is called the Treasure Coast after a look at the collection in

this museum that tells the story of 11 Spanish ships that wrecked in 1715 near this site. A 35-minute starts the story of the treasure fleet, then the museum showcases coins, pottery, a cannon and other artifacts from the ships. An outdoor walkway takes you to an overlook of the site of the 1715 survivor's camp.

Shopping

Tanger Outlets (1824 94th Drive, Vero Beach; (772) 770-6097; www.tangeroutlet.com) has more than 65 stores including nationally acclaimed manufacturers such as Polo Ralph Lauren, Ann Taylor, Versace, Dooney-Burke, and Mikasa. If you're traveling on I-95, take Exit 147.

Dining

Black Pearl Riverfront Restaurant

4445 North A1A, Vero Beach; (772) 234-4426

Meals served Dinner nightly **Cuisine** Continental **Entree range** $21–$29 **Reservations** Yes **Payment** All major credit cards

Comments Award-winning Black Pearl has been serving wonderful continental cuisine for 14 years, with starters like lobster bisque and pan-seared diver scallops, and entrees that include onion-crusted grouper, veal piccata and filet of beef Wellington. Also a great selection of martinis and wines by the glass.

Monte's of Vero Beach

1517 South Ocean Drive, Vero Beach; (772) 231-6612

Meals served Dinner **Cuisine** Italian/American **Entree range** $14–$23 **Reservations** Strongly recommended **Payment** All major credit cards accepted

Comments We were intrigued when we discovered that former Dodger manager Tommy Lasorda frequented this restaurant during his days at spring training camps in Vero Beach. If anyone knows Italian food, it's Tommy. A great, authentic Italian meal.

Pearl's Bistro

56 Royal Palm Boulevard, Vero Beach; (772) 778-2950

Meals served Lunch daily; dinner Thursday, Friday, and Saturday nights **Cuisine** Island-style seafood **Entree range** Lunch $6.25–10.25; dinner $12.95–22.95 **Reservations** Suggested for dinner; accepted at lunch for five or more **Payment** V, MC, AmEx

Comments Authentic Delicious Caribbean-inspired food—Jamaican jerk shrimp, coconut fried shrimp, barbecued Key West–style dolphin steak—is served in this tiny restaurant tucked away in a strip mall.

Nightlife

Riverside Café

Who goes there Locals and visitors of all ages who want to see the sunset

1 Beachland Boulevard, Vero Beach; (772) 234-5550

Cover No **Minimum** No **Mixed drinks** $4.25–$6 **Food available** Fresh local seafood, American cuisine

What goes on On the Intracoastal Waterway, this is a terrific spot to watch the sun set on the open-air deck.

Comments This seafood grill has a lively late-night bar. In contrast to the mega-clubs further south, the atmosphere is casual and the company more interested in having a good time than being seen.

Palm Beach County

In the 1890s, visionary Henry Flagler, a founding partner of Standard Oil, built the Florida East Coast Railway system from Jacksonville to Key West in order to open the state as a winter paradise. In Palm Beach, he also built two large hotels, the Royal Poinciana Hotel and the Breakers, plus his own winter home, Whitehall, which is now the Flagler Museum.

The Town of Palm Beach, located on a barrier island, was incorporated in 1911. The area continued to grow as a fashionable winter retreat, and workers arrived to supply the needs of wealthy vacationers.

Today, Palm Beach's Ocean Boulevard is lined with millionaires' estates. Perhaps the most recognizable is Donald Trump's 118-room mansion, Mar-a-Lago, built for cereal heiress Marjorie Merriweather Post. But, because the beaches are public, there's nothing to stop you from accessing Palm Beach Municipal Beach—say, at the foot of Worth Avenue—and strolling along for some mansion-gazing and celeb-watching. Just don't expect public bathrooms.

Many other stops along Flagler's railroad route blossomed as well. For instance, Boca Raton was settled in 1896. It became noteworthy because of the foresight of architect Addison Mizner. His 100-room hotel, the Cloister, built in 1925, is now part of the world-renowned Boca Raton Resort and Club.

Unfortunately, visitors can't pop into the Boca Raton Resort and Club to glimpse the period opulence unless they're registered guests. However, as a non-guest you may view the amazing lobby and public rooms of the Breakers in Palm Beach, and even dine there.

There's more to Palm Beach County than those bastions of affluence, however. With a land mass larger than Delaware, Palm Beach has 37 municipalities and unincorporated areas. The county has 47 miles of beaches, on the east, and Lake Okechobee and the Everglades on the west.

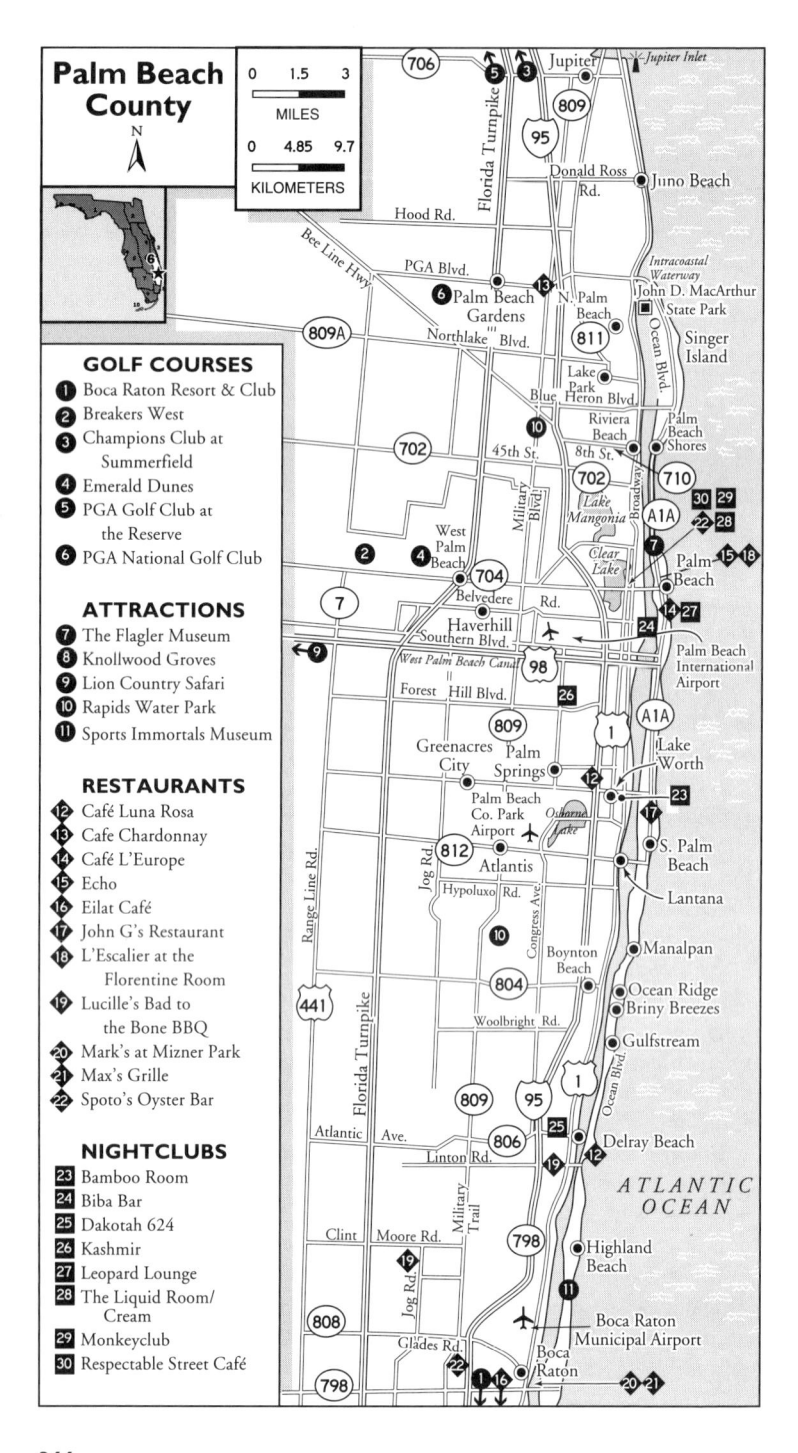

Palm Beach County

N

GOLF COURSES
1. Boca Raton Resort & Club
2. Breakers West
3. Champions Club at Summerfield
4. Emerald Dunes
5. PGA Golf Club at the Reserve
6. PGA National Golf Club

ATTRACTIONS
7. The Flagler Museum
8. Knollwood Groves
9. Lion Country Safari
10. Rapids Water Park
11. Sports Immortals Museum

RESTAURANTS
12. Café Luna Rosa
13. Cafe Chardonnay
14. Café L'Europe
15. Echo
16. Eilat Café
17. John G's Restaurant
18. L'Escalier at the Florentine Room
19. Lucille's Bad to the Bone BBQ
20. Mark's at Mizner Park
21. Max's Grille
22. Spoto's Oyster Bar

NIGHTCLUBS
23. Bamboo Room
24. Biba Bar
25. Dakotah 624
26. Kashmir
27. Leopard Lounge
28. The Liquid Room/Cream
29. Monkeyclub
30. Respectable Street Café

Golf

Boca Raton Resort & Club, Resort Course

501 East Camino Real, Boca Raton; (561) 395-3000; www.bocaresort.com

Established 1997 | **Designer** Gene Bates and Fred Couples | **Holes** 18

Tees Championship/Men's/Ladies **Par** 71/71/7 **Slope** 128/124/107
Fees $260–$600 per person
Specials 9-hole and twilight rates **Cart rental** Included **Club rental** $85 per set **Payment** Major credit cards **Tee times** Available with no restrictions **Facilities** Driving range, clubhouse, locker rooms, and restaurant.
Comments Available only to registered guests and club members, this brand-new course is in the shadow of one of the nation's most historic hotels. This is not a particularly easy course despite its miniscule yardage. But this can be a fun course for every class of player, especially intermediates.

Breakers West

1550 Flagler Parkway, West Palm Beach; (561) 653-6320; www.thebreakers.com

Established 1896 then redesigned in 2000 | **Designer** Alexander Findley in 1896 then Brian Silva in 2000 | **Holes** 18

Tees Blue/White/Gold/Red **Par** 71/71/71/72 **Slope** 135/131/123/131
Fees $169 **Cart rental** Included **Club rental** $55 per set **Payment** All major credit cards **Tee times** Available in advance to guests **Facilities** Driving range, pro shop, restaurant, Todd Anderson Golf Academy
Comments You have to be a guest of The Breakers hotel, ten miles to the east, to gain access to the course. So if you are a guest, don't miss this one. The course is relatively long and poses a good challenge, especially from the back tees.

Champions Club at Summerfield

3400 Southwest Summerfield Way, Stuart; (772) 283-1500; www.thechampionsclub.com

Established 1994 | **Designer** Tom Fazio | **Holes** 18

Tees Gold/ Blue/White/Green **Par** 72/72/72/72
Slope 131/125/117/116
Fees $25 before noon, $20 after noon, $15 after 4 p.m.
Specials None **Cart rental** Included **Club rental** $25 per set **Payment** V, MC, AmEx, D **Tee times** Up to 7 days in advance **Facilities** Modest but handsome pro shop/clubhouse and a first-rate driving range and putting green.
Comments This is not an easy course, with more than 90 sand traps, and situated among surrounding wetlands. Champions is a very good value, and a terrific opportunity to play a Fazio creation.

Emerald Dunes

2100 Emerald Dunes Drive, West Palm Beach; (561) 684-4653; www.emeralddunes.com

Established 1990 | **Designer** Tom Fazio | **Holes** 18

Tees Gold/Blue/White/Green/Red
Par 72/72/72/72/72
Slope 133/129/125/126/115
Fees $65 Monday–Thursday, $75 Friday–Sunday (fees vary duirng the year)
Specials 9-hole and twilight rates **Cart rental** Included **Club rental** $40 per set **Payment** All major credit cards **Tee times** Up to 60 days in advance
Facilities $2.5 million clubhouse
Comments If you are on a budget, you may consider Emerald Dunes well out of your price range, especially since it is a public course. Though we agree it tends to be a tad pricey, it is no typical public course—in fact, it is one of Florida's best public golf courses, a blend of Scottish-style links and a rolling, mounded Carolina-like layout.

PGA Golf Club at The Reserve

1916 Perfect Drive, Port St. Lucie; (800) 800-GOLF; www.pgavillage.com

North Course

Established 1996 | **Designer** Tom Fazio and Pete Dye | **Holes** 18

Tees Championship/Blue/White/Red
Par 72/72/72/72 **Slope** 133/129/124/118

South Course

Established 1996 | **Designer** Tom Fazio and Pete Dye | **Holes** 18

Tees Championship/Blue/White/Red
Par 72/72/72/72 **Slope** 141/137/129/123
Fees $26 Monday–Thursday, $33 Friday–Sunday
Specials After 3 p.m. everyday $16 **Cart rental** Included **Club rental** $40 **Payment** All major credit cards **Tee times** Up to 9 days in advance **Facilities** Restaurant, golf shop, PGA learning center
Comments The Reserve is Tom Fazio's creation, but golf almost takes a back seat to the environment here. These courses have earned the highly coveted "signature" status from the Audubon Society, and honor that has only been given to a handful of courses nationwide. Visually stunning with lush flora and fauna, both courses have distinct personalities. The South Course is the most impressive of the two and will no doubt intimidate the average golfer. The North Course tends to be less demanding, but you will find more sand traps as well as fairways that have more mounding. Both courses are designed to challenge but not overpower.

PGA National Golf Club, Champion Course

1000 Avenue of the Champions, Palm Beach Gardens; (561) 627-1800; www.pgaresorts.com

Established 1981 | **Designer** Tom Fazio | **Holes** 18

Tees Black/Gold/Blue/White/Red

Par 72/72/72/72/72 **Slope** 142/133/129/124/123

Fees $225 (prices may vary throughout the year)

Specials None **Cart rental** Included **Club rental** $40–$80 per set **Payment** V, MC, AmEx **Tee times** Tee times can be made up to a year in advance, but you must be a guest of the resort **Facilities** Clubhouse, pro shop, lockers, restaurant, bar, nine putting greens, two driving ranges.

Comments PGA National is the headquarters of the PGA of America, and it is fitting that the Champions Course is dedicated to Jack Nicklaus, a man who personifies golf. In 1990 he redesigned the Fazio creation, making it more playable and spectator friendly. This is one course where you really need all aspects of your game to by in sync to score well.

Attractions

Flagler Museum

Cocoanut Row and Whitehall Way, Palm Beach; (561) 655-2833; www.flagler.org

Hours Tuesday–Saturday, 10 a.m.–5 p.m.; Sunday, noon–5 p.m.

Admission Adults, $10; children ages 6–12, $3; children under age 6 free

Appeal by Age Group

Pre-school ★	Teens ★★	Over 30 ★★★
Grade school ★★	Young Adults ★★★	Seniors ★★★

Touring Time 1–2 hours

Rainy-Day Touring Recommended

Author's Rating ★★★

Description and Comments Here's a peek at how the wealthy once wintered. Henry Morrison Flagler bought and combined several railroad companies, so his Florida East Coast Railway opened the state for development as far as Key West. Flagler built this 55-room mansion, Whitehall, in 1902—in the Beaux-Arts style—as a wedding gift for his third wife. The *New York Herald* then called it... "grander and more magnificent than any other private dwelling in the world." After the family left and before it was reopened as a museum (in 1960), the property opened as the Whitehall Hotel in 1925.

Most visitors take the 45-minute guided tour which reveals the country's largest marble room during the Gilded Age, silk-covered walls, gilded period furnishings, Baccarat crystal chandeliers, and frescoed ceilings.

Knollwood Groves

8053 Lawrence Road, Boynton Beach; (561) 734-4800

Hours Daily, 8:30 a.m.–5:30 p.m.; closed holidays and Sundays in July and August

Admission Groves are free; $1 for wagon train tour; alligator show $6 adults, $4 children

Appeal by Age Group

Pre-school ★★	Teens ★★	Over 30 ★★
Grade school ★★★★	Young Adults ★★	Seniors ★★

Touring Time *Average* 1½ hours; *minimum* 1 hour

Rainy-Day Touring Not recommended

Author's Rating ★★; a living history lesson

Description and Comments Knollwood Groves is another pre-Disney attraction that's a wonderful, old-fashioned adventure. The orange and grapefruit trees were planted in the 1930s, and they still harvest the trees.

Visitors tour 30 acres of orange groves and a juice processing plant. The half-hour tram ride through the groves demonstrates how fruits are grown, while the one-and-a-half-hour show in the simulated Seminole village exhibits Native American life and culture. Little ones also enjoy seeing the live deer, rabbits, and three little pigs.

Lion Country Safari

Southern Boulevard West (SR 80), 18 miles west of I-95 Exit 50 in West Palm Beach; (561) 793-1084; www.lioncountrysafari.com

Hours Daily, 9:30 a.m.–5:30 p.m.

Admission $17 for adults, $13 for seniors ages 65 or older, $15 for children ages 3–9; children under age 3 free

Appeal by Age Group

Pre-school ★★★★	Teens ★★★★	Over 30 ★★★★
Grade school ★★★★	Young Adults ★★★★	Seniors ★★★★

Touring Time *Average* 1 hour to drive through, but plenty to keep you busy for at least three hours

Rainy-Day Touring OK, but not recommended

Author's Rating ★★★★

Description and Comments More than 1,300 animals—including chimps and zebras—roam this cageless 500-acre drive-through zoo. It has been wowing guests since 1967. Kids of all ages are thrilled as hippopotamuses walk past their car, or a group of elephants surround a baby for protection when a feeding truck arrives. Kiddie rides, paddle boats, a walk-through section for smaller animals (stroller accessible), and miniature golf add further appeal; there's even a real, live elephant ride. Guests remain in their cars and slowly drive through seven habitats—such as Serengeti Plain and Lake Nakuru—of elephants, lions, ostriches, and other major animals.

Rapids Water Park

6566 North Military Trail, West Palm Beach; (561) 842-8756; www.rapidswaterpark.com

Hours Park opens at 10 a.m.; closes at sunset, 5–8 p.m.; open daily March 17–April 22 and May 19–Labor Day, weekends only April 23–May 18.

Admission $25; children under age 2 free

Appeal by Age Group

Pre-school ★★	Teens ★★★	Over 30 ★★
Grade school ★★★	Young Adults ★★	Seniors ★★

Touring Time 4–5 hours

Rainy-Day Touring Not recommended

Author's Rating ★★

Description and Comments All sorts of water-related amusements on 22 acres, including water slides, a wave pool, and rubber tube flumes. Participants must wear bathing suits—cutoff jeans not permitted—but cannot wear water shoes on the rides (must go barefoot).

Sports Immortals Museum

6830 North Federal Highway, Boca Raton; (561) 997-2575; www.sportsimmortals.com

Hours Monday–Friday, 10 a.m.–6 p.m.; Saturday, 11 a.m.–5 p.m.; closed Sunday

Admission Ground floor, free; 2nd floor, $5 for adults, $3 for children ages 12 and under

Appeal by Age Group

Pre-school ★	Teens ★★★	Over 30 ★★★
Grade school ★★★	Young Adults ★★★	Seniors ★★★

Touring Time *Average* 1½ hours; *minimum* 1 hour

Rainy-Day Touring Recommended

Author's Rating ★★★; tops for sports fans

Description and Comments This museum showcases the largest sports memorabilia collection in the world—1 million pieces at last count—from Ty Cobb's spikes to Muhammad Ali's championship belt. They don't play favorites in this wide array of collectibles, recognized by the Smithsonian Institution as "absolutely the most outstanding single collection of sports."

Shopping

Worth Avenue on the island of Palm Beach is one of the country's most glamorous shopping streets on par with Rodeo Drive. Most buildings are only one or two stories high, and the architecture is Mizner-style Mediterranean, with blooming bougainvillea all about. There are street-side meters and valet parking at the eastern end near **Saks Fifth Avenue** (172 Worth Avenue, Palm Beach; (561) 694-9009). And don't miss the famous doggie watering trough outside **Phillips Galleries** at 318 Worth Avenue.

For world-class shoppers, Worth Avenue boasts such recognizable names as Chanel, Armani, Cartier, Hermes, Brooks Brothers, Gucci, and Ungaro. Along with antique and other collectibles shops are some long-standing icons, such as **Trillion** (315 Worth Avenue; (561) 832-3525), which has featured a splayed rainbow display of men's sweaters for 16 years; the individual garments are changed frequently to showcase different colors. **Morgan Terry Hats** (5 Via DeMario; (561) 659-0771) is the spot to find the absolutely perfect Palm Beach straw hat. The whimsical chapeaux range from about $130 to $200. Worth Avenue businesses often host unadvertised after-season sales starting in April.

Mizner Park (407 Plaza Real, Boca Raton; (561) 362-0606; **www.miznerpark.org**) is a beautiful outdoor shopping area anchored by Jacobson's and filled with fashionable boutiques, galleries, and restaurants. A standout is **Liberties Fine Books, Music & Cafe** (309 Plaza Real, Boca Raton; (561) 368-1300)—a fabulous store that regularly hosts book signings by famed authors.

In West Palm Beach, the new **CityPlace** on Okeechobee Boulevard (**www.cityplaceweb.com**; (561) 366 1000) is a shopping/entertainment/dining/residential complex. Preserved in the 1926 Spanish Colonial Revival church is the Harriet Himmel Gilman Theatre. The theater features original details such as pecky cypress doors and beams and is used for cultural events. Outside at Palladium Plaza is a set of fountains, choreographed to provide watery displays announced by the church bell. Free outdoor concerts are held Friday and Saturday nights. A complimentary trolley service connects with Clematis Street; it transports 40,000 people a month.

This largely suburban area is, naturally, not without mall shopping. The **Gardens of the Palm Beaches** (3101 PGA Boulevard, Palm Beach Gardens; (561) 775-7750) is a lovely two-story mall with open, airy garden styling that's all bright and sunny. Among its 175 stores are anchors Macy's, Burdines, Sears, Bloomingdale's, and Saks Fifth Avenue.

Town Center at Boca Raton (6000 Glades Road, Boca Raton; (561) 368-6000). This upscale enclosed center has recently been expanded with even more glamorous shops for shopaholics, now totaling 220. Anchors include Bloomingdale's, Saks Fifth Avenue, Burdines, Sears, Lord & Taylor, and Nordstrom. Valet parking is available.

Antiques

Do you think all South Florida residents decorate their homes in modern pastels? Think again. You'll find a gaggle of antiques stores (about 43) located on **Antique Row,** on South Dixie Highway (two blocks north of Southern Boulevard) in West Palm Beach. Pop into any of the stores on the six-block stretch for a printed map showing locations and types of merchandise. **Peter Werner, Ltd.** (3709 South Dixie Highway; (561) 832-0428) offers eighteenth- to twentieth-century furnishings and paintings. **Boomerang Modern** (3301 South Dixie Highway; (561) 835-1865) specializes in mid-twentieth-century furnishings, glass, and ceramics. **Cassidy's Antiques** (3621 South Dixie Highway; (561) 832-8017) boasts museum-quality seventeenth- and eighteenth-century Spanish and Italian pieces.

Longtime names around tony Worth Avenue include **Christian Du Pont Antiques** (352 Peruvian Avenue, Palm Beach; (561) 655-7794), specializing in seventeenth- through nineteenth-century intricate French marquetry and sparkling crystal chandeliers, and **Yetta Olkes Antiques** (332 South County Road, Palm Beach; (561) 655-2800), which has been on the scene for about 20 years. She specializes in nineteenth- and twentieth-century porcelains and small decorative objects.

Bargains

Long familiar to savvy New York shoppers of discounted ladies' clothing off the rack, **Loehmann's** has two locations (8903 Glades Road, Boca Raton; (561) 852-7111 and 4100 PGA Boulevard, Palm Beach Gardens; (561) 627-5575). Don't forget to pop into The Back Room for special occasion glam. Near Palm Beach's Worth Avenue awaits a high-class consignment shop, **Déjà Vu,** where shopaholics might find a cast-off glitzy gown formerly owned by a local celeb. The most popular items requested are Chanel designs; the shop sells bouclé suits for $500–$1,000 that were originally $3,000. Savvy shoppers might save enough to pay for some outrageous dinners.

Flea Markets

The **Delray Swap Shop & Flea Market** (2001 North Federal Highway, Delray Beach; (561) 276-4012) is a bargain-lovers paradise with 124 merchants indoors and 76 outdoors. Open Thursday–Monday, 9 a.m.–4 p.m. Closed on Monday in summer.

At the **Uptown Downtown Flea Market & Outlet Mall** (5700 Okeechobee Boulevard, West Palm Beach; (561) 684-5700), approximately 200 merchants vie for sales in an enclosed mall. The outlet is open Monday–Thursday, 10 a.m.–6 p.m.; Friday and Saturday, 10 a.m.–8 p.m.; and Sunday, noon–6 p.m. The flea market is open Tuesday–Friday, 10 a.m.–5 p.m.; Saturday, 10 a.m.–6 p.m.; and Sunday, noon–6 p.m. Hours are reduced in the summer.

Dining

Caffé Luna Rosa

34 South Ocean Boulevard, Delray Beach; (561) 274-9404, www.caffelunarosa.com

Meals served Breakfast, lunch and dinner **Cuisine** Italian **Entree range** $15–$35 **Reservations** Not accepted **Payment** MC, V, AmEx

Comments A favorite with locals and snow birds alike, Luna Rosa offers good service and gastronomically smart Italian. The restaurant makes all of its pastas fresh in-house. It's located right on the ocean; seating is offered outside. Luna Rosa gets busy. So if you want a quieter meal, come early on weekends or during the week. There is live entertainment Monday–Friday, 7–11 p.m.

Cafe Chardonnay

4533 PGA Boulevard, Palm Beach Gardens; (561) 627-2662

Meals served Lunch and dinner **Cuisine** New American **Entree range** $22–$35 **Reservations** Required in season **Payment** V, MC, AmEx, D

Comments At this bilevel restaurant where modern paintings provide a sophisticated background, wine lovers often sit at the wine bar, choosing among 500 selections.

Start with a pesto-crusted goat cheese tart with grilled eggplant, roasted portabella mushrooms, and marinated pepper, and follow with a rack of roasted Australian lamb enhanced by a rosemary-scented port reduction.

Café L'Europe

331 South County Road, Palm Beach; (561) 655-4020

Meals served Lunch and dinner **Cuisine** Continental **Entree range** $22–$36 **Reservations** Required **Payment** V, MC, AmEx, DC

Comments In this elegant dining room with swagged drapes and divine accoutrements, a pianist provides soft background music, while dancers enjoy a jazz quartet on Friday and Saturday nights.

A caviar bar appeals to old-time Palm Beachers. Start with fried sweetbreads with poached pear, followed by a grilled veal chop in a tarragon reduction served with potato-scallion cake. Dessert may star a flourless chocolate cake swathed with praline, served with butter pecan ice cream.

Echo

230 Sunrise Avenue, Palm Beach; (561) 802-4222

Meals served Dinner **Cuisine** Pan Asian **Entree range** $16–$30 **Reservations** Suggested **Payment** V, MC, AmEx, D, DC

Comments The menu, which features Chinese, Japanese, Thai, and Vietnamese, is divided into five elements: wind, fire, water, earth, and flavor. Exquisitely fresh sushi and sashimi are available by the piece. Outstanding interpretations include steamed sea bass with a soy and ginger glaze, pad Thai with chicken and shrimp, Peking duck for two, and Vietnamese roasted chicken with lemon grass–chili sauce. A "sharing menu" for a table for four at $60 per person provides an exotic Asian trip.

Eilat Cafe

6853 Southwest 18th Street, Boca Raton; (561) 368-6880

Meals served Lunch and dinner **Cuisine** Kosher dairy **Entree range** $10–$17 **Reservations** Not accepted **Payment** V, MC, AmEx, D, DC

Comments This bright and airy restaurant offers dairy dishes for its observant Jewish clientele. Tables—sans tablecloths—are inside and on the patio. Favorites include Israeli classics like hummus and falafel, plus gourmet pizzas, sesame-seared salmon with mesclun greens, and St. Peter's fish marsala with shiitake mushrooms.

John G's Restaurant

10 South Ocean Boulevard, Lake Worth; (561) 585-9860

Meals served Breakfast and lunch **Cuisine** American/seafood **Reservations** Not accepted **Entree range** $5–$18 **Reservations** No **Payment** Cash only

Comments Bring along patience for waiting in line at this popular breakfast and lunch eatery at the Lake Worth public beach, family owned since 1973. Seafood is immaculately fresh and portions huge. French toast is lipsmacking here with cinnamon and sliced almonds cooked in. Jumbo shrimp is crispy fried and served with fries, cole slaw—and corn fritters.

L'Escalier at the Florentine Room

The Breakers Hotel, 1 South County Road, Palm Beach; (561) 659-8480

Meals served Dinner **Cuisine** French **Entree range** $32–$40 **Reservations** Recommended **Payment** V, MC, AmEx, D, DC

Comments This regally appointed dining room under a 24-foot-high frescoed ceiling serves arguably the county's best-prepared and elegantly served meals. Under the creative skills of dining room chef Matthew Sobon, cuisine has soared in the last few years. At the meal's finale, the cheese presentation of 18 varieties appears on a cart; the server then describes each, peppering the history with humorous anecdotes. The wine selection is exceptional—6,500 selections, up to an $1,800 bottle, running $8–$24 by the glass.

Lucille's Bad to the Bone BBQ

3011 Yamato Road, Boca Raton; (561) 997-9557
710 Linton Boulevard, Delray Beach; (561) 330-6705

Meals served Lunch and dinner **Cuisine** Southern **Entree range** $5–$13 **Reservations** Not accepted

Comments Decor in this fun spot is funky Dixie roadhouse, where farm implements such as watering troughs and washboards provide local color. All-you-can-eat ribs draw bushels of regulars on Tuesday, but locals bring the youngsters on Wednesdays, when kids under 12 eat free; a clown keeps them busy by painting faces and making balloon animals. Rotisserie-roasted chicken and St. Louis ribs are major choices, served with zippy barbecue sauce, baked sweet potato, and pecan pie.

Mark's at Mizner Park

344 Plaza Real, Boca Raton; (561) 395-0770

Meals served Lunch and dinner **Cuisine** Mediterranean fusion **Entree range** $14–$31 **Reservations** Accepted **Payment** V, AmEx, D, DC

Comments Mark Militello, who started out with restaurateur Dennis Max and branched off with his own highly successful hotspots, created this popular eatery next to Max's Grille in Mizner Park. The interior is dramatically contemporary, featuring ultra-high booth backs, but many choose to sit at outdoor tables at the seven-seat chef's table to watch the culinary whizzes in action.

Dishes that seem commonplace are taken to new heights: lobster and asparagus pizza; grilled chicken Caesar salad with focaccia croutons; pork chop stuffed with pignoli and spinach; and duckling with mashed sweet potatoes and braised greens.

Max's Grille
404 Plaza Real, Boca Raton; (561) 368-0080

Meals served Lunch and dinner daily **Cuisine** American/contemporary **Entree range** $13–$30 **Reservations** Necessary for 6 or more **Payment** V, MC, AmEx

Comments Dennis Max, the restaurateur responsible for many of the area's culinary innovations (starting with Pompano Beach's Cafe Max), created this more casual spot in Mizner Park. Imaginative dishes are served within its dramatic, dark-wood interior or at tables for dining al fresco—and people-watching—at this European-style cafe with Pacific Rim influences. The stylish bar sees plenty of action.

Spoto's Oyster Bar
125 Datura Street, West Palm Beach; (561) 835-1828

Meals served Lunch and dinner **Cuisine** American/seafood **Entree range** $13–$25 **Reservations** Not accepted **Payment** V, MC, AmEx, D, DC

Comments Around the corner from Clematis Street, near the Intracoastal Waterway, Spoto's has a lively bar and tables inside the wood-paneled, brick-floored area and outside. The staff is extremely gracious.

Arts and Culture

Outstanding art museums include the **Norton Museum of Art** (1451 South Olive Avenue, West Palm Beach; (561) 832-5196; **www.norton.org**), an ever-expanding art museum that boasts a permanent but small collection of gems, including works by Monet, Gauguin, Picasso, Cezanne, Bellows, O'Keeffe (whose sister lived in Palm Beach), Hopper, Shahn, and Pollock. The **Boca Raton Museum of Art** (501 Plaza Real, Mizner Park, Boca Raton; (561) 392-2500) has a few items representing well-known artists such as Matisse and Picasso, plus nineteenth- and twentieth-century modern masters. Fun for funny paper aficionados awaits at the nearby **Cartoon Art Museum** (201 Plaza Real, Mizner Park, Boca Raton; (561) 391-2200; **www.cartoonart.org**) featuring more than 100,000 original drawings and cartoon videos in permanent and changing exhibitions.

Nightlife

Bamboo Room

Who Goes There People who like blues with their beers

25 South J Street, Lake Worth; (561) 585-BLUE

Cover Free on weekdays, varies according to artist on weekends **Minimum** None **Mixed drinks** $7; $3 cocktail specials **Food available** "Booze and blues only" (with salty snacks) **Hours** Daily, 4 p.m.–2 a.m.; happy hour 4–7 p.m. with half priced drafts, house wines, and certain drinks

What goes on Live music holds the fort Wednesday–Sunday, including a Texas blues band, contemporary jazz, and classic R&B; Bo Diddley has stopped by.

Comments Bamboo lines the walls and the bar is topped with a collection of copper shakers. This is George Thorogood's kind of bar, with a 'trademark acoustic blues act' that's worth the trademark. Unpretentious music and drinking with a cool, intimate atmosphere.

Biba Bar

Who Goes There People who speak three languages and own sneakers with more separate parts than are in your DVD players (attractive internationals), young Palm Beachers

320 Belvedere Road, West Palm Beach; (561) 832-0094

Cover None **Minimum** None **Mixed drinks** $7–$19, $65–$325 bottle service **Food available** None **Hours** Opens at 6 p.m. daily, open until 2 a.m. Wednesday, Friday, and Saturday, midnight Tuesday and Thursday, and 11 p.m. Sunday and Monday

What goes on More chillin' than dancing

Comments Located in the swanky Hotel Biba, Biba Bar is on the high end of cool, but too small to be a ridiculous scene. The decor is lovely—a minimalist decorating scheme that is novel for the way it belies the hotel's island colonial exterior. Even Floridians feel like they are on vacation when they walk into Biba Bar.

Dakotah 624

Who Goes There 30–60-something single yuppies

270 East Atlantic Avenue, Delray Beach; (561) 274-6244

Cover None **Minimum** None **Mixed drinks** $6 and up; martinis $7 and up **Food available** Full restaurant offers New American cuisine utilizing local ingredients, such as macadamia-crusted dolphin, and often with a Southern influence. **Hours** Sunday, 4–11 p.m.; Monday–Wednesday, 4 p.m.–1 a.m.; Thursday–Saturday, 4 p.m.–2 a.m.

What goes on One of three DJs spins Thursday–Saturday 11 p.m.–2 a.m. Blues and dance music is featured; sometimes one DJ plays top 40 selections on the sax.

Comments The spot is decorated in warm tones of butterscotch and caramel, with trompe l'oeil swags and sconces; its popularity has grown and it now offers 75 different martini choices. The most popular is the traditional martini, although 12–15 olive choices are offered as enhancement. Nontraditional types choose chocolate martinis.

Kashmir

Who Goes There Boys who like boys and girls who like girls

1651 South Congress Avenue, West Palm Beach; (561) 649-5557; www.clubkashmirwpb.com

Cover Varies with the night **Minimum** None **Mixed drinks** $3 and up **Food available** None **Hours** Wednesday: Sunday 10 p.m.–5 a.m.
What goes on Where Palm Beach County's gay and gay friendly drink, cruise, and dance
Comments One of the oldest gay bars in the area.

Leopard Lounge

Who Goes There Palm Beachers, internationals, and celebrities

The Chesterfield Hotel, 363 Cocoanut Row, Palm Beach; (561) 659-5800

Cover None **Minimum** $5 **Mixed drinks** $6–$8, martinis $9; check out cognac and cigar menu: servings run from "affordable" $8 for some single-malt Scotch up to $125 for Louis XIII by Remy Martin. **Food available** An adjacent dining room serves steaks and nut-crusted fish; more casual items are available in the lounge; true to the hotel's British influence, fish and chips are available. **Hours** Daily, 5 p.m.–1 a.m.
What goes on A mix of middle-aged couples and singles hit the dance floor—which lights up as areas are trod upon—to the accompaniment of a pianist, classical guitarist, or vocalist nightly. A younger crowd hangs out during the nightly happy hour (5–7 p.m.), when drinks are half-price and complimentary hors d'oeuvres are served.
Comments Though the hotel is charmingly British, the carpet is leopard-spotted, as is the ceiling-height border, and a hand-painted fresco spotlights sensual frolicking nymphets. No jeans or shorts are permitted, and jackets are suggested for gentlemen. Young Palm Beach kids dress in preppy style; older guests dress up, particularly in season. There's complimentary valet parking.

The Liquid Room/Cream

Who Goes There Club Goers with a capital "Prada," gay and straight, 20s and 30s

313 Clematis Street, West Palm Beach; (561) 655-2332

Cover Saturday, $10 for men and $5 for women, free before midnight **Minimum** None **Mixed drinks** $7 and up **Food available** Just about every dish imaginable at one of many neighboring restaurants **Hours** Thursday–Saturday, 10 p.m.–4 a.m.

What goes on DJs, dancing, drinking—a parade of fabulousness

Comments The most upscale dance club on Clematis, Liquid is still a place where A-listers can go when they don't want to drive to SoBe. A couple can reserve a table in the VIP room, Cream, for about $105, which includes a bottle of champagne—but the doorman can always refuse to lift the velvet rope for anyone who shows up looking shoddy or ill-mannered. There are occasional college nights, but mostly it's a 21 and over crowd.

Monkeyclub

Who Goes There Twenty-something singles who like to shake a tail feather, the occasional celebrity

219 Clematis Street, West Palm Beach; (561) 833-6500; www.monkeyclub.com

Cover Varies, Saturdays average $5 for women (18 and up), $10 for men (21 and up) **Minimum** None **Mixed drinks** $3 and up **Food available** None **Hours** Tuesday, 9 p.m.–3 a.m.; Thursday, 8 p.m.–3 a.m.; Friday and Saturday, 8 p.m.–4 a.m.

What goes on Rump shaking, glass draining

Comments Most people don't realize that South Florida, especially Palm Beach County, was ground zero for 'booty rap' in the 1990s, but it's a tradition the area continues proudly to this day and especially at the jungle-themed Monkeyclub. The dress code prohibits: head gear, words, pictures, logos of any kind, jerseys, sleeveless shirts, baggy pants, shorts, beach attire, or sandals; Friday night ladies get in free and drink free until 11 p.m.

Respectable Street Café

Who Goes There musical melting pot—metal heads, goth kids, punks, Manolo Blahnik-istas, National Enquirer editors, you name it.

518 Clematis Street, West Palm Beach; (561) 832-9999; www.respectablestreet.com

Cover None unless you're under 21, then it's $5; cover also varies with performers **Minimum** None. **Mixed drinks** $4–$6 **Food available** None

What goes on The longest running alternative dance club in the Southeast and one of the best venues in Palm Beach County for live music.

Comments Built in a renovated Salvation Army in 1987, Respectable Street is a watering hole for animals of the underground music scene. "Respectables," as it's known, originally made a name for itself by staging the Red Hot Chili Peppers on the eve of their fame (a hole that the Peppers' drummer put in the wall remains there to this day).

Side Trips

Lake Okeechobee A 45-minute drive west on US 441 from Palm Beach takes you into the heart of sugarcane country and to Lake Okeechobee, the second-largest freshwater lake in the country, covering more than 700 square miles in five counties. The lake, only about 12 feet deep, is famous for its bass and speckled perch. You can also walk, bike, or Rollerblade along the Lake Okeechobee Scenic Trail, a 140-mile-long trek along a 35-foot levee encircling the lake. There are parks along the way and several marked entrances.

The first burg you'll drive through is Belle Glade, and you can see the huge farms that produce much of Florida's fresh produce—sugarcane, sweet corn, green beans, lettuce, carrots, radishes, and rice. If you want to sample some fresh-picked produce, it's usually on the menu at **Linda's** (232 South Main Street; (561) 996-0300). The locals head here for baked chicken and dressing, smoked turkey, turnip and collard greens, black-eyed peas and rice, yams, potato salad, and more. You won't leave hungry, and a complete dinner is just $6.

Fort Lauderdale/Broward County

Broward County was, for many years, a bedroom community for Miami workers. Suburban in setting, the area began to attract migrants from the Northeast and Midwest in the 1950s and '60s. While originally Broward was—like Miami Beach to the south—a community of retirees, current statistics indicate the average age of residents is now under 40.

In recent years, Fort Lauderdale has emerged as a business center on par with others in the South. Redevelopment and renewal projects have revitalized downtown Hollywood.

Downtown Fort Lauderdale has become a center of fine-dining opportunities, home to the Broward Center for the Performing Arts (and with it, the Florida Philharmonic), and some outstanding museums. And Las Olas seems almost as lively as Miami Beach's Lincoln Road; just not as international. Realtors have revived the popularity of these older communities with the addition of new amenities that attract younger buyers.

Greater Fort Lauderdale boasts the second-highest hotel occupancy in the state (Orlando and the mighty mouse, Disney World, rank number one). In recent years, there's been a boom in tourism and recreation-relation programs in Greater Fort Lauderdale. A $300 million Seminole Hard Rock Hotel & Resort, the renovated 1,000-room, 39-story Diplomat, and, the $470 million Convention Center Hotel are among the newer properties.

Golf

Bonaventure Country Club

200 Bonaventure Boulevard, Weston;
(954) 389-2100; www.golfbonaventure.com

West Course

Established 1969 | Holes 18

Tees Championship/Men's/Ladies' **Par** 70/70/70 **Slope** 118/116/114

East Course

Established 1969 | Holes 18

Tees Championship/Mens'/Ladies'/Seniors
Par 72/72/72/72 **Slope** 132/127/122/117
Fees Monday–Thursday, $80 for West, $90 for East; weekend rates are $20 higher
Specials Florida residents discounts **Cart rental** Included **Club rental** $25 per set **Payment** Major credit cards **Tee times** Up to 90 days in advance **Facilities** Pro shop, restaurant and lounge, banquet facilities for 150, lessons, equipment rental.
Comments These two popular 18-hole courses are in good shape. They are frequented year-round by locals and guests at nearby Wyndham Resort and Spa, which some may remember as Bonaventure.

Club at Emerald Hills

4100 North Hills Drive, Hollywood; (954) 961-4000;
www.theclubatemeraldhills.com
Established 1968 | **Holes** 18

Tees Championship/Men's/Ladies' **Par** 72/72/72 **Slope** 142/137/116
Fees $100–$150 high-season, $50–$75 low-season **Cart rental** Included **Club rental** $40 per set (new); $15 per set (used) **Payment** V, MC, AmEx, D **Tee times** Up to 5 days in advance **Facilities** Catering services, restaurant, pro shop.
Comments This course was completely redone in 2000 and is considered top-quality. It's a qualifying course for Honda and Doral tournaments.

Colony West Country Club

6800 Northwest 88th Avenue (Pine Island Avenue), Tamarac;
(954) 721-7710; www.colonywestcc.com
Established 1970 | **Holes** 18

Tees Championship/Men's/Ladies **Par** 71/71/71 **Slope** 146/142/135
Fees $75
Specials Florida residents, $43 weekends until 10 a.m., $25 10 a.m.–4 p.m., $25 Monday–Friday **Cart rental** Included **Club rental** $25 per set **Payment** All major credit cards accepted **Tee times** Up to 7 days in advance **Facilities** Pro shop, restaurant, snack bar, banquet capacity for 250, outdoor area for parties.
Comments A cart is required on the Championship Course, golfers can walk the Glades Course. This course caters to locals and is popular year-round.

Diplomat Resort Country Club & Spa

501 Diplomat Parkway, Hallandale; (954) 883-4444; www.diplomatresort.com
Established 2000 | **Holes** 18

Tees Championship/Men's/Ladies' **Par** 72/72/72 **Slope** 136/129/119
Fees $150 per day

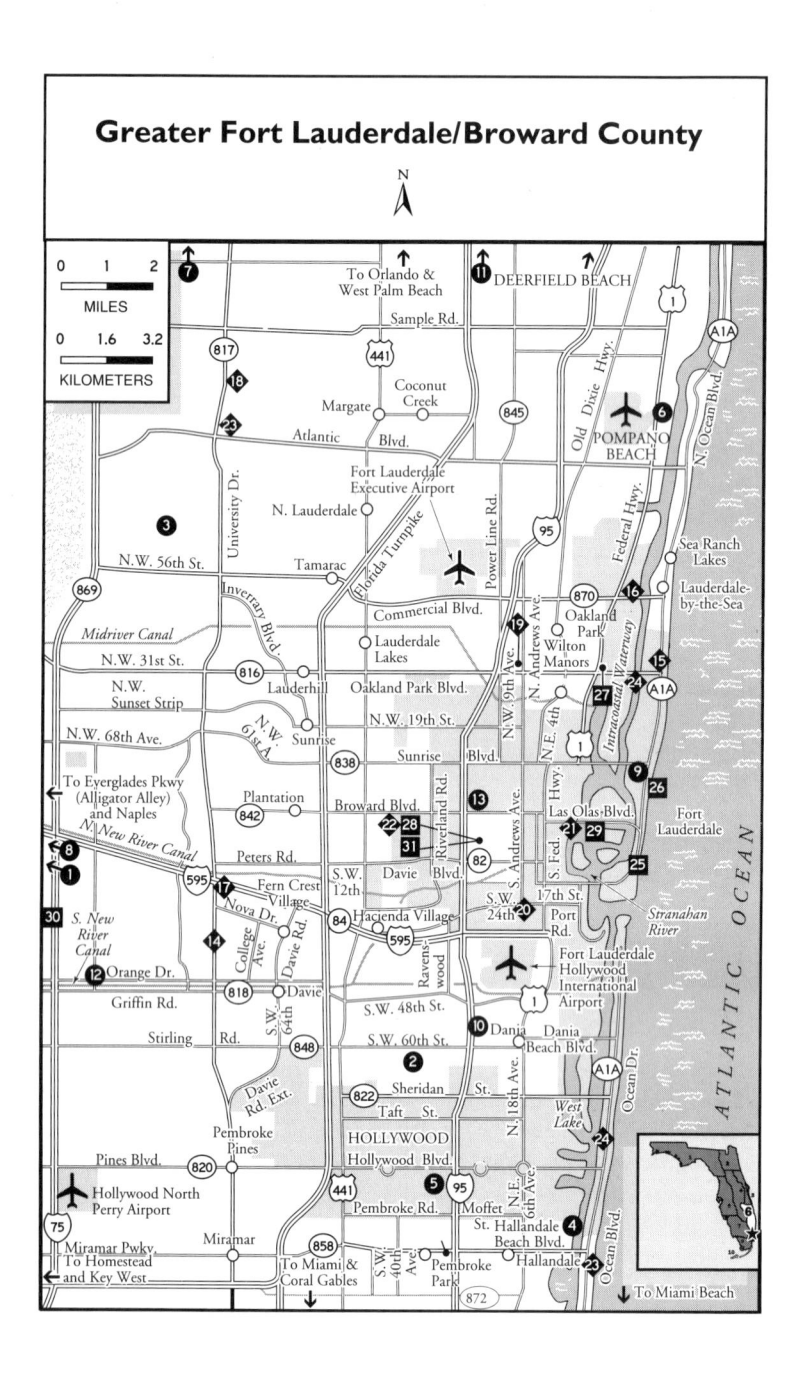

Greater Fort Lauderdale/Broward County

Greater Fort Lauderdale/Broward County

GOLF COURSES
1. Bonaventure Country Club
2. Club at Emerald Hills
3. Colony West Country Club
4. Diplomat Resort Country Club & Spa 501
5. Orangebrook Golf Club
6. Pompano Beach Municipal Golf Course
7. Tournament Players Club at Heron Bay

ATTRACTIONS
8. Ah-Tah-Thi-Ki Museum
9. Bonnet House
10. Boomers/Dania Beach Hurricane
11. Butterfly World
12. Flamingo Gardens
13. Museum of Discovery & Science/Blockbuster IMAX 3-D

RESTAURANTS
14. Armadillo Café
15. Café Martorano
16. Eduardo de San Angel
17. 84 Diner
18. Hobo's Fish Joint
19. India House
20. Lester's Diner
21. Mark's Las Olas
22. Max's Grille
23. Padrino's
24. Tavena Opa

NIGHTCLUBS
25. Bahia Cabana
26. Café Iguana
27. Christopher's
28. Himmarshee Side Bar
29. Howl at the Moon/Sloppy Joe's
30. Swig Bartini
31. Voodoo Lounge

Specials Florida residents, 60 before 2 p.m., $40 after 2 p.m. all week long; prices may vary throughout the year **Cart rental** Included **Club rental** $30 per set **Payment** All major credit cards **Tee times** up to 30 days in advance **Facilities** Country club complex, two restaurants, 60 guest rooms, meeting space and yacht slips, pro shop, and two air-conditioned convenience stations.

Comments This beautiful course, redesigned by golf architect Joe Lee, is state-of-the-art.

Orangebrook Golf Club

400 Entrada Street, Hollywood; (954) 967-4653; www.orangebrook.com

West Course

Established Early 1950s | **Holes** 18

Tees Championship/Men's/Ladies **Par** 71/71/71 **Slope** 122/118/123

East Course

Established Early 1950s | **Holes** 18

Tees Championship/Men's/Ladies' **Par** 71/71/71 **Slope** 120/114/119 **Fees** Vary by season; about $40 high season, $25 low season **Cart rental** Included **Club rental** $15 per set **Payment** V, MC, AmEx **Tee times** Up to 3 days in advance **Facilities** Pro shop, restaurant, lessons available

Comments One of Hollywood's oldest, most popular courses, Orangebrook is just one-half mile west of I-95.

Pompano Beach Municipal Golf Course

1101 North Federal Highway, Pompano Beach; (954) 786-4142;
www.ci.pompano-beach.fl.us/parksrec/golf/

Pines

Established 1967 | **Holes** 18

Tees Championship/Men's/Ladies **Par** 72/72/72 **Slope** 120/116/113

Palms

Established 1967 | **Holes** 18

Tees Championship/Men's/Ladies **Par** 71/71/71 **Slope** 113/111/109
Fees $35 to walk and $45 to share cart; afternoons, $23 to walk, $35 to share cart; $3 more weekends and holidays.
Specials $18 after 1 p.m. every day **Cart rental** Included in green fee quotes (they do not quote carts separately) **Club rental** $15 per set **Payment** V, MC **Tee times** First-come, first-served **Facilities** Driving range, practice greens, restaurant and bar, locker rooms and showers, pro shop, and instruction.
Comments A recent $2 million renovation has improved the course. Carts are not required. The Pines course is long, and Palms course, with more doglegs, requires "position golf."

Tournament Players Club at Heron Bay

11801 Heron Bay, Coral Springs; (954) 796-2000;
www.tpc.com/daily/heron_bay/index.html
Established 1996 | **Holes** 18

Tees Championship/Men's/Ladies' **Par** 72/72/72 **Slope** 133/128/114
Fees $51
Specials Twilight rate, $41 after 2 p.m. **Cart rental** Included **Club rental** $60 per set **Payment** V, MC, Diners **Tee times** up to 60 days in advance **Facilities** Golf shop, full service restaurant and lounge, locker rooms, club and shoe rentals.
Comments This excellent course is the permanent home of the Honda Classic. Expect a challenging day on the green.

Attractions

Ah-Tah-Thi-Ki Museum

17 miles north of Alligator Alley (I-75), Exit 14 on the Seminole Big Cypress Reservation; (863) 902-1113; www.seminoletribe.com/museum
Hours Tuesday–Sunday, 9 a.m.–5 p.m.
Admission Adults, $6; seniors and students, $4; children under age 6 free

Fort Lauderdale/Broward County

Appeal by Age Group

Pre-school ★★★	Teens ★★★	Over 30 ★★★★
Grade school ★★★	Young Adults ★★	Seniors ★★★★

Touring Time 2 hours

Rainy-Day Touring Not recommended

Author's Rating ★★★; a great way to learn about some of the original Floridians and their many contributions to the region. There's are exhibits, artifacts, films, nature trails, and a "living" village.

Description and Comments No traditional alligator wrestling (which most people associate with Seminoles), and that's the whole point of this museum. A 17-minute orientation film and gallery, plus a mile-and-a-half walk through a Seminole village, impart knowledge graciously and thoroughly. Don't miss the opportunity to watch Native American arts and crafts being constructed.

The Seminoles continue to maintain a vibrant presence throughout the area (including a Hard Rock Cafe Resort and Casino); two ongoing Indian gaming halls in the county offer bingo and video poker 24 hours a day.

Bonnet House

900 North Birch Road, Fort Lauderdale; (954) 563-5393; www.bonnethouse.org

Hours Wednesday–Friday, 10 a.m.– 3 p.m. for house tours, but grounds are open until 4 p.m.; Saturday, 10 a.m.–4 p.m.; Sunday, noon–4 p.m.; closed Monday and some holidays

Admission Adults, $10; seniors, $9; students ages 6–18, $8; children under age 6 free; grounds only, $6

Appeal by Age Group

Pre-school ★	Teens ★★	Over 30 ★★★★
Grade school ★★	Young Adults ★★★★	Seniors ★★★★

Touring Time 2 hours

Rainy-Day Touring Recommended

Author's Rating ★★; great for history buffs who enjoy Old Florida

Description and Comments This is a quintessentially lush attraction, and a not-to-be missed Florida estate. Watch for the monkeys swinging through the banyan trees, and the black swans in the pool. The house is illustrates a wealthy Florida lifestyle from the early twentieth century. Built by painter Frederick Clay Bartlett, the 35-acre beachfront home is a turn-of-the-nineteenth-century beauty. The art is excellent, the grounds gorgeous, and the mansion typically Floridian.

Boomers/Dania Beach Hurricane

1801 Northwest First Street, Dania Beach; (954) 921-1411; www.boomersparks.com

Hours Sunday–Thursday, 10 a.m.–2 a.m.; Friday and Saturday, 10 a.m.–4 a.m. (The actual Hurricane coaster is open Sunday–Thursday, 10 a.m.–1:30 p.m., and Friday and Saturday, 10 a.m.–2 a.m.)

Admission Per-ride basis, about $6 each; multiple-ride passes available, $18–$22

Appeal by Age Group

Pre-school ★	Teens ★★★	Over 30 ★★★★
Grade school ★★	Young Adults ★★★★	Seniors ★★

Touring Time 2–3 hours
Rainy-Day Touring Not recommended
Author's Rating ★★
Description and Comments The wooden roller coaster called the Hurricane is popular with aficionados. It's the largest wooden roller coaster in the state and reaches speeds up to 60 mph—you can see it from I-95. Other than the Hurricane, this is a standard amusement park with midway rides and arcade games. Go-cart racing, mini-golf, batting cages, bumper cars, and a bungee-like Sky Coaster ride are popular attractions.

Butterfly World

3600 West Sample Road, Coconut Creek (in Trade Winds Park, just west of the Florida Turnpike); (954) 977-4400; www.butterflyworld.com

Hours Monday–Saturday, 9 a.m.–5 p.m.; Sunday, 1–5 p.m.
Admission Adults, $16; children ages 4–12, $11; children under age 4 free

Appeal by Age Group

Pre-school ★★	Teens ★★★	Over 30 ★★★
Grade school ★★★	Young Adults ★★	Seniors ★★★★

Touring Time 2 hours
Rainy-Day Touring Not recommended
Author's Rating ★★★
Description and Comments On three acres of gardens and waterfalls, thousands of multi-hued butterflies flutter by. There are also fish, birds, and an insectarium. This is a tour for the whole family—colorful, beautiful, tropical, and interesting. Little ones love the color, and everyone enjoys the lush foliage.

Flamingo Gardens

3750 South Flamingo Road, Davie/Fort Lauderdale; (954) 473-2955; www.flamingogardens.org

Hours Daily, 9:30 a.m.–5:30 p.m.; closed Monday in summer
Admission Adults, $12; children ages 4–11, $6; discounts for seniors and AAA members

Appeal by Age Group

Pre-school ★★	Teens ★★★	Over 30 ★★★★
Grade school ★★★	Young Adults ★★★	Seniors ★★★★★

Touring Time 2–3 hours

Rainy-Day Touring Not recommended
Author's Rating ★★★
Description and Comments Everything from a subtropical rain forest to a free-flight aviary, nature trails, and wilderness animals, coexist on 60 acres of botanical gardens. Rare, exotic plants abound. The tram tour is a comfortable way to see everything, and kids love it. The gardens are outstanding; a profusion of tropical flora. One of the prettiest sites in Broward. Take your time. Go early and explore the grounds. Check out the 200-year-old oak hammock.

Museum of Discovery & Science/Blockbuster IMAX 3-D Theater

401 Southwest Second Street, Fort Lauderdale; (954) 467-6637; www.mods.org
Hours Monday–Saturday, 10 a.m.–5 p.m.; Sunday, noon–6 p.m.; closed Thanksgiving and Christmas
Admission Adults, $14; seniors and students, $13; children, $12; all prices include museum exhibits and one IMAX feature

Appeal by Age Group

Pre-school ★★★	Teens ★★★	Over 30 ★★★
Grade school ★★★	Young Adults ★★★★	Seniors ★★★★

Touring Time At least 3 hours—more if you see the film
Rainy-Day Touring Recommended
Author's Rating ★★★★; an outstanding museum—sure to be enjoyed by all
Description and Comments This well-designed, hands-on, interactive facility with a five-story 3-D IMAX theater is kid-friendly without boring adults. In addition to rotating exhibits, be sure to see Florida Ecoscapes, which features live coral, turtles, and alligators.

Shopping

Fort Lauderdale's **Las Olas Boulevard** is where the savvy shopper finds cutting-edge fashion and boutiques, art galleries, charming restaurants, sidewalk cafes, and jazz houses. Las Olas means "the waves" in Spanish, and it makes them indeed for South Florida shoppers.

Zola Keller (818 East Las Olas Boulevard; (954) 462-3222) has clothed the area's best-dressed for years with outstanding women's wear from around the globe. Across the street, **Call of Africa's Native Vision Galleries** (807 East Las Olas Boulevard; (954) 767-8737) offers rare and exotic African art; and at **Maus & Hoffman** (800 East Las Olas Boulevard; (954) 463-1472) men's clothing appeals to shoppers from all over the world.

Genesis Fine Art (803 East Las Olas Boulevard; (954) 467-6066) specializes in landscapes and representational paintings; you'll see watercolors, acrylics, and oils and modern and postmodern schools, but few abstract works.

A variety of gift shops and galleries—some funky, some fabulous—make Las Olas a great day's activity. Diverse eateries range from moderately priced to expensive.

The **Shops & Restaurants of Downtown Hollywood** (Hollywood Boulevard and Harrison Street; (954) 921-3016) is a renovated downtown area similar to Las Olas, with old cinemas and banks reincarnated as restaurants and shops. Hollywood has created a collection of clothing boutiques, art galleries and studios, and intimate cafes, as well as a growing array of nighttime live entertainment.

Mall Shopping

We strongly recommend a visit to **Sawgrass Mills** outlets (12801 Sunrise Boulevard, Sunrise; (954) 846-2300) just to ooh and aah at its size. Consider Saks Fifth Avenue and Neiman Marcus outlets, add Ann Taylor and Carter's children's wear, Levi Strauss, Benetton, Spiegel, American Tourister, Nine West, Joan & David, and DKNY, and you've got a trunkful of bargains. The values are there—it just takes some looking.

Sawgrass opened in 1992 is a major tourist attraction. The Oasis features a 300,000-square-foot entertainment area with more than 30 stores and restaurants. Valet parking is available.

Galleria Mall (2414 East Sunrise Boulevard, Fort Lauderdale; (954) 564-1015) is a high-end mall with glitzy stores (Saks Fifth Avenue and Neiman Marcus), designer boutiques, and a huge parking garage—valet service is available.

Antiques

Dania Beach is known for blocks of antique shops with fine glassware, furniture, jewelry, and more. Like Las Olas, this is a stroll-and-window-shop area, so take the time to explore some of the 250 shops.

One way to go about it is to visit the **Antique Center Mall of Dania** (3 North Federal Highway, Dania Beach; (954) 922-5467) with a selection including **Paula Schimmel's** for antique and period jewelry, **Dick's Toys, E & F** for antiques and collectibles, and **Madeleine France's 19th and 20th Century Past and Pleasure** for perfume bottles, furniture, housewares, and gold.

For antique art, try **Kodner Gallery** (45 South Federal Highway, Dania Beach; (954) 925-2550), or **Athena Gallery,** which buys antiques and estates (19 South Federal Highway, Dania Beach; (954) 921-7697). Also visit **Attic Treasures** (32 North Federal Highway, Dania Beach; (954) 920-0280), with goodies from the first half of the twentieth century.

Flea Markets

Festival Flea Market (2900 West Sample Road, Pompano Beach; (954) 979-4555) and **Swap Shop of Fort Lauderdale** (3291 West Sunrise Boulevard, Fort Lauderdale; (954) 791-7927) are popular with bargain-hunters.

Festival Flea Market features upscale bargains, food court, and full-service beauty salon. The Swap Shop features a circus, food court, and a carnival-like ambience with more than 2,000 vendors, and they offer shuttle bus service from hotels and downtown locations.

SOME SURPRISING (FUN!) BROWARD THINGS

- **Davie Rodeo** The wild west in Southeast Florida. Yes, the fourth weekend of every month you can enjoy a rodeo. Who needs Texas? 4271 Davie Road; (954) 384-7075; www.fivestarrodea.com.

- **Fort Lauderdale Museum of Art** A permanent collection of artworks from Copenhagen, Brussels, Amsterdam, and Cuba, and a new wing housing the world's largest collection of works by American Impressionist William Glackens is just the start. Watch for exciting visiting exhibits in this downtown Fort Lauderdale museum, near Riverwalk; (954) 525-5500; www.museumofart.org.

- **Royal Horsedrawn Carriages** Central Park has nothing on Fort Lauderdale's Las Olas. You can ride in style Wednesday–Sunday nights, starting at 7 p.m., from carriage stands at Southeast Eighth Avenue and Las Olas Boulevard.

- **Goodyear Blimp Base** Get up close to that huge bag of wind, The Stars and Stripes Blimp, at 1500 Northeast Fifth Avenue (at Copans Road), Pompano Beach.

- **Pompano Park Racing** Trotters and pacers thunder down the stretch of Florida's only nighttime horse track, which offers simulcast thoroughbred and harness racing as well as jai alai; fine dining and light fare; and free admission and parking. One block south of Atlantic Boulevard, on Powerline Road, Pompano Beach; (954) 972-2000.

- **Stranahan House** Broward's oldest building is beautifully restored and furnished in period antiques. Built in 1901 for Fort Lauderdale's founder, it's one of several turn-of-the-last-century pioneer buildings by the river (335 Southeast Sixth Avenue; (954) 524-4736). Others along Southwest Second Avenue, including the King Cromartie House (1907) and New River Inn (1905).

    Strolling by these dwellings—ancient by Florida standards—is a good way to enjoy the early morning balmy breezes and get some exercise. Nearby is the Third Avenue Arts District (phone (954) 763-8982). And if you enjoy breakfast out, stop by another classic, the Riverside Hotel, Broward's oldest (620 East Las Olas Boulevard; (954) 467-0671).

- **Billie Swamp Safari** A real Everglades experience and a great way to learn about the land, history, and culture of the Seminole Indians on Big Cypress Seminole Reservation; (800)-949-6101; www.seminoletribe.com/safari. Swamp buggy eco-tours, airboat rides, and snake and gator educational shows operate daily. You can even spend a night in a real Seminole thatch hut.

- **A One-Day Cruise to the Bahamas** Discovery Cruise Lines lets you experience cruising, gambling, and award-winning cuisine, daily, between Port Everglades and Grand Bahama Island; (800) 866-8687; www.discoverycruiseline.com.

Dining

Armadillo Café

3400 South University Drive, Davie; (954) 423-9954

Meals served Dinner **Cuisine** Southwestern **Entree range** $15 $33 **Reservations** Yes **Payment** AmEx, V, MC, D, DC

Comments The strip-mall exterior of this restaurant can be deceiving. This is one of the best restaurants in Broward—and one of the few longstanding, reliable Southwestern restaurants in South Florida. Try cedar-planked salmon with a chipotle-mango barbecue sauce, roasted corn-jalapeño fritters, house-smoked duck quesadillas, or chocolate fritters.

Café Martorano

3343 East Oakland Park Boulevard, Fort Lauderdale; (954) 561-2554; www.cafemartorano.com

Meals served Dinner **Cuisine** Italian **Entree range** $12–$40 **Reservations** Not accepted; entire party must be present to be seated **Payment** V, MC, AmEx

Comments No menu. You eat what Martorano tells you to eat, capiche? This is known as the place the Sopranos would eat, if they were in town. (The cast actually did eat here during a press junket.) Pics of Sinatra and other Italian-Americans line the walls. Martorano prepares what comes in freshest each day. The atmosphere is charming, and the food is delicious and simple.

Eduardo De San Angel

2822 East Commercial Boulevard, Fort Lauderdale; (954) 772-4731

Meals served Lunch and dinner weekdays; dinner only weekends **Cuisine** Mexican **Entree range** $12–$15 **Reservations** Recommended for weekends **Payment** MC, V, AmEx, DC

Comments This gourmet Mexican menu includes crispy roasted duck with sauce made with pumpkin seeds and green chilies (the recipe is more than 200 years old). The garlic shrimp are also spectacular. This romantic restaurant has been designed to look like a small hacienda.

84 Diner

11432 SR 84, Davie; (954) 370-8217; www.84diner.com

Meals served Breakfast, lunch, dinner **Cuisine** American diner **Entree range** $7–$27 **Reservations** Not needed **Payment** Cash only (ATM on site)

Comments A real diner's diner. This place takes up about several store slots, which means you will almost never have a hard time getting seated in a booth. The servers and staff make the place—hurried, friendly, quick witted. A great place to have breakfast for dinner.

Hobo's Fish Joint

Palm Spring Plaza, 10317 Royal Palm Boulevard, Coral Springs; (954) 346-5484

Meals served Dinner **Cuisine** Seafood **Entree range** $19–$30 **Reservations** Recommended **Payment** V, MC, AmEx, D

Comments Skip the menu—pay attention to the chalkboard on the wall by the kitchen. Some think it's overpriced, but the restaurant enjoys a loyal following and steady praise for a selection of fresh fish you can find only in South Florida.

India House

563 Oakland Park Boulevard, Fort Lauderdale; (954) 565-5701; www.indiahouserestaurant.com

Meals served Lunch and dinner **Cuisine** Indian **Entree range** $9–$19 **Reservations** Yes **Payment** V, MC, AmEx, D, DC

Comments India House has a great daily lunch buffet for just $7. And the food tastes as lovely as it looks.

Lester's Diner

150 SR 84, Fort Lauderdale; (954) 525-5641

Meals served Open 24 hours **Cuisine** American **Entree range** $5–$12 **Reservations** No **Payment** V, MC, AmEx, D, DC

Comments A Fort Lauderdale tradition, Lester's is a cavernous 1950s-style diner with food to match. Soups are filling and taste like homemade, sandwiches are large enough for two, and desserts are big enough for three or four to share. Daily specials are a great value.

Mark's Las Olas

1032 East Las Olas Boulevard, Fort Lauderdale; (954) 463-1000

Meals served Lunch and dinner **Cuisine** Continental **Entree range** $13–$40 **Reservations** Suggested **Payment** V, MC, AmEx, D, DC

Comments A restaurant favored by Lauderdale's power players and foodies alike. The progressive menu is matched by almost whimsical decor. An excellent place to people watch on Las Olas.

Max's Grille

Las Olas Riverfront, 300 Southwest First Avenue; (954) 779-1800

Meals served Lunch and dinner **Cuisine** Continental **Entree range** $11–$30 **Reservations** Recommended **Payment** V, MC, AmEx, D, DC

Comments A great all-around experience, Max's is located in a popular area, serves well-crafted dishes, and offers happy-hour drink specials to keep fickle patrons from roaming to other, newer bars. Menu recommendations include maple-ginger glazed salmon, pistachio grouper, and New York strip steak.

Padrino's

2500 East Hallandale Beach Boulevard, Hallandale; (954) 456-4550

Meals served Lunch and dinner **Cuisine** Cuban **Entree range** $10–$15 **Reservations** Not accepted **Payment** V, MC, AmEx, D, DC

Comments Cuban restaurants are not a novelty in South Florida, and Padrino's is one of the best in the moderate price range. The decor is pleasant, the service fairly good, and the music can make it a bit loud—which is good if you have a rowdy bunch of niños and want to blend. Try the *ropa viejo* (shredded beef in a piquant tomato sauce) or the shrimp in garlic sauce.

Taverna Opa

3051 Northeast 32nd Avenue, Fort Lauderdale; (954) 567-1630
410 North Ocean Drive Hollywood; (954) 926-4010

Meals served Dinner **Cuisine** Greek **Entree range** $9–$20 **Reservations** No **Payment** MC, V, AmEx

Comments Broward's beloved big fat Greek restaurant has a waterfront view (in Hollywood), inexpensive Greek fare, music, singing, dancing on tables, and breaking dishes—plenty of opa! for everyone.

Arts and Culture

Generally, in Greater Fort Lauderdale most art, entertainment and nightlife is concentrated in clusters east of I-95:

Second Street is in close proximity to the Broward Center for the Performing Arts and the Science Museum. Of all four locales, it's probably the least touristy.

Las Olas Riverfront (www.riverfrontfl.com) is an outdoor mall that has a 15-screen movie theater and Riverfront Cruises, as well as a charter service that tours the city's intracoastal.

Las Olas Boulevard (www.lasolasboulevard.com) offers art galleries, antique shops, and salons. It's the most gentrified commercial area of Fort Lauderdale. It's also the city's location of choice for street festivals.

Nightlife

South Florida is a grab bag if international influences. The Miami area is filled with Latin dance clubs. Fort Lauderdale has far fewer, but **Café Samba** (350 East Las Olas Boulevard, Fort Lauderdale; (954) 468-2000) has a Latin beat nightly. One of Fort Lauderdale's primo tourist attractions is **Mai Kai Polynesian Restaurant and Dinner Show** (3599 North Federal Highway, Fort Lauderdale; (954) 566-9533). For more than three decades, the hula show—featuring fire twirlers and dancers from Tahiti and Samoa, as well as Hawaii—has told stories via carefully choreographed movements complemented by the songs, costumes, and island artifacts. Irish tunes and a thick brogue are on tap at **Maguire's Hill #17** (535 North Andrews Avenue, Fort Lauderdale; (954) 764-4453), with live music

Thursday–Sunday, and **Dicey Riley's** (217 Southwest Third Street, Fort Lauderdale; (954) 524-2202), a pub with blues and Irish music nightly. The joint is jumpin' at **Sushi Blues** (1836 South Young Circle, Hollywood; (954) 929-9560), with dinner at 6 p.m. and live music Thursday–Saturday.

Bahia Cabana

Who Goes There Young people, college students, yuppies who fondly remember spring break, tourists, occasionally a celebrity or two.

3001 Harbor Drive, Fort Lauderdale, behind the Bahia Cabana Beach Resort; (954) 524-1555

Cover None **Minimum** None **Mixed drinks** $4–$5 **Food available** Full menu available, but lots of sandwiches and burgers **Hours** Sunday–Thursday, 7 a.m.–2 a.m.; Friday and Saturday, 7 a.m.–3 a.m.

What goes on This great outdoor bar has a wonderful view of the yacht harbor and either a DJ or live music nightly.

Comments This is a Fort Lauderdale tradition—a kind of coming-of-age bar for locals—and the nightly action appeals to laid-back tourists of all ages. T-shirts and shorts are the most common outfit for guys and gals, but you'll run into a couple of suits who come by after work as well.

Café Iguana

Who Goes There Tourists, locals looking for popular dance music

Where: 17 South Atlantic Boulevard, BeachPlace, Fort Lauderdale; (954) 763-7222

Cover Varies according to specials and events **Minimum** None **Mixed drinks** $3 and up **Food available** None **Hours** Daily, noon–4 a.m.

What goes on Baila, baila! Musica, musica! Salsa lessons and Latin house music and rap are the norm—radio stations broadcast from the lizard twice a week

Comments Overlooking the Atlantic Ocean from the third floor of Beach-Place, it's like a little bit of Cancun in South Florida. Open until 4 a.m., seven nights a week. Iguana is a favorite with tourists. Parking can be difficult, and during the winter season crowds are pretty thick at BeachPlace. On the weekend, this place is open later than the (expensive) third-floor garage, which closes at 2 a.m.

Christopher's

Who Goes There Singles ages 25–55—a mature, upscale, professional crowd

2587 East Oakland Park Boulevard, Fort Lauderdale; (954) 561-2136; www.christophersnightclub.com

Cover Generally none (although there is an admission cost for special nights, like Hot Latin Sunday) **Minimum** None **Mixed drinks** $3–$8, $80–$1,000 bottle service **Food available** Full restaurant—American/continental, upscale restaurant **Hours** Weekdays 8 p.m.–2 a.m., weekend 8 p.m.–3 a.m.

What goes on Singles swinging Tom Jones style.

Comments This is possibly the oldest, most reliable over 30 singles scene in South Florida (especially on Sunday, when the club has a singles party and complimentary buffet starting at 8 p.m.). Ladies must be 23 and over, guys 25.

Himmarshee Side Bar

Who Goes There Lauderdale's young professionals and singles

210 Southwest Second Avenue, downtown Fort Lauderdale; (954) 524-1818

Cover None **Minimum** None **Mixed drinks** $5–$10 **Food available** The menu from neighboring Himmarshee Bar and Grille offers favorites like chorizo taquitos and seviche of yellowtail snapper; guests can order upstairs on Friday and Saturday **Hours** Friday–Saturday, 5 p.m.–2:30 a.m.; Monday–Thursday, 5 p.m.–midnight

What goes on Nouveau yuppies getting their drink on.

Comments A good all-in-one spot for night-crawling: food, drinks, acoustic music, and people who need people. Parking is difficult on this corner—give yourself time to find a space or valet on Second and Second in front of Tarpon Bend.

Howl at the Moon/Sloppy Joe's

Who Goes There Tourists and locals who enjoy Beach Place or the area

17 South Atlantic Boulevard, BeachPlace, Fort Lauderdale; (954) 522-5054

Cover Seasonal, $5 on Friday and Saturday **Minimum** None **Mixed drinks** $4.25 and up **Food available** Finger food, appetizer-like items including chicken fingers and conch fritters from Sloppy Joe's menu (a branch of the famous Key West bar founded in 1931 by Ernest Hemingway) **Hours** Sunday–Thursday, 7 a.m.–2 a.m.; Friday and Saturday, 7 a.m.–4 a.m.

What goes on Dueling pianos play everything from classic rock to pop favorites, show tunes, current hits, classic rock, and country—basically anything that the masses can sing along to—and they do so with great passion. Sloppy Joe's pumps reggae and "high-energy dance music."

Comments Parking can be difficult, and during the winter season crowds are pretty thick at BeachPlace. On the weekend, this place is open later than the (expensive) third-floor garage, which closes at 2 a.m.

Swig Bartini

Who Goes There Mature, chic west-Broward professionals

1744 Main Street, Weston; (954) 349-2102; www.swigbartini.com

Cover None **Minimum** None **Mixed drinks** $4.75 and up, martinis $8–$11 **Food available** Eclectic menu with pizzas, pastas, appetizers—spinach dip, escargot, and fresh vegetable pizza are popular dishes; kitchen stops serving at 1:30 a.m. on weekends **Hours** 3 p.m.–3 a.m.

What goes on Sometimes Circ X performs with "erotic fire acts, stage shows, dancing divas," check the website for events and promotions.
Comments This is one of your best bets in West Broward.

Voodoo Lounge

Who Goes There The kind of people you see in music videos set in clubs—attractive and well-dressed (or half-dressed) club kids in their 20s–40s

111 Southwest Second Avenue (Moffat Street), downtown Fort Lauderdale; (954) 522-0733; www.voodooloungeflorida.com

Cover Varies by the night; generally none before 12:30, after that it averages $5 for women and $10 for men **Minimum** None **Mixed drinks** $4–$7, $140–$1,000 bottle service **Food available** None **Hours** 10 p.m.–4 a.m. Wednesday, Friday, Saturday, and Sunday

What goes on DJs play hip-hip, house, electronica, and the occasional '80s night. Party 93.1 FM broadcasts live from Voodoo Lounge on Ladies night (Wednesday when women get in free and get well and domestic drinks free midnight–4 a.m.) and on Fridays from 10 p.m. to midnight.

Comments A local favorite and one of Fort Lauderdale's "velvet rope" clubs.

Part Eight

Southwest Florida: Fort Myers, Sanibel and Captiva Islands, Naples, and Marco Island

Welcome to Southwest Florida

Southwest Florida, the destination on the Gulf of Mexico that many people know best as Fort Myers and Naples, has been referred to as an "ecological Disneyland." More laid-back than its cousins along the Atlantic Coast, Southwest Florida doesn't offer a lot of glitz, but is nevertheless home to outstanding oceanfront golfing and shopping.

What the southwest coast does offer is miles of beaches famous for rare shells, and the calm, shallow waters of the Gulf of Mexico. Off the coast, Sanibel and Captiva islands are popular for their excellent shelling and beaches. On the lush island of Sanibel, where all the buildings must be lower than the tallest palm, the sites are best seen by cycling along Periwinkle Way's canopy of whispering pines and expansive banyans.

Due south are affluent Naples and nearby Marco Island, best known for beaches and fishing. Boat and ferry services from Marco Island can take you on a journey through the surrounding ancient mangroves and marshes.

Peak season in Southwest Florida runs January through April, and reservations are essential throughout the area during those months.

A Brief History

Located on the Caloosahatchee River, Fort Myers has a history tied strongly to Native Americans, Spanish colonials, and Cubans who fished the rich waters of the Gulf of Mexico. One such Cuban fisherman, Manuel Gonzalez, sailed from Spain for Cuba. He missed the island nation and settled in the Fort Myers area, later moving on to Key West.

In 1839, the area was home to little more than alligators, a few bears, and Cubans who fished off the barrier islands. Two years later, the U.S. military built a fort near the mouth of the Caloosahatchee River to supply a prexisting fort that had been hit badly by a hurricane. Eventually the new fort was named for Lieutenant Colonel Abraham Charles Myers, an Army quartermaster.

Fort Myers blossomed and soon earned a nationwide reputation as a center for citrus, shipping 20 boxcars of fruit a day during the picking season. The historic freeze that struck Florida in 1894 spared citrus in the Caloosahatchee region, and prices soared to as much as $200 for fruit from one tree.

One early tourist was inventor Thomas Edison, who came to Fort Myers on doctor's orders after a rainy cold spell in St. Augustine sent him scurrying for sunshine and warmth during the winter of 1884. He spent 46 winters in Lee County, enjoying the mild climate and encouraging friends such as Henry Ford and Harvey Firestone to come visit.

However, the area never achieved—or was spared, depending on your perspective—the fame of more cosmopolitan South Florida destinations on the Atlantic. During World War II there were more military personnel than residents in the Fort Myers area. And many of those service men and women chose to return to the area and set up their post-war homes. Southwest Florida today is home to world-class resorts along its powdery beaches, but thanks largely to local conservationists and preservationists, retains a relaxed, fishing-village air.

HIGHLIGHTS

- J. N. "Ding" Darling National Wildlife Refuge on Sanibel Island
- Edison and Ford Winter Estates in Fort Meyers
- Shelling and sunset on Bowman's Beach, Sanibel Island
- Wildlife viewing boat trip from Marco Island
- Cayo Costa Island State Park

Visiting Southwest Florida

Gathering Information

Lee Island Coast Visitor and Convention Bureau, Tourist Development Council, 2180 West First Street, Suite 100, Fort Myers 33901; (800) 237-6444; **www.leeislandcoast.com**

Greater Naples Marco Island Everglades Convention and Visitors Bureau, 3050 North Horseshoe Drive #210, Naples 34104; (800) 688-3600; **www.classicflorida.com**

Charlotte Country Visitor's Bureau, 18501 Murdock Circle, Suite 502, Port Charlotte 33948; (941) 743-1900; **www.pureflorida.com**

Getting There

By Plane The major airport in Southwest Florida is aptly called Southwest Florida International Airport and is located approximately one mile east of Exit 131 off I-75. A new terminal is under construction, opening in 2005. Flying into Southwest Florida are Air Canada, Air Tran, Air Transat, America West, American, American Eagle, American Trans Air, Balair-CTA,

Canada 3000 Airlines, Cape Air, Condor German Airlines, Continental/Continental Connection, Delta, Delta Express, JetBlue, LTU, Midwest Express, Northwest/KLM, Pro Air, Spirit Airlines, Sun Country, TWA, United Airlines, and US Air. To reach Marco Island and the Everglades from the airport, take I-75 South to Exit 101. To reach Naples, take I-75 south to Exit 101, 107, or 111.

Visitor Services Centers are located near the baggage claim areas at the airport to help travelers with questions regarding attractions, accommodations, beaches, and parks. German is spoken at the center in the LTU International Airway Terminal, reflecting the sizable percentage of area tourism that nation provides. For more information, call (239) 768-1000.

Naples Municipal Airport offers commuter and direct flights, private charters, and regularly scheduled flights to the Florida Keys, Key West, and Miami. For more information, call (239) 543-0733. Marco Island Executive Airport offers commuter and charter flights to and from nearby international airports. For more information, call (239) 394-3355.

Taxi and limousine services are available at the airports. Taxi fares to beach resorts are about $40 from Southwest Florida International Airport and about $20 from Naples Municipal Airport. Fares from Miami International Airport run to $150.

Rental car companies include: Alamo, Avis, Budget, Cape Coral, CarTemps, Dollar, Enterprise, Hertz, National, Ro-Lin, and Thrifty. Reservations are not required for taxis and limos. Travelers simply make arrangements upon arrival at the ground transportation booth located in the median between the airport terminal and the parking lot.

By Car Many people choose to drive to Southwest Florida from their northern homes. Others head to the Gulf Coast after visiting other Florida cities. From Palm Beach, for example, take Florida's Turnpike (also known as the Ronald Reagan Expressway) south to US 595/Alligator Alley, or the Sawgrass Expressway to I-75 North, then straight into Fort Myers. I-75 South from the Tampa Bay area is a major roadway into the Fort Myers area. This latter route is the road most often taken from the Midwest, a primary source of area tourism.

Miami's Tamiami Trail (US 41) leads into Fort Myers and Naples. It's a two-lane road through much of the route. While this highway is picturesque, it takes about three hours to get from Miami to Naples on the Tamiami. I-75 and US 41 are major north-south arteries into the region, and Alligator Alley and US 41 east of Naples are the key east-west highways.

By Train Amtrak makes stops in Port Charlotte, Fort Myers, and Naples; (800) USA-RAIL, **www.amtrak.com**.

Getting Around

Probably the best advice we can provide anyone choosing to rent a car and drive in Southwest Florida (or anywhere in sprawling Florida, for that matter) is to request driving instructions from your hotel, motel, or host. Let them know where you will be picking up a car and get complete directions to the property.

US 41 (also known as the Tamiami Trail) is a major highway running to Naples from Miami. At Naples, US 41 runs north and south between Naples and Fort Myers. It is very slow-going and heavily traveled. For many years, this was the only highway connecting the east and west coasts. Construction along US 41 is pandemic. Although I-75, which also runs north-south from Naples, was built to handle the overflow and speed traffic through Collier and Lee Counties, it doesn't do the job. Rush hours can find both major roadways clogged.

Fort Myers and Surrounding Areas US 41 and I-75 carry the bulk of the north-south traffic here (they also lead northwest to the Tampa Bay area). East-west streets vary in the amount of traffic they see; a series of one-way streets in downtown Fort Myers tend to confuse visitors, but signage is clear if you pay attention.

The Caloosahatchee and Edison Bridges span the Caloosahatchee River, and SR 80 (also called Palm Beach Road) parallels the curve of the bay. SR 80 accesses I-75 at Exit 141.

The major routes to Fort Myers Beach and Sanibel and Captiva Islands are McGregor Boulevard and Summerlin Road, both of which lead to the Summerlin Bridge. You can also take San Carlos and Estero Boulevards to Fort Myers Beach; Estero Boulevard, SR 865, also leads to Bonita Beach.

Naples and Marco Island Three exits from I-75 reach Naples: Exit 101 is Golden Gate, a main Naples exit; Exit 107, Pine Ridge Road, leads directly to US 41; and Exit 111, Immokalee Road, leads to North Naples to the west and the National Audubon Society's famed Corkscrew Swamp Sanctuary 18 miles northeast of Naples. To get to Marco Island, take Exit 101 (Golden Gate) off I-75 and head south on Collier Boulevard for 20 miles.

Naples' Third Street South is a remnant of the town's old central commercial district. Third Street is at the western edge of Fifth Avenue South, Naples' Main Street. It is the heart of old Naples, and legend has it that Charles and Anne Morrow Lindbergh often landed their plane on a strip at the corner of Fifth Avenue and Third Street to have Sunday lunch at the Naples Hotel. Today, Third Street sits on the National Register of Historic Places and is home to more than 100 shops, galleries, outdoor cafes, and restaurants.

Marco Island is a serene outpost on the Gulf of Mexico where you can get around by bicycle or trolley. You can get there via FL 951 (Isle of Capri Road). Day cruises leave from Marco Island to Key West (Key West Shuttle, 1079 Bald Eagle Drive #3, Marco Island; (941) 394-7979).

Public Transportation

LeeTran offers local bus service Monday–Saturday from 5 a.m.–9:45 p.m. and limited service to the beach on Sunday from 6 a.m.–9 p.m. LeeTran also offers airport service hourly, 6 a.m.–10 p.m., to a transfer point at Daniels Parkway and US 41 with connections to other routes. Fare is $1 for adults, 50 cents for seniors and disabled citizens, and free for children under 42 inches tall. For more information on LeeTran, call (239) 275-8726 or check www.rideleetran.com.

If you don't want the hassle of parking in Fort Myers, consider other means of getting around the area: Tolleys (for 25 cents) run up and down Estero Boulevard the length of Fort Myers Beach. This trolley serves only as transportation, providing no narration or sight-seeing, but it may be better than trying to park along the beach.

Island Hopping

This part of Florida, from Charlotte County to Fort Myers, has dozens of little islands just off the coast, everything from uninhabited beaches to seaside resorts. Some are accessible by roads, other only by boat. We focus on activities and establishments on the major islands of Marco, Sanibel, and Captiva. But don't miss the chance to tour some of the regions unique and charming islets.

If you don't have your own boat and want to get to the less inhabited spots, try one of these:

Tropic Star Nature Cruise, is a water taxi that drops you off and comes back for you, like clockwork, at specified times. The boats depart from Four Winds Marina at Bokeelia on the north end of Pine Island, east of Sanibel and Captiva, and offer cruises to Cabbage Key, Cayo Costa, and other islands daily at 9:30 a.m., 11 p.m., and 2 p.m., with the last shuttle returning at 4:30 p.m. You can bring a picnic if you're headed to Cayo Costa or the other beaches, or have lunch at Cabbage Key. The cost is $25 for adults, $15 for children ages 11 and under, (239) 283-0015; **www.tropic starcruises.com.**

Shell Seekers works out of the bayside of South Seas Resort on Captiva and offers a two-hour excursion to Cayo Costa for seashell hunts. They depart at 9 a.m. and 1 p.m. every day, and if you can make the early trip, you'll find more treasures. The fare is $35 for adults, $17.50 for children ages 4–11; (239) 472-5111.

Captiva Cruises generally carries a crowd, but it's a reliable, enjoyable way to see the Gulf Coast islands. Cruises to Cabbage Key and Useppa islands are $27.50 for adults, $15 for children ages 12 and under. Cruises to Boca Grande and Cayo Costa islands (during the winter months only) are $35 for adults, $17.50 for children ages 12 and under. Dolphin-watch cruises depart every day at 4 p.m.; they cost $20 for adults, $10 for children ages 12 and under. Sunset cruises depart daily according to sunset times, costing $17.50 for adults, $10 for children ages 12 and under. There are two daily shelling cruises on Tuesday, Thursday, and Saturday: 9 a.m.–noon and 1–4 p.m.; the cost is $35 for adults, $17.50 for children ages 12 and under. All cruises depart from South Seas Plantation on Captiva; (239) 472-5300; **www.captivacruises.com.**

Gasparilla Island

Gasparilla Island is 43 miles northwest of Fort Myers, with powdery white beaches and a historic lighthouse. The island is named for notorious pirate Jose Gaspar, and it's said that his treasure still is buried on the island. But today Gasparilla is most famous for the tarpon that run here in spring and summer, and since the early 1900s the rich and famous have come here to fish. Many fourth- and fifth-generation families still live on the island as fishing and sightseeing guides.

Most of the public beaches are at **Gasparilla Island State Recreation Area** at the bottom end of the island, where there are summertime turtle walks with park rangers in the morning and beach nature walks and shelling walks in the fall and winter. You can also explore the town of Boca Grande by bike, on a 6.5-mile bike path (13 miles round-trip) that follows the trail of the original Seaboard Airline Railroad and passes the historic Boca Grande Railroad Depot.

The rail-trail is well maintained, the terrain is flat, and there's always an ocean breeze. Beware, traffic does cross at some points, so stop at all road crossings. To get to the trail, take the toll bridge to Gasparilla Island and downtown Boca Grande. From Park Avenue, turn right onto First Street and left onto Gulf Boulevard. The bike path is on the opposite side of the road. Bikes are for rent for $7 an hour at **Island Bike 'n Beach** (333 Park Avenue; (941) 964-0711). The shop is open Monday–Saturday, 9 a.m.–6 p.m., and on Sunday, 10 a.m.–5 p.m.

Clothing boutiques, art galleries, gift stores and restaurants are in the center of town, with more shops in historic Whidden's marina and along Park Avenue. There is expensive and limited lodging at the Gasparilla Inn.

To get there by car, take I-75 to Exit 179, then west to the end of Toledo Blade Boulevard. Right onto SR 776, left on SR 771 to Placida and the Boca Grande Causeway. There are also boat trips from Pine and Captiva Islands.

Cayo Costa

South of Gasparilla Island and Boca Grande Pass, Cayo Costa is 2,225 acres—one of the largest undeveloped barrier islands in Florida, with Cayo Costa State Park occupying most of the island.

You can only get there by private boat or ferry, but the journey is worth it: seven miles of undeveloped beaches, acres of pine forest, oak palm hammocks, mangrove swamps, and a spectacular display of bird life. Shelling is especially good during the winter months. There are 12 cabins for rent and tent camping, but no drinking water or electricity. In the fall, park rangers lead guided beach walks; in the summer, rangers offer morning programs about sea turtles.

Palm Island Resort

Escape to a barrier island that's only accessible by a 15-minute ferry ride: you load your car on the barge in Placida and park it at the entrance to the resort. After that it's a golf cart, bicycle or your own two feet, as no cars are allowed past the reception parking lot.

If you're looking for a laid-back, beach-only environment, Palm Island has one- to three-bedroom villas (160 in all), with screened porches, full kitchens, and washers and dryers. There are five pools, eleven tennis courts, an island store, a full-service marina with boat rentals, two playgrounds, and a nature center. We recommend taking your own groceries or for a dinner out, take the ferry over to **Johnny Leverock's Seafood House** in Cape Haze.

Shelling is bountiful on the beach—you can stroll to the end of the island where a pass connects the Intracoastal Waterway to the Gulf of Mexico (and where dolphins love to frolic).

Visitors can fish, snorkel, bicycle, canoe, go kayaking, or just read a good book. Most days of the week there are morning and afternoon nature activities, from family bicycle tours to kid fishing and canoe nature tours. Villas start at $205 in the summer, $305 in the winter. Palm Island Resort is located at 7092 Placida Road, Cape Haze; (941) 697-4800 or (800) 824-5412; **www.palmisland.com**.

Cabbage Key

Built on top of an ancient Calusa Indian shell mound, rustic **Cabbage Key Restaurant, Bar, and Inn** (www.cabbagekey.com) is about all you find on this 100-acre island, accessible only by boat from Bokeelia on Pine Island or from Captiva Island. The rustic watering hole was built in 1938 by the children of mystery novelist Mary Roberts Rinehart.

Julia Roberts has dined here, as well as Sean Connery, and it's rumored that Jimmy Buffett wrote "Cheeseburger in Paradise" after a burger at the Cabbage Key Inn. You can eat on the screened porch or have a drink in Mrs. Rinehart's library, plastered with $1 bills left by former guests—it's estimated that there's more than $50,000 on the walls.

There is no beach and are just six rooms at the inn (down the hall from the bar and restaurant, so the noise level can make it nearly impossible to sleep). Better to opt for one of the seven air-conditioned cottages among the live oaks and mangroves. Some overlook the water, and some have kitchens. Accommodations range from one to eight guests.

Pine Island

Crossing the bridge to the charming Matlacha area on Pine Island is like stepping back into time, when fishing was the area's largest industry. This quaint island just east of Sanibel continues to be a fisherman's paradise, and also features some of the most funky, fun shops and galleries in the area—the best in Matlacha (Mat-la-shay). Along with anglers, it's mostly residential and agricultural, with mangoes, guavas, and other fruit harvested. Contact **Gulf Coast Kayak Company** (phone (239) 283-1125; **www.gulfcoastkayak.com**) trips for guided tours of local natural areas, including the Matlacha Aquatic Preserve. The cost is $35 per person; reservations are required.

Useppa Island

Millionaire Barron G. Collier bought this island in 1911, and it's been the refuge of the rich and famous ever since. Today it's a chichi island country club. **Captiva Cruises** (see above) takes day guests over for a two-hour stay with lunch at the Collier Inn, but you can't stay the night unless you're a member or know a member of this private vacation club. If your children are teenagers, you'll enjoy the day trip, catching a glimpse of the lifestyles of the rich and famous.

The Best Beaches

Fort Myers Area

Bonita Beach Park A low-key, full-service beach with plenty of parking. Alternatively, you can park at the K-Mart at Bonita Beach Road and US 41 in Bonita Springs and take the bus or trolley for 25 cents.

Bowditch Point Regional Park This 17-acre park was designed to provide a total day at the beach. Free parking is at Main Street on Fort Myers Beach, or ride the trolley for 25 cents; handicapped parking is available inside the park. Located on Estero Boulevard, Fort Myers Beach; (239) 463-1116.

Bowman's Beach This is a remote, city-operated beach on the west end of Sanibel Island, one of the best for shelling and sunsets. Also picnic areas and showers. Parking is available.

Gulfside City Park, Sanibel Island Located off Casa Ybel Road in central Sanibel Island, the beach offers swimming, picnicking, showers, and rest rooms.

Lakes Regional Park This park consists of 279 acres of Florida foliage and summertime fresh-water swimming. Other water sports and picnic tables are also available. Expect a $2 per person fee to ride the miniature train. Parking is 75 cents per hour, $3 maximum per day. Locate at 7330 Gladiolus Drive in Fort Myers; (239) 432-2000.

Lover's Key State Recreation Area Accessible by tram or footpath, Lover's Key is just two miles south of Fort Myers Beach. The recreation area also includes adjacent Inner Key and Carl. E. Johnson County Park for an expansive 712 acres. There are nearly three miles of pristine beach (no lifeguards) reachable by tram or footpath from a paved parking lot. There are rest rooms, canoe and kayak rentals, and a beach concession. Several short nature walks are marked near the beach. And the shelling is great if you get there early enough. The park is open daily 8 a.m.–sunset; admission is $2–$4 per vehicle. On CR 865 between Fort Myers Beach and Bonita Beach; (239) 463-4588.

Sanibel Lighthouse Park Beach, Sanibel Island The beach at this 100-year-old lighthouse on Sanibel's eastern tip offers picnic facilities and pier fishing. It is not a great swimming beach, however, because of the currents.

Turner Beach This is a big-time shelling area between Sanibel and Captiva Islands. Foot showers and handicapped parking and rest rooms are available. This is one of the most popular beaches for sunset watching, and parking is limited. If you've ever heard the expression "Sanibel Stoop," this is where it originated, with dedicated shellers looking for the best. Swimmers, beware of strong currents.

Naples and Marco Island

Barefoot Beach Preserve, North Naples There's not much here but the a 1.5-mile beach, the sea, and wide-open spaces—no lifeguards, but rest rooms, concessions, and nature trails. Barefoot Beach is open 8 a.m.–sundown. Location is off Bonita Beach Road to Lily Road, north of Naples. Entry costs $3 per vehicle.

Clam Pass County Park Another outstanding natural beach at the south end of Naples has gentle waves and a shallow, sandy bottom, making it a good place to take children. Located at the end of Seagate Drive in Pelican Bay, just north of Naples. Entrance costs $3; open from 8 a.m. to sunset with concessions, rest rooms, and showers.

Delnor-Wiggins Pass State Recreation Area This 166-acre preserve is on a narrow barrier island north of Old Naples, separated from mainland Naples by mangrove swamps and tidal creeks. It's the perfect setting for all-day family fun, with lifeguards, a boat launch, barbecue grills and picnic tables in the shade, and showers. Be sure to swim near the lifeguards and avoid Wiggins Pass, where currents can be swift. Native gopher tortoises, manatees, dolphins, osprey, and a wide variety of wading birds are commonly seen; a lookout station provides a view of the beach, and woods. From June to August, there's a Sea Turtle Beach Walk Program at 9 a.m. every Friday and other ranger programs throughout the year, from native plant walks to talks on marine mammals and beach habitats. To make reservations for any programs, call (239) 597-6196. Hours are 8 a.m.–sunset; admission is $4 per car for 2–8 people. Located six miles south of Bonita Springs, off CR 901, off US 41.

Lowdermilk Park In the middle of Naples, this municipal beach is a favorite of the locals, with 1,000 feet of beach, lifeguards, a playground, shady picnic spots, sand volleyball, showers, and rest rooms. Special attractions are the duck ponds and complementary sand chairs for wheelchair-bound beachgoers. Location is at Gulf Shore and Banyan Boulevards neighboring Old Naples. Parking is metered. The park is open daily from dawn to dusk.

Tigertail Beach County Park This beach on the northern end of Marco Island stretches 1.5 miles with a sandbar, known as Sand Dollar Island, that creates a shallow lagoon for young swimmers. There are rest rooms, showers, a children's playground, and volleyball nets. You can get impromptu windsurfing lessons or rent a pontoon boat for nature and shelling tours. They also rent cabanas, chairs, umbrellas, and other toys. And there's a beach restaurant serving hot dogs and sandwiches from 10 a.m. to 4 p.m. Parking is $4. The park is on Hernando Drive and is open daily 9 a.m.–5 p.m.; (239) 642-8414.

BEST SHELLING

Southwest Florida is known for shelling, with nearly 300 varieties washing up on the beaches. Where are the best spots to find a perfect specimen? We talked with Captain Mike Fuery, author of *New Florida Shelling Guide*, who says the easiest shelling is on Cayo Costa or North Captiva, both only accessible by boat.

If you haven't got a boat, he recommends Blind Pass between Sanibel and Captiva, or Bowman's Beach smack in the middle of Sanibel. Gasparilla Island is another good spot. If you're looking for shark's teeth, Manasota Key is the place, he says.

Nearly all the beaches on Sanibel and Captiva offer decent shelling but nowhere to park. And if you're on a good shelling beach with parking, like Lighthouse Beach, it's probably going to get crowded. Fuery recommends traveling the two islands by bicycle and stopping whenever the urge strikes. The best time of day is early morning, around seven, finishing by ten when the sun starts to scorch. Shelling is best after a storm.

Though shelling is great year-round, he loves the summertime when he can introduce kids to the joys of snorkeling for shells in 2–3 feet of water. "It opens a whole new world," says Fuery.

Note: A 2002 ordinance prohibits beachcombers throughout the coastal county from keeping any shells containing live creatures, including sand dollars, star fish, and sea urchins.

Outdoor Adventures and Sports

Recommended Excursions

Fort Myers

Babcock Wilderness Adventures Just 23 miles north of Fort Myers, get a real Florida experience on this 90-minute swamp buggy tour of the Crescent B Ranch. Or if you're an off-road cyclist, Babcock offers guided off-road biking tours for both novice and experienced bikers. Experienced guides point out alligators, panthers, American bison, native birds, wild turkeys, snakes, and other animals. Cost is $18 for adults, $10 for ages 3–12. Reservations required. November–May, 9 a.m.–3 p.m.; morning tours only June–October. Two three-hour tours are given per day, at 9 a.m. and 1 p.m. No handicap access is available. Located at 8000 SR 31, Punta Gorda; (800) 500-5583; **www.babcockwildnerness.com**.

Estero Bay Boat Tours If you're vacationing at Fort Myers Beach, this is a nice experience to get back to nature, with an expert guide to help you spot dolphin, manatee, birds, and other Florida wildlife in the state's first aquatic preserve. Tours depart three times a day, at 10:30 a.m., 1:30 p.m., and in the evening (2 hours before sunset), last for 2 hours, and are recommended for all ages; cost is $15 for adults, $10 for children ages 12 and under. The launching point is five miles north of Bonita Beach Road, off US 41 at the end of Coconut Road, Bonita Springs; (239) 992-2200.

Manatee Park You can observe the endangered West Indian manatee in its natural habitat from three observation decks in the park from November through March. Naturalists are there to answer questions, and you can rent kayaks for $10 an hour from 9 a.m. to 3 p.m. to cruise the Orange River. To find out if the manatees are there, call (239) 694-3537; **www.leeparks.org** for updates. Parking is 75 cents an hour, $3 maximum. Located on SR 80, 1.5 miles east of I-75, Fort Myers.

Six Mile Cypress Slough ("Slew") Take a stroll with your family on this mile-long boardwalk through a 2,200-acre wetlands ecosystem to see subtropical ferns, wild ferns, wild orchids, and birds such as herons, storks, spoonbills, and egrets. Admission is free, and the park is open 8 a.m.– 5 p.m. daily October-March, and 8 a.m.–8 p.m. April-September, with guided tours Wednesdays at 9:30 a.m on alternating days. Parking is 75 cents an hour or $3 a day. Located at 7751 Penzance Crossing, Fort Myers; (239) 432-2004.

Sanibel and Captiva Island

Canoe Adventures Highly recommended by the locals, guide Mark "Bird" Westall formerly was the mayor of Sanibel, and now he leads excellent environmental tours, three that are appropriate for children. One heads for The J. N. "Ding" Darling Wildlife Refuge, a second to the Sanibel River, and a third to Buck Key. You can reach Westall at (239) 472-5218, and he'll discuss the best trip for you, from a one-hour tour ($35 for adults, $15 for children up to age 18) to a two- or three-hour trip ($40 for adults, $20 for kids up to age 18).

J. N. "Ding" Darling National Wildlife Refuge This 6,000-acre wildlife refuge on the southern end of Sanibel Island is part swamp, part prairie, crisscrossed with elevated boardwalks, hiking trails, and streams. More than 238 bird species and 50 types of reptiles live in the spongy shallows— roseate spoonbills and otter are often spotted. You can stay in your car and take the five-mile scenic drive, but the best way to see it is on foot, by bicycle, or in a canoe.

Even inexperienced boaters can maneuver a canoe through the shallows and mangroves, where you may even see an occasional manatee.

First-timers might want to take the two-hour tram tour narrated by a naturalist. You can catch the tram at the Tarpon Bay Recreation Center at the north end of Tarpon Bay Road. Cost is $10 for adults, $9 for ages 12 and under; call (239) 472-8900 for tour times.

The best time to visit, when you'll see the most wildlife, is just after sunrise or late afternoon. Gates open half an hour after sunrise and close about half an hour before sunset. Admission is $5 per vehicle. The visitors center is open daily, 9 a.m.–4 p.m.; (239) 472-1100; **http://dingdarling.fws.gov.** Darling, by the way, was a Pulitzer Prize–winning cartoonist and a conservationist.

For more back-to-nature fun, visit the **Sanibel-Captiva Conservation Center** with nature trails and interpretive tours; (239) 472-2329. Also, **Care and Rehabilitation of Wildlife** (CROW), where kids can see rescued animals, offers a tour at 11 a.m., Monday–Friday. The cost is $5 for adults, children under age 12 free; (239) 472-3644. Both centers are nearby.

Tarpon Bay Explorers This is the easiest way to see the spectacular "Ding" Darling Wildlife Refuge, with tram tours, guided canoe tours, and kayak trips through the refuge. Tram tours are two hours long and cost $10 for adults, $7 for children ages 12 and under. The one-hour canoe and kayak guided trips, departing at 10:30 a.m. and 1:30 p.m., are $30 per Adult, $15 for Children. Located inside the J. N. "Ding" Darling Wildlife Refuge, 900 Tarpon Bay Road, Sanibel; (239) 472-8900; **www.tarponbayexplorers.com.**

Wildside Adventures McCarthy's Marina on Captiva is home to Wildside, where you can take your pick of kayaking, sailing, and canoe tours with a guide, many trips as short as two hours. A two-hour day trip or a two-hour moonlight trip in kayaks is $35 or $45 for adults, $25 or $35 for teens, $20 or $35 for children. Located at 11401 Andy Rosse Lane, Captiva; (239) 395-2925.

Naples

Corkscrew Swamp Sanctuary Managed by the National Audubon Society, this 11,000-acre natural preserve is mecca for bird-watchers. A two-mile boardwalk trail takes you past the world's largest remaining stand of virgin bald cypress. Some of the trees are more than 700 years old, soaring 13 stories. You might also see native wildlife, including alligators, bobcats, and otters, and you'll always be entertained by a symphony of birds and frogs. Corkscrew is the nesting site for the largest colony of wood storks in the United States.

There are picnic tables and a small welcome center. Hours are 7 a.m.–5:30 p.m. from October through April, and 7 a.m.–7:30 p.m. from April through September. Admission is $8 for adults, $5.50 for students with ID, $3.50 for minors. Located at 375 Sanctuary Road, about 20 miles north of Naples and 14 miles west of Immokalee; (239) 348-9151.

Don Pedro Island State Recreation Area, Cape Haze At the southern end of Little Gasparilla Island, you can only get here by private (or chartered) boat, but the shelling and swimming along the 1.3-mile beach are worth the adventure. There's nothing man-made here except picnic tables and rest rooms, so come prepared.

Naples Nature Center/Briggs Nature Center These two nature centers are part of the Conservancy, a nonprofit organization dedicated to the preservation of Southwest Florida's fragile ecosystem. The Naples Nature Center (1450 Merrihue Drive; (239) 262-0304) includes the Conservancy Museum of Natural History, where kids can touch a snake, count an alligator's teeth, and explore Southwest Florida's underwater world; a wildlife rehabilitation center where recuperating patients like owls, eagles, and hawks are on display; guided trail walks; guided electric boat tours through a mangrove forest; and canoe and kayak rentals for exploring the Gordon River.

At the Briggs Nature Center (401 Shell Island Road, off SR 951 six miles north of Marco Island; (239) 775-8569), located on 12,700 acres in the Rookery Bay National Estuarine Research Reserve, you'll find a butterfly garden, an interpretive center where you can meet some estuary residents including fish and snakes, and a half-mile boardwalk through the reserve. Briggs is also the launching point for canoe and boat rides in Rookery Bay and for guided bird-watching and shelling on Key Island in the bay. Dolphins often breach the water and follow the boat, with egrets guarding the shoreline, and pelicans diving for mouthfuls of fish. Children must be 6 or older to go along on the afternoon shelling trip to Key Island. Cost is $35 per person.

Admission is $7.50 for adults, $2 for children ages 3–12. Admission is good for both the Naples Nature Center and Briggs Nature Center if you visit both within 7 days. Both are open year-round Monday–Saturday, 9 a.m.–4:30 p.m.

Canoeing and Kayaking

Southwest Florida's Sanibel and Captiva islands have found their way onto *Paddler* magazine's list of ten best kayaking destinations in the nation. *Paddler* publisher and editor Eugene Buchanan kayaked on the Lee Island Coast and says, "besides the islands having a strong community feel, the area's temperate climate is great for year-round kayaking, and its easy access and close proximity to other areas are ideal for paddlers." For more information, contact the following: **Captiva Kayak and Wildside Adventures** (11401 Andy Rosse Lane, Captiva Island; (239) 395-2925); **Estero River Outfitters** (20991 South Tamiami Trail, Estero; (239) 992-4050); **Gulf Coast Kayak** (The Olde Fish House Marina, 4530 Pine Island Road, Matlacha; (239) 283-1125); **Canoe Adventures, Inc.** (716 Rabbit Road, Sanibel Island; (239) 472-5218); **Briggs Nature Center** (401 Shell Island Road, Naples; (239) 775-8569); and **Naples Nature Center** (1450 Merrihue Drive, Naples; (239) 262-0304).

Scuba Diving and Snorkeling

The Gulf of Mexico along the Southwest Florida coast offers some dive sites with visibility approaching 50 feet. Artificial reefs are plentiful and made up of old culverts, the old Edison Reef, and a ship called the Pegasus. The Caloosa Dive Club has been exploring underwater sites for three decades. For more information, contact **Scuba Quest** (11705-3 Cleveland Avenue, Fort Myers; (239) 936-7106) or **Seahorse Scuba** (15600 No. 19 San Carlos Boulevard, Fort Myers; (239) 454-3115).

Sailboats and Sailing Schools

Sailing on the Gulf of Mexico is an exhilarating experience, and thousands of sailors have learned their skills at the **Offshore Sailing School** (16731

Outdoor Adventures and Sports

McGregor Boulevard, Fort Myers; (239) 454-1700; **www.offshoresailing.com**). It was founded 28 years ago by Olympic and America's Cup winner Steve Colgate. Offshore teaches at South Seas Resort on Captiva Island (call (239) 454-1700) as well as at other locations throughout the Caribbean and United States. Other sailboat rentals and schools include: **Captiva Kayak and Wildside Adventures** (11401 Andy Rosse Lane, Captiva Island; (239) 395-2925); **Florida Sailing and Cruising School** (3444 Marinatown Lane, North Fort Myers; (239) 656-1339).

SOUTHWEST FLORIDA MARINAS

Marina	Location	Phone
Sanibel and Captiva Islands		
Captiva Cruises	South Seas Plantation	(239) 472-5300
Captain Jim's Charters	Tween Waters Marine	(239) 472-1779
Castaways Marina	6460 Sanibel-Captiva Road	(239) 472-1112
Sanibel Marina	634 North Yachtsman Drive	(239) 472-2723
South Seas Plantation	Yacht Harbor (1.5 miles west of IWC)	(239) 472-5111
Tarpon Bay Recreation, Inc.	900 Tarpon Bay Road	(239) 472-8900
Fort Myers Beach (Estero Island)		
Captain Tony's Fishing	416 Crescent Street	(239) 463-4166
Fish Tale Marina	7225 Estero Boulevard	(239) 463-3600
Island Lady Deep Sea Fishing	702 Fisherman's Wharf	(239) 482-2005
Moss Marine	450 Harbor Court	(239) 463-6137
Fort Myers		
Adventures in Paradise	14341 Port Comfort Road	(239) 472-8443
Sanibel Harbour Marina	15051 Punta Rassa Road	(239) 454-0104
Cape Coral		
Cape Coral Yacht & Racket Club	5819 Driftwood Parkway	(239) 574-0806
Lazy Day Charters	1428 SW 53rd Lane	(239) 549-9366
Bonita Springs and Beaches		
Bonita Bay Marina	27598 Marina Point Drive SE	(239) 495-9009
Captain Ron LePree	9971 Puopolo Lane	(239) 498-9992
Estero Bay Boat Tours	5231 Mamie Street SW	(239) 992-2200

Fishing

Fishing on the Gulf coast can be fishing from almost anywhere. It can be by boat in the backcountry, inshore or offshore. Called a fisherman's paradise by those in the know, the opportunities are so varied that they appeal to anyone who loves the water and has ever picked up a fishing rod. Snook, redfish, spotted sea trout, sheepshead, jack, crevalle, mangrove snapper, and other species can be caught in mangrove shorelines; over the open flats;

around bridges, piers, and docks; and by wading. Shark, grouper, bonito, barracuda, permit, black fin tuna, cobia, and Spanish and king mackerel can be caught over natural or artificial reefs offshore.

During the months of April, May, and June, tarpon migrate by the thousands from Boca Grande Pass to the reefs off Sanibel Island and Fort Myers Beach. In Boca Grande Pass (known as the world capital of tarpon fishing), anglers in 20- or 30-foot boats employ a controlled drift-fishing technique with heavy tackle using live bait. Along the beaches as well as in the backcountry, anglers pursue tarpon in smaller boats and flat skiffs using light tackle with live crabs or 11 to 15 weight fly rods with various flies are used.

Anyone can fish from beaches, piers, bridges, or docks. A saltwater license is required for nonresidents over the age of 16 and can be obtained from the Lee County Tax Collector (phone (239) 339-6000) or through Florida Marine Patrol (phone (239) 332-6966), which provides information on fishing regulations and closed seasons for specific types of fish.

Party Boats

No fishing license is required on party boats, and fishers of any age can go out. Tackle is supplied, and boats are usually 60–100 feet with rest room and small galley. Average cost for a half day is $25 per person ($40 for full day).

Charter Boats

No fishing license is required to arrange a charter boat, and anglers can charter a captain and boat for a half-day or full day. Tackle is supplied; costs range from $150 for half-day to $400 for a full day.

More than 50 marinas are available on the Lee Island Coast alone. See the previous page for a sampling, offering bait, charters, fishing equipment, and customized trips.

Biking

Bike rentals are available all across the islands, and customers are provided with a detailed map and highlighted waypoints. Though routes and trails for serious cyclists are rare in Southwest Florida, especially on the islands, the area is very bike friendly. Biking is an excellent way to sightsee and, oftentimes, a suitable transportation alternative. We suggest **Bike Route, Inc.** (locations at 2330 Palm Ridge Road, Sanibel Island; (239) 472-1955 and 14530 South US 41, Fort Myers; (239) 481-3376); **Finnimore's Cycle Shop** (2353 Periwinkle Way, Sanibel Island; (239) 472-5577); **www.finnimores.com**; and **Trikes, Bikes, & Mowers, Inc.** (3451-53 Fowler Street, Fort Myers; (239) 936-1851). For information on Boca Grande's 6.5-mile rail-trail, see "Gasparilla Island," above.

Spectator Sports

Baseball

The first baseball team in Lee County was organized in January 1896, playing its first game the following July 4. Baseball continued as a major player in the region, and in 1924, the Philadelphia Athletics became the first major league club to train in Fort Myers. Cornelius McGillicuddy, better known as Connie Mack, was the team manager. Mack's grandson and namesake was a U.S. senator from Lee County. From 1939 to 1940, the Cleveland Indians made Fort Myers their spring training headquarters. And in 1955 the Pittsburgh Pirates came to town.

Terry Park is not a "park" in the true meaning of the word—it's comprised of four baseball fields. Don't expect playground equipment or picnic facilities. This is the headquarters for Lee County Parks and Recreation (3410 Palm Beach Boulevard, Fort Myers; (239) 338-3288). Terry Park does have quite a history, including its role as the site of the annual Lee County fair for some 50 years. It was also home to Kansas City Royals spring training from 1968 to 1988.

The Lee County Sports Complex in south Fort Myers (which includes the William H. Hammond Stadium) is spring training headquarters for the **Minnesota Twins,** the fifth team in more than 65 years to train in Lee County (phone (239) 768-4210) and the summer home to the **Fort Myers Miracle,** the Twins Class-A affiliate co-owned by Bill Murray and Jimmy Buffet. The 7,500-seat stadium opened in 1994 and boasts four regulation major league practice fields, two half-fields, four softball practice fields, ten indoor batting cages (four in the main stadium), and 30 practice pitching areas with mounds. The handicapped-accessible stadium is located at 14400 Six Mile Cypress Parkway, Fort Myers; (239) 768-4210.

The City of Palms Park (2201 Edison Avenue, Fort Myers; (239) 334-4700) in downtown Fort Myers is the spring training home of the **Boston Red Sox.** The ten-year-old, 6,800-seat stadium resembles Chicago's Wrigley Field or Boston's Fenway Park.

Hockey

The Everblades belong to the East Coast Hockey League and compete with 26 other franchises in the eastern half of the country. They play at the 71,000-square-foot Fort Myers Skatium; (239) 461-3145.

MONEY TO BURN?

Gamblers should hit the Naples-Fort Myers Greyhound Track in Bonita Springs (10601 Bonita Beach Road; (239) 992-2411); the Big "M" Casino at Moss Marine (45 Harbour Court, at the end of Third Street, Fort Myers Beach; (239) 765-7529), a boat that spends a few hours in international waters; and the Seminole Casino (506 South First Street, Immokalee; (239) 658-1313 or (800) 218-0007), specializing in video gaming, poker, and bingo.

Fort Myers and Fort Myers Beach

The Caloosahatchee River is an appealing backdrop for the historic city of Fort Myers, long considered an ideal spot for winter homes with majestic palms lining McGregor Boulevard, the main thoroughfare. Thomas Edison

Fort Myers and Fort Myers Beach

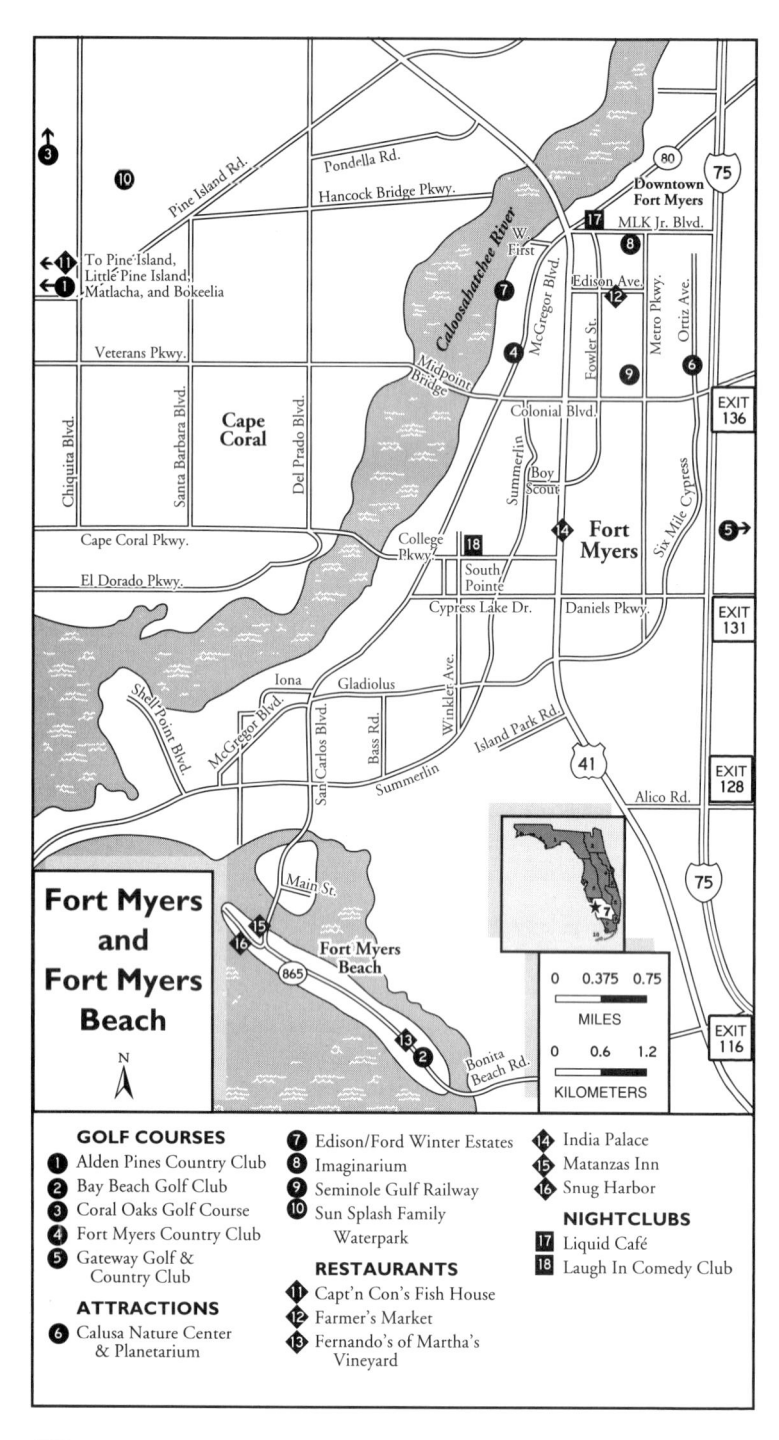

GOLF COURSES
1. Alden Pines Country Club
2. Bay Beach Golf Club
3. Coral Oaks Golf Course
4. Fort Myers Country Club
5. Gateway Golf & Country Club

ATTRACTIONS
6. Calusa Nature Center & Planetarium
7. Edison/Ford Winter Estates
8. Imaginarium
9. Seminole Gulf Railway
10. Sun Splash Family Waterpark

RESTAURANTS
11. Capt'n Con's Fish House
12. Farmer's Market
13. Fernando's of Martha's Vineyard
14. India Palace
15. Matanzas Inn
16. Snug Harbor

NIGHTCLUBS
17. Liquid Café
18. Laugh In Comedy Club

lived here in the late 1800s on his 14-acre winter estate, laboratory, and botanical garden beside the Caloosahatchee, which today is a premier stop for visitors on their way to the beach. Fort Myers Beach is really an adjacent barrier island, Estero Island, about 30 minutes from downtown, considered one of the "world's safest beaches" because of its gently sloping shoreline and powdered-sugar-like soft sand. During winter months, the area is home port for a large shrimp and fishing fleet. It's also the gateway to the two most popular Gulf Coast islands, Sanibel and Captiva.

Golf

Alden Pines Country Club

14261 Clubhouse Drive, Bokeelia; (239) 283-2179; www.aldenpines.org
Established 1980 | **Designer** Gordon Lewis | **Holes** 18

Tees Championship, 5,596/Men's, 4,971/Ladies', 4,333
Par 71/71/71 **Slope** 121/116/114
Fees $35
Specials April–October, $13 weekdays, $15 weekends **Cart rental** Included **Club rental** $10 per set **Payment** V, MC, D **Tee times** Available 3 days in advance **Facilities** Snack bar, bar, club rental, GPS on each cart.
Comments Gorgeous course with paved cart paths. Alligators and wildlife share the fairways. The greens, nurtured by brackish water, are beautiful.

Bay Beach Golf Club

4200 Bay Beach Lane, Fort Myers Beach; (239) 463-2064; www.baybeachgolfclub.com
Established 1973 | **Designer** Gordon Lewis | **Holes** 18

Tees Men's/Ladies **Par** 61/61 **Slope** 99/99
Fees Before 12:30 p.m., $23 (with electric cart, $37); after 12:30 p.m., $19 (with electric cart, $30); after 3:30 p.m., $12 (with electric cart, $22). No electric carts after 5 p.m.
Specials Summer rates, $17 before 12:30 p.m. (with electric cart, $25); $12 after 12:30 p.m. (with electric cart, $20) **Cart rental** Pull carts are available for $3.25 **Club rental** $14 per set **Payment** V, MC, D **Tee times** Available 4 days in advance **Facilities** Snack bar, driving range.
Comments On lovely and serene Estero Island, Bay Beach, one of the area's oldest courses, is set in one of the prettiest beach communities in Florida. The course makes creative use of minimal yardage (3,091 Mens, 2,632 Ladies).

Coral Oaks Golf Course

1800 Northwest 28th Avenue, Cape Coral; (239) 573-3100; www.coraloaks.com
Established 1988 | **Designer** Arthur Hills | **Holes** 18

Tees Championship, 6,623/Middle, 6,078/Forward, 4,803

Par 72/72/72 **Slope** 123/118/117
Fees $59 before noon; $47 afternoon (winter)
Specials $22 before noon; $17 after noon (summer) **Cart rental** Included in greens fees **Club rental** $12 per set **Payment** V, MC, D, AmEx **Tee times** Available two days in advance **Facilities** Snack bar, driving range
Comments This layout plays through trees and features rolling fairways that vary in width. Greens range in size from small to large, with some undulated and other flat. This course is not too challenging, but the price is hard to beat—if you are on a budget and looking for a solid course, Coral Oaks may just be the ticket.

Fort Myers Country Club

3591 McGregor Boulevard, Fort Myers; (239) 936-3126; www.cityftmyers.com/attractions/golf/fmcc.htm

Established 1917 | **Designer** Donald Ross | **Holes** 18

Tees Championship/Men's/Ladies **Par** 71/71/71 **Slope** 118/115/119
Fees $28 before 11 a.m., $23 11 a.m.–2 p.m., $18 after 5 p.m.
Specials Walking, $15, $10 after 2 p.m. **Cart rental** Included in standard fees **Club rental** $15 per set **Payment** V, MC **Tee times** Available 1 day in advance **Facilities** Clubhouse, pro shop, restaurant, practice facilities
Comments This is the oldest course in southwest Florida, with terrain that tends to be flat, and fairways relatively wide open. There are two ponds and a meandering canal, which can be found on eight holes and adds a definite bite to the course. But it is on the greens where the course snaps like an alligator. The putting surfaces are small domes, thus approaches need to be struck delicately and perfectly. You are hard pressed to find another opportunity to play a Donald Ross design at the low greens fees you pay here.

Gateway Golf & Country Club

11360 Championship Drive, Fort Myers; (239) 561-1010; www.gatewaygolf.com (members only website)

Established 1989 | **Designer** Tom Fazio | **Holes** 18

Tees Championship/Men's/Ladies **Par** 72/72/72 **Slope** 129/121/123
Fees $90 morning tee times in high season, $30 in low season
Specials $40 afternoons before 2 p.m.; $30 after 2 p.m. **Cart rental** Included; no walking allowed **Club rental** $15 per set **Payment** V, MC **Tee times** Beginning at 7:22 a.m. **Facilities** Pro shop (lessons available), restaurant, driving range.
Comments Gateway offers superior service and top-notch amenities. Gateway's fairways are open and forgiving, but they also feature mounding, so level stances can be hard to find. Unusual are Fazio's mounded bankers, which he calls "Cape Cod style." The front side is a links-style layout with only a few trees, but a beachful of sand. Conversely, the back nine features

an abundance of trees.

Attractions

Calusa Nature Center and Planetarium

3450 Ortiz Avenue, Fort Myers; (239) 275-3435; www.calusanature.com

Hours Monday–Saturday, 9 a.m.–5 p.m.; Sunday, 11 a.m.–5 p.m.
Admission Museum: adults, $4; children ages 3–12, $2.50

Appeal by Age Group

Pre-school ★★	Teens ★★	Over 30 ★★
Grade school ★★	Young Adults ★★	Seniors ★★

Touring Time *Average* 2–3 hours
Rainy-Day Touring Recommended for museum and planetarium
Author's Rating ★★ ; plenty of wildlife and outdoor amusements
Description and Comments A great display of Southwest Florida's history, including information on the Calusa Indians who ruled the area from 800 to 1700 A.D. If you have little ones, take the stroller onto the mile-long boardwalk.

Edison and Ford Winter Estates

2350 McGregor Boulevard, Fort Myers; (239) 334-3614;
www.edison-ford-estate.com

Hours Monday–Saturday, 9 a.m.–5:30 p.m.; Sunday, noon–5:30 p.m.
Admission Adults, $14; children ages 8–12, $7.50; children under age 6 free

Appeal by Age Group

Pre-school ★	Teens ★★	Over 30 ★★★
Grade school ★★	Young Adults ★★★	Seniors ★★★

Touring Time *Average* 2–3 hours; *minimum* 1 hour
Rainy-Day Touring Feasible, but you will miss the incredible landscaping
Author's Rating ★★★; authentic and educational
Description and Comments In 1884, Thomas Alva Edison, whom we thank for inventing the light bulb, phonograph, and dozens of other things electrical, decided to make his winter home in Fort Myers. The home was built in 1886 and donated to the city of Fort Myers in 1947 by Edison's widow Mina Miller Edison. See not only his home, laboratory, experimental gardens, and museum but also rare antique cars and some 200 Edison phonographs among the memorabilia. Edison convinced his buddy Henry Ford to visit Fort Myers, and Ford also became a winter resident. A gate between the two properties is called the "Friendship Gate."

The 90-minute tour takes you through both homes, but Edison's is the focus; you can see the first modern swimming pool in Florida, Edison's laboratory, a guest house, grounds and gardens, and a museum. Quick-paced, guided tours depart every 30 minutes. No unguided touring is permitted, but you can browse in the museum, loaded with Edison's inventions, possessions, and artifacts, at the completion of the tour.

Imaginarium

2000 Cranford Avenue, Fort Myers (four miles west of I-75, Exit 23 in downtown Fort Myers); (239) 337-3332; www.cityftmyers.com/attractions/imaginarium.htm

Hours Monday–Saturday, 10 a.m.–5 p.m.; Sunday, noon–5 p.m.

Admission Adults, $7; students and seniors, $6; children ages 3–12, $4; children under age 3 free

Appeal by Age Group

Pre-school ★★★	Teens ★★	Over 30 ★★
Grade school ★★★	Young Adults ★★	Seniors ★★

Touring Time 2–3 hours

Rainy-Day Touring Recommended

Author's Rating ★★★; great entertainment for a rainy day

Description and Comments Good for all ages. See a giant Pipe-O-Saurus at the wetland area entry, stand in a Florida thunderstorm without getting wet, and surf the Internet or broadcast the weather from a TV center. Take your time. This can be fun for the whole family.

Seminole Gulf Railway

Metro Mall Station, at Colonial Boulevard and Metro Parkway, Fort Myers; (239) 275-8487 or (800) 736-4853; www.semgulf.com

Hours In summer the train operates Wednesday– Sunday; call for departure times

Admission $50–$60

Appeal by Age Group

Pre-school ★	Teens ★	Over 30 ★★★
Grade school ★	Young Adults ★★	Seniors ★★★

Touring Time Varies, whether you take the dinner tour, murder mystery tour, or train ride; evening tours are 3 hours long.

Rainy-Day Touring Recommended

Author's Rating ★★; take the evening trip—it leaves around 6:30 p.m., so you can still see the passing scenery.

Description and Comments Get a unique take on the area's history while riding in a 1930s–1950s vintage railroad car. The dinner tour offers a five-course meal with wine and other beverages. The daytime tour provides narration and a snack bar.

Sun Splash Family Waterpark

400 Santa Barbara Boulevard, Cape Coral; (239) 574-0557; www.sunsplashwaterpark.com

Hours Open March–September: Friday, 11 a.m.–5 p.m.; Saturday and Sunday, 10 a.m.–5 p.m.
Admission Adults and children 48 inches and taller, $11; smaller children, $9; seniors, $6; children under age 2, $3
Appeal by Age Group

| Pre-school ★★★ | Teens ★★★ | Over 30 ★★ |
| Grade school ★★★ | Young Adults ★★ | Seniors ★ |

Touring Time 2–3 hours
Rainy-Day Touring Not recommended
Author's Rating ★★
Description and Comments Zoom Flume, Cape Fear (a popular tube slide), and the Electric Slide are the main attractions here, but don't overlook the inner-tube river and children's play area. Outside food and beverages are not allowed in the water park proper; however, you can eat and drink all you want at the picnic area outside the gates. U.S. Coast Guard life jackets are the only ones approved for use in the park (a limited supply is available at the park).

SKATE OF THE ART

Too rainy, too cold, too sunburned for another beach day? Head for the Fort Myers Skatium where everyone can burn up energy on the ice and in-line rinks, along with laser tag, indoor soccer, and volleyball. Skating prices range from $4 to $5; skate rentals are $2 (for groups). Hours vary. The Skatium is at 2250 Broadway in downtown Fort Myers; (239) 461-3145; **www.fortmyersskatium.com**.

Behind the Skatium is the Sanctuary Skate Park, a $500,000 outdoor skate park with 20 pieces of equipment for skateboarding and in-line skating. Sessions are $6 for non-members and last two hours; $2 per helmet, wrist pad, or knee pad (protective gear is required). Open daily; (239) 337-5297.

Shopping

Edison Mall (4125 Cleveland Avenue; (239) 939-5464) is the largest mall in the region and includes Florida-based Burdines and Dillard's plus the usual mall fare in more than 150 shops. **Tanger Outlets** (20350 Summerlin Road, just before the Sanibel Causeway; (239) 454-1974 or (888) 471-3939; **www.tangeroutlets.com**) offers 55 shops like Liz Claiborne, Corning Revere, Coach, Jones New York, and Reebok. The upscale, **Mediterranean-style Bell Tower Shops** (13499 US 41, corner of US 41 and Daniels Parkway; (239) 489-1221) houses Saks Fifth Avenue, dozens of other name retailers like Banana Republic and Ann Taylor, eight restaurants, and a 20-screen multiplex. **Miromar Outlets** (10801 Corkscrew Road, Estero; (239) 948-3766; **www.miromar.com**) hosts DKNY, Ellen Tracy, Nike, Fila, and Bose outlets; and **Promenade Shops** at Bonita Bay (26811 South Bay Drive off US 41, Fort Myers; (239) 261-6100; **www.bonitasprings.com/promenade**) are also not to be missed on a rainy day.

Swim World (13300-53 South Cleveland Avenue, Fort Myers; (239) 481-3350) offers a variety of swimwear in the latest styles, fabrics, and colors.

Historic downtown Fort Myers has a fledgling shopping district on and around First Street with art galleries, and clothing and jewelry shops. Out on Fort Myers Beach, colored cobblestone leads to **Seafarer's Village** (1113 Estero Boulevard; (239) 463-9919), stocked with souvenirs and "Florida casual" clothing. And the north end of the beach is **Times Square** (1010 Estero Boulevard; (239) 463-3739) with restaurants, shops, and clubs.

Flea Markets

Visit **Fleamasters Flea Market** (S4135 Dr. Martin Luther King Boulevard, one-and-one-quarter mile west of I-75 at Exit 23, Fort Myers; (239) 334-7001) for Florida souvenirs, T-shirts (tacky and trendy alike), produce, and craft items. Also, **Ortiz Flea Market** (Ortiz Avenue; (239) 694-5019) has an emphasis on locally grown produce.

Fruit

Sun Harvest Citrus (14810 Metro Parkway at Six Mile Cypress Parkway; (239) 768-2686 or (800) 743-1480) sells gift packs and fresh Florida fruits and food for shipping to the folks back home.

SHE SELLS SEASHELLS

An institution in southwest Florida for more than 60 years, the **Shell Factory** (2787 North Tamiami Trail, North Fort Myers; (239) 995-2141) is billed as the "world's largest collection of rare shells, corals, sponges, and fossils from the seven seas."

This gargantuan shop sprawls across more than 65,000 square feet, with shell jewelry (ranging from costume to fine) and shell magnets, T-shirts, night lights, chimes, mobiles, key chains, towels, candles, and other kitsch items. There's also a video game area, a glass blower, a seafood restaurant, a live animal area called "Journey into Africa," the Railroad Museum, and bumper and paddle boats. Not as pretty as Sanibel Island, but the shells are easier to find.

Dining

Bistro 41

Bell Tower, 13499 South Cleveland Avenue, Fort Myers; (239) 466-4141

Meals served Lunch and dinner **Cuisine** Eclectic American **Entree range** $5–$30 **Reservations** Yes **Payment** V, MC, AmEx

Comments Located in the trendy Bell Tower shopping center, Bistro 41 serves both classic comfort food and cutting-edge cuisine. Many dishes are offered in half portions. Tables can feel somewhat close when the dining room is full, but when the weather is good, the covered outdoor dining area affords great people-watching. Try the roasted chicken or meatloaf with mashed potatoes. The chocolate-bourbon bread pudding is a favorite.

Capt'n Con's Fish House

8421 Main Street, Bokeelia (on Pine Island); (239) 283-4300

Meals served Breakfast, lunch, and dinner **Cuisine** American/seafood **Entree range** $4.50–$16 **Reservations** Accepted for parties of ten or more **Payment** All major credit cards accepted

Comments Try the seafood chowder and the grouper prepared any way you like.

Farmers Market Restaurant

2736 Edison Avenue; (239) 334-1687

Meals served Breakfast, lunch, and dinner **Cuisine** Southern **Entree range** $6–$10 **Reservations** Not accepted **Payment** No credit cards

Comments This no-frills eatery is right next door to the State Farmers Market, with heaping helpings of classic down-home fare. Smoked beef, pork barbecue, and country-fried steak are favorites. Don't be discouraged if the small dining room is full, turnover is fairly rapid. Arrive hungry. Large entrees come with three vegetables plus rolls.

Fernando's of Martha's Vineyard

4675 Estero Boulevard, Fort Myers Beach; (239) 463-0026

Meals served Dinner daily **Cuisine** Italian/seafood **Entree range** $12–$18 **Reservations** Yes **Payment** All major credit cards accepted

Comments In a region rich in Italian restaurants, Fernando's sets itself apart with a menu that includes both the classics and lesser-known dishes. The Fort Myers Beach location has a waterfront view. Favorites include stuffed eggplant appetizer, chicken Saporito (with olives, sun-dried tomatoes, garlic, and white wine), gamberi alla Toscana (grilled shrimp over Tuscan-style beans), and tiramisu.

India Palace

Dragon Plaza, 11605 Cleveland Avenue, Fort Myers; (239) 939-2323

Meals served Lunch and dinner **Cuisine** Indian **Entree range** $7–$17 **Reservations** For groups larger than 4 **Payment** All major credit cards accepted

Comments The restaurant sits back quite a distance from the highway, so look for the Dragon Plaza sign. With numerous meatless dishes, it's a prime pick for vegetarians. Take care when ordering dishes hot; even the mild dishes have a distinct bite. Service can be a bit slow on busy weekends, but customers are never rushed out of their tables, either.

Matanzas Inn

416 Crescent Street, Fort Myers Beach; (239) 463-3838

Meals served Lunch and dinner **Cuisine** American/seafood **Entree range** $6–$20 **Reservations** Not accepted **Payment** All major credit cards accepted

Comments If it's a nice day, request a table dockside or on the deck. Try the gator tail or the conch chowder. Fish any way you like it is a good bet, and they cook up some interesting seafood specials.

Snug Harbor

645 Old San Carlos Boulevard, Fort Myers Beach; (239) 463-4343

Meals served Lunch and dinner **Cuisine** American/seafood **Entree range** $8–$17 **Reservations** Accepted for groups of 4 or more **Payment** V, MC, AmEx, D

Comments Seafood doesn't get any fresher, as Snug Harbor has its own fishing fleet. Their most popular creation is Grouper Popeye, steamed fish with spinach in a lemon-butter sauce.

Arts and Culture

Southwest Florida offers an increased awareness of the fine arts with numerous venues and opportunities. A center for many performances is the **William R. Frizzell Cultural Center** (10091 McGregor Boulevard, Fort Myers; (239) 939-2787; www.artinlee.org) with an exhibition gallery, the 200-seat Claiborne and Ned Foulds Theatre, an outdoor amphitheater, and art education classrooms. Many festivals are set at the Frizzell, in addition to a professional equity theater group, the Film Society of Southwest Florida, the Southwest Florida Historical Society, and the Lee County Art in Public Places program.

Nightlife

Liquid Café

Who Goes There Downtown workers, musicians, music lovers, Goths, hippies, theater people

2236 First Street, Fort Myers; (239) 461-0444; www.liquidcafe.com

Cover No **Minimum** No age minimum since they serve food **Mixed drinks** Beer and wine only ($3 and up) **Food available** Salads and sandwiches ($6 average) **Hours** 11 a.m.–2 a.m.

What goes on Wine, beer, and song are dispensed in generous quantities (and usually at high volume) in this popular downtown hangout.

Comments For less smoke and lower volume, there is seating outside—prime people-watching right in the heart of the city's burgeoning arts and entertainment district. If there's live music, as there is most evenings, the entertainers will set up wherever they can fit in the stage-less room.

Laugh In Comedy Café

Who Goes There Locals looking for a laugh

8595 College Parkway, Fort Myers; (239) 479-5233; www.laughincomedycafe.com

Cover $10 **Minimum** 21 **Mixed drinks** $5 and up **Food available** Full menu; crowd pleasers are Liberace's Ring (onion rings), Gilligan's Island (fish filet), and Bye Bye Miss American Pie (apple pie) **Hours** 7 p.m.–2 a.m. Friday–Saturday; Thursday 8 p.m. shows

What goes on Comedians perform on Thursday, Friday and Saturday nights. The venue features both headliners and up-and-coming comedians, typically for $5 per show.

Comments The Saturday show is smoke-free, while Thursday night is half-price comedy night.

Side Trips

Estero and Bonita Springs If you're heading south to Naples, ten miles south of Fort Myers the two small towns of Estero and Bonita Springs are worth a look. Shops in Estero include international designers, and **Miromar Outlets** (10801 Corkscrew Road; (239) 948-3766) with more than 100 shops. And nearby Bonita Springs has **The Promenade** (26811 South Bay Drive; (239) 261-6100), a European-style shopping center with restaurants, shopping, and lovely gardens.

Bonita Springs is home to **Everglades Wonder Gardens** (27180 Old US 41; (239) 992-2591), and if you ever wondered what Florida was like in the early days of tourism, this time warp attraction hasn't changed much since the 1930s. The gardens are actually an old-fashioned zoo featuring Florida wildlife including bears, otters, deer, wading birds, birds of prey, the Florida panther, and endangered Everglades crocodiles. Rather quaint, evoking nostalgic thoughts of the days when tourism was on a smaller scale and less plastic, the attraction is appealing to all ages if you try not to make comparisons with Busch Gardens or Disney World. There are alligator feedings and otters who perform throughout the day. It's open daily, 9 a.m.–5 p.m.; admission $12 for adults, $6 for children ages 3–12.

Sanibel and Captiva Islands

At one time, the only way to get to tiny Sanibel or Captiva Islands 20 miles off the coast of downtown Fort Myers was by boat or ferry. Today, a three-mile-long causeway connects the islands to the mainland.

Sanibel offers world-class shelling opportunities with some 200 varieties found on the beach. The posture one assumes looking for shells has been named the "Sanibel Stoop," and dedicated shellers have been known to attach flashlights to their heads to try to be the first on the beach after an especially high or low tide and capture an especially exotic prize shell. Inland, nature reserves give Sanibel star status among nature lovers.

Sanibel and Captiva Islands

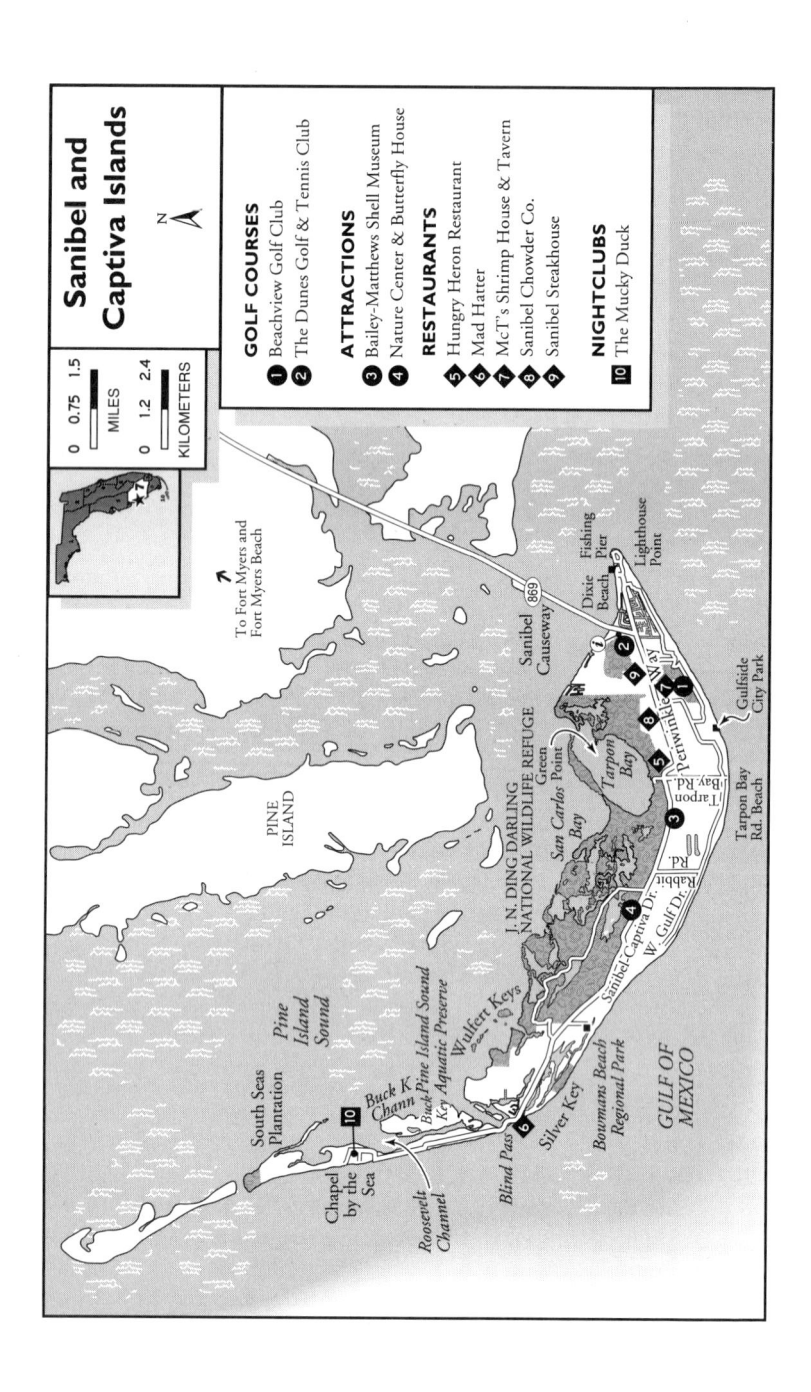

GOLF COURSES
1. Beachview Golf Club
2. The Dunes Golf & Tennis Club

ATTRACTIONS
3. Bailey-Matthews Shell Museum
4. Nature Center & Butterfly House

RESTAURANTS
5. Hungry Heron Restaurant
6. Mad Hatter
7. McT's Shrimp House & Tavern
8. Sanibel Chowder Co.
9. Sanibel Steakhouse

NIGHTCLUBS
10. The Mucky Duck

Captiva, a half-hour drive north across a two-lane bridge, is a six-mile-long island with outstanding natural beauty. The late Anne Morrow Lindbergh wrote her best-selling memoir *A Gift from the Sea* on the island.

Golf

Beachview Golf Club

1100 Parview Drive, Sanibel; (239) 472-2626; www.beachviewgolfclub.com
Established 1974 | **Designer** Truman Wilson | **Holes** 18

Tees Championship/Men's/Ladies **Par** 71/71/71 **Slope** 127/118/116
Fees Vary by season and time of day $46–$101
Specials Afternoons, $36 **Cart rental** Included with greens fees **Club rental** Yes **Payment** V, MC, D **Tee times** Available 7 days in advance **Facilities** Pro shop, restaurant, lockers.
Comments This pretty course, located one block from the Gulf of Mexico, is dotted with little ponds and lakes and provides one of the most natural golf settings in the country.

The Dunes Golf & Tennis Club

949 Sandcastle Road, Sanibel; (239) 472-3355; www.dunesgolfsanibel.com
Established 1973; redesigned in 1995 | **Designer** Mark McCumber | **Holes** 18

Tees Championship/Men's/Ladies **Par** 70/70/70 **Slope** 123/111/111
Fees $57–$122 depending no time of year
Specials No **Cart rental** Included in greens fees **Club rental** $25 per set **Payment** V, MC, AmEx, D **Tee times** 7 a.m.–5:30 p.m. daily **Facilities** No lockers, large pro shop (lessons available).
Comments Two minutes from the beach, the course is set on 140 acres in a wildlife area; alligators, bald eagles, and other local species are always evident. This is a popular course and features 70 acres of water.

Attractions

Bailey-Matthews Shell Museum

3075 Sanibel-Captiva Road, Sanibel Island; (239) 395-2233; www.shellmuseum.org
Hours Tuesday–Sunday, 10 a.m.–4 p.m.
Admission $5 for adults, $3 for children ages 8–16, free for children ages 7 and under

Appeal by Age Group

Pre-school ★	Teens ★★★	Over 30 ★★★
Grade school ★★	Young Adults ★★★	Seniors ★★★

Touring Time *Average* 2 hours; *minimum* 1 hour
Rainy-Day Touring Recommended

Author's Rating ★★

Description and Comments Visitors can see how nature has created shells with a breathtaking variety of colors, patterns, and shapes in this museum devoted entirely to shells of the world. The centerpiece is a six-foot revolving planet surrounded by shells from around the world. You can hear the sounds of the Florida Everglades while walking through the Kingdom of the Landshells, learn about the relationship between shells and the web of life in the habitat exhibits, and discover why shells wash ashore in abundance on Sanibel and Captiva.

A play area for children has hands-on displays and a live shell tank. Kids 17 and younger get to choose two free shells to take home.

Nature Center & Butterfly House

3333 Sanibel-Captiva Road, Sanibel Island; (239) 472-2329

Hours Nature Center is open December–mid-April, 9 a.m.–4 p.m.; mid-April–November, 9 a.m.–3 p.m.

Admission $3, 17 and under free

Appeal by Age Group

Pre-school ★★★	Teens ★★	Over 30 ★★★
Grade school ★★★★	Young Adults ★★	Seniors ★★★

Touring Time Minimum 1 hour if you want to stroll the trails.

Rainy-Day Touring Not recommended

Author's Rating ★★

Description and Comments Sanibel-Captiva Conservation Foundation Inc. is a not-for-profit organization dedicated to the preservation of natural resources and wildlife habitat on and around Sanibel and Captiva, and the Nature Center is the hub of activities. The interpretive area hosts a live touch tank and exhibits of history, plants and animals. A nature trail meanders along the Sanibel River The 12 x 12-foot Butterfly House is a favorite, where native butterflies flit about nectarine plants before they are released to the wild. The best time to visit is springtime, when you'll find an abundance of butterflies during wildflower season.

Shopping

Periwinkle Place (2075 Periwinkle Way, Sanibel Island; **www.periwinkle-place.com**) offers a dozen shops, mostly women's clothing, in a park-like setting with covered walkways and Banyan trees. **The Village** (2340 Periwinkle Way, Sanibel Island) has fine art stores that carry original aboriginal artifacts of the native people of Africa, Australia, the Americas, and the Arctic. The site of the original Sanibel Post office is now **Old Sanibel Shoppes** (630 Tarpon Bay Road, Sanibel Island), with a collection of fine gifts, custom jewelry, and clothing. **Captiva Village Square** (Captiva Drive, Captiva Island) has several galleries that feature turn-of-the-century antiques and art from the area's heyday when it hosted inventors like Thomas Edison and Henry Ford, as well as the work of local artists. **Chadwick's Square** (5400 Plantation Road, Captiva Island) features contemporary craft stores, clothing, and small art galleries.

Dining

Hungry Heron Restaurant

2330 Palm Ridge Road, Sanibel; (239) 395-2300

Meals served Lunch and dinner (Saturdays, breakfast buffet) **Cuisine** American/seafood **Entree range** $9–$19 **Reservations** Preferred seating available **Payment** All major credit cards accepted

Comments Try the homemade sweet potato chips. Sandwiches are huge, so you can share. The restaurant has big-screen TVs and often pops in a cartoon video for the kids.

Mad Hatter

6460 Sanibel-Captiva Road, Sanibel (239) 472-0033

Meals served Dinner daily **Cuisine** New American **Entree range** $26–$36 **Reservations** Yes **Payment** MC, V, AmEx

Comments *Alice in Wonderland* decor lends an air of whimsy and informality, while the food and service measure up to this restaurant's prime beachfront real estate. Sunsets are visible through large windows that run the length of the smoke-free dining room. Standouts include bibb salad with gorgonzola dressing; yellowfin tuna with sweet-chili glaze and toasted macadamia nuts; beef tenderloin; and anything on the dessert tray.

McT's Shrimp House and Tavern

1523 Periwinkle Way, Sanibel; (239) 472-3161

Meals served Dinner **Cuisine** Seafood/steaks **Entree range** $15–$30 **Reservations** Not accepted **Payment** All major credit cards accepted

Comments This is casual seafood dining, and if you're among the first 100 to show up between 5 and 6 p.m., you get the early-bird special for $10 (your choice of peel-and-eat shrimp, grouper fingers, seafood pasta, chicken romano, or prime rib). They also serve good barbecue, along with the requisite all-you-can-eat shrimp and crab platters.

Sanibel Chowder Co.

2075 Periwinkle Way, Sanibel Island; (239) 472-2525

Meals served Breakfast, lunch, and dinner **Cuisine** American/seafood **Entree range** $7–$10 lunch, $13–$19 dinner **Reservations** Accepted **Payment** V, MC, AmEx, D

Comments Great breakfast. The restaurant is located in a small shopping center, so you can shop and eat at the same time. And if the kids finish first, there's a children's playground in front of the restaurant so parents can watch children from inside.

Sanibel Steakhouse

1473 Periwinkle Way, Sanibel Island; (239) 472-5700

Meals served Dinner only **Cuisine** Steakhouse **Entree range** $20–$26
Reservations Yes **Payment** All major credit cards accepted
Comments As is the case at many steakhouses, everything on the menu is à la carte. Raised panels, muted colors, and subtle lighting create a clubby feel. The food is hearty and old-fashioned: shrimp cocktails, oysters Rockefeller, sautéed lump crab cakes, dry-aged prime rib-eye steak, and Porterhouse steak for two.

FUN AND FREE

A fabulous place to watch the sunset is the 1,000-foot-long Naples Pier, listed on the National Register of Historic Places. The pier and adjacent beach make a great gathering spot all day long for fishing, swimming, walking, and just relaxing. There's a bait shop, snack bar, rest rooms, and showers, with concessions open from 8:30 a.m. until 5 p.m. Parking is metered, and it's can be tough to find a spot.

Nightlife

The Mucky Duck

Who Goes There Families for dinner, boistrous locals for drinks

1546 Andy Rosse Lane, Captiva Island; (239) 472-3434

Cover None **Minimum** None **Mixed drinks** $5 and up, but beer is the drink of choice **Food available** Steaks, seafood in a British-style pub **Hours** Daily, 11 a.m.–2 a.m.

What goes on There's almost always a lively crowd—with charismatic owner Victor Mayeron often leading the pack—at this popular waterfront pub. Because of its prime sunset view, seats are hardest to get just before sunset.

Comments Outdoors, tables overlook the beach. Within, it's filled with wood and British memorabilia. Locals recommend the grouper sandwich.

Naples and Marco Island

Naples is just 30 minutes south of Fort Myers in Collier County. It has always appealed to wealthy tourists and residents who look for fine dining, cultural events, and upscale shopping opportunities. Naples is also called the "Golf Capital of America," with more courses per capita than anyplace else in the world. The Collier County region is considered one of the fastest growing in the country.

The affluent city was surveyed, plotted, and lots were sold beginning in 1887. Debt brought further development to a screeching halt until

Memphis-born millionaire Barron Gift Collier used his fortune to introduce paved roads, electricity, and other conveniences to the town in the 1920s. Collier County was incorporated in 1923. Five years later, Collier completed the Tamiami Trail (connecting Miami-Dade County with the state's west coast), expanding the potential for agriculture and tourist. Development took off after World War II. Major hotels, such as the Ritz-Carlton in Naples, came into the region in the late 1980s.

Naples is more than just a material girl. Eleven miles of beach and nature preserves line the Gulf of Mexico.

The area is working hard to shake its image as a winter-only retreat, and is reaching out for families and eco-tourists, taking advantage of its proximity to the Everglades, the barrier islands, and the cypress swamps.

Marco Island, 20 miles south of Naples, is the largest of Florida's Ten Thousand Islands, secluded until the 1960s, now jammed with two miles of high rises. Another golfer's delight, Marco has also established a reputation as an angler's paradise. Backwater fishing is especially popular.

MARCO ISLAND TROLLEY TOURS

Learn a little history from the humorous drivers on this casual tour of the island. You can jump on and off as often as you like as the trolley takes you past some of the earliest sites of cultural contact between Europeans and Native Americans. There are 11 historical markers, including the Cushing Archaeological site where 3,500-year-old Native American artifacts were unearthed. You'll also see burial mounds of the Calusa Indians who settled this island more than 6,000 years ago. Park at the Chamber of Commerce near the island's north bridge on Collier Boulevard. The cost is $16 for adults, $7 for children under age 12; (239) 394-1600.

Golf

Lely Resort Golf and Country Club

8004 Lely Resort Boulevard, Naples; (800) 388-4653 or (239) 793-2223; www.lely-resort.com

Lely Flamingo Island Club Course

Established 1990 | **Designer** Robert Trent Jones Sr. | **Holes** 18

Tees Championship/Green/Ladies **Par** 72/72/72 **Slope** 136/128/123

Lely Mustang Golf Club Course

Established 1996 | **Designer** Lee Trevino | **Holes** 18

Tees Championship/Green/Ladies **Par** 72/72/72 **Slope** 141/125/120
Fees May 1–May 15, $45 before 3 p.m., $35 after 3 p.m.; May 15–Oct. 31, $27
Specials Replays available for $27 (must have card); also reduced summer memberships available **Cart rental** Included in greens fees **Club rental** $20–$40 per set **Payment** All major credit cards accepted **Tee times**

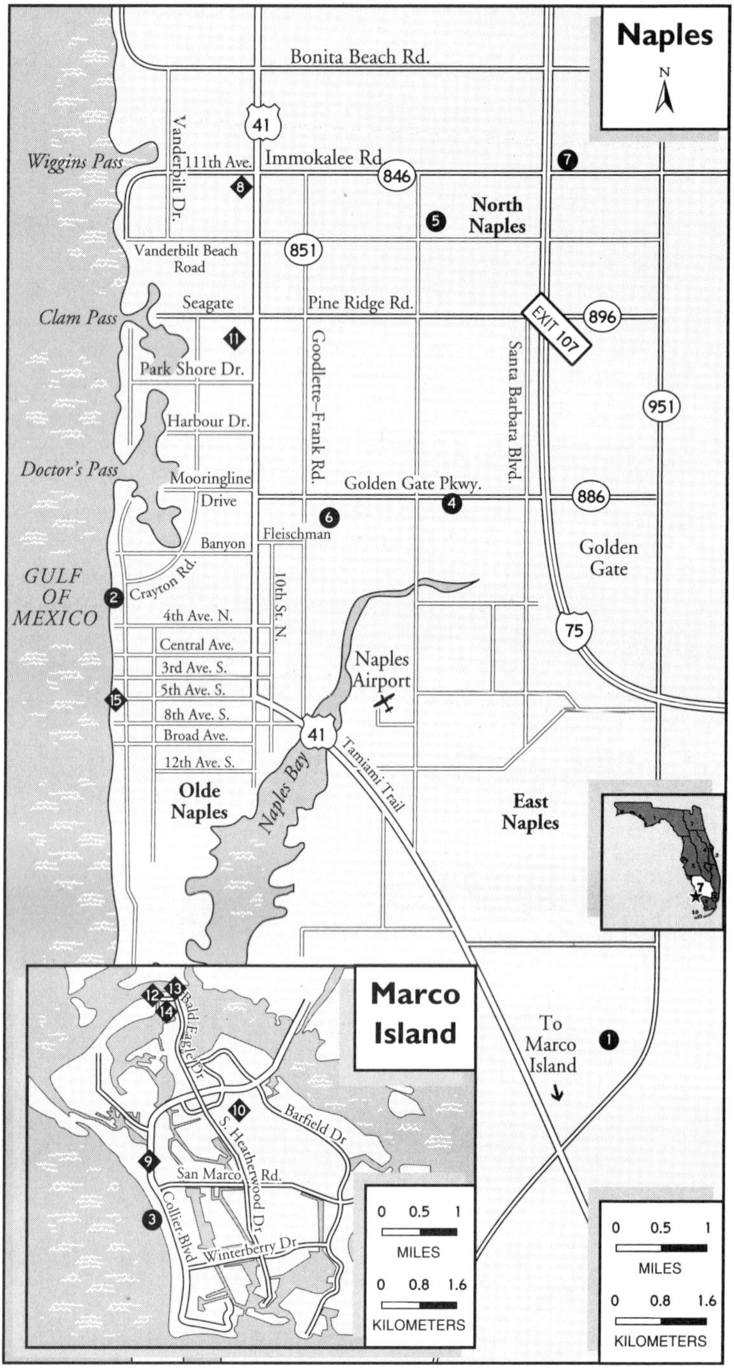
Naples
N
Bonita Beach Rd.
41
Vanderbilt Dr.
Wiggins Pass
111th Ave.
Immokalee Rd.
846
North Naples
851
Vanderbilt Beach Road
Seagate
Pine Ridge Rd.
Clam Pass
EXIT 107
896
Park Shore Dr.
Goodlette–Frank Rd.
Santa Barbara Blvd.
951
Harbour Dr.
Doctor's Pass
Mooringline Drive
Golden Gate Pkwy.
886
Fleischman
Banyon
Golden Gate
GULF OF MEXICO
Crayton Rd.
10th St. N.
4th Ave. N.
75
Central Ave.
3rd Ave. S.
Naples Airport
5th Ave. S.
8th Ave. S.
Broad Ave.
Tamiami Trail
12th Ave. S.
Olde Naples
Naples Bay
East Naples
To Marco Island
Marco Island
Bald Eagle Dr
Barfield Dr
S. Heatherwood Dr
San Marco Rd.
Collier Blvd
Winterberry Dr
0 0.5 1
MILES
0 0.8 1.6
KILOMETERS

> ## Naples and Marco Island
>
> **GOLF COURSES**
> 1. Lely Resort Golf and Country Club
> 2. Naples Beach Hotel and Golf Club
> 3. Marco Island Marriott Resort, Golf Club & Spa (The Rookery at Marco)
> 4. Naples Grande Golf Club
> 5. Tiburon Golf Club
>
> **ATTRACTIONS**
> 6. Caribbean Gardens: The Zoo in Naples
> 7. The Teddy Bear Museum
>
> **RESTAURANTS**
> 8. Bha! Bha! A Persian Bistro
> 9. Café de Marco
> 10. Kretch's
> 11. Le Bistro
> 12. Olde Marco Island Inn
> 13. Snook Inn
> 14. Verdi's
> 15. Yabba Street Grill

Reservations required from 7 a.m. **Facilities** Golf shop, locker room, Flamingo Island Grille, Flamingo Bar

Comments Lely Flamingo is not your typical public golf course. This is Naples's premier course and is truly one of southern Florida's hidden gems.

Marco Island Marriott Resort, Golf Club & Spa (The Rookery at Marco)

3433 Marriott Club Drive, Naples; (239) 793-6060; www.rookeryatmarco.com

Established 1991, renovated in 2002 | **Designer** Robert Cupp Jr. | **Holes** 18

Tees Championship/Back/Middle/Forward/Front
Par 72/72/72/72/72 **Slope** 143/137/128/117/108
Fees May 27–September, $55 before noon, $35 after noon; October–December, $100 before noon, $65 after noon; January–April, $140 before noon, $99 after noon
Specials Hotel guest special rates available **Cart rental** included in greens fees **Club rental** $40 per set **Payment** All major credit cards accepted **Tee times** 7 days in advance **Facilities** Award-winning pro shop; clubhouse; private instructions at Nick Faldo School of Golf.
Comments This course is a prime example of Lee's architectural philosophy: the simpler, the better. Greens, although well protected by both sand and water, are large and very puttable.

Naples Beach Hotel and Golf Club

851 Gulf Shore Boulevard North, Naples; (800) 237-7600 or (239) 434-2475; www.naplesbeachhotel.com

Established 1920; updated in 1980, 1993, and 1998 by Ron Garl | **Holes** 18

Tees Blue/White/Red **Par** 72/72/72 **Slope** 134/130/121
Fees $57 before 3 p.m., $36 after 3 p.m.
Specials Discounts for guests of the hotel **Cart rental** Included in greens fees **Club rental** $30 per set before $3 p.m.; $20 after 3 p.m. **Payment** All major credit cards accepted **Tee times** Hotel guests 3 months in advance/ nonguests 3 days in advance **Facilities** Pro shop, driving range, locker room, restaurants
Comments This is one of the oldest courses in the area and offers a traditional layout and good, old-fashioned golf. The tree-lined fairways are very generous and tend to be rolling.

Naples Grande Golf Club

7760 Golden Gate Parkway, Naples; (239) 659-3710; www.naplesgrande.com
Established 2000 | **Designer** Rees Jones | **Holes** 18

Tees Championship/Back/Members, /Seniors/Forward
Par 72/72/72/72/72 **Slope** 143/135/128/124/119
Fees June–August, $60 before 1:30 p.m., $40 after 1:30 p.m.; October– May, $175
Specials None **Cart rental** Included in greens fees **Club rental** $60 per set **Payment** V, MC **Tee times** Open to guests of The Registry and Edgewater Resorts only (90 days in advance) **Facilities** Professional practice facility, TPGS Golf School, restaurant, locker room
Comments This contemporary course layout, which makes liberal use of elevation changes and water hazards, has garnered praise from *Golf Digest* and is an emerging area favorite.

Tiburon Golf Club

2620 Tiburon Drive, Naples; (239) 594-2040; www.wcigolf.com

Gold Course

Established 1998 | **Designer** Greg Norman | **Holes** 18

Tees Championship/Back/Middle/Forward
Par 72/72/72/72 **Slope** 137/129/117/113

Black Course

Established 1998 | **Designer** Greg Norman | **Holes** 18

Tees Championship, 7,005/Back, 6,323/Middle, 5,624/Forward, 4,909
Par 72/72/72/72 **Slope** 147/138/119/119
Fees $200–$225 in high season; $60–$85 in low season; call for specific dates
Specials Group and twilight rates **Cart rental** included in greens fees **Club rental** $55 per set **Payment** V, MC, AmEx **Tee times** 10 days in advance **Facilities** Putting green, chipping green, golf academy, restaurants, bar, locker rooms.

Comments This 7,179-yard Greg Norman design is home of the 2003 Franklin Templeton Shootout. A top-notch facility, it draws golfers from throughout the country.

Attractions

Caribbean Gardens: The Zoo in Naples

1590 Goodlette-Frank Road, Naples; (239) 262-5409; www.napleszoo.com

Hours Daily, 9:30 a.m.–4:30 p.m.; closed Thanksgiving, Christmas, and Easter

Admission $16 for adults, $10 for children ages 4–15, free for ages 3 and under; annual membership available

Appeal by Age Group

Pre-school ★★★	Teens ★★★★	Over 30 ★★★★
Grade school ★★★	Young Adults ★★★★	Seniors ★★★

Touring Time *Average* 4 hours; *minimum* 2 hours

Rainy-Day Touring Not recommended

Author's Rating ★★★; family-owned and a piece of the real Florida

Description and Comments "Jungle Larry, Friend of the Beasts" (a.k.a. Colonel Lawrence Tetzlaff) opened his private menagerie to the public in 1969 as Jungle Larry's African Safari Park.

The colonel died in 1984, and his two sons, Tim and David, now run the place, and the collection has expanded to more than 200 animals, ranging from rare golden tigers to graceful impala antelope. Though it's not a state-of-the-art operation (many large animals, for example, are in cages), the animals are well cared for.

The Primate Expedition Cruise glides past islands where monkeys, lemurs, and apes live in natural habitats. There are also elephant rides and a petting farm. Coolers and picnic lunches are welcome.

The Teddy Bear Museum

2511 Pine Ridge Road, Naples (two miles west of I-75, Exit 107); (239) 598-2711; www.teddymuseum.com

Hours Tuesday–Saturday, 10 a.m.–5 p.m.; closed Sunday and Monday

Admission Requested donations are $8 for adults, $6 for seniors ages 60 and older, $3 for children ages 4–12

Appeal by Age Group

Pre-school ★★★	Teens ★★	Over 30 ★★
Grade school ★★★	Young Adults ★★	Seniors ★★

Touring Time *Average* 1 hour; *minimum* 30 minutes

Rainy-Day Touring Recommended

Author's Rating ★★; "beary" fun for little ones on a rainy afternoon

Description and Comments This one-of-a-kind museum is extra fun for kids who love their stuffed bears. There are more than 5,000 teddy bears and "bearaphenalia" from around the world, miniature to giant, crystal to mohair.

There's a reading "libeary" with books about bears and a replica of the Three Bears' house that kids love to explore. Saturday morning is storytime.

Shopping

Naples has two premier shopping districts. **Fifth Avenue South,** with its wonderfully colorful array of shops, galleries, boutiques, and restaurants is a world-class shopping destination. **Third Street South** is home to a group of stores now on the National Register of Historic Places. Most clothing stores feature a collection of pricey leisure and golf wear (in bright Florida-deco hues).

Fifth Avenue South is home to **Back of the Bay** (555 Fifth Avenue South; (239) 263-4233), offering one-of-a-kind women's sweaters and outerwear, plus hand-painted apparel, shoes, and jewelry. **GH Collections** (727 Fifth Avenue South; (239) 649-4356) features men's and women's clothing and original artwork by Guy Harvey, a famous marine wildlife artist. **Glad Rags Etc.** and **Glad Rags Too** (655 and 757 Fifth Avenue South; (239) 262-3222) are a pair of stores hawking bright colors and Lily Pulitzer and Fresh Produce resort wear for women; they also sell sportswear featuring floral and sea life prints in bright and cheery colors. Like lime green and turquoise? Purple and pink? Blue and yellow? This one's for you.

Other shops include **Giggle Moon** (720 Fifth Avenue South, Suite 105; (239) 643-3833), a children's boutique featuring local and European designs; and **The Paddle** (300 Fifth Avenue South; (239) 262-4688), a menswear retailer with a local flavor.

For rare shells and a coral gallery, try the upscale shop **The Blue Mussel** (478 Fifth Avenue South; (239) 262-4814). **World Antiques** (1111 Fifth Avenue South; (239) 263-0609) features global antique furniture and decorative arts for serious collectors and gift-buyers alike. **Antique Mall at Treasure Island** (950 Central Avenue; (239) 434-7684) is another good local option.

For an area with so many golf courses, what would you expect but a huge collection of women's golf wear? The best selection awaits the shopper at **For the Love of Golf** (976 South Tamiami Trail; (239) 566-3395), where you can find all the newest and sharpest gear for the next 18 holes.

Naples on the Run (2128 Ninth Street North; (239) 434-9786) has a good selection of running shoes. And **Pratt's Shoe Salon of Naples** (1183 Third Street South; (239) 261-7127) has a wide assortment of dressy and casual shoes.

Tin City in Naples on US 41 (1200 Fifth Avenue South and East Goodlette Road; (239) 262-4200) is a collection of 40 waterfront restaurants and shops catering to tourists. And just across US 41 is the new **Bayfront** (on the Gordon River at Goodlette-Frank Road and US 41 East), featuring Cerruti, Valentino, Jennings of Naples, and other upscale shops. The **Village at Venetian Bay** (4200 Gulf Shore Boulevard North; (239) 261-6100) has nearly 60 shops, galleries, and restaurants on the waterfront.

Other Naples shopping opportunities include: **Coastland Center** (1900

Tamiami Trail North; (239) 262-7100), built in a Key West style, and **Waterside Shops** (5415 Tamiami Trail North; (239) 598-1605), an upscale mall anchored by Saks Fifth Avenue and Jacobson's department stores. **Prime Outlets** (7222 Isle of Capri Road; (239) 775-8083) offer more than 40 stores, including Mikasa (6060 Collier Boulevard, Suite 112; (239) 793-7171); Harry & David (6060 Collier Boulevard, Suite 26; (239) 417-5530); and Dansk (6070 Collier Boulevard, Suite 4; (239) 793-5533).

Marco Island Though area shopping is concentrated in Naples, you can expect to find numerous resort boutiques and bathing suit shops, as well as stores for sandals, sunglasses, and sunscreen on Marco Island. These include **The Beach House** (1300 Third Street South; (239) 261-1366) and **The Cricket Shop** (326 13th Avenue South; (239) 262-2260).

Dining

Bha! Bha! A Persian Bistro

Pavilion Shopping Center, 847 Vanderbilt Beach Road, Naples; (239) 594-5557

Meals served Lunch, dinner **Cuisine** Middle Eastern **Entree range** $15–$26 **Reservations** Yes **Payment** V, MC, AmEx

Comments Except during the busiest winter months, expect entertainment by a belly dancer on Thursdays and a fortune teller on Fridays. The menu includes Middle Eastern classics as well as innovative creations. The decor reflects that diversity. Try the roasted butternut squash soup; duck in pomegranate sauce; charbroiled lamb drizzled with homemade yogurt; or Persian ice cream with saffron and rose water.

Café de Marco

244 Palm Street, Marco Island; (239) 394-6262

Meals served Dinner **Cuisine** Seafood **Entree range** $16–$37 **Reservations** Yes **Payment** V, MC, AmEx

Comments Café de Marco has been satisfying its clientele since 1983, with the finest and most diverse selection of fresh seafood available on Marco Island. Non-seafood items also offered such as rack of lamb, filet mignon and chicken dishes for the "land lovers."

Kretch's

527 Bald Eagle Drive, Marco Island; (239) 394-3433

Meals served Lunch, Monday–Friday; dinner, Monday–Saturday **Cuisine** Seafood/Mexican **Entree range** Lunch, $8–$13; dinner, $8–$25 **Reservations** Recommended in the winter **Payment** V, MC, D

Comments Decadent sauces accompany Ketch's fresh seafood, or you can go local with great grilled fish. The prime rib is also recommended. "Mexican Friday" lunches are popular, with cheap spicy eats like tacos and burritos.

Le Bistro

842 Neapolitan Way, Naples; (239) 434-7061

Meals served Dinner **Cuisine** Country French **Entree range** $20–$34
Reservations Yes **Payment** All major credit cards
Comments Worth finding in a busy shopping center, Le Bistro's Mexican tile floors, crisp linen tablecloths, and bubbling fountain soothe the soul. Service is friendly and efficient without being chummy. Traditional French selections include lobster bisque; mussels with cream sauce; bouillabaisse Marseillaise; roasted duck l'orange; grilled swordfish; crème caramel; and poached pear with vanilla ice cream and cinnamon sauce.

Olde Marco Island Inn

100 Palm Street, Marco Island; (239) 394-3131

Meals served Dinner **Cuisine** American **Entree range** $19–$29 **Reservations** Accepted **Payment** All major credit cards accepted
Comments Though it's a little pricey, the locals favor Olde Marco for fresh seafood and an interesting selection of international dishes from Wiener schnitzel and sauerbraten to crisp roast duckling and veal Madagascar. Kids love their Southern fried chicken with honey.

Snook Inn

1215 Bald Eagle Drive, Marco Island; (239) 394-3313

Meals served Lunch and dinner **Cuisine** Seafood **Entree range** $10–$29
Reservations Not accepted **Payment** All major credit cards accepted
Comments On the Marco River, the inn has myriad seafood choices, all fresh and prepared every way imaginable. You can even bring your own catch and they'll cook it for you with all the trimmings for $13. Save room for a slice of the Milky Way Pie.

Verdi's

241 North Collier Boulevard, Marco Island; (239) 394-5533

Meals served Dinner, Monday–Saturday **Cuisine** American bistro **Entree range** $16–$27 **Reservations** Yes **Payment** V, MC, D
Comments Verdi's specializes in contemporary American fare, with dishes emphasizing fresh ingredients served in a casual resort atmosphere.

Yabba Street Grill

711 Fifth Avenue, Naples; (239) 262-5787

Meals served Dinner **Cuisine** Caribbean **Entree range** $15–$20 **Reservations** Yes **Payment** All major credit cards accepted
Comments Eat indoors or out at this trendy, high-volume restaurant in Old Naples. Inside, the dining room sports a tin-ceiling and walls awash in vivid azure and lime. Service can suffer during peak times, such as weekend nights. This isn't the place for an intimate dinner for two, but it fills the bill for a lively night out and is next door to the Sugden Theatre. Try the Bahamian conch chowder or the tuna Negril appetizer, and save room for the flourless chocolate cake with rum and raspberry sauce.

Part Nine

Miami and Miami Beach

Welcome to Miami

Mention Miami and most folks are hit with a flood of impressions: a stunning city by the sea, with broad, white beaches and towering palms; candy-colored Art Deco palaces fronting sidewalks jammed with gorgeous fashion models and Lycra-clad rollerbladers; a hotbed of dance clubs and party-goers; and, also, a city awash in illegal money that proudly wears its reputation for crime and violence like a cheap perfume.

Vivid impressions, all, and totally in sync with this Miami Chamber of Commerce message: "Miami is the sun-and-fun capital of the universe, a jet-setter's paradise with a bad-boy reputation, a sun-drenched escape from the winter cold."

All of which is true. Yet Miami is something else. It's a city of two million where more people speak Spanish than English, a multicultural collage representing 158 ethic backgrounds and speaking 25 different languages. For Americans, Miami is an international destination that doesn't require a passport.

HIGHLIGHTS
- A stroll in the Art Deco district on Miami Beach
- Venetian Pool in Coral Gables
- Bill Baggs Cape Florida Recreation Area
- Vizcaya Museum & Gardens
- Sunning, swimming, and people watching on Miami Beach

A Brief History

When Henry Flagler, a founding partner in Standard Oil, first brought his rail line to Palm Beach in 1893, he chose not to continue south into Miami—a distance of some 65 miles. Cleveland-born Julia Tuttle, born, settled on the north bank of the Miami River in 1891, determined to create a city at the mouth of the river, or so the story goes. She searched in vain

Miami

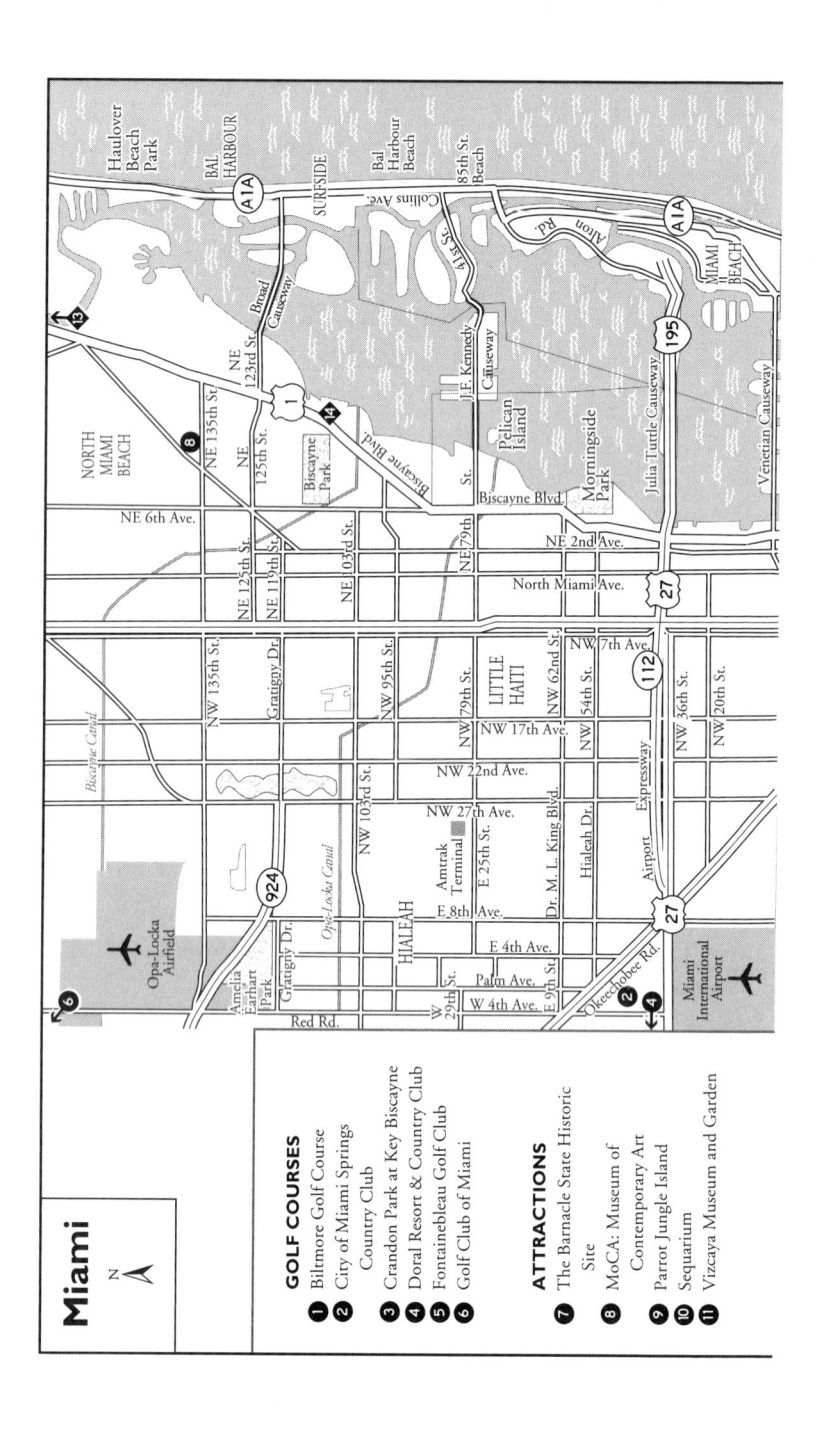

GOLF COURSES
1. Biltmore Golf Course
2. City of Miami Springs Country Club
3. Crandon Park at Key Biscayne
4. Doral Resort & Country Club
5. Fontainebleau Golf Club
6. Golf Club of Miami

ATTRACTIONS
7. The Barnacle State Historic Site
8. MoCA: Museum of Contemporary Art
9. Parrot Jungle Island
10. Sequarium
11. Vizcaya Museum and Garden

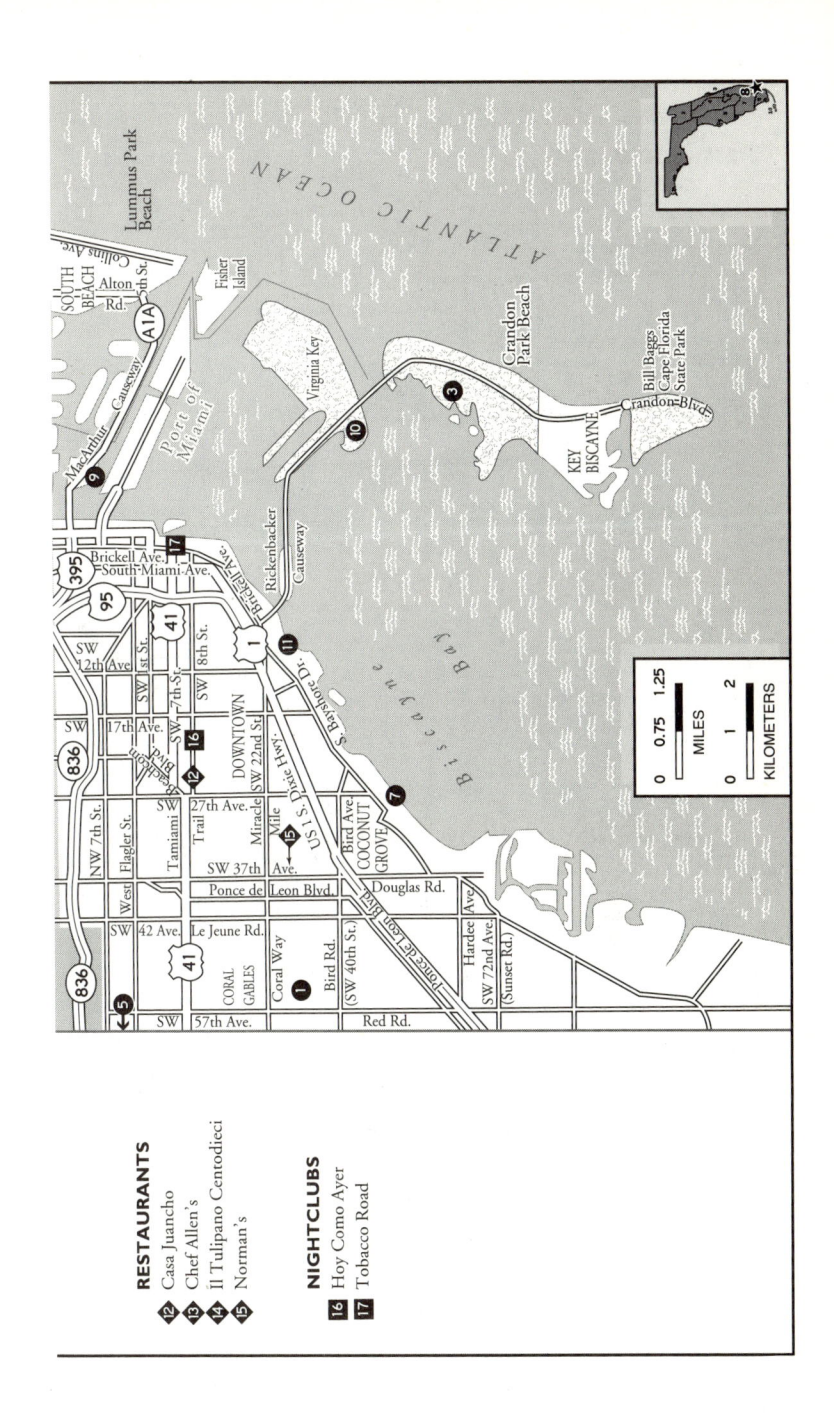

RESTAURANTS
- 12 Casa Juancho
- 13 Chef Allen's
- 14 Il Tulipano Centodieci
- 15 Norman's

NIGHTCLUBS
- 16 Hoy Como Ayer
- 17 Tobacco Road

South Miami Beach

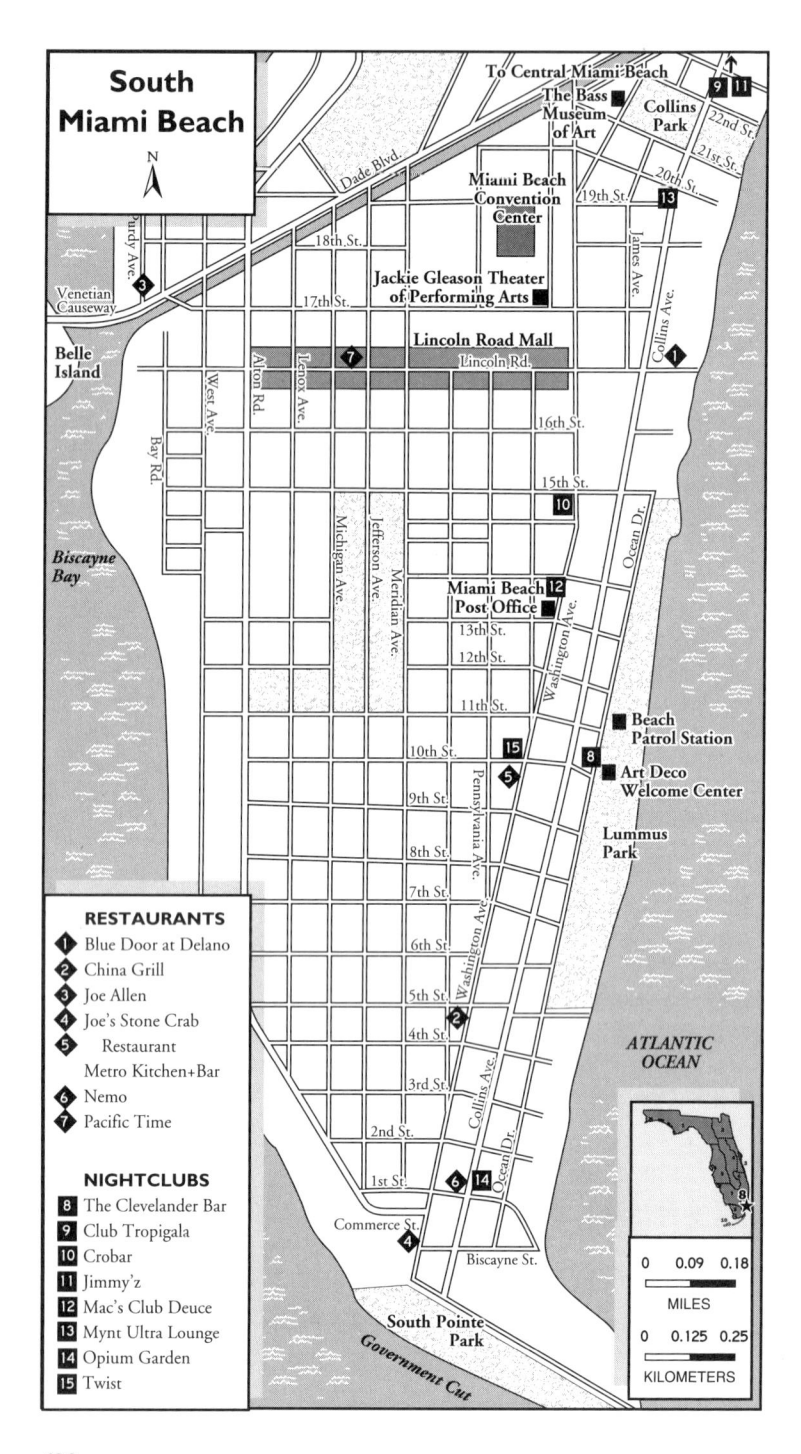

RESTAURANTS
1. Blue Door at Delano
2. China Grill
3. Joe Allen
4. Joe's Stone Crab Restaurant
5. Metro Kitchen+Bar
6. Nemo
7. Pacific Time

NIGHTCLUBS
8. The Clevelander Bar
9. Club Tropigala
10. Crobar
11. Jimmy'z
12. Mac's Club Deuce
13. Mynt Ultra Lounge
14. Opium Garden
15. Twist

Southern Miami–Dade County

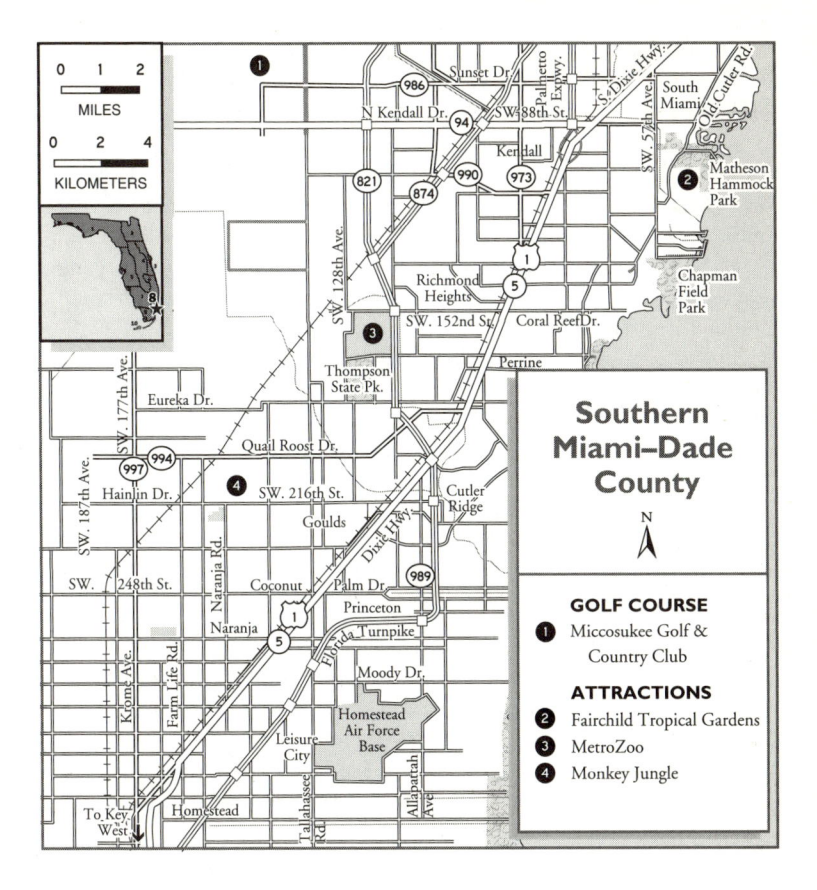

GOLF COURSE
1. Miccosukee Golf & Country Club

ATTRACTIONS
2. Fairchild Tropical Gardens
3. MetroZoo
4. Monkey Jungle

for a railroad mogul who would bring a line south. When the frost of 1894–1895 depleted citrus crops in Palm Beach, Tuttle sent a simple but eloquent message to Flagler—a single orange blossom. The frost hadn't touched Miami-area crops, and in spite of himself, Flagler completed the line to Miami on April 15, 1896, and all 300 Miami residents turned out to greet the locomotive.

Once the railroad arrived, Miami real estate was as hot as the Florida sun. Before the turn of the century, Miami had a newspaper. Soon churches and schools were established, and the city was calling itself "America's sun porch." Flagler extended his railroad on to the southern tip of Florida, Key West, in 1912.

During Prohibition, rum-runners thrived in Miami and mobsters operated with reputed immunity. A 1926 hurricane killed 100 Miami residents and thousands more fled northward rather than rebuild. Following the Depression, however, Miami experienced a resurgence that saw the construction of Miami Beach's famous Art Deco District. During World War II, the army converted 147 Miami hotels to makeshift barracks, and with the baby boom that followed the war, the city's population approached one million. New hotels, many with exotic, even outlandish themes, rose along the coast.

In 1960, Fidel Castro came to power in Cuba, triggering Miami's first wave of Cuban immigration, a tide that has yet to turn. Miami is today what many consider the most Latin city in the United States, where strong, hot café Cubano is the wakeup drink of choice for more than half the population.

In the 1970s, Miami become a major player in international banking and business. As the gateway to Latin America, huge office buildings began dotting the Miami skyline.

Growth continued, Miami's South Beach was redeveloped, and the Art Deco District attracted travelers from around the globe, primarily Latinos and Europeans.

Devastating Hurricane Andrew hit South Florida in 1992, causing nearly $20 billion in damages. But in the new century, the area has made tremendous efforts to rebuild itself and become a world-class tourist destination.

Visiting Miami

Gathering Information

Miami-Dade County Visitor Service Center at Greater Miami Convention and Visitors Bureau, 701 Brickell Avenue, Suite 2700, Miami 33131; phone (800) 933-8448 or (305) 539-3034; **www.tropicoolmiami.com**

Miami Beach Chamber of Commerce Visitor Center, 1920 Meridian Avenue, Miami Beach 33139 (305) 672-1270; **www.miamibeachchamber.com**

Greater Miami and the Beaches Hotel Association, 407 Lincoln Road, Suite 10G, Miami Beach 33139; (305) 531-3553 or (800) SEE-MIAMI; **www.gmbha.org**

Coconut Grove Chamber of Commerce, 2820 McFarlane Road, Coconut Grove 33133; (305) 444-7270; **www.coconutgrove.com**

Getting There

By Plane Virtually all international visitors fly into Miami International Airport, but domestic flyers, have a choice: Fort Lauderdale/Hollywood International Airport, a smaller facility, is well worth considering. It's only 30 minutes north of downtown Miami, close to I-95, and convenient for folks headed to Miami Beach because you can skip the major highways by taking US A1A south. While not as close to most Miami-destinations as its big brother to the south, this airport offers peace of mind to visitors who are anxious about safety when they drive to and from Miami International Airport. For more information, see "Part Seven: The Gold and Treasure Coasts."

Miami International Airport (MIA) is the ninth-largest airport in the United States, and third in the number of international passengers it handles. More than 33 million passengers fly in and out of MIA each year.

Visiting Miami   441

More airline companies fly into MIA (100) than to any other airport in the country, averaging more than 1,400 take-offs/landings a day. MIA has service to every major city in Latin America and the Caribbean, as well as connections to Europe and the Middle East. All tolled, MIA makes connections to about 200 cities on five continents.

The Dade County–owned facility has embarked on a $5.4 billion expansion program scheduled to be completed in 2007. Improvements will increase the number of gates to nearly 140, add three new passenger concourses, upgrade baggage-handling systems, and double the amount of retail space. But the second-floor departure level of the horseshoe-shaped terminal is already jammed with boutiques, bookstores, a hotel (with 260 rooms), bars, gift shops, restaurants, and a culturally diverse flow of people from around the world.

In spite of its size, however, MIA is an easy airport to navigate. From your gate, follow signs to the baggage area on the lower level; bus, taxi, and shuttle service, passenger car pickup, and rental car limos are outside the door. Directly across the street is a multilevel garage for short-term parking. If you're faced with a long walk between terminals, take the elevator to Level 3, for a "horizontal escalator" that will save wear and tear on your feet.

By Car   Most drivers to Miami arrive from the north via I-95, the major north-south expressway on the East Coast. Florida's Turnpike, a toll highway that starts near Orlando and Walt Disney World, runs down the center of the Florida peninsula, then heads east to Fort Pierce on the Atlantic coast. From there, the turnpike parallels I-95 south to Miami. The Homestead Extension of Florida's Turnpike skirts Greater Miami to the west. It's the route to take if you're headed to the Keys.

Another major highway, I-75, funnels motorists to Miami from Naples, Fort Myers, St. Petersburg, Tampa, and other points along Florida's west coast. It's better known as the Everglade Parkway. US 41, also called the Tamiami Trail and Alligator Alley, connects Miami and the Everglades to the west.

US 1 is the stoplight-laden road that I-95 and Florida's Turnpike replaced, but the old highway is still intact, a diversion from highway driving. Though it's not a practical route for visitors on a tight schedule (traffic lights, shopping centers, and congestion often slow traffic to a crawl, and the road is regarded as one of the most unpleasant driving experiences in South Florida), US 1 still affords glimpses of beaches, palm trees, occasional Florida kitsch, and plenty of strip shopping centers.

US A1A, Alternate Route 1, is even better for folks weary of interstates—and even slower. Much of this venerable old highway runs directly along the beach. For visitors who fly into Fort Lauderdale/Hollywood International Airport and are headed to Miami Beach, A1A is the way to go . . . if you're not in a rush.

Driving north to Miami from the Keys on US 1, take Florida's Turnpike, Homestead Extension in Florida City; US 1 between here and Miami is often unpredictably congested. Then take Route 874 north (the Don Shula

Expressway) to Route 826 north (the Palmetto Expressway); next, go east on the Dolphin Expressway (Route 836), which goes past Miami International Airport and links up with I-95 near downtown Miami. It may sound complicated, but this route is much faster.

By Train Amtrak operates a small, modern terminal near Hialeah Park, northwest of downtown Miami. It's not very convenient if your destination is the beach or downtown Miami—and the neighborhood is a bit rough.

The terminal is located at 8303 Northwest 37th Avenue; for recorded arrival and departure information, call Amtrak at (800) 872-7245. For ticket prices and reservations, call (305) 835-1222. To reach the station by car from I-95, take Northwest 79th Street west to Northwest 37th Avenue and turn right; the station is a few blocks north where the street dead-ends. Signs will help direct you.

A Metrorail station (call (305) 770-3131 for transit information) is about eight blocks away. Outside the terminal, board Metrobus "L," which takes you to the elevated-train station; the fare is $1.25 plus $.25 for a transfer to the above-ground train. TriRail also offers commuter trains to Miami from Palm Beach and Broward counties. Call (800) 874-7245 for details.

Via the Port of Miami

One of Miami's great sights is cruise ships floating from the port down Government Cut toward the Atlantic. Miami is the "Cruise Capital of the World," with more than three million passengers a year sailing from the Port of Miami, the home of about two dozen cruise ships—the world's largest year-round fleet. Cruise passengers can choose from the world's most popular ports of call on sea vacations ranging from three-and-four-day excursions to voyages up to eleven days. Destinations include exotic ports in the Caribbean, South America, the coastal resorts of Mexico, the Bahamas, and Key West. Year-round, passengers enjoy tropical weather virtually from the start of their voyages—a big attraction for vacationers from northern climates and a key to Miami's leadership in the cruise industry.

For cruise passengers flying into Miami International Airport who booked a cruise with airfare included, getting to the ship is easy: Representatives from cruise ship operators, holding signs, greet passengers as they enter the passenger terminal. Luggage is transferred automatically to the ship and passengers board motorcoaches for the quick trip (less than 30 minutes) to the dock. Your luggage is later delivered to your stateroom.

If you booked your own flight to Miami, don't expect to be greeted by an official from the cruise line. Instead, proceed to the lower level, pick up your luggage, step outside, and take a cab to the Port of Miami. Taxi rates are $12–$16 for up to five passengers.

If you're driving, the Port of Miami is easy to find: It's located on Dodge Island in Biscayne Bay between Miami and Miami Beach, and can be reached from Miami via Port Boulevard. From I-95, take Exit 3 to downtown and follow the signs to Biscayne Boulevard; Port Boulevard is next to

Bayside Marketplace. From I-395 (Exit 5 east on I-95, toward Miami Beach), take the Biscayne Boulevard exit south to downtown and follow signs to the Port of Miami. Parking is located in front of the terminals for $10 a day, payable prior to embarking. Have your cruise tickets handy and drop off your luggage at the terminal before parking; the luggage will be sent to your cabin.

Getting Around

The Major Highways

Immediately south of downtown, I-95 ends and merges with US 1, also called South Dixie Highway. US 1 swings southwest along Biscayne Bay through congested suburbs that include the cities of Coral Gables, Coconut Grove, Kendall, South Miami, Perrine, Cutler Ridge, and Homestead. South Dixie Highway is infamous for its seemingly endless number of traffic lights and horrendous traffic jams.

Forming Greater Miami's western border is Florida's Turnpike, Homestead Extension. Folks heading south from Miami and Miami Beach to visit southern Dade County's attractions—or to tour the Florida Keys, Key Biscayne, or the Everglades—should skip US 1 and take Route 836 (the Dolphin Expressway) to Florida's Turnpike and head south toward Homestead on this toll road.

Other major highways that visitors to Miami need to know about are: Route 112, the Airport Expressway, a toll road that links Miami International Airport with I-95 and Miami Beach; Route 836, the major east-west link connecting Florida's Turnpike, MIA, I-95, downtown Miami, and South Miami Beach; Route 826, the Palmetto Expressway, a major commuter route that runs north to south between MIA and Florida's Turnpike before heading east to I-95 in North Miami; Route 874, the Don Shula Expressway, which links the Palmetto Expressway and Florida's Turnpike in South Miami.

Taxis, Shuttles, and Public Transportation

Taxis With a population highly reliant on private cars, Miami isn't an easy place to hail a cab. If you need one, a phone call is your best bet.

Taxis are usually plentiful outside the terminals at Miami International Airport, however; the rate is $1.75 a mile. Expect to pay about $18 for a trip from the airport to downtown and $23 to Coconut Grove. Flat-rate fares are available to Miami Beach south of 63rd Street ($22–$24), Miami Beach between 67th Street and 87th Terrace ($29), Miami Beach between 87th Terrace and Haulover Park ($34), Miami Beach between Haulover Park and the Broward County line ($41), and Key Biscayne ($31). Trips to other destinations in and around Miami can range from $25 on up.

Metromover A ride on downtown's Metromover—called the "People Mover" by almost everyone—should be on every visitor's list of things to do on a Miami visit. The Disneyesque, automated monorail scoots people around downtown, treating them to spectacular views of the city, Biscayne Bay, and, off in the distance, the Atlantic Ocean. The system has recently been expanded with two out-and-back connections (in spite of their names, they're not "loops") to the Brickell Avenue business district to the south (Brickell Loop) and to the Omni Hotel to the north (Omni Loop). It's a very practical, clean, and safe system for getting around downtown Miami. Plus, it's air-conditioned.

Priced at a quarter per trip, the "People Mover" is the best tourist bargain in South Florida—and it hooks up with the Metrorail system. But unless you're staying downtown and don't plan to venture to other parts of Miami, this small transportation system won't replace your need for a car.

Visitors can cruise South Beach on the **ElectroWave**, Florida's first electric shuttle system. Shuttles stop every 6 to 11 minutes at 38 designated stops on Washington Avenue between 16th Street and South Pointe Drive and along Collins Avenue between 16th Street and Dade Boulevard. The shuttle operates 20 hours a day every day of the year. The fare is cheap, too: a quarter each way.

The Best Beaches

Bill Baggs Cape Florida State Recreation Area, Key Biscayne This beach is less crowded than Miami Beach, with five miles of sand and a more laid-back atmosphere. It's a great place for picnics, with plenty of tables in the shade. To get there, take Rickenbacker Causeway ($1 toll). Head for the southern tip of Key Biscayne. There's a lighthouse to explore (the oldest building in South Florida); bikes, sailboats, kayaks, jet skis, and water toys are for rent. Lifeguards are on duty. There's even a restaurant serving delicious Cuban food. Admission is $4 per car; open daily, 8 a.m.–sunset. Cape Florida State Recreation Area is located at 1200 Crandon Boulevard; (305) 361-5811.

Crandon Park Beach There's usually a crowd on sunny days, but Crandon has four miles of beach shaded by palms and sea grapes, with restaurants nearby and plenty of parking ($4 per vehicle). An offshore sandbar protects swimmers from crashing surf, and lifeguards are on patrol. The Marjory Stoneman Douglas Nature Center (phone (305) 361-6767; **www.biscayne naturecenter.org**) is part of the 1,200-acre park, located at 4000 North Crandon Park Boulevard, Key Biscayne; (305) 361-5421.

Miami Beach This barrier island, linked to downtown Miami by several bridges, is arguably the penultimate Florida beach—it is what many people envision when they hear "Miami," or even "Florida." However, Miami Beach is home to several distinct stretches of sand, which are best described by the kinds of folks who congregate at them.

The War Zone is the old name for the tip of land below Fifth Street down to Government Cut (the shipping channel leading to the Port of Miami). Now it's called **SoFi** (south of Fifth). This used to be mostly surfer turf, but the neighborhood is undergoing rapid change as the Art Deco

District trendiness, chains and boutiques, and high-rise and loft luxury condos push south. There's a park on the ocean-side between Second and Third Streets where folks gather at sunup for tai chi, and **South Pointe Park** is great for sunsets.

The renowned **South Beach,** or SoBe, especially 10th through 12th Streets, is topless-friendly, and gays tend to favor the beach around 18th Street. South Beach also attracts Germans, Italians, Hispanics (naturally), the young and the restless, Eurotrash, and glitterati from the world over.

Families going to the beach tend to flock to blocks numbered in the 20s, 30s, and 40s—and north. A wooden boardwalk extends from the 20s to the 50s behind many of the huge hotels that line the beach; you'll see a wide array of people strolling and jogging.

Mid-Miami Beach, centered around 41st Street, is a main commercial strip and has one of the largest concentrations of Lubovitch Jews in the state. Farther north, **Surfside** attracts an older population and is also a popular destination for Canadian and Scandinavian tourists. The epicenter of Canadian tourism is Hollywood, Florida, just over the line in Broward County.

For folks looking to sunbathe in the raw, **Haulover Beach Park** (just past Bal Harbour) has a "clothing optional" section along its more than one-mile length. It's a beautiful park that features a marina and plenty of parking.

Sunny Isles, located above Haulover Beach, has a lovely park beach with sea grape trees and sand dunes (which are about as high above sea level as you'll get in Miami). It's a popular spot for families.

Outdoor Adventures and Sports

Recommended Excursions

Biscayne National Park   More than 180,000 acres of underwater reefs, islands, and the closest coral reef snorkeling to Miami (about an hour's drive). There are guided and self-guided tours. A park concession offers three-hour glass-bottom-boat tours of the bay and reef. The cost is $20 for adults and $13 for children ages 12 and under; the trips leave at 10 a.m. daily. Three-hour snorkeling trips to the reef are $30 per person and include all equipment; the boat leaves at 10 a.m. and 1 p.m. daily. Two-tank scuba dives for certified divers are offered at 8:30 a.m. and 1 p.m. on weekends only; the cost is $45. Advance reservations for the boat tour and the snorkel trip are strongly advised; reservations are required for the scuba dives. Canoe rentals are $8 an hour, and kayak rentals are $16 an hour; prices include paddles and life jackets. Location is the Convoy Point Visitor Center, the only part of the park accessible by car, about 25 miles south of Miami and six miles east of US 1 and Homestead. From the Florida Turnpike Extension, take Southwest 328th Street (North Canal Drive) to the park entrance on the left. Admission is free. Open daily, 8:30 a.m.–5 p.m. (305) 230-7275; for reservations for snorkel, scuba, and boat trips, call (305) 230-1100.

Oleta River State Recreation Area   The 854-acre park is virtually surrounded by high-rises, but visitors can rent canoes and explore the quiet waters—and possibly sight a manatee. Admission to the park is $4 per car (up to eight people); canoe and paddleboat rentals are $12 per hour. One-person kayaks rent for $12 per hour. A $20 deposit and a driver's license are also required. Boat rentals are available weekdays, noon–5 p.m.; and weekends, 9 a.m.–5 p.m. The park is located off Sunny Isles Boulevard between Miami Beach and the mainland (North Miami Beach). For more information, call (305) 919-1846.

Venetian Pool   Created from rock quarry in 1923, the spring-fed pool was originally excavated to supply limestone for early Coral Gables homes, and is now on the National Register of Historic Places. Coral rock caves, waterfalls and stone bridges are quite a sight, surrounded by pink stucco towers, candystick Venetian poles, and a cobblestone bridge. Open Tuesday–Friday, 11 a.m.–4:40 p.m., closed Monday (with extended hours in the summer). Admission is $8 adults, $4.50 for children ages 12 and under; children under age 3 not permitted. A café offers a full lunch menu (2701 DeSoto Boulevard, Coral Gables; (305) 460-5356; **www.venetianpool.com**).

Canoeing and Kayaking

Visitors to Miami can rent canoes and kayaks to explore the backwaters of Biscayne Bay. The visual rewards range from close-up views of gorgeous waterfront estates to glimpses of Everglades-worthy wilderness located in Miami's backyard.

While 854-acre **Oleta River State Recreation Area** (see above) is virtually surrounded by high-rises, visitors can rent canoes and explore the quiet waters that surround the park—and possibly sight a manatee, a gentle, giant water mammal. At **Haulover Beach Park,** the **Urban Trails Kayak Company** offers guided and unguided tours of the Oleta River area and its mangrove-shrouded waterways and uninhabited islands. That's not all: to the south, on Key Biscayne, kayakers can explore the man-made backwaters and sumptuous estates bordering Biscayne Bay. Guided group tours ($45 per person) are by appointment; self-guided trips can start anytime. One-person kayak rental rates are $8 an hour, $20 for a half day, and $25 a full day. Tandem (two-person) kayaks are $12 an hour, $30 a half day, and $35 all day; no paddling experience is required. Call (305) 947-1302 for more information.

Some of the world's most extensive mangrove forests can be explored by canoe at **Biscayne National Park** (see above) near Florida City in southern Dade County. Canoe rentals are available 9 a.m.–4:30 p.m. for $8 an hour, $22 a half-day, and $32 a full day; the price includes paddles and life jackets. Folks with their own canoes can launch for free. Call (305) 230-1100 for more information.

Scuba Diving and Snorkeling

For more experienced certified divers, Miami is a destination that offers a chance to explore an extensive line of natural reefs that parallels the entire length of Dade County. Miami is also home to one of the largest artificial reef programs in the world.

It started in 1972 with the sinking of the *Biscayne,* a 120-foot-long freighter that formerly hauled bananas from South America. The ship was the first of many wrecks (including barges, tugboats, naval vessels, and private yachts) that have been sunk for the enjoyment of sport divers. While the shallowest reefs near Miami are 30 feet down, wreck diving starts at 35 feet and goes down to about 130 feet. Private dive boats can lead visiting divers on tours of the wrecks and reefs, including night dives.

Up the coast in Sunny Isles, the **Diving Locker** (phone (305) 947-6025) offers a three-and-a-half-hour, two-dive trip every morning and afternoon, weather permitting. The cost, including tanks and weights, is $45. Most trips visit a wreck and a shallow reef. In addition, the shop offers a certification course (a four-day private course is $350) and a one-hour introduction to scuba diving ($45, pool only). **H2O Scuba** (phone (305) 956-3483) offers four-hour, two-tank dive trips at 8:30 a.m. and 1 p.m. on weekends and at noon on weekdays; the cost is $48 per person without equipment, $58 with two tanks, and $85 with all equipment. A certification course is $239.

The closest place to Miami with shallow reefs for snorkelers to enjoy is **Biscayne National Park** (see above), an underwater park located a few miles east of Florida City in southern Dade County; it's about an hour's drive from downtown Miami. The requirements for snorkeling are minimal: the ability to swim and a desire to see aquatic life up close.

At Biscayne National Park, three-hour snorkeling trips (two hours of travel, one hour exploring the reef) leave daily at 1:30 p.m., weather permitting; the cost is $29.95 per person and includes all the equipment you need. Call (305) 230-1100 to make a reservation. See our profile of Biscayne National Park (page 445) for more information.

A small reef is located off Miami Beach between Third and Sixth Streets in South Beach, 70 yards offshore and 16 feet down. Check with a lifeguard for the exact location and be sure to take out a diving flag to warn boaters that you're swimming in the area.

Sailboats and Boating

To set sail on the calm, shallow waters of Biscayne Bay, head for Sailboats of **Key Biscayne** (Crandon Park Marina, Key Biscayne; (305) 361-0328 or (305) 279-7424). Catalina 22-footers rent for $35 an hour and $110 a half day; each additional hour is $20; Catalina 25-foot, J-24, and Hunter 23-foot sailboats rent for $35 an hour, $110 for a half day, and $170 for a full day. Bareboat (no crew) charters on sailboats from 30 to 54 feet are also available.

Never sailed? Then sign up for a ten-hour sailing course offered at Sailboats of Key Biscayne that will turn you into a certified skipper. There's no classroom time—all instruction is on the water—and graduates of the course qualify for a 15 percent discount on boat rentals. The cost of the private, one-on-one course is $250; add $100 for a spouse or friend for one-on-two instruction. After completing the course, graduates are qualified to rent a cruising sailboat and embark on an overnight sailing trip.

Another option: Dinner Key in Coconut Grove is another nearby destination well known for sailing, and it is a good jumping off point for sailing Biscayne Bay.

For the nautically inclined, a sure bet is a two-hour cruise on Biscayne Bay aboard the *Heritage of Miami II,* an 85-foot topsail schooner. Once out on the placid waters of the bay, the engine goes off and wind fills the crimson sails. If the weather cooperates, the skipper might let passengers take the helm for a few minutes while under sail.

Two-hour sails depart at 1:30 p.m. and 4 p.m.; a one-hour trip leaves at 6:30 p.m. In the winter, sign up for the 4 p.m. sail, which turns into a sunset cruise. All sails depart daily from Bayside Marketplace in downtown Miami. The cost is $15 for adults and $10 for children under age 12. One-hour sails depart on Friday, Saturday, and Sunday at various times. Call ahead for specific schedules on weekends or for more information, (305) 442-9697.

MIAMI AREA MARINAS AND CHARTER SERVICES		
Marina	Location	Phone
Action Charters		(305) 361-2131
Blue Waters Fishing	Bayside Marketplace	(305) 944 4531
Captain Bouncer	16850-112 Collins Avenue #291	(305) 945-5114
Crandon Park Marina	4000 Crandon Boulevard	(305) 361-1281
Free Spool Sportfishing Charters, Inc.	Haulover Marina	(305) 947-8844
Haulover Marina	10800 Collins Avenue	(305) 947-3525
Matheson Hammock Marina	9610 Old Cutler Road	(305) 665-5475
Miami Beach Marina	300 Alton Road	(305) 673-6000
Pelican Harbor Marina	1275 Northeast 79th Street	(305) 754-9330

Fishing

Deep-sea fishing is a popular pastime for Miami guests and residents alike. Many serious anglers opt to head south to the Keys, but charters are readily available at the city's marinas. Expect to pay from $400 to $1000 for a charter trip, depending on length, destination, and the size of your party. If that sounds too expensive, consider a drift boat, or party boats. For $30–$45, you'll join fellow aspiring anglers on a half-day outing with all gear supplied; often the crew will bait your hook and clean your catch. One reputable outfit is the **Kelley Fishing Fleet** (Haulover Marina, Sunny Isles; (305) 945-3801.

If you're looking to fish from shore, try **Haulover Beach Park** (108000 Collins Avenue, Sunny Isles; (305) 947-3525), with a nearby tackle shop, or

Southe Pointe Park (1 Washington Avenue, Miami Beach; (305) 673-7224), with its lengthy pier. Fishing from bridges such as Rickenbacher Causeway is also common. Remember, a Florida fishing license is required if casting from shore (call (800) FISH-FLORIDA for details).

Biking

Mountain bikes and beach cruisers are available for rental at **Miami Beach Bicycle Center** (601 Fifth Street; (305) 674-0150). Rental rates start at $20 per day or $70 per week. **Grove Cycles** (3226 Grand Avenue, Coconut Grove; (305) 444-5415) rents beach cruisers, tandems, and in-line skates. Beach cruisers and in-line skates rent for $5.50 an hour, $15 a day, and $25 for 24 hours; tandems rent for $10 an hour and $45 a day. Helmets rent for $1 an hour or $3 a day; children 15 years old and younger receive free helmet rental. **Mangrove Cycles** (260 Crandon Boulevard, Key Biscayne; (305) 361-5555) rents one-speed bikes for $7 for two hours, $10 a day, and $35 a week; mountain bikes rent for $12 for two hours, $18 a day, and $45 a week. The shop, otherwise open 10 a.m.–6 p.m., is closed Mondays.

For eye-pleasing scenery and enough tree cover to ward off the subtropical sun, most riders head for Coconut Grove. For a longer spin, follow the bike path south along Bayshore Drive, Main Highway, Ingraham Highway, and Old Cutler Road—although the paved path is often broken up by tree roots and is better suited for fat tires and one-speed rental bikes. For a more energetic ride with stunning view—and the biggest climb in Dade County—take the Rickenbacker Causeway to Key Biscayne.

The premier off-road destination is just over the line in Broward County: **Markham County Park** (phone (954) 389-2000), located near the intersection of I-75 and I-59, west of Fort Lauderdale. The park features single-track trails, jeep roads, low hills in the woods, and black, sticky mud guaranteed to keep intermediate and advanced riders entertained. There's a $1 entrance fee to the park on weekends and holidays.

Dade County offers three smaller destinations for off-road rambles. **Amelia Earhart Park** in Hialeah offers easier trails. **Greynolds Park,** off West Dixie Highway in North Miami Beach, has a 1.6-mile course that local riders like to jam around. **Haulover Park** offers three short rides in the woods—but avoid riding through the field or you'll be picking thorns out of your inner tubes.

Spectator Sports

Football

Leading the list of attractions is the AFC East **Miami Dolphins** football team, which packs 'em in every season at Pro Player Stadium (formerly Joe Robbie Stadium). The Dolphins have played in the Super Bowl five times and in 1972 achieved everlasting glory with the only all-win, no-tie season in NFL history. The season runs from August through December; ticket prices range from $24 to $130 and are available from the stadium box office or TicketMaster at (954) 523-3309. The stadium is located at 2269 Northwest 199th Street in North Miami; (305) 620-2578.

Top-flight collegiate sports teams in South Florida include the University of **Miami Hurricanes,** who play football at the famous Orange Bowl from September through November. Sit high up in the stands and you'll get a great view of Miami while watching the gridiron action. The stadium is located at 1400 Northwest Fourth Street, west of downtown. Tickets are $18 and $22. For tickets and game information, call (305) 284-CANE or (800) GO-CANES.

Baseball

Pro Player Stadium, which hosted its second Super Bowl in 1995, also hosts the annual Blockbuster Bowl college football championship. It's also home to the **Florida Marlins,** 1997 and 2003 World Series champs. General admission tickets for Marlins games range from $2 to $125, but average $10–$25. Call the stadium at (305) 626-7400 for home game dates and other information.

Basketball

The 20,000-seat AmericanAirlines Area, located at 601 Biscayne Boulevard, hosts the **Miami Heat,** an NBA team offering fast-paced basketball action. The squad debuted in 1988 and has been to the NBA's Eastern Conference Finals. Ticket prices are $15–$135. Call (305) 577-HEAT for ticket information.

The University of Miami basketball squad plays at the Miami Arena, 701 Arena Boulevard in downtown Miami. Tickets are $9–$18 (call (305) 284-2263). Florida International University's **Golden Panthers** basketball team plays November through March at the Golden Panther Arena, Southwest 8th Street and 112th Avenue in Miami. For a schedule, call (305) 348-4263.

Hockey

The National Hockey League's **Florida Panthers,** who made an incredible run to the Stanley Cup finals in just their third season, play in Sunrise at the Office Depot Area (2555 Southwest 137th Way). Ticket prices are $14–$100. For information, call (954) 835-7000.

THE GRAND PRIX

The **Grand Prix of Miami** is South Florida's premier auto racing event. Each spring, international drivers compete at speeds of more than 100 mph at Metro-Dade Homestead Motorsports Complex in Homestead. Tickets for three days of racing action range from $40 to $200. For ticket information, call the Homestead-Miami Speedway ticket office at (305) 230-RACE.

The Betting Sports: Horse Races, Greyhounds, and Jai Alai

South Florida is home to several sports that permit pari-mutuel wagering, in which you bet against other wagerers, not the house. While no one under age 18 may bet in Florida, children may accompany adults to horse races, greyhound races, and jai alai games.

Horse Racing For more than 75 years Florida has been a center of thoroughbred horse racing. Classy **Hialeah Park** (2200 East Fourth Avenue, Hialeah; (305) 885-8000), built in 1925, is no longer a venue for racing, but can be visited just to enjoy the gorgeous grounds and coral clubhouse listed on the National Register of Historic Places, and a flock of 400 pink flamingos on the track's infield. **Calder Race Course** (21001 Northwest 27th Avenue, Miami; (305) 625-1311) has a weatherproof track that permits racing during the rainy summer.

Dog Racing Greyhounds reach speeds of more than 40 miles an hour and you can see the action at **Flagler Greyhound Track** (401 Northwest 38th Court; (305) 649-3000). In Broward County, the Hollywood Greyhound Track is located on US 1 a mile east of I-95, just over the county line in Hallandale; phone (954) 924-3200.

Jai Alai Teams compete in the world's fastest sport, a Basque game dating from the fifteenth century. The hard ball (called a pelota) flung and caught in a long, curved wicker basket (a cesta) has been clocked at 180 mph. Teams of two or four compete and the first team to score seven points wins. You can watch the game for $1 at the **Miami Jai Alai Fronton** (3500 Northwest 37th Avenue; (305) 633-6400). A fronton, by the way, is the 176-foot-long court where jai alai (pronounced "high lie") is played; Miami's court, built in 1926, is the oldest in the United States.

A CUBAN COFFEE PRIMER

You'll see crowds huddling around open windows in front of the restaurants that line Calle Ocho in Little Havana and dot the rest of Miami. From these café windows wafts the aroma of Cuban coffee.

In the mornings, workers stop by the windows for a cup of espresso with steamed milk. In late afternoon, the men in their *guayaberas* (loose-fitting shirts) gather to talk politics and drink thimblefuls of black, sweetened espresso that the locals call it "jet fuel."

Here's a java glossary of *café Cubano* in ascending order of potency.

- *Café con leche* usually a morning drink. About one part coffee to four parts steamed whole milk. Usually served *con azucar* (with sugar) and very sweet. Ask for it *sin azucar* (without sugar) to add your own to taste. For more of a kick, drink it *oscuro* (dark).
- *Cortadito* smaller than a café con leche. About one part espresso to two parts milk.
- *Colada* a cup of straight, hypersugared espresso served with about five plastic thimble-sized cups for sharing. Only the truly intestinally fortified would venture to drink one solo.

What to See and Do in Miami

Miami Neighborhoods

The following list of Miami's most popular neighborhoods (all of which are safe for exploration by visitors on foot, except where noted) starts in South Miami Beach, continues north along the ocean to Sunny Isles, crosses Biscayne Bay to North Miami and Aventura, and turns south to Little Haiti, downtown and Coral Gables.

South Beach

Created years ago as a place for Northerners to escape cold winters and the Great Depression, South Miami Beach (now usually called South Beach or SoBe) is a 23-block area on the southern tip of Miami Beach. The architecture is intentionally whimsical—a collage of Art Deco, streamlined moderne, and Spanish Mediterranean–revival styles adapted to the South Florida climate.

Over the decades, the neighborhood had its problems, but today, South Beach is sizzling. A preservation movement that began in the 1970s has produced a kaleidoscope of restored buildings—mostly hotels, but some apartment buildings, restaurants, and condos—in lollipop colors. The streets are filled with fashion models and photographers, young Europeans, fitness fanatics, and a few retirees hanging on as prices keep going up. South Beach is also a popular stop with Hollywood celebs. No wonder it's been dubbed the "American Riviera."

SoBe has drawbacks. On weekends, traffic slows to a crawl, and finding a place to park induces heartburn. While South Beach has a reputation for being safe, car break-ins are a problem. Don't leave anything of value in your car. And keep a couple of dollars handy for valet parking. Many Miami residents taxi to South Beach to avoid the hassle.

Thinking of renting a room? Accommodations tend toward the funky, with small rooms right out of the 1950s. Don't assume that a South Beach hotel's recently renovated exterior is an indication that the rooms got a facelift, too. The nightclub and street scene goes on all night, seven nights a week. If you're a light sleeper, rent a room on the upper floors, away from the elevator and street.

Don't miss an evening stroll down **Ocean Drive,** where the best Art Deco architecture faces the Atlantic and the beautiful people strut their stuff. Or Sundays in season, when **Lincoln Road** becomes a fun fair of art, artifacts, food, and plantings, all sold al fresco. Walk down the hotel side for up-close, elbow-to-elbow people-watching, then cruise back on the **Lummus Park** (Atlantic) side for the best views of the architecture.

Central Miami Beach

While the architecture of South Beach is rooted in the 1930s, the mile-long stretch of Miami Beach above 21st Street has its feet firmly planted in the 1950s. Outrageous, ostentatious hotels loom over the beach and Collins

Avenue, most notably the **Fontainebleau Hilton** at 4441 Collins Avenue, a curving mass of 1950s kitsch designed by Morris Lapidus.

Across Collins Avenue and Indian Creek is an area where Miami Beach's wealthiest residents live. Drive, stroll, or rent a bike to view exclusive homes along tree-lined roads such as Alton Road, Pine Tree Drive, Bay Drive, and La Gorce Drive. Boat cruises of Biscayne Bay are available at the marina across from the **Eden Roc Hotel.**

Miami Beach's mix of commercial properties—hotels, restaurants, bars, grocery stores, travel agencies, etc.—and residential properties—mostly large condominium and apartment buildings testify that Miami Beach is a year-round working city, not just a vacation mecca.

The 21st Street area, with the **Bass Museum,** an enhanced new library, and the **Miami City Ballet Rehearsal Hall** (where you can watch the dancers practice through big windows) has become a new cultural epicenter.

North of Miami Beach

North of the procession of glitzy 1950s hotels in central Miami Beach, the scenery gets less . . . interesting. This stretch resembles the Miami Beach of 20 years ago, and lets up on the unrelenting trendiness to the south.

The communities of **Surfside, Bal Harbour,** and **Sunny Isles** are dominated by Jewish and Canadian tourists and retirees, living in an exclusive enclaves alongside tourists who care most about easy access to the beach. With their seemingly endless succession of high-rise buildings, these neighborhoods comprise what's often called the "condo corner" of Miami.

The **North Shore State Recreation Area** (between 91st and 95th Streets), is one of the few places in Miami to allow topless bathing—although European women tend to ignore local conventions and doff their tops all along Miami Beach's shoreline.

Haulover Beach Park is where boats were once hauled over to the Intracoastal from the Atlantic. Today it features uncrowded beaches—including a nude beach—a marina, kayak rentals, and a great place to fly kites.

Bal Harbour Shops, a famed outdoor/indoor mall, offers expensive designer goods as tony as any on Rodeo Drive.

At the northern end of Miami Beach, Sunny Isles was, until about ten years ago, a busy, tacky commercial strip along Collins Avenue filled with theme-motif motels. Now, luxury high-rise condos line the Atlantic across from strip malls targeting condo residents. Enjoy the whimsy of the remaining theme structures before chain hotels and luxury condos buy them out.

Wolfie Cohen's Rascal House, a restaurant and sandwich shop in Sunny Isles, is considered by many to be one of Miami Beach's quintessential monuments to eating (along with Joe's Stone Crab in South Beach).

Little Haiti

Immigrants from Haiti are a major ethnic group in Miami, and a visit to Little Haiti gives visitors a chance to encounter this rich Caribbean culture.

Yet the neighborhood's name promises more than it can deliver: This is no well-defined Chinatown or Little Italy, but an amorphous community with few architectural features to make it stand out from the rest of sprawling Miami. Look for bright paintings and wall art, in a typically Haitian style.

The best bet for first-time visitors is the **Caribbean Marketplace** (5927 Northeast Second Avenue). The open-air marketplace designed to resemble the Iron Market in Port-au-Prince houses food booths, record stores and arts-and-crafts vendors. During the day, the neighborhood is safe, but unfortunately we can't recommend visiting at night.

Downtown Miami

Downtown Miami is easily identifiable by its distinctive skyline, but it is not yet a 24/7 area. Streets are lined with cut-rate shops hawking electronics, luggage, jewelry, and clothes. Festivals like the great **Miami Book Fair,** at the downtown campus of Miami Dade Junior College, draw many to the downtown area.

Bayside Shopping Center on Biscayne Boulevard, next to the American Airlines Sports Center, offers boat rides and a festive atmosphere. Small shopping malls, exotic eateries offering Brazilian fare, small Cuban cafés, and a few honest-to-God tourist attraction—the **Metro-Dade Cultural Center** is the best—are what you should seek out.

At night, alas, downtown Miami is as dead as last night's salsa and chips—except for glorious **Gusman Hall,** with stars on the ceiling and a peacock perched on a backlit Moorish facade surrounding the stage. The landmark former Olympia movie palace from the 1920s has been refurbished, and is home to the Florida Philharmonic, the Maximum Dance Group, and the Miami Film Festival.

But Gusman is slowly acquiring new neighbors. Museums are moving to Bicentennial Park along the bay. New downtown condos, proposed entertainment areas, the new performing arts center between the MacArthur and the Venetian Causeways, improved landscaping and lighting, and a revitalized river walk are beginning to make this city pulse at night as well as day.

South of Downtown Miami/Brickell Avenue

This is Miami's Fifth Avenue and Wall Street in one. Running from the Miami River (the southern border of downtown) to Coconut Grove along Brickell Avenue is the largest group of international banks in the United States, partially the result of political instability throughout Latin America in the late 1970s, when Miami became a safe haven for corporate money and a new corporate banking center.

A little farther on Brickell Avenue, along Biscayne Bay, is a collection of impressive high-rise condominiums, home to seasonal Latin American visitors, and long-time locals—it's upscale and dramatic, with primary colors, tropical gardens and bold designs, The most famous condo is the **Atlantis,** designed by the famed Architectonica Group; its gaping square includes a palm tree, Jacuzzi, and a red spiral staircase. New buildings include the Millennium, the city's highest.

What to See and Do in Miami 455

Nearby **Brickell Key** has luxury condos and the Mandarin Oriental Hotel, and nearby **Brickell Village** is a new pedestrian friendly neighborhood, with condos, restaurants, galleries, and boutiques going up, just west of Brickell Avenue.

Little Havana
Cubans have made a tremendous impact on Miami over the last three decades; they are unquestionably the largest and most visible ethnic group in the city. However, the streets of Little Havana (located a few miles west of downtown, centered on Southwest Eighth Street) offer mostly neighborhood shops, not tourist destinations. In fact, the name "Little Havana" is misleading; while the words suggest a self-contained, ethnic enclave; the reality is a neighborhood without strict boundaries that doesn't look a whole lot different from other parts of Miami.

Yet, old men in guayaberas play dominoes in the park, and you'll also see plenty of examples of what locals call "Spanglish": signs and billboards that charmingly mix English and Spanish, like one motel's boast, "Open 24 Horas."

The best place for a stroll in Little Havana is **Calle Ocho** (pronounced KAH-yeh OH-cho, Spanish for Eighth Street), where streetside counters sell café Cubano, and the odor of cigars being rolled and baking bread fills the air.

You can visit Little Havana for lunch or dinner at **Versailles Restaurant** (3555 Southwest Eighth Street; (305) 444-0240), open Sunday–Thursday, 8 a.m.–2 a.m.; Friday, 8 a.m.–3:30 a.m.; and Saturday, 8 a.m.–4:30 a.m. A Little Havana institution that shouldn't be missed, Versailles offers great Cuban fare, it's cheap, it's easy to find, and parking is ample.

Coral Gables
One of America's first planned communities, dating from the 1920s, Coral Gables is a gracious, Spanish-styled enclave, filled with gorgeous homes, manicured lawns, and lush foliage. The layout of the place, however, resembles a maze, with street names in Spanish written on small white stones at ground level that are hard to read. Yet this classy old neighborhood, where many of Miami's most successful citizens live, is perfect for exploration by foot or bicycle.

Coral Way is the banyan-shaded commercial street that connects from Miami to the Gables, with some of the oldest homes in the area.

Intriguing sights include the **Venetian Pool,** a freshwater coral rock lagoon called the best swimming hole in the world (bring a swimsuit, a towel, and five bucks); the **Biltmore Hotel,** fabulously restored after decades of neglect (with one of the largest pools anywhere, and a famous Sunday brunch around the fountain in the courtyard); and the **Miracle Mile,** a four-block stretch of expensive shops and boutiques. Peek inside the restored **Omni Colonnade Hotel**. The building was the former office of George Merrick, the man who built Coral Gables.

Merrick Park, a vast new indoor/outdoor shopping area, rivals Bal Harbour for fashionable shops, fine restaurants, and high-end atmosphere.

Coconut Grove

"The Grove." Miami's former Bohemian quarter is today a mix of expensive shops, trendy bars and restaurants, galleries and boutiques, and young crowds. Although not as outrageous as South Beach, Coconut Grove offers people-watchers another outstanding opportunity to sit at an outdoor café and watch fashion magazine victims strut their stuff and in-line skaters weave through bumper-to-bumper traffic. The west section of the Grove also includes an area originally settled by Bahamians, one of the oldest African-American communities in Florida.

Shoppers can browse in New Age bookstores, lingerie shops, a surfboard boutique, a Harley-Davidson dealership, and flower shops. **CocoWalk,** a multilevel mall done in pink and beige, features a courtyard with live music on evenings and weekends.

The outrageous **Mango Strut,** where gays dress up and parade, the huge, famed **Grove Art Fair,** and the now-venerable **Coconut Grove Theater** all add luster and creative energy to the area.

Key Biscayne

This tropical island is just ten minutes from downtown via the Rickenbacker Causeway ($1 toll). The island, more like the New York's Hamptons than SoBe, features some of the best beaches in the Miami area—broad, duned, with calmer waters than Miami Beach—and most are open to the public. **Seaquarium,** Miami's sea-mammal emporium, is located on Virginia Key, the Island the causeway crosses before reaching Key Biscayne (and until the 1950s the only area where black residents could swim and sunbathe legally). On the five-mile-long causeway, visitors can pull over, park, and rent sailboards and jet skis for zooming around. A note for those who travel with their pets: These are the only beaches in the Miami area that allow dogs.

Two state parks are located on Key Biscayne. At the tip is **Bill Baggs Cape Florida State Park**. The 406-acre park is tipped with a nineteenth-century lighthouse, one of the oldest structures in South Florida. For swimming, we recommend **Crandon Park,** with its wide beaches, as a better bet for visitors. Pack a lunch and swimming gear. Public rest rooms are available for changing.

Golf

Biltmore Golf Course

1210 Anastasia Avenue, Coral Gables; (305) 460-5364; www.biltmorehotel.com
Established 1926 | **Designer** Donald Ross | **Holes** 18

Tees Championship/Men's/Ladies **Par** 71/71/71 **Slope** 119/116/122
Fees $76
Specials Twilight (after 2 p.m.), $48; 9-holes, $9 **Cart rental** Included
Club rental $50 per set **Payment** V, MC, AmEx **Tee times** up to 48 hours

in advance **Facilities** Clubhouse, full-service pro shop with custom club-building and club repair capabilities, restaurant, locker rooms, driving range, putting greens, sand trap area, lessons from pros, tennis courts, Biltmore Hotel.

Comments Redesigned in 1992, the Biltmore Golf Course is in excellent shape. The fairways are wide open, so you can swing away—be careful not to hit one of the million-dollar homes that line the fairways. The hardest hole if the Sixth, a 391-yard par-4.

City of Miami Springs Country Club

650 Curtiss Parkway, Miami Springs; (305) 863-0980
Established 1923 | **Holes** 18

Tees Championship/Men's/Ladies **Par** 71/71/72 **Slope** 120/116/122
Fees $30
Specials Weekdays, $20 after noon; weekends, $25 after noon. **Cart rental** Included **Club rental** $15 per set **Payment** V, MC, AmEx **Tee times** up to 1 day in advance **Facilities** Pro shop, restaurant, banquet facility for up to 700, lounge, lighted driving range, lessons from pros.

Comments The Country Club in Miami Springs was opened by the City of Miami in 1923. The course features challenging sand traps and a tropical ambience throughout its 6,741 yards. Home of the original Miami Open from 1925 until 1955, Miami Springs is now the annual host of the prestigious North-South Tournament. Less than five minutes from Miami International Airport and area hotels, Miami Springs has become a favorite among business travelers in Miami.

Crandon Park at Key Biscayne

6700 Crandon Boulevard, Key Biscayne; (305) 361-9129;
www.golfersweb.com/crandon.htm
Established 1972 | **Designers** Robert von Hagge and Bruce Devlin | **Holes** 18

Tees Blue/White/Forward **Par** 72/72/72 **Slope** 139/125/129
Fees $52.97 (7 days a week)
Specials Twilight, $29 after 4 p.m. (Dade County residents specials available) **Cart rental** Included **Club rental** $32 per set **Payment** V, MC, AmEx **Tee times** up to 5 days in advance **Facilities** Municipal-like clubhouse, pro shop, and practice facilities

Comments This is one of Florida's best public courses, and may well be the best value around. The course was rebuilt by von Hagge (one of the original designers) after Hurricane Andrew in 1992, and is now much more demanding than the original. Water is the prevalent theme, with 13 holes featuring water and five playing right along Biscayne Bay.

Doral Resort & Country Club

4000 Northwest 87th Avenue, Miami; Silver Course Clubhouse: 5001 Northwest 104th Avenue; (305) 592-2000; www.doralresort.com
Established 1961 | **Designer** Dick Wilson

The Blue Monster

Holes 18 **Tees** Championship/Men's/Ladies **Par** 72/72/72
Slope 130/125/124

The Gold Course

Holes 18 **Tees** Championship/Men's/Ladies **Par** 70/70/70
Slope 129/124/123

The Red Course

Holes 18 **Tees** Championship/Men's/Ladies **Par** 70/70/70
Slope 121/118/118

The White Course

Holes 18 **Tees** Championship/Men's/Ladies **Par** 72/72/72
Slope 128/113/130

The Silver Course

Holes 18 **Tees** Championship/Men's/Ladies **Par** 71/71/71
Slope 131/128/117

The Green Course

Holes 9 **Par** 3

Fees Hotel guests: Blue course, $225; White course, $225; Red course, $180; Gold course, $195; Silver course, $195. Non-guests: Blue course, $250; White course, $250; Red course, $200; Gold course, $225; Silver course, $225. In season valid December 22–May 3. Green course, $25 all the time for all guests.
Specials Greens fees are significantly lower off-season, call for details **Cart rental** Included **Club rental** $85 per set **Payment** All major credit cards **Tee times** Guests of the resort can make tee times when they make their reservations; nonguests can make tee times 30 days in advance **Facilities** One of the world's largest pro shops, driving range, four putting greens, world-class Doral Spa, on-course snack bar, three full-service restaurants, 15-court tennis facility, Doral golf learning center with Jim McLean, caddies available, fishing in the course lakes; the clubhouse for the Silver Course was under renovation at press time—the new facilities will be extensive.
Comments The home of the famous Doral "Blue Monster" and the Doral-Ryder Open. This is one of the premier golf courses in the country. The Gold Course has recently been redesigned by Raymond Floyd (original

designer of the "Blue Monster"). With the tropical Miami climate and four championship courses, this Florida destination is one that should not be missed by the avid golfer. Serene lakes and cypress trees line the fairways of this wonderful setting.

Fontainebleau Golf Club

9603 Fontainebleau Boulevard, Miami; (305) 221-5181;
www.fontainebleaugolfclub.com

East Course

Established 1970 | **Designer** Mark Mahanna | **Holes** 18

Tees Championship/Men's/Ladies **Par** 72/72/72 **Slope** 122/117/119

West Course

Established 1970 | **Designer** Mark Mahanna | **Holes** 18

Tees Championship/Men's/Ladies **Par** 72/72/72 **Slope** 120/118/118
Fees Fees valid for two people. Winter: weekdays, $50 ($40 after noon); weekends, $60 ($46 after noon). Call for summer rates. **Cart rental** Included **Payment** V, MC, AmEx, DC **Tee times** up to 30 days in advance **Facilities** 36-hole championship course, driving range, snack bar, pro shop, lessons from PGA professional.
Comments Affordable and convenient to the airport, Fontainebleau is a good choice for business travelers looking to squeeze in a couple of rounds. The course also hosts tournaments for private companies and clubs.

Golf Club of Miami

6801 Miami Gardens Drive, Miami; (305) 829-4700
Established 1990 | **Holes** 18

East Course

Established 1990 | **Holes** 18

Tees Championship/Men's/Ladies **Par** 70/70/70 **Slope** 124/120/118

West Course

Established 1990 | **Holes** 18

Tees Championship/Men's/Ladies **Par** 72/72/72 **Slope** 132/128/124
Fees in season (December–April 15): weekdays, $55; weekends, $75. Off-season (April 16–December): $22–$55. All fees subject to 6.5% Florida tax.
Specials Twilight fees available **Cart rental** Included **Club rental** $15 **Payment** All major credit cards **Tee times** Up to 7 days in advance **Facilities** Two grass driving ranges (one lighted), two pro shops, on-course beverage service, lessons from PGA professionals, Turn Key tournament operation, full service restaurant, banquet room, men's and women's locker rooms.

Part Nine Miami and Miami Beach

Comments South Florida's premier public golf facility. Site of former National Airlines Open, the 1991 Senior PGA Tour National Qualifying School, and Regional USGA events such as the Mid-AM qualifier.

Miccosukee Golf & Country Club (formerly Miami National Golf Club)

6401 Kendale Lakes Drive, Miami; (305) 382-3930; www.miccosukeeresort.com

Marlin Course

Established 1970 | **Holes** 18

Tees Blue/White/Red **Par** 36/36/37 **Slope** 129/124/119

Dolphin/Barracuda Course

Established 1970 | **Holes** 18

Tees Blue/White/Red **Par** 36/36/36 **Slope** 130/125/119

Barracuda/Marlin Course

Established 1970 | **Holes** 18

Tees Blue/White/Red **Par** 36/36/37 **Slope** 132/126/118
Fees Winter: $39–$45; $35–$45 after 10 a.m.; $20–$25 after 2 p.m.
Specials Call for summer rates. **Cart rental** $20 weekdays; $30 weekends **Club rental** $20 per set **Payment** All major credit cards **Tee times** up to 7 days in advance **Facilities** Three championship 9-hole courses, 40-stall driving range (lighted), 12-court tennis facility (6 lighted), 2 Olympic-size pools, infant wading pool, swimming lessons from professionals, men's and women's locker rooms, banquet facility, and grill bar.
Comments Miami National Golf Club was built was remodeled after Hurricane Andrew, with $2 million going to repair the clubhouse and golf course. It was purchased by the Miccosukee Tribe in 2001 to augment their gaming resort. The course has hosted several LPGA tour events and PGA qualifiers for the Doral-Ryder Open and the Honda Classic.

Attractions

The Barnacle State Historic Site

3485 Main Highway, Coconut Grove; (305) 448-9445
Hours Friday–Sunday, 9 a.m.–4 p.m.; closed Monday–Thursday and Thanksgiving, Christmas, and New Year's Days
Admission $1
Appeal by Age Group

Pre-school ★	Teens ★	Over 30 ★★★
Grade school ★	Young Adults ★★	Seniors ★★★

Touring Time 1 hour

Rainy-Day Touring Recommended

Author's Rating ★★; a real find for history buffs and folks interested in how the landed gentry lived in South Florida a century ago. It's also a terrific picnic spot with a drop-dead view of Biscayne Bay.

Description and Comments Dade County's oldest home was built in 1891 by yacht designer and wrecker (a person who salvages ships that run aground) Ralph Middleton Munroe, who first visited South Florida in 1877 and returned in 1886 to purchase 40 acres facing Biscayne Bay. He built his home, called the "Barnacle," a one-story structure raised off the ground on wood pilings with an octagonal central room. Today, visitors can tour the unique house filled with nautical touches; the building provides a glimpse of a way of life that no longer exists. Outside, a tropical hardwood "hammock" gives way to a gorgeous view.

Fairchild Tropical Garden

10901 Old Cutler Road, Miami; (305) 667-1651; www.ftg.org

Hours Daily, 9:30 a.m.–4:30 p.m.; closed Christmas

Admission $10 per adult, $9 for seniors, $5 ages 3–12, free for children under age 3

Appeal by Age Group

Pre-school ★★	Teens ★★	Over 30 ★★★★
Grade school ★★★	Young Adults ★★★	Seniors ★★★★

Touring Time *Average* a half-day; *minimum* 2 hours

Rainy-Day Touring Not recommended

Author's Rating ★★★★★; this manicured park filled with lush palms and exotic trees and dotted with man-made lakes is a knockout

Description and Comments Fairchild Tropical Garden is the largest tropical botanical garden in the United States, with 83 beautifully landscaped acres containing plants from tropical regions around the world; its mission is education, scientific research, and display. The grounds and plant life are stunning, in spite of the beating they took from Hurricane Andrew in 1992. You don't have to be a certified tree hugger to appreciate the beauty and tranquility found here.

MetroZoo

12400 Southwest 152nd Street, Miami (take the Florida's Turnpike Extension to Southwest 152nd Street and follow the signs); (305) 251-0400 or 251-0401; www.miamimetrozoo.com

Hours Daily, 9:30 a.m.–5:30 p.m.; open every day of the year

Admission $12 for adults, $11 for seniors, $7 for children ages 3–12, under age 3 free

Appeal by Age Group

Pre-school ★★★★	Teens ★★★	Over 30 ★★★
Grade school ★★★★	Young Adults ★★★	Seniors ★★★

Touring Time *Average* a half-day; *minimum* 2 hours
Rainy-Day Touring Not recommended
Author's Rating ★★★★★; it's no surprise that this is rated by experts as one of the best zoos in the world. And no cages mean that people who normally hate zoos may love this one
Description and Comments This "new style" zoo features cageless animals that roam on plots of land surrounded by moats. Start your visit with a trip on the air-conditioned Zoofari monorail, which makes a complete loop of MetroZoo in about 25 minutes. Then begin at Station 1 or Station 4 (the last stop). Along the way you'll pass exhibits featuring gorillas, chimpanzees, elephants, Himalayan black bears, a white Bengal tiger, and other exotic animals. Some exhibits feature "viewing caves" that let you view animals through plate glass windows on their side of the moat. In all, there are about 260 species with more than 900 reptiles, birds, and mammals.

There's also a narrated behind-the-scenes tram tour and a new petting zoo.

Try to time your visit for early morning or late afternoon; when it's cooler the animals are most active.

Monkey Jungle

14805 Southwest 216th Street; (305) 235-1611

Hours Daily, 9:30 a.m.–5 p.m.; ticket office closes at 4 p.m.
Admission $14 for adults, $11 for seniors ages 65 and older, $8 for children ages 4–12, under age 4 free

Appeal by Age Group

Pre-school ★★★★	Teens ★★★★	Over 30 ★★★
Grade school ★★★★	Young Adults ★★★	Seniors ★★★

Touring Time *Average* 2 hours; *minimum* 1 hour
Rainy-Day Touring Not recommended
Author's Rating ★★★★; a lot of fun—and it's OK to feed the primates
Description and Comments Founded in the 1930s, when admission was just ten cents, this old-fashioned park features gibbons, spider monkeys, orangutans, a gorilla, chimpanzees, and more, all close at hand as you tour screened walkways winding through a tropical forest. While not all the monkeys roam free—a lot of them reside in large cages located along the walkways—many primates can be seen when you pass through the larger jungle habitat. Four different shows featuring swimming monkeys, a gorilla, twin chimpanzees, and orangutans start at 10 a.m. and run continuously at 45-minute intervals.

Museum of Contemporary Art (MoCA)

770 Northeast 125th Street, North Miami.; (305) 893-6211

Admission Adults, $5; seniors and students, $3; children under age 12 free

Hours Tuesday–Saturday, 11 a.m.–5 p.m.; Sunday, noon–5 p.m.; closed Monday

Appeal by Age Group

Pre-school ★	Teens ★★	Over 30 ★★★★
Grade school ★	Young Adults ★★★★	Seniors ★★★

Touring Time 1 hour or more

Rainy-Day Touring Recommended

Author's Rating ★★★★; never a dull moment in Miami's newest museum—a gem

Description and Comments After moving from cramped quarters and undergoing a name change, MoCA is still basically a one-room exhibition hall. But the room's a heck of a lot bigger, allowing MoCA to stage larger shows of cutting-edge contemporary art. Expect to be stimulated (or, at least, amused) by whatever is on display during your visit. Films, lectures, artists' talks, and excursions are also offered. The exhibits change, so the ratings above are generalizations. Docent-led tours are available on weekends. You can listen to jazz in the courtyard one night a month; check with the museum.

Parrot Jungle Island

1111 Parrot Jungle Trail, Watson Island; 305-2-JUNGLE; www.parrotjungle.com

Hours Daily, 9:30 a.m.–6 p.m.

Admission $15 for adults, $10 for children ages 3–12, under age 3 free

Appeal by Age Group

Pre-school ★★★★★	Teens ★★★★	Over 30 ★★★★
Grade school ★★★★★	Young Adults ★★★★	Seniors ★★★★

Touring Time *Average* 3 hours; *minimum* 2 hours

Rainy-Day Touring Not recommended

Author's Rating ★★★★★; what a hoot—or, better yet, screech. Don't miss it

Description and Comments An South Florida attraction since 1936, Parrot Jungle is finally in its new $47 million home on Watson Island between downtown Miami and South Beach, where you'll find a lot more than a zillion parrots (actually, about 1,000 varieties of birds) and a huge collection of reptiles and amphibians, including a rare albino alligator. Don't-miss exhibits include the giant aviary, Everglades Habitat, animal shows in the Jungle Theater, and hilarious bird shows in the Parrot Bowl.

Seaquarium

4400 Rickenbacker Causeway (on Virginia Key between Key Biscayne and Miami); (305) 361-5705

Hours Daily, 9:30 a.m.–6 p.m.; ticket office closes at 4:30 p.m.

Admission $24 for adults, $19 for children ages 3–9, under age 3 free; parking is $3 and the causeway toll is $1

Appeal by Age Group

Pre-school ★★★★	Teens ★★★	Over 30 ★★★
Grade school ★★★★	Young Adults ★★★★	Seniors ★★

Touring Time *Average* 4 hours; *minimum* 2 hours
Rainy-Day Touring Not recommended
Author's Rating ★★; expensive, and a bit worn around the edges
Description and Comments Unquestionably, the hottest attraction at this tropical marine aquarium is Lolita, Seaquarium's killer whale. It's an adrenaline rush you don't want to miss when this 20-foot-long behemoth goes airborne—and lands with a splash that drenches the first ten rows of spectators. Plan your visit around the *Killer Whale Show,* which generally takes place at 11:45 a.m. and 3:40 p.m. (Call to verify the schedule.)

Other performances include the *Flipper Show,* a reef aquarium presentation, the *Top Deck Dolphin Show,* the *Golden Dome Sea Lion Show,* and a shark presentation. There's also a rain forest, a sea life touch pool, a wildlife habitat, a crocodile exhibit, and a tropical aquarium to view between shows.

The Seaquarium shows are slick and well orchestrated. But like the disco music played during the performances, this marine-life park struck us as a little worn and dated. (It's about 40 years old.)

Vizcaya Museum and Garden

3521 South Miami Avenue, Miami; (305) 250-9133; www.vizcayamuseum.org

Hours Daily, 9:30 a.m.–5 p.m.; ticket office closes at 4:30 p.m. and the gardens close at 5:30
Admission $10 for adults, $5 for children ages 6–12, under age 6 free
Appeal by Age Group

Pre-school ★	Teens ★★★	Over 30 ★★★★
Grade school ★★	Young Adults ★★★	Seniors ★★★★

Touring Time *Average* 2 hours; *minimum* 1 hour
Rainy-Day Touring Not recommended
Author's Rating ★★★, the mansion; ★★★★★, the gardens
Description and Comments Chicago industrialist James Deering built his winter home on the shores of Biscayne Bay in 1916, and Vizcaya's 34 rooms are loaded with furniture, textiles, sculptures, and paintings from the fifteenth century through the early nineteenth century. The effect is that of a great country estate that's been continuously occupied for 400 years.

Most visitors go on a guided tour of the first floor that lasts 45 minutes. Highlights of the magnificent rooms include a rug that Christopher Columbus stood on, an ornate early telephone booth, and dramatic carved ceilings and patterned marble floors.

Mr. Deering didn't like doors slamming from the continuous breeze off the bay, so many doors were hung at off-angles so they would close slowly. The breeze is not as much of a problem today: The proliferation of high-rise condos on Biscayne Bay blocks much of the wind.

Shopping

South Beach

The current hotspot of South Florida, South Beach is a fine destination for shopping on foot. While the entire district spans a mere 17 blocks, with trendy boutiques and quaint galleries in unlikely places such as hotel lobbies, there are certain streets the *au courant* shopper will not want to miss.

Lincoln Road runs from the ocean to Biscayne Bay, with nine blocks of shopping. In the 1940s, Lincoln Road was a chi-chi strip of elite retail stores, including Bonwit Teller, Saks Fifth Avenue, and Lillie Rubin. Today, like everything else on South Beach, it's hip again. With a nod to New York's SoHo, Lincoln Road is a revamped, open-air, pedestrian mall that is home to artists, boutiques both funky and chic, chain stores such as **Pottery Barn** (1045 Lincoln Road; (786) 276-8889) and **Anthropologie** (1108 Lincoln Road; (305) 695-0775), and sidewalk cafés. Don't overlook the side streets, which are scattered with worthwhile stores, salons, and cafés one block north and south of Lincoln Road.

Espanola Way intersects Washington Avenue and is situated between 14th and 15th Streets. This quaint block of shops includes adorable gift and vintage boutiques, as well as avant-garde art galleries. **South Beach Makeup** (439 Espanola Way; (305) 538-0805) carries a plethora of makeup as well as the Kiehl's line of products.

Washington Avenue is South Beach's main commercial artery and is brimming with upscale boutiques, trendy restaurants, and the occasional hardware store. One of the can't-miss stops is **My Uncle Deco Shop** (1570 Washington Avenue; (305) 534-4834) for preworn Levis and other gear favored by models and locals.

Ocean Drive, at once scenic and chaotic, is fine for people-watching while sipping overpriced cappuccino, but as far as serious shopping is concerned, you're better off searching out the small boutiques located along its side streets. One exception is

Island Life (1332 Ocean Drive; (305) 673-6300) is where you'll find fun items such as bamboo bracelets and colorful sarongs for women to wrap over a bikini.

One block west is the **Collins Avenue** fashion district, a three-block stretch (from Sixth to Ninth Streets) littered with national boutiques including **Nicole Miller** (656 Collins Avenue; (305) 535-2200), **Banana Republic** (800 Collins Avenue; (305) 674-7079), **Urban Outfitters** (653 Collins Avenue; (305) 535-9726), **Intermix** (634 Collins Avenue; (305) 531-5950), and **Arden B.** (600 Collins Avenue; (305) 534-0317).

Alton Road, South Beach's quietest retail street, is getting increasingly popular as rents in other areas skyrocket. Music buffs will want to check out **Revolution Records** (1620-A Alton Road; (305) 673-6464) for new and used CDs, cassettes, and hard-to-find LPs. Also on Alton Road, try **Spiaggia** (1624 Alton Road; (305) 538-7949) for an eclectic and ever-changing offering of new and vintage home decor.

Coral Gables

A picturesque business and residential area, Coral Gables contains one of Miami's most historic shopping areas, Miracle Mile. This four-block stretch of outdoor shopping (don't neglect the side streets) contains more than 150 boutiques, with something to satisfy everyone's taste and budget. The area is probably the safest in Miami, as well as the best manicured. Favorite destinations include **Leather World** (339 Miracle Mile; (305) 446-7888), for every type of small leather good imaginable; **Luminaire** (2331 Ponce de Leon Boulevard; (305) 448-7367), for contemporary furnishings and accessories; and **Books & Books** (265 Aragon Avenue; (305) 442-4408), Miami's favorite independently owned bookstore.

Coconut Grove

Miami's hotspot hippie village of the 1970s, Coconut Grove has retained its anti-establishment charm while continuing to attract young sophisticates. Follow narrow sidewalks down the shady streets and browse the afternoon away. Our favorites include **IOS** (3109 Commodore Plaza; (305) 442-7166), offering sleek hip-chick attire, and **Silvia Tcherassi** (3403 Main Highway; (305) 447-4540), which features the elegant and modern clothing of its Colombian designer-owner.

Miami Design District

This 18-square-block area centers on the intersection of Northeast First Avenue and Northeast 40th Street just north of downtown (phone (305) 573-8116; www.miamidesigndistrict.net) with more than 50 high-end galleries and showrooms with kitchens, baths, furniture, fabrics, antiques, and more. Many of the shops are only open weekdays, so plan your discount shopping spree accordingly.

Mall Shopping

If it's a big, generic mall you want, Miami's got plenty. **Dadeland** and **Aventura** malls will do just fine, located respectively at 7535 North Kendall Drive (phone (305) 665-6226) and 19501 Biscayne Boulevard #450, North Miami Beach (phone (305) 935-1110). Probably Miami's most beautiful mall, **The Falls** (US 1 and Southwest 136th Street, Miami; (305) 255-4570) is tropical and serene, with lots of wood, waterfalls, and leafy foliage. Bloomingdales is the big draw, but there are also 60 specialty and national boutiques, including Banana Republic, Crate and Barrel, Pottery Barn, and Ann Taylor. But it's that Miami flavor you crave, right? Okay, we know just where to send you.

If the thought of a $3,000 knit day dress doesn't send you into convulsions, you'll feel right at home at **Bal Harbour Shops** (9700 Collins Avenue, Bal Harbour; (305) 866-0311). A charming, two-floor mall with valet parking (self-parking by the hour is also available), a fleet of security guards, and French cafés serving $35 pasta entrees, Bal Harbour Shops is

Miami's toniest mall. Offerings include Tiffany, Gucci, Chanel, Prada, Hermes, Saks Fifth Avenue, Neiman Marcus, Yves St. Laurent, and Versace. For the label-conscious, this is paradise found.

The Village of Merrick Park (358 San Lorenzo Avenue; (305) 529-0200) is Miami's newest addition to the upscale mall scene, this sprawling open-air Coral Gables mall has all the heavy hitters: Donald J Pliner, Jimmy Choo, Diane von Furstenberg, Neiman Marcus, Nordstrom, Gucci, Sonia Rykiel, Etro, and Hogan, among others.

Fruit

What's a trip to Florida without a box of rosy oranges and grapefruit to ship back home? **Norman Brothers Produce** (7621 Southwest 87th Avenue, South Miami; (305) 274-9363) will ship anything you wish from their amazing array of culinary exotica, which includes obscurities such as the dwarfed doughnut apple. Then there's always our favorite standby, **Publix** (numerous locations throughout Miami), which will do the shipping honors for you in season, November through February.

Dining

Blue Door at Delano

Delano Hotel, 1685 Collins Avenue, Miami Beach; (305) 674-6400

Meals served Breakfast, lunch, and dinner **Cuisine** French **Entree range** $25–$46 **Reservations** Recommended **Payment** AmEx, V, MC, DC

Comments A walk through the long lobby of the well-hyped Delano takes the visitor past white, gauzy draperies defining seating alcoves with chinchilla throws covering uniquely fashioned chaises. Eventually one reaches the all-white restaurant, a setting you must see to believe. It is a magnet to celebrities and large crowds. Consulting chef Claude Troisgros seasonally re-creates the menu, and the prompt and friendly waitstaff make dining here a pleasure.

Casa Juancho

2436 Southwest Eighth Street, Miami; (305) 642-2452

Meals served Lunch and dinner **Cuisine** Spanish **Entree range** $14–$40 **Reservations** Accepted **Payment** V, AmEx, MC, DC

Comments This is a popular, Spanish-style themed dining spot for active members of the Hispanic community. The mood at night is festive, and the rooms are crowded. Specialties include Spanish roasted peppers stuffed with codfish mousse; garlic soup Castillian-style; chilled whole two-pound Florida lobster with two salsas; grilled snapper fillet over flaming oak logs splashed with fiery garlic and vinegar sauce; and rabbit cured in sherry and baked with thyme and creamy brown sauce.

Chef Allen's

19088 Northeast 29th Avenue, Miami; (305) 935-2900

Meals served Dinner **Cuisine** New American **Entree range** $25–$39
Reservations Accepted **Payment** V, AmEx, MC, DC
Comments Operating in a stylish, contemporary setting, Chef Allen is one of the most daring interpreters of bold New American cuisine, embellishing his dishes with Florida-Caribbean tastes, flavors, and ingredients. A tasting menu of five courses is $75. Creations include Bahamian lobster and crab cakes with tropical fruit chutney and vanilla beurre blanc; yellowfin tuna tartar with sevruga caviar; Chai tea–cured salmon gravlax with cucumber raita; and telecherry pepper seared French foie gras.

China Grill

404 Washington Avenue, Miami Beach; (305) 534-2211

Meals served Lunch and dinner **Cuisine** Pan Asian **Entree range** $18.50–$49 **Reservations** Accepted, necessary **Payment** AmEx, V, MC, DC
Comments China Grill's "world cuisine" is delicious and as extraordinarily beautiful as the setting. Though not inexpensive, portions are enormous and meant to be shared family-style. There's a separate VIP area with gold-threaded draperies. Ordinary folk are equally welcome. The new Dragon, a sushi den, serves the most surprising and creative sushi in town. Menu favorites include broccoli rabe dumplings; crackling calamari salad; Peking duckling salad; sashimi tempura with wasabi champagne cream; and lobster pancakes.

Il Tulipano Centodieci

11052 Biscayne Boulevard, Miami; (305) 893-4811

Meals served Dinner **Cuisine** Italian **Entree range** $15–$25 **Reservations** Accepted **Payment** V, AmEx, MC, DC
Comments Now that the original Il Tulipano team is back, things are better than ever. With Chef Sandrino Benitez and owner Philipo Il Grande at the realm, Il Tulipano Centodieci is serving the best Italian food in Miami. Try the tricolored roasted peppers; risotto verde with baby asparagus spears; Mediterranean red prawns with olive oil, garlic, and thyme; or the veal cutlet Valdostana with prosciutto, fontina cheese, and tomato sauce.

Joe Allen

1787 Purdy Avenue, Miami Beach; (305) 531-7007

Meals served Lunch and dinner **Cuisine** American **Entree range** $8.50–$24 **Reservations** Accepted 1 week in advance **Payment** V, MC
Comments Legendary restaurateur Joe Allen, owner and operator of a string of successful namesake establishments—including the original in the

New York's theater district—brings his signature style of informal dining to South Florida. The values are great, and the service is friendly. Favorites include gazpacho with spicy croutons; arugula salad with grilled portobello mushrooms, roasted red peppers and gorgonzola dressing; and hamburgers or New York sirloin with french fries.

Joe's Stone Crab Restaurant

11 Washington Avenue, Miami Beach; (305) 673-0365; www.joesstonecrab.com

Meals served Lunch and dinner **Cuisine** Seafood **Entree range** $5–$60 **Reservations** Not accepted **Payment** V, AmEx, MC, DC

Comments South Florida's most popular and famous restaurant is open from mid-October to mid-May. A must for tourists and a hang out for locals, Joe's is busy, a bit noisy, but always an exciting experience. Though other restaurants serve stone crabs, none seem to taste quite like those at Joe's. Nearly essential accompaniments are the generous plates of hash browns and coleslaw. Also try the fried soft-shell crabs; blue crab cakes; ginger salmon; fried or grilled pompano, swordfish, or grouper; and New York sirloin or broiled lamb chops for non-fish eaters.

Metro Kitchen+Bar

Astor Hotel, 956 Washington Avenue, Miami Beach; (305) 672-7217

Meals served Breakfast, lunch, and dinner **Cuisine** New American **Entree range** $12–$30 **Reservations** Accepted **Payment** AmEx, V, MC, DC

Comments Formerly known as Astor Place, this new name and menu replaced it's Florida-Caribbean precursor with the modern American vision of chef Rob Boone. Owner Karim Masri has spared no expense in creating his vision of the ideal restaurant within a sophisticated hotel. Try the spicy octopus carpaccio accompanied by a garlic and citrus sauce with Asian vegetables; beef short rib ravioli with cipolline onion broth; or pan-seared snapper with Udon noodles in a ginger-lime-scallion sauce.

Nemo

100 Collins Avenue, Miami Beach; (305) 532-4550

Meals served Lunch and dinner **Cuisine** New American **Entree range** $23–$33 **Reservations** Accepted **Payment** AmEx, V, MC, DC

Comments Continuing on the footsteps of creator and previous chef/owner, Michael Schwartz, new executive chef Mike Sabin, applies a fusion of culinary techniques to his cooking in an unusual and pleasant atmosphere best described as "South Beach casual."

The polenta fries are a must; other recommendations include garlic- and ginger-cured salmon rolls with tobiko caviar and wasabi mayo; crispy prawns with spicy salsa cruda and mesclun greens; and spicy pork loin with caramelized onions and papaya relish.

Nobu

1901 Collins Avenue, Miami Beach; (305) 695-3232

Meals served Dinner **Cuisine** Japanese **Entree range** $24–$38 **Reservations** Accepted **Payment** V, MC, AmEx, D

Comments There's no view of Miami Beach in this oceanfront hotel dining room, but most of the patrons are here for sushi, thanks to the reputation of the original Nobu in Manhattan, and Chef Nobu Matsuhisa. The pristine sushi is costly, but delicious. And, oddly enough, Peruvian cuisine shares the menu, including a spicy ribeye steak topped with chimichurri sauce. Trendy and packed most nights.

Norman's

21 Almeria Avenue, Coral Gables; (305) 446-6767

Meals served Dinner **Cuisine** New world **Entree range** $30–$40 **Reservations** Accepted **Payment** AmEx, V, MC, DC

Comments Norman Van Aken is considered one of the country's finest and most inventive chefs, a forerunner of Florida's New World cuisine. Often called a Picasso in the kitchen, he sets a stylish, sophisticated, and unique tone with both his cuisine and restaurant setting. Try the foie gras wafers on a Cuban bread "shortstack" with exotic fruits; jerk chicken skewer on pigeon-pea salsa; yucca-stuffed shrimp with sour orange mojo, greens, and tartar salsa; or the rum- and pepper-painted grouper on mango-habanero mojo with boniato-plantain mash en poblano.

Pacific Time

915 Lincoln Road, Miami Beach; (305) 534-5979

Meals served Dinner **Cuisine** Pacific Rim **Entree range** $19.50–$34 **Reservations** Accepted; recommended on weekends **Payment** V, AmEx, MC, DC

Comments Owner Jonathan Eismann came to this pleasant, pastel-toned setting by way of Manhattan's China Grill. He combines his Oriental skills with the tastes of the Caribbean with fascinating results and artistic presentations. Try the grilled giant squid with local Asian greens and hot-and-sour vinaigrette; pan-seared Hudson Valley foie gras with California port, red, and plum wines; or whole ginger-stuffed Florida yellowtail snapper tempura with steamed ribbon vegetables and sizzling fish dipping sauce.

Arts and Culture

When you're ready for a break from the sunshine or it's a rainy day, there are several museums worth a look. The **Lowe Art Museum** (just off US 1 on the Coral Gables campus of University of Miami; (305) 284-3535; **www.lowemuseum.org**) has a collection of 7,000 works ranging from antiquities to Renaissance, traditional, contemporary, and non-Western works. The **Jewish Museum of Florida** (301 Washington Avenue, Miami

Beach; (305) 672-5044; **www.jewishmuseum.com**) showcases 230 years of Florida Jewish life in a 1936 Art Deco–style building that once served as Miami Beach's first Orthodox synagogue. The **Wolfsonian-Florida International University** (1001 Washington Avenue, Miami Beach; (305) 535-2625, **www.wolfsonian.fiu.edu**) is a sophisticated museum dedicated to architecture, design, and cultural history circa 1885–1945. Also on Miami Beach, the **Bass Museum of Art** (2121 Park Avenue; (305) 673-7530; **www.bassmuseum.org**) recently reopened after an $8.8-million expansion that tripled the exhibition space, with a collection highlighting European painting from the Renaissance on.

Nightlife

Miami offers not only the unusual small concert clubs, but also the café-cum-club, and these are some of the best nightlife bets in the area. Restaurants that feature live performances of salsa, jazz, and just about everything else run rampant. Impromptu dancing on tabletops is not uncommon. Local, regional, and less mainstream national talent can be found every night. Miami being Miami, the Latin music is unbeatable. **Yuca** (501 Lincoln Road, Miami Beach; (305) 532-9822), a restaurant whose name is not only a popular root vegetable used in Cuban cuisine but also an acronym for its clientele (Young Urban Cuban Americans), serves up Latin vocalists in its upstairs concert space.

In the café club category, **Monty's Raw Bar** (2550 South Bayshore Drive, Coconut Grove; (305) 856-3992) is an oasis of fun with calypso and reggae throughout the week, right on the waterfront. **John Martin's** (253 Miracle Mile, Coral Gables; (305) 445-3777) features fantastic and hard-to-find Irish music on Saturdays and Sundays. The intimate upstairs space at the **Van Dyke Café** (846 Lincoln Road, Miami Beach; (305) 534-3600) offers live jazz nightly in a candlelit setting. **Satchmo Blues Bar & Grill** (60 Merrick Way, Coral Gables; (305) 774-1883) is a music lover's venue that varies its live jazz line-up weekly. **Café Iguana** (8505 Mills Drive, Miami; (305) 274-4948) sheds its modern disco duds on Sundays with a wild Western Night, featuring food, music, and costume contests; line dance lessons start at 6 p.m. **Taurus** (3540 Main Highway; (305) 443-5553), in the heart of Coconut Grove, showcases blues talent and more in its terraced locale, Tuesday through Saturday. On weekends, the tropically appointed **Cardozo Cafe**—within the Cardozo Hotel—features live music and a DJ until 1 a.m. (1300 Ocean Drive, Miami Beach; (305) 695-2822). **Globe Café & Bar** (377 Alhambra Circle, Coral Gables; (305) 445-3555) features live jazz on Thursdays and is home to a very popular happy hour on Fridays.

In the heart of South Beach, check out **Mango's Tropical Cafe** (900 Ocean Drive; (305) 673-4422), **Clevelander Hotel Bar** (1020 Ocean Drive; (305) 531-3485), and **I Paparazzi** (940 Ocean Drive; (305) 531-3500). The exotic restaurant/lounge **Tantra** (1445 Pennsylvania Avenue; (305) 672-4765), is swarming with models, trendies, and movie stars on any given night; of special note is the Sod Lounge with the tented banquettes and fresh grass floor. In a similar vein, **Touch** (910 Lincoln Road; (305) 532-8003) serves up glamour and belly dancing with its $34 entrees. At the "it" spot, **Pearl** (at Penrod's Beach Club, One Ocean Drive; (305) 673-1575), the modern orange-and-white interior and round champagne bar are a suitable backdrop for a fashionable crowd. At the wildly popular **Rumi** (330 Lincoln Road; (305) 672-4353), trendies dine downstairs in chic Zen surroundings, then sojourn to the upstairs lounge for DJ-enhanced cocktailing. Enjoy a saketini and the spicy shrimp appetizer at **Nobu Bar**—adjacent to Nobu restaurant at the Shore Club Hotel (1901 Collins Avenue; (305) 695-3232)—where Miami Beach's jet-set scene is at its glamorous best.

Concert clubs in Miami feature an eclectic and diverse line-up. **Tobacco Road** (profiled) is undeniably lively, and even holds the title of Miami's oldest club. The nightly live music ranges from Latin jazz to rock and R&B. Hardcore rock fans will appreciate **Churchill's Hideway** (5501 Northeast Second Avenue, Miami; (305) 757-1807), an English-themed rock 'n' roll pub showcasing local bands and serving traditional pub grub. For live jazz and R&B in a dimly-lit boite, check out **Jazid** (1342 Washington Avenue, Miami Beach; (305) 673-9372), which offers cabaret acts downstairs and billiards upstairs. For live Latin music with dancing, **Hoy Como Ayer** (profiled), a tiny club in Little Havana, is full of youthful Latinos moving to Afro-Cuban grooves. At **Mr. Moe's** in Coconut Grove (3131 Commodore Plaza; (305) 442-1114), in addition to live country music you'll find a mechanical bull, karaoke, billiards, 30 TVs and yummy slow-cooked barbecue.

The Clevelander Bar

Who Goes There Ages 21–45; restless youth, locals, European tourists, Causeway crawlers, bikini babes

1020 Ocean Drive, Miami Beach; (305) 531-3485

Cover None **Minimum** None **Mixed drinks** $6–$8 **Food available** Full menu until 3 a.m., from burgers to surf 'n' turf; live lobster tank **Hours** Daily, 11 a.m.–5 a.m.

What goes on A high-energy melting pot of nationalities, scantily clad babes and bronzed hunks parade around the pool/bar of this popular oceanfront hotel. Live bands nightly and omnipresent DJs keep the rambunctious spirit going. Needless to say, this is prime cruising territory.

Comments Smack on trendy Ocean Drive, this outdoor bar is studded with palm trees and cartoonish, Jetsonian obelisks. Ten TVs inside and out ensure you'll never miss a music video or major sporting event, not that you won't get distracted by the physical beauty on display. You'll see all forms of beachwear, from bikinis with sarongs to Levis. This is one place where less is more. Also, a good spot to start the night before you hit the clubs. Weekday happy hour, 5–7 p.m., offers two-for-one drinks.

Club Tropigala

Who Goes There Ages 21–60; Latinos who know how to dance, stylemongers, tourists, condo groups, locals with a sense of adventure

Fontainebleau Hilton Resort and Spa, 4441 Collins Avenue, Miami Beach; (305) 538-2000

Cover Show only, $20; dinner and show, prices vary **Minimum** None **Mixed drinks** $7–$8 **Food available** Full menu, Tapas menu available; continental standards **Showtimes** Wednesday, Thursday, and Sunday, 8:30 p.m.; Friday and Saturday, 8 and 10 p.m.; dancing until the wee hours

What goes on This world-renowned supper club draws an eclectic crowd of all ages and looks, from discerning trendies who think it's the ultimate in camp to older Latin couples who've made it their Saturday night tradition for years. Club Tropigala features 30 performers, special acts, and an orchestra led by famous director Gaby Gabriel, who has been there for 20 years.

Comments It's right out of the *Jungle Book,* with extravagant tropical murals, palm fronds, bamboo, waterfalls, and color-enhanced dancing fountains. And, according to management, "the best lighting system in the Miami area." The truly huge room is successfully tiered for greater intimacy. What's really amazing is that every seat is filled. Men should wear jackets, while ladies' dress is semiformal.

Crobar

Who Goes There Celebrities, models, locals, and beautiful people with plenty of lunch money; on Sunday's gay night, shirtless go-go boys and bewigged gender illusionists jockey for space on the dance floor

1445 Washington Avenue, Miami Beach; (305) 531-5027

Cover $20 Thursdays, Sundays, and Mondays; $25 Fridays and Saturdays **Minimum** None, except at tables where there is a two-bottle minimum **Mixed drinks** $7–$12 **Wine** $7 and up **Beer** $4 and up **Food available** None **Hours** Thursday–Monday, 10 p.m.–5 a.m.

What goes on The scene doesn't get much trendier in South Beach, especially on weekends. On Mondays, the local's party Back Door Bamby goes full tilt till the wee hours. The Show, Thursdays at Crobar, is a well-known hip-hop party. Expect to wait in line, as this branch of the Chicago club is the perennial favorite of visiting celebrities and local hipsters. DJs from around the country can often be found spinning the latest house music.

Comments Industrial-chic architects have transformed the historic Art Deco Cameo Theater into a complex, voyeuristic space. There is plenty of tucked-away seating within its two levels so that you'll never feel spied upon, plus a large strobe-lit dance floor and requisite VIP room.

Hoy Como Ayer

Who Goes There Ages 25–45; an international and artistic Latin crowd; sexy gringos with happy feet

2212 Southwest Eighth Street, Miami; (305) 541-2631

Cover $7–$15, price depends on artist performing **Minimum** None **Mixed drinks** $6–$8 **Wine** $5–$6; bottle service available **Beer** $4–$5 **Food available** Tapas menu until 2 a.m. **Hours** Thursday–Sunday, 9 p.m.–5 a.m.; call for events schedule

What goes on Cuban-Americans reminisce about the heyday of Havana, even those born stateside. In Miami, Café Hoy Como Ayer, the small club that translates, appropriately, to "Today Like Yesterday," is located in trendy-but-still-in-transition Little Havana. People come for comfort, entertainment, or to dance madly to live Afro-Cuban bands that take the stage at 10:30 p.m. on Fridays and Saturdays. At Thursday night's party, known as Fuácata, a DJ mixes Afro-Cuban rhythms with hip-hop and reggae accompanied by an improvising trio of saxophone, trombone, and timbales that packs the house.

Comments All nightclubs once looked like this—tiny tables, dark corners, intimate lighting, and an inviting bar. Cuban songsters from the 1950s, such as Celia Cruz and Cachao, are featured in original campy videos on an overhead screen. Spanish is by far the language of choice among patrons and staff, but feel free to order your drinks in English. Glowing from the club's dark walls are painted takes of La Caridad del Cobre, Cuba's patron saint, depicted in the nude. The newest addition to the club, the bar known as *El Cuarto de Tula,* is a quieter spot for those who want a private area to chat and smoke cigarettes or cigars.

Jimmy'z

Who Goes There Ages 21–50; A Fellini-esque mix of models, Euroboys in crested blazers, celebs, upscale barflies, young women with bionic décolleté, and hip-hop-lovers on certain nights

432 41st Street, Miami Beach; (305) 604-9798

Cover $10–$20 **Minimum** Yes **Mixed drinks** $8–$10 **Food available** Yes; ladies receive complementary dinner on Thursdays **Hours** Tuesday–Saturday, 10 p.m.–5 a.m.

What goes on Regine Choukroun, the legendary Queen of the Night, is the impresario of the club, which caters to the junior jetset. There are theme nights galore, from combos and full Latin bands to whimsical soirees named for exotic destinations. Wednesday is alarmingly popular, with a loyal contingent for the weekly theme party, as well as spill-over from the adjoining luxury restaurant, The Forge.

Comments Sophisticated yet full of character—like Regine herself—Jimmy'z doesn't lack for color. There are red walls, gilt-edged mirrors, a

What to See and Do in Miami

chandelier as large as a Mustang, and a bed done up in rich jewel tones by one of the bars. Concerning attire, the wilder the better for this sexy crowd.

Mac's Club Deuce

Who Goes There Hip and not-so-hip locals, pool junkies, barflies, tattooed bikers, drag queens, film crews, unfazed normal folk, New Yorkers

222 14th Street, Miami Beach; (305) 673-9537

Cover None **Minimum** None **Mixed drinks** $2.50 and up **Food available** Miniature pizzas, pickled eggs **Hours** Daily, 8 a.m.–5 a.m.—365 days a year
What goes on Since 1926, the constant stream of nightcrawlers taking their place at the wraparound bar has served as the main attraction. The best training a novice barfly could get.
Comments Assorted neon beer signs dot the walls; a worn pool table sits off to a corner, and a decently stocked juke box and cigarette machine get lots of use. The big-screen TV is the only trace of modernism. Dress is inexplicably casual, although we once saw a woman wearing a pink taffeta pea coat. Weekday happy hours offer two-for-one drink specials.

Mynt Ultra Lounge

Who Goes There Ages 21–50; models, visiting celebrities, hip locals, young women with a penchant for dancing on couches for the amusement of their dates.

1921 Collins Avenue, Miami Beach; (786) 276-6132

Cover $20; Thursday, none **Minimum** 2 bottles for a VIP table on Fridays and Saturdays **Mixed drinks** $10–$12 **Food available** None **Hours** Wednesday–Saturday, 11 p.m.–5 a.m.
What goes on The Grand Lounge, complete with 40-foot-long bar, is open to all, but the Plexiglas-shrouded Ultra Lounge is reserved for the famous and connected. DJs spin grooves so danceable that couch and tabletop gyrations are an inevitable occurrence as the night advances. An aromatherapy system infuses the air with a variety of 50 scents. Even the most beautiful and trendy of mortals may have to suffer temporarily at the hands of the handsome yet attitudinal doormen, but celebrities such as Lenny Kravitz, "P.Diddy" Combs, Enrique Iglesias, Martin Lawrence, Justin Timberlake, and Cameron Diaz glide in via the heavily guarded back alley entrance.
Comments The later it gets, the harder it is to get in. If you're staying at a hotel with a concierge, by all means have him/her call for you to put you on the guest list, which, by the way, is no guarantee. Dress sharp, show up by midnight, and walk up to the doorman with confidence. You'll leave with enough stories to last you a year.

Opium Garden

Who Goes There Sprite models with deeply tanned playboys; urban sophisticates from 21 to 40; visiting celebs and rock stars after their Miami concert gigs

136 Collins Avenue, Miami Beach; (305) 531-7181

Cover $20 **Minimum** On Fridays and Saturdays, a two-bottle minimum for table service **Mixed drinks** $9–$13 **Food available** None **Hours** Thursday–Sunday, 11 p.m.–5 a.m.

What goes on Dancing, necking, and often indiscreet displays of affection—even among the famous—are not an unusual scene at Opium. The young revelers are gorgeous and know it, so everyone's basically happy, if rather clannish, preferring that you keep to your side of the double banquette, thank you very much. Celebrity sightings include Cindy Crawford with designers Roberto Cavalli and Esteban Cortazar, Jay-Z, Britney Spears, "P.Diddy" Combs, Daisy Fuentes, Beyonce Knowles, Anna Kournikova, and Justin Timberlake.

Comments As its name implies, the spacious club is addictive, with an infectious energy and cozy VIP table area for those craving some privacy. The catch, though, is that you have to buy a bottle (vodka or champagne are typical), and it doesn't come cheap—champagne starts at $165, spirits at $210. The lighting is mercifully dim, given the rampant hedonism in this crowd. Wearing Gucci, Prada, or Chanel will cut down the risk of your having to wait in line, an unfortunate (and unfortunately very common) occurrence here. And don't even think of wearing denim.

Tobacco Road

Who Goes There Ages 21–45; hep cats, rockers, bikers, modern bohemians

626 South Miami Avenue, Miami; (305) 374-1198

Cover Usually $5–$6, weekends only **Minimum** None **Mixed drinks** $3.25–$3.75 **Wine** $3.25 **Beer** $2.75–$3.25 **Food available** Lunch and dinner in the American vein: steaks, burgers, chicken wings, and nachos, plus daily specials **Hours** Daily, 11:30 a.m.–5 a.m.; kitchen open until 2 a.m.

What goes on A Miami hot spot since 1912, this New Orleans–type bar is the city's oldest, and holds Miami's first liquor license. Perennially popular with locals, The theme nights are among the best: Monday night is a blues jam; Wednesday, live jazz. Once a year, in October, the bar sponsors Blues Fest, showcasing 20 bands in the rear parking area.

Comments Charmingly quaint, the wooden frame structure has the feel of a roadhouse. There are two stories, each with a stage. Often, both stages are in use simultaneously. Outside, the wooden deck is shaded by a huge oak tree; thatched tiki-style huts and colored patio lights complete the bohemian picture. Rags range from tuxedoes to Harley gear—anything goes. Weekday happy hour is 5–8 p.m. with $1–$2 appetizer plates.

Twist

Who Goes There Ages 21–45; the young, tan, and built—your basic gay Greek gods

1057 Washington Avenue, Miami Beach; (305) 538-9478

Cover None **Minimum** None **Mixed drinks** $4 and up **Food available** None **Hours** Daily, 1 p.m.–5 a.m.

What goes on Twist yourself into a quiet corner or contort yourself on the dance floor. This gay bar/club offers a number of very different atmospheres to suit your mood; depending on which of the six bars you select, it can be a place for a romantic drink on a first date or a spot to let loose to throbbing music on the packed dance floor. And, of course, this being Florida, there is an outdoor deck bar that makes you realize Key West is only hours away.

Comments There are detailed painted murals combined with eclectic decor—but, frankly you won't remember much about the decor because it will be packed to the gills. Don't end your experience at the first-level bars, which is where the chatty locals hang out. Venture up the staircase, and you can scam drinks, play pool, or dance before heading outside to the terrace. Attire is South Beach casual—jeans, T-shirts (frequently removed), or more exotic apparel announcing availability, such as a scrap of leather.

Part Ten

Everglades National Park

Welcome to Everglades National Park

The Spaniards called it "El Laguno de Espiritu Sanctu"—The Lake of the Holy Spirit. In this vast, mysterious expanse of hammocks and mangroves, big-city noise is replaced by the cries of herons, the splash of leaping anhinga fish, and the wind rippling through sawgrass. Manatees, bob-tailed deer, and rare Florida panthers all reside here.

Originating south of Lake Okeechobee, the 1.5-million-acre Everglades National Park, the second-largest in the lower 48 (after Yellowstone), is set within an ecosystem seven times its size. This huge expanse of grass and water is a vast, slow-moving, shallow river that's flowing over land nearly as flat as a pool table. For eons, the overflow of Lake Okeechobee to the north has moved south slowly over this land into Florida Bay, nourishing millions of acres of sawgrass as the water ebbs and flows. This 50-mile-wide river is only two or three feet deep, and moves so slowly that a drop of water may take eight months to travel between its northern and southern ends.

In her best-selling 1947 book, *The Everglades: River of Grass,* Florida environmentalist Marjory Stoneman Douglas popularized the notion of the Everglades as a river. Douglas, who died in 1998 at the age of 107, continued to write and speak out about preserving this unique ecosystem until the end of her life.

What was once disparaged as a mosquito-filled swamp has been designated a World Heritage Site, an International Biosphere Preserve, and a Wetland of International Importance. Nevertheless, the Everglades remains imperiled by advancing civilization.

The Everglades once encompassed all of Florida south of Lake Okeechobee, but encroaching civilization has pushed its perimeter back. Today, the Everglades is only a fraction of its former size.

Initiatives to save this unique ecosystem include $200 million in funds provided by Congress in 1996 and a $7.8 billion, 30-year restoration plan approved by Congress in 2000. But true restoration, experts say, is a long-term goal and will be extremely expensive. Pick up almost any edition of the *Miami Herald* and you'll find articles reporting the raging controversies surrounding efforts to protect the remaining—and seriously threatened—portions of this unique environment.

The Everglades may seem like just another swamp standing in the way of development. But in actuality, the Everglades encompasses vast expanses of water, sawgrass prairies, clumps of trees called "hammocks," and pockets of tropical jungle. It is also an unparalleled wildlife sanctuary, containing an astounding variety of animals, including roseate spoonbills, egrets, wood storks, osprey, and both alligators and crocodiles—it is the only place in the world where both reside.

Our advice: Travelers who enjoy the outdoors and thrill to seeing wildlife in its natural environment should put the Everglades on their "A" list during a visit to South Florida.

You've Got to Get Out of Your Car

Admittedly, the Everglades doesn't look like very much when viewed through a car window: Seemingly endless expanses of grass and water fade into the distance, with only an occasional clump of trees to break the monotony. These apparently empty spaces, however, are deceiving; the landscape is teeming with life and activity. The Everglades is the complex, ever-evolving product of climate, topography, and vegetation.

To find out what's so special about it, you've got to get out of your car.

We don't recommend visiting the Everglades April through October, when mosquitoes and other biting insects make a visit difficult. In the winter you'll see more wildlife; it's the dry season, and a vast array of animals—especially alligators and birds—congregate near the remaining water.

Visiting Everglades National Park

Gathering Information

For details on access to and activities in Everglades National Park, contact the park headquarters: 40001 SR 9336, Homestead, FL 33034; (305) 242-7700; **www.nps.gov/ever.** The headquarters can send you a copy of *Parks and Preserves,* a newsletter with information on park programs and schedules.

Getting There

By Plane   The closet airports are Miami, Fort Lauderdale, and Fort Myers. For details on each, see the appropriate section.

By Car   To reach the Shark Valley entrance on US 41 (Tamiami Trail) 25 miles west of Florida's Turnpike (Route 821), take the exit for Southwest Eighth Street. From the Naples area, take US 41 (Tamiami Trail) east to Shark Valley.

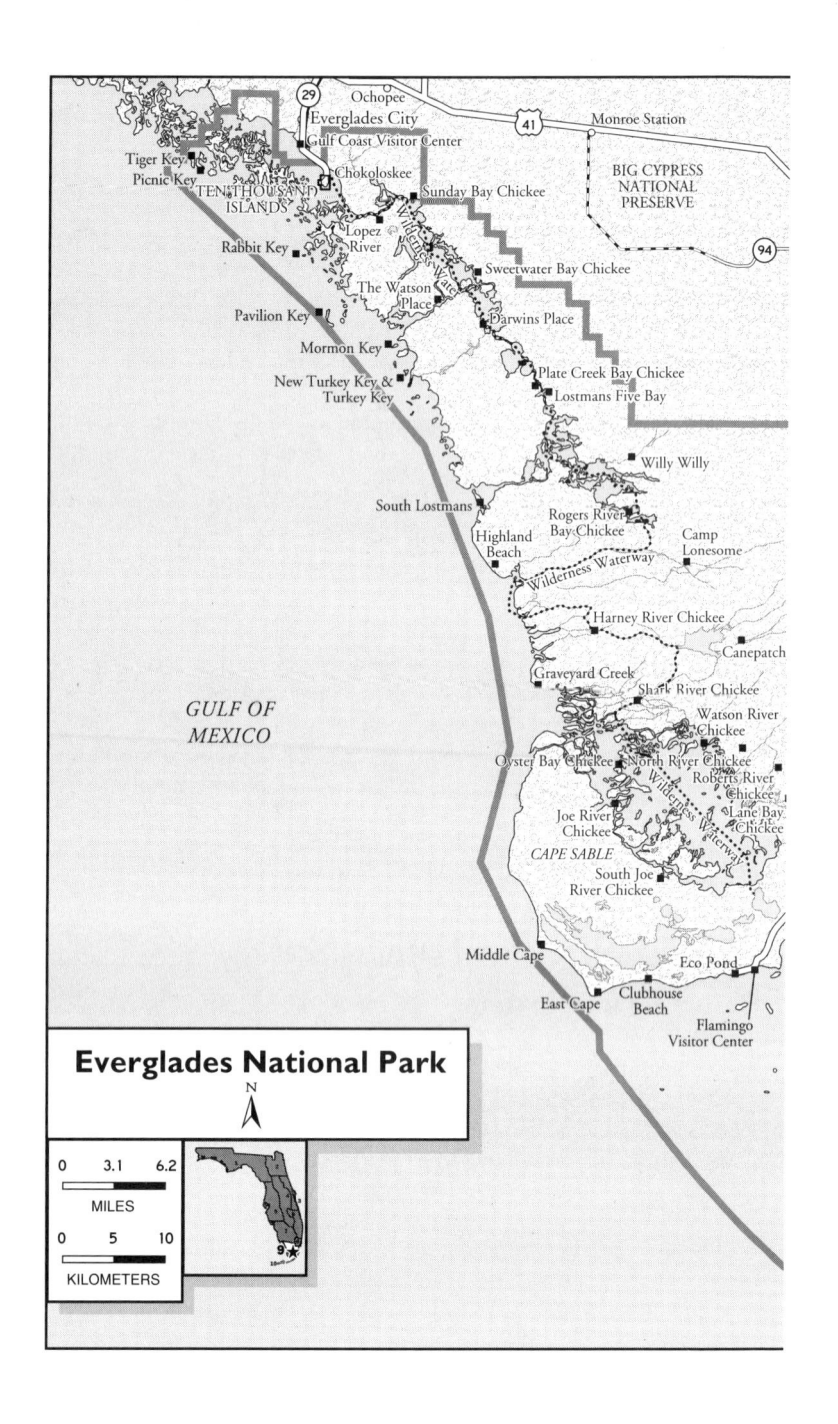

Everglades National Park

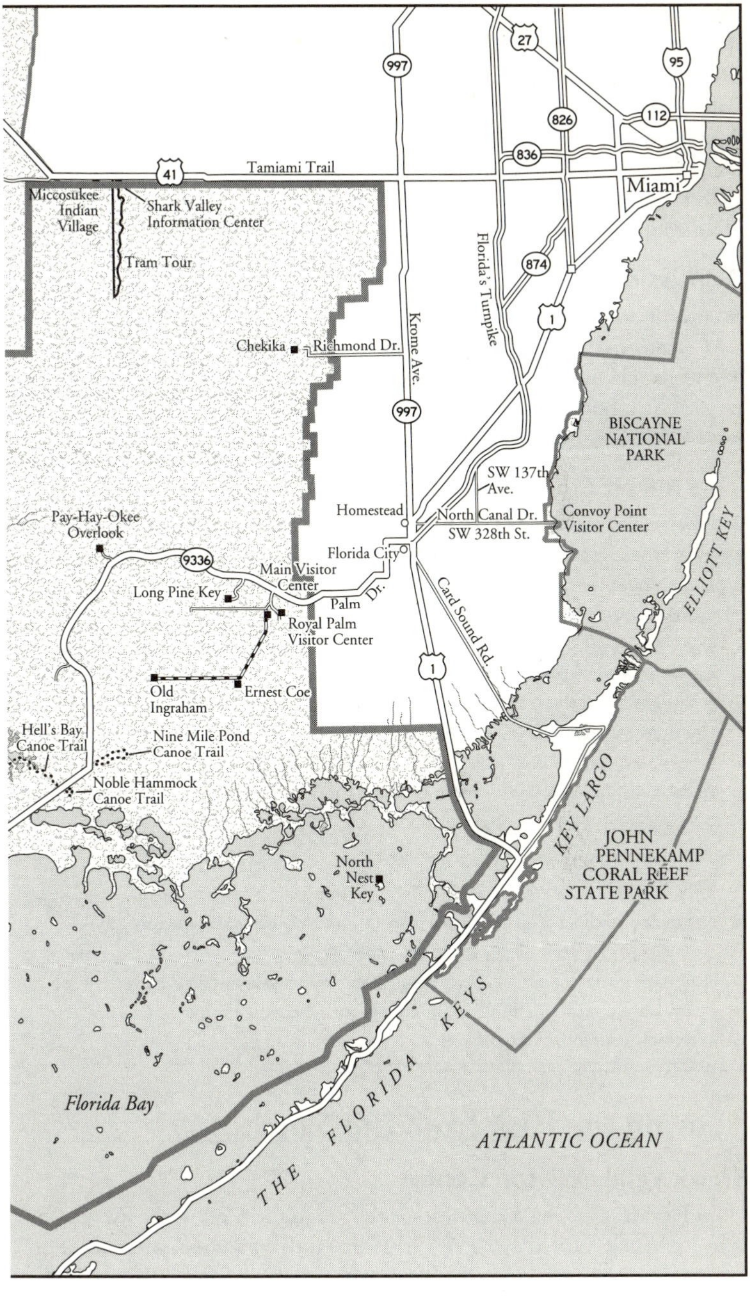
27
95
997
826
112
836
41
Tamiami Trail
Miami
Miccosukee Indian Village
Shark Valley Information Center
Tram Tour
874
Florida's Turnpike
1
Krome Ave.
Chekika
Richmond Dr.
997
BISCAYNE NATIONAL PARK
SW 137th Ave.
Homestead
North Canal Dr.
SW 328th St.
Convoy Point Visitor Center
Pay-Hay-Okee Overlook
Florida City
9336
Main Visitor Center
ELLIOTT KEY
Long Pine Key
Palm Dr.
Royal Palm Visitor Center
Card Sound Rd.
1
Old Ingraham
Ernest Coe
Hell's Bay Canoe Trail
Nine Mile Pond Canoe Trail
Noble Hammock Canoe Trail
KEY LARGO
JOHN PENNEKAMP CORAL REEF STATE PARK
North Nest Key
THE FLORIDA KEYS
Florida Bay
ATLANTIC OCEAN

To reach the main park entrance and the village of Flamingo, visitors coming from the Miami area and points north may take Florida's Turnpike (Route 821) south until it ends, merging with US 1 at Florida City. Turn right at the first traffic light onto Palm Drive (SR 9336/Southwest 344th Street) and follow the signs to the park. Visitors driving north from the Florida Keys should turn left on Palm Drive in Florida City and follow the signs to the park. From the Gulf Coast, continue five miles south of US 41 (Tamiami Trail) on US 29, south of Everglades City.

Admission

Admission to Everglades National Park is $10 per car ($8 at the Shark Valley entrance), $5 per pedestrian, bicyclist, or motorcyclist, and is good for one week. There is no admission charge at the Gulf Coast entrance. Hours vary slightly, but generally are 8:30 a.m.–4:30 p.m. For information, contact (305) 242-7700; **www.nps.gov/ever.**

Tips for an Optimum Visit

The best time to visit is November through March, when it's dry and the low water levels attract wading birds and their predators. The wet season is June to November, when the mosquitoes are peskier, migratory birds have left, and wildlife is harder to find.

- Don't forget mosquito repellent, hats, and sunscreen. Mosquitoes and biting flies can be severe during the summer months, so wear long-sleeved clothing and avoid grassy areas and shady places where mosquitoes often lurk.
- Get out of the car and onto a trail, even if it's just for a walk.
- Bring binoculars or rent them at a visitor center. While you're there, pick up guidebooks that explain the park's natural variety and beauty.
- Take a boat ride with a guide.
- Take the tram tour, or better yet, rent a bike.
- Bring bottled water and snacks along.
- Never approach an alligator closer than 15 feet; they can easily outrun you. And do not feed alligators or any other wild animals. Elevated boardwalks, like Anhinga Trail, offer good opportunities to view gators from a safe distance. Never try to catch baby alligators (which are undeniably cute) because mother gators are extremely protective of their young.

Touring the Park from the North

Shark Valley Visitor Center

From Florida's east coast, the closest entrance to the heart of the Everglades is Shark Valley, located on US 41 (the Tamiami Trail) about 35 miles west of downtown Miami. If you are coming from Miami, to avoid a seemingly endless procession of traffic lights on Southwest Eighth Street (US 41 in the city), take Route 836 (the Dolphin Expressway) west to the Florida Turnpike, and go south one exit to US 41 West.

When visiting Shark Valley, consider renting a bicycle at the visitor center. Single-speed bikes rent for $5.25 an hour between 8:30 a.m. and 3 p.m.; bikes must be returned by 4 p.m. And don't forget to bring binoculars when you visit; although if you do, you can rent a pair at the visitor center.

Take the Tram

If a day trip to Shark Valley is your only visit to the Everglades, our advice is to take the two-hour tram tour that leaves from the Shark Valley parking lot on the hour from 9 a.m. to 4 p.m. daily in the winter and at 9:30 a.m., 11 a.m., 1 p.m., and 3 p.m. daily in the summer. The cost is $12 for adults, $11 for seniors, and $7.25 for children under age 12. Try to arrive early; the parking lot is small and this is a popular visitor destination. Reservations are recommended for tram tours; call (305) 221-8455.

Soon after the open-air tram leaves the visitor center, you'll discover what all the excitement is about as you view an incredible number of birds, alligators resting beside the narrow road, and a surreal, endless landscape of open sky and shallow, vegetated water. Well-informed and enthusiastic guides do a good job of explaining the unique topography and pointing out the unusual fauna. The tram stops often to let visitors view and photograph the wildlife and terrain.

The tram follows a 15-mile paved loop. At the halfway point, visitors disembark at an observation tower for one of the best views in South Florida: a 360°, 18-mile panorama of the Everglades. Rest rooms, vending machines, and water fountains are available at the 20-minute stop.

Airboats

Another highlight of a Shark Valley excursion is taking an airboat ride. While the motorized contraptions are illegal inside the national park, small airboat operations found all along US 41 offer visitors 30-minute rides into the 'Glades for $7–$10. Airboats are so incredibly loud that customers are given wads of cotton to stuff in their ears. You need them. Very small children may be frightened by the noise. Detractors claim the large boats disturb the environment, but proponents say the rides are fun and educational—and that operators have a vested interest in preserving the Everglades natural state.

Most drivers make a stop at a hammock (a small, wooded island) that features a re-creation of an Indian village. Your driver will often try to locate some alligators, tossing marshmallows or pieces of bread into the water to attract the critters.

Dining

Blue Crab Café

39395 Tamiami Trail, Ochopee; (239) 695-2682
Meals served Lunch and dinner **Cuisine** Seafood **Entree range** $7–$20 **Reservations** Not necessary **Payment** V, MC, D

Comments The blue-crab sandwiches and the Everglades swamp dinner—gator, frog legs, and Indian fry bread—are legendary at this roadside landmark. The swamp-shack atmosphere invites guests to kick back with beer.

Side Trips

An Indian Village The Miccosukee Indians are descendants of Seminole Indians who retreated into the Everglades to escape forced resettlement during the nineteenth century. They lived on hammocks in open-sided "chickees"—thatched-roof huts built from cypress—and hunted and fished the Everglades by canoe. They also learned how to handle alligators.

At the Miccosukee Indian Village, on US 41 a mile or so west of the Shark Valley entrance to Everglades National Park, alligators are the stars of the show—and if this is your chance to see an alligator do more than snooze in the sun. Alligator wrestling exhibitions are offered at 11 a.m., 12:30 p.m., 1:30 p.m., 3 p.m., and 4:40 p.m.; admission to the attraction is $5 for adults, $4 for seniors, and $3.50 for children ages 4–12. Airboat rides are $10 per person. The hours are 9 a.m.–5 p.m. daily. For more information, call (305) 223-8380.

In addition to seeing a Miccosukee Indian put a live gator through its paces, you'll get a peek at Miccosukee culture and life on a tour of the village and small museum. Lots of crafts and souvenirs are also offered for sale.

Ochopee If you're looking for quirky old Florida, another stop near the Shark Valley entrance on the Tamiami Trail is the little town of Ochopee (a Native American term meaning "big field"), best known as home of the much-photographed "world's smallest post office." Measuring just 8 feet, 4 inches by 10 feet, 6 inches, the building has been featured on CNN and written about in both *Smithsonian* and the *National Enquirer*. It's so small because it was once the shed behind a general store and post office, and when the store burned down in 1953, they just moved into the shed. You can get your mail postmarked, then stop for lunch a quarter mile down the road at the Blue Crab Café. The post office is located at 38000 Tamiami Trail; (239) 695-4131.

Touring the Park from the South

Ernest F. Coe Visitor Center

This visitor center, named for the man who proposed making a park out of the Everglades, is also park headquarters, located at the main park entrance west of Homestead and Florida City. Though no trails originate here, there are plenty of interactive exhibits and films providing an overview of the park, and naturalists give talks and demonstrations year-round. Inside, you can pick up a telephone and hear differing viewpoints on the Everglades water debate, or watch a movie about hurricanes, or check out park-wide activities on computer monitors. A gift shop has insect repellent in case you forgot.

Royal Palm Visitor Center

Another option for both day-trippers to Everglades National Park and folks who want to spend a few days in the Everglades is to start south of Miami near Florida City at the Royal Palm Visitor Center, located at the park's main entrance. To get there, take Route 9336 from US 1 at Homestead for ten miles to the gate; admission is $10 per car and is good for a week.

The new visitor center (it replaced one destroyed by Hurricane Andrew) features interactive displays, a small theater, and an enclosed walkway to a "borrow"—a water-filled pit, created by coral excavation. Visitors can pick up free brochures, view educational displays, obtain information on boat tours and canoe rentals, and get a map to the many trails that intersect with the 38-mile main road that leads to Flamingo.

Two easy trails, the Gumbo Limbo Trail and the Anhinga Trail originate here. (See "Easy Walks" below.)

Flamingo

At the end of the road is the village of Flamingo, which offers boat rides on Florida Bay, canoe rentals, birding cruises, backcountry boat excursions, a restaurant, a small store, a marina, and a motel—the only overnight sleeping facilities in the park besides primitive camping. While Flamingo is a stretch for day-trippers, the village there is the park's largest visitor complex. If you've got the time and interest, it's a great place for an extended visit. Note, however, that services are limited in Flamingo during the sweltering summer.

Overnight visitors should plan to take a sunset cruise on the **Bald Eagle,** a large pontoon boat that cruises Florida Bay for 90 minutes several times a day. Huge flocks of birds fly across the water to roost on uninhabited keys. The views of the bay, dense mangrove forests, and the shoreline are spectacular, and naturalist guides offer insight. The sight-seeing tour of the bay is $18 for adults and $10 for children ages 6–12.

Other services visitors can use to explore the Flamingo area include canoe rentals ($27 for a half-day and $43 for a full day) and bicycle rentals ($8 for a half-day and $14 all day).

Rates at the Flamingo Lodge Marina & Outpost Resort's comfortable (but not fancy) motel range from $100 to $135. Fully equipped cottages and houseboats are also available for rent. Call the lodge at (239) 695-3101 for more information and at (800) 600-3813 to make reservations.

Easy Walks

Anhinga Trail, which begins just behind the Royal Palm Visitor Center, is a half-mile long and takes about 30 minutes round-trip. It is named for a large black fishing bird. One of the most popular trails in the park, children especially enjoy this leisurely walk, but remind them that the animals will be frightened by loud noises and will go into hiding if alarmed. A paved road leads to the boardwalk, which traverses a sawgrass marsh where you might spot alligators, turtles, river otters, herons, and egrets.

Gumbo Limbo Trail, three miles from the Flamingo entrance and right next to Anhinga Trail, is named for the gumbo limbo tree. Less than a half-mile, it makes for a 30-minute round-trip walk through a shaded and junglelike hammock of royal palms, gumbo limbo trees, lush ferns, and orchids. You'll encounter lots of mosquitoes, lizards, snails, tree frogs, and birds, as well as orchids, ferns, and bromeliads.

Pa-Hay-Okee Trail, 11 miles from the main entrance, features a quarter-mile-long boardwalk with interpretive signs. The walk takes only 15–30 minutes round-trip. An observation tower at the end of the boardwalk offers a great view of the Everglades. Pa-hay-okee is the name the native Americans given the Everglades; it means "grassy waters."

Mahogany Hammock Trail, 18 miles from the main entrance, has an elevated boardwalk. Also half a mile, a walk on the trail takes 30 minutes and passes through a subtropical hardwood forest that is home to the largest living mahogany tree in the United States. This trail is lush and junglelike; owls, frogs, insects, small birds, and bald eagles may be sighted.

Ranger-led hikes and other programs are available year-round, but schedules are limited in summer months. Call ahead for current schedules; (305) 242-7730.

Dining

Flamingo Restaurant

Flamingo Lodge; (239) 695-3101

Meals served Lunch and dinner **Cuisine** Seafood **Entree range** $11–$22
Reservations Recommended in season **Payment** V, MC, D
Comments Located at Flamingo Lodge, this dining room has spectacular views of Florida Bay and specializes in fresh fish, served grilled, blackened, or fried. Entrees come with salad or their famous conch chowder as well as vegetables. There is also a kid's menu.

Side Trips

An Alligator Farm Outside the park entrance near Florida City, the Everglades Alligator Farm is a small, private attraction worth a look. Among the creatures residing in this minizoo are more than 3,000 alligators (most of them little guys in "grow out" pens), a collection of snakes and crocodiles (including an eight-and-a-half-foot-long speckled caiman), two mountain lions, two lynxes, and a black bear. The farm is located on Southwest 192nd Avenue; follow the signs out of Florida City.

The two main attractions are a 20-minute alligator show (a handler "wrestles" a gator and answers questions from visitors) and the only airboat rides on this end of the Everglades (no airboats are allowed in the national park). Alligator feedings, alligator shows, and snake shows alternate on the hour. Don't plan to stick around for all three shows, though. This attraction is too small to invest that much time.

The farm is open 9 a.m.–6 p.m. daily; admission is $14.50 for adults, $8 for children ages 4–12, and free for children ages 3 and under, including a 30-minute airboat ride. Skip the ride and admission is $14.50 for adults and $8 for kids 4–12. For more information, call (800) 644-9711 or (305) 247-2628.

Touring the Park from the Gulf Coast

Everglades City, off the Tamiami Trail and just above the western edge of Everglades National Park is a good place to start an Everglades adventure from the Gulf Coast. Here you'll find the park's Gulf Coast Visitor Center, with narrated boat rides into the water and mangrove island portion of the park. An observation tower rises 400 steps from a boardwalk, offering a 360° panorama of the surrounding bay. Within Everglades City (or nearby) are Native American reservations; the world's smallest post office, in Ochopee; famed Everglades photographer Clyde Butcher's Big Cypress Gallery; airboat rides and swamp buggy tours; canoe and kayak adventures; alligator farms; and great backcountry fishing.

The weathered **Museum of the Everglades** is just off the circle in the center of town, near US 41 and SR 29. It presents the story of 2,000 years of human habitation with Indian artifacts, period photographs, and palm-thatched chickee huts. Education programs, lectures, and events are presented throughout the year. The museum is open Tuesday through Saturday, 11 a.m.–4 p.m. and is located at 105 West Broadway. Call (239) 695-0008 for more information.

Opened in 1998, the museum is in the Old Laundry building, which dates to 1927, when the Tamiami Trail was under constructed. Built by Barron Gift Collier as part of his planned community, the laundry served the people of the new city of Everglades.

Ten Thousand Islands

Everglades City is also a great starting point for visiting one of the "Ten Thousand Islands" (give or take a thousand or so) that hug the tip of Florida, from the Gulf of Mexico to Florida Bay. You can take an airplane ride from a landing strip here for an overview of this unspoiled wetlands of rugged, isolated keys and mangrove isles.

Chokoloskee Island has been called one of Florida's last frontiers. About 2,000 years ago, the earliest inhabitants began altering the landscape with mounds of oyster shells and with canals. Native Americans expanded the mounds, fished the Gulf, hunted, and farmed the rich soil. Moving south from conflict in North Florida and Georgia, the Seminole Indians were the last native peoples to make the Everglades their home.

Near the end of the nineteenth century, plume, hide, and fur hunters arrived, quickly followed by families who combined seasonal hunting, fishing, and farming. The settlement brought a need for goods and mail, and in

1906 the Smallwood Store trading post began serving the remote area, buying hides, furs, and farm produce and providing goods.

Ted Smallwood's store was placed on the National Register of Historic Places in 1974, and remained open and active until 1982. When the doors were shut, 90 percent of the original goods remained. Ted's granddaughter has reopened **Smallwood's Store** (360 Mamie Street, Chokoloskee Island; (941) 695-2989) as a museum, a time capsule of Florida pioneer history. The hide room has been turned into exhibit space, telling the history of the pioneers of Southwest Florida. The museum is open 10 a.m.–5 p.m. December–April and 11 a.m.–5 p.m. May–November. Admission is $2.50.

Gulf Coast Water Tours

Everglades National Park Boat Tours This tour docks in the Everglades National Park on the Chokoloskee Causeway (SR 29). There are two-hour guided tours with a naturalist through the Ten Thousand Islands starting every 30 minutes, 9 a.m.–4:30 p.m. daily. The cost is $16 for adults, $8 for children ages 6–12, and free for ages 5 and under. No reservations are needed. Canoe rentals are also available; call (239) 695-2591 or (800) 445-7724 for details.

Everglades Eco Adventures The Harraden family operates tours from December through April. Their Everglades Eco Adventures (107 Camelia Street, Everglades City; (239) 695-4666; **www.iveyhouse.com**) also rents canoes for $35 a day and kayaks starting at $45 a day. Guided trips range from $50 to $500 a day, lunch included.

Jungle Erv's Airboat World Jungle Erv's is another old-time airboat ride, open daily 9 a.m.–5 p.m., with pontoon boats departing every hour from 11 a.m. until 4 p.m. Large airboat tours lasting half an hour are $19.50 for adults, $8 for children under age 10. Private hour-long rides in smaller airboats are $30 for adults, $20 for children under age 10. Safari rides on pontoon boats are $19.50 for adults, $8 for children under age 10. Jungle Erv's is located in Everglades City just two miles south of US 41 on SR 29; (239) 695-2805.

Wooten's Everglades Adventures Wooten's started offering airboat rides in 1953 and today is one of the oldest companies offering excursions in the area. They're open daily, 9 a.m.–4:30 p.m. Airboat and swamp buggy rides are $16; a trip through their animal sanctuary is $8, and you'll see more than 350 alligators, crocodiles, panthers, jaguars, sea turtles, otters, and snakes. Private airboat tours are $35 per person. Wooten's is on US 41; (239) 695-2781.

Dining

Rod and Gun Club
200 Broadway, Everglades City; (239) 695-2101

Meals served Lunch and dinner **Cuisine** American **Entree range** $7–$30
Reservations Not necessary **Payment** No credit cards
Comments This 130-year-old historic lodge caters mostly to fishermen, but kids are awed by the wildlife "trophies"—giant tarpon, turtles, wild hogs, bears, and more—displayed all over the place. The movie *Gone Fishin'* with Joe Pesci and Danny Glover was filmed here. The restaurant is a great stop after a day in the Everglades, with fresh seafood (there's always grouper on the menu, and Southern-fried is the best), lobster salad, stone crabs, and frog legs. The tart Key lime pie is the real thing.

Part Eleven

The Florida Keys and Key West

Welcome to the Keys

Together, the Florida Keys are a tourist, diving, and sportfishing mecca that draws over a million visitors each year. The archipelago of fossilized coral stretches more than 100 miles beyond the tip of mainland Florida, forming a natural barrier between the Atlantic Ocean and the Gulf of Mexico and ending in Key West, closer to Cuba than to the U.S. mainland.

The Keys' mystique—Humphrey Bogart in *Key Largo*, Ernest Hemingway at Sloppy Joe's, and 1960s-era Key West bohemianism—comes from a never-ending flow of fiction, film, and public-relations hype. That earthy, rum-soaked image has been largely pushed aside by restoration, revitalization, and the good intentions of the tourist industry.

And while the PR copy overstates the romance, intrigue, and hipness to be found in the Keys, there remains an end-of-the-road feel. Here you'll find a sense of escape into the exotic, a feeling that your next step might be the jungles of South America. While the Keys are increasingly touristy and overdeveloped, they still afford a comfortable abode for misfits and dropouts, artists and writers, gays and lesbians, and anyone else not in lockstep with the conventional American dream.

HIGHLIGHTS

- Snorkeling at John Pennekamp State Park
- Swimming with dolphins
- Sunset celebration in Key West's Mallory Square
- Beach camping at Bahia Honda State Park
- Boat or seaplane to the Dry Tortugas

A few miles offshore lies the jungle of the sea, the coral reef. Thousands of sea plants and animals thrive in and around the coral reef in water anywhere from 10 to 60 feet deep. The cracks and holes in the reef provide protection or homes for all types of marine animals. The variety of life on display makes

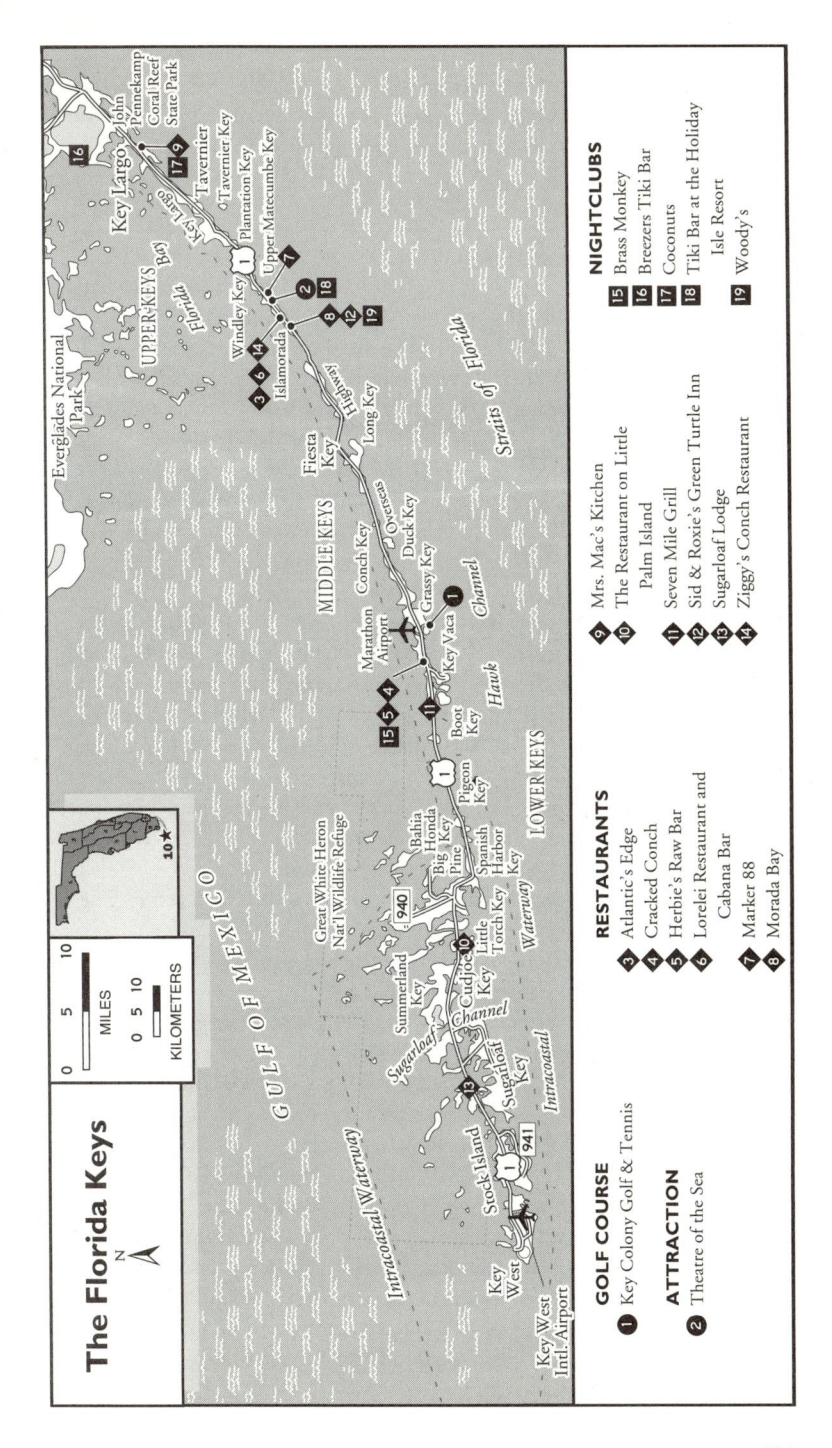

The Florida Keys

GOLF COURSE
1. Key Colony Golf & Tennis

ATTRACTION
2. Theatre of the Sea

RESTAURANTS
3. Atlantic's Edge
4. Cracked Conch
5. Herbie's Raw Bar
6. Lorelei Restaurant and Cabana Bar
7. Marker 88
8. Morada Bay
9. Mrs. Mac's Kitchen
10. The Restaurant on Little Palm Island
11. Seven Mile Grill
12. Sid & Roxie's Green Turtle Inn
13. Sugarloaf Lodge
14. Ziggy's Conch Restaurant

NIGHTCLUBS
15. Brass Monkey
16. Breezers Tiki Bar
17. Coconuts
18. Tiki Bar at the Holiday Isle Resort
19. Woody's

for a moving kaleidoscope of colors and shapes—and a wonderland for divers and snorkelers. The living, slow-growing reef is very fragile, however, and visitors must be careful not to stand on, sit on, or touch the coral, because it will die. Doing so, by the way, almost always results in a painful scratch.

A Brief History

Not long after Christopher Columbus set foot in the New World in 1492, Spanish explorers Ponce de Leon and Antonio de Herrera were the first Europeans to sight the Florida Keys, on May 15, 1513. In the seventeenth and eighteenth centuries, pirates buried treasure here, fortunes were made scavenging sea wrecks on the reef, and smugglers and slave merchants plied their trades, finding cover in the lush, dark hardwood hammocks located on the islands.

Key West was not settled until 1822, and development in the rest of the Keys came even later. Early settlers farmed productive groves of Key limes, tamarind, and breadfruit. In the Lower Keys, pineapple farms flourished, and a large pineapple processing factory supplied canned pineapple to most of the eastern United States.

The real money, however, was in salvaging cargo from ships sunk on nearby reefs. As a result of the efforts of the "wreckers," Key West became one of the wealthiest U.S. cities in the early nineteenth century. Later, sponge fishermen developed a thriving market for the high-quality sponges harvested in the waters off Key West. Later still, cigar makers from Cuba built factories in the city.

Henry Flagler, the associate of John D. Rockefeller who opened up the east coast of Florida at the end of the nineteenth century with his railroad, extended his tracks to the Keys in 1905. The Overseas Railroad—also called "Flagler's Folly"—was an incredible engineering feat for its time. The greatest technical achievement was the Seven Mile Bridge, which links Marathon to the Lower Keys. The railroad reached Key West in 1912 and wealthy visitors took the train to vacation here.

The Depression years were bleak in the Keys, and Key West declared bankruptcy in 1934. More bad luck followed while Flagler's bridges took everything Mother Nature threw their way, the Labor Day hurricane of 1935 tore up the railroad; the bridges later were adapted for roadways. In 1938, the Overseas Railroad became the Overseas Highway.

The new road opened up hope for the renewal of tourism, but World War II intervened. During the war, the opening of a submarine base in Key West started an economic revival, as boosted by the development of a commercial shrimp industry. Ernest Hemingway and other notable writers and artists called Key West home—at least some of the year—and enhanced its reputation as a mecca for creative types. The most recent, tourist-fueled economic upswing began in the early 1980s—and, judging by the size of the crowds on Duval Street, it shows no signs of letting up.

Visiting the Florida Keys

Gathering Information
Monroe County Tourist Development Council, P.O. Box 866, Key West 33041-0866; (800) FLA-KEYS; **www.fla-keys.com.** If you're planning on visiting Key West, for example, you can request free guides listing hotels, motels, bed-and-breakfasts, rental properties, and real estate agents.

Why and How to See the Florida Keys
The Florida Keys are the primary vacation destination for about 1.5 million people who visit South Florida each year. Most, but not all, are outdoorsy people who come to enjoy the islands' unique location between two large bodies of water: the Atlantic Ocean and the Gulf of Mexico. The mingling of these waters results in a fantastic array of marine life—and world-class sportfishing. Some visitors come to dive and snorkel in gin-clear waters and view the only coral reef in the continental United States. Others explore the Keys' unusual and beautiful backcountry that is full of birds and marine life. Finally, Key West is a popular tourist destination that draws over a million visitors each year.

One reason not to come to the Keys is to savor miles and miles of gleaming white beaches: Though there are a handful of decent beaches, there's no naturally occurring sand. It takes waves to make sand, and the offshore reef eliminates the surf action.

Day-Tripping to the Keys
For folks on a visit to Miami who can spare a day or two out of their schedule, the Keys offer a dramatic—and usually appreciated—contrast to the high-octane pace of hot, hot, hot Miami. The Upper Keys aren't much more than an hour's drive away from the city. Most folks who take a day trip to the Keys don't get below the Upper Keys; if you only have a day yet must visit Key West, we suggest taking a bus tour. See the section on specialized tours, page 506, for information on commercial tours to Key West.

When to Visit
The tourist season in the Florida Keys roughly mirrors that of Miami and the rest of South Florida. The winter season begins in mid-November and ends around Easter; both Christmas and Easter are periods when hotels, motels, restaurants, and other tourist-dependent facilities are jammed.

While the summer months are off-season, keep in mind that the Keys are a popular destination for many South Florida residents seeking relief from the intense heat and humidity; the Keys are typically ten degrees cooler than Miami and much breezier. As a result, a lot of native Floridians crowd US 1 on Friday afternoons and evenings during the summer for a weekend escape; most of them return on the following Sunday evening. Out-of-state visitors should try to avoid the weekend traffic crushes.

The summer months are also increasingly popular with foreign visitors, especially those from Asia and Germany. Increasingly, Key West's popularity as a port of destination on minicruises out of Miami and Fort Lauderdale is resulting in many people returning to the town for a summer vacation.

Summer visitors discover that rooms are cheaper and Key West is less crowded. A note to anglers: While migrating tarpon swim past the Keys April through June, don't expect to find a fishing guide who's available; they're booked at least a year in advance—unless you get lucky and there's a cancellation.

Locals say the best months to visit the Keys are September and October: the weather is warm, crowds are nonexistent, and lodging is cheaper.

Arriving

By Plane   While both Key West (at the end of the string of islands) and Marathon (located in the Middle Keys) have small commercial airports, most folks headed to the Keys by air arrive at Miami International Airport, rent a car, and drive to their final destination.

A glance at a map shows why: MIA is located west of Miami near Route 836, a major east-west highway that connects with Florida's Turnpike Homestead Extension. You can literally be in the Upper Keys within an hour after landing at MIA—if you didn't check any baggage and the line at the rental car agency is short. If your final destination is Key West, figure on about a three-hour drive from the airport, or longer if it's a Friday afternoon.

For folks concerned about Miami's reputation for crime against tourists, we have good news: getting to the Keys from MIA takes you away from high-crime areas, not through them. At the rental car agency, get explicit driving directions. Most people will take LeJeune Road south to Route 836 west. After you get on Route 836, it's about 6 miles to Florida's Turnpike. Take it south to Homestead, another 20 miles or so.

By Car   From the end of Florida's Turnpike at Florida City, US 1 heads south toward the tip of Florida through stands of tangled mangrove and thick trees; Mile Marker 127, just south of Homestead, counts down to Mile Marker 00 in Key West.

Say good-bye to four-lane expressways: US 1 is a mostly two-lane road as it heads over land and water on its way to Key West. Traffic on the narrow road can be a bear, especially around weekends and holidays, when many South Floridians and tourists head for Key West and other points along the way. During the winter, avoid driving to the Keys on Friday afternoons and evenings, and on Sunday evenings. The traffic is usually horrendous and multihour backups are routine.

And don't think that off-season is any better. That's when Miami residents and other South Floridians descend on the Keys by the thousands to escape the heat and humidity that bakes Miami in the summer. Try to leave on Friday morning and return on Monday to beat the worst of the weekend traffic.

After passing Florida City, you can make a more dramatic entrance to the Keys than ho-hum US 1 by hanging a left onto Card Sound Road (Route

905A). You'll miss most of the tourist traffic heading south and the toll bridge over Card Sound offers a great view of undeveloped Key Largo and Florida Bay. Savor the view—farther south on Key Largo, the commercialism is rampant.

The Best Beaches

Cannon Beach in John Pennekamp Coral Reef State Park. There's not much sand on this manmade beach, but a replica of a seventeenth century shipwreck attracts lots of fish for snorkelers. Also at Pennekamp is Far Beach with palm trees for shade. Both have concessions, rest rooms, picnic tables, showers, and a visitor center. Admission is $2.50 each for a vehicle's first two passengers and 50 cents for each additional passenger; open 8 a.m.–sunset. Located at MM102.5 in Key Largo; (305) 451-1202.

Anne's Beach At MM 73.5 on Lower Matecumbe Key, this is a pretty two-mile beach with a wooden walkway above the dunes. Calm water make it a nice spot for swimming. There are rest rooms and free parking; (305) 664-2345.

Bahia Honda State Park The longest natural beach in the keys in on Big Pine Key at MM 36.5. Though the sand is only about ten yards wide, but the water is shallow and gin clear. The beach has concessions, rest rooms, showers, and a visitor's center. There are a handful of coveted cabins, often booked a year in advance, and beach campsites. Entry is $4 per vehicle plus 50 cents per person. Open 8 a.m.–sunset; (305) 872-2353.

Smathers Beach At MM 3 in Key West, this is a good beach for snorkeling, but the best show is on the beach along South Roosevelt Boulevard where vendors sell food, snorkeling equipment, beach chairs, even seashells out of their vans alongside the road. Metered street parking; (305) 292-8190.

Clarence S. Higgs Memorial Beach At MM 1 in Key West along Atlantic Avenue, this beach has plenty of action, from bike paths to tennis and volleyball courts, plus showers and rest rooms. Free street and lot parking; (305) 292-8190.

Outdoor Adventures and Sports

Recommended Excursions

Dolphins Plus, Key Largo Visitors get to do more than just swim with the dolphins here. A special marine orientation program includes a one-hour swim seminar that gives a general awareness of the plight of dolphins. You get to swim with the mammals, then participate in a question-and-answer session with researchers. Children must be at least 7 years old to participate in the swim. The cost is $160. Located at Corrine Place, MM 99, Key Largo; (305) 451-1993; www.dolphinsplus.com.

Dolphin Research Center You can touch, play, and swim with dolphins here, but the main goal of the center is to educate the public. About 15 dolphins swim in a 90,000-square-foot coral natural saltwater tide pool carved out of the shoreline. Guided tours are $17.50 for adults, $14.50 for seniors over age 55, and $11.50 for children ages 4–12; ages 3 and under get in free. To swim with the dolphins, children must be at least 5 years old and those under 13 must be accompanied by a paying adult. Cost is $155; reservations are taken the first day of the month for the following month (reservations for July can be made starting June 1, for instance). And it's pretty difficult to get one of the prized spots to swim with the mammals. Located at MM 59, Grassy Key; (305) 289-1121; **www.dolphins.org.**

John Pennekamp Coral Reef State Park The 78 miles of living coral reef in this park is only a small portion of one of the most beautiful reef systems in the world. But because it's all underwater, the best way to see it is snorkeling or diving. Pennekamp is the first undersea preserve in the United States and a sanctuary for 55 species of coral and more than 650 species of fish.

First-time snorkelers, especially children, will not believe their eyes when they get their first glimpse of the underwater world. After a 30-minute boat ride to the reef, it's over the side for up-close views of a fantastic array of aquatic life. The boat crew gives plenty of coaching to novices and a ten-minute mini-course on how to snorkel. The fee includes rental of a mask, flipper, and snorkel (and you get to keep the snorkel). All snorkelers must wear inflatable life vests, which are provided. Snorkeling tours are $27 for adults, $22 for children ages 17 and under; rental for (required) equipment is $6. Tour times are 9 a.m., noon, and 3 p.m.

If swimming with the fishes doesn't appeal or non-swimmers are in your family, take a two-hour glass-bottom boat tour. Cost is $20 for adults, $12 for children ages 11 and under. For reservations, call (305) 451-1621.

Other facilities in the park include hiking trails, a small swimming beach, an aquarium, canoe rentals, and a visitors' center featuring ecological displays of Keys flora and fauna. There are 47 campsites, but be prepared for the heat and mosquitoes. Cost is $26. Nature walks and campfire lectures by camp rangers are held. The park is open daily, 8 a.m.–sunset; admission is $2.50 each for a vehicle's first and second passengers, 50 cents each additional passenger. Located at MM 102.5, Key Largo; (305) 451-1202; **www.pennekamppark.com.**

Looe Key National Marine Sanctuary This five-square-mile area of submerged reef six miles southwest of Big Pine Key is considered the best reef in the Keys for snorkeling, diving, fishing, and boating. Its gin-clear waters reveal underwater sights such as brain coral, tall coral pillars rising toward the surface, and other interesting formations. Make arrangements to visit at any dive shop; prices vary. MM 27.5, Looe Key; (305) 292-0311.

National Key Deer Refuge Come early in the morning or near sunset to watch the tiny deer come out to graze on 2,300 acres. Stand quietly near the Blue Hole, where alligators, birds, and turtles hang out. A nature preserve, called Watson's Hammock, and the Great White Heron Refuge are also part of the park. Open from sunrise to sunset. Located at MM 30.5, Big Pine Key; (305) 872-2239.

Canoeing and Kayaking

Reflections Nature Tours in Big Pine Key guides visitors on kayak trips to the Keys' backcountry. No experience is necessary to paddle the calm, shallow waters in stable, easy-to-paddle sea kayaks on tours that emphasize seeing wildlife. On the trip you'll view birds, animals, and marine life in Great White Heron and Key Deer wildlife refuges; snorkeling is another popular option on the tours. Trips are $50 per person and last about three hours. Big Pine Key is 30 miles from Key West. Reflections Nature Tours is based at Old Wooden Bridge Fishing Camp adjacent to No Name Key Bridge. For more information or to make a reservation, call (305) 872-4688 or visit **www.floridakeyskayaktours.com.**

Diving and Snorkeling

Numerous kiosks and dive shops in Key West offer half-day snorkeling and diving trips to the reef. Shop around for the best price and most convenient departure time. If you have your own gear, you can snorkel right from the beach at **Fort Zachary Taylor State Historic Site,** located in the Truman Annex at Whitehead and Southard streets in Old Town Key West.

Certified scuba divers, however, can dive anywhere on their own. The Keys offer both beginning and experienced divers plenty of great scenery in protected waters that are relatively shallow (60 feet deep and less). At the only living coral barrier reef in North American continental waters, giant brain coral grows up to six feet high, elkhorn corals six to ten feet high, and mountainous star coral to five feet or more across and up to ten feet high.

Popular dive sites include John **Pennekamp Coral Reef State Park,** in Key Largo, **Looe Key National Marine Sanctuary** (near Big Pine Key in the Lower Keys), and the **Marquesas** (22 miles west of Key West). Snorkeling is an option at these parks as well. For those in need of rental equipment, dive shops are located all along US 1 and throughout Key West.

Seaplanes of Key West offers full- and half-day flights to Fort Jefferson and the Dry Tortugas that include coolers, ice, sodas, and snorkeling gear—all you need to bring is a towel and a camera. The 70-mile flight is 40 minutes each way; the plane flies at low altitude so passengers can view the clear waters, shipwrecks, and marine life. You spend two hours on the island. Four-hour trips leave at 8 a.m. and noon daily; prices are $179 for adults, $129 for children ages 7–12, and $99 for children ages 2–6. Full-day trips are $305 for adults, $225 for children ages 7–12, and $170 for children ages 2–6. For reservations, call (800) 950-2359.

Another option for visiting Fort Jefferson and the Dry Tortugas is the **Fort Jefferson Ferry,** which sails out of Lands End Marina (251 Margaret Street in Key West) for full-day excursions. The 100-foot *Yankee Freedom II* boasts a large, air-conditioned salon with a chef's galley, a cash bar, a snack bar, a large sundeck, and freshwater showers for swimmers, snorkelers, and divers. The ferry departs daily at 8 a.m. and returns at 5:30 p.m.; it's three hours each way, and visitors can enjoy about four hours on the island (including a complete tour of the fort). The price for the all-day trip is

$119 for adults, $109 for seniors ages 62 and older, and $79 for children ages 16 and under; breakfast and lunch included in price. For schedule and booking information, contact (800) 634-0939 or (305) 294-7009; **www.yankeefreedom.com.**

Boating

The ***MV Discovery,*** a glass-bottom boat with an underwater viewing room that puts you at eye level with marine life, offers trips at 10:30 a.m., 1:30 p.m., and (in winter) sunset. Tickets for the two-hour trip are $30 for adults and $16 for children (plus tax); kids sail free on the first trip of the day. The ship is located at the Lands End Marina, 251 Margaret Street in Key West. For more information, call (800) 262-0099 or (305) 293-0099.

Sebago Watersports offers catamaran cruises and solo or tandem parasailing. Call (305) 292-4768.

Fishing

Anglers looking for some recommendations for reputable guides and fishing boat charters available at Key West marinas can stop by the **Saltwater Angler** at the Hilton Resort and Marina, 243 Front Street, and talk to Captain Jeff Cardenas, who spent ten years guiding flats fishermen in the Keys before opening his custom rod shop. He's an expert on the outdoors around Key West and happy to offer advice. The phone number is (800) 223-1629 or (305) 296-0700.

Little Green Signs

Those signs on the side of the road are mile markers (MM), making it easy to find places along US 1 from Key Largo to Key West. The numbers begin with 1 in Key West and got to 113 in Key Largo. If there's an O beside any address, it means Oceanside; B is for bayside.

The Upper Keys

After merging back with US 1 (now also called the Overseas Highway), continue south on to Key Largo. The name is pure hype: The eponymous, late 1940s flick starring Bogart and Robinson wasn't filmed here. The local flacks changed the name of the island from Rock Harbor to Key Largo to cash in on the publicity generated by the movie.

More tenuous links with Tinseltown are on tap at the local Holiday Inn, where the original *African Queen,* the small, steam-powered boat used in the film of the same name starring Bogie and Katharine Hepburn, is on display in the hotel's marina (when it's not on promotional tours). Needless to say, that movie wasn't made here either—it was filmed in England and Africa.

From US 1, don't expect a whole lot in the way of legendary Keys' ambience. Key Largo is close enough to Homestead and the southern 'burbs of Miami to serve as a bedroom community to the city, and strip malls, restaurants, gas stations, and fast-food joints line the highway. To find anything interesting to see, you've got to get off the island.

Luckily, that's easy to do. John Pennekamp Coral Reef State Park, located at MM 102.5, offers visitors an easy escape to snorkeling, diving, and glass-bottom-boat trips. In addition, a small sandy beach (a rare commodity in the Keys) and a visitor center make this unusual park a worthwhile stop. The park is also a major draw for the million-plus divers who come to Key Largo each year, making it the "Diving Capital of the U.S."

Tavernier is the next town traversed as you continue south on US 1. Harry Harris Park, located on the left at MM 92.5, is a county park offering a sandy beach, a tidal pool, barbecue pits, picnic tables, a playground—and an excuse to pull over and relax.

Past Tavernier is a 20-mile stretch of islands collectively known as Islamorada (pronounced EYE-la-ma-RAHD-a), which touts itself as the "Sportfishing Capital of the World." Indeed, this is big-time deep-sea fishing country, as the many marinas and bait-and-tackle shops along the road attest; folks with other interests should keep driving south. An exception: As with all the Keys, the snorkeling and diving at offshore reefs is excellent. Stop in any dive shop along the highway for more details.

Theatre of the Sea, a fish-and-sea-mammal emporium at MM 84.5, is the second-oldest marine park in the world. Sea lions, dolphins, glass-bottom-boat tours, saltwater aquariums, and ongoing shows make this a worthwhile stop, especially for kids. See below for more information.

ROBBIE'S PET TARPON

If you don't want to go deep-sea fishing, here's a chance to see, and even feed, a tarpon or two. Robbie's 200-pound pets hang around the docks just waiting for a snack. Open daily, 8 a.m.–5 p.m. Admission is $1 per person; it's $2 for a bucket of fish food. Robbie's Marina is at MM 77.5, Islamorada; (305) 664-9814; **www.robbies.com**.

Attractions

Theater of the Sea

MM 84.5 on US 1, Islamorada; (305) 664-2431; www.theaterofthesea.com

Hours Daily, 9:30 a.m.–4 p.m. Holiday hours vary.

Admission $18.50 for adults, $11.50 for children ages 3–12, free for children under age 3. Group rates are available. Price of admission does not include the Dolphin Swim, boat rides, or snorkeling trips.

Appeal by Age Group

Pre-school ★★★	Teens ★★★	Over 30 ★★★
Grade school ★★★	Young Adults ★★★	Seniors ★★★

Touring Time *Average* a half-day; *minimum* 1½ hour

Rainy-Day Touring Not recommended

Author's Rating ★★★; plenty of interaction with all sorts of sea creatures

Description and Comments Established in 1946, Theater of the Sea is the world's second-oldest marine park. Here, you can explore the surroundings of the deep in a natural lagoon setting. Activities at the park such as bottomless-boat rides, aquatic shows, and lagoon tours will entertain guests of all ages, as well as educate them about marine life. Children are especially drawn to the touch tank, where they can pet a shark or kiss a sea lion. Also, children of all ages are invited to take part in the shows.

Theater of the Sea will let you swim with their dolphins for $140 and with the sea lions for $95. Participants must be at least 5 years old to swim with a parent and at least 13 years old to swim without a parent. You need to call ahead for reservations. They also offer a snorkel cruise.

Shopping

There's not much shopping until Key West, and the best shopping in the Upper Keys is around Islamorada and Tavernier. **The Rain Barrel** (MM 86.7; (305) 852-3084) in Islamorada features artists at work in the tropical gardens, with eight to ten artists in residence and shops showcasing the works of nearly 100 artists—everything from stained glass and jewelry to sculpture. There's also a wonderful little vegetarian café on the premises. A 35-foot lobster points the way across the street to **Treasure Village** (MM 86.7; (305) 852-0511), with ten shops in a small shopping mall built to look like a fort, offering unusual gifts and original art including pottery, glass, tropical clothing, and children's toys. There's also a bakery with gourmet coffee.

More retail in Islamorada includes **Hooked on Books** (MM 82.6; (305) 517-2602), where you'll find best-sellers, lots of Florida books, children's books, and great deals on used books—but no newspapers or magazines. For impromptu clothes shopping, **Latitude 25** (MM 82.7; (305) 664-4421) carries Tommy Bahama as well as fun gifts. Nearby competition is **Island Silver & Spice** (MM 82; (305) 664-2714) a Keys-style department store with men and women's clothing, a children's department, toys, jewelry, watches, even home decor.

Sports enthusiasts won't want to miss **World Wide Sportsman** (81576 Overseas Highway, MM 81.5; (305) 664-4615), the largest fishing store in the Keys with two stories of shopping, everything from rods and reels to kids' clothing, and a full-service marina. They'll even arrange charter trips and tours. On the second floor, a genteel bar called **Zane Grey Lounge** offers a nice view of the bay and live music on the weekends (with no cover charge).

Dining

Atlantic's Edge

Cheeca Lodge, Overseas Highway, MM 82, Islamorada; (305) 664-4651

Meals served Dinner only **Cuisine** American/Caribbean **Entree range** $17 and up **Reservations** Necessary **Payment** All major credit cards accepted
Comments This upscale, award-winning restaurant offers views of the ocean with seating indoors and outdoors, and a menu focused on seafood with many of the inspired by the resort's Avanyu Spa. Favorite starters include the coconut conch chowder, or pan-seared jumbo scallops over goat cheese whipped potatoes with sherry vinegar, brown butter, and white truf-

fle oil. Locally caught fish is the star, and can be ordered grilled, braised, sauteed, meunière, steamed, blackened, onion-crusted, plantain-crusted, or deep fried. Veal, chicken, beef, and tofu also are on the diverse menu.

Lorelei Restaurant and Cabana Bar

Overseas Highway, MM 82; Islamorada; (305) 664-4656

Meals served Dinner nightly except Monday **Cuisine** Seafood **Entree range** $15–$24 **Reservations** For parties of five or larger **Payment** All major credit cards accepted

Comments On the beach with live music by locals "Paul and Billy," this family-friendly spot is the place to watch the sunset and dine on fresh fish, Florida lobster, and conch.

Marker 88

Overseas Highway, MM 88; (305) 852-5503

Meals served Lunch and dinner daily **Cuisine** Continental/Caribbean **Entree range** Lunch $7–$9; dinner $13–$30 **Reservations** Highly recommended **Payment** V, MC, AmEx, D

Comments Almost every famous person who has visited the Keys has also visited Marker 88, a rustic, weathered building that overlooks the Florida Bay. An interesting mix of dishes, from conch fritters to such longtime French classics as rack of lamb Provençale, is available here. Also great Cuban black bean soup, conch steak, and local fish.

Morada Bay

Overseas Highway, MM 81, Islamorada; (305) 664-0604

Meals served Lunch, dinner **Cuisine** American/Mediterranean **Entree range** Lunch, $10–$15; dinner, $21–$29 **Reservations** Not accepted **Payment** All major credit cards accepted

Comments Morada Bay's tasteful main dining room overlooks Florida Bay and the mangroves, with an impressive beach-and-water view from the back terrace. The contemporary menu features tapas and interesting Keys fare, but best bet is always catch of the day. There's a solid wine list and snazzy tropical drinks at the bar. Live entertainment under the stars is featured on weekends.

Mrs. Mac's Kitchen

99336 Overseas Highway, MM 99.4, Key Largo; (305) 451-3722

Meals served Breakfast, lunch, and dinner **Cuisine** American **Entree range** Breakfast, $5–$8; lunch, $3–$8; dinner, $8–$16 **Reservations** Not accepted **Payment** No credit cards

Comments This kitschy little roadside joint has been serving hungry diners for decades, and we think the home cookin' beats the fast-food outlets that line the highway. Sun and saltwater make you hungry, so try their stuffed pitas, burgers, or shrimp baskets.

Sid and Roxie's Green Turtle Inn
Overseas Highway, MM 81.5, Islamorada; (305) 664-9031

Meals served Lunch and dinner, Tuesday–Sunday **Cuisine** Seafood/American **Entree range** Lunch, $12–23; dinner, $14–$39 **Reservations** Recommended for dinner only **Payment** All major credit cards accepted
Comments You can't miss the giant turtle that marks the spot for Sid and Roxie's eatery. Though Sid and Roxie are long gone, the place hasn't been updated much since the 1950s (it opened in 1947), and the food is plain and a bit old-fashioned—fresh fish or a steak with soup, potatoes, and salad. Lots of diners ask for the turtle soup, which comes from the cannery right behind the inn. Breads and pies are made from scratch.

Ziggy's Conch Restaurant
Overseas Highway, MM 83, Islamorada; (305) 664-3391

Meals served Dinner daily **Cuisine** American **Entree range** $11–$25 **Reservations** Recommended **Payment** V, AmEx, MC, D
Comments Open since 1962, Ziggy's original chef was French, a fact that continues to be reflected in the menu. The present executive chef has been there for over 30 years and continues the French touches. Fresh, native fish, however, is the main attraction here. Favorites include conch: in a chowder; raw and marinated in lime juice with peppers and onions; as fritters, or breaded and fried. Oysters, native fish and lobsters are recommended.

Nightlife

Breezers Tiki Bar
Who Goes There Locals and hotel guests

Marriott Key Largo, Overseas Highway, MM 103.8, Key Largo; (305) 453-0000; www.marriottkeylargo.com

Cover No **Minimum** No **Mixed drinks** $5.50 **Food available** Hot dogs, hamburgers, chicken fingers, and more **Hours** 4–11 p.m.
What goes on Live entertainment featuring island-style music.
Comments The full menu is complemented by specials.

Coconuts
Who Goes There Primarily 30-and 40-something and locals

529 Caribbean Drive, MM 100; (305) 453-9794; www.coconutsrestaurant.com

Cover No **Minimum** No **Mixed drinks** $7 **Food available** Seafood, beef, salads, pastas, and more **Hours** 11 a.m.–2 a.m.
What goes on Monday is football night (in season), Tuesday is blues night, Wednesday through Saturday it's Top 40. Other regular events include Locals Jam Night, Karaoke Night, and Ladies Night.
Comments This is the place locals go for dancing and live music, one of the hottest spots in the Florida Keys.

Tiki Bar at the Holiday Isle Resort

Who Goes There Bikini-clad boaters, divers, sport fishermen

Overseas Highway, MM 84; (305) 664-2321

Cover No **Minimum** No **Mixed drinks** $6 **Food available** No **Hours** 10 a.m.–12:30 Weekdays; 10 a.m.–2 a.m. Weekends

What goes on Holiday Isle is a popular spot for boaters, and the bar comes to life around noon and stays packed most of the day. There's live music nightly for a partying crowd.

Comments A quintessential Keys experience—drinking, dancing, bikinis.

Woody's

Who Goes There Locals and tourists looking for fun—or who don't know better

Overseas Highway, MM 82; (305) 664-4335; www.keysdining.com/woodys/index.htm

Cover No **Minimum** No **Mixed drinks** $5 **Food available** Pizza and bar food **Hours** 6 p.m.–4 a.m.

What goes on Raunchy humor from the house band, Big Dick and the Extenders, on stage Tuesday through Sunday. Big Dick is a 300-pound Native American who doesn't mind embarrassing anyone in the place with lewd jokes, so be forewarned. But the place is usually packed with partiers.

Comments If you're looking for quiet, skip Woody's. And if you go, refuse a seat at a front table unless you're prepared to be harangued by Big Dick.

The Middle and Lower Keys

South of Long Key are the Middle Keys, about halfway to Key West. Views of water on both sides of the highway start to appear and you get the feeling that you're actually off the North American continent and out to sea.

The next town is Marathon, the second-largest community in the Keys; it even has an airport. While the waters offshore are a big draw with the fishing and boating crowd, the town itself doesn't exude a lot of personality.

Next is the Seven Mile Bridge connecting Marathon to the Lower Keys, built in the early 1980s at a cost of $45 million. To the right is the original bridge, built by Henry Flagler for his Overseas Railroad in the early years of the twentieth century. The fine structure took all the weather the Keys could throw its way, but the infamous Labor Day hurricane of 1935 destroyed the railroad and the bridge was converted into a highway. Now it's a fishing and jogging pier par excellence.

Entering the Lower Keys is like stepping back in time; it's easy to imagine that the rest of the Keys, now so commercial, must have looked like this 30 years ago. These islands are heavily wooded, primarily residential, and decidedly noncommercial.

The Lower Keys are where you find Bahia Honda State Park, located at MM 37 and one of the loveliest spots in the Keys. Attractions in the 300-acre park include a nationally ranked white sand beach, nature trails, plentiful bird life, snorkeling, and diving. It's a popular day-trip destination for Key Westers—or Conchs (pronounced "conks"), as they're called—with a yen for the feel of sand between their toes.

Big Pine Key is home to canine-sized Key deer, an endangered species under federal protection since 1952; the miniature white-tailed deer are only found on Big Pine Key and 16 surrounding keys.

Golf

Key Colony Golf & Tennis

MM 53.5, Eighth Street, Key Colony Beach; (305) 289-1533; www.keycolonybeach.net
Established 1952 (resort) | **Holes** 9

Fees $8.50 **Cart rental** $1 for pull cart **Club rental** $2 per person **Payment** All major credit cards accepted **Facilities** Small golf shop

Comments There are no tee times available at this 9-hole course, which is open for play from 7:30 a.m. until dusk. Built as part of the City of Key Colony Beach development, the course, one of few in the area, makes creative use of limited land. This is the place for duffers who can't last a weekend without swinging a club. It's also a great halfway break for families en route to Key West.

Shopping

KeyBana (Key Colony Beach Causeway in Marathon, MM 53.5; (305) 289-1161) carries a wide selection of brand name sportswear, swimwear, and accessories for men and women. There's also a good selection of women's shoes. It's another great place to stop if you're en route to Key West and looking for a leg stretcher—or if you forgot your bathing suit.

Dining

Cracked Conch Café

Overseas Highway, MM 49.5; (305) 743-2233

Meals served Lunch, dinner **Cuisine** American **Entree range** Lunch and dinner, $3–$20 **Reservations** Accepted **Payment** All major credit cards accepted

Comments For 24 years, Cracked Conch has been serving simple fare, including conch—conch Parmesan, cracked conch, conch chowder—and local seafood. There's also decent Cuban coffee, and authentic Key lime pie. You can dine indoors or outside on a shady little patio.

Herbie's Raw Bar

Overseas Highway, MM 50.5, Marathon; (305) 743-6373

Meals served Lunch, dinner **Cuisine** American **Entree range** Lunch $2–$6; dinner $9–$24 **Reservations** Not accepted **Payment** No credit cards

Comments Like a step back in time, this little restaurant offers outdoor picnic tables, an indoor bar, and a screened porch. The locals have frequented

Herbie's for nearly 30 years, since the days it was just a raw bar serving oysters and cold beer. Now the expansive menu includes ice-cold oysters, Florida lobster, and fresh catch—try the blackened grouper for a real treat.

The Restaurant on Little Palm Island

Overseas Highway, MM 28.5, Little Torch Key; (305) 872-2551

Meals served Breakfast, lunch and dinner **Cuisine** New American/Caribbean **Entree range** $25–$32 **Reservations** Required **Payment** V, MC, AmEx, DC

Comments Located on a hidden island—a 30-mile drive from Key West and a 20-minute boat ride provided by the management—the resort's restaurant building sits amid a profusion of tropical plants, an exclusive retreat for the rich and famous, including an occasional president. Lobster is the big seller, from a lobster martini to the chili-spiced chilled lobster, and lobster fettuccine with tarragon vanilla emulsion. Also recommended: Adam's crab cakes, the pan-seared yellow snapper, and red-lobster dumplings with watermelon relish and tamarind-pineapple jus.

Seven Mile Grill

Overseas Highway, MM 47, Marathon; (305) 743-4481

Meals served Lunch and dinner **Cuisine** American **Entree range** Lunch, $4–$8; dinner, $8–$12 **Reservations** Not accepted **Payment** V, MC

Comments Opened in 1954, the grill is one of the most popular home-style eateries along the Overseas Highway. Located right at the foot of the Seven Mile Bridge, this place is as basic as it gets—20 seats at the bar and it's open to the outside no matter what the weather. Try the conch chowder or any of the fried fish. And the Key lime pie is the real thing.

Sugarloaf Lodge

Overseas Highway, MM 17, Sugarloaf Key; (305) 745-3741

Meals served Breakfast, lunch, and dinner **Cuisine** American **Entree range** Breakfast, $4–$6; lunch, $7–$10; dinner, $10–$25 **Reservations** Not accepted **Payment** All major credit cards accepted

Comments Most of the clientele are hungry fishermen, and if you catch a fish, the restaurant will gladly cook it for you. Hearty breakfasts, burgers, sandwiches, and salads.

Nightlife

Brass Monkey

Who Goes There Watering hole frequented by locals

Marathon, MM 50; (305) 743-4028

Cover No **Minimum** No **Mixed drinks** $3.50–$5 **Food available** Lunch only **Hours** 10:30 a.m.–4 a.m.

What goes on Local live music, classic rock

Comments Beer and drinks are reasonably priced, entertainment is provided by a house band or juke box, and you dance wherever you can find the space (which may be next to the pool table). It attracts a fun-loving, friendly group of people. If you enjoy people-watching, this is definitely the place. If you like good, basic, loud rock 'n' roll music from the '60s through the '90s, Freddy Bye and his band provide the perfect background for a night of partying. Just tell Freddy what you want to hear—this guy can play just about anything that has been recorded. You don't need to get there early to reserve a table—this is a late-night place, and many of the Monkey's patrons arrive after other joints have closed.

Key West

As the Overseas Highway enters Key West, a sign for the far right lane reads: "Right Lane Go At All Times." Follow it to North Roosevelt Boulevard and on to Duval Street and Old Town Key West, full of bars, restaurants, hotels, bed and breakfasts, museums, galleries, blocks of charming old homes, and congested, narrow streets. If you go left as you enter Key West, you'll pass Houseboat Row, the Atlantic Ocean, snazzy resorts, Key West International Airport, Southernmost Point, and then Old Town.

If you're a first-time visitor, you might want to get oriented before you drive right into town. Park at the Welcome Center near the intersection of US 1 and North Roosevelt Boulevard and sign up for the next **Conch Tour Train:** an open-air, narrated "trolley"—really an open-air bus—that transports visitors around Key West and gives them an overview of the town.

Is it corny? You bet. The train's "engine" is a diesel-powered truck disguised as a locomotive, and even has a whistle. But the 90-minute tour is fun and informative.

With its rich, complicated history, Key West can be difficult for first-time visitors to grasp. A ride on the Conch Tour Train can help you understand why this city was once the wealthiest per capita in the United States, show that it once was the largest producer of natural sponges and cigars, explain its roles during the Civil War and the Cuban missile crisis of 1962, and reveal insights into why people such as John James Audubon, Ernest Hemingway, Harry Truman, Tennessee Williams, and Robert Frost came to identify with Key West.

You'll also gain some insight into the ups and downs this town of 30,000 people has endured over the centuries—from the boom years of the wreckers in the early 1800s to the depths of the Great Depression of the 1930s (the city declared bankruptcy in 1934), to its attempted secession from the United States in the 1980s. The tour will also help you understand the town's physical layout and show you attractions that you can go back and visit later on your own.

The Conch Tour Train leaves every 30 minutes from 9 a.m. to 4:30 p.m. daily. You can board at the Roosevelt Boulevard location or in Old Town's

Key West 507

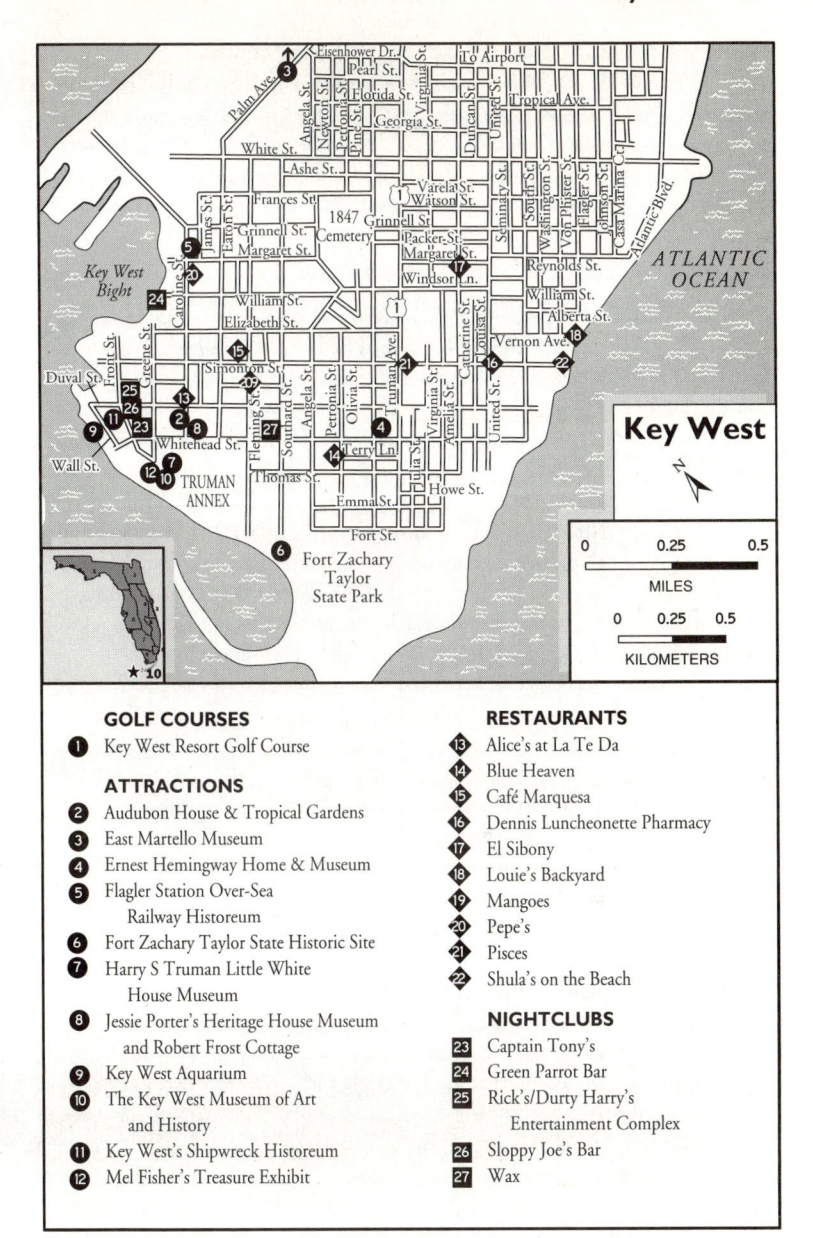

GOLF COURSES
1. Key West Resort Golf Course

ATTRACTIONS
2. Audubon House & Tropical Gardens
3. East Martello Museum
4. Ernest Hemingway Home & Museum
5. Flagler Station Over-Sea Railway Historeum
6. Fort Zachary Taylor State Historic Site
7. Harry S Truman Little White House Museum
8. Jessie Porter's Heritage House Museum and Robert Frost Cottage
9. Key West Aquarium
10. The Key West Museum of Art and History
11. Key West's Shipwreck Historeum
12. Mel Fisher's Treasure Exhibit

RESTAURANTS
13. Alice's at La Te Da
14. Blue Heaven
15. Café Marquesa
16. Dennis Luncheonette Pharmacy
17. El Sibony
18. Louie's Backyard
19. Mangoes
20. Pepe's
21. Pisces
22. Shula's on the Beach

NIGHTCLUBS
23. Captain Tony's
24. Green Parrot Bar
25. Rick's/Durty Harry's Entertainment Complex
26. Sloppy Joe's Bar
27. Wax

Mallory Square. Tickets are $20 for adults and $10 for children ages 4–12. Passengers can disembark in Old Town, wander around or get lunch, and catch the next "train" 30 minutes later. Call (305) 294-5161 for more information.

Another option for a guided tour is **Old Town Trolley,** open-air buses that shuttle visitors on a 90-minute, narrated tour of Key West. Unlike the Conch Tour Train, passengers can depart at any of 12 marked stops on the tour route and reboard another trolley later; many hotels are on the route. The tours depart every 30 minutes from 9:00 a.m. to 4:30 p.m. from Mallory Square. The tour is $20 for adults and $10 for children ages 5–12. For more information, call (305) 296-6688.

Old Town Key West

Compact Old Town, a square mile of restored houses that makes up the heart of Key West, is best viewed on foot or by bicycle. While main avenues such as Duval Street are frequently jammed with tourists, the side streets still ooze with the peculiar Key West charm that's made the town famous. As the many bike rental shops attest, Key West is a very bicycle-friendly town. Do yourself a favor and don't attempt driving a car down the narrow streets; walk or ride a bike.

While there's little evidence of anything but unbridled tourist schlock on the main drags, the residential streets frequently reveal glimpses of the anarchic spirit of its residents—even if it's only the sound of Bob Dylan's "Blonde on Blonde" blasting from a hippie crash pad at nine in the morning. And much of the architecture is beautiful, iconoclastic, and fun to look at.

Key West's tolerant spirit has made the town a mecca for gay people. The large population of homosexuals in Key West has given support to restoration efforts, pushed up the price of real estate, and given the town a solid economic boost.

Today's main tourist strip is the once-seedy Duval Street, renovated with well-manicured boutiques, T-shirt shops, bars, T-shirt shops, restaurants, T-shirt shops, galleries, beachwear shops, and other essentials to vacationing tourists. (Do your duty and buy a T-shirt!) For folks unfamiliar with the layout of Old Town, Duval Street serves as an anchor as it cuts a swath across the island from the Gulf of Mexico to the Atlantic Ocean.

On the Gulf end of Duval Street is **Mallory Square,** famous for its daily sunset celebration. The "square" is in fact a cramped old concrete wharf that hosts a mini street festival late each afternoon. During high tourist season, it's shoulder-to-shoulder along the dock with tourists, cruise-ship passengers, and street vendors selling anything from fruit-and-yogurt shakes to "Southernmost" falafels.

Key West–style free entertainment includes a troupe of trained cats (most impressive), a bowling ball juggler, an escape artist, innumerable Dylan clones strumming guitars, and the "Southernmost Bag Piper" (least impressive). You'll have trouble seeing any of this, though, because of the throngs.

For folks expecting a re-creation of Haight-Ashbury during the mid-1960s, Mallory Square is a letdown: No hippies pass joints to toast the setting sun, and no seafaring bohemians pass around a bottle of rum to mark the end of another day. Our opinion is that this famous "ritual" is touristy and overrated . . . at least when the crowds are overpowering. If crowds are not your thing, get up early one morning and check out the Key West sunrise on the east side of the island, over the Atlantic. Just as beautiful as the sunset, and a lot less noisy.

On the Atlantic side of Duval Street—actually, a block over on parallel Whitehead Street—is **Southernmost Point,** another example of Key West hype. A huge buoy perched on land and a placard mark the most southern point in the continental United States. But, as any schoolchild will readily point out, the land continues south a few yards to the water's edge—the real southernmost point. Still, you can't deny the draw of this otherwise undistinguished place: It's usually packed with tourists getting their picture taken in front of the buoy.

Behind the tourist schlock and commercialization, Key West still retains its quixotic charm. Our advice: To really enjoy Key West, get off Duval Street, wander its back roads, visit its unique and interesting museums, and get a handle on its rich history and local culture. Stop at an outdoor café for a two-hour lunch and hang out in bars that don't have T-shirt shops on the premises (which rules out Sloppy Joe's and Jimmy Buffett's Margaritaville). See a play at the Waterfront Playhouse or The Red Barn Theatre. Slow the pace, give it a chance, and you'll soon discover Key West's charms away from the crowds.

Cruise Ships

Speaking of crowds: Keep an eye peeled for huge cruise ships docked at the foot of Whitehead Street, near Mallory Square. Not that you'll have any trouble seeing them—the bigger ships tower over the docks and look like they could accommodate the entire population of Key West. The presence of one or more of the big ships could mean even bigger crowds along Duval and Whitehead streets, so try to tour away from the dock area until the ships leave. Restaurants, however, aren't usually affected: many of the cruise passengers return to their ships for meals.

Golf

Key West Resort Golf Course

6450 East College Road, Key West; (305) 294-5232; www.keywestgolf.com

Established 1960s; redesigned in 1983 | **Designer** Rees Jones | **Holes** 18

Tees Back/Middle/Forward **Par** 70/70/70 **Slope** 124/113/118

Fees $80 June–mid-October; $140 mid-October–May

Specials Twilight rates, $80 and $55 (seasonal) **Cart rental** Included in fees **Club rental** $30 **Payment** Credit cards accepted **Tee times** Taken seven days in advance **Facilities** Clubhouse with beverages, snacks, lunch. Lessons and golf school available.

Comments Key West's only public golf course covers 200 acres with palms, mangroves, and lakes. The infamous "Mangrove Hole" (#8, par 3) is played completely over a field of thickly intertwined tropical mangroves.

Attractions

Audubon House

205 Whitehead Street, Key West; (305) 294-2116

Hours Daily, 9:30 a.m.–5 p.m. (last tour at 4:30 p.m.)
Admission $9 for adults, $8 for seniors, $6.50 for students, $5 for children ages 6–12
Appeal by Age Group

Pre-school ★	Teens ★	Over 30 ★★★
Grade school ★	Young Adults ★★★	Seniors ★★★★

Touring Time *Average* 45 minutes; *minimum* 30 minutes
Rainy-Day Touring Recommended
Author's Rating ★★★; a beautifully restored house and gardens
Description and Comments Audubon House is the restored home of an early nineteenth-century Key West harbor pilot and wrecker, Captain Geiger. He and his heirs lived in the house for more than 120 years, but in 1958 the deteriorating structure was slated for demolition. Through the efforts of local conservationists, the house was saved and restored, decorated with exquisite period pieces collected in Europe, and dedicated as a museum commemorating the visits of painter and ornithologist John James Audubon. The restoration inaugurated a movement that saved many historically significant Key West buildings.

Though you must walk up, don't miss the children's room on the third floor; two pairs of nineteenth-century roller skates look like forerunners of in-line skates popular today. Outside, orchid-filled trees evoke the wealthy, cosmopolitan lifestyle of early Key West residents. Check out the duplex outhouse in the corner of the garden.

East Martello Museum

3501 South Roosevelt Boulevard, Key West; (305) 296-3913

Hours Daily, 9:30 a.m.–4:30 p.m. (last admission at 4 p.m.)
Admission $6 for adults, $4 seniors, $3 for students, $2 for children ages 7–12, free for military and for children under age 6.
Appeal by Age Group

Pre-school ★★★	Teens ★★★	Over 30 ★★★
Grade school ★★★★	Young Adults ★★★	Seniors ★★★

Touring Time *Average* 2 hours; *minimum* 1 hour
Rainy-Day Touring Recommended
Author's Rating ★★★; a bizarre museum with a little bit of everything
Description and Comments It might be easier to catalog what you won't find in this Civil War fort converted to an eclectic museum, but we'll give it a try. The low brick ceilings and arches of this old fort house a horse-drawn hearse and wicker casket (circa 1873), ship models, exhibits on

Native Americans, Civil War and Spanish American War military artifacts, a hotel safe, "junkyard" art, a deep-sea diver's air suit and a wooden air pump, and a crude raft used by Cubans to escape the Castro regime. Kids can play in the "junior museum"—a tiny house that adults must stoop over to enter—located on the well-manicured grounds. The climb up the lookout tower requires negotiating a steep spiral staircase. There's also an art museum that features temporary exhibits.

Ernest Hemingway Home and Museum

907 Whitehead Street, Key West; (305) 294-1575

Hours Daily, 9 a.m.–5 p.m.
Admission $10 for adults, $6 for children ages 6–12
Appeal by Age Group

Pre-school ★	Teens ★★	Over 30 ★★★★
Grade school ★★	Young Adults ★★★	Seniors ★★★★

Touring Time *Average* 1 hour; *minimum* 30 minutes
Rainy-Day Touring Recommended
Author's Rating ★★★★; an interesting slice of American literary history
Description and Comments Ernest Hemingway owned this Spanish-Colonial house, built in 1870, from 1931 until his death in 1961. In his study in the loft of his pool house he wrote some of his most famous novels and short stories, including *A Farewell to Arms*, *The Snows of Kilimanjaro*, and *For Whom the Bell Tolls*. The spacious mansion gives visitors a glimpse into genteel life in the 1930s. Much (but not all) of the furniture and memorabilia on display belonged to Hemingway, as well as the alleged descendants of his cats—about 40 roam the one-acre grounds. Go early in the morning, as the house isn't air conditioned, and take the 30-minute guided tour; the leaders are witty, literate and tell great stories about Hemingway.

Flagler Station Over-Sea Railway Historeum

901 Caroline Street, Key West; (305) 295-3562

Hours Daily, 9 a.m.–5 p.m.
Admission Adults, $2.50; children ages 12 and under, $1.75
Appeal by Age Group

Pre-school ★	Teens ★★	Over 30 ★★★
Grade school ★★	Young Adults ★★★	Seniors ★★★

Author's Rating ★★★; good films tout an interesting piece of not-so-widely-known history
Description and Comments This small collection of clothing, contracts, photos, building materials, and other bits of history are accented by three highly enjoyable and informative films about Henry Flagler's goal to build the first railway from Miami to Key West. The first film is 13½-minutes long and runs continuously—it makes the most sense to see it from the

beginning, but you can pick it up at any time and watch through the loop. It takes four minutes to rewind between showings, so it is relatively easy to catch it at the beginning. The film, entitled *The Day the Train Arrived,* is about Flagler's personal drive and the actual building of the railway. The second film, *The Seven-Mile Bridge,* lasts about three minutes and is a quick synopsis of bridge and railroad construction—especially as it related to this specific project. The last film, *A Trip down the Florida Keys,* is an eight-minute narrative of life in the Keys before and after construction of the railway. There are limited seating/viewing areas, and since it doesn't matter which order films are viewed, choose based on which screen you can see best.

Fort Zachary Taylor State Historic Site

Southard Street (in the Truman Annex), Key West; (305) 292-6713

Hours Daily, 8 a.m.–sundown

Admission $2.50 for a car with one person, $5 with two people, 50 cents for each additional person

Appeal by Age Group

Pre-school ★★★★	Teens ★★★★	Over 30 ★★★★
Grade school ★★★★	Young Adults ★★★★	Seniors ★★★★

Touring Time *Average* a half-day; *minimum* 2–3 hours

Rainy-Day Touring Not recommended

Author's Rating ★★★★; a triple hit: a neat fort, interesting history, and a beach you can snorkel from. Free guided tours of the fort are offered at noon and 2 p.m., daily. And there's a great view of the sunset.

Description and Comments For 145 years Fort Zachary Taylor defended the harbor of Key West. During the Civil War it was one of four Union forts in Confederate territory that never fell into Southern hands. As a result, hundreds of cannon trained on the nearby shipping lanes kept ships bottled up in Key West throughout the Civil War. The workmanship of the exquisite brickwork throughout the fort couldn't be duplicated today.

Over the years the old fort structure has become landlocked, creating a pleasant man-made beach for swimming and snorkeling. There's also a great view of the Gulf of Mexico from the top of the fort.

Harry S Truman Little White House Museum

111 Front Street (one block up Caroline Street through the presidential gates), Key West; (305) 294-9911

Hours Daily, 9 a.m.–4:30 p.m.; guided tours leave every 15 minutes or so

Admission Adults, $10; children ages 12 and under, $5

Appeal by Age Group

Pre-school ★	Teens ★	Over 30 ★★
Grade school ★	Young Adults ★★	Seniors ★★★

Touring Time 1 hour

Rainy-Day Touring Recommended

Author's Rating ★★; a nostalgia trip for folks old enough to remember "Give 'Em Hell" Harry.

Description and Comments President Harry Truman spent 175 vacation days during his presidency (1945–53) at this house in Key West. Today the building is completely redone to posh 1949 standards, although most of the furnishings aren't original. One exception is the custom-made mahogany poker table. The guide tells visitors that while Truman disapproved of gambling in the White House, poker playing with "the boys" was a major form of relaxation for the president when he was vacationing in Key West.

The tour, which includes some steep stairs, begins with a ten-minute video that evokes the Truman era and primes visitors for the tour. The guides offer interesting tidbits about Truman's personal life when vacationing in Key West. For example, Bess Truman didn't often accompany her husband because she preferred their home in Independence, Missouri. Don't miss the gift shop, which sells aprons inscribed, you guessed it, "If you can't stand the heat, get out of the kitchen."

Jessie Porter's Heritage House and Robert Frost Cottage

410 Caroline Street, Key West; (305) 296-3573

Hours Monday–Saturday, 10 a.m.–4 p.m.; Closed Sundays.

Admission Adults, $7; seniors, $5; students, $3; children under age 12, free

Appeal by Age Group

Pre-school ★	Teens ★★	Over 30 ★★★
Grade school ★	Young Adults ★★★	Seniors ★★★

Touring Time 30 minutes

Rainy-Day Touring Recommended

Author's Rating ★★★; fascinating stuff—worth a look

Description and Comments Jessie Porter, a granddaughter of one of Key West's founders, was a friend to famous writers such as Ernest Hemingway, Tennessee Williams, and Robert Frost. In addition to photos of a few of America's great literary stars and some original manuscripts, the 1830s sea captain's home is filled with priceless artifacts, unique furnishings, musical instruments, exquisite silk kimonos . . . the list goes on and on. In the backyard is a small cottage where poet Robert Frost spent many winters. While it's not open to the public, the tour guide plays a tape of Frost reading one of his poems. Touring tips: Look for the marijuana leaves imprinted in the handmade tiles around the fireplace. The freshwater well outside the front door was used by Native Americans as early as the twelfth century.

Key West Aquarium

1 Whitehead Street, Key West; (305) 296-2051

Hours Daily, 10 a.m–6 p.m.; guided tours and feedings at 11 a.m. and 1, 3, and 4:30 p.m.

Admission $9 for adults, $4.50 for children ages 4–12. Tickets are good for 2 days

Appeal by Age Group

Pre-school ★★★	Teens ★★	Over 30 ★★
Grade school ★★★	Young Adults ★★	Seniors ★★

Touring Time *Average* 1½ hours; *minimum* 1 hour
Rainy-Day Touring Recommended
Author's Rating ★★; great for the kids, but otherwise a bit ho-hum
Description and Comments This old-fashioned aquarium is small but comfortable and will especially please younger children. At the touch tank, kids can handle conch, starfish, and crabs. You'll probably never get closer to a shark unless you hook one. This aquarium has been around since 1932, the first tourist attraction built in the Florida Keys.

Key West Lighthouse Museum

938 Whitehead Street, Key West; (305) 294-0012

Hours Daily, 9:30 a.m.–5 p.m.; closed Christmas
Admission Adults, $8; children ages 6–12, $4

Appeal by Age Group

Pre-school ★★	Teens ★★★★	Over 30 ★★★★
Grade school ★★★★	Young Adults ★★★★	Seniors ★★★

Touring Time *Average* 1½ hours; *minimum* 1 hour
Rainy-Day Touring Not recommended
Author's Rating ★★★★; a great view and interesting history in an 1848 lighthouse
Description and Comments Folks who aren't in shape or don't like heights should skip this climb to the top of a 90-foot lighthouse. But the 88 steps to the top lead to an impressive view of the Atlantic Ocean, the Gulf of Mexico, and cruise ships docked in the harbor. The nearby museum (formerly the Keeper's Quarters when this was an operating lighthouse) is small, dark, cool, and filled with fascinating artifacts from the days when the big light atop the tower guided navigators through the treacherous waters outside Key West.

The Key West Museum of Art and History

281 Front Street, Key West; (305) 295-6616

Hours Daily, 9 a.m.–5 p.m.
Admission Adults, $6; seniors and locals, $5; children ages 7–17, $4; children ages 6 and under free

Appeal by Age Group

Pre-school ★★	Teens ★★	Over 30 ★★★
Grade school ★★	Young Adults ★★	Seniors ★★★

Touring Time 1 hour

Rainy-Day Touring Recommended

Author's Rating ★★★; beautiful architecture housing varied and interesting works

Description and Comments The Key West Museum of Art and History at the Custom House has several permanent exhibits. These include a room dedicated to (and funded by) Wilhelmina Harvey, who calls herself Key West's most famous political celebrity. You can also find the work of Stanley Papio, sculptor of amusing characters from all sorts of scrap metal junk, and the woodcarvings of local artist Mario Sanchez. He creates intricately carved three-dimensional scenes representing different aspects of life in Key West in a folk art style. Additionally, the permanent collection of art and history of Key West, including the history and restoration of the Custom House will be completed by fall 2001. This will also include pieces of the past permanent exhibit "The U.S.S. Maine" as it relates to the history of Key West.

Key West Shipwreck Historeum

1 Whitehead Street at Mallory Square, Key West; (305) 292-8990

Hours Daily, 9:45 a.m.–4:45 p.m.; shows begin 15 minutes before and after the hour

Admission $8 for adults, $4 for children ages 4–12, free for children under age 4

Appeal by Age Group

Pre-school ★★	Teens ★★★	Over 30 ★★★★
Grade school ★★★	Young Adults ★★★★	Seniors ★★★★

Touring Time *Average* 1 hour; *minimum* 45 minutes

Rainy-Day Touring Recommended

Author's Rating ★★★★; talented actors, interesting history

Description and Comments Drift back in time as Asa Tift, a famous nineteenth-century Key West wrecker, greets you in his warehouse as a potential crew member. Listen to the story of how Key West became the "richest city in the U.S.A." when the vessel Isaac Allerton sank in 1856. A 20-minute video depicts the life of the wreckers and their fight to save lives and precious cargo from ships doomed by the dangerous reefs. Much of the story is told through comments and stories from some of Key West's prominent figures of the time. The Historeum is not wheelchair accessible. You must descend several stairs to where the movie is shown, and the museum tour involves several flights of stairs. The lookout tower provides a bird's eye view of the historic district and the barrier reef, but it requires visitors to climb nine flights of stairs. Those afraid of heights might want to skip this part of the attraction. But if you're up for the climb, you will be rewarded with a spectacular vista.

Mel Fisher's Treasure Exhibit

200 Greene Street, Key West; (305) 294-2633

Hours Daily, 9:30 a.m.–5 p.m.; the last video presentation is at 4:30
Admission $9 for adults, $4.50 for children ages 6–12
Appeal by Age Group

Pre-school ★★★	Teens ★★★★	Over 30 ★★★
Grade school ★★★★	Young Adults ★★★★	Seniors ★★★

Touring Time *Average* 1 hour; *minimum* 45 minutes
Rainy-Day Touring Recommended
Author's Rating ★★; impressive booty, a small exhibit, and plenty of self-promotional schlock
Description and Comments Ever dreamed of finding a trove of treasure worth millions? Well, Mel Fisher, the best-known salvager in the Keys, did—a bar of solid silver, a solid gold dinner plate, pieces of eight in a cedar chest, and cannon and sailors' artifacts from the seventeenth century are among the items on display in this small museum. Exhibits also explain how modern treasure hunters find the ancient wrecks and bring the loot up from the bottom of the sea. Yet the relentless self-promotion and commercialism of this private museum—not to mention its small size—are a letdown.

R.I.P.

For a look at a wacky side of Key West that's managed to avoid the rest of the island's commercialism, spend an hour in the early morning or late afternoon in the Key West Cemetery, the final resting place of many prominent—and unusual—Key West residents. You can wander on your own, but guides can explain how the high water table and tough coral rock created the unusual burial practices in this corner of paradise—everyone here is "buried" above ground. As a result, the cemetery is filled with coffin-shaped tombs, many of them stacked on top of one another like mortuary condominiums. In addition, pets are often interred next to their owners.

The main gate is at Margaret and Angela streets. Guided tours depart the main gate Tuesday and Thursday mornings at 9:30 a.m.; the cost is $10 per person. The most inspired headstone inscription in the cemetery may be that of a famous Key West hypochondriac, Mrs. B. P. Roberts: "I told you I was sick."

Shopping

Shopping is major sport in Key West, from T-shirt shops (too many) to chic boutiques. Start your spree on Duval Street, home to everything from national retailers to unusual boutiques and galleries. Strolling Duval you'll find the **Key Lime Pie Factory** (1209 Truman Avenue; (305) 293-6667); **Fast Buck Freddie's** (500 Duval Street; (305) 294-2007), the city's most renowned department store with imaginative gifts, bathing suits, casual clothes and imported decorative items from around the world; **Gingerbread Square Gallery** (1207 Duval Street; (305) 296-8900); **Island Store** (712-B Duval Street; (305) 292-0409), featuring one of the largest collections of handcrafted Haitian metal sculpture in the U.S; **Key West Havana Cigar Co.** (1117 Duval Street; (800) 217-4884); casual cotton clothes in **The Official Conch Republic Store** (817 Duval Street; (305) 296-1976); **Sloppy Joe's Store** (201 Duval Street West; (305) 294-5717); **Wings of Imagination** butterfly shop (291 Front Street; (305) 296-2922); and **Wyland Gallery** (719 Duval Street; (305) 292-4998).

Two blocks north, Simonton Street has the **Pelican Poop Shoppe** (314 Simonton Street; (305) 296-3887) for Caribbean art and **Key West Handprint Fashions** (201 Simonton Street; (305) 294-9535) with original copyrighted prints designed by Key West artists for more than 30 years.

Near the waterfront, a true Key West experience is a stop at **Key West Aloe** (524 Front Street; (800) 445-2563), which has sold popular, lightly scented aloe vera products since 1971. **The Original Key West Cigar Factory** (306 Front Street; (305) 294-3470) opened in 1963 when there were few cigar factories remaining in Key West from the turn of the century. All of the cigars, including the popular El Hemingway, are still hand rolled using the traditions of the past.

Other shops we like: **Blue Island Store** (718 Caroline Street; (305) 292-5172) features super-sleek, sophisticated women's clothing—classic linen or silk pants, chic shoes, great handbags for a blend of classy and cool. **Half Buck Freddie's** (726 Caroline Street; (305) 294-2007) is the discount store for Fast Buck Freddie's, carrying out-of-season bargains. And for art, one of the best shops is **Haitian Art Co.** (600 Frances Street; (305) 296-8932), where there's something for most any budget.

And some finds for foodies: **Baby's Coffee** (US 1, MM 15; (800) 523-2326) roasts 23 varieties of coffee beans in small batches and ships it all over the world. The name, by the way, comes from the original location on Duval Street, owned by a Cuban family who christened it "Baby's Place" in the 1920s. The coffee shop outgrew the original storefront, but it's worth the trek for a cup. **Key West Lime Shoppe** (200-A Elizabeth Street; (800) 376-0806) is a real treat, featuring cookies, candy, salad dressings, even bath and body products made with Key limes.

Dining

Alice's at La Te Da

1125 Duval Street, Key West; (305) 296-6706; www.aliceskeywest.com

Meals served Breakfast, lunch, and dinner; Sunday brunch **Cuisine** New world fusion **Entree range** $8–$25 **Reservations** Yes **Payment** All major credit cards accepted

Comments The restaurant's name comes from the original name of the building, La Terraza de Marti, shortened to La Te Da. Once a hotel with dubious credentials, La Te Da has been spiffed up and is now more mainstream. Chef and owner Alice Weingarten chooses the best local produce and seafood, then unleashes her creativity with dishes like a sublime Tahitian pan-roasted chicken scented with vanilla, or a ceviche martini appetizer with gazpacho. Alice prefers to choose a wine to accompany your selection.

Blue Heaven

729 Thomas Street, Key West; (305) 296-8666

Meals served Breakfast, lunch, and dinner **Cuisine** Fine American **Entree range** Breakfast, $4–$12; lunch, $7–$12 lunch; dinner, $20–$40 **Reservations** Not accepted, and the wait can be long **Payment** V, MC, D

Comments This restaurant's backyard is intriguing—heroic roosters from the days when the restaurant offered a cockfighting pit are buried in a graveyard behind the dining area. Today, cats and birds still roam around the dirt-floored patio among the tables. It's the kind of place that inspires songs—like Jimmy Buffett's "Blue Heaven Rendezvous."

The breakfast is ethereal; they're famous for their homemade pancakes with pure maple syrup and their homemade granola (served with cow's milk or soy milk). For lunch or dinner, try the delectable Caribbean shrimp dinner, the jerk chicken, or anything from the large selection of vegetarian items. Just save room for the flamed Banana Heaven dessert. Expect a wait.

Café Marquesa

600 Fleming Street, Key West; (305) 292-1919

Meals served Dinner **Cuisine** American **Entree range** $27–$37 **Reservations** Yes **Payment** TK

Comments One of Key West's most elegant, popular restaurants to celebrate a special occasion because it's regarded the best. Situated in the charming, well-appointed Marquesa Hotel, the open kitchen is set behind a giant trompe l'oeil wall painting of a kitchen scene. Large mahogany framed mirrors give diners a larger perspective on this small 50-seat dining room. The menu changes daily, featuring seafood, beef and poultry.

Dennis Pharmacy Luncheonette

1229 Simonton Street, Key West; (305) 294-1577

Meals served Breakfast and lunch **Cuisine** Spanish/American **Entree range** $4–$11 **Reservations** Not necessary **Payment** All major credit cards accepted

Comments A Key West landmark for 35 years, this classic drugstore lunch counter is famous for daily specials and the "Cheeseburger in Paradise." They also make an excellent picadillo, with spicy ground beef spiked with olives, and traditional Cuban sandwiches. Kids love the rotating barstools and visiting the drugstore's toy department while the food is prepared.

El Siboney

900 Catherine Street, Key West; (305) 296-4184

Meals served Lunch and dinner **Cuisine** Cuban **Entree range** $7–$16 **Reservations** Not accepted **Payment** No credit cards

Comments Not much to look at, but step inside this family-style restaurant for traditional Cuban cuisine. The Siboneys were Cuban Indians, and this authentic eatery is a tribute to them. The heaping portions of roast pork and grilled garlic chicken keep the locals coming back, as do traditional Cuban side dishes like crusty fried plantains and garlicky yucca. Waitresses are happy to guide you through the menu.

Louie's Backyard

700 Waddell Street, Key West; (305) 294-1061

Meals served Lunch and dinner **Cuisine** Seafood **Entree range** Lunch $9–$18; dinner $28–$39 **Reservations** Yes **Payment** All major credit cards accepted

Comments Nestled among a profusion of tropical foliage, flowering bougainvillea, and hibiscus, the restaurant looks out on a dockside dining deck that sits on the sandy beach. This is a popular, attractive restaurant that typifies the laid-back Key West character. The menu changes three to four times a year, but favorite you'll often find include Gulf shrimp and shellfish paella with sausage; boar, rabbit and quail with polenta; lamb; Bahamian conch chowder with bird pepper hot sauce salad.

Mangoes

700 Duval Street, Key West; (305) 292-4606

Meals served Lunch and dinner **Cuisine** Caribbean **Entree range** Lunch $6–$15; dinner $12–$25 **Reservations** Not accepted **Payment** All major credit cards accepted

Comments Quaint Mangoes is on touristy Duval Street, but the locals love the family-friendly place. Creative Florida seafood dominates the menu, and pizza prepared in the wood-burning oven is a favorite.

Pepe's

806 Caroline Street, Key West; (305) 294-7192

Meals served Breakfast, lunch, and dinner **Cuisine** American **Entree range** $5–$27.25 **Reservations** Not accepted **Payment** V, MC, D

Comments This marina-front landmark has been around since 1909. Parents might want to order Pepe's Steak Dinner for Two, their most-requested dish. And don't pass up the warm coconut bread if they've been baking that day. The Sunday night barbecue is a weekly tradition, as well as a full Thanksgiving dinner every Thursday. And there's a toy box to keep kids happy.

Pisces

1007 Simonton Street, Key West; (305) 294-7100

Meals served Dinner **Cuisine** French/Caribbean **Entree range** $26–$55 **Reservations** Recommended **Payment** V, MC, AmEx

Comments This restaurant, said to have been built by one of the Al Capone gang in 1934, offers an opportunity—rare in the Keys—to dine elegantly on French food that contains interesting Caribbean nuances. Though there are no windows, walls are decorated with colorful art.

Shula's on the Beach

Wyndham Reach Resort, 1435 Simonton Street, Key West; (305) 296-5000

Meals served Dinner **Cuisine** Steakhouse **Entree range** $20–$30 **Reservations** Strongly recommended **Payment** All major credit cards accepted

Comments Excellent service and fine china and crystal add to the elegance of the decor, while huge cuts of meat and larger-than-life lobsters can be savored while watching the sunset far in the distance. Try the Oysters Rockefeller, lobster bisque, barbecue shrimp stuffed with fresh basil wrapped in applewood bacon, or the certified Angus beef selections, including 16-ounce New York strip, 12-ounce filet mignon, 24-ounce porterhouse steak, and 22-ounce cowboy steak. Also good are the gigantic lobsters and steak Mary Anne—two 5-ounce filet mignons with a creamy peppercorn sauce.

Arts and Culture

Key West has a lively arts community, with more than three dozen art galleries showing notable works. The Key West Art Gallery Association publishes a brochure with a map and brief descriptions of the specialty of each of its 22 members. **Key West Art Center** (301 Front Street) is a non-profit artist cooperative where members, who must be local property owners, show their work. **Gingerbread Square** (1207 Duval Street), the oldest private gallery in Key West, represents many of the best artists.

Nightlife

In Key West, where laid-back bars—many of which feature a combination of reggae and karaoke—rule over the flashy disco scene favored in Miami, some of the more popular haunts include the open-air **Schooner Wharf Bar** (202 Williams Street; (305) 292-9520), open 8 a.m.–4 a.m. with live music Thursday–Saturday. The **Green Parrot Bar** (see below) is another good choice for a little piece of Key West, with prime people-watching. The Sunday evening tea dance at the **Atlantic Shores Motel** (510 South Street; (305) 296-2491) features a disco overlooking the pier and a largely gay clientele. Martini bars such as **Wax** (422 Appelrouth Lane; (305) 296-6667) and cocktail lounges such as **Virgilio's** (Appelrouth Lane; (305) 296-8118) offer an alternative to the traditional Margaritaville scene.

Captain Tony's

Who Goes There Ages 25–40; locals and tourists, spring breakers

428 Greene Street, Key West; (305) 294-1838

Cover None **Minimum** None **Mixed drinks** $4 and up **Food available** None
Hours Monday–Saturday, 10 a.m.–2 a.m.; Sunday, noon–2 a.m.

What goes on This is one of the Keys' legendary bars, owned since the 1960s by local character Captain Tony, who is 77, has been married seven times, has 13 children, and was even elected mayor (1988–91). Captain Tony, who originally came to the Keys as a fisherman in the 1940s, occasionally drops by the bar, amusing patrons with incredible stories, such as how he used to give Jimmy Buffett $10 a day, plus all he could drink. In case Captain Tony doesn't show, there are live musical acts daily, starting in the afternoons. Music is truly eclectic, ranging from Nirvana to the Top 40 hits of the 1950s. In case you experience déjà vu, the bar site is the former location of the original Sloppy Joe's, before it moved to Duval Street.

Comments An amusing hodgepodge of bar patrons past, with mementos stuffed everywhere. Wall-to-wall business cards, musical instruments, license plates, celebrity bar stools, a plane propeller, and even a bra dangling from the ceiling. Folklore has it that the bar's tip bell was stolen from an old Key West fire truck by none other than Hemingway himself, according to Captain Tony. You can wear cut-offs and flip flops, but shoes and shirts are requested at night. Try the house pirate's punch, a gin/rum/fruit-juice concoction served in a 22-ounce souvenir jug.

Green Parrot Bar

Who Goes There 21–75; locals, tourists, New Yorkers escaping the rat race

601 Whitehead Street, Key West; (305) 294-6133

Cover None **Minimum** None **Mixed drinks** $3 and up **Food available** None **Hours** Monday–Saturday, 10 a.m.–4 a.m.; Sunday, noon–4 a.m.

What goes on Open since 1890, this popular bar features live entertainment every Saturday with reggae, rock, and blues from 10 p.m. to 4 a.m. Once a month, poetry slams liven up Sundays with open readings. Occasionally, single acts perform on Saturday afternoons. Several years back, the bar's propensity for attracting the most eligible bachelors in town was noted in *Playboy* magazine.

Comments This is an open-air bar, known to display bold (if not quality) art, with the outside walls covered in various themes (i.e., sports, slice-of-life, Jamaica). Two pool tables, two deluxe pinball machines, three dart boards, and an eclectically stocked jukebox add to the bar's breezy, laid-back charm. Dress is Key West casual. Happy hour runs 4–7 p.m., seven days a week, with $2.25 mixed drinks, $1 draft, and $1.50 domestic beer.

Rick's/Durty Harry's Entertainment Complex

Who Goes There A cross-section of Key West humanity, 20- to whatever-somethings, college-aged karaokeaholics, thirsty tourists

200 Duval Street, Key West; (305) 296-4890

Cover None **Minimum** None **Mixed drinks** $3.25 and up **Food available** Peanuts **Hours** Monday–Saturday, 11 a.m.–4 a.m.; Sunday, noon–4 a.m.

What goes on You'll never be bored in this five-bars-in-one entertainment complex, which features live performers daily 3–11 p.m. in Durty Harry's Bar; karaoke at Rick's downstairs bar from 11 p.m. to closing (4 a.m.); dancing with three bars and an open deck upstairs at Rick's upstairs bar; adult entertainment with two stages, a bar, and a private dance floor at the 21-and-older Red Garter Saloon; and al fresco cocktailing at the Tree Bar, which fronts Duval Street. Local comedian/musician Steven Neil performs Thursday through Monday evenings. Music offerings are typically reggae and rock.

Comments New rustic. Dark wood bars—the one in the Tree Bar is so massive it spans the entire length of the space—and dim lighting pretty much sum up the decor, which relies on the local color for aesthetics.

Sloppy Joe's Bar

Who Goes There A mix of humanity, from local barflies to Midwestern tourists

201 Duval Street, Key West; (305) 294-5717

Cover None, unless it's a special event **Minimum** None **Mixed drinks** $4.25 and up **Food available** Light menu including appetizers, salads, and sandwiches **Hours** Monday–Saturday, 9 a.m.–4 a.m.; Sunday, noon–4 a.m.

What goes on Famed for being the local watering hole of Ernest Hemingway, this bar has gained a following with both locals and the international tourist crowd. The Hemingway Days Festival, which originated at the bar in 1981, has now become a world-renowned week-long event. The bar continues to host the outrageous Hemingway Look-A-Like Contest in mid-July. Entertainment goes on all day and night, with a varied selection of country duets, rock, and blues vocalists.

Comments Everything about the bar reads "sit back, relax, and have fun." There is an enormous amount of memorabilia on Hemingway and George Russell (Hemingway's friend and owner of the bar). The original long, curving bar, ceiling fans, and jalousie doors open on busy Duval Street. Note the Depression-era mural of Russell, Hemingway, and Skinner. Check out the constant drink specials, including the bar's Hemingway Hammer and Key Lime shooter, priced from $3–$7.

Wax

Who Goes There 25–35, hip out-of-towners and locals, both gay and straight, looking for a little bit of urban decorum (or not) in relaxed Key West

422 Appelrouth Lane, Key West; (305) 296-6667

Cover On weekends and special events **Minimum** None **Mixed drinks** $5 and up **Food available** None **Hours** Monday–Sunday, 9 p.m.–4 a.m.

What goes on Evenings start on a relatively mellow note at this two-year-old establishment, with well-dressed patrons sipping cocktails and oversized martinis. The scene gradually progresses into a frenzied nightclub, with self-liberated souls dancing on banquettes and every other available surface. Local DJs spin house music every night, with national DJs making guest appearances when in the area.

Comments This urban cocktail-lounge-meets-dance-club is tiny but packs in 250 people on a weekend night. Chinese red–lacquered walls, plush red velvet benches, and steel tables and bar give Wax the look of a sleekly modern bordello. An outside courtyard bar in the back provides relief for those needing to escape the chaos and remember they are indeed in tropical Key West.

Side Trips

Fort Jefferson and the Dry Tortugas For a little adventure, take a day trip to Fort Jefferson and the Dry Tortugas, a nineteenth-century coastal fortification 70 miles west of Key West that's only accessible by boat or seaplane.

Fort Jefferson is on Garden Key, a national monument administered by the National Park Service. You can explore the stone fort that was begun in 1846 and never completed, though in the late 1800s it was used as a prison.

Most visitors take the trip to snorkel or dive in the warm waters, abundant with fish and corals, and inhabited by four species of endangered sea turtles. (Tortugas is Spanish for "turtle.") If you're not a snorkeler, try the bird-watching, which is fabulous, with more than 100 species spotted, partly because Garden Key is in the path of migration for birds between North and South America.

Seaplanes of Key West offers full- and half-day flights to Fort Jefferson and the Dry Tortugas that include coolers, ice, sodas, and snorkeling gear—all you need to bring is a towel and a camera. Half-day trips depart daily in the mornings and afternoons; prices are $179 for adults, $129 for children ages 7–12, and $99 for children ages 2–6. The 70-mile flight is 40 minutes each way; the plane flies at low altitude so passengers can view the clear waters, shipwrecks, and marine life. You spend two hours hours on the island. Full-day trips are $305 for adults, $225 for children ages 7–12, and $170 for children ages 2–6. For reservations, call (305) 294-0709.

Another option for visiting Fort Jefferson and the Dry Tortugas is the **Fort Jefferson Ferry,** which sails out of Lands End Marina (251 Margaret Street in Key West) for full-day excursions. The 100-foot *Yankee Freedom* boasts a large, air-conditioned salon with a chef's galley, a large sundeck, and freshwater showers for swimmers, snorkelers, and divers. The ferry departs seven days a week (weather permitting) at 8 a.m. and returns at 5:30 p.m.; it's three hours each way, and visitors can enjoy about four hours on the island (including a complete tour of the fort). The price for the all-day trip is $119 for adults, $109 for seniors ages 62 and older, and $79 for children ages 16 and under. For schedule and booking information, call (800) 634-0939 or (305) 294-7009.

Accommodations Index

Adam's Mark Hotels, 32, 36
Agustin Inn, St. Augustine, 34
Alexander Hotel, Miami Beach, 47
All-Star Resort, Walt Disney World, 38–40
Ambassador Beach Condominium, Panama City, 27
Ambrosia House, Key West, 55
Amelia Island hotels and resorts, 30
Americano Beach Resort, Daytona Beach, 36
AmericInn Hotel & Suites, Sarasota, 44
AmeriSuites, 38–40
Amy Slate's Dive Resort, Florida Keys, 53
Anastasia Inn B&B, St. Augustine Beach, 35
Anchor Court Apartments & Motel, St. Petersburg, 41
Anchorage Inn, St. Augustine Beach, 35
Animal Kingdom Lodge, Walt Disney World, 38–40
Apalachicola hotels and resorts, 28
Artist House, Key West, 55
Ash Street Inn, Amelia Island, 30
Atlantic Shores Motel, Key West, 55
Avalon Bed & Breakfast, Key West, 55
Avalon Majestic Hotel, South Beach, 52

Bailey House, Amelia Island, 30
Bal Harbor, Sheraton, 50–51
Bambi Motel, Gainesville, 31
Bay Beach Inn, Pensacola, 23
Baymont Inn & Suites
  Broward County, 48
  Gainesville, 31
  Miami, 50–51
  Space Coast, 37
  Walt Disney World, 38–40
Baymont Inn, Naples, 58
Baymont Tampa, Brandon, 42–43

Baymont Tampa Fairgrounds, Tampa, 42–43
Baymont Tampa Inn & Suites, Tampa, 42–43
Beach & Yacht Club Resort, Walt Disney World, 38–40
Beach Club Villas, Walt Disney World, 38–40
Beach House, Destin, 25
Beach Landing Motel, Jacksonville, 32
Beach Palms, Sarasota, 44
Beach Plaza Hotel, South Beach, 52
Beach Street Cottages, Destin, 25
Beach Suites Resort, St. Petersburg, 41
Beach Tower Resort Motel, Panama City, 27
Beach View Cottages, Sanibel Island, 59
Beachbreak by the Sea, Panama City, 27
Beachcomber, Daytona Beach, 36
Beachcomber by the Sea, Panama City, 27
Beachcomber Motel, Daytona Beach, 36
Beacher's Lodge Oceanfront Suites, St. Augustine Beach, 35
Beachside Inn, Destin, 25
Beachside Motel, Amelia Island, 30
Beachside Motel, Daytona Beach, 36
Beachside Resort & Conference Center, Pensacola, 23
Beachwood Motel on the Ocean, Treasure Coast, 45
Beacon Motel & Gift Shop, Fort Myers Beach, 57
Bel Mar Resort, Naples, 58
Bentley Hotel, South Beach, 52
Best Value Inn Beach Resort, Panama City, 27
Best Western
  Airport Inn, Walt Disney World, 38–40
  All Suites, Treasure Coast, 45
  Apalach Inn, Apalachicola, 28

Accommodations Index 525

Beach Resort, Fort Myers Beach, 57
Beach Resort, Miami Beach, 47
Beach Resort, Sanibel Island, 59
Beachcomber, Broward County, 48
Beachfront Hotel, Fort Walton, 24
Beachfront Resort, St. Petersburg, 41
Casa Loma Motel, Panama City, 27
Del Coronado, Panama City, 27
Gateway to the Keys, Florida Keys, 53
Hibiscus Motel, Key West, 55
Historical Inn, St. Augustine, 34
Inn, Amelia Island, 30
Key Ambassador, Key West, 54
Lake Buena Vista South, Walt Disney World, 38–40
Mainsail Inn & Suites, Daytona Beach, 36
Marathon, Florida Keys, 53
Mayan Inn, Daytona Beach, 36
Naples, 58
Navarre, 24
Oceanfront, Jacksonville, 32
Oceanfront Resort, Miami, 50–51
Oceanfront Resort, Space Coast, 37
Oceanside Inn, Broward County, 48
Pelican Beach Resort, Broward County, 48
Pink Shell Beach Resort, Fort Myers Beach, 57
Resort, Pensacola, 23
Sea Wake Beach Resort, Clearwater, 41
Seminole Inn, Tallahassee, 29
Siesta Beach Resort, Sarasota, 44
Space Shuttle Inn, Space Coast, 37
St. Augustine I-95, 34
Suites at Key Largo, Florida Keys, 53
Summer Place Inn, Destin, 25
Treasure Island, St. Petersburg, 41
University Inn, Palm Beach, 46
Vero Beach, 45
Waterfront, Fort Myers, 56
Bikini Beach Resort, Panama City, 27
Bilmar Beach Resort, St. Petersburg, 41
Biltmore Hotel, Miami, 50–51
Biscayne Bay hotels, 50–51
Blue Marlin, Key West, 55
Blue Moon, South Beach, 52
Boardwalk Inn & Suites, Daytona Beach, 36
Boardwalk Inn & Villas, Walt Disney World, 38–40
Boat House Motel, Marco Island, 60
Boca Raton hotels and resorts, 46
Bonita Beach Resort, Naples, 58
Bonita Springs lodging, 58

Brandon lodging, 42–43
Breakers Beach Oceanfront Motel, Daytona Beach, 36
Breakers Palm Beach, Palm Beach, 46
Brigham Gardens, South Beach, 52
Broward County hotels and resorts, 48
Bryant House B&B, Apalachicola, 28
Bucaneer Inn, Apalachicola, 28
Budget Inn, 31, 35
Buena Vista, Apalachicola, 28
Buttonwood Cottages, Sanibel Island, 59

Cabbage Key Restaurant, Bar and Inn, 402
Cabot Lodge, Gainesville, 31
Canopy Palms Resort, Palm Beach, 46
Captiva Island lodging, 59
Cardinal Inn, Daytona Beach, 36
Cardozo Hotel, South Beach, 52
Caribbean Beach Resort, Walt Disney World, 38–40
Caribe Beach Resort, Sanibel Island, 59
Casa de la Paz B&B, St. Augustine, 34
Casa Grande Suite Hotel, South Beach, 52
Casa Loma Inn, Fort Myers, 56
Casa Marina Inn, Jacksonville, 32
Casa Playa Beach Resort, Fort Myers Beach, 57
Casa Ybel Resort, Sanibel Island, 59
Casablanca Inn B&B, St. Augustine, 34
Cayo Costa, 401
Celebration Hotel, Walt Disney World, 38–40
Celebration World Resort, Walt Disney World, 38–40
Chase Suites Hotel, Tampa, 42–43
Chateau Motel, Panama City, 27
Cheeca Lodge, Florida Keys, 53
Chesapeake Resort, Florida Keys, 53
Chesterfield Palm Beach, Palm Beach, 46
Civic Inn, Pensacola, 22
Clarion Hotel, 37–40, 50–51
Clarion Inn & Suites, Naples, 58
Clarion Maingate, Walt Disney World, 38–40
Clarion Suites Resort and Convention Center, Pensacola, 23
Clearwater hotels and resorts, 41
Clinton Hotel South Branch, South Beach, 52
Club Destin Resort, Destin, 25
Cocoa Beach Oceanside Inn, Space Coast, 37
Coconut Palms Beach Resort, Daytona Beach, 36
Collier Inn, Useppa Island, 403

Accommodations Index

Colonial Resort Motel & Apartments, Fort Myers, 56
Colony Hotel & Cabana Club, Palm Beach, 46
Colony Palm Beach, Palm Beach, 46
Comfort Inn
  Airport, Fort Lauderdale, 48
  on the Beach, Miami Beach, 47
  Boatways Rd., Fort Myers, 56
  Bonita Springs, 58
  Destin, 25
  Downtown, Naples, 58
  Florida Keys, 53
  Key West, 54
  Maingate, Walt Disney World, 38–40
  Oceanfront, Jacksonville, 32
  Oceanside, Broward County, 48
  Orange Park, Jacksonville, 32
  Ormond Beach, Daytona Beach, 36
  Pensacola, 23
  S. Cleveland Ave., Fort Myers, 56
  Space Shuttle Inn, Space Coast, 37
  St. Augustine, 34
  Tallahassee, 29
  University, Gainesville, 31
  West, Gainesville, 31
Comfort Inn & Suites
  Airport, Miami, 50–51
  Daytona Beach, 36
  Tampa, 42–43
Comfort Suites
  Airport, Jacksonville, 32
  Airport, Walt Disney World, 38–40
Comparisons, hotel, 63–95
Condominiums
  Miami Beach, 19
  reservations, 61
Consulate, The, Apalachicola, 28
Contemporary Resort, Walt Disney World, 38–40
Coombs House Inn, Apalachicola, 28
Coral Beach Resort, Daytona Beach, 36
Coral Gables
  Hyatt Regency, 50–51
Coral Reef Motel, Treasure Coast, 45
Coronado Springs Resort, Walt Disney World, 38–40
Country Inn & Suites
  Destin, 25
  Fort Myers, 56
  Jacksonville, 32
  Sarasota, 44
  Universal, Walt Disney World, 38–40
  Walt Disney World, 38–40
Countryside Lodge, Walt Disney World, 38–40
Coupons, discount, 61

Courtyard
  Airport, Jacksonville, 32
  Airport South, Miami, 50–51
  Airport West, Miami, 50–51
  Disney Village, Walt Disney World, 38–40
  Downtown, Miami, 50–51
  Downtown, Orlando, 39
  Fort Myers, 56
  Gainesville, 31
  Jacksonville, 32
  Jensen Beach, Treasure Coast, 45
  Key West, 54
  Lake Lucerne, Orlando, 39
  Naples, 58
  Space Shuttle Inn, Space Coast, 37
  Villas on the Ocean, Broward County, 48
Cove Motel, Daytona Beach, 36
Creek, The, South Beach, 52
Crowne Plaza
  Airport, Walt Disney World, 38–40
  Grand Hotel, Pensacola, 22
  La Concha, Key West, 55
  Miami, 50–51
  Sawgrass, Broward County, 48
  Singer Island, Palm Beach, 46
  Tampa, 42–43
  Universal, Walt Disney World, 38–40
  West Palm Beach, 46
Curry Mansion Inn, Key West, 55

David William Hotel, Miami, 50–51
Days Inn
  Airport, Tampa, 42–43
  Airport, Walt Disney World, 38–40
  Airport North, Miami, 50–51
  Airport West, Palm Beach, 46
  Bahia Cabana, Broward County, 48
  Beach, Panama City, 27
  Fairground, Tampa, 42–43
  Fort Pierce Beach, Treasure Coast, 45
  Fort Pierce, Treasure Coast, 45
  Gainesville I-75, 31
  Island Beach Resort, Fort Myers Beach, 57
  Kennedy Space Center, Space Coast, 37
  Key West, 54
  North, Fort Myers, 56
  North, Tallahassee, 29
  Oceanside, Miami Beach, 47
  Oceanside, Space Coast, 37
  Pensacola, 22
  South, Fort Myers, 56
  St. Augustine, 34
  Suites, Treasure Coast, 45
  University, Gainesville, 31

Accommodations Index 527

Days Suites Maingate East, Walt Disney World, 38–40
Daytona Beach hotels and resorts, 36
Del Prado Inn, Fort Myers, 56
Delray Beach, Marriott Hotel, 46
Desert Inn, Daytona Beach, 36
Destin lodging, 25
Dewey House, Key West, 55
DiamondHead All Suite Beach Resort, Fort Myers Beach, 57
Discount coupons, 61
Dockside Harborlight Resort, Treasure Coast, 45
Dolphin Inn, Fort Myers Beach, 57
Dolphin Resort, Walt Disney World, 38–40
Don Cesar Beach Resort and Spa, St. Petersburg, 41
Don Shula's Hotel & Golf Club, Miami, 50–51
Doubletree Guest Suites
  Boca Raton, 46
  Broward County, 48
  Naples, 58
  Tampa Bay, 42–43
  Walt Disney World, 38–40
Doubletree Hotel
  Club Hotel, Miami, 50–51
  Coconut Grove, Miami, 50–51
  in the Gardens, Palm Beach, 46
  Grand Hotel, Miami, 50–51
  Space Shuttle Inn, Space Coast, 37
  Surfcomber, South Beach, 52
  Tallahassee, 29
Driftwood Inn, Apalachicola, 28
Driftwood Lodge, Panama City, 27
Dunes, The, Pensacola, 23
Duval House, Key West, 55

Eaton Lodge, Key West, 55
Eaton Manor Guesthouse, Key West, 55
Econo Lodge
  Clearwater Beach, Clearwater, 41
  Fort Myers, 56
  Fort Pierce Beach, Treasure Coast, 45
  Space Shuttle Inn, Space Coast, 37
  University, Gainesville, 31
  West, Gainesville, 31
Eden House, Key West, 55
Eden Roc Hotel, Miami Beach, 47
Eden Roc, Miami Beach, 19
Edgewater Beach Resort, Panama City, 27
Edgewater Inn, St. Augustine Beach, 35
Edison Beach House, Fort Myers Beach, 57
El Caribe Resort & Conference Center, Daytona Beach, 36
El Govenor Motel, Apalachicola, 28

Elizabeth Pointe Lodge, Amelia Island, 30
Embassy Suites
  Airport, Miami, 50–51
  Boca Raton, 46
  Deerfield Beach Resort, Broward County, 48
  Downtown, Orlando, 39
  Fort Lauderdale, 48
  Miramar Beach, Destin, 25
  Palm Beach, 46
EO Inn Spa, Orlando, 39
Esquire Beach Motel, Daytona Beach, 36
Essex House Hotel, South Beach, 52
Extended Stay America, Jacksonville, 32

Fairbanks House, Amelia Island, 30
Fairfield Destin, South Walton, 26
Fairfield Inn
  Airport, Jacksonville, 32
  Airport, Walt Disney World, 38–40
  Gainesville, 31
  Orange Park, Jacksonville, 32
  Pensacola, 23
  Tallahassee, 29
Fairway Inn, Florida Keys, 53
Farrell's Motel, Treasure Coast, 45
Fawlty Towers, Space Coast, 37
Fiesta Motel, Panama City, 27
Fiesta Motel, St. Petersburg, 41
Five Flags Inn, Pensacola, 23
Flamingo, Motel, Panama City, 27
Flamingo Motel, Naples, 58
Florida House Inn, Amelia Island, 30
Florida Keys
  "best" hotel deals in the, 99
  hotel comparisons, 94–95
  lodging, 53
Florida Motel, Gainesville, 31
Florida Panhandle
  "best" hotel deals in the, 96
  hotel comparisons, 65–69
  overview, 14–15
Fontainebleau, Miami Beach, 19
Fontainebleau Terrace, Panama City, 27
Fort Lauderdale Beach Resort, Fort Lauderdale, 48
Fort Lauderdale hotels and resorts, 48
Fort Myers Beach
  Beacon Motel & Gift Shop, 57
  Best Western Beach Resort, 57
  Best Western Pink Shell Beach Resort, 57
  Casa Playa Beach Resort, 57
  Days Inn Island Beach Resort, 57
  DiamondHead All Suite Beach Resort, 57
  Dolphin Inn, 57
  Edison Beach House, 57
  Grand View All Suite Resort, 57

Accommodations Index

Fort Myers Beach *(continued)*
  GuestHouse Inn Mariner's Lodge & Marina, 57
  Gullwing Beach Resort, 57
  Hidden Harbor Inn, 57
  Holiday Court Motel, 57
  Holiday Inn, 57
  Howard Johnson Beachfront, 57
  Island Motel, 57
  Kahula Beach Club, 57
  Lighthouse Island Resort, 57
  Neptune Inn, 57
  Outrigger Beach Resort, 57
  Pointe Estero Resort, 57
  Quality Inn & Suites at the Lani Kai, 57
  Ramada Inn Beachfront, 57
  Sandpiper Gulf Resort, 57
  Sandy Beach Hideaway, 57
  Ti Ki Resort, 57
  Tropical Inn Resort, 57
Fort Myers hotels and resorts, 56
Fort Myers Inn, Fort Myers, 56
Fort Walton hotels and resorts, 24
Fort Wilderness Resort, Walt Disney World, 38–40
Forty/Fifteen Resort, Sanibel Island, 59
Four Seasons Resort, Palm Beach, 46
Frances Street Bottle Inn, Key West, 55

Gainesville hotels and resorts, 31
Garden House, Key West, 55
Gardens Hotel, Key West, 55
Gasparilla Inn, Gasparilla Island, 401
Gator Lodge, Gainesville, 31
Georgian Terrace Motel, Panama City, 27
Gibson Inn, Apalachicola, 28
Gilbert's Resort, Florida Keys, 53
Gold Coast
  "best" hotel deals in the, 98
  hotel comparisons, 82–86
Governor's Inn, Tallahassee, 29
Grand Floridan Resort, Walt Disney World, 38–40
Grand Seas Resort, Daytona Beach, 36
Grand View All Suite Resort, Fort Myers Beach, 57
Grosvenor Resort, Walt Disney World, 38–40
Grove Isle Club & Resort, Miami, 50–51
GuestHouse Inn Mariner's Lodge & Marina, Fort Myers Beach, 57
Gulf Beach Motel, Sarasota, 44
Gulf Coast
  "best" hotel deals in the, 97–98
  hotel comparisons, 79–82
Gulf Strand Beach Front Resort, St. Petersburg, 41

Gulf View Motel, Apalachicola, 28
Gulf View Motel, Panama City, 27
Gullwing Beach Resort, Fort Myers Beach, 57

Hampton Inn
  Airport, Jacksonville, 32
  Airport/Cordova Mall, Pensacola, 23
  Bonita Springs, 58
  Central, Jacksonville, 32
  Clearwater, 41
  Cocoa Beach, Space Coast, 37
  Destin, 25
  Florida City, Florida Keys, 53
  Fort Walton, 24
  Gainesville, 31
  Historic, St. Augustine, 34
  I-10, Tallahassee, 29
  Key West, 54
  Naples, 58
  Orange Park, Jacksonville, 32
  Pensacola Beach, Pensacola, 23
  Sarasota, 44
  St. Augustine, 34
  St. Augustine Beach, 35
  West Palm Beach, 46
Hampton Inn & Suites
  Amelia Island, 30
  Broward County, 48
  Florida Keys, 53
Harbour Beach Resort, Daytona Beach, 36
Hard Rock Hotel, Walt Disney World, 38–40
Hawk's Cay Resort, Florida Keys, 53
Hawthorn Suites, 38–40, 58
Heart of Palm Beach Hotel, Palm Beach, 46
Helmsley Sandcastle Hotel on the Beach, Sarasota, 44
Heron House, Key West, 55
Hibiscus House B&B, Palm Beach, 46
Hidden Dunes Beach & Tennis Resort, South Walton, 26
Hidden Harbor Inn, Fort Myers Beach, 57
High Noon Beach Resort, Broward County, 48
Hillsmoore Oceanfront Inn, Jacksonville, 32
Hilton
  Airport, Miami, 50–51
  Airport, Palm Beach, 46
  Beach Resort, Marco Island, 60
  Clearwater Beach Resort, Clearwater, 41
  Cocoa Beach Resort, Space Coast, 37
  Fontainebleau Resort & Spa, 47
  Garden Inn, Fort Myers, 56
  Garden Inn, Jacksonville, 32
  Garden Inn, Pensacola, 23

Accommodations Index 529

Garden Inn, St. Augustine Beach, 35
Garden Inn, Walt Disney World, 38–40
Garden Inn, Ybor City, 42–43
Longboat Key Beach Resort, Sarasota, 44
Oceanfront Resort, Daytona Beach, 36
Riverfront, Jacksonville, 32
Sandestin Beach Resort & Spa, 26
Singer Island Oceanfront Resort, Palm Beach, 46
Tampa Bay N. Redington Beach, St. Petersburg, 41
Hilton Towers, Naples, 58
Historic Inn, St. Augustine Beach, 35
HoJo Holiday Isle Resort & Marina, Florida Keys, 53
Holiday Court Motel, Fort Myers Beach, 57
Holiday Inn
   Airport, Jacksonville, 32
   Airport, Palm Beach, 46
   Airport North, Miami, 50–51
   Airport Select, Fort Myers, 56
   Airport Select, Walt Disney World, 38–40
   Beach Resort, Sanibel Island, 59
   Beach Resort, Sarasota, 44
   Beachfront Resort, St. Petersburg, 41
   Beachside, Key West, 54
   Cocoa Beach Resort, Space Coast, 37
   Downtown, Orlando, 39
   Family Suites Resort, Walt Disney World, 38–40
   Fort Lauderdale, 48
   Fort Myers Beach, 57
   Highland Beach, Palm Beach, 46
   Hollywood Beach, 48
   Hotel & Suites, Daytona Beach, 36
   Hotel & Suites, New Smyrna Beach, 36
   Jensen Beach, Treasure Coast, 45
   Kennedy Space Center, Space Coast, 37
   Key Largo Resort, Florida Keys, 53
   Lido Beach, Sarasota, 44
   Marathon, Florida Keys, 53
   Marina Park, Miami, 50–51
   Naples, 58
   Navarre, 24
   Nikki Bird Resort, Walt Disney World, 38–40
   Northwest, Tallahassee, 29
   Oceanside, Broward County, 48
   Orange Park, Jacksonville, 32
   Pensacola, 23
   Riverwalk, Fort Myers, 56
   Select, Tallahassee, 29
   St. Augustine Beach, 35
   Staybridge Suites, Naples, 58
   Stuart, Treasure Coast, 45
   Suites, St. Augustine, 34
   Sun Spree Resort, Clearwater, 41
   Sun Spree Resort, Fort Walton, 24
   Sun Spree Resort, Panama City, 27
   Sun Spree Resort, St. Petersburg, 41
   Sun Spree Resort, Walt Disney World, 38–40
   Town Center, Boca Raton, 46
   Treasure Island, St. Petersburg, 41
   University Center, Gainesville, 31
   Vero Beach, 45
   West, Gainesville, 31
Holiday Inn Express
   Brandon, 42–43
   Downtown, Boca Raton, 46
   Florida Mall, Walt Disney World, 38–40
   Fort Pierce, Treasure Coast, 45
   Naples, 58
   Palm Beach, 46
   Pensacola, 23
   Space Coast, 37
   St. Augusstine, 34
   Tampa, 42–43
Holiday Terrace, Panama City, 27
Hollywood Beach hotels and resorts, 48
Homestead Studio Suites
   Miami, 50–51
   Tampa, 42–43
Homewood Suites
   Fort Myers, 56
   Pensacola, 23
   Summy Isles, Miami, 50–51
Hotel, The, South Beach, 52
Hotel Astor, South Beach, 52
Hotel Delano, South Beach, 52
Hotel Escalante, Naples, 58
Hotel Impala, South Beach, 52
Hotel Intercontinental, Miami, 50–51
Hotel Ocean, South Beach, 52
Hotel Place St. Michel, Miami, 50–51
Hotel Sofitel, Miami, 50–51
House of Tarts, Apalachicola, 28
Howard Johnson
   Airport, Miami, 50–51
   Beachfront, Fort Myers Beach, 57
   Boardwalk Resort, Panama City, 27
   Edison Mall, Fort Myers, 56
   EnchantedLand Resort Hotel, Walt Disney World, 38–40
   Express Inn & Suites, Tampa, 42–43
   Express Inn, Destin, 25
   Express Inn, Fort Myers, 56
   Express Inn, Gainesville, 31
   Express Inn, Sarasota, 44
   Express Inn, Space Coast, 37
   Express Inn, Tallahassee, 29
   Ocean's Edge, Fort Lauderdale, 48

Accommodations Index

Howard Johnson *(continued)*
  Plaza Resort, Broward County, 48
  Port, Miami, 50–51
  Resort Hotel, St. Petersburg, 41
  Resort Key Largo, Florida Keys, 53
  Treasure Coast, 45
Hoyt House, Amelia Island, 30
Hurricane House, Sanibel Island, 59
Hyatt Regency
  Coral Gables, 50–51
  Orlando, 38–40
  Pier Sixty-six, Broward County, 48
  Sarasota, 44
  Tampa, 42–43
  West Resort & Marina, Key West, 55
  Westshore, Tampa, 42–43

Ibis Bed & Breakfast, Tampa, 42–43
Imperial's Hotel & Conference Center, Space Coast, 37
Indian Creek Hotel, Miami Beach, 47
Inn at Cocoa Beach, Space Coast, 37
Inn at Pelican Bay, Naples, 58
Inn on Fifth, Naples, 58
Inns of America, Palm Beach, 46
Internet. *see* Websites
Ireland's Inn Beach Resort, Broward County, 48
Island Breeze, Panama City, 27
Island City House Hotel, Key West, 55
Island Inn, Sanibel Island, 59
Island Motel, Fort Myers Beach, 57
Island View, Aplachicola, 28
Ivanhoe Beach Resort, Daytona Beach, 36

Jacksonville hotels and resorts, 32
Jefferson Motel, St. Petersburg, 41
Jensen Beach Motel, Treasure Coast, 45
Jensen's Twin Palms Cottages & Marina, Captiva Island, 59
Jensen's Waterfront Cottages, Treasure Coast, 45
Jupiter Waterfront Inn, Treasure Coast, 45
JW Marriott Hotel, Miami, 50–51

Kahula Beach Club, Fort Myers Beach, 57
Key West hotels and resorts, 55
Kingsail Resort Motel, Florida Keys, 53
Kona Kai Resort and Gallery, Florida Keys, 53

La Fiesta Ocean Inn & Suites, St. Augustine Beach, 35
La Flora, South Beach, 52
La Mer Hotel, Key West, 55
La Playa Beach Resort, Naples, 58

La Quinta Inn
  Airport, Walt Disney World, 38–40
  Baymeadows, Jacksonville, 32
  Fort Myers, 56
  Gainesville, 31
  Inn & Suites, Tampa, 42–43
  Orange Park, Jacksonville, 32
  Pensacola, 23
  St. Augustine, 34
  Tallahassee, 29
  Tampa, 42–43
  West Palm Beach, 46
La Te Da Hotel, Key West, 55
Landmark Holiday Beach Resort, Panama City, 27
Legacy by the Sea, Panama City, 27
Lemon Tree Inn, Naples, 58
Lighthouse Inn, Naples, 58
Lighthouse Island Resort, Fort Myers Beach, 57
Lily Guesthouse, South Beach, 52
Lion Inn, St. Augustine Beach, 35
Loews Miami Beach Hotel, South Beach, 52
Luna Sea B&B Motel, Space Coast, 37
Luxury Crowne Plaza Grand Hotel, Pensacola, 14

Magic Carpet Motel, Daytona Beach, 36
Majestic Sun beach Resort, Destin, 25
Makai Beach Lodge, Daytona Beach, 36
Mandarin Oriental, Miami, 50–51
Marco Island hotels and resorts, 60
Marina Bay Resort, Fort Walton, 24
Marlin, South Beach, 52
Marriott Hotel
  Airport, Miami, 50–51
  BeachPlace Towers, Broward Conty, 48
  Biscayne Bay, 50–51
  Boca Raton, 46
  Delray Beach, 46
  Downtown, Orlando, 39
  Downtown, Tampa, 42–43
  Fort Lauderdale, 48
  Harbor Beach Resort, Broward County, 48
  Key Largo Beach Resort, Florida Keys, 53
  Marco Island, 60
  Resorts Suites, Walt Disney World, 38–40
Marriott Village, Walt Disney World, 38–40
Maverick Resort, Daytona Beach, 36
Merida Motel, St. Augustine, 34
Miami
  "best" hotel deals in, 99
  hotel comparisons, 91–93

Accommodations Index 531

hotels and resorts, 50–51
Miami Beach
    Art Deco District, 18–19
    "best" hotel deals in, 99
    Condominiums, 19
    hotel comparisons, 91–93
    hotels and resorts, 19, 47
Microtel Inn & Suites, 29, 38–40
Miramar Resort, St. Petersburg, 41
Mitchell's Sand Castles, Sanibel Island, 59
Motel 6
    Fort Myers, 56
    Gainesville, 31
    International Drive, Walt Disney World, 38–40
    Jacksonville, 32
    Pensacola, 23
    Space Shuttle Inn, Space Coast, 37
    Treasure Coast, 45

Naples Beach Hotel & Golf Club, Naples, 58
Naples hotels and resorts, 58
Nassau Suite Hotel, South Beach, 52
National Hotel, South Beach, 52
Navarre, 24
Neptune Inn, Fort Myers Beach, 57
New World Inn, Pensacola, 14, 22
Newport Beachside Resort, Miami, 50–51
Northeast Florida
    "best" hotel deals in, 96
    hotel comparisons, 70–73

Oak Haven River Retreat, Tampa, 42–43
Oasis Resort Siesta Key, Sarasota, 44
Ocean Inn, Daytona Beach, 36
Ocean Key Resort & Marina, Key West, 55
Ocean Suite Hotel, Space Coast, 37
Ocean View Inn, Amelia Island, 30
Ocean Walk Resort, Daytona Beach, 36
Oceanaire Lodge, Treasure Coast, 45
Oceania Beach Club, Daytona Beach, 36
Old Carrabele Hotel, Apalachicola, 28
Old Florida River Tours Black Tie Yacht B&B, Fort Myers, 56
Old Key West Resort, Walt Disney World, 38–40
Old Pier Motel, Destin, 25
Omni Colonnade Hotel, Miami, 50–51
Omni Jacksonville Hotel, Jacksonville, 32
Orlando
    "best" hotel deals in, 97
    hotel comparisons, 76–78
    hotels and resorts, 38–40
    see also Walt Disney World

Outrigger Beach Resort, Fort Myers Beach, 57
Overview by geographic region, 14–20

Palm Beach hotels and resorts, 46
Palm Island Resort, Cape Haze, 402
Palm Plaza Oceanfront Resort, Daytona Beach, 36
Palm View Motel, Sanibel Island, 59
Palmetto Motel, Panama City, 27
Palms, The, Miami Beach, 47
Palms Hotel, Key West, 55
Palms Inn & Suites, Treasure Coast, 45
Palms of Sanibel, Sanibel Island, 59
Panama City
    Ambassador Beach Condominium, 27
    Beach Tower Resort Motel, 27
    Beachbreak by the Sea, 27
    Beachcomber by the Sea, 27
    Best Value Inn Beach Resort, 27
    Best Western Casa Loma, 27
    Best Western Del Coronado, 27
    Bikini Beach Resort, 27
    Chateau Motel, 27
    Days Inn Beach, 27
    Driftwood Lodge, 27
    Edgewater Beach Resort, 27
    Fiesta Motel, 27
    Flamingo, Motel, 27
    Fontainebleau Terrace, 27
    Georgian Terrace Motel, 27
    Gulf View Motel, 27
    Holiday Inn Sun Spree Resort, 27
    Holiday Terrace, 27
    Howard Johnson Boardwalk Resort, 27
    Island Breeze, 27
    Landmark Holiday Beach Resort, 27
    Legacy by the Sea, 27
    Palmetto Motel, 27
    Panama City Resort & Club, 27
    Peeks Beach Motel, 27
    Pier 99 Waterfront Motel, 27
    Quality Inn Beach Front, 27
    Ramada Limited, 27
    Sandpiper Beacon Beach Resort, 27
    Southwind Condominiums, 27
    Wind Drift Motel, 27
Panama City Resort & Club, Panama City, 27
Paradise Beach Resort, Broward County, 48
Paramount Resort & Conference Center, Gainesville, 31
Park Central Imperials Hotel, South Beach, 52
Parmer's Resort, Florida Keys, 53

532 Accommodations Index

Peeks Beach Motel, Panama City, 27
Pelican Cove Resort, Florida Keys, 53
Pelican Rest Motel, Treasure Coast, 45
Peninsula Inn & Spa, St. Petersburg, 41
Pensacola
  Bay Beach Inn, 23
  Beachside Resort & Conference
    Center, 23
  Best Western Resort, 23
  Civic Inn, 22
  Clarion Suites Resort and Convention
    Center, 23
  Comfort Inn, 23
  Crowne Plaza Grand Hotel, 22
  Days Inn, 22
  The Dunes, 23
  Fairfield Inn, 23
  Five Flags Inn, 23
  Hampton Inn Airport/Cordova Mall, 23
  Hampton Inn Pensacola Beach, 23
  Hilton Garden Inn, 23
  Holiday Inn, 23
  Holiday Inn Express, 23
  Homewood Suites, 23
  hotel maps, 22–23
  La Quinta Inn, 23
  Luxury Crowne Plaza Grand Hotel, 14
  Motel 6, 23
  New World Inn, 14, 22
  Pensacola Lodge, 23
  Red Roof Inn, 23
  Residence Inn, 22–23
  Seville Inn and Suites, 22
  SpringHill Suites, 23
Pensacola Lodge, Pensacola, 23
PGA National Resort, Palm Beach, 46
Pier 99 Waterfront Motel, Panama City, 27
Pier House, Key West, 55
Pirate Haus Hostel, St. Augustine, 34
Plaza Beach Resort Motel, Clearwater, 41
Plaza Hotel & Suites, Boca Raton, 46
Plaza Resort & Spa, Daytona Beach, 36
Pointe Estero Resort, Fort Myers Beach, 57
Polynesian Resort, Walt Disney World,
  38–40
Port Inn, Apalachicola, 28
Port of the Islands, Marco Island, 60
Port Orleans Resort, Walt Disney World,
  38–40
Portofino Bay Hotel, Walt Disney World,
  38–40
Profiles, hotel, 3

Quality Hotel, Fort Myers, 56
Quality Hotel on the Beach,
  St. Petersburg, 41

Quality Inn
  Beach Front, Panama City, 27
  Clearwater, 41
  Gainesville, 31
  Gulfcoast, Naples, 58
  Key West, 54
  Nautilus, Fort Myers, 56
  Pompano Beach, Broward County, 48
  Space Shuttle Inn, Space Coast, 37
Quality Inn & Suites, 38–40, 57
Quality Suites, 32, 38–40
Quayside Inn, Sarasota, 44

Radisson
  Airport Suite Inn, Palm Beach, 46
  Bahia Mar Beach Resort, Broward
    County, 48
  Barcelo Inn International, Walt Disney
    World, 38–40
  Bay Harbor Hotel, Tampa, 42–43
  Beach Resort, Fort Walton, 24
  Beach Resort, Marco Island, 60
  Beach Resort, Treasure Coast, 45
  Bridge Resort, Boca Raton, 46
  Fort Myers, 56
  Hotel Tallahassee, 29
  Key West, 54
  Lido Beach Resort, Sarasota, 44
  New Hotel, Miami, 50–51
  Resort, Daytona Beach, 36
  Resort at the Port, Space Coast, 37
  Resort Parkway, Walt Disney World,
    38–40
  Riverwalk Hotel & Conference Center,
    Jacksonville, 32
  Riverwalk Hotel, Tampa, 42–43
  Sanibel Gateway, Fort Myers, 56
  Suite Resort on SAnd Key, Clearwater,
    41
Rainbow Motel Resort, Fort Myers, 56
Ramada Inn
  Beachfront, Fort Myers Beach, 57
  Fort Myers, 56
  Kennedy Space Center, Space Coast, 37
  Ocean Beach Resort, Broward, 48
  Plaza Beach Resort, Fort Walton, 24
  Plaza Hotel, Broward County, 48
  Plaza Marco Polo, Miami, 50–51
  Resort, Miami Beach, 47
  Resort Hotel, Hollywood Beach, 48
  Satellite Beach, Space Coast, 37
  Sea Club Resort, Broward County, 48
  St. Augustine, 34
  Tallahassee, 29
  Treasure Coast, 45
  Treasure Island, St. Petersburg, 41

Accommodations Index   533

Ramada Limited
  Destin, 25
  Florida Keys, 53
  Fort Myers, 56
  Gainesville, 31
  Jacksonville, 32
  Panama City, 27
  St. Augustine, 34
  St. Augustine Beach, 35
Ramada Plaza, Naples, 58
Rancho Inn, Apalachicola, 28
Randolph Inn, Space Coast, 37
Raney Guest Cottage, Apalachicola, 28
Rates and reservations, 20–21, 61–63
Ratings, hotel, 63–95
Red Carpet Inn, Daytona Beach, 36
Red Roof Inn
  Airport, Jacksonville, 32
  Gainesville, 31
  Orange Park, Jacksonville, 32
  Pensacola, 23
  Southpoint, Jacksonville, 32
  Tampa, 42–43
Regency Inn, 24, 35
Registry Resort, Naples, 58
Renaissance Hotel Airport, Orlando, 38–40
Reservations and rates, 20–21, 61–63
Residence Inn
  Airport, Jacksonville, 32
  Convention Center Walt Disney World, 38–40
  Fort Myers, 56
  Gainesville, 31
  Naples, 58
  Pensacola, 22–23
  Tampa, 42–43
Resort on Cocoa Beach, Space Coast, 37
Riande Continental, South Beach, 52
Ritz Plaza Hotel, South Beach, 52
Ritz-Carlton
  Amelia Island, 30
  Coconut Grove, Miami, 50–51
  Naples, 58
  Palm Beach, 46
  Sarasota, 44
River Palm cottages, Treasure Coast, 45
Riverside Hotel, Broward County, 48
Riverside Inn, Space Coast, 37
Rolling Waves Cottages, Sarasota, 44
Rosemary Beach Rentals, South Walton, 26

Safety Harbor Resort & Spa, Tampa Bay, 42–43
Sandestin Inn, South Walton, 26
Sandpiper Beacon Beach Resort, Panama City, 27

Sandpiper Gulf Resort, Fort Myers Beach, 57
Sandpiper Inn, Sanibel Island, 59
Sands Motel, Gainesville, 31
Sandy Beach Hideaway, Fort Myers Beach, 57
Sanibel Island lodging, 59
Sarasota hotels and resorts, 44
Scottish Inns
  Daytona Beach, 36
  Gainesville, 31
  St. Augustine, 34
Sea Aire Motel, Space Coast, 37
Sea Breeze Manor B&B Inn, St. Petersburg, 41
Sea Breeze Resort, South Walton, 26
Sea Castle Inn, Broward County, 48
Sea Court Hotel, Naples, 58
Sea Horse Beach Resort, Sarasota, 44
Sea Oats Motel, South Walton, 26
Sea View Hotel, Miami, 50–51
Seagarden Inn, Daytona Beach, 36
Seagate, The, Palm Beach, 46
Seagrove Cottages, South Walton, 26
Seagrove Villa Motel, South Walton, 26
Seahorse Cottages, Sanibel Island, 59
Seahorse Cottages, St. Petersburg, 41
Seaside Rentals, South Walton, 26
Seven Seas Resort, Daytona Beach, 36
1735 House, Amelia Island, 30
Seville Beach Hotel, Miami Beach, 47
Seville Inn and Suites, Pensacola, 22
Shalimar Resort, Sanibel Island, 59
Sheldon Ocean Resort, Broward County, 48
Sheraton
  Airport, Fort Lauderdale, 48
  Bal Harbor, 50–51
  Biscayne Bay, 50–51
  Four Points, Miami Beach, 47
  Key West, 54
  Royal Safari, Walt Disney World, 38–40
  Sand Key Resort, Clearwater, 41
  Vistana Resort, Walt Disney World, 38–40
  West Palm Beach, 46
  World Resort, Walt Disney World, 38–40
  Yankee Clipper, Broward County, 48
  Yankee Trader, Broward County, 48
Shoney's Inn, Tallahassee, 29
Siesta Holidays, Sarasota, 44
Siesta Key Suites, Sarasota, 44
Siesta Sands on the Beach, Sarasota, 44
Silver Beach Club, Daytona Beach, 36
Silver Beach Resort, Sarasota, 44

534 Accommodations Index

Silver Shells Beach Resort & Spa, Destin, 25
Sleep Inn
    Miami, 50–51
    St. Augustine Beach, 35
    Suites, Airport, Fort Lauderdale, 48
    Suites, Walt Disney World, 38–40
Sonesta Beach Resort, Miami, 50–51
South Beach lodging, 52
South Walton lodging, 26
Southernmost on the Beach, Key West, 55
Southwest Florida
    "best" hotel deals in, 98–99
    hotel comparisons, 86–90
Southwind Condominiums, Panama City, 27
Space Coast
    "best" hotel deals in the, 97
    hotel comparisons, 73–76
    hotels and resorts, 37
Spanish Gardens, Key West, 55
Sportsman's Lodge, Apalachicola, 28
SpringHill Suites
    Broward County, 48
    Palm Beach, 46
    Pensacola, 23
    Walt Disney World, 38–40
St. Augustine Beach lodging, 35
St. Augustine lodging, 34
St. George Inn, Apalachicola, 28
St. Petersburg hotels and resorts, 41
Suburban Extended Stay Hotel, Treasure Coast, 45
Suburban Lodge, Fort Myers, 56
Sugar Beach Inn B&B, South Walton, 26
Suite Dreams, Key West, 55
Summer Beach Resort, Amelia Island, 30
Summerfield Suites, Miami, 50–51
Sundial Beach Resort, Sanibel Island, 59
Sundy House, Palm Beach, 46
Sunrise Inn, St. Augustine Beach, 35
Super 8
    Fort Myers, 56
    Gainesville, 31
    Kissimmee Lakeside, Walt Disney World, 38–40
    Maingate, Walt Disney World, 38–40
    St. Augustine, 34
    St. Augustine Beach, 35
    University Hospital, Gainesville, 31
Surf, The, Amelia Island, 30
Surf Studio Beach Resort, Space Coast, 37
Surfside, Destin, 25
Surfside Inn, Apalachicola, 28
Surfside Inn, Jacksonville, 32
Surfside Resort & Suites, Daytona Beach, 36
Surfview Motel, Sarasota, 44

Swan Resort, Walt Disney World, 38–40
Symphony Beach Club, Daytona Beach, 36

Tahitian, St. Petersburg, 41
Tallahassee hotels and resorts, 29
Tampa Bay hotels and resorts, 42–43
Tampa hotels and resorts, 42–43
Ti Ki Resort, Fort Myers Beach, 57
Tides, The, South Beach, 52
Trade Winds Island Resorts, St. Petersburg, 41
Tradewinds, Naples, 58
Trapon Tale Inn, Sanibel Island, 59
Travelodge
    Eastgate Suites, Walt Disney World, 38–40
    Florida Keys, 53
    Gainesville, 31
    Key West, 54
    Maingate Suites, Walt Disney World, 38–40
    Orlando, 39
Treasure Coast
    "best" hotel deals in the, 98
    hotel comparisons, 82–86
    hotels and resorts, 45
Treasure Island resorts, 36, 41
Trianon, Bonita Bay, Naples, 58
Tropical Breeze Resort of Siesta Key, Sarasota, 44
Tropical Inn Resort, Fort Myers Beach, 57
Tropical Manor Motel, Daytona Beach, 36
Tropical Winds Cottages, Sanibel Island, 59
Tropical Winds Oceanfront Hotel, Daytona Beach, 36
Trump International Sonesta Beach Resort, Miami, 50–51
Tudor Hotel, South Beach, 52
Turtle Crawl Inn, Sarasota, 44
Tween Waters Inn, Captiva Island, 59

Vanderbilt Beach Resort House, Naples, 58
Vero Beach hotels, 45
Vero Beach Inn, Vero Beach, 45
Villager Lodge, Gainesville, 31
Villamar Inn, Broward County, 48

Wakulla Suites, Space Coast, 37
Waldorf Towers Hotel, South Beach, 52
Walt Disney World hotels and resorts, 38–40
    see also Orlando
Watercolor Inn, South Walton, 26
Waterside Inn on the Beach, Sanibel Island, 59
Websites, lodging and travel, 61–62
Wellesley Inn & Suites, 44, 56

Accommodations Index 535

West Palm Beach hotels, 46
West Wind Inn, Sanibel Island, 59
Westgate Resort, Walt Disney World, 38–40
Westgate Towers, Walt Disney World, 38–40
Westin hotels and resorts, 39, 48
Westwinds, Key West, 55
Whale's Tale B&B, St. Augustine, 34
White Sands Resort Club, Naples, 58
Wilderness Lodge and Villas, Walt Disney World, 38–40
Wind Drift Motel, Panama City, 27
Windjammer Resort & Beach Club, Broward County, 48

Wingate Inn, Jacksonville, 32
Winterhaven, South Beach, 52
Wright by the Sea, Palm Beach, 46
Wyndham
    Airport, Fort Lauderdale, 48
    Airport, Miami, 50–51
    Beach Resort, Key West, 55
    Casa Marina Resort, Key West, 55
    Grand Bay, Miami, 50–51
    Resort, Miami Beach, 47
    Westshore, Tampa, 42–43

Ybor City, Hilton Garden Inn, 42–43
Yellowtail Inn, Florida Keys, 53

Subject Index

Accommodations. *see* Accommodations Index
Amelia Island, 159–61
Animals. *see* Guide dogs; Wildlife
Apalachicola, 15, 146–47
Apalachicola National Forest, 7
Aquariums
   Florida Aquarium, Tampa, 320
   Gulf Specimen Marine Laboratories, Wakulla Springs, 106
   Gulfarium, Fort Walton, 128
   Key West Aquarium, 513–14
   Marine Aquarium, Clearwater, 330
   Marine Science Center, New Symrna Beach, 222
   Mote Marine Aquarium, 340
   Seaquarium, Miami, 463–64
Art Deco District, Miami Beach, 18–19
Arts
   Alexander Brest Museum, Jacksonville, 171–72
   Daytona Bandshell, 217
   Florida Heritage MuseumSt. Augustine, 187
   Harn Museum of Art, Gainesville, 195
   Museum of Art, Fort Lauderdale, 389
   Museum of Contemporary Art, 462–63
   Norton Museum of Art, West Palm Beach, 376
   see also Museums; Performing Arts
Attractions and outings
   Amelia Island, 160–62
   Cocoa Beach, 226, 229–33
   Daytona Beach, 212–15
   Destin, 127–29
   Florida Keys, 495–96
   Florida Panhandle, 105–09

Fort Lauderdale, 384–87
Fort Myers, 405–06, 415–17
Fort Walton, 123, 127–29
Gainesville, 190–93
Gold Coast, 352–55
Gulf Coast, 303–08
Key West, 507, 510–16
Miami-Miami Beach, 445–46, 460–65
Naples, 407–08, 431–32
New Symrna Beach, 221–23
Northeast Florida, 151–56
Orlando, 278–79, 281–88
Orlando area dinner shows, 294
Palm Beach, 369–71
Panama City, 136–37
Pensacola, 116–18
Sanibel-Captiva Islands, 406–07
Sarasota, 338–43
St. Augustine, 177–84
St. Petersburg-Clearwater, 326–27, 330–32
Tallahassee, 143
Tampa, 314–21
Treasure Coast, 352–55
Vero Beach, 361–64
Audubon Society Corkscrew Swamp Sanctuary, 20

Bal Harbour, 19
Beaches
   "Best of" lists for, 10
   Florida Keys, 495
   Florida Panhandle, 103–05
   Gold Coast, 352–53
   Gulf Coast, 303–06
   Miami-Miami Beach, 444–45
   Northeast Florida, 151–52

Resorts and Hotels are listed separately in the Accommodations Index (p. 524).

536

Subject Index

Beaches *(continued)*
  precautions, 9-10, 12
  Southwest Florida, 403-05
  Space Coast, 201-02
  Treasure Coast, 352-53
Biking
  Daytona Beach, 209
  Florida Panhandle, 107-08, 111
  Gainesville- Hawthorne Rail Trail, 153
  Gold Coast-Treasure Coast, 359
  Gulf Coast, 311
  Miami Beach, 449
  Orlando, 245-46
  Southwest Florida, 410
  Bird watching
  Audubon Society Center for Birds of Prey, 242
  Dry Tortugas, 523
  Parrot Jungle Island, 463
  St. George Island State Park, 107
  Suncoast Seabird Sanctuary, 308
Biscayne Bay, 18
Biscayne National Park, 7, 445, 447
Boating. *see* Sailing and boating
Bonita Springs, 20
Broward County. *see* Fort Lauderdale
Busch Gardens, Tampa Bay, 316-19

Calder Race Track, 19
Camping, 8
Canaveral National Seashore, 201, 204
Canoeing and kayaking
  Florida Keys, 497
  Florida Panhandle, 107-09
  Gold Coast-Treasure Coast, 355-56
  Gulf Coast, 308
  Little Manatee River State Recreation Area, 307
  Miami-Miami Beach, 446
  Northeast Florida, 156
  Pine Island, 402
  Southwest Florida, 406-08
  Space Coast, 205
Captiva Island
  attractions and outings, 406-07
  overview, 396-99
  overview and maps, 421-23
Cautions. *see* Precautions; Safety
Caves, Florida Caverns State Park, 106
Children
  museums for, 11
  precautions for, 8-10
  vacationing with, 11-13
Choctawhatchee National Forest, 7
Clearwater, 325-32

Cocoa Beach, 225-33
Coconut Grove, 18
Convention Center, Miami Beach, 18-19
Coral Gables, 18
Corkscrew Swamp Sanctuary, 20

Dania Beach, 18
Daytona
  attractions and outings, 210, 212-15
  golf courses, 209-12
  maps, 4-5
  overview, 2
  overview and maps, 209-10
Destin, 121-27
Dining. *see* separate Restaurant Index
Disabled visitor information, 7
Disney. *see* Walt Disney World

Elgin Air Force Base, 14
Entertainment, 3
  see also Attractions and outings; Nightlife
Everglades City, 20
Everglades National Park
  Corkscrew Swamp Sanctuary and, 20
  overview and maps, 3-5, 478-81
  touring, 482-88
  wheelchair access, 7

Fairchild Tropical Garden, 18
Fernandina Beach. *see* Amelia Island
Fishing
  "Best of" lists for, 10-11
  Destin, 122
  Florida Keys, 498
  Florida Panhandle, 110
  Gold Coast-Treasure Coast, 358-59
  Gulf Coast, 309-10
  Miami-Miami Beach, 448-49
  Northeast Florida, 157-58
  Southwest Florida, 409-10
  Space Coast, 207
  Walt Disney World, 245
Florida Attractions Association, 6
Florida City, 20
Florida geographic regions, map of, 3-4
  see also specific region by name
Florida Keys
  attractions for children, 13
  beaches, 495
  golf courses, 504
  Middle and Lower Keys, 503-06
  overview and maps, 3-5, 490-92
  Upper Keys, 498-500
  see also Key West

Subject Index

Florida Panhandle
  attractions and outings, 105–09
  attractions for children, 12
  beaches, 103–05
  maps, 4–5
  overview, 2, 100–101
Foreign visitor information, 6
  see also Tourist information
Fort Lauderdale
  attractions and outings, 384–87
  golf courses, 380–84
  overview, 347–49
  overview and maps, 380, 382
Fort Myers
  attractions and outings, 405–06, 415–17
  beaches, 403–04
  golf courses, 412–14
  overview and maps, 396–99, 411–13
Fort Myers Beach, 20
Fort Walton, 121–27

Gainesville
  attractions and outings, 190–93
  golf courses, 189–91
  overview and maps, 189–90
  University of Florida, 16
Gambling. *see* Wagering
Gardens
  Alfred B. Maclay Gardens, 105
  Cummer Museum of Art and Gardens, Jacksonville, 167–68
  Fairchild Tropical Garden, Miami, 461
  Flamingo Gardens, Fort Lauderdale, 386–87
  Harry P. Leu Gardens, Orlando, 242–43
  Jungle Gardens, Sarasota, 342–43
  Kanapaha Botanical Gardens, 154
  Marie Selby Botanical Gardens, Sarasota, 338–40
  McKee Botanical Garden, 363
  Morikami Museum and Japanese Gardens, 355
  Sugar Mill Gardens, New Symrna Beach, 223
  Sunken Gardens, St. Petersburg, 332
  Vizcaya Museum and Garden, Miami, 464
  Washington Oaks State Gardens, 155–56
  see also Museums
Geographic regions, map of Florida, 3–4
  see also specific region by name
Gold Coast
  attractions and outings, 352–55
  attractions for children, 13
  beaches, 352–53
  maps, 4–5
  overview, 3, 347–49
Golden Shores, 19
Golf courses
  Amelia Island, 160–61
  "Best of" lists for, 10
  Fort Lauderdale, 380–84
  Fort Myers, 412–14
  Key West, 507, 509
  Miami-Miami Beach, 456–60
  Naples-Marco Island, 427–31
  Orlando, 276–81
  overview, 3
  Palm Beach, 366–69
  Pensacola, 112, 114–16
  Sanibel Island, 422–23
  St. Petersburg-Clearwater, 326–29
  Tampa, 312–16
  Tournaments, 360–61
Guide dogs, 7
Gulf Coast
  attractions and outings, 306–08
  attractions for children, 13
  beaches, 303–06
  maps, 4–5
  overview, 3, 300–301
Gulf Island National Seashore, 14, 103–04, 111–13

Handicap access information, 7
Hazards. *see* Precautions
Health considerations, 9–10, 12
Historical sites
  Amelia Island, 160–62
  Art Deco District, Miami Beach, 18–19
  Barnacle State Historic site, 460–61
  "Best of" lists for, 11
  Bulow Plantation Ruins State Historic Site, 152
  Cassadaga, 299
  Duval Street, Key West, 20
  Everglades National Park, 484
  Fort Jefferson, 523
  Fort Lauderdale Beach, 18
  Gainesville, 192–93
  Hillsborough River State Park, 306
  information, 6
  Jacksonville, 168–69
  Key West, 510–16
  Pensacola, 14, 114, 116
  St. Augustine, 15–16, 177–84, 187
  Tallahassee, 141–42
  Ybor City, 312
  see also Museums
Hot air ballooning, 205–06
Hotels. *see* Accommodations Index

Subject Index

Internet. *see* Websites

Jacksonville, 164–69
Juno, 17
Jupiter, 17

Kayaking. *see* Canoeing and kayaking
Kennedy Space Center, 226, 231–32
Key Biscayne, 18, 444
Key West
  attractions and outings, 510–16
  golf courses, 507, 509
  overview and maps, 506–09
  see also Florida Keys
Keys. *see* Florida Keys
Kissimmee, 299

Lake Okeechobee, 379–80

Maps, Florida geographic regions, 3–4
Marco Island
  beaches, 404–05
  golf courses, 427–31
  overview and maps, 20, 396–99, 426–29
Matlacha, 19
Miami
  attractions and outings, 460–65
  attractions for children, 13
  beaches, 444–45
  golf courses, 456–60
  neighborhood overview, 452–56
  overview and maps, 3–5, 435–40
Miami Beach
  attractions and outings, 460–65
  attractions for children, 13
  beaches, 444–45
  maps, 4–5
  overview, 3
  overview and maps, 435–40
Museums
  Ah-Tah-Thi-Ki Museum, 384–85
  Air Force Armament Museum, 127–28
  Alexander Brest Museum, Jacksonvill, 171–72
  Amelia Island Museum of History, 160–62
  Bailey-Matthews Shell Museum, 423–24
  "Best of" lists for, 11
  Cedar Key Historical Museum, 147
  Classic Car Museum, Sarasota, 341–42
  Cummer Museum of Art and Gardens, Jacksonville, 167–68
  Flagler Museum, 369
  Florida International Museum, 330
  Great Explorations, 331
  Key West, 510–16
  Lightner Museum, St. Augustine, 178
  McLarty Treasure Museum, 238
  Museum of Discovery & Science, 387
  Museum of Natural History Education and Exhibition Center, 191–92
  Museum of Science and Industry, Tampa, 321
  Museum of Southern History, Jacksonville, 172
  National Museum of Naval Aviation, Pensacola, 117
  Navy Frogman Museum, Fort Pierce, 353
  Ormond Memorial Art Museum and Gardens, 214–15
  Pensacola Museum of Art, 120
  Ringling Museum of Sarasota, 340–41
  Ripley's Believe It Or Not Museum, 180
  Salvador Dali Museum, 17, 331–32
  Sebastian Fishing Museum, 238
  Sports Immortals Museum, 371
  St. Augustine Lighthouse and Museum, 181
  Tallahassee Museum of History and Natural Science, 143
  Teddy Bear Museum, 431
  Valiant Air Command Warbird Air Museum, 232–33
  Vero Beach, 363–64
  Ybor City State Museum, 312
  see also Arts; Gardens; Historical sites

Naples
  attractions and outings, 407–08, 431–32
  beaches, 404–05
  golf courses, 427–31
  overview and maps, 396–99, 426–29
National Forest, Ocala, 7, 239, 243–44
National Parks
  Biscayne National Park, 7, 445, 447
  Everglades National Park, 3, 7
  Fort Jefferson, 523
National Seashores. *see* Canaveral National Seashore; Gulf Island National Seashore
Nature viewing
  Anne Kolb Nature Center, 353–54
  "Best of" lists for, 10
  Calusa Nature Center and Planetarium, 415
  Gumbo Limbo Nature Center, 354
  Morningside Nature Center, 154
  Tree Hill Nature Center, 155
  see also Attractions and outings
New Symrna Beach, 220–23

540 Subject Index

Nightlife
  Amelia Island, 164
  Cocoa Beach, 236–37
  Daytona, 218–19
  Florida Keys, 502–03, 505–06
  Fort Lauderdale, 392–95
  Fort Myers, 420–21
  Fort Walton-Destin, 132–33
  Gainesville, 190, 196
  Jacksonville, 172–73
  Key West, 520–23
  Miami-Miami Beach, 471–77
  New Symrna Beach, 221, 225
  Orlando and Walt Disney World, 295–98
  Palm Beach, 377–79
  Panama City, 139–41
  Pensacola, 120–21
  profiles, 3
  Sanibel Island, 426
  Sarasota, 346
  St. Augustine, 187–89
  St. Petersburg-Clearwater, 335–36
  Tallahassee, 146–47
  Tampa, 323–25
  Vero Beach, 365
Northeast Florida
  attractions and outings, 151–56
  attractions for children, 12–13
  beaches, 151–52
  maps, 4–5
  overview, 2, 148–51

Ocala National Forest, 7, 239, 243–44
Orange Bowl, 18, 450
Orlando
  attractions and outings, 242–44, 278–79, 281–88
  attractions for children, 13
  golf courses, 276–81
  maps, 4–5, 278
  overview, 2, 239–41, 276
  see also Universal Orlando; Walt Disney World
Osceola National Forest, 7

Palm Beach
  attractions and outings, 369–71
  golf courses, 366–69
  overview and maps, 347–49, 365–66
Panama City, 133–36
Panhandle. *see* Florida Panhandle
Parasailing, 205–06
Parking permits, handicap, 7
Parks and recreation areas
  Florida Panhandle, 103–09
  Gold Coast, 352–55

  Gulf Coast, 303–08
  information, 6
  Northeast Florida, 152–56
  Space Coast, 202–05
  Treasure Coast, 352–55
  see also National Forests; National Parks
Parrot Jungle, 18
Pensacola, 111–16
Performing Arts, 11, 18
Pets. *see* Guide dogs
Pine Island, 19
Poynter Institute for Journalism, 17
Precautions
  beach, 9–10
  for children, 11–12
  weather, 8–9
Pro Player Stadium, 18–19

Regions, geographic. *see* Geographic regions
Rosemary Beach, 15

Safety. *see* Precautions
Sailing and boating
  Florida Keys, 498
  Florida Panhandle, 109–11
  Gold Coast-Treasure Coast, 357–59
  Gulf Coast, 309–10
  Key Biscayne, 447–48
  Northeast Florida, 156–58
  Southwest Florida, 408–10
  Space Coast, 207–08
Salvador Dali Museum, 17
Sanibel Island
  attractions and outings, 406–07, 423–24
  beaches, 403–04
  golf courses, 422–23
  overview, 396–99
  overview and maps, 421–23
Santa Rosa Island, 14
Sarasota, 338–43
Scuba diving and snorkeling
  Biscayne National Park, 445, 447
  Blue Springs State Park, 219–20
  DeLeon Springs State Recreation Area, 220
  Dry Tortugas, 523
  Epcot, 257
  Florida Keys, 496–98
  Florida Panhandle, 109
  Gold Coast-Treasure Coast, 356–57
  Gulf Coast, 309
  Miami-Miami Beach, 446–47
  Northeast Florida, 156
  Orlando, 244
  SeaWorld Orlando, 285
  Southwest Florida, 408
  Space Coast, 206

Subject Index 541

Sea shells. *see* Shelling
Seaquarium, Miami, 18
Seaside, 15
SeaWorld Orlando, 283–86
Shelling
  Bailey-Matthews Shell Museum, 423–24
  "Best of" lists for, 10
  Florida Panhandle, 122
  Sea Life Safari, 308
  Southwest Florida, 400–402, 404–05
Shopping
  Amelia Island, 162
  "Best of" lists for, 11
  Cocoa Beach, 233–34
  Daytona, 215
  Florida Keys, 500, 504
  Fort Lauderdale, 387–89
  Fort Myers, 417–18
  Fort Walton-Destin, 129–30
  Gainesville, 193–94
  Jacksonville, 169–70
  Key West, 516–17
  Miami-Miami Beach, 465–67
  Miracle Mile, Coral Gables, 18
  Naples-Marco Island, 432–33
  New Symrna Beach, 223–24
  Orlando, 288–90
  Palm Beach, 371–73
  Panama City, 137
  Pensacola, 118
  Sanibel-Captiva Islands, 424–25
  Sarasota, 343
  St. Augustine, 184
  St. Petersburg-Clearwater, 333
  Tallahassee, 143–44
  Tampa, 321–22
  Vero Beach, 364
  Walt Disney World, 267–69
Snorkeling. *see* Scuba diving and snorkeling
South Walton Beach, 15, 121–27
Southwest Florida
  attractions for children, 13
  beaches, 403–05
  island hopping overview, 400–403
  maps, 4–5
  overview, 3, 396–97
Space Coast
  attractions and outings, 202–05
  attractions for children, 13
  beaches, 201–02
  maps, 4–5
  overview, 2, 197–200
Sport fishing. *see* Fishing
Sports teams and facilities
  baseball spring training, 246, 311, 360, 410–11
  Calder Race Track, 19
  Daytona International Speedway, 198, 208–09, 213–14
  The Everblades hockey, 411
  Florida Gators football, 158
  Florida Marlins baseball, 450
  Florida Panthers hockey, 360, 450
  Jacksonville Barracuda hockey, 159
  Jacksonville Jaguars football, 158
  Jacksonville Suns basketball, 158
  Miami Dolphins football, 449–50
  Miami Heat basketball, 450
  Orange Bowl, 18
  Orlando Magic basketball, 246
  Pro Player Stadium, 18–19, 449–50
  Tampa Bay Buccaneers football, 311–12
  Tampa Bay Lightning hockey, 312
  University of Miami Hurricanes, 450
St. Augustine, 7
  attractions and outings, 174, 177–84
  golf courses, 174–76
  overview and maps, 173–75
St. George Island, 15
St. Petersburg
  attractions and outings, 326–27, 330–32
  golf courses, 326–29
  museums, 330–32
  overview and maps, 325–28
State Parks. *see* Parks and recreation areas
Stuart, 17
Sunny Isles, 19
Surfing
  Fort Pierce, 353
  Northeast Florida, 156
  Space Coast, 206–07
Swimming precautions, 9–10

Tallahassee, 141–43
Tampa, 312–21
Tarpon Springs, 337
Tourist information
  "Best of" lists for, 10–11
  Everglades National Park, 479–82
  Florida Keys, 493–95
  Florida Panhandle, 101–03
  Gold Coast, 349–51
  Gulf Coast, 301–03
  Miami-Miami Beach, 440–44
  Northeast Florida, 149
  Orlando, 240–41
  sources for, 6–7
  Southwest Florida, 397–400
  Space Coast, 198–200
Treasure Coast, 349–51

Subject Index

Treasure Coast
  attractions and outings, 352–55
  attractions for children, 13
  beaches, 352–53
  maps, 4–5
  overview, 3, 347–49

Universal Orlando
  Islands of Adventure, 274–76
  overview and maps, 269–72
  Universal Studios, 272–74
  Universal Studios CityWalk, 276
  see also Orlando; Walt Disney World
University of Florida, 16, 158
University of Miami, 18, 450
University of South Florida, 17

Vero Beach
  attractions and outings, 361–64
  golf courses, 361
  overview, 347–49
  overview and maps, 361–62
Vizcaya, 18

Wagering, 360, 411, 450–51
Walt Disney World
  Disney Animal Kingdom, 257–60
  Disney Water Theme Parks, 261–64
  Disney-MGM Studios, 260–61
  Downtown Disney, 264–66
  Epcot, 254–57
  Magic Kingdom, 252–54
  overview and maps, 239–41, 246–52, 278

  see also Orlando
Weather considerations, 7–9, 11–12
Websites
  Disney, 247
  Everglades National Park, 482
  handicap information, 7
  lodging and travel, 61–62
  SeaWorld Orlando, 285
  Universal Orlando, 272
Welcome Centers, Florida, 6–7
Wheelchair access, 7, 303
Wildlife
  beach precautions and, 9–10
  Blue Springs State Park, 219–20
  Dolphin Research Center, 495–96
  Everglades Alligator Farm, Florida City, 486–87
  Gulf Coast, 306–08
  Lion Country Safari, 370
  Merritt Island National Wildlife Refuge, 204
  Monkey Jungle, 462
  Pelican Island National Wildlife Refuge, 238
Winter Park, 299

Zoos
  Alligator Farm and Zoological Park, St. Augustine, 180–81
  Brevard Zoo, Melbourne, 230
  Caribbean Gardens, Naples, 431
  Everglades Wonder Gardens, 421
  Gatorland Zoo, Kissimmee, 282
  Jacksonville, 168–69
  Lowry Park Zoo, Tampa, 320–21